AF378416

VINCENT'S CHOICE
Van Gogh's Musée Imaginaire

CHRIS STOLWIJK, SJRAAR VAN HEUGTEN, LEO JANSEN AND ANDREAS BLÜHM (EDS.)

with the assistance of Nienke Bakker

VINCENT'S CHOICE

Van Gogh's Musée Imaginaire

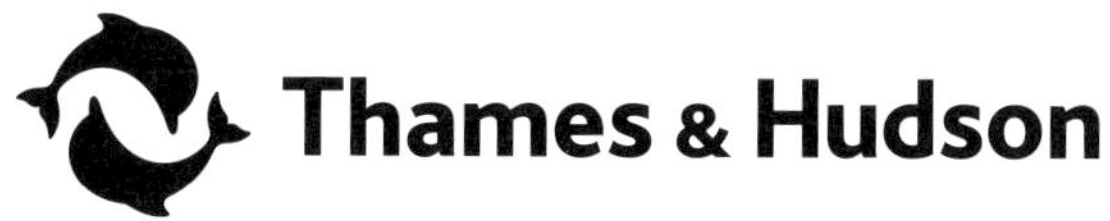

Thames & Hudson

This catalogue is published in conjunction with the exhibition
Vincent's choice: the Musée imaginaire of Van Gogh, organised by
the Van Gogh Museum, Amsterdam (14 February - 15 June 2003).

The quotations from Van Gogh's Dutch correspondence are taken
from the new transcriptions of the letters compiled by Leo Jansen
and Hans Luijten for the forthcoming complete edition of the
correspondence (Amsterdam, Van Gogh Museum, & The Hague,
Constantijn Huygens Instituut). The quotations from the French
letters are drawn from *De brieven van Vincent van Gogh*, ed. Han
van Crimpen and Monique Berends-Albert, 4 vols., The Hague 1990,
and verified against the new transcriptions.

References to Van Gogh's letters are given in the form of two
numbers. The first refers to *De brieven van Vincent van Gogh*,
ed. Han van Crimpen and Monique Berends-Albert, 4 vols., The
Hague 1990, the second to *Verzamelde brieven van Vincent van
Gogh*, 4 vols., Amsterdam & Antwerp 1952-54.

The b and t numbers in the notes refer to archival material (mainly
family correspondence) kept in the Van Gogh Museum (Vincent
van Gogh Foundation) in Amsterdam.

References to Van Gogh's works are given in the form of two
(catalogue) numbers. The first (F or SD) refers to J.-B. de la Faille,
The works of Vincent van Gogh. His paintings and drawings,
Amsterdam 1970 (1st edition 1928) and the second (JH) to Jan
Hulsker, *The new complete Van Gogh. Paintings, drawings,
sketches*, Amsterdam/Philadelphia 1996 (1st edition 1977).

First published in the United Kingdom in 2003 by
Thames & Hudson Ltd, 181A High Holborn, London WC1V 7QX

British Library Cataloguing-in-Publication Data
A catalogue record for this book is available from the British Library

ISBN 0-500-23806-5

Printed and bound in Belgium

Vincent van Gogh was born 150 years ago, on 30 March 1853. To mark this anniversary the Van Gogh Museum has organised a range of events and activities throughout the year as a special tribute to the artist and his achievement. This book and the exhibition it accompanies form the centrepiece for these festivities. Our intention is to offer the public a unique opportunity to sample the artist's taste in fine art. Visitors to our museum can normally only catch glimpses of the enthusiasms that informed Van Gogh's art – a copy after Rembrandt perhaps, or references to Millet or Delacroix. Here, for the first time, we reveal the full panoply of his passions, so that the world's largest collection of works by Van Gogh is joined temporarily by Vincent's *Musée imaginaire.*

There are few Western artists who have left such a comprehensive record of their likes and dislikes in art as Vincent van Gogh. His letters crackle with zest for art and literature. In his correspondence we can follow his taste as it developed, from his youthful observations as an art dealer through to his days as a combatant in the avant-garde and the urgent reflections of his final months. Like most painters, Van Gogh looked at pictures through the tinted filter of his own ambitions, so that the refinement of his taste became inextricably linked with the course of his own art.

In the exhibition and the essays in this book we have attempted to demonstrate this resonance between Vincent's taste and his own art. Where possible, we have borrowed or illustrated works that he actually saw and described. However, our search was not so much for direct visual correspondences or art-historical influences. Rather, using a broadly thematic approach we have tried to reveal the qualities that Van Gogh looked for in the art of his predecessors and contemporaries, and to set out the criteria against which he judged the art he admired or dismissed.

The preparation of this book and exhibition has made heavy demands on all the curatorial and exhibition departments at the museum, and I am grateful to all the staff who have worked so hard to make this project a success. I am also grateful to our outside authors, Joan Greer, Cornelia Homburg, Evert van Uitert and Wouter van der Veen, for their contributions to this book. We had the privilege to work with Thierry W. Despont on this project, and his stunning design for the exhibition also influenced the look and feel of this publication. Our greatest debt of gratitude is to the lenders. The success of this undertaking depended on obtaining particular works rather than generic examples, and we are grateful to the many museums and private collectors who responded so willingly to our requests.

Finally, I would like to offer a special thank you to our sponsoring partner, the Rabobank. Their generous sponsorship made this project possible on a scale that befits a 150th anniversary and has allowed us to offer this fulsome tribute to an artist whose work and imagination remain extraordinarily vivid and alive a century and a half after he first opened his eyes.

John Leighton
Director

Vincent's choice: the Musée imaginaire of Van Gogh would not have been possible without the generous cooperation of a large number of people.

In the first instance we would like to thank those lenders and museum colleagues without whose efforts this exhibition would not have been possible: Clifford S. Ackley, Robert G.W. Anderson, Jean-Pierre Angremy, Hugo Bongers, Christopher Brown, Françoise Cabioc'h, Blandine Chavanne, Arland Christ-Janer, Michael Clarke, Jean-Pierre Cuzin, Benoît Decron, Yolande Deckers, Chris Dercon, Danièle Devynck, Søren Dietz, Dominique Ducassou, Jean-Luc Dufresne, Frits Duparc, Larry J. Feinberg, Jan-Piet Filedt Kok, Bruno Foucart, Flemming Friborg, Gerbert Frodl, Rudi Fuchs, Josette Galiegue, Catherine Goeres, Antony Griffiths, Aron H. De Groft, Gloria Groom, Dorothee Hansen, Anne d'Harnoncourt, Wulf Herzogenrath, Michel Hilaire, Paul Huvenne, David Jaffé, Gerda Jansen, Guido M.C. Jansen, Theo Jansen, Hervé Joubeaux, Kyriakos Koutsomallis, Wim van Krimpen, Fred Leeman, Ronald de Leeuw, Serge Lemoine, Henri Loyrette, Ger Luijten, Neil MacGregor, Françoise Maison, Evan M. Maurer, Bernhard Mendes Bürgi, Danielle Molinari, Philippe de Montebello, Emmanuelle Mutricy, Sandy Nairne, Jacques Perot, Jacques T. Quentin, Janice Reading, Bernard Renaud, Pierre-Lin Renié, Malcolm Rogers, Axel Rüger, Laurent Salomé, George T. M. Shackelford, Hans-Werner Schmidt, Peter Schoon, Kate M. Sellers, Sir Nicholas Serota, Peter Sigmond, Howard Smith, Susan Alyson Stein, Virginia Tandy, Gary Tinterow, Guy Tosatto, Kees van Twist, Theo Vermeulen, Marie-José Villadier, O.B. Vos, Mark S. Weil, Eliane De Wilde and James N. Wood.

The exhibition design lay in the hands of Thierry W. Despont and his colleagues at the The Office of Thierry W. Despont in New York. We are particularly grateful to Thierry W. Despont, Manoocher Akhtarshenas, Luis E. Gonzalez, Eric G. Hilton, Chris Kelly, Matthew Maddalene, Mark Sohn and Milly Wilson. Under the enthusiastic and inspiring direction of Thierry W. Despont they were able to create an extraordinary and beautiful design for the exhibition installation. Its practical execution was the work of our trusted collaborator Bart van der Linden. Bill Schwinghammer was responsible for the lighting design.

The driving forces behind the production and publication of the accompanying catalogue were Jan Martens (Antwerp, Mercatorfonds), Ann Mestdag (Antwerp, Mercatorfonds), Ronny Gobyn (Ghent, Tijdsbeeld) and Petra Gunst (Ghent, Tijdsbeeld). Frederik de Wal incorporated word and image into a lucid and attractive design.

We would like to extend a special word of thanks to Rachel Esner and Michael Hoyle, who were responsible for the English translations, and to Jan Robert and Michael Reaburn for their careful editing. We are also indebted to Joan Greer, Cornelia Homburg, Evert van Uitert and Wouter van der Veen, and our colleagues Nienke Bakker, Hans Luijten and Roelie Zwikker for their contributions to the catalogue. In preparing the catalogue we could not have done without the cooperation of our colleagues Nienke Bakker, Suzanne Bogman and Monique Hageman.

The exhibition was prepared by a large team drawn from the staff of the Van Gogh Museum. For their efforts 'behind the scenes' we would like to thank: Edwin Becker, Saskia Beukers, Caroline Breunesse, Arda van Dam, Josette van Gemert, Esther Hoofwijk, Ton Hoofwijk, Ruth Kervezee, Martine Kilburn, Adrie Kok, Evelien Lafaille, Alex Nikken, Rianne Norbart, Fieke Pabst, Mario Penzen, Kees Posthuma, Jan Samuelsz, Frans Stive, Heidi Vandamme, Marije Vellekoop, Sara Verboven, Melanie Verhoeven, Berber Vinckemöller, Anita Vriend and Marije Wissink.

Finally, the Van Gogh Museum expresses its gratitude to the Rabobank, for their generous sponsorship.

Andreas Blühm, Sjraar van Heugten, Leo Jansen and Chris Stolwijk

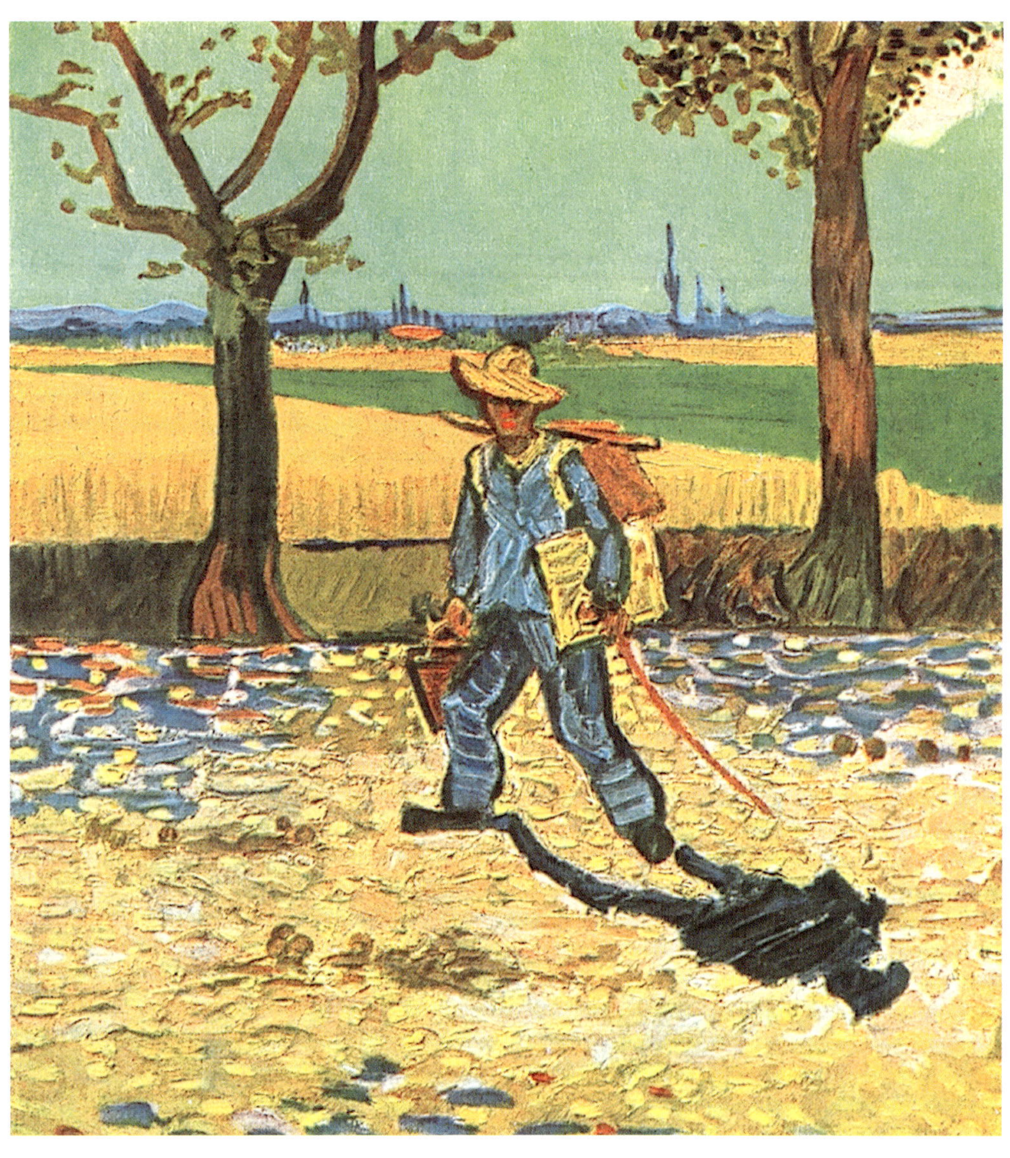

1. Vincent van Gogh, *The painter on the road to Tarascon* (F 448 JH 1491), 1888, destroyed (formerly Magdeburg, Kaiser Friedrich Museum)

SJRAAR VAN HEUGTEN AND CHRIS STOLWIJK

A PASSION FOR ART – VINCENT VAN GOGH'S TASTE

Art and literature were Vincent van Gogh's great loves from early on in his life. His correspondence and his own work offer abundant testimony to this. Although his father and mother might perhaps not be described as artistic, they did take a reasonable interest in literature and the visual arts, and two of his uncles were actually in the art trade. Both Vincent and his brother Theo entered the world of art while still young, and they spurred each other on in their artistic explorations. One of Van Gogh's earliest surviving letters, written in mid-January 1873, provides a good example of this. He was 19 at the time, and was working at the Hague branch of the art dealers Goupil & Cie. He urged Theo, who had become the junior employee at Goupil's Brussels branch a few weeks earlier: 'You must write to me in particular about what kind of paintings you see & what you find beautiful' [3/3]. ❧ From then until his death on 29 July 1890 in Auvers-sur-Oise, he reported constantly and in detail about what he saw and read, and made it very clear which works of art and literature he found 'beautiful', and which he did not. His correspondence is a 'gallery' bursting at the seams with more than 1,100 works of art by the most diverse artists. A curator could very easily use this stock of 485 paintings, 52 drawings, 567 sheets of graphic art, 10 sculptures and 3 murals to put together a string of exhibitions illustrating different periods and movements. They would be variable in quality, however, for Van Gogh's preferences, based not on the logic of a museum curator but on strongly held, personal views, are not always easy for a modern viewer to comprehend. ❧ The correspondence also contains the titles of more than 300 books and magazine articles, and once again one is struck by the wide range of favourite authors and styles.

❧ Van Gogh's sheer determination to absorb all of this was prompted in part by his ambition constantly to improve and refashion himself, and his eagerness to learn is typical of that. In the period 1869-80 the ideal he envisaged for his cultural development was still almost entirely in line with the very clear wish that his parents had for him, which was that he climb the social ladder to an established position as a respectable member of 19th-century society, either as an art dealer or as a clergyman. His role model was his father. After 1880, when he decided to become an artist having proved a failure at several different occupations, he utilised his need for intellectual and artistic sustenance mainly to help him develop into an artist with his own distinctive signature. His parents looked on in sorrow as their eldest son, struggling to gain a place for himself in the art world, strayed further and further from the path they had envisaged. The breakdown in their relationship, which came in 1882, was inevitable. ❧ In 1869, however, when Van Gogh took his first job at Goupil & Cie in The Hague, that estrangement was far in the future. He was young, and prepared to follow the path that his parents had charted for him in close consultation with his father's brother, the art dealer Vincent van Gogh. There is no indication that he had a particular interest in the visual arts before he joined the famous art dealers. ❧ His uncle Vincent and another uncle, Cor van Gogh, probably gave the young Vincent his first real introduction to the subject. Both headed flourishing businesses dealing in books and art, in The Hague and Amsterdam respectively, and had built up a large, contemporary collection. ❧ Moreover, as an employee of Goupil's, he had a superb opportunity to broaden his artistic horizons, for every day he came into contact with contemporary paintings, drawings and prints in the firm's branches in The Hague, London and Paris, at which he worked successively from 1869 to 1876 (fig. 2).

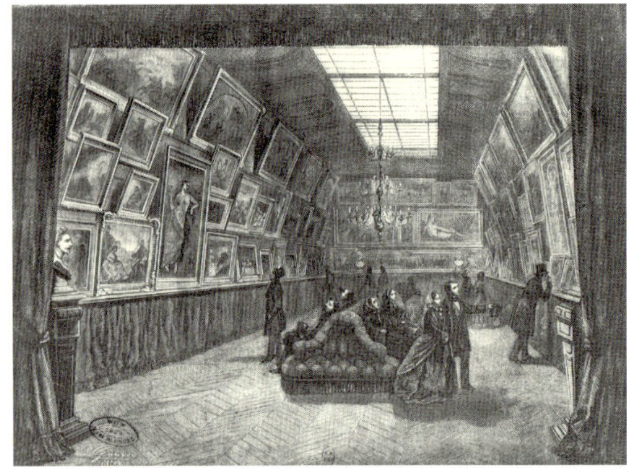
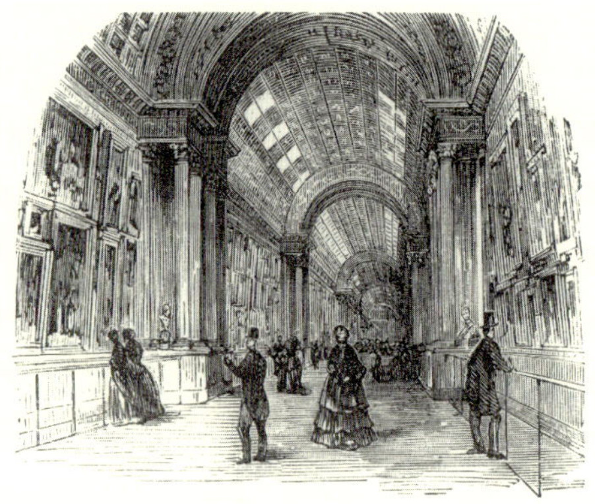

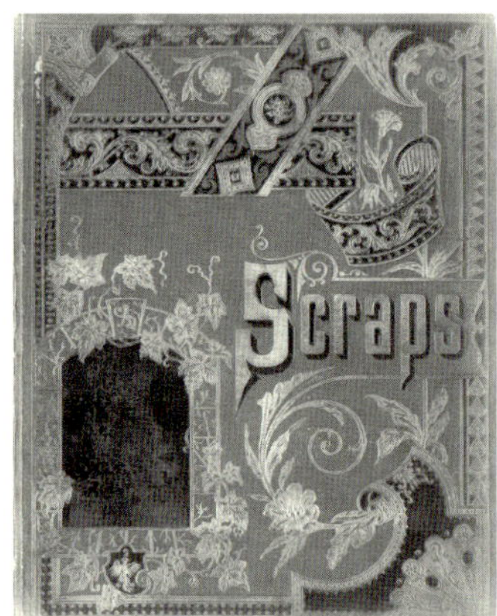

THE DEVELOPMENT OF VAN GOGH'S TASTE

The chronology presented later in this book provides a factual overview of what Van Gogh saw and appreciated during his life, including literature. The main aim of this introduction is to give a brief sketch of the development of his taste in the realm of the visual arts. ❧ The young Vincent grew up in a circle where religious faith conditioned people's appreciation of art. As the son of a Protestant minister he received a sound education influenced by the teachings of the Groningen School, a moderate variant of Protestantism whose principle tenets were love of one's fellow man and of the nature created by God. A knowledge of art and literature may have been an important part of his upbringing, but they were subordinate to religion and had no roles in themselves. Art was valued above all for the ethical, civilising function it could fulfil. That was not to deny that beauty could be found in it, but beauty merely buttressed the implicit ethical and religious message. The influential clergyman and writer J.J.L. ten Kate was the chief exponent of the writing enjoyed in those circles, and the *Kunstkronijk*, a cultural periodical not noted for its adventurous approach, was a good example of a popular art magazine. Religious pictures by artists like Ary Scheffer, genre scenes, and the works of the Hague and Barbizon schools exemplified the more or less contemporary art that was prized, while the tone for earlier art was set by the masters of the Dutch 17th century. ❧ Van Gogh's knowledge and taste developed rapidly when in 1869, aged 16, he started work at the Hague branch of Goupil & Cie. It was a house that dealt in the work of established painters, and kept a safe distance from anything vaguely innova-

tive. There Van Gogh was able to admire real paintings, and his knowledge was broadened considerably by the reproductions published and sold by Goupil, which constituted one of the concern's prime sources of income. ❧ Van Gogh remained with Goupil until April 1876, serving for four years in the Hague branch, almost three in London (spread over two postings) and more than a year in Paris (also two postings). This gave him the chance to acquaint himself with art both old and new in the Royal Acadamy and in museums like the Mauritshuis, the National Gallery, the Louvre (fig. 3) and the Musée du Luxembourg. Despite those influences, his taste remained much the same, as can be seen from a list of around 60 contemporary artists he valued that he drew up for his brother in January 1874. It contains the names of masters of the Hague School and the School of Barbizon, and of other established artists of that and slightly earlier generations, like De Groux, Rochussen, Meissonier, Koekkoek and Schelfhout [17/15]. The same picture is provided by a scrapbook he filled in those years, mainly with reproductions, including some prints after 17th-century masters (fig. 4). His love of the work of Jean-François Millet began to manifest itself around this time. An important influence on his taste came from the books of Théophile Thoré (who also wrote under the pseudonym of W. Bürger), an eloquent champion of the School of Barbizon and of the Dutch masters of the Golden Age. ❧ Between April 1876 and the autumn of 1880 Van Gogh worked in various places as, in turn, a teacher, a book dealer, a student and an evangelist, but these experiences added little to his cultural outlook. When he started out as an artist in 1880, therefore he still had the same preferences as four years previ-

---

2. Gallery of Goupil & Cie in the rue Chaptal, Paris, c. 1860

3. The Grande Galerie of the Louvre, Paris, c. 1856

4. Scrapbook with prints collected by Van Gogh, Amsterdam, Van Gogh Museum ously. However, from the moment when he began to marshal his thoughts about the nature of his own work, in the course of 1881, it is clear that he formed a hierarchy of artists whom he rated highly, headed by painters of the peasant genre like Millet, Léon Lhermitte and Jules Breton, and in Holland by realists such as Jozef Israëls and Anton Mauve. Millet, above all, presented a reality in his scenes of the harsh life of peasants, which also stood for something loftier, a 'quelque chose là-haut', as Van Gogh often put it, quoting his predecessor. Millet's *Sower* [plate 45], who creates new life with his yearly, almost ritual activity, is an image that Van Gogh admired immensely, so much so that it became an icon in his own work. However, he only knew it from reproductions and never saw any of the variants that Millet painted. ❧ Van Gogh's idealistic preference for a realism centred on the daily lives of workers and peasants emerges ever more clearly, as can be seen from the collection he built up of illustrations from magazines like *The Graphic, The Illustrated London News* and *L'Illustration*. Most of them were prints in the genre of social realism. ❧ A similar picture is found in the literary choices of his Dutch years, when he was evolving into a rather old-fashioned artist in the tradition of the School of Barbizon. Realistic English novels by Charles Dickens and George Eliot, and the naturalist works of French authors like Emile Zola and the Goncourts, are good examples of his reading matter. ❧ Compared to the wealth of art that Van Gogh had seen earlier, when in the art trade, his opportunities in the Netherlands were severely limited, especially after he left The Hague in 1883. His growing knowledge and the resulting appreciation for certain artists was mainly based on books and black-and-white illustrations. It was thus, for instance, he developed a marked preference in 1884-85 for Eugène Delacroix as a colourist, without ever seeing a single work by him in real life during that period. ❧ With a visit to Amsterdam's Rijksmuseum in the autumn of 1885 (fig. 5) and his departure for Antwerp soon afterwards, his love of old masters like Frans Hals, Rembrandt and (in Antwerp) Rubens was rejuvenated. This was mirrored in his work, for example in his strong interest in portraiture and more colourful palette. ❧ He left Antwerp in March 1886 for Paris, where he spent two years. There, at last, he could see works by the artists whom for years he had only been able to read about – Millet, Breton, Delacroix. This forced him to revise quite a few of his artistic opinions in a change of course that took on dramatic

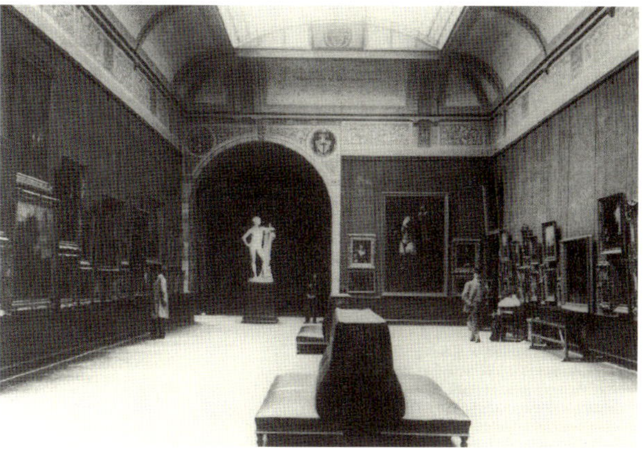

forms when he got to know and appreciate the modern art of the impressionists and the young avant-garde of Paris. The work of older painters like Monet and Pissarro, and of such young innovators as Seurat, Gauguin and Bernard, supplemented with his beloved Japanese prints, were in fact the first truly *new* additions in many years to his pantheon of cherished masters. Puvis de Chavannes, who was not really a member of the avant-garde but was highly respected by it, was also installed there. However, that in no way meant that Van Gogh abandoned his earlier loves. Although he distanced himself from the use of colour by such painters as Israëls and Mauve, which he had defended so stubbornly for years, his love for the content of their works remained as strong as ever. His guiding lights continued to be Millet and Delacroix, the former for his highly charged subject matter, the latter for his insights into colour (which Van Gogh also detected in the more modern painter Adolphe Monticelli). This continuity in his taste and appreciation remained to the end of his life, and it is a remarkable phenomenon in an artist whose oeuvre underwent one of the greatest transformations in the history of art. ❧ When he left for the south of France in 1888, Millet, Delacroix and Puvis de Chavannes continued to give direction to the work he produced there. The arrival of Gauguin in Arles in the autumn of 1888 provoked an often heated artistic confrontation, which, on closer analysis, ultimately confirmed him in his old preferences. The visit they made together to the Musée Fabre in Montpellier played a great part in their discussions, and fanned the flames of Van Gogh's old love of Delacroix (fig. 6).

5. Van der Hoop Gallery in the Rijksmuseum, Amsterdam, 1885

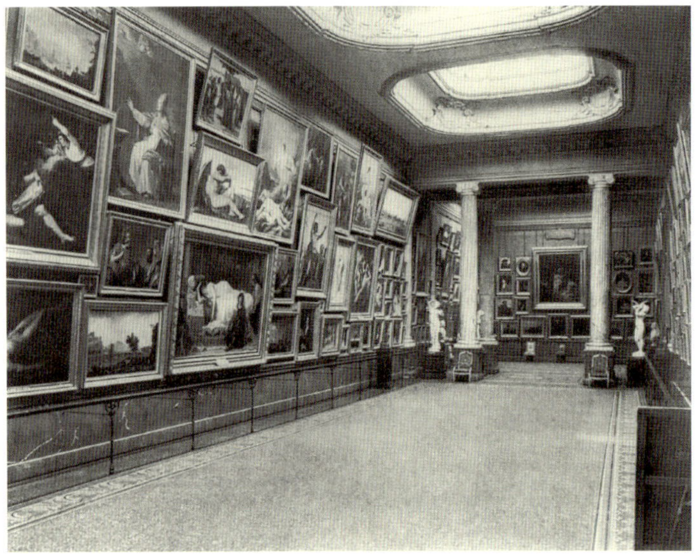

COMPONENTS OF A PERSONAL TASTE

Taste is a complex subject, certainly in the case of someone who improved himself on so many fronts as Vincent van Gogh did. As shown by the brief survey outlined above, there were numerous factors at work, and for that reason we felt that a richly chequered approach in the form of several essays would do more justice to the subject than an attempt at a simple analysis and synthesis. This book contains ten essays divided into four sections. That subdivision came about on the basis of a reading of Van Gogh's letters, with a special emphasis on the reasons he gives for valuing particular works of art. The extensive research into the letters that has been taking place in the Van Gogh Museum over the past few years in the framework of a new, scholarly edition of the correspondence, was of vital importance here.

❧ The first section examines the way in which Van Gogh experienced art: the 'sentiment' – a word he uses often – that he found in specific works. Sentiment in his day did not have the somewhat melodramatic connotations that it does now. It stood for a true feeling for art, the genuine emotion and often comforting effect that a work can convey. The essays in this section deal with the consolation that Van Gogh sought in art, and the experience of nature that plays such an important role in his oeuvre. The second section focuses on the artists and writers whom he found worthy of emulation, paying particular attention to the painters who trained him in art, as if they were his teachers. Section three is devoted to his views about art, and investigates the issues, chiefly ethical, that shaped his taste. Here a central position is reserved for religious matters and for Van Gogh's preference for art derived from everyday reality. The fourth and final section deals with the practice of art, and explores the influence of Van Gogh's print collection on his thinking and work, his artistic reaction on encountering the Parisian avant-garde, and his appreciation of the technique and use of colour of certain artists – Delacroix paramount among them. These four themes broadly shape the form of the exhibition itself. ❧ This approach has inevitably led to overlaps, if only because Van Gogh did not, of course, always appreciate works of art for just a single aspect. Sometimes they could easily have been fitted into almost all of the categories. This is accepted as being inevitable, with no attempt to disguise it with artful editing, for in a sense it is symbolic of the cohesion between all the components of Van Gogh's highly personal but consistent taste.

❧

6. The Grande Galerie of the Musée Fabre, Montpellier, c. 1904

VINCENT VAN GOGH'S BELIEF IN ART AS CONSOLATION

LEO JANSEN

Life is misery and existence is affliction. Every sensitive person will agree with this assessment, and only the most incurable optimist can continually face the world with both good humour and conviction: for example, the character Pangloss from Voltaire's *Candide*, who – with his 'metaphysico-theologo-cosmolo-nigology' – never tires of proclaiming that 'All is for the best in the best of all possible worlds'. Vincent van Gogh may have been fond of quoting this profundity in later years, but on his deathbed he is said to have commented: 'La tristesse durera toujours'[1] – a statement more in keeping with his intrinsic nature. His repeated invocation of Voltaire's pseudo-philosopher was in essence a contrived counterweight to his own despair, a way of putting things in perspective and preventing the trials and tribulations of life from overpowering him. ❧ Characteristic of this psychological expedient is the passage in a letter to Theo of 26 May 1888 in which Van Gogh attempts with a mixture of sincerity and light-heartedness to explain away the failings of creation: 'More and more I believe we mustn't judge God by this world, as it is a study that has turned out badly. What do you do if you like an artist – you don't complain about his faulty sketches, you keep your mouth shut. However, you do have the right to demand better. But we need to see other work by the same hand. This world was obviously made in a hurry, at an inopportune moment when the creator didn't know what he was doing, when his mind was elsewhere. According to legend, the Good Lord did his best with his study for the world. I'm inclined to believe that's true, but that the thing then got spoiled in many ways. Only the greatest masters can afford to make mistakes like that; that's perhaps the greatest consolation, because it leaves you reason to believe that the same creating hand might one day come up with something better'

[615/490]. Van Gogh often wrote about such deeply felt doubts and fears, and the guise of raillery and irony only makes his remarks all the more poignant. ❧ Van Gogh's image of the Supreme Being as artist is intriguing, but the quote reveals another important aspect of his way of thinking about life. Assuming the fiasco of creation is the fault of a 'master', then, according to Van Gogh, we as mortals have the right to hope for a better version in the future – and this is a kind of *consolation*, even the *greatest* consolation ('la meileure consolation'). His sequence of argumentation is not logical, but rather teleological; one could almost say that he here reveals himself a worthy student of Pangloss. But this does nothing to detract from the gravity and scope of his comments. Van Gogh suffered from severe and insistent existential malaise, and it was only natural that he should have felt an urgent need for solace. The outcome of his reasoning was a foregone conclusion: He *needed* consolation and therefore sought, with his own particular 'logic', to prove to himself and to Theo that such consolation was possible. ❧ Consolation is thus not surprisingly a regularly recurring theme in Van Gogh's correspondence, both during his years as an artist – from 1880 onwards – and before. And because art and literature were central to his life and work, it follows that the notion played an important role in his approach to literary works, paintings and drawings. As for the first, two examples will suffice to demonstrate that in principle the younger Van Gogh was in search of the same thing as the older. In the autumn of 1875, in a frenzy of moral purification, Vincent repeatedly asked his younger brother Theo to dispose of all his books by 'Michelet, Renan, etc.' On 14 October he wrote to him from Paris: 'I advised you to get rid of your books and I advise you to do so again, certainly – just do it; it will make you feel calmer; but even in doing so, make sure you don't become too narrow-minded and timid to read what is well written; on the contrary: that is *a comfort in life*. "Whatsoever things are true, whatsoever things are honest, whatsoever things are just, whatsoever things are pure, whatsoever things are lovely, whatsoever things are of good report; if there be any virtue, and if there by any praise, think on these things". Look for enlightenment and freedom and don't involve yourself too deeply in the *mire* of the world' [55/43]. The biblical quotation is borrowed from the epistle to the Philippians by the apostle Paul, author of the letters to the Corinthians, which Van Gogh would cite time and again later in life. Having emerged from his religious phase, Van Gogh would once again return to Michelet and Renan, critics of the Church and the traditional concept of Christ. But in 1875 they were incompatible with his newfound devotional zeal, and he could only allow Theo reading matter such as Erckmann-Chatrian, which he judged to be 'simpler' (i.e. innocuous); and he reassured him: 'it's alright to relax now and then' [54/42]. ♣ Thirteen years later his view of literature was not only much broader, but his opinions had also become more personal. In the intervening period he had become a great admirer of naturalism, and he compares two modern writers of a completely different cut: Jean Richepin, whose recently published *Césarine* he had just read, and Guy de Maupassant. Comparing the rather gloomy Richepin with the more ironic Maupassant, he writes to Theo: 'I much prefer Guy de Maupassant to Richepin; he is far more consoling' [712/555]. As much as his preferences and ideas have changed, they are still based on the same criterion. ♣ A closer examination, however, reveals that Van Gogh drew this consolation from Maupassant's work under somewhat false pretences – yet another demonstration of how much he needed it. In a letter to Theo of 18 March 1888 he praises the programmatic foreword to *Pierre et Jean*, entitled 'Etude sur le Roman': 'I'm busy reading *Pierre et Jean* by Guy de Maupassant. It's lovely – have you read the foreword, which clearly explains that the artist has the liberty to exaggerate, to create in his novel a nature more beautiful, more simple, more consoling than ours' [589/470]. Although Maupassant does indeed allow the writer a certain freedom 'to adapt events in aid of probability and at the expense of reality' – reality, after all, 'is sometimes improbable'[2] – Van Gogh pushes the author a step further in his own direction: in fact, the word 'consolant' – consoling – is never employed here in the way he suggests. Maupassant does use it once, namely in his rather condescending list of things 'the public' expects of the novelist, where it appears as item number one: 'Consolez-moi' – 'Console me'.[3] In short, Van Gogh's reason for

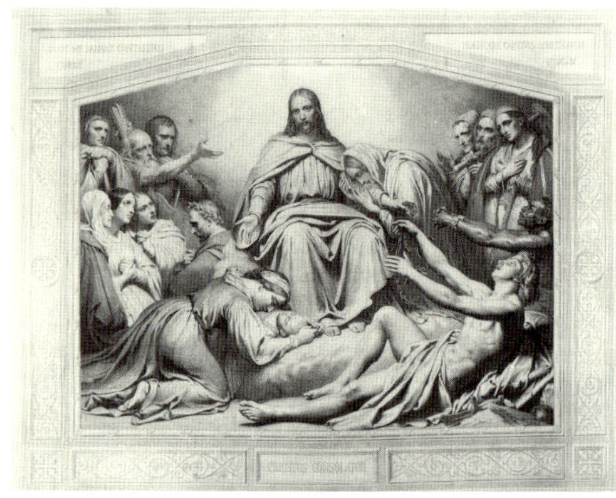

praising the author of *Bel-Ami* is at odds with Maupassant's own intentions – which, incidentally, Van Gogh could have known from the very same introduction. There are numerous other examples of Van Gogh's selective (to say the least) understanding of the ideas of others. ♣ As far as painting was concerned, in Van Gogh's early years consolation was easily found: Ary Scheffer's *Christus consolator* was one of his undisputed favourites (fig. 7, plate 9). It is mentioned repeatedly in the correspondence – sometimes together with its pendant, *Christus remunerator* – not only in his religious period but even as late as 1882. The painting enjoyed enormous popularity at the time, and the large number of available reproductions in varying formats only contributed to the phenomenon. More important, however, is that Van Gogh's unconditional admiration was for the depiction itself: whether a painting or reproduction, in colour or black and white, large or small, was irrelevant: this was a true representation of 'the consoler of the agitated spirit' and as such had a consoling effect.[4] ♣ In later years this is still the greatest compliment Van Gogh could bestow on a painting or its maker. In January 1890, for example, he writes: 'If I had the chance to travel, I would so love to copy the work of Giotto, a painter who would have been just as modern as Delacroix if he hadn't been a primitive, and who is yet so different from the other primitives. I haven't seen much of his work, but he is one of those who provide consolation' [841/623]. Once again, the need for consolation predicates reality. ♣ He used consolation not only as the yardstick by which to measure the work of others; Van Gogh, never one to go easy on himself, also made it his own goal to offer his viewers some form of comfort. This ambition is frankly stated in an important letter to Theo, written from the Saint-Paul de Mausole hospital at Saint-Rémy in June 1889. Theo had just informed him that he had not sent Vincent's work to an exhibition organised by the so-called 'Groupe impressionniste et synthétiste' to be held at the Café Volpini on the Champ-de-Mars, where works by Paul Gauguin and Emile Bernard, among others, would be on display. The planning of the event had been somewhat chaotic and Vincent agrees with Theo's decision not to participate. At the same time, however, he praises Gauguin and Bernard, both of whom he considers promising artists, for letting their voices be heard rather than 'turning their canvases to the wall until people are ready to admit them to one or another official circle' [784/595]. Like them, he, too, was striving for a kind of personal expression, in which the exact depiction of nature or the elegance of the sitter was only secondary. Taking Delacroix and Daumier as their models, he writes, their aim is to achieve a new kind of purity and serenity. 'Gauguin, Bernard or I – we may well all go down in the end and fail to conquer, but at the same time we won't be conquered either. Perhaps we weren't made for one or the other because we're here instead to comfort and to prepare the way for a more consoling kind of painting' [784/595]. The notion of consolation is thus linked to the deepest driving force behind Van Gogh's art.

'BEYOND THE PAINT'

This approach to art, literature and personal ambition, with its focus on consolation, has one important consequence: it draws attention away from the more or less objective characteristics or qualities of the work of art itself, revolving instead around the susceptibility of the viewer. In other words, what we are dealing with here has more to do with psychology than technique and aesthetics. ✿ A painting is an image created through form, lines and colour. The choices the artist makes and the way he presents them determine the artistic success or failure of the work. Naturally, whether or not the viewer appreciates it depends entirely on his or her personal preferences and criteria, but in any case its inherent qualities are always the starting point for judgment. Van Gogh, too, defines artistic quality in terms of external characteristics when he writes: 'When, stylistically, the object depicted is in complete harmony and union with the way in which it is depict-

ed, isn't that what makes for excellence in a work of art?' [781/594]. How Van Gogh evaluated these aspects in the art of others and how he applied them to his own creations will be dealt with elsewhere in this volume.[5] Important here, however, is that the properties of the work as such are apparently viewed as mere *means* in the service of a higher goal, namely consolation, i.e. something 'beyond the paint' [537/426], as it was expressed at the time.

✿ From this we may draw a second conclusion. If it is not the execution or structure or technique of the work that provides the consoling effect, what is it? One is tempted to suggest that it must be the subject matter. But this does little justice to the essence of the problem and shifts the accent to what Van Gogh instead refers to as 'sentiment'. He uses this word time and again, and almost always in a way that fails to reveal its exact meaning. Something can 'be done with sentiment'; have 'a truly Dutch character and sentiment'; or a modern artist must 'have sentiment when he paints' and so on. Obviously, we need to take the word and its application at face value; for Van Gogh it had none of the negative connotations it has today. A passage from a letter to Emile Bernard proves enlightening in this context. The young artist had sent Van Gogh a number of sonnets, with the latter offering his opinion in a letter of circa 21 April 1888. Leaving aside the details of the discussion, here inlies the vital point of Van Gogh's critique: 'it seems to me you haven't said clearly enough what you would like to *let be felt*' (emphasis added) [601/484]. 'Sentiment' is thus the mood or emotion the artist seeks to conjure up in the viewer: feelings of dismay, compassion, tranquillity, happiness. Naturally – for the 19th century – subject matter is crucial to this process, while the artist also has further recourse to colour, line, composition and style. ✿ Not only do we thus unwittingly arrive once again at the means, but it has also become clear that consolation is *not* one of those feelings that can be evoked by a work of art – at least not directly. By and large it seems safe to say that a successful work makes clear which emotions the artist seeks to arouse; whether or not we want to give in to them is an entirely different question. For a work to provide *consolation*, however, the viewer must in some sense be predisposed; he must find himself in an existential crisis or have endured setbacks or anxieties that might be ameliorated by aesthetic experience. He who does not suffer from the world and life needs no comforting and would be incapable of experiencing comfort anyway, just as only the thirsty can truly savour the refreshment of water. The solace the viewer finds is thus a *projection* – something of a quite different order from the 'sentiment' inherent in the painting; the consolation the artist hopes to provide by means of his work, is to effect this projection in a like-minded group. In his ambition to provide relief, then, the later Van Gogh is essentially in search of the chosen individual. One finds this most clearly expressed in a letter to Paul Gauguin: 'an art that offers consolation for broken hearts! There are only a few who can feel it, such as you and I!!!' [743/GAC VG/PG].[6]

CONSOLATION FROM FAITH

One needs little imagination to understand why Van Gogh was in such dire need of consolation. Even without construing him as a man whose genius had gone unrecognised since childhood, there can be no doubt that the path of his life was paved with misfortune and disappointment. ♣ Although we know little about Van Gogh's youth, it seems certain that his school years were not without their troubles and that in any case he was never a child like all the others, so that those around him were led to perceive him as strange or eccentric. His various attempts to give his life a purpose failed again and again. This must have been extremely frustrating; moreover, it meant that he could never live up to the social expectations of either the period or his milieu. As the letters up to 1885 demonstrate, the battle he fought against parental authority – sometimes openly, sometimes furtively – was both a rebellion and a striving for recognition. Art offered him the foothold he so desperately sought, but his work was either ignored or received with disdain; only at the very end of his career would it find some small acknowledgment. ♣ He was equally unhappy in his love life. Partly nourished by the idealistic and moralising work of Jules Michelet, Van Gogh was convinced that a man was incomplete without a woman at his side. His adolescent passions remained unrequited. His deep feelings for his cousin Kee Vos led to protracted conflict and alienation from his family, to the threat of institutionalisation and a broken heart that mended only slowly. His affair with Sien Hoornik was based more on a feeling of solidarity than on real mutual affection. His relationship with his Nuenen neighbour, Margot Begemann, and their plans to marry encountered stark opposition from her family; it drove her to attempt suicide and made Van Gogh's life in the

village impossible. To add to this litany, in the last years of his life he was the victim of successive mental breakdowns. ♣ There was thus more than enough reason to seek some form of consolation. Still, such causality does little to explain his understanding of the term. For this we must return to his youth and the values instilled in him at home. Victorian morality and Protestant faith were the two determining factors in his early life. Socially speaking, the aim was to become a successful member of the middle class and, if possible, to reach new heights through hard work and a life of sobriety, restraint and piety. Although Van Gogh's father had achieved a respectable position as the pastor of a small Dutch Reformed congregation in a predominantly Roman Catholic part of the country, his rich uncle, Vincent, had risen from a small-time art dealer to become a partner in the international firm Goupil & Cie, proof that material wealth and social status were eminently attainable. One abided by strict behavioural norms and never indulged in fantasies or whims. Art had a civilising, decorative and – above all – edifying function. Meanwhile, life in a country vicarage at Zundert necessarily brought with it a sustained focus on Christian belief, and this inevitably played a fundamental role in forming Vincent's disposition. Reverend Van Gogh belonged to a relatively moderate school of Protestant thought, the so-called Groningen school.[7] This meant, among other things, that he considered dogma less important than the practice of Christian charity, and believed that God revealed himself not only in the Word, but also in creation itself, that is, in man and nature. All this culminated in a single exemplary figure, namely Christ. He was viewed as the personification of consolation in the biblical sense: the Consoler of the poor and weak. By extension, he was thought to fulfil this function for all mankind, since according to Christian doctrine every mortal bears the mark of original sin and is thus in need of succour. This conception of Christ naturally helps explain the immense popularity of Ary Scheffer's *Christus consolator* in Christian circles. ♣ In Van Gogh's letters, words like 'consolation' and 'solace' initially appear only in this biblical sense, although not in his very first years, indicating that on this point his parents had less influence than one might expect.[8] The early reports of his reading and the surviving albums in which he copied his favourite poems demonstrate rather that he channelled his gloominess and melancholy into the romantic verse of Goethe, Uhland, Heine and Longfellow, as well as Edmond Roche, whom he empatheti-

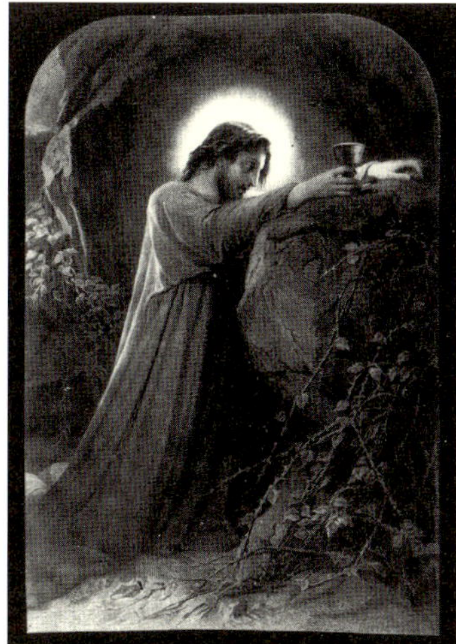

cally referred to as beautiful, grave and sad, citing the following stanza [32/25]:

> J'ai gravi triste & seul, la dune triste & nue,
>
> Où la mer fait gémir sa plainte continue,
>
> La dune où vient mourir la vague aux larges plis
>
> Monotone sentier aux tortueux replis.⁹

In this period, art and literature were undoubtedly Van Gogh's greatest passions, but he experienced them in terms of 'recognition'. The exposure to their 'sentiment' sufficed; one cannot yet speak of a deeper, more existential lack. ♣ Following his unsolicited transfer from the London branch of Goupil & Cie to the firm's headquarters in Paris in mid-1875, Van Gogh became caught up in issues of religion. He re-engaged with the ideas of his youth, taking them to new extremes. It is in this period that he began incorporating edifying texts into his letters. Among the most frequently cited works is the book of the prophet Isaiah; nowhere in the Bible is the word 'consolation' used so often as here. His father became his role model – to such an extent, in fact, that one is involuntarily reminded of the 'imitatio patris'. Religious images were given an important place in the decoration of his room. Time and again he mentions Scheffer's *Christus consolator*, a print of which he had received from Theo as a gift and which he himself would eventually give to many others. Other works include *Christ in the Garden of Olives* by Paul Delaroche (fig. 8) and a picture of the same subject by Ernest Hébert. Once again, the significance of these works lies exclusively in the fact that they are representations of Christ, and thus

recall the promises of the gospel to those who are like-minded and can understand the pictorial language. In an almost iconographic manner, then, they *refer* to something that lies outside the image itself. The most important thing about these works was not their aesthetic quality, but their message.¹⁰ ♣ As Van Gogh perceived it, existence had by now become a burden of biblical proportions: 'It seems that every day has its own evil and also its own good. But what is life worth, particularly for the future – as far as things of the world are concerned, the evil grows greater every day – it must be terrible without the support and comfort of faith' [97/80]. Following his failed attempt to join the clergy, his convictions led him to try and bring consolation to the miners of the Borinage, not only through the word of God but with a personal commitment to the poor and sick. ♣ As the letters up to 1880 demonstrate, Van Gogh's obsession with religion grew steadily, making tragically palpable the kind of psychological pressure he slowly but surely found himself under. If in the early stages his sufferings were of a more 'romantic' sort, by the late 1870s they were deeply and truly felt. According to his own convictions, he could not humble himself enough: 'Man is naturally evil, at his best nothing more than a thief' [136/116]. The only solution was to follow Christ, the Consoler. Reverend Van Gogh had little tolerance for this kind of rigid absolutism. Van Gogh's parents were greatly concerned; realising their son was living and thinking beyond the bounds of reality, they nonetheless offered him what little support they could. For years Vincent struggled to find a place within traditional religious institutions, no matter how modest. But, as is well known, the Borinage period ended with a definitive break with ecclesiastical authority and its representatives, and a rigorous rejection of all forms of dogmatism.

FROM FAITH TO ART

The letters clearly illustrate this rupture. The word 'consolation' is last used in its religious sense in a letter to Theo of 26 December 1878, written from the Borinage: 'At one of the meetings this week I spoke about Acts 16:9: "And a vision appeared to Paul in the night; There stood a man of Macedonia and prayed him, saying, Come over into Macedonia, and help us." And they all listened attentively as I tried to describe what that Macedonian was

8. After **Paul Delaroche,** *Christ in the Garden of Olives*, 1855, Bordeaux, Musée Goupil

like who needed and longed for the consolation of the gospel and for knowledge of the One True God. How we should imagine him as a workman with traces of pain and suffering and fatigue on his face, without fame or glory but with an immortal soul that needs the food that never perishes, that is, the Word of God, because man shall not live by bread alone, but by every word that comes from the mouth of God. How Jesus Christ is the Master who can give strength, consolation and enlightenment to a man like the Macedonian, a workman and labourer whose life is hard. Because he himself is the great Man of Sorrows who knows our ills, who is also called the Son of a carpenter although he was the Son of God, the great Healer of sick souls. Who laboured for 30 years in a humble carpenter's workshop in order to fulfil God's will; and God wills that in imitation of Christ man should live and walk humbly on the earth, not striving for higher things but bowing down to that which is humble, learning from the gospel to be meek and humble at heart' [148/127]. ♣ The next time Van Gogh wrote about consolation he had just decided to try and become a draughtsman or illustrator, and to seek employment with a magazine or newspaper. His change of course, which must have taken place in early 1880, was radical and definitive: suddenly it was art that was to provide consolation. On 24 September 1880 he wrote a long letter to Theo in which, among other things, he describes his journey to the northern French town of Courrières, where Jules Breton had his house and studio. He had failed to meet the great master, found the painter's atelier ugly and the village itself of little artistic interest: 'Not a trace of a living artist, but a café called the Café des Beaux-Arts, also of a new, inhospitable and abhorrent brick – the café is decorated with a kind of fresco or mural depicting episodes from the life of that illustrious knight, Don Quixote. To be honest, at the time the frescos seemed to me a rather poor consolation and pretty mediocre. I don't know who painted them' [157/136]. Although it is true he rejects the frescos because they *cannot* offer consolation, nonetheless the link is made. ♣ At the same time, however, this did not mean he rejected Christianity as a whole.[11] Van Gogh was certainly neither atheist nor agnostic, and the humanitarian, charitable spirit of the gospels always remained one of his personal articles of faith. The same letter that marks the change in his concept of consolation demonstrates that he had not entirely abandoned his evangelical preoccupations. He comments with great compassion on the poverty of the rural population and the miners, here and

there weaving in a characteristic, more or less unadulterated, biblical quotation. Looking ahead to the artistic difficulties he knew he would encounter and somehow have to conquer, he writes: 'Strait is the gate and narrow is the way, and few there be that find it' – a quote from the gospel of St Matthew. Although much had changed, much had also remained the same – which, in fact, is exemplary for Van Gogh's entire development. ♣ Clearly, however, traditional faith no longer represented the path to solace. The total devotion with which Van Gogh threw himself into his art is well known. Still, in the early part of his new career he rarely wrote on the subject of consolation. This seems inconsistent, but may be explained by circumstances. Van Gogh's first mature work was *The potato eaters* (April/May 1885) (plate 44), and the years leading up to it should be regarded as a necessary period of apprenticeship. Naturally, Van Gogh must have taken comfort in the fact that he had finally found his true calling; but his passionate battle with paper, pencil, pen and chalk, with canvas and paint, had first to be won and the tools of the trade mastered before he could consider attempting to achieve the effect he so admired in others. He thus reflects less often on the meaning and function of art, concentrating instead on the 'sentiment' that he hoped to incorporate into his pictures and that he regarded as a precondition for the creation of something lasting. It is thus this quality in the work of his great models that engages him above all. ♣ Latently, however, the notion of art as consolation must have worked on unabated. In these same Dutch years, Van Gogh developed his idea of an art for the people. Inspired by Hubert von Herkomer's famous pronouncement to the public, 'For you it is really done' [285/R19], at the end of 1882 he devised a plan to set up an association whose aim was to produce inexpensive lithographs, not for trade but as charity.[12] Nothing ever came of this venture, but it occupied him for some time, and he did, in fact, execute a few lithographs. There can be no doubt that Van Gogh's aim was to create appealing prints that would offer people some consolation for the hardships they were forced to endure. It must have been with some secret pride that he wrote to Theo regarding an incident at the Smulders printing plant involving his lithograph *Pensioner with a stick* (fig. 9): 'I don't know if you'll find it self-satisfied or the like of me when I tell you I derived some pleasure from the following: the boys from Smulders […] saw the stone with the orphan man and asked the printer if they could get a copy to hang up. No result could be more pleasing to me than

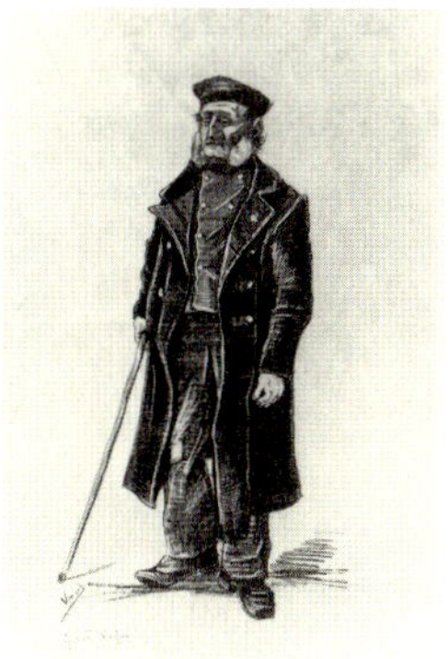

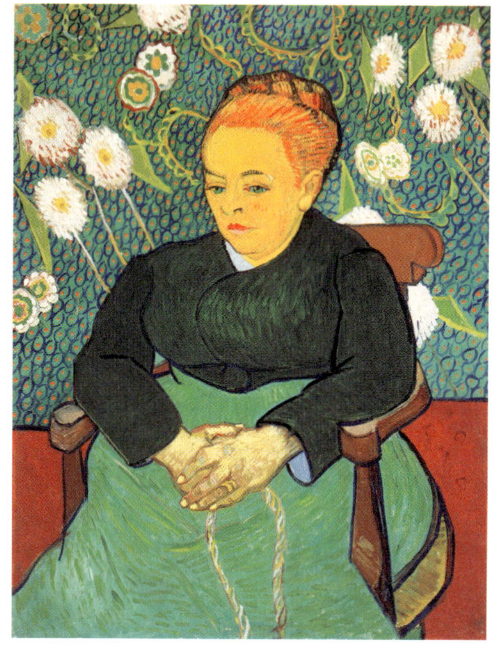

that regular working people should hang up something of mine in their room or workshop. *For you – the public – it is really done – Herkomer's words really ring true'* [286/245]. ✍ Van Gogh was still thinking along the same lines when six years later, in early 1889, he had just finished the first version of *Augustine Roulin ('La berceuse')* (fig. 10, plate 84): 'I have just said to Gauguin about this picture that when he and I were talking about the fishermen of Iceland and of their mournful isolation, exposed to all dangers, alone on the sad sea [...] the idea came to me to paint a picture in such a way that sailors, who are at once children and martyrs, [...] would feel the sense of being rocked come over them, reminding them of their own lullabies. Now, it may be said that it looks like a chromolithograph from a cheap shop' [747/574]. It was also in reference to the same painting that Van Gogh heaved his afore-mentioned sigh for 'an art that offers consolation to broken hearts'.[13] ✍ In the period between the pensioner and the cradle-rocker, Van Gogh had also changed his ideas about the role of subject matter in the work of art. A more symbolic treatment had come to replace the earlier, purely iconographical one. The image no longer denoted something specific, but suggested it instead. This does not make Van Gogh a symbolist in the sense of – for example – a Gauguin or a Redon, but the associative had now unmistakably become more important than the concrete. This change of attitude is embodied in the following passage from a letter to Theo: 'In my pictures I want to say something consoling, like music. I want to paint men and women with something of the eternal, whose symbol used to be the halo, and that we try to achieve through radiance itself, through the vibran-cy of our colouring. Portraits conceived in this way won't turn into an Ary Scheffer just because there is blue sky in the back-

ground, as in the St Augustine. Ary Scheffer is hardly what one would call a colourist' [677/531]. With these last lines Van Gogh bids a definitive farewell to the traditional approach, and thus also to the *Christus consolator*.[14] Van Gogh's comparison between the effects of colour and music are typical and oft repeated: 'Ah! My dear friend [Gauguin], to achieve in painting what the music of Berlioz and Wagner has done before us' [743/GAC VG/PG]. It is worth noting in passing that, when music is mentioned, ideas of consolation or rest and peace are often not far behind. In linking music and the visual arts Van Gogh takes up the romantic con-cept of synaesthesia, first developed in the work of Schiller and Novalis and the basis for the notion of the *Gesamtkunstwerk*. The more artists come to appreciate the abstract qualities of their var-ious media, the easier it is to relate them to one another. This explains Van Gogh's repeated references to Berlioz and Wagner. He was, however, no expert in music theory, and it is not impossi-ble that he merely latched onto these concepts in order to stress his own modernity.[15] ✍ Finally, as regards music and in reference to *Memory of the garden at Etten* (fig. 80), he wrote to his sister, Wil: 'I don't know if you understand that one can create poetry merely by arranging the colours in the right way, just as you can say something consoling in music. Likewise, the numerous and deliberately bizarre lines winding their way over the whole can-

9. Vincent van Gogh, *Pensioner with a stick* (F 1658 JH 256), 1882, Amsterdam, Van Gogh Museum (Vincent van Gogh Foundation)

10. Vincent van Gogh, *Augustine Roulin ('La berceuse')* (F 508 JH 1671), 1888-89, Boston, Museum of Fine Arts, Bequest of John T. Spaulding vas are not meant to create a banal likeness of the garden, but rather to show it as it would be seen in a dream, comparable in character, but much stranger than in reality' [725/W9]. One must keep in mind here, however, that this passage was written under the influence of his collaboration with Gauguin, who in this respect cherished ideas that went much further than Van Gogh would in the end be willing to go himself.

THE ARTIST VERSUS SOCIETY

Rather than continuing to seek a place for himself within society, from mid-1880 onwards Van Gogh began to focus on finding one beyond it. Perhaps he eventually succeeded more in this endeavour than he wanted. Little by little he came to conform completely to the modernist myth of the romantic artist, with all its inherent schizophrenia in both conception and ambition: the artist purposefully placing himself outside society and simultaneously feeling misunderstood; being anti-academic, having the creation of art for oneself as one's sole aim, refusing to make concessions or to express anything but one's own vision and experience of reality. For Van Gogh, the artist's psyche was something atypical and extraordinary; 'la névrose artistique' was a necessary precondition for artistic creation [635/B8]. As he commented to Theo: 'we artists in today's society are nothing but broken pitchers' [754/579]. ♣ This did not, however, mean that traditional faith had simply been replaced by a post-romantic high-priesthood of art or by a 'l'art pour l'art' cult of beauty. For Van Gogh art was never the *summum bonum*, nor had it become value-free. Whenever he refers explicitly to 'l'art pour l'art' he appears to conceive it as a kind of stopgap with which to compensate for his disappointment: 'work for work's sake – energy for energy's sake'; 'persistence' because 'society won't thank you for it' [559/448].[16] In other words, for Van Gogh, devotion to art was a form of … consolation. There are a number of instances in the correspondence in which he describes art's meaning for him in this way: 'It's some consolation that we continue to work with raw materials, not speculating but just trying to produce' [687/539], he told Theo in September 1888. This is virtually the same opinion as that expressed by old Martin in Voltaire's *Candide*, who thus provides the hero with the insight that leads to the novel's famously sober moral conclusion that 'we must cultivate our garden'.[17] And in the letter to his

brother in which he announces his plan to commit himself to the hospital in Saint-Rémy de Provence, it once again becomes clear how much painting gave him something to hold on to: 'You of course understand that I wouldn't have chosen mental illness if I'd had a choice, but if you've got it, at least you can't get it anymore! All the same, there's the one consolation that I can work a bit on my painting' [763/585]. At the time, the difference between Vincent's and Theo's situations could not have been greater. The letter was written around 21 April 1889; Theo had just got married and was a particularly happy bridegroom. Vincent saw this as his brother's path to consolation: 'I regard all your goodness towards me as more admirable than ever. I can't tell you how I feel it, but I assure you this goodness has been of the best sort, and even if you don't see the results of it, my dear brother, don't worry, your goodness is forever. But give as much of your affection as you can to your wife. And even if we write to each other less, you'll see – if she's like I think she is – that she'll console you. That's what I hope' [763/585]. While Theo took part in real life and thus contributed to its continuation, Vincent had to content himself with a place outside it, in art. Several weeks later, in his last letter before departing for Saint-Rémy, he wrote: 'As an artist you're nothing but a link in the chain and, whether you succeed or not, this is a kind of consolation' [771/590]. ♣ In some of Van Gogh's statements such confidence is occasionally and emphatically undermined by the fact that he seems to draw consolation from nothing more than the *hope* of a better future. Around six months after leaving Paris, sick, fed up and overworked, and shortly before Gauguin's arrival at the Yellow House in Arles, with the prospect of a shared studio, he had apparently regained his courage. He wrote to his long-awaited guest: 'Now I see a bit of hope on the horizon, however, the hope that flares up in fits and starts and that has often consoled me in my lonely life' [699/553a]. The link between hope and consolation is given a concrete manifestation in a reference to Puvis de Chavannes's *Hope* (fig. 11), which Van Gogh introduced as proof that it was possible to find relief from one's artistic 'neurosis'.[18] For him, Puvis was an exemplary artist, who offered a counter to the hastiness and cruelty of modern life; this is shown by his exuberant praise for the calm and delicate colouration and the composition of Puvis's *Inter artes et naturam (Between art and nature)* (plate 94), one of the very few works by other artists after which he made a letter-sketch (fig. 12).[19] ♣ In addition to those already mentioned, there

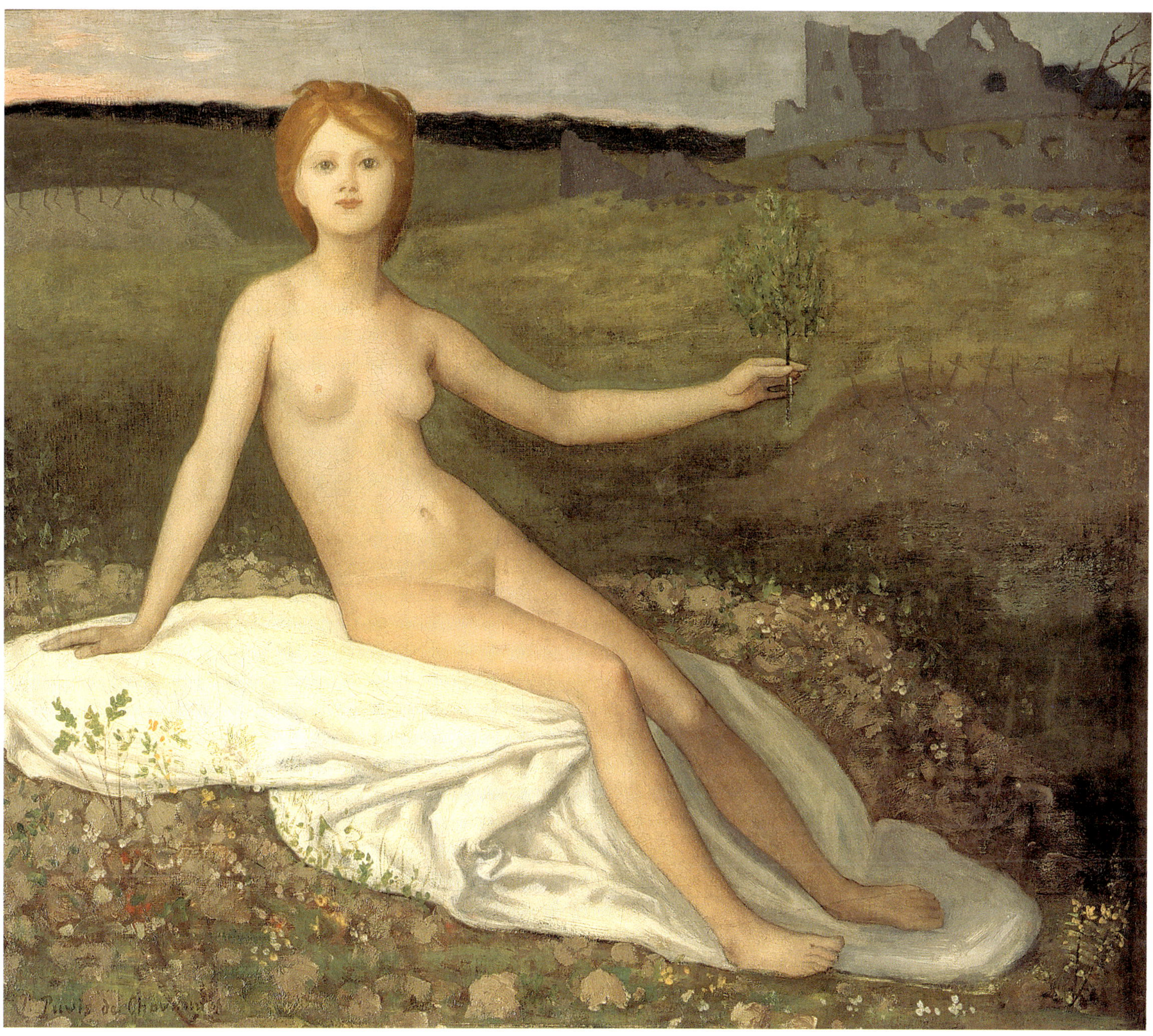

11. **Pierre Puvis de Chavannes,** *Hope*, c. 1872, Paris, Musée d'Orsay

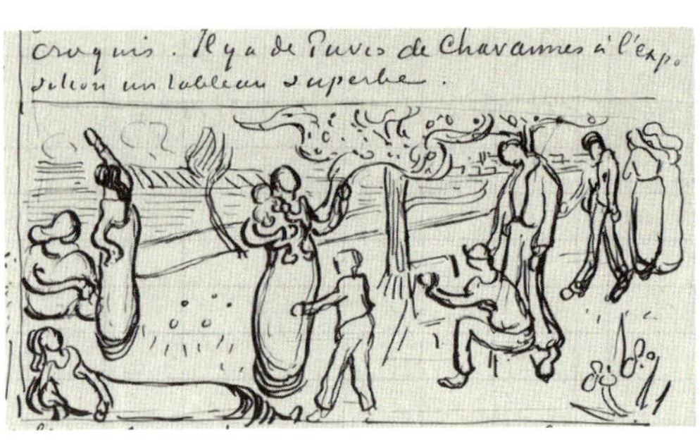

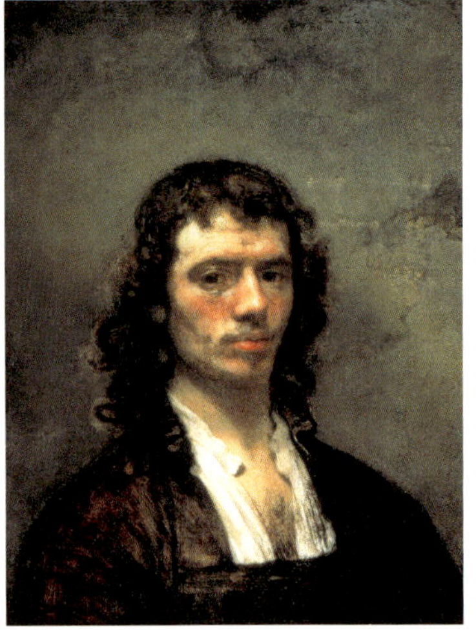

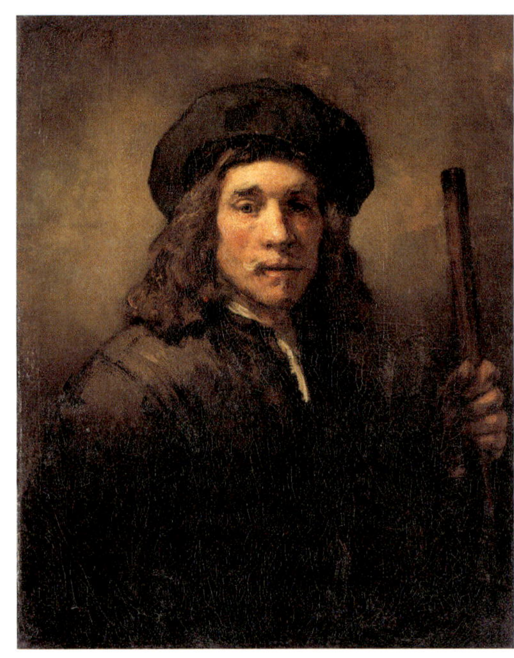

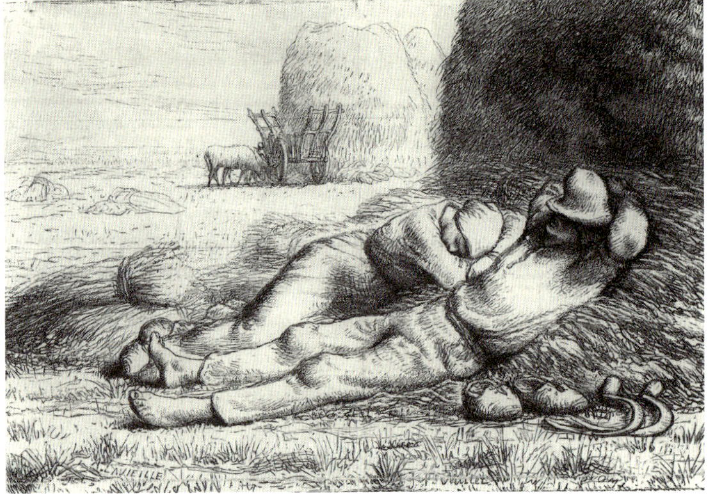

are several other works or artists that Van Gogh found 'consoling'. It is certainly no surprise that Jean-François Millet was among them. Van Gogh wrote about his idol in one of his fatherly letters to his sister; she was in Paris at the time, helping Theo's wife Johanna with her newborn son. Vincent notes his own preference for the countryside because it allows him to work outdoors, and he continues: 'Millet is such a master! He who is so wise, so moving, he paints the countryside in such a way that you feel it even in the city. Moreover, there is something so unique and so fundamentally good in his works that they are a consolation to look at, and you have to ask yourself if he didn't paint them just to comfort us' [843/W19]. Van Gogh does not mention any picture in particular, but a short time earlier he had made painted copies (fig. 13, plate 54) of three Lavieille prints after Millet's series *The four times of the day* (plates 55-58), and this undoubtedly resonated as he was writing the letter to his sister. ✍ As with this individual artist, Van Gogh gave a special place to one particular genre: portraiture. Writing once again from Saint-Rémy, where his need for consolation was undoubtedly greater than usual, he thanked Theo for an etching after Rembrandt (probably *The archangel Raphael*), which he classified in 'a special category of portraiture, in which the likeness is given something unspeakably radiant and consoling,' together with 'the portrait by Fabritius from Rotterdam [and] the traveller from the Lazace gallery' [799/602] (figs. 14, 15).[20] ✍ The praise is similar for two works Van Gogh saw during the Exposition de tableaux, pastels, dessins par M. Puvis de Chavannes, held at Durand-Ruel's gallery from 20 November to 20 December 1887: *Portrait of Eugène Benon* (fig. 16, plate 90) and *Portrait of Princess Maria Cantacuzène* (fig. 17). Regarding the male portrait, Van Gogh wrote that as far as he was concerned this was 'an ideal figure': 'That is consoling: seeing modern life clearly, despite the inevitable sorrow' [830/617]. ✍ It was undoubtedly the intransigence and serenity of these portraits – emanating the kind of calm he himself was seeking between his mental breakdowns – that made him particularly

---

12. **Vincent van Gogh,** letter-sketch [883/W22] after Pierre Puvis de Chavannes, *Inter artes et naturam*, 1890, Amsterdam, Van Gogh Museum (Vincent van Gogh Foundation)

13. After **Jean-François Millet,** *The four times of the day. Noon: rest,* 1873, Amsterdam, Van Gogh Museum (Vincent van Gogh Foundation)

14. **Carel Fabritius,** *Portrait of a man (self-portrait?),* c. 1648-50, Rotterdam, Museum Boijmans Van Beuningen

15. **Rembrandt van Rijn** (attributed), *Young man with a walking stick,* 1651, Paris, Musée du Louvre

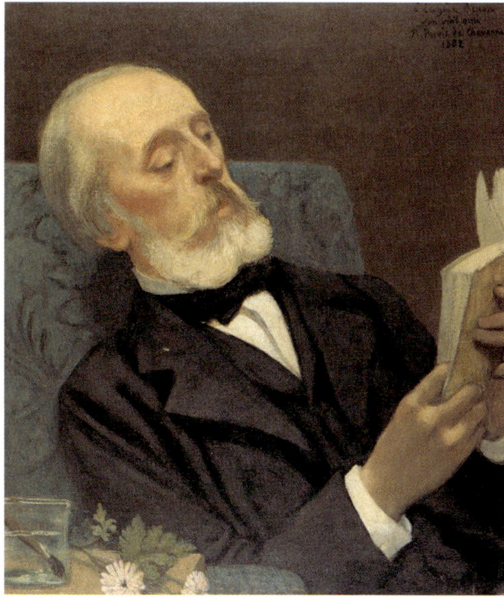

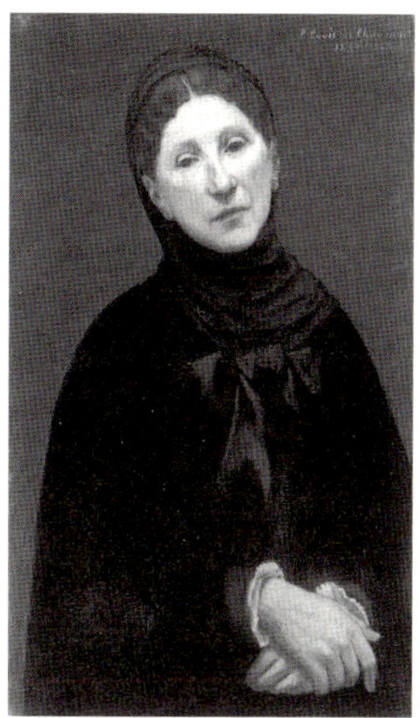

sensitive to them. This underlines once more that the consoling effect of a painting is conditioned by the viewer's susceptibility.

VAN GOGH'S AIMS

Did Van Gogh believe his work succeeded in offering consolation?[21] There can be no doubt that he hoped – or, if one reads the relevant passages carefully, almost dared to expect – to achieve something with his work that would give people relief from their troubles. Despite the unmistakable insecurity regarding the future, his letter of late January 1889 is nonetheless relatively self-confident in tone, and in this mood he even goes so far as to write to Theo: 'If I'm not crazy, then the time will surely come when I can send you what I promised you at the outset. Well, the paintings will perhaps one day be irrevocably separated, but looked at as a whole you'll see what I've been striving for, then, I hope, you'll have a comforting impression of it' [747/574]. ✍ Van Gogh is never specific regarding the consoling effect of his individual drawings or paintings, however. The *Berceuse* has already been mentioned above. In a letter to Emile Bernard of August 1888 he writes regarding his series of *Sunflowers*, the first versions of which he had just begun. The letter once again makes clear that in painting Van Gogh sought compensation for the fact that artists like himself were forced to live in misery and consid-

ered 'madmen' ('toqués'). But when he then remarks that by looking at 'the sunflowers' he hopes to find consolation for his not being able to join Gauguin and Bernard in the Breton village of Pont-Aven, he seems to be speaking of the *models* for his paintings – i.e. nature itself – rather than of his own painted depiction of them: 'How I wish I could pass these days in Pont-Aven. But no matter, I can console myself with the sight of the sunflowers' [669/B15]. ✍ In reference to another work, however, he explicitly states his intention to express something consoling. This example also demonstrates the extent to which Van Gogh had lost interest in the directly referential in the image. He first described *The garden of Saint Paul's Hospital* (F 659 JH 1850), in which he sought to convey feelings of anxiety as he and his fellow patients in the hospital at Saint-Rémy knew them, the feeling of what he calls 'voir rouge'. Going back to their discussion about modern religious art, he then tried to make it clear to Bernard 'that you can express fear without having to refer to the historical Gesthemane.' He had sought the opposite with his *Enclosed field with young wheat and rising sun* (fig. 18), which could be regarded as the emotional pendant to *The garden of Saint Paul's Hospital* and illustrated 'that one can express something consoling and sweet without having to paint figures from the Sermon on the Mount' [824/B21]. ✍ It is not surprising that, otherwise, the meaning his own work might have for others remained more or less outside the scope of the letters. After all, this is more a question of reception than an aspect of his ideas about art. Whether or not he was really able to offer comfort to others depended – and depends –

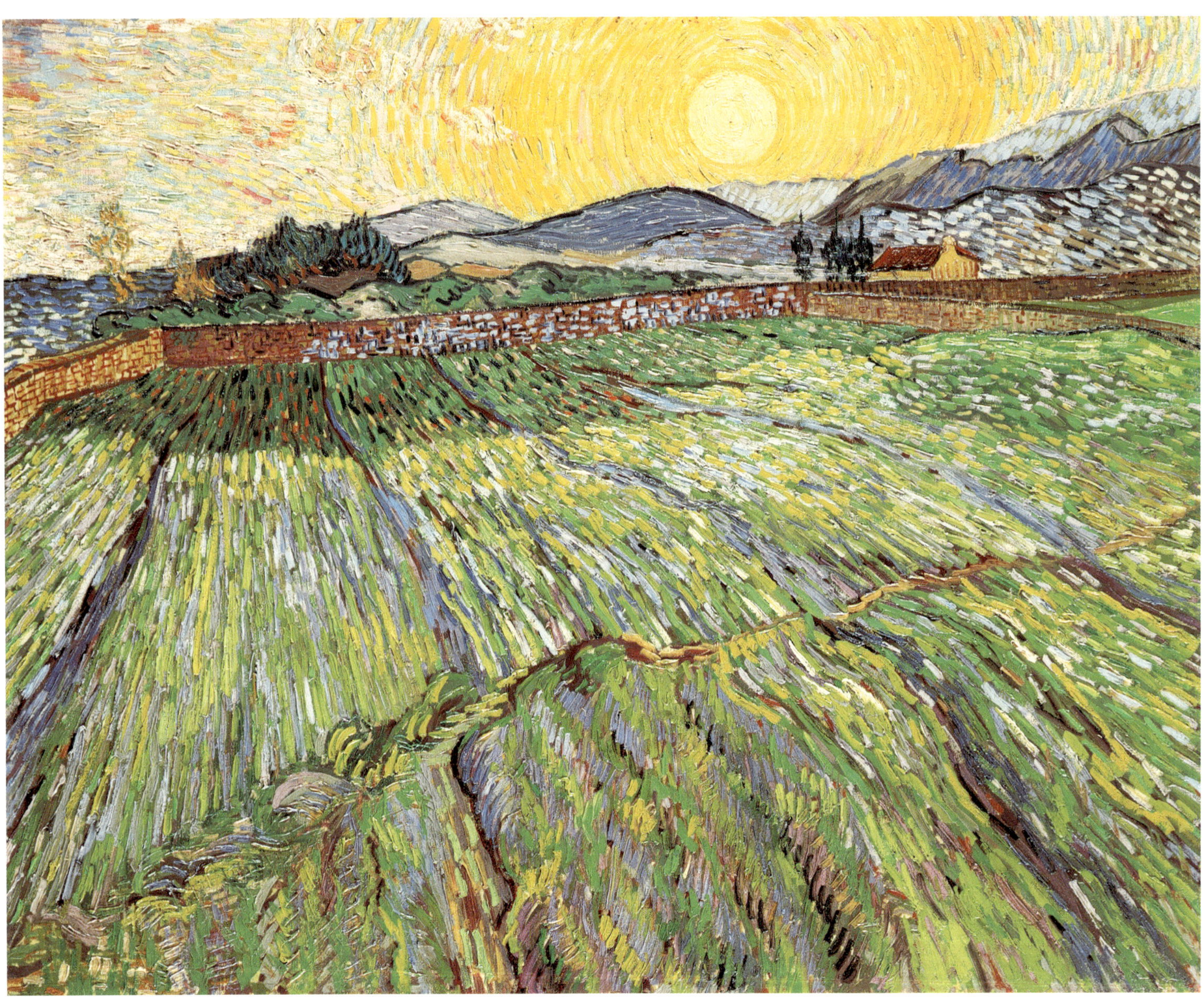

on the perception and mental constitution of the viewer, on his or her existential (or religious) privations and need for solace, as already discussed above. But Van Gogh was correct in his assumption that there are enough people in the world in need of relief from life's troubles and who find that which they seek in art – in his as well, as history since 1890 has shown.

18. Vincent van Gogh, *Enclosed field with young wheat and rising sun* (F 737 JH 1862), 1889, private collection

VAN GOGH'S NATURE

CHRIS STOLWIJK

Now that the silence in the woods and fields of Van Gogh's native land has been lost forever in the thunderous roar of yet another new century, it is possible that his letters and art might give us a chance briefly to return to a vanished age. There is perhaps no other 19th-century artist who has given a more personal and penetrating testimony to his natural environment. Nature puts in an appearance in many of his letters, ranging from a brief aside to lengthy, detailed and evocative descriptions. ✍ In his letters, Van Gogh combined his gift for language and his keen but selective view of nature with his own experiences and general ideas about the roles expected of art, artists and literature. He spoke of nature in his own way, and as such his work projects an image of his own *experience of nature* and of the way in which he tried to adopt a position vis-à-vis nature, both as a human being and as an artist. Consequently, although that image does say something about nature itself, it says more about Van Gogh's relationship to it. A study of Van Gogh's experience of nature is also a study of his image of nature and his image of self.[1] ✍ This essay associates Van Gogh's ideas about nature with his appreciation for landscape painting. It examines the wellsprings of his experience of nature, and what landscape and its depiction signified for him as *lieu de mémoire*. His ideas about the role of landscape painting and his personal preferences are also dealt with. The essay ends with a discussion of how Van Gogh's evolving view of art led to his use of colour as the supreme means of expression for capturing the essence of landscape.

NATURE LOVER

Van Gogh's Protestant upbringing in the countryside of Brabant had a profound influence on his experience of nature and his appreciation of landscape painting. He grew up in Zundert,

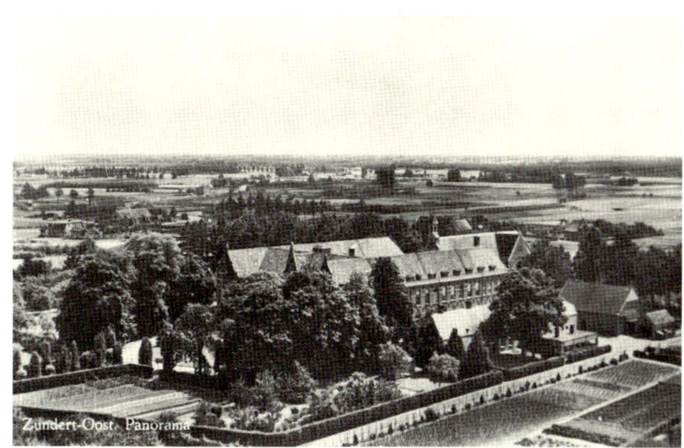

a sprawling rural community close to the Dutch-Belgian border. The village, where his father was the minister of the Reformed Church, was surrounded by agricultural land given over to rye, oats and potatoes, and by untouched moorland, marshes and pine forests. It was in this countryside that Van Gogh went on long walks from an early age, either alone or with his father or brother. This was the most direct way of coming into contact with nature and experiencing it (fig. 19). ✍ It was there that Van Gogh heard the lark sing 'above the black fields with the young green corn', and saw 'the sparkling blue sky with the white clouds above' [102/85]. Here he acquired his lifelong love of the country and nature: 'everything there speaks a distinct language, everything is firm, everything explains itself' [843/W19]. And although he lived and worked for long periods in Europe's largest cities, he said time and again that the Brabant countryside had shaped him and continued to exert a hold over him. The landscape of his youth and of his early years as an artist (1881; 1883-85) remained 'inexpressibly dear' [791/603]. ✍ Whenever he got the chance, even in later life, he would go out into the countryside or a park or garden to refresh himself,[2] or to look for suitable subjects to paint.[3] He repeatedly reported on these explorations in his letters. As an enthusiastic walker and nature lover he constantly urged Theo to continue going out on walks and to

19. The surroundings of Zundert, c. 1900

retain his love of nature, in part because the experience and observation of nature were 'the true' ways 'to come to understand art more and more' [17/13]. ✇ His attitude to the city, on the other hand, was decidedly ambivalent. As a young man he could still see 'a strange beauty' in the streets of London [92/76], have some sympathy with the pleasant neighbourhood where he lived in Montmartre, or later be amazed at the 'unfathomable confusion' he encountered in the docks and on the quays in Antwerp [548/437]. He found it reassuring that he could occasionally get a feeling of the countryside in the city, and could visit the parks and gardens that he loved so much. He also realised that in order to promote and sell his work he was dependent on the opportunities offered by a metropolis like Paris, with its artists, art dealers, societies and collectors. ✇ Early in his career, however, the balance tilted in favour of the countryside. In October 1883 he wrote to tell his parents that there was more chance of 'meeting a reasonable person in the country than in the city', which he associated with degeneration, stupidity and wickedness [400/334]. In later years he was to rail against cities for their lack of civilised values. His ideas about life in the pernicious city and the healthy countryside was part of a *topos* current in classical antiquity, which became topical again in the second half of the 19th century as a result of rapid industrialisation and urbanisation.[4] It was nourished by Van Gogh's reading of authors like Zola and Dickens, who denounced the social evils of the cities in their novels, and by Alfred Sensier's *La vie et l'oeuvre de J.-F. Millet* of 1881, which presented an idealised picture of that painter's life in the midst of countryfolk.

WALKING WITH GOD

Van Gogh's upbringing was governed by the precepts of the moderate Groningen school of theologians, and that too fostered his attachment to nature. In contrast to the strict teachings prevalent in traditional Protestant circles, the Groningen theologians advocated a more liberal, evangelical and individualistic experience of faith, in which Christ's humanity was a central tenet. Jesus's example of humility, service to others and humanity was the most important guiding principle for a virtuous life under the Lord, who manifested himself in his Son and in his Word, in history, and in the beauty of nature.[5] ✇ God's creation was hymned

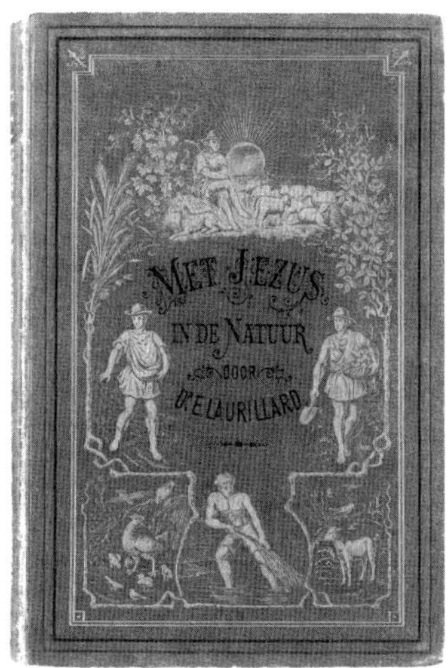

in numerous psalms and in the writings of popular and influential theologians and preachers of other, even more progressive, Reformed movements with which Van Gogh came into contact, particularly during his period of study in Amsterdam (1877-78). They included *Met Jezus in de natuur* by the Reverend Eliza Laurillard (fig. 20), several of whose sermons Van Gogh heard in Amsterdam. According to Laurillard, the beauty of nature was 'abundant and of many forms', and in addition to delightful repose and uplifting and bewitching song it offered above all the opportunity to 'hear the Lord God walk through the garden' and 'to understand the symbolism of nature bearing God's imprint'.[6] ✇ One finds a similarly undogmatic, more symbolic and personal view of nature as a revelation of God in Van Gogh's letters until the early 1880s. It was related to romantic idealism. However, to him it did not mean that a feeling for nature was the same as religious feeling; it was not 'everything' to him [71/57]. Faith prevailed, for the time being anyway. A love of nature was certainly a wonderful thing to have, offering the opportunity to meet God. This, and his own artistry, enabled Van Gogh to reform and improve himself, as he wrote from the province of Drenthe in November 1883: 'Our purpose is in the first place self-reform by means of a handicraft and of intercourse with nature, believing as we do that this is our *first duty* in order to be able to continue doing right by others and to be consistent. Our aim is "walking with God"[7] – the opposite of living amidst the doings of the big

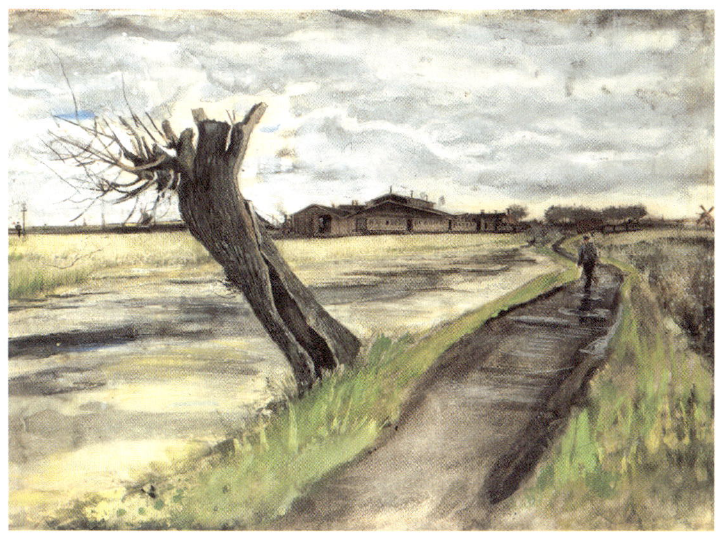

Man's position in the presence of nature, and the attendant alien-ation, disharmony and strife, did not prevent Van Gogh from going out into the countryside in an attempt to record it. As a young artist he was still convinced that art could bridge the gap between man and nature if the artist set out with the aim of restoring the lost harmony, which he also referred to in pastoral terms like 'peace'. He mentioned Jules Dupré, Van Goyen, Millet and Jozef Israëls as artists who had succeeded in doing this,[10] and above all Corot, who like no other artist could depict 'a still-ness, a mystery, a peace' [407/340]. The landscapes themselves could also elicit similar feelings in him. ✹ A few years later, when his life had taken several dramatic turns, there was little of this conviction left. In July 1889 he felt that his endeavours to portray the landscape of the south of France were doomed to failure, although working outdoors did bring him some comfort, in the sense that contact with nature could help him regain his strength, feel less lonely, and make him sense 'the ties that unite us all' [790/599].[11] The unfathomable richness and contrasts of nature continued, as ever, to touch him deeply, but at the same time forced him to face facts. 'From time to time there are mo-ments when nature is superb, autumn effects glorious in colour, green skies contrasting with foliage in yellows, oranges, greens, earth in all the violets, heat-withered grass among which, how-ever, the rains have given a last energy to certain plants, which again start putting forth little flowers of violet, pink, blue, yellow. Things that one is very sad not to be able to reproduce' [810/610].

Various authors have recently posited a direct link between Van Gogh's religious background and its resonance in his approach to art.[12] That background was important for his love of landscape painting, certainly in the years when he was 'walking with God', but he rarely interpreted nature in an overtly religious way. He reserved that primarily for history painting and figurative art.[13] That is remarkable, considering his religiosity at the time, partly because the potential religious function of landscape painting was being emphasised increasingly around the middle of the century, certainly in Protestant art appreciation in the Nether-lands.[14] ✹ In December 1877, however, Van Gogh did refer to the work of Ruisdael and to Millet's *The church of Gréville* (1871-74) (fig. 22), which he believed perfectly illustrated 'the church of God standing on a rock', a phrase from Hymn 243 in the Dutch Reformed Church hymnal, to which he had listened approvingly

cities' [402/337]. ✹ As a man and an artist, Van Gogh was opposed to an animistic and meaningful nature that could 'tell' him the 'truth'. As he saw it, nature would only yield up that secret after a constant, bitter struggle.[8] For example, he encountered an ani-mistic nature at the end of July 1882 near The Hague, where he saw a pollard willow hanging over a pool, 'all alone and melan-choly'; he intended to 'attack' it the following day [252/220] (fig. 21). He also anthropomorphised nature. For instance, he associated a row of pollard willows with a procession of pensioners ('orphan men', as he called them), young corn with the expression on a sleeping child's face, flattened grass with the exhaustion of those living in a working-class neighbourhood, and a row of cab-bages, 'standing frozen and benumbed' in the snow, with a group of women he had once seen standing in a cellar [282/242]. ✹ That same year he wrote that a painter could only be happy if he lived in harmony with nature and was able to depict 'a little of what he sees' [290/248]. According to him, the moment when an artist suc-ceeds in revealing the truth and beauty that nature conceals within itself, he can create something that ultimately rises above nature. He spoke of 'something up above' ('quelque chose là-haut'), a phrase he borrowed from Sensier.[9] In June 1879 he be-lieved that the work of painters of the Hague School, especially Mauve (plate 68), Jacob Maris (fig. 25) and Jozef Israëls (plates 64-65), met this criterion. Their art spoke 'more clearly than nature herself' [151/130].

21. **Vincent van Gogh,** *Pollard willow* (F 947 JH 164), 1882,
present whereabouts unknown

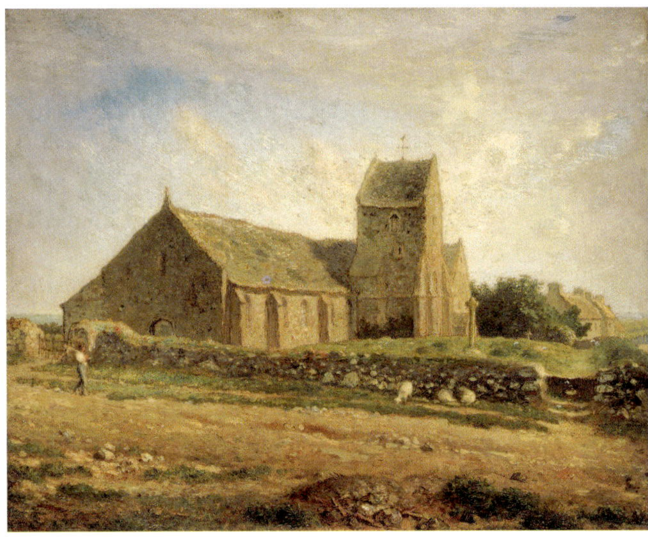

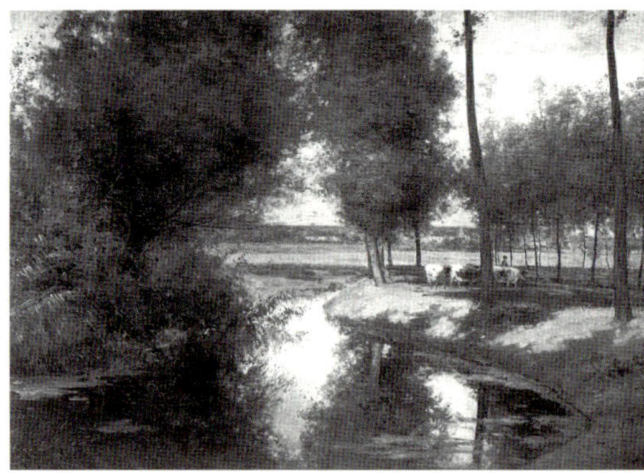

on one of his many visits to churches in Amsterdam. However, he described even an historicised landscape like Corot's *Agony in the garden* of 1849 (plate 12), which he admired in Paris in 1875, in strictly formal terms.[15] More than 14 years later he referred to it again in a letter to Emile Bernard, stressing that Corot, in this work (which he called 'sublime'), may have made a biblical painting 'with Christ and the evening star', but it was not so much a revelation of God as of the feelings of modern man [824/B21].

LANDSCAPE AND MEMORY

Landscapes can help us recall specific events and episodes in our lives, particularly from childhood, when the child is simultaneously discovering itself and the world around it.[16] This interweaving of an individual life with nature is also found in Van Gogh's love of landscape painting. ✒ He felt himself to be a traveller 'going somewhere and to some destination' [660/518], even though it was an uncertain one.[17] He left home at an early age and, after many wanderings in the Netherlands, England and France, he eventually chose the fields near Auvers-sur-Oise as his destination. His journey of discovery took him further and further away from 'home', and a few months before his death he wrote that he had actually become a 'degenerate child' [857/W20]. ✒ In 1873,

Johan Hendrik Weissenbruch's *View of the Trekvliet* of 1870 (plate 2) reminded him of a particular walk he and Theo had taken on the Rijswijk road near The Hague, during which they had discussed important philosophical questions.[18] Then, in 1874, when he was working at the London branch of Goupil & Cie, he longed 'so much for Holland, and especially Helvoirt' [22/16], and was delighted when a colleague brought back drawings of Dutch towns and meadows.[19] ✒ The love of Brabant and his precious memories of that province emerge in the praise he had in 1874 for the Belgian painter César de Cock and his poetic landscapes, the refined tonality of which relates them to the work of Corot: 'He is one of the few painters to have understood in an intimate enough way *our Brabant*' [23/17] (fig. 23). ✒ In 1882 Van Gogh rediscovered that province in drawings of the moors of Drenthe made by Mauve and Ter Meulen. To him, those painters of the Hague School captured the atmosphere of the still unspoiled North Brabant, of '*when I was young*, some 20 years ago. [...] But since then that part of Brabant with which I was acquainted has changed enormously as a consequence of agricultural developments and the establishment of industries' [257/R11]. When he saw those drawings, he had not yet set foot on the soil of Drenthe, but a month later he did so in the hope of rediscovering his lost Brabant. ✒ As the years passed, with that beloved countryside receding in both time and distance, Van Gogh came to the painful realisation that it had become impossible for him ever to return there. What remained was a vain longing and the sometimes harrowing yet comforting memories, as during his illness from December 1888 to January 1889 in Arles, when he saw Zundert in 'every path, every plant in the garden, the immediate surroun-

22. **Jean-François Millet,** *The church of Gréville,* 1871-74, Paris, Musée d'Orsay

23. **César de Cock,** *Landscape near the Leie. The road to the Patijntje,* 1863, Ghent, Museum voor Schone Kunsten

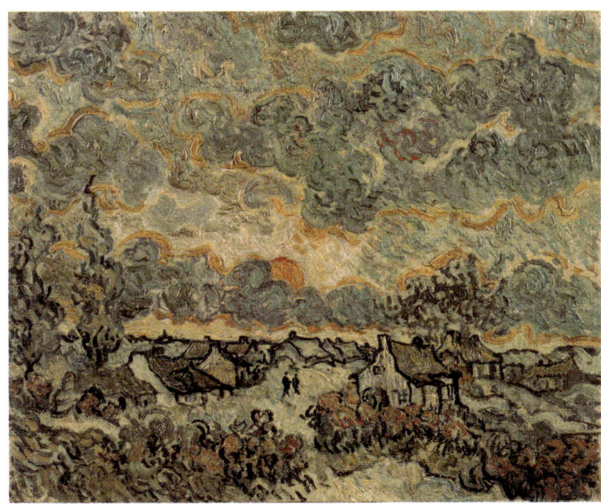

dings, the fields' [744/573]. In the early spring of 1890 he incorporated those memories in his *Recollection of Brabant* (fig. 24), 'hovels with moss-covered roofs and beech hedges on an autumn evening with a stormy sky, the sun setting red amid ruddy clouds' [865/629a]. ✍ So Van Gogh never forgot the country of his birth. As soon as he arrived in Arles in February 1888 he was comparing it to Breda, and for the next two years in Provence he repeatedly harked back to the Netherlands.[20] At first he imagined himself to be in Japan, but as time passed 'Holland' came increasingly to the fore, to the extent, in fact, that one might wonder whether he was actually able to see the real Provence, conditioned as he was by his own expectations and memories. ✍ In May 1888 he wrote to say that many of the subjects in Arles and its surroundings 'are exactly like Holland', the only difference being the colours [612/488]. The association with his native country often recurs in subsequent letters. The flat land of the Camargue and the Crau was 'exactly like Ruisdael' [626/496], that is to say 17th-century Holland. And in June 1888 he began work on *The harvest* (plate 113), which he said was done 'exactly' in the manner of Philips Koninck (plate 112), 'you know, the pupil of Rembrandt who painted vast level plains' [626/496]. ✍ Initially he had nothing but praise for 'the land of the good Tartarin'.[21] He even believed that he would find a new fatherland in the south of France. He had not had so much faith in the future for years. But the failure of his collaboration with Gauguin in October to December 1888 and his mental crises in the spring of 1889 undermined his optimism, and memories of the Netherlands

came more sharply to the fore. In July 1889 he mused wistfully: 'Here there are very beautiful fields with olive trees, which are silvery grey in leaf, like pollard willows. Then I never tire of the blue sky. One never sees buckwheat or rape here, and perhaps there is in general less variety than with us. And I should so much like to paint a buckwheat field in flower, or the rape in bloom, or flax. [...] Also here one never sees those moss-covered roofs on the barns or cottages as at home, nor the oak coppices, nor spurrey, nor beech hedges with their reddish brown leaves and white tangled old stems. Nor the real heather, nor the birches which were so beautiful in Nuenen' [787/598]. ✍ The south of France eventually exhausted him completely. Resigned, he said that the pictures he had produced there remained 'just as if they had been painted in Zundert or Kalmthout'; in short, work that could give the viewer the idea that it would have been simpler if he 'had stayed quietly in North Brabant' [828/616]. In May 1890 he headed north again, but never reached Brabant.

As shown by the above passage about his time in the south of France, Van Gogh's experience of nature was governed to a large extent by literature and art (here conceived as a specific form of remembering). The large arsenal of images, motifs and quotations that he had assembled over the years blurred the boundary between the real landscape that he saw and the imaginary landscape that he made of it through free association.[22] ✍ He took to heart what he had told Theo in 1874: 'Painters understand nature and love it, and teach us to see' [17/13].[23] He also listed the painters who did so: the Dutch romantics Barend Cornelis Koekkoek and Andreas Schelfhout, forerunners, masters and followers of the School of Barbizon like Emile Breton, César de Cock, Corot, Daubigny, Decamps, Diaz, Jules Dupré, Huet, Jacque, Rousseau and Troyon, and painters of the Hague School like Jacob Maris, Anton Mauve and Johan Hendrik Weissenbruch. It was a list as extensive as it was heterogeneous, and as the year passed he added the names of the 17th-century Aelbert Cuyp, Van Goyen, Hobbema, Koninck and Jacob van Ruisdael; the Englishman Constable; the French Delacroix and Monticelli; and the impressionists and post-impressionists Cézanne, Monet, Seurat and Signac. ✍ Van Gogh had a great facility for association. He not only had an apt quotation for every personal experience, but also a striking image in his mind's eye from his canon of landscape painters for almost every encounter with nature. To give some examples:

24. **Vincent van Gogh,** *Recollection of Brabant* (F 675 JH 1921), 1890, Amsterdam, Van Gogh Museum (Vincent van Gogh Foundation)

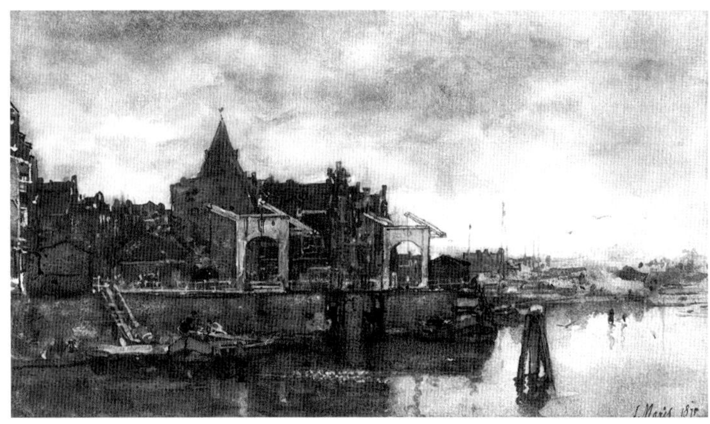

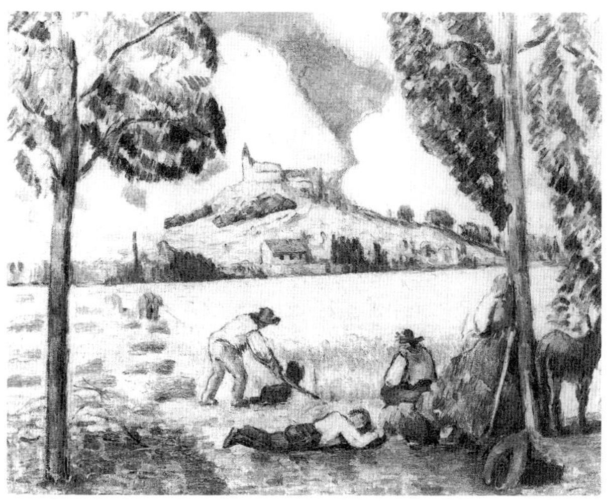

in Dordrecht he saw in the reflection of the setting sun in the
water a golden glow that was reminiscent of a painting by Cuyp
(plate 110);[24] walks in a rainy Amsterdam reminded him of the art
of August Allebé and the brothers Jacob (fig. 25) and Matthijs
Maris, (plate 4), while the evening twilight recalled Georges
Michel (plate 31); near The Hague he saw Corot and Van Goyen
'in an infinity of delicate, soft green, miles and miles of flat meadow, and a grey sky' [251/219]; in Loosduinen he found a spot in the
autumn rain where everything was Ruisdael, Daubigny or Jules
Dupré;[25] one moment Drenthe was more Daubigny (plates 34-35)
for him than Corot, the next it was 'absolutely Michel' [404/339];
and in the south of France, finally, he saw 'the harsh side of
Provence' [627/497] in Cézanne's *Harvest* of c. 1877 (fig. 26), and in
the landscape itself the contrasting range of colours used by
Japanese artists, particularly the printmakers, and by Delacroix
(plates 117, 123-124) and Monticelli (plate 126).[26]

LANDSCAPE AS A GENRE

Van Gogh's appreciation of landscape as a genre was subject to
change. He said that in the years when he worked for the art
dealers Goupil & Cie (1869-76) he was struck more by it than by
figure painting.[27] As a novice artist, however, the latter grew more
in his estimation. In March 1882 he even wrote that he was
'decidedly' not a landscape painter, although that in no way
meant that landscape played no further role for him. He did
believe that the genre was less able to evoke certain emotions in

the viewer than figure painting. And if a landscapist did succeed
in doing so, as Jules Dupré had done in his *Autumn* of c. 1865
(plate 36), he approvingly quoted Jozef Israëls, who had supposedly said of this picture that it was like a figure painting.[28] Van
Gogh's changing opinion about the symbolic and aesthetic potential of landscape and figure painting are typical of the changes
taking place in the systematisation of the arts in his day. Since
time immemorial, landscape had been ranked lower in the hierarchy of genres than the figure. It was felt that figure painting
– especially the depiction of Christian, classical and historical
subjects – was better able to inspire the beholder to uplifting
thoughts about such matters as good, truth and beauty. Landscape painting, with its (allegedly) slavish imitation of nature,
could not generate such loftiness of thought.[29] It could move and
please, true, and make the viewer feel calm and restful, and
those were qualifications that Van Gogh used as well.[30] In the
last quarter of the 19th century, however, the realistic approach
of art argued for a freer choice of subject and vocabulary of form,
and for a more personal and time-specific view of landscape
painters.[31] From then on, in principle, any spot on earth was eligi-
ble for depiction on paper or canvas. A portrayal of nature could
nevertheless evoke an ideal of beauty in the viewer through the
use of selection, ordering and formal vocabulary. In the
Netherlands, that latter view could be found in the writings of an
author like Carel Vosmaer. In Nuenen in 1884, Van Gogh read
Vosmaer's *Eene studie over het schoone en de kunst* of 1856. He

25. **Jacob Maris,** *The Buitenkant with the Schreierstoren,* Amsterdam, 1875,
Amsterdam, Rijksmuseum

26. **Paul Cézanne,** *The harvest,* c. 1877, private collection

found it 'awfully dull' and written in an 'academic, sermonising tone' [455/373]. Johannes van Vloten's *Aesthetica of schoonheids-kunde, in losse hoofdtrekken, naar uit- en in-heemsche bronnen voor Nederlanders geschetst* of 1865, which Van Gogh had read back in the early 1870s, also failed to win his approval.[32] One important element in the book may have appealed to him, in that the author made no distinction in principle between the experience of nature in real life and the experience of nature in art, and accordingly no longer classified landscape as an inferior genre. According to Van Vloten, the receptive viewer could find beauty in it too. [33] ❧ Van Gogh discovered a more individual experience of nature and art in the views of Théophile Thoré, Charles Blanc and Eugène Fromentin, and of Emile Zola, who emphasised in his novels and art criticism that it was the artist's duty to depict nature, or a part of it, as seen through his own temperament.[34] ❧ Thoré and Fromentin argued for a re-evaluation of 17th-century Dutch landscape painting.[35] The influential Thoré, in the words of his Dutch apologist Van Santen Kolff, found that it contained 'a truth of characterisation and scene, sobriety of composition and harmony', a 'spirit of simplicity and truth', and a 'healthy realism'.[36] In Thoré's view, painting could be elevated to a higher plane if the painter was of his own day, free in his choice of subject matter, and if he painted what he saw and above all *felt*. The rest was 'genius', by which Thoré meant the painter's ability to observe and depict nature in a personal and original way.[37] Van Gogh shared this view. In June 1879 he wrote that an artist had to depict nature by giving it 'a significance, a conception, a character' [151/130].

MOOD, SENTIMENT, EFFECT

The emphasis on an artist being of his own time, and on his personality and originality, had important implications. In theory, those characteristics could be recognised by viewers with a discerning eye and sensibility. This led to a reassessment of the landscape genre and a new canon of landscape artists who depicted the spirit of their times and worked with *contemporary* feelings. Van Gogh, with an apparently playful ease, associated Japanese art with that of the ancient Greeks, the Flemish primitives and 17th-century Dutch painters like Rembrandt, Hals, Vermeer, Adriaen van Ostade and Jacob van Ruisdael.[38] ❧ Like

Thoré, Van Gogh found truth and authenticity in his own day in artists of the School of Barbizon, and in the 17th century among the Dutch landscape painters.[39] In Van Goyen's *Landscape with two oaks* of 1641 (plate 111), for example, which he saw in 1885 in the newly opened Rijksmuseum in Amsterdam, he admired not only the monochrome use of colour but especially 'the honesty, the naivety, the truth' [293/251]. According to Van Gogh, the painter gave his own vision of a landscape and did not imitate it literally – 'nature in a mirror' [542/451].[40] ❧ He also praised Jacob van Ruisdael, who was regarded as an important innovator in landscape painting from an early date for canvases that are both monumental and ingeniously composed and detailed.[41] Van Gogh saw an exhibition of five of Ruisdael's works in London in 1875, and from then on the 17th-century master became an important point of reference. Van Gogh was impressed not so much by Ruisdael's 'waterfalls and the grand forest views' as by 'more commonplace things' [527/R50] like *The storm* of c. 1660 (plate 3) and *Dune landscape near Haarlem (Le buisson)* of 1647-50 (fig. 27), *The windmill at Wijk bij Duurstede* of c. 1670, and the *View of Haarlem with bleaching grounds* (plate 30).[42] The *Dune landscape near Haarlem*, in particular, which Van Gogh first admired in the Louvre in 1875, made an indelible impression on him.[43] This painting of a walker out with his dogs, with its unorthodox composition and abundance of chiaroscuro effects and atmospheric mood, expressed for Van Gogh 'that moment and that place in nature to which one can repair alone, without company' [363/299]. ❧ The characteristics of honesty, naivety and truth cited by Van Gogh in his appreciation of Dutch landscape painting apply to the internalisation of the observation and depiction of landscape. One also finds this internalisation in Van Gogh himself, when he wrote in 1881 that he paid as much attention to the personality of the artist as to the work in question.[44] ❧ Associated with this was the idea that a landscape painter could only truly observe nature and then discover and depict its 'truth' if he was a true nature lover himself. In 1882 Van Gogh regarded it as an artist's duty 'to be entirely absorbed by nature and to use all his intelligence to express his sentiment in his work, so that it becomes intelligible to other people' [253/221]. That ideal could only be achieved if the artist lived and worked surrounded by nature, as had been done by the painters of the School of Barbizon, but also by Cézanne, Monticelli and Pissarro. His admiration for Japanese artists, the printmakers in particular, can in part be traced back to this idea.

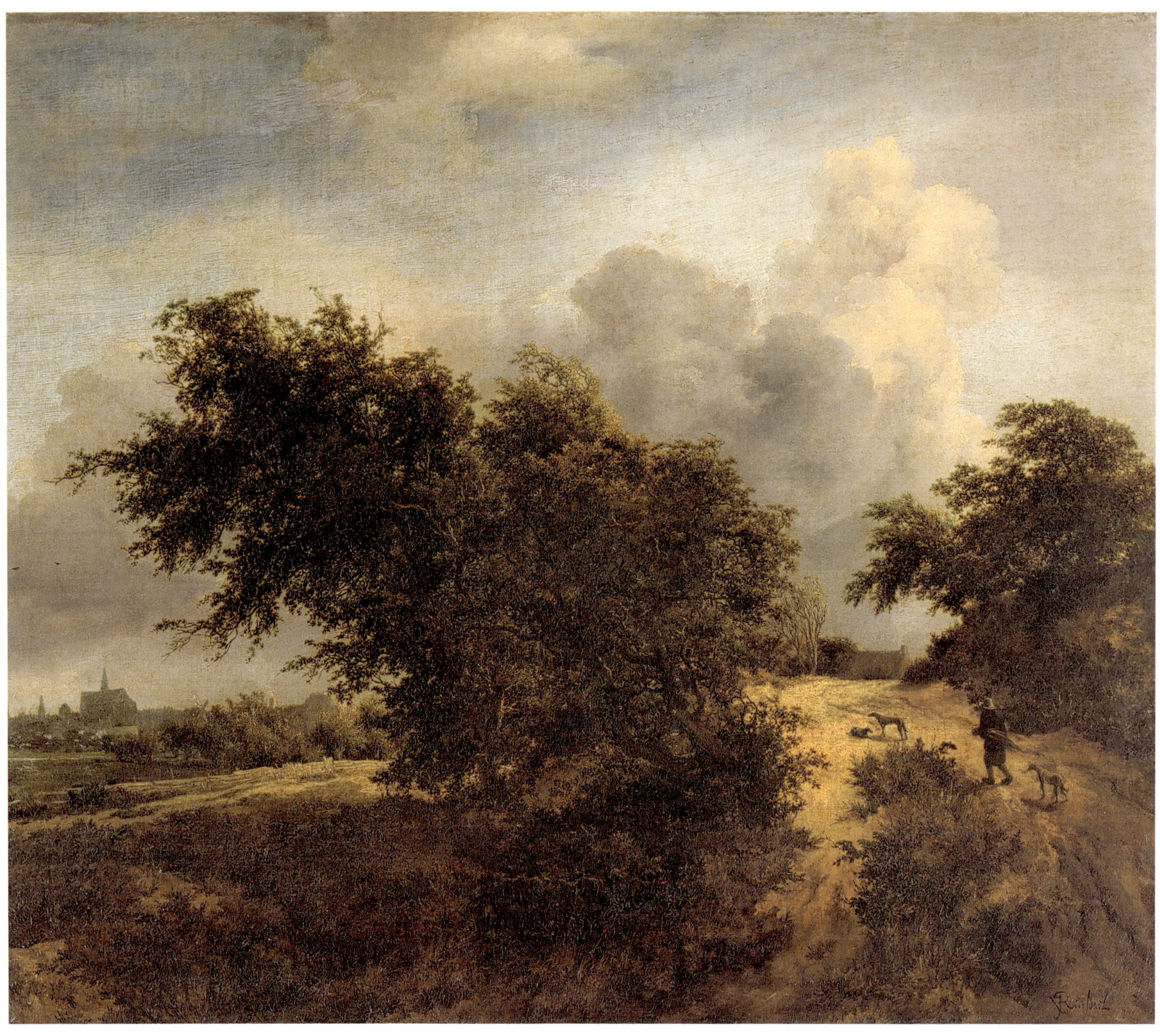

27. Jacob van Ruisdael, *Dune landscape near Haarlem (Le buisson),* 1647-50, Paris, Musée du Louvre

Van Gogh believed that they had lived in perfect harmony with nature, 'as if they were flowers themselves' [690/542].

The freer choice of subjects and the dual observation – of nature and of the artist's innermost feelings – turned the depiction of landscape into a continuous process. The idea of a 'definitive' image of a landscape, that is to say one that is harmonious, belonged to the past. From now on, in a manner of speaking, the depiction of a single blade of grass was sufficient. The very act of painting and the personal signature of the artist became extremely important.[45] The emotion, the artist's sentiment and the chosen subject could be read in that signature – a conviction that had already emerged in Van Gogh's appreciation of Van Goyen and Ruisdael.[46] ✐ The terms 'mood', 'sentiment' and 'effect' recur repeatedly in Van Gogh's discussions of the landscape painters he prized. He was neither stinting nor unique in his use of these terms, for they were part of the standard vocabulary of art and literary criticism in the second half of the 19th century. 'Mood' and 'sentiment' had multiple meanings for Van Gogh, referring to a landscape, a landscape painting or drawing, and to the emotions of a landscape painter.[47] The concept of 'effect' did not have that latter connotation, but was reserved for an atmospheric rendering and to individual motifs in nature.[48] Van Gogh used it mainly for picturesque, landscape (or urban) and pictorial elements: a morning or evening effect, a moorland effect, a seasonal effect, a colour effect. ✐ The proper sentiment enabled a painter to call an effect to life and evoke a specific emotion or feeling – of drama, hope, comfort – in the viewer.[49] When Van Gogh looked out of the window of his room in the Saint-Paul de Mausole hospital in Saint-Rémy in June 1889 and observed the landscape 'long before sunrise, with nothing but the morning star', he was reminded of Daubigny and Rousseau, who had achieved similar effects, 'but expressing all that it has of intimacy, all that vast peace and majesty, but adding as well a sentiment so heartbreaking, so personal. I have no aversion to emotions of that kind' [780/593]. ✐ Nowadays the word 'sentiment' has a rather negative connotation. For Van Gogh, however, it was a very valid concept for distinguishing between good and bad, true and phoney art and artists, and for establishing a hierarchy in the personal feelings of artists. Emile Breton's sentiment was 'far superior to that of many others' [293/251], while Mesdag had not 'felt' enough in his conception of a large marine [257/R11]. In 1882 it also ena-

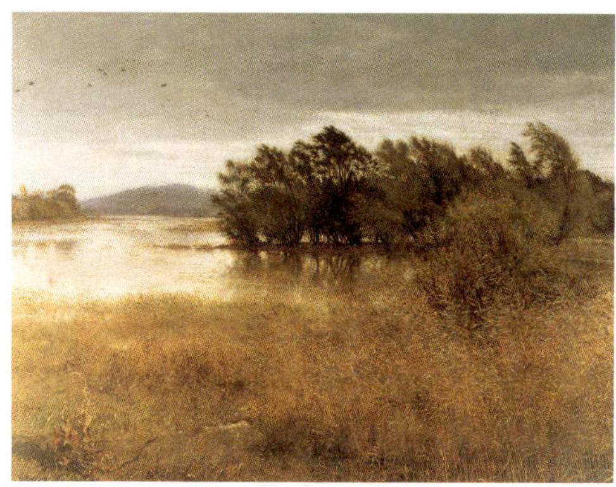

bled Van Gogh to make a distinction between the sentiment of old and contemporary masters. According to him, Rembrandt and Jacob van Ruisdael were 'sublime', but the work of several modern landscapists – among those he singled out was John Everett Millais, with his *Chill October* (fig. 28) – were 'more personally intimate' [250/218]. ✐ Which other artists did he place in that last category? To put it in a nutshell, like Thoré he was charmed above all by painters whom he believed had successfully carried on the tradition of the 17th-century Dutch landscape, and had managed to incorporate that tradition in a new, contemporary, painterly idiom. In the Netherlands it was the painters of the Hague School who met these requirements, more especially Jacob Maris and Anton Mauve.[50] They had 'restored nature' with their painting instead of working in the style and convention of the romantic school, preferring 'sentiment and impression over academic platitudes and dullness' [503/406]. In France he perceived a truthful and personal assimilation of nature in the art of 'Barbizon', which was very popular in the third quarter of the 19th century, examples of which he had seen daily in the galleries of Goupil & Cie. In 1883 he described the history of Barbizon as 'sublime' [404/339]. Five years later he said that he loved making work in the manner of Corot, Decamps, Diaz, Dupré and Jacque (fig. 29), although by then they belonged to the previous generation.[51] ✐ These 'faithful veterans' [257/R11] lived up to almost all his ideals. They had left the city to go and live in the countryside and record nature 'en plein air'. They did not shy away from painting fragments of a landscape as they saw and experienced them, presenting studies as marketable works, applying new compositional schemes, and also showing that they were colourists. Dupré, according to Van Gogh, could express

28. John Everett Millais, *Chill October*, 1870, private collection 'symphonies of colour' and an 'enormous variety of mood' [540/429]. His work was 'simple, and as infinitely deep as nature itself' [453/371].

THE COLOUR OF LANDSCAPE

Van Gogh experienced the shock of the new in Paris in 1886. Back in the Netherlands he had been cut off from the recent developments in French landscape painting, which reached their culmination in the 1870s in the work of the impressionists Monet, Pissarro and Sisley.[52] He had heard something of this new 'school' from Theo, who had been dealing in the impressionists' work since the mid-1880s in the Paris gallery of Boussod, Valadon & Cie, but in 1884-85 he certainly had no clear idea of what they were producing. He did deduce from his brother's reports that the landscapist Monet must be a 'colourist' [529/R57], and that immediately made him sympathetic. Nevertheless, he believed that the impressionists would never attain the level of Corot, Delacroix, Millet and his other cherished masters of Barbizon. For him they were still the axis around which peasant and landscape painters would revolve [499/402]. ✒ On arriving in Paris, he discovered that impressionist painting had now become the norm against which a younger generation of painters was trying to measure itself – no longer, as Van Gogh had done, against the yardstick of Barbizon. That school had become canonised as a praiseworthy part of the French landscape tradition.[53] The modern landscape presented by the impressionists had a quality that Van Gogh had also admired in Barbizon painting, namely an internalised vision of nature. But the painterly idiom and the subjects of the impressionists differed radically from those of their predecessors from the Forest of Fontainebleau. ✒ Up until the mid-1880s, the impressionists preferred subjects in the immediate vicinity of Paris. They combined landscape with motifs like trains, railway bridges and strolling city-dwellers that reflected the social and technological changes of the day. They did so in unprecedentedly bright colours and with a virtuoso, loose brush, suggesting speed in order to express the fleeting landscape and the hectic existence of the late 19th-century bourgeois.[54] Then, in the late 1880s, they sought their subjects further afield, out in the French countryside, which had been opened up by the railways (and had been discovered by tourists), depicting it in an extreme-

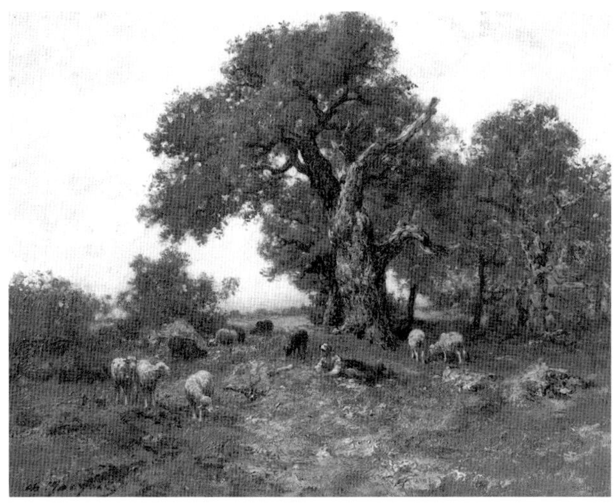

ly colourful and atmospheric way. Monet, in particular, established his reputation with the portrayal of constantly changing weather conditions and light. It was mainly paintings of this kind that Theo sold in his gallery (fig. 30).[55] ✒ Van Gogh admired luminous impressionism, especially the work of Monet (plates 129, 138) and Pissarro (plate 137) for their colour effects, and Renoir for 'that pure, clean line of his' [605/481]. Personally, however, he was looking for something different, in both style and content. Like his colleagues of the 'Petit Boulevard' – Angrand, Anquetin, Bernard, Gauguin, Seurat, Signac and Toulouse-Lautrec – he longed to depict more than just the innate sensation of the landscape with a bright palette and a rapid brushstroke. He found impressionism too subjective, and too tightly focused on visual effects. ✒ One important stimulus for his development as a painter was his discovery in Paris of the *pointillé*, based on the science of optics, which was being developed by Seurat and Signac, whose *La Grande Jatte* and 'broadly stippled landscapes' (plate 133) respectively he described as personal and original in 1888 [673/528]. The paintings of Anquetin (plate 146), Bernard (plate 86) and Gauguin (plates 131, 141) also prompted him to strike out in a new direction. Partly under the influence of Japanese prints, they used a sketchy line and a solid division of surfaces and colour in order to give art a firmer basis and to capture the essence of the chosen subject. ✒ Van Gogh sought his subjects in the city landscape – gardens, parks, Montmartre – and, in its outskirts, he experimented with his own variant of pointillism, simplified his vocabulary of form even further, and 'opened up' his

29. Emile Jacque, *Landscape with sheep,* c. 1870, The Hague, Museum Mesdag

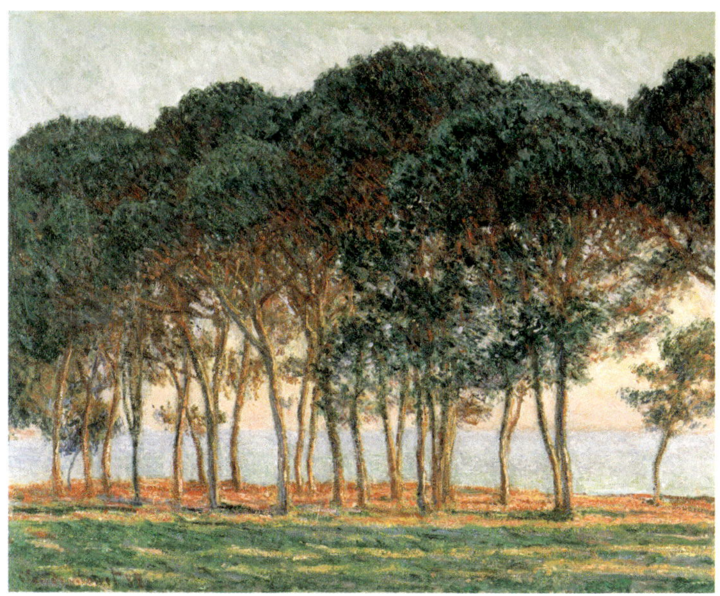

palette (plates 130, 134, 136). The close observation of nature remained a constant, because in his view it was there that a true and real 'character' could be found [692/541]. ✿ After two years of experimentation Van Gogh left for the south of France with the lessons he had learned in Paris in his baggage, his head filled with ideas of what he could expect in the way of colour and subjects. And he certainly found colour. Barely had he arrived in Arles than, in March 1888, he wrote that the region 'struck me as being as beautiful as Japan for the limpidity of the atmosphere and gay colour effects. The water makes patches of a beautiful emerald and a rich blue in the landscape. [...] The pale orange setting sun making the land appear blue. Splendid yellow suns' [590/B2]. Capturing the southern landscape in colour eventually became the task he set himself. ✿ In June 1888 he approvingly quoted a saying of Pissarro's that 'you must boldly exaggerate the effects of either harmony or discord which colours produce' [623/500]. However, he now condemned the impressionists because they merely used colour effects to reproduce what they saw. For his part, he wanted to use colour 'more arbitrarily' in order to express himself 'forcefully' [663/520]. His discussions with Bernard and Gauguin had strengthened him in this view. They pointed out to him the importance of a more schematised vocabulary of form and a resolute use of colour. 'They do not ask the

correct shape of a tree at all, but they do insist that one can say if the shape is round or squared, and honestly, they are right, exasperated as they are by certain people's photographic and empty perfection. They will not ask the correct tone of the mountains, but they will say: By God, the mountains were blue, were they? Then chuck on some blue and don't go telling me that it was a blue rather like this or that, it was blue, wasn't it? Good – make them blue and be done with it' [806/607]. ✿ Colour for Van Gogh in the south of France became an autonomous, symbolically charged means of expression, and at the same time the norm for depicting the essence of the Provençal landscape as he experienced it. According to him, those who had previously succeeded in doing so were above all the colourists Delacroix, Monticelli and Cézanne. ✿ However, Van Gogh did not regard art as a vehicle for the representation of abstract ideas. This is clear, among other things, from his downright rejection in November 1889 of Bernard's *Christ in the Garden of Olives* (fig. 31) and *The road to Calvary* (plate 14), and of Gauguin's *Christ in the Garden of Olives* (fig. 40). Rather than wallow in biblical interpretations of this kind he preferred to paint women picking olives (fig. 81), which the viewer might then perhaps associate with Christ in the Garden of Olives.[56] He remained rooted in the soil and clung to reality. In contrast to his dismissal of Bernard's Christ, he greatly admired the natural and simple subject, the clear shapes and the contrasting, pure colours of his *Red poplars* (fig. 32), which Gauguin had told him about. He found it 'splendid' [824/B21]. ✿ In May 1890 Van Gogh headed back north, to Auvers-sur-Oise, where he intended to devote himself to the 'study of peasants and landscapes from nature' [867/632]. Although his time in the asylum in Saint-Rémy had left him depressed, he parted from the south of France with pain in his heart. His last days there were 'a revelation of colour' [871/633]. On the point of departure he was deeply struck once again by the countryside, which looked 'fresh and full of flowers' after a shower, and he sighed: 'What things I could still have done' [873/634]. ✿ In Auvers he realised that his time in the south had not been wasted after all, and believed that he was now in a better position to see the north.[57] He worked feverishly and intensely, expressing the speed and haste of modern life.[58] As a counterweight to that frantic bustle, he composed his monumental, spacious landscapes with a bright palette, like the *Landscape with a carriage and train in the distance* (fig. 33) and the *Wheat field under thunderclouds* (plate 29). He intended the latter

30. Claude Monet, *Under the pine trees at the end of the day,* 1888, Philadelphia Museum of Art, Gift of Mrs F. Otto Haas

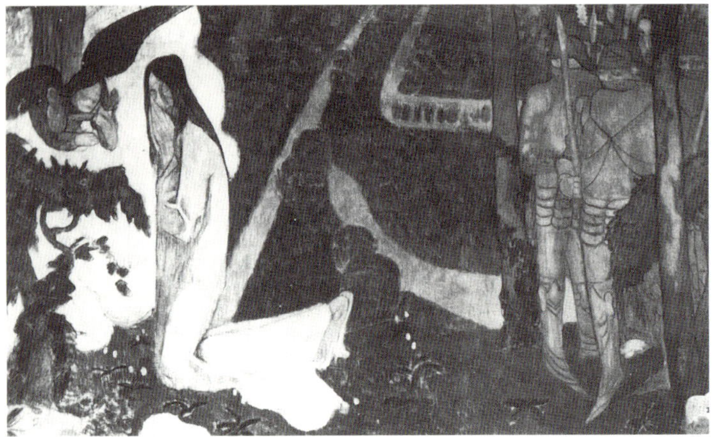

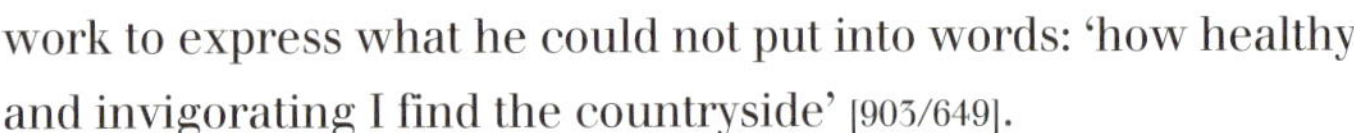

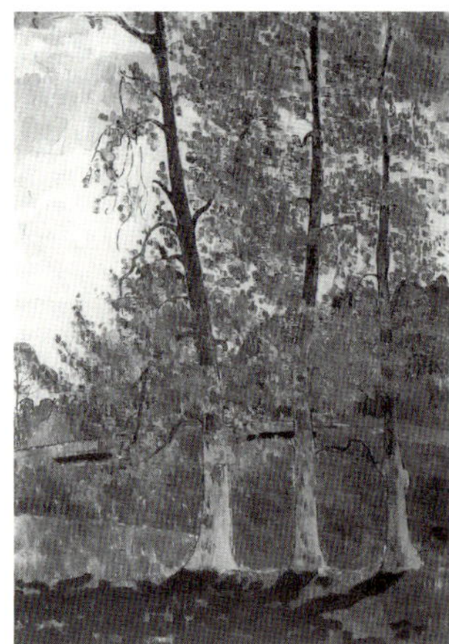

work to express what he could not put into words: 'how healthy
and invigorating I find the countryside' [903/649].

Van Gogh in fact followed an 'evolutionary' curve from a realistic
to a more symbolic conception of art, in which colour was the
supreme means of expression for capturing the essence of landscape. His personal vision of nature, and his depiction of landscape in a vibrant, glowing and contrasting range of colours, has
given him a unique place in the tradition of landscape painting.
In doing so it underscores one of his convictions, which was that
'feeling and love for nature sooner or later always find a response
from people who are interested in art' [253/221].

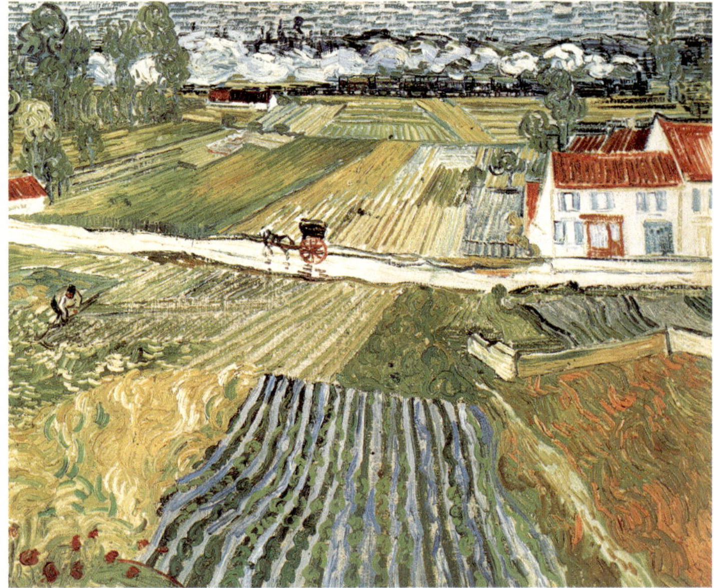

31. **Emile Bernard,** *Christ in the Garden of Olives,* 1889,
present whereabouts unknown

32. **Emile Bernard,** *Red poplars,* 1887, present whereabouts unknown
33. **Vincent van Gogh,** *Landscape with a carriage and train in the distance*
(F 760 JH 2019), 1890, Moscow, Pushkin Museum

VAN GOGH'S TEACHERS

ROELIE ZWIKKER

Van Gogh's eagerness to learn runs like a golden thread through his correspondence. There are numerous passages where he writes that he has to learn, wants to learn more and wants constantly to improve himself. He only started out as an artist at the age of 27 and, unlike most of his contemporaries who had completed a recognised training at an academy or in a studio, he was essentially self-taught. He needed guidance, and set out to find it. He got to know several teachers, some of them personally, but by far the most important for him were his 'paper tutors', with whom he came into contact solely in the pages of books about them or their work (sometimes in the form of reproductions). ❦ Van Gogh speaks so vividly about his great role models – Delacroix, Millet and Rembrandt – that it is almost as if they were physically present. Such a relationship between the autodidact and his teachers was once summarised as follows: 'The autodidact, too, has his teachers. However, he has never met them; he has created their form and voice from the best that they, in his belief, left behind: their work, and probably above all from the apparent effortlessness of it, from the style and the erudition it contains.'[1] In contrast to a few teachers from whom he did actually take lessons, like Eugène Siberdt and Fernand Cormon, he remained true to some of those teachers at a distance his whole life long. ❦ Although Van Gogh's friendships with fellow artists did contribute to his development, only the intense relationship with Paul Gauguin will be touched on in passing. My central theme is the artists with whom Van Gogh had a pupil-master relationship. With what kinds of teacher did he come into contact, and in what way were they important for his work and life?

IN SEARCH OF TEACHERS

From the moment, sometime around the summer of 1880, when Van Gogh decided to become an artist, he desperately wanted to live in an artistic milieu. He knew that it was essential for his development to see artists at work and 'to have good things to look at', so that he could see his own shortcomings and remedy them [158/137]. He was looking for people and models who would teach him something and help him achieve his goal, for 'how can one learn to draw unless someone shows one how,' he sighed on 1 November 1880. 'With the best will in the world, one cannot succeed without coming into contact with artists who are more advanced. Good intentions alone are not sufficient without some opportunity for development' [159/138]. ❦ His dearest wish was to work in an artist's studio. At first he did not want to have anything to do with an academy, for he believed that there was no empathy in people who followed that kind of training, which had the reputation of being old-fashioned. The main reason why he nevertheless enrolled at the academy (October 1880-April 1881) during his stay in Brussels was probably because he had been advised to do so by the landscape painter Willem Roelofs, whom he greatly respected. However, he took the step rather reluctantly, and it is not known whether he ever actually attended the classes.[2] He does, though, mention that he was taking drawing lessons from a painter.[3] ❦ In practice, then, Van Gogh studied largely on his own, using manuals by Armand Cassagne, Charles Bargue and others.[4] At the same time he tried, using Theo and his contacts in the art world, to get in touch with people who could have a lot to teach him.[5] In doing so, it seems that he was open to anyone who crossed his path. In a letter to Theo he said that one could learn a great deal indirectly 'even from relatively bad artists', specifically mentioning Wouter Verschuur Sr – an artist with little to recommend him, in Van Gogh's

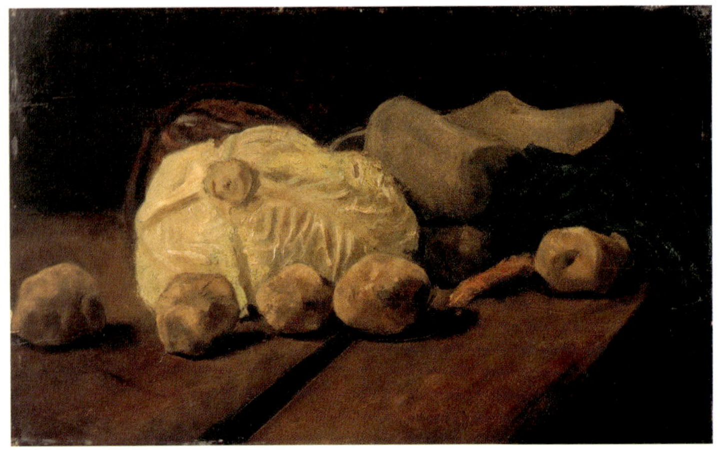

opinion, but who had given lessons in perspective to Anton Mauve, one of the most famous modern landscape painters of his day.[6]

ANTON MAUVE

Not long after committing that thought to paper, Van Gogh, to his great delight, became a pupil of Mauve, a cousin by marriage, whom he admired above all the other painters of the Hague School as 'a great interpreter of the delicate, grey Dutch nature' [750/-].[7] According to him, Mauve had the ability to add 'a significance, a conception, a character' to a realist subject, with the result that a painting by him 'says more, and says it more clearly, than nature herself' [151/130]. Van Gogh saw that, for instance, in Mauve's *Fishing boat on the beach* (plate 68). He was particularly impressed by the resignation with which 'those poor, broken-down old nags' [210/181] accepted their fate and did their work with no other prospect than of being packed off shortly to the knacker's yard. ⚜ When Van Gogh visited Mauve in his Hague studio, probably in August 1881, he was given some bits of advice. Then, at the end of the year, he spent a little over three weeks taking drawing and painting lessons from him.[8] It must have been encouraging for the inquiring and ambitious Van Gogh, who up until then had mainly been practising his drawing, that Mauve immediately allowed him to paint still lifes in oils so that he could get a feeling for colour and handling the brush (fig. 34). Van Gogh was so enthusiastic about this teaching method

that he recommended the painting of still lifes when giving lessons to some amateurs a few years later.[9] ⚜ In addition to allowing Van Gogh to gain experience with oil paint, Mauve taught him about the watercolour technique, introduced him to colleagues who were members of the Pulchri Studio artists' society, and also gave him a lesson in perseverance. As an experienced teacher, he showed his pupil that at first he would make mistakes in his drawings before he had mastered the proper working method. Van Gogh resolved to work with as much 'composure' as he could muster, and not to be disheartened by his mistakes.[10] ⚜ In his correspondence Van Gogh mainly wrote about Mauve's work with admiration and love.[11] He trusted his mentor and valued his opinions highly, but he was also open to other influences. He had no intention of following Mauve blindly.[12] Although their relationship came to an abrupt end in early 1882 as a result of personal and artistic differences, he always spoke about 'the excellent Mauve' with great respect [854/626a]. He was very upset when his teacher died unexpectedly on 8 February 1888, and to commemorate him he painted *Pink peach trees, 'Souvenir de Mauve'* (fig. 35) for Mauve's widow.[13] ⚜ Van Gogh worked hard on his figure studies while he was in The Hague, and drew inspiration from English and French wood engravings, which he admired both for their social commentary and their technique. He experimented with black-and-white effects in his own drawings and lithographs in imitation of those prints.[14] ⚜ From the autumn of 1883 to the end of 1885 he worked successively in Drenthe and Nuenen, where he recorded the rustic surroundings and worked intensively from live models, as Mauve had advised him to do. He immersed himself in his studies with the aid of books but without the inspirational, personal supervision of a more experienced artist. He did not always find that easy, as he wrote in June 1884. He needed 'to talk to people occasionally who *know* how to give advice, and from whom one *learns* and gets *light* – without them playing the schoolmaster' [452/370]. ⚜ Van Gogh knew that he still had a lot to learn, but he was gaining confidence in his own abilities as a result of his intensive self-tuition, in the course of which he learned about the theories of Eugène Delacroix (particularly as regards colour), the importance of which will be discussed below. And although he was perhaps forced to rely on himself, it seems that he preferred to work alone than to make do with a dominating teacher whom he did not like. After a while he be-

34. Vincent van Gogh, *Still life with cabbage and clogs* (F 1 JH 81), 1881, Amsterdam, Van Gogh Museum (Vincent van Gogh Foundation)

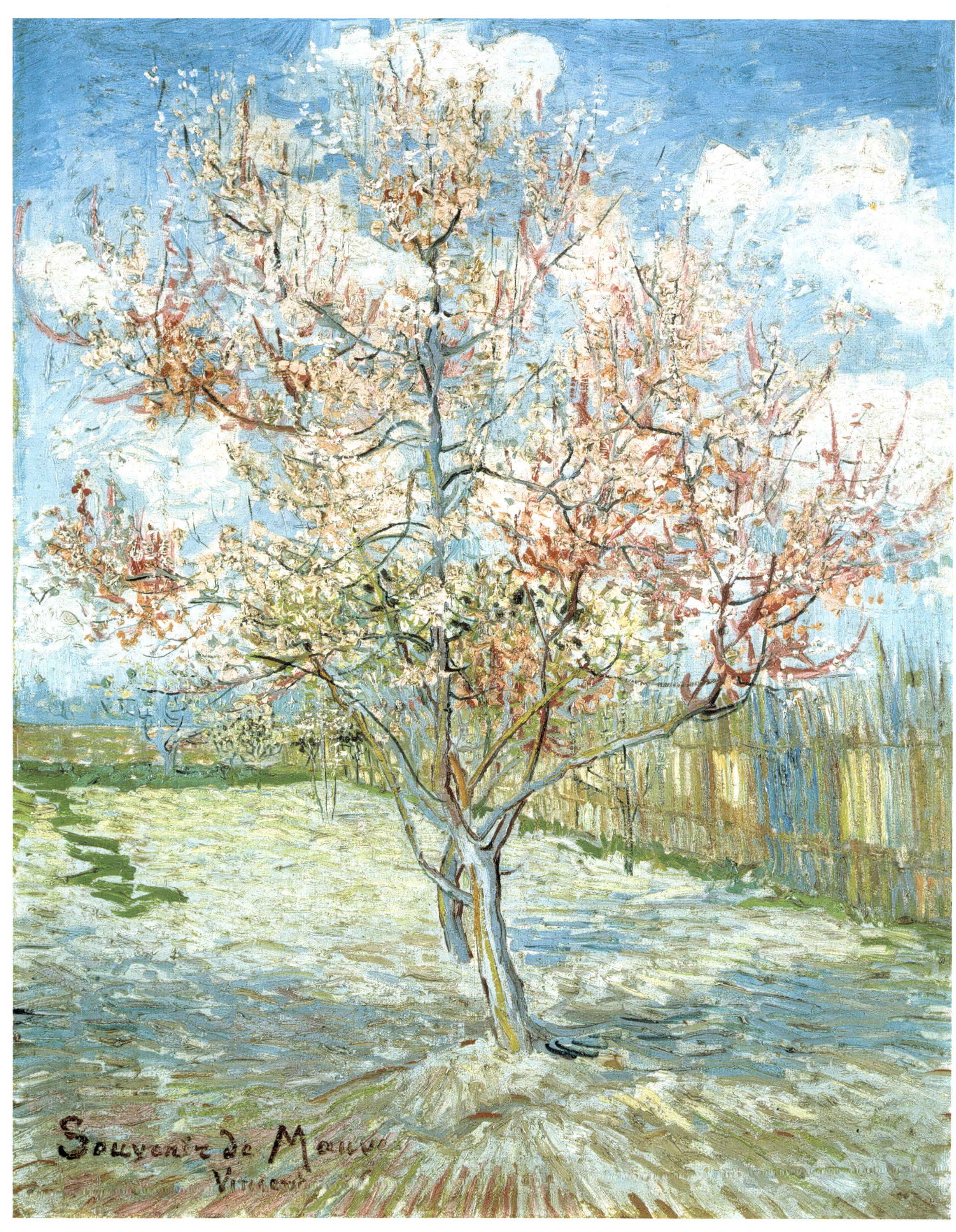

35. Vincent van Gogh, *Pink peach trees, 'Souvenir de Mauve'*
(F 394 JH 1379), 1888, Otterlo, Kröller-Müller Museum

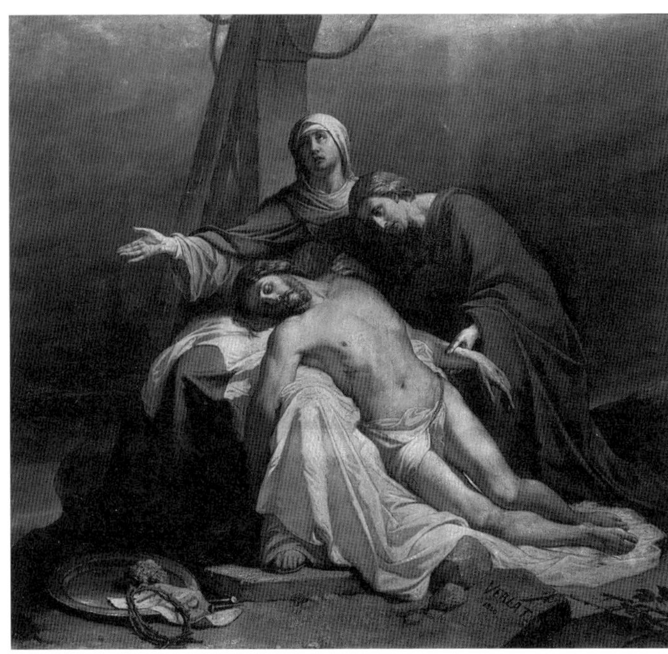

came increasingly convinced that he had his own way of working, and that he had to preserve his own originality, no matter how.*15*

ACADEMIC TRAINING

The encouragement of originality did not appear to be the credo of the Royal Academy of Fine Arts in Antwerp, at which Van Gogh enrolled in January 1886. Given his scathing criticism of the academic system, in which, he said, originality was hard to find, this seems an odd step to have taken. Van Gogh, however, was looking at the practical side. After studying peasant life in Nuenen he realised that he still had much to learn about figure studies, and the quickest way to do so just happened to be the academy. There he could study the human body and its proportions at length, using plaster casts of classical sculpture. Another reason for joining was the opportunity it gave him to meet other artists who worked in different ways. He also felt that the experience would stand him in good stead if he wanted to carry on with his studies in Paris.*16* ✍ Once he got started, he was enthusiastic about making studies after classical models. He spoke with his fellow students about his drawings, and found

the 'friction of ideas' he was looking for [558/447]. This enabled him to take a fresh look at his own work, note his weak points, and try to overcome them. That being said, he was pretty dismissive about the work of his teachers Karel Verlat (fig. 36) and François Vinck. Their 'fault' was 'in the colour, which [...] isn't right' [558/447].*17* ✍ The relationship between teacher and student at the academy was very much a one-way street. The teacher passed on his knowledge, and there was little room for discussion. This method did not remotely resemble the approach of the English graphic artist Hubert von Herkomer, which Van Gogh so admired. He had read how Herkomer, when he opened his own school for artists who had already mastered technique, politely asked his students not to paint as he did but 'in their own way'. Van Gogh greatly admired Herkomer's aim 'to set original spirits free, not to recruit disciples for Herkomer's *doctrine*' [440/R43].*18* ✍ By contrast, according to Van Gogh, the best student was the obedient one who did exactly what he was told, which was to place the emphasis of a drawing on the outlines instead of on form and colour. This produced results that Van Gogh loathed, for all the studies looked the same, no matter who had made them. In general the drawings were 'flat', 'lifeless' and 'insipid' [563/452], the figures were 'top-heavy' [558/447] – in short: 'hopelessly bad – and absolutely wrong' [556/445]. He saw that his own studies were totally different; 'time must tell who is right,' he wrote in January 1886 [556/445]. ✍ The way of drawing propagated by the academy was at complete loggerheads with Delacroix's method, which Van Gogh had learned about when reading Jean Gigoux's *Causeries sur les artistes de mon temps* (1885). That approach was based on the idea that the main mass of a body had to be depicted first, before the outlines were drawn, and it was this method that Van Gogh invariably used, much to the frustration of his teacher Eugène Siberdt (fig. 37). ✍ Knowing that it would be futile to argue the point, Van Gogh decided to go his own way and 'play the innocent, as if one would really like to be rid of this bad habit, but unfortunately one falls back into it all the time' [558/447]. He was not bothered by his deteriorating relationship with Siberdt and, although he liked to be corrected by a teacher in principle, he believed that he was capable of continuing to study classical models on his own. All in all, he was pleased with his Antwerp experience. At the end of February 1886 he left for Paris.

36. Karel Verlat, *The descent from the Cross,* Antwerp, Sint-Andrieskerk

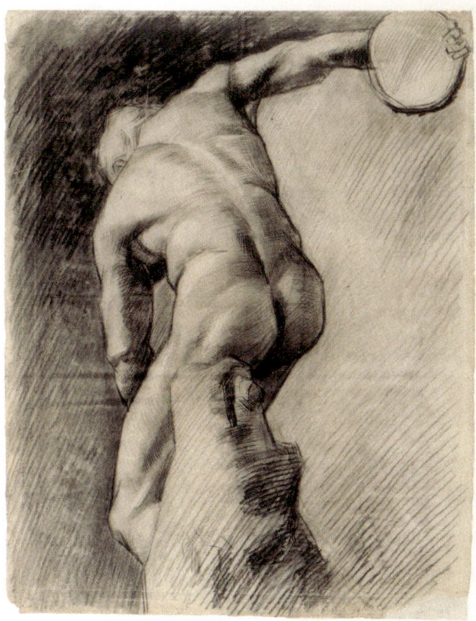

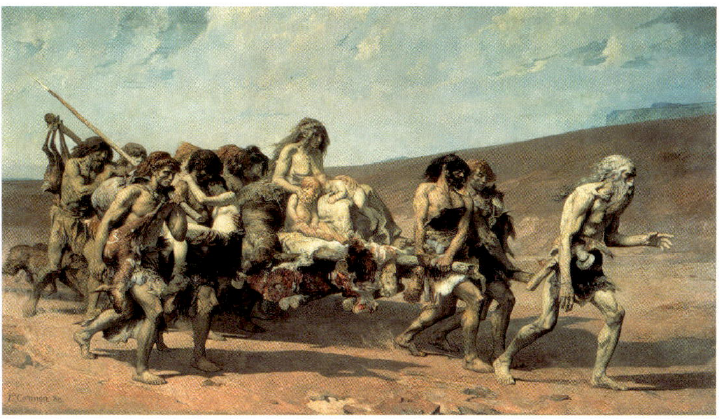

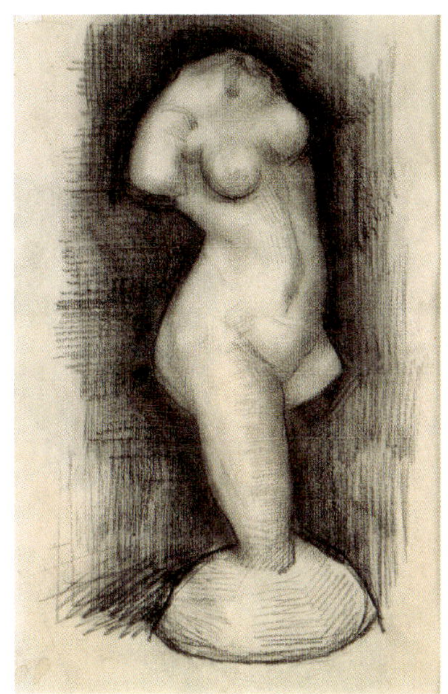

PARIS

In Paris (1886-88) Van Gogh enrolled in the studio of the history
painter Fernand Cormon, resolved as he was to immerse himself
in a study of the human figure. It was here that he got to known
the avant-garde artists Henri de Toulouse-Lautrec and Emile
Bernard. Cormon used a classical teaching method, and his goal
was to see his pupils represented at the annual Salon. He himself
was a celebrated exhibitor there each year, but one really wonders
whether Van Gogh was much taken with a work so decidedly un-
modern as *Cain* (fig. 38), which his teacher had exhibited in 1880.
Cormon encouraged his pupils to work outside the studio as
well, submitting their results later for correction.[19] The lessons in
drawing probably did not differ very much from those given at the
Antwerp academy, and once again Van Gogh took the opportunity
to continue his study of the proper contour. In addition to drawing
and painting from classical models, he was now also given the
chance to work from the nude. It seems that he had greater
opportunities in Cormon's studio to follow his own artistic ideas,
which chiefly concerned the use of colour, than he had had in
Antwerp.[20] However, Cormon's academically inclined teaching
also failed to satisfy him. He abandoned his studies after about
three months and went his own way once again.[21] He continued
his study of classical models from his own plaster casts, but now

in a freer manner than he had used at Cormon's (fig. 39). In addition, he worked a great deal out of doors. After his experiences
with Cormon he never again took a lesson in a studio or an
academy.

THE SOUTH

Van Gogh's eagerness to learn remained unabated after he departed for Arles in the south of France in February 1888. It was
there, eight months later, that the remarkable and by now famous collaboration with Paul Gauguin was to start – an artistic

37. Vincent van Gogh, *The discus thrower* (F 1364e JH 1080), 1886,
Amsterdam, Van Gogh Museum (Vincent van Gogh Foundation)

38. Fernand Cormon, *Cain,* 1880, Paris, Musée d'Orsay
39. Vincent van Gogh, *Torso of Venus* (F 1363cr JH 1070), 1887,
Amsterdam, Van Gogh Museum (Vincent van Gogh Foundation)

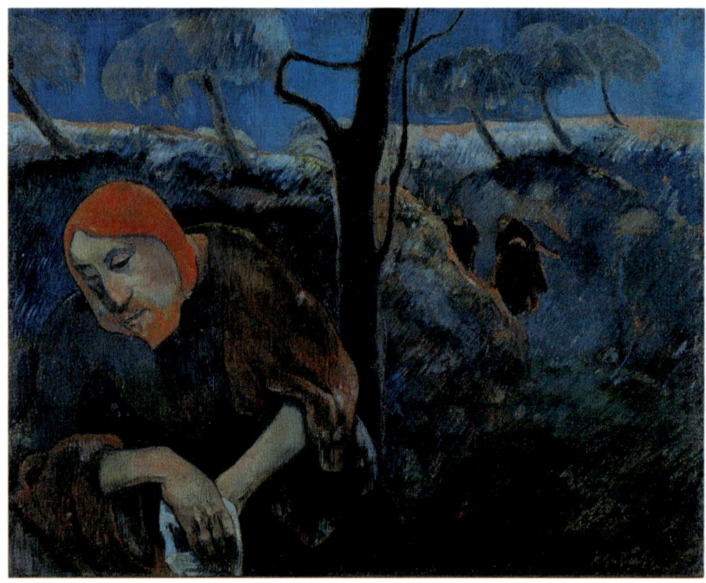

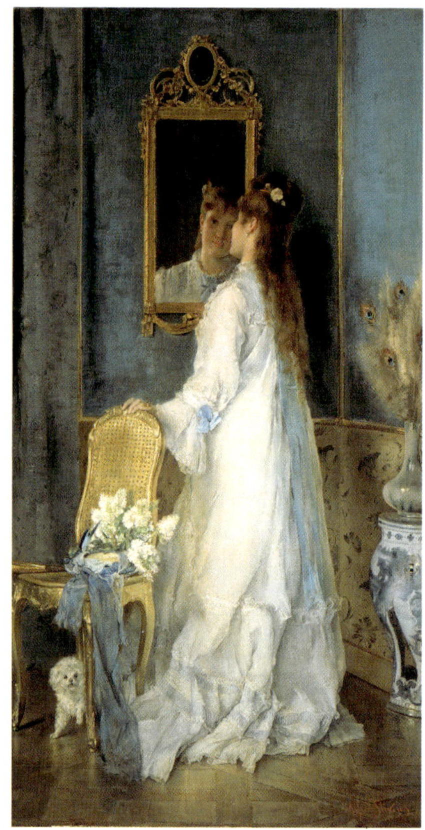

exchange of views which, more than any teacher-pupil relationship, was to be of decisive importance in his search for a style all his own. Van Gogh had an almost boundless admiration for his friend, and called his paintings of black women 'high poetry' [614/B5] (plate 141).[22] Gauguin encouraged and inspired him to experiment, and he in turn underwent Van Gogh's influence. Their different basic principles, with Gauguin believing that an artist should work from his imagination while Van Gogh wanted to work from nature or the model, sometimes led to heated discussions. Van Gogh did not approve of a work like *Christ in the Garden of Olives* (fig. 40), in which nothing was based on the observation of reality.[23] He eventually arrived at a synthesis of Gauguin's love of mysticism and abstraction and his own desire to be faithful to reality by continuing to look for his subjects in nature, while developing an original style characterised by large areas of colour, stronger contours and intense colours. Despite turning further and further away from Gauguin's artistic ideas after their dramatic break at the end of December 1888, he still respected him very much indeed.[24]

TEACHERS AT A DISTANCE

Van Gogh got to know several important teachers by looking at their art, collecting reproductions of their work, and reading a

great deal. Their importance to him was not so much for his technique, which he had honed by studying on his own and at the academy and Cormon's studio, as for his view of art – his artistic ideals. They gave him direction, and his admiration for them knew few bounds. ⚘ What was he looking for in these teachers? To start with he felt most attracted to those artists who worked with love and passion or, as he put it, with 'the soul' [440/R43]. He felt that a good technique alone was not enough. Moreover, his appreciation did not depend on the fame of the artist or of the movement he represented.[25] Although he made no secret of the fact that what he loved most were works illustrating life on the land, a fashionable woman by Alfred Stevens (fig. 41), according to him, could in theory be just as beautiful as a peasant by Léon Lhermitte (fig. 42, plates 151-52): 'If there is life and feeling in it, then it is good' [503/406]. As far as his own work was concerned, Van Gogh also found that expression, life, was more important than correct anatomy or perspective. Since he believed that in years gone by there was more passion, both in making and

40. **Paul Gauguin,** *Christ in the Garden of Olives,* 1889, West Palm Beach, Norton Museum of Art, Gift of Elizabeth C. Norton

41. **Alfred Stevens,** *A girl in front of a mirror,* Amsterdam, Netherlands Institute for Cultural Heritage (on loan to the Van Gogh Museum, Amsterdam)

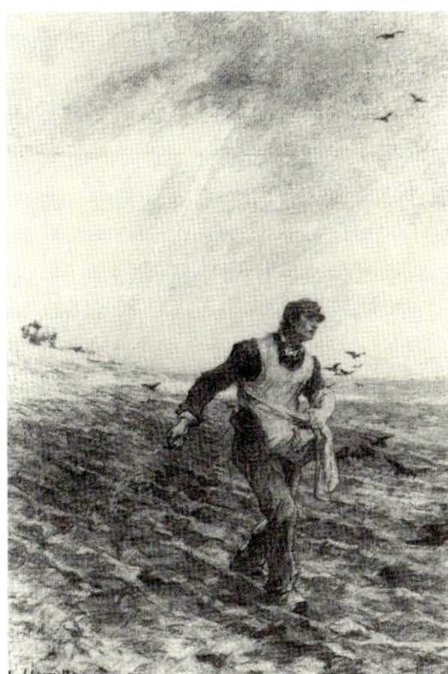

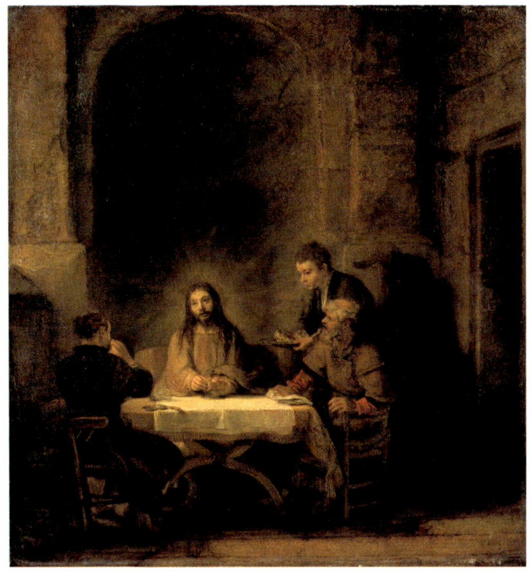

assessing work, it is only natural he was most attracted to teachers from earlier generations.[26] He looked for and found inspirational models in several art movements, some better known than
others, ranging from 17th-century Dutch painting to the School of
Barbizon, and by extension from that the Hague School, as well
as in the illustrations he collected of working-class types taken
from magazines like *The Graphic*. Those prints formed a kind of
Bible for him, one which every artist, he believed, should have in
his studio.[27] ❦ What those favourites had in common was the
importance they attached to realism.[28] He made it clear to Theo
in December 1883 how much that generation of 19th-century
artists meant to him: 'You see, dear brother – I feel a deep, deep,
deep respect for Millet, Corot, Daubigny, Breton, Herkomer,
Boughton, Jules Dupré &c. &c., Israëls, in short, the painters.
I am far from confusing myself with them – I do not consider
myself their equal – no – but yet say, even if people find it priggish
of me, or whatever else – yet I say: you will show me the way, and
I pay more heed to your example than to that of Father, a schoolmaster or anyone else' [347a, enclosed with 416/347]. Even his discovery of impressionism in Paris did not make him forget his 19th-
century predecessors. Quite the reverse, he wrote in August 1888:
he wanted 'to make things which the *previous* generation,
Delacroix, Millet, Rousseau, Diaz, Monticelli, Isabey, Decamps,
Dupré, Jongkind, Ziem, Israëls, Meunier, a lot of others, Corot,
Jacque... could understand' [661/519]. As he said, 'I hardly think
that impressionism will ever do more than, say, the romantics'
[780/593]. ❦ Of all the people who had some kind of influence on
Van Gogh's artistic development, there were three who played

a pivotal role: Rembrandt van Rijn, Eugène Delacroix and Jean-
François Millet – artists after whom he also made copies (plates
74, 125, 46, 49, 51, 52, 54). Other models whom he considered
important were either related to these idols or were associated
with them in some way by Van Gogh himself. For example, he
found a similar honesty in the work of Lhermitte, Honoré Daumier and the 'minor master' Jean-François Raffaëlli. It was alive,
even if it was perhaps not entirely correct in the eyes of the aca-
demics.[29]

REMBRANDT

Van Gogh had got to know Rembrandt's work well in the 1870s.
In February 1875 he saw *The lamentation of Christ* (c. 1650), now
attributed to the Rembrandt workshop, at the Royal Academy in
London (plate 69), and found it full of 'sentiment' [29/22]. Three
months later he visited the Louvre, where he saw *The pilgrims at
Emmaus* of 1648 (fig. 43), and the two pendant paintings of *A scholar in a room with a winding staircase* (1632 and c. 1640-45, neither of which is now attributed to Rembrandt). Finally, in the Trippenhuis in Amsterdam, which in those days housed the nucleus of
what would later become the Rijksmuseum, he admired *The syndics of the drapers' guild* (1662), which he considered to be 'the
most beautiful Rembrandt' [537/426], *The night watch* (1642) and

---

42. After **Léon Lhermitte,** *Rural labours. November: the sower,* 1886,
Amsterdam, Van Gogh Museum (Vincent van Gogh Foundation)

43. Rembrandt van Rijn, *The pilgrims at Emmaus,* 1648, Paris,
Musée du Louvre

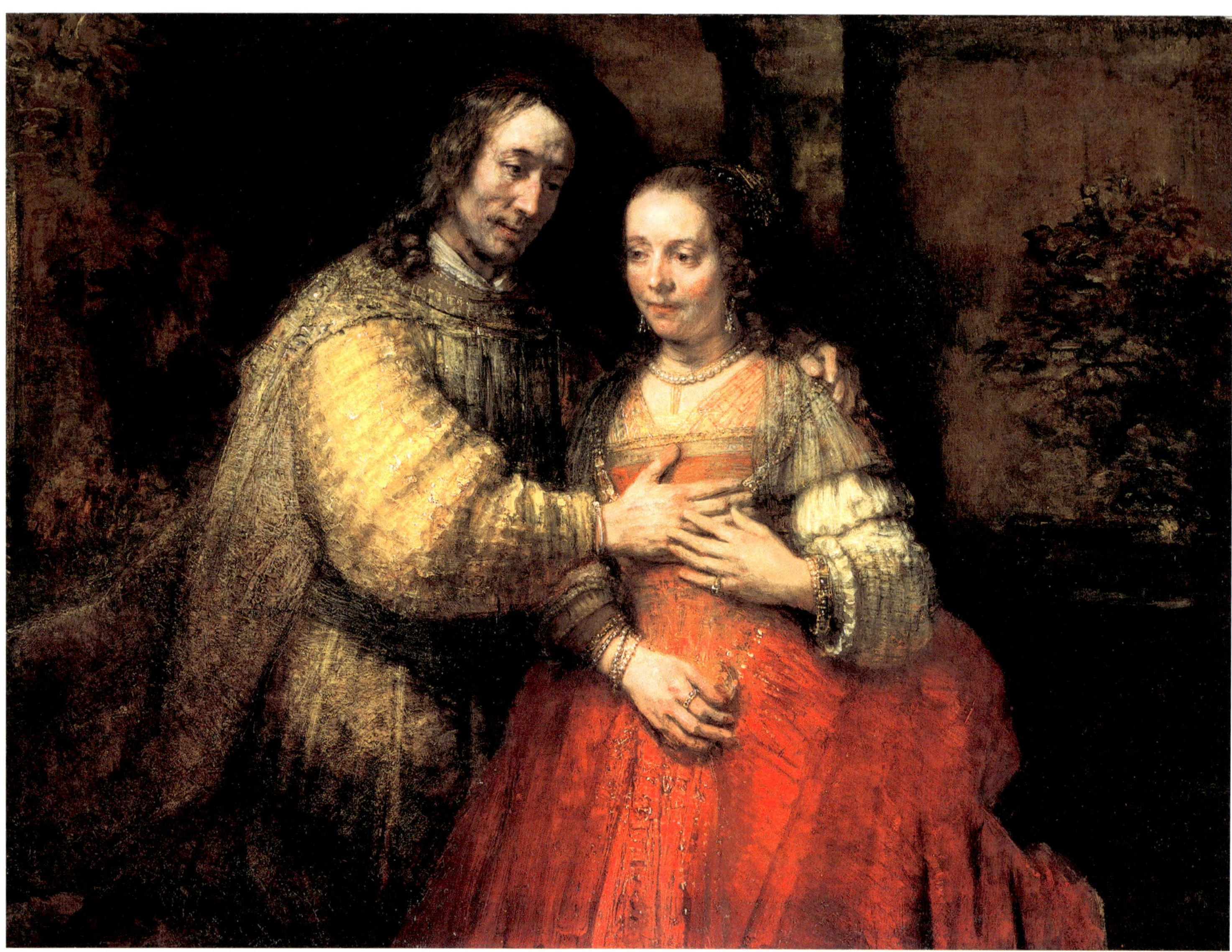

The Jewish bride (c. 1666) (fig. 44), which he called 'an intimate, [...] infinitely sympathetic painting'. According to him, Rembrandt demonstrated with this portrait that he was a true 'poet, that is to say Creator', 'what a noble sentiment, infinitely deep' [537/426]. 🌿 Rembrandt, that 'magician of magicians' [553/442], played a prominent part in Van Gogh's artistic development. 'I am thinking more about Rembrandt than might appear from my studies' [727/558a], he wrote at the end of November 1888, and it is indeed true that at first sight there seems to be no direct connection between the work of the two artists. From a technical point of view, Van Gogh was extremely attracted to the way in which Rembrandt, like other 17th-century artists, succeeded in capturing the essence of a subject. Colour and form were one, details served the overall effect, and a rapid working method breathed life into the painting. 'What especially struck me on seeing the old Dutch paintings again is that most of them were *painted quickly*,' he wrote in 1885. 'That these great masters like a Hals, a Rembrandt, a Ruisdael – so many others – set a thing down with the first stroke and did not return to it so very much. And – this too, if you please – *that if it was right they left it as it was*. I have especially admired the hands

44. **Rembrandt van Rijn,** *The Jewish bride,* c. 1666, Amsterdam, Rijksmuseum

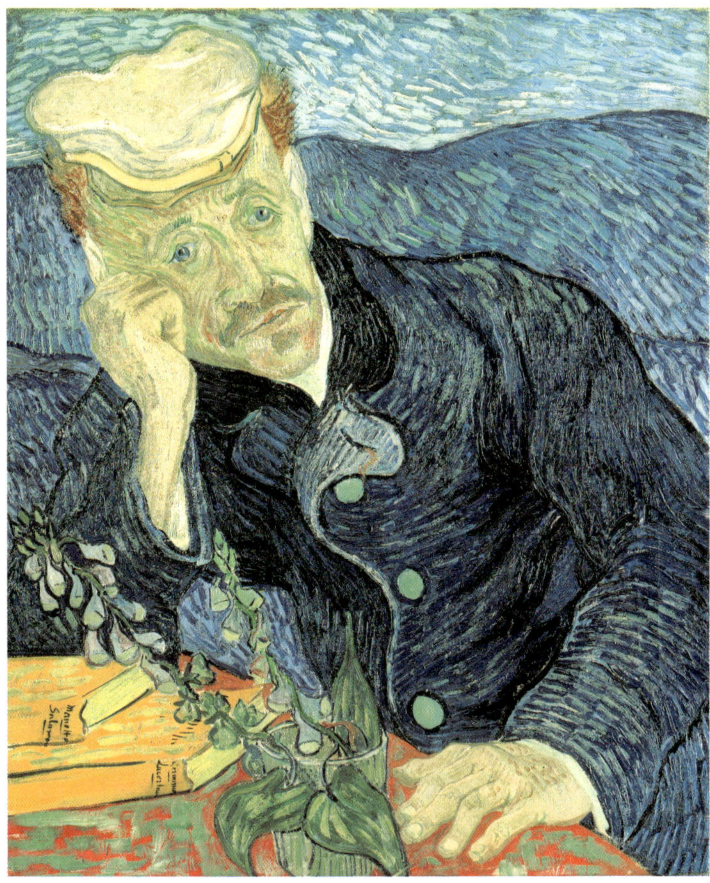

bution to its development. Rembrandt, whom he also described as the 'great and universal, master portrait painter of the Dutch Republic' [653/B13], acted as his guide. Just as the Barbizon painter Théodore Rousseau added something personal to his landscapes, so Rembrandt's portraits were, to Van Gogh, 'more than nature, something of a revelation' [363/299]. His great role model had succeeded in giving everyday reality a deeper significance, mixing observation of reality with imagination. Moreover, the viewer could recognise himself or herself in the figures, even though they had been painted hundreds of years ago. ❧ Van Gogh set himself a similar goal. He wanted to take nature as his point of departure, but add something distinctive to it. In a portrait, according to him, one should be able to see the thoughts, the 'soul', of the sitter [677/531]. He wanted 'to paint portraits which would appear after a century to people living then as apparitions'. 'By which I mean that I do not endeavour to achieve this by a photographic resemblance, but by means of our impassioned expressions, that is to say, using our knowledge of and modern taste for colour as a means of arriving at the expression and the intensification of the character' [883/W22]. In 1890 he painted the *Portrait of Doctor Gachet* (fig. 45), in which he set out to capture the passion and expressiveness that he considered to be the hallmarks of his own day. Although there was a contrast with the calm portraits of previous centuries, Van Gogh believed that certain human qualities remain the same for centuries.[30]

by Rembrandt and Hals – hands that lived, but *were not finished* in the sense they demand nowadays. Certain hands, even in *The syndics*, in the *Jewish bride*, in Frans Hals. And heads too – eyes, nose, mouth done with the first brushstrokes, without any retouching whatever' [538/427]. Van Gogh found it a pleasure to see precisely these works, in contrast to the many paintings 'in which everything has been carefully smoothed down in the same way' [538/427]. ❧ In a way that was similar to Rembrandt's working method, he himself sought to 'exaggerate the essential and purposely leave the incidentals vague' [615/490]. In addition, there was never any idealisation of the subject. Van Gogh was impressed by the way Rembrandt depicted himself so directly and with so much simplicity, 'old, toothless, wrinkled' [651/B12] (plate 72). Van Gogh painted his own *Self-portrait as an artist* (plate 73) in the same spirit as that of his idol. ❧ Portraiture was the genre that fascinated Van Gogh the most. According to him it had an important part to play in modern art, and he intended to make a serious contri-

EUGÈNE DELACROIX

Van Gogh often mentioned Rembrandt in the same breath as Eugène Delacroix, and he was not alone in doing so, for both were popular artists in the second half of the 19th century, and a great deal was written about them. They closely matched the prevailing image, coloured largely by romanticism, of the painter as a genius who followed his own ideas instead of those of the academy. And it was for that stance that they were revered by the avant-garde. ❧ One of the things that drew Van Gogh to Delacroix was that, like Rembrandt, his work was founded on reality, and that at the same time he had the talent to make an everyday subject expressive.[31] Van Gogh himself tried to achieve this effect in Nuenen by talking to his peasant models while painting them, so as to 'keep their faces animated' [550/439]. Delacroix's belief that

45. Vincent van Gogh, *Portrait of Doctor Gachet* (F 753 JH 2007), 1890, private collection naturalistic figures were more important than academically cor-rect drawing was a great support to Van Gogh when his mistakes in drawing were pointed out to him. ❧ He had known Dela-croix's work since his days in Paris in the 1870s. His enthusiasm for the master's technique was fanned even further in 1885, when he was working alone in Nuenen, by what he read about him in various books, among them Charles Blanc's *Les artistes de mon temps* of 1876 and the book by Gigoux mentioned above. He followed Delacroix's example by constructing his figures from large forms reproducing the main mass of the body, and only then drawing the contours. He used this method in order to de-pict his figures with 'great *expression* [...] In short: life' [505/408]. As shown by his peasant figures from the summer of 1885, this method fitted in very well with his expressive style of drawing. It is not surprising, then, that he embraced Delacroix's approach wholeheartedly at the beginning of 1886, when his teacher at the Antwerp academy tried to convince him of the correctness of a method that was the very opposite. Delacroix, who was dismis-sive of the academic routine, but who always considered drawing after classical models important, had according to Van Gogh cor-rectly understood how that study should be interpreted.[32] Even when he started giving more prominence to the contours in his later work, he emphasised the importance of giving things mass 'by means of a drawing style which tries to express the interlock-ing of the masses', as in Delacroix's *Jacob wrestling with the an-gel* [818/613] (plate 123).[33] ❧ Although Delacroix's theories about drawing were an important guide for Van Gogh, his colour theo-ry, in which complementary colour contrasts played an important part, made the greatest impression on him. The basic principle was that 'the MOOD *of the colours and the tone [be] at one with the meaning*' [533/R58]. Because at first he had no chance of seeing the master's paintings, Van Gogh found it difficult to form a prop-er idea of what this meant. It was only in Paris in 1886-88 that he saw Delacroix's work again, and could finally discover whether he had understood his theories correctly. For instance, in 1886 he and Theo saw *Christ asleep during the tempest* (plate 124), which he described in 1888 as 'an inspired sketch': 'Oh, what a beautiful painting that is by Eug. Delacroix, Christ in the boat on the Sea of Gennesaret! He – with his pale lemon-yellow aureole, sleeping, luminous in the dramatic violet, dark-blue, blood-red patch of the group of bewildered disciples – on that terrible emerald-green sea, rising, rising, right to the top of the frame' [635/B8].

❧ An analysis of the way the impressionists and Delacroix used colour was decided in the latter's favour. Van Gogh was forced to conclude that his own way of working 'has been fertilised by Delacroix's ideas rather than theirs. Because instead of trying to reproduce exactly what I have before my eyes, I use colour more arbitrarily, in order to express myself forcefully' [663/520]. In the asylum at Saint-Rémy, where he had no live models, he copied works by Delacroix in his own original way. It was an exercise he needed, because he wanted to learn.[34] Although he had only black-and-white reproductions, he painted with impassioned brushstrokes in accordance with the theory of colour contrasts (plate 125).[35] ❧ With his goal of working from reality, while mak-ing the fullest possible use of colour as a means of expression, he saw Delacroix's journey to Africa as confirmation of his own decision to move to Arles in February 1888.[36] Moreover, he felt heartened by Delacroix's attitude to life. The fact that his role model did not give up in despair when a large number of his paintings were rejected for the Salon, but on the contrary carried on working, must have been a help for Van Gogh at times when his own work was not understood. He loved to identify with his teacher, who had also devoted his entire life to art.[37]

JEAN-FRANÇOIS MILLET

Van Gogh adored Rembrandt for the way in which he fused reali-ty with the imagination. His inspiration for form and colour was Delacroix. What struck him most about Millet was his depiction of peasant life.[38] 'Put off thy shoes from off thy feet, for the place whereon thou standest is holy ground' [36/29] was his conviction when he saw his first drawings by Millet at a commercial exhibi-tion in Paris in 1875. His enthusiasm and admiration for the work of this artist of the Barbizon School became even greater in 1882 when he read Alfred Sensier's *La vie et l'oeuvre de J.-F. Millet* (1881). From then on, his opinion about Millet was heavily col-oured by this book, which gives a highly romanticised picture of the artist by present-day standards. ❧ In Nuenen, especially, he tried to follow in the footsteps of Millet, whom he regarded as the 'perennial master' of the peasant genre and 'the very heart of modern art' [522/418], in order to gain an understanding of peasant life. Deeply affected by the idea that Millet had painted agricul-tural labourers in the colour of the earth in which they sowed, he

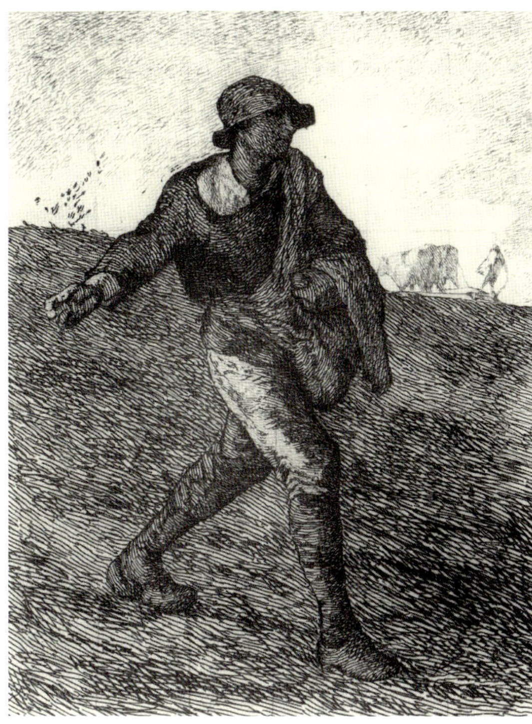

used a similar earth-coloured palette for his *Potato eaters* (plate 44). This, together with the expressive hands and the almost animal-like heads, was designed to show the peasants in their most primitive, pure form, living in harmony with nature.[39] ❦ The copies that Van Gogh made after works by Millet have a special place in his oeuvre. Early on in his career he used black-and-white reproductions as models for his drawings (fig. 46), and in 1889 he again took Millet as his source of inspiration, not for literal copies but for original, expressive translations in colour (plates 49, 54).[40] ❦ In addition to using Millet in his own work, he also involved him in assessing other art by imagining what his teacher's reaction would have been. For example, he saw in his mind's eye how Millet would have stood for a long time in front of Mauve's *Fishing boat on the beach* (plate 68), before muttering to himself: 'There is heart in that painter'.[41] ❦ As with Delacroix, Millet's influence was not restricted to matters of art. For Van Gogh, who did not make a strict distinction between life and art, Millet was his role model *par excellence*. He drew strength from his teacher, not only for persevering in the face of lack of success and adhering to the idea of being original.[42] He also waxed lyrical about Sensier's picture of Millet as an uncommercial artist who

lived as a peasant among the peasants. According to Van Gogh, all artists should take this as their example. In his eyes, Millet, 'set an example to painters *as a human being*, which Israëls and Mauve, for instance, who live rather luxurious lives, have *not*, and I repeat – Millet is – FATHER Millet, that is, counsellor and mentor in everything to the younger painters' [496/400].

EXOTIC TEACHERS

Van Gogh was enthralled by Japanese prints from the very moment when he first set eyes on them in Antwerp. He began collecting them furiously, especially during his time in Paris, and also read articles and books touching on Japanese art and culture. He put the Japanese on a pedestal, right alongside his favourite 17th-century masters, Rembrandt and Hals.[43] ❦ His plan to produce work in the manner of Japanese prints resulted in a way of painting characterised by stylised areas of colour, asymmetrical compositions and unexpected truncations.[44] Like his Japanese models, he longed to set down a figure 'in a few sure strokes as if it were as easy as buttoning up your waistcoat' [690/542]. The precision with which a Japanese artist drew a single blade of grass (fig. 47) encouraged Van Gogh to make similar studies (fig. 48). ❦ His fascination, however, did not end with making work in the manner of Japanese prints, for as with Millet his idols were a model for life itself. He was drawn to the (apparent) simplicity that was so characteristic of work, domesticity and Japanese life in general. His plan of forming an artists' community in Arles was inspired in part by his idea that Japanese artists had achieved the same ideal. Although his 'studio of the south' never became a reality, he did succeed in firing Bernard, Gauguin and Charles Laval with enthusiasm for the idea of making artists' portraits along Japanese lines and exchanging them among themselves as a mark of friendship (plates 170-172).[45]

CONCLUSION

Van Gogh's attitude towards his teachers was ambivalent. On the one hand he wanted their comments on his work, but on the other he inevitably ended up arguing with them. It seems that he

46. After **Jean-François Millet,** *The sower,* Amsterdam (Vincent van Gogh Foundation)

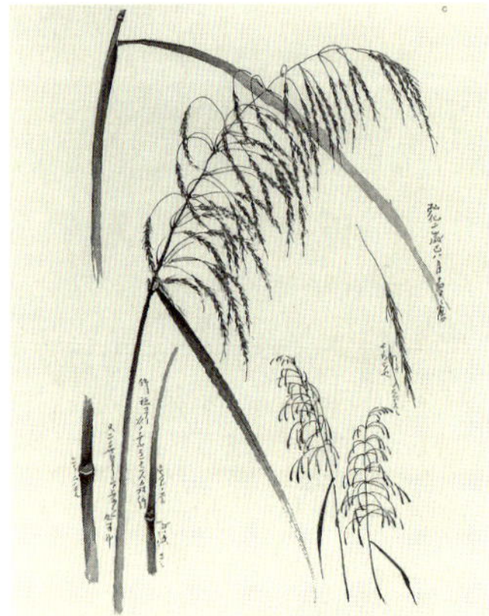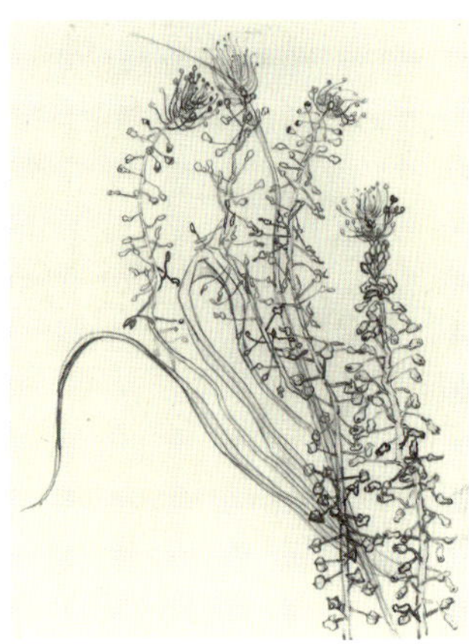

had to have sufficient distance from them if he was to appreciate them. For example, very soon after leaving Mauve he was again speaking of him in adoring tones. ❧ Although he was by and large satisfied with the technical skills he acquired on academic courses, the bond with the teachers there was never more than superficial. There was little development in his relationship with them, nor did they impress him very much. With Mauve it was different, the teacher he had deliberately sought out himself. He was far more of a mentor than a teacher. ❧ It is not surprising that Van Gogh, who had great difficulty in accepting authority, found his true teachers among artists whom he never met. This enabled him to create an image of their life and work as he saw

fit, and then draw on it freely. ❧ And yet, all his teachers were only partly responsible for Van Gogh's artistic development. The circles in which he moved and the contacts he made there were at least as important. For example, his transformation into a modern artist would not have been possible if he had not met his impressionist contemporaries in Paris, who made him realise how old-fashioned his own, dark palette really was. ❧ Van Gogh had only a few years' experience as an artist when, in 1883-85, he himself was placed in the position of teacher, advising a few amateurs.[46] However, he did not regard teaching as his calling; it was more of a sideline. His main concern was his own development as an artist. ❧ It was only after his death that he began to play his true role as a teacher. He was soon being regarded by a new generation of artists as a major forerunner of modern art.[47] He was admired for his unique style and his total dedication to art. Just as he had interpreted the lessons of his teachers in his own way, so his own artistic ideas and expressions have formed an important source of inspiration for artists right up to the present day. And although he did not think much of 'the *future* life of artists *through their works*' in his day, with his own work he did indeed pass on 'the torch' [660/518].

❧

47. **Anonymous artist,** *Study of grass,* in: *Le Japon Artistique* (May 1888)

48. **Vincent van Gogh,** *Study of sprigs of feather hyacinth* (Muscari comosum) (F 1612 JH 2059), 1890, Amsterdam, Van Gogh Museum (Vincent van Gogh Foundation)

AN AVID READER –
VAN GOGH AND LITERATURE

WOUTER VAN DER VEEN

Writing from his self-imposed exile in the hospital at Saint-Rémy in July 1889, Vincent van Gogh reported to his sister Wil: 'I'm becoming quite engrossed in reading the Shakespeare Theo sent me; here, I finally have the peace and quiet necessary to tackle something difficult. I've started with the histories [...]. But you know, I don't think I should encourage you to read such dramatic tales; whenever I finish I always have to contemplate a blade of grass, a branch of pine, an ear of corn in order to calm down' [788/W13]. The intensity with which he apparently experienced the plays was not only a result of his mental state at that particular moment; Van Gogh's correspondence reveals that he was always fascinated and deeply touched by the written word. Paul Gauguin, who met him during his second stay in Paris (1886-88), described him as a man possessed by literature.[1] Seven years earlier, while in the Borinage in Belgium, Van Gogh had written to his brother Theo of his 'consuming passion for books', claiming that he needed them for study as much as he needed his daily bread [154/133]. And the poetry albums compiled by the young Vincent for his friends and family, comprising poems and prose passages he had selected himself, bear witness to both his very early interest and his long-standing desire to share his enthusiasm with others.[2] ❧ In May 1877 he wrote to Theo that he had recently seen a portrait of the historian Jules Michelet (fig. 50), whom he greatly admired, and that the likeness had made him think of the Frenchman's life of 'ink and paper' [114/95]. And indeed, Michelet's existence had been almost entirely dominated by reading and writing: this son of a printer not only studied and filled countless pages, but had also worked the printing press himself. At the time, Van Gogh's own life consisted of little more than ink and paper. He was busy learning Greek and Latin and studying the

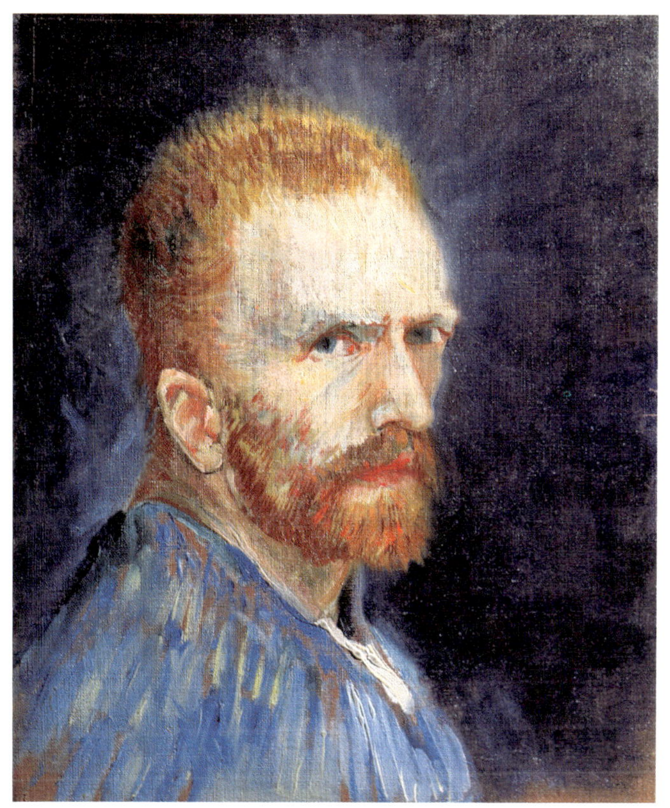

Bible and other religious writings in order to join the theological seminary at the university of Amsterdam. He was well aware that this new path would be a difficult one, but he trusted in God and in his own calling and capacity for work. 'Just as the ivy climbs along the wall, so must the pen along the paper,' he wrote with confidence [114/95]. In this respect he saw Michelet as a model and mentor. ❧ When several years and disappointments later Van Gogh finally decided to become an artist – in 1880 – ink and paper still remained important: he used these ingredients not only for his hundreds of drawings but also for writing his innu-

49. **Vincent van Gogh,** *Self-portrait* (F 268 JH 1299), 1887, Hartford, Wadsworth Atheneum Museum of Art, Gift of Philip L. Goodwin in memory of his mother, Josephine S. Goodwin

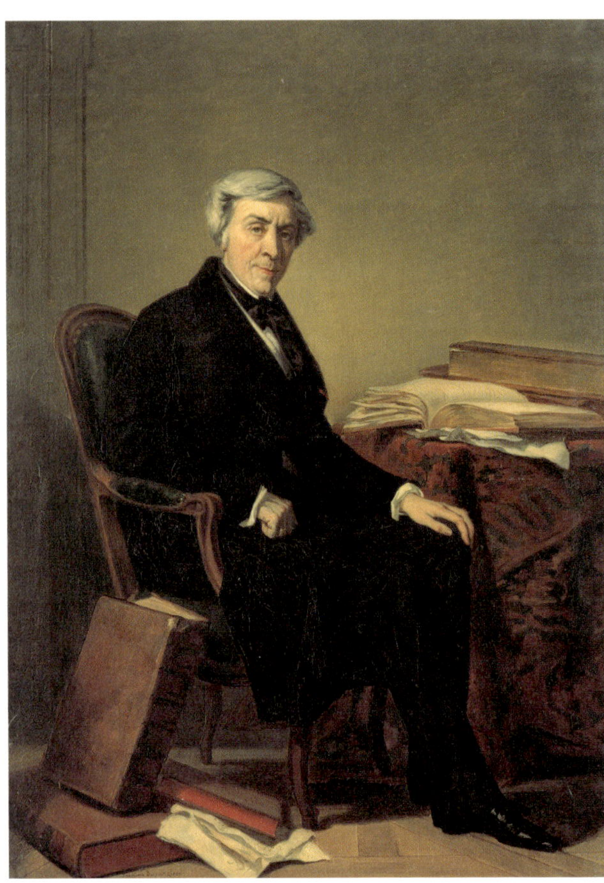

merable letters. And he continued to read ceaselessly, with both devotion and enthusiasm.

Van Gogh's surviving correspondence includes around 800 references to literary works by more than 150 authors.[3] It is obvious that he loved to read, and to read as much as possible. From Arles, for example, he wrote of his intention to reread all of Balzac.[4] The Frenchman had published no fewer than 80 novels and even for a fanatic like Van Gogh such a project would undoubtedly have proved extremely difficult. The plan was comparable in scope to several others that many today would consider doomed to failure, but which Van Gogh undertook with both fervour and aplomb: a transcription of *De imitatione Christi* by Thomas à Kempis (c. 1379-1471); reading all the works of Emile Zola, Michelet and Shakespeare; and the execution of a thousand studies before daring to call himself a painter. ❧ Despite this

avidity, however, Van Gogh was not what one would call a connoisseur of literature. He was rather a true amateur. This meant that he took little notice of 'official' terminologies and theories – if he was even aware of them. His use of the term 'naturalists', for example, is extremely unclear. It covers not only the oeuvres of Honoré de Balzac and Gustave Flaubert, but also the non-naturalistic stories of Guy de Maupassant and Alphonse Daudet. He uses the designation 'naturalists' and 'modern French authors' interchangeably, thus drawing an obscure boundary between the romantic Victor Hugo and the realist Flaubert, while leaving Balzac dangling somewhere in the middle. It appears that for Van Gogh modernity in literature began where romanticism left off. There is of course no exact date marking the end of romantic influence, which does not help in making Van Gogh's approach any clearer. ❧ The classification of works of literature into movements, schools or 'isms' was entirely irrelevant to Van Gogh, and these therefore had no influence on his choice of reading material. This makes research into the possible effects of various literary theories on his art, for example, extremely difficult. Nonetheless, it is perhaps revealing to attempt to characterise his literary world, as this may provide insight into his opinions and taste. Van Gogh read the way he wrote and painted: abundantly and often, and although he attached great importance to the relationship between contemporary ideas and his own artistic activity, he refused to be distracted from what he felt to be essential by stringent formal precepts or other artistic dogmas. ❧ Thanks to the innumerable literary references it contains, Van Gogh's correspondence allows us to trace fairly closely his intellectual development and interest in books. In the years for which letters have survived he read mainly British, American and French (including Belgian) literature.[5] From 1881 onwards, French authors became his clear favourites, and this predilection only grew once he had moved to France in 1886. It even seems that from May 1890 Van Gogh – who probably no longer read Dutch except in the letters from his family and friends in the Netherlands – preferred not to speak or write his mother tongue if he could use French instead.[6]

IMITATION OF CHRIST

The lack of documents pertaining to the first half of Van Gogh's life makes it impossible to reconstruct which Dutch-language

50. **Emile Dupont-Zipcy (**after **Thomas Couture),** *Jules Michelet,* late 19th century, Versailles, Musée National du Château et des Trianons

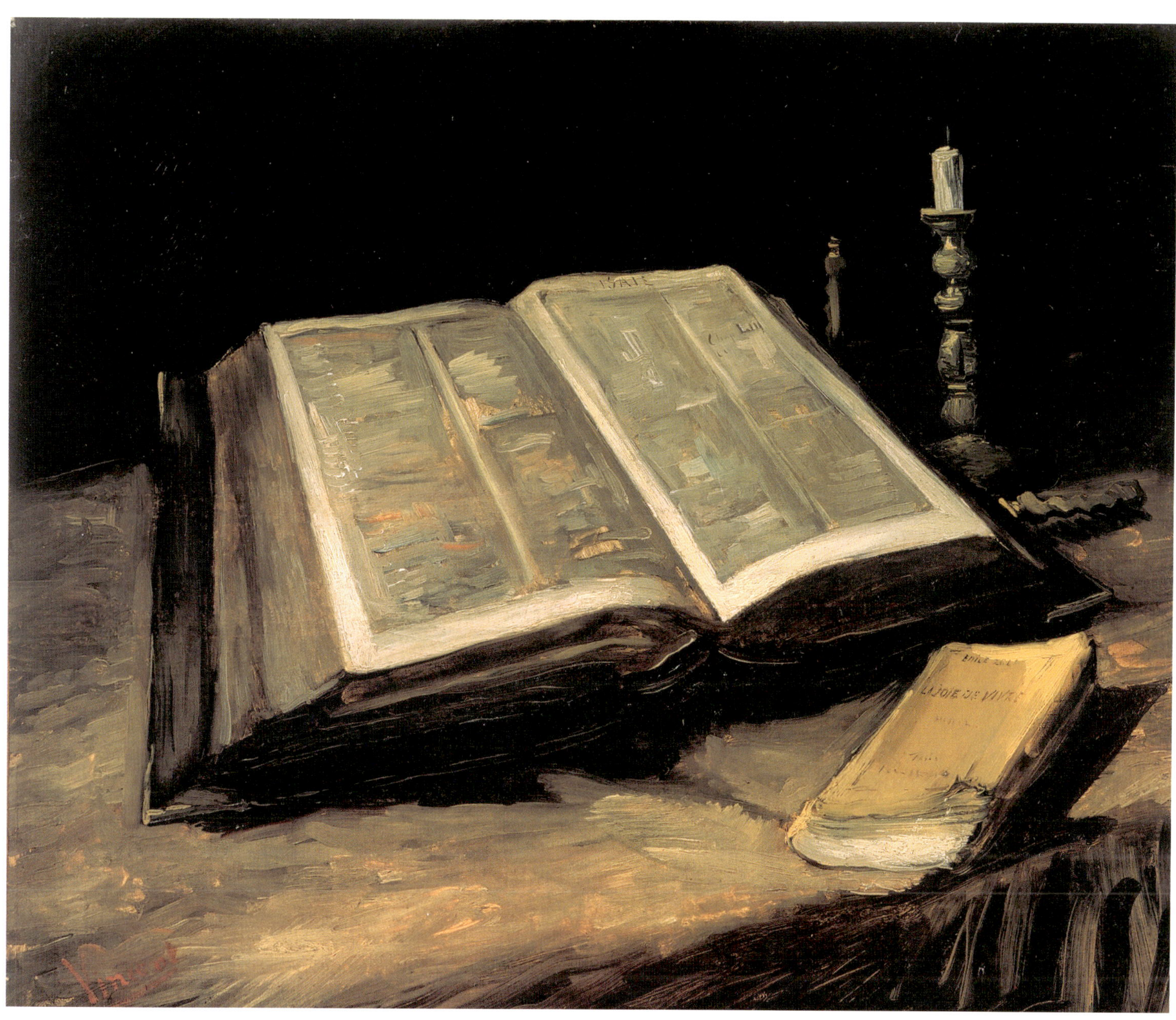

51. Vincent van Gogh, *Still life with Bible* (F 117 JH 946), 1885,
Amsterdam, Van Gogh Museum (Vincent van Gogh Foundation)

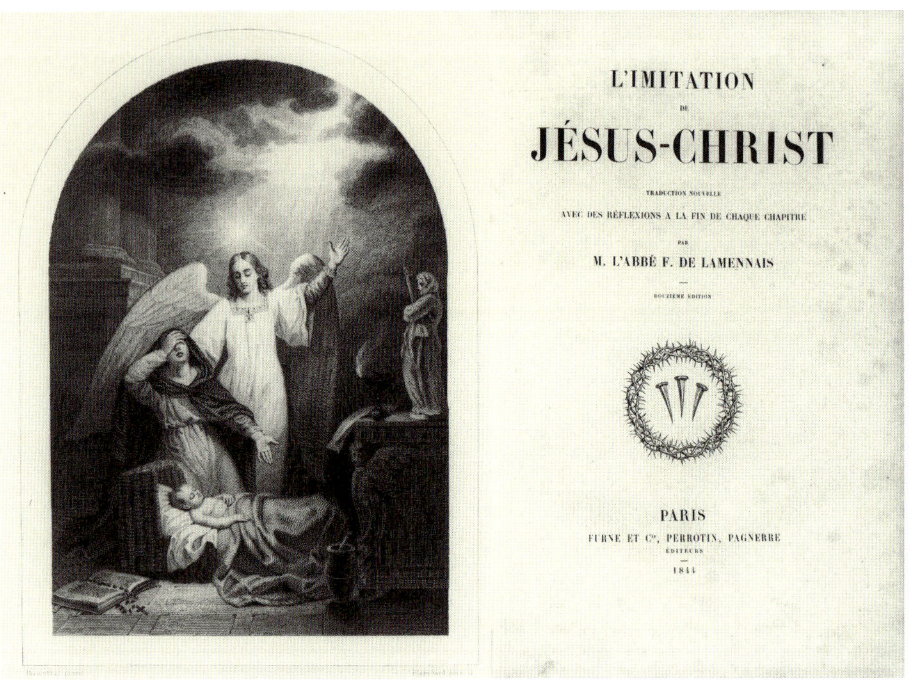

authors he favoured in his youth. It also makes it difficult to judge what role his upbringing played in the development of his passion for literature. We can be certain, however, that a lot of reading was done in the Van Gogh household in Zundert, as indicated by the family correspondence.[7] Among the books available to Van Gogh in this period, the Bible was undoubtedly the most important (fig. 51). It thus comes as no surprise that the Holy Scripture is the most quoted work in the first 150 letters; in fact, some of these early epistles are little more than a succession of biblical quotations, and often seem more like prayers than letters. ❧ Everything Van Gogh experienced between the ages of 17 and 23, everything he saw or felt, was brought into direct relation with the biblical text, particularly with the New Testament: 'To cherish the thought of Christ at every turn and under all circumstances is an excellent thing,' he wrote [108/88]. The possibility of renewal through Christ and the consolation the 'living Christ' could offer mankind continually occupied his thoughts. Nowhere, however, does Van Gogh provide a clear definition of what he understood by the latter term. For him, the 'living Christ' appeared to manifest himself above all in melancholy, a power that offers rejuvenation, hope and solace to the sorrowful. In February 1877 he wrote to Theo from Dordrecht: 'If we allow ourselves to be taught by the experience of life and to be led to God through sorrow, then a new kind of vitality will spring from our weary hearts. Once we have become drained enough we will come to believe still more firmly in God, and will find a Friend and Consoler in Christ and His word' [102/85]. ❧ It thus goes almost without saying that Van Gogh's early preferences tended towards literature in which ethics were more important than aesthetics; in this particular area *l'art pour l'art* was entirely lost on him. Writing, for example, about the poet Henry Wadsworth Longfellow, he expressed his admiration not for the American's poetic style but rather for the feelings his poems conveyed. Van Gogh's interest was in content, the themes treated, the descriptions (in which he often literally saw paintings or drawings) and, not least, in the relevance of what he read for his own life and the lessons that could be learned from it. With his religious background and unrestrained love of God it is thus no wonder that until 1878 references to books other than the Bible were mainly to various works of a devotional or edifying nature. ❧ The young Van Gogh's sources of knowledge, wisdom and faith were, among others, Thomas à Kempis's *De imitatione Christi* (1441), John Bunyan's *The pilgrim's progress: from this world to that which is to come* (1678), Jacques-Bénigne Bossuet's *Oraisons funèbres*

52. Thomas à Kempis, *L'imitation de Jésus-Christ,* ed. M. L'Abbé
F. de Lamennais, Paris 1844

(1669) and, finally, François de Salignac de la Mothe Fénelon's *Les aventures de Télémaque* (1699). What he sought in these texts was an uplifting message, and he therefore cared little for the form in which this was transmitted. None of these titles would be amiss in a reverend's bookcase, and indeed it seems likely that Vincent first became acquainted with them through his father. ❧ According to Van Gogh, *De imitatione Christi* was a 'sublime' work (fig. 52). He was deeply impressed by its clarity and sincerity, and in 1877 even began transcribing a French translation of it.[8] He found the same probity and imperturbable faith in Bunyan's *Pilgrim's progress*, which is chiefly a series of mystical visions and dreamlike parables. Central to Bunyan is mankind's base, impious and guilty nature – a sharp contrast to God's unconditional love for even the lowest of creatures. Given his Calvinist upbringing, this aspect must have particularly appealed to Van Gogh. ❧ Van Gogh also read the French theologian, philosopher and historian Bossuet's *Oraisons funèbres*, a collection of various funeral orations in which the author describes his ideas about religion and the love of God. The young Vincent found in him a moderate and reassuring author with respect to the traditions of the Church, quite the opposite of his contemporary and compatriot Fénelon. The work of the latter – a priest – is highly didactic in tone and content, and was particularly well suited to an unfledged believer in search of his intellectual and spiritual footing. Fénelon's *Télémaque*, written as a manual for the grandson of Louis XIV – and from which Van Gogh even in later life would continue to derive much wisdom – provoked a small revolution in the highly conservative France of the late 17th century. Fénelon emphasises not the sacred traditions of the Church but rather and above all man's inner spiritual life, and he defends a kind of sentimental mysticism of which many of his peers, among them Bossuet, disapproved. In his youth Van Gogh sought to construct a spiritual frame of reference and found an abundance of material in both Bossuet and Thomas à Kempis. Moreover, he could reflect his personal religious experience through Bunyan's striding pilgrim, Christian, and Fénelon's doubting Telemachus.

In addition to these religious authors, in this period Van Gogh read Harriet Beecher Stowe, Thomas Carlyle, George Eliot, Jules Michelet and Charles Dickens. The last two in particular have little in common with the devout and traditional Bunyan and

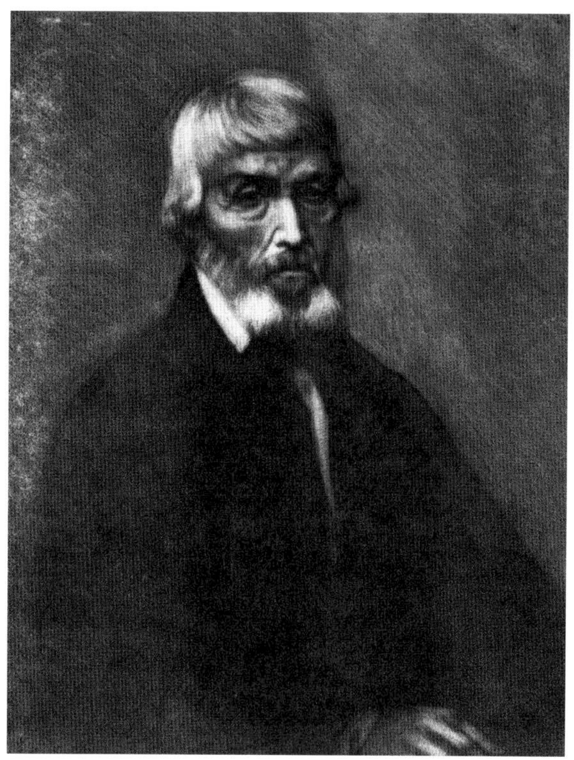

Bossuet, and their work would seem to conflict with Van Gogh's love of the Church and the Bible. Nonetheless, for Van Gogh this hotchpotch of authors formed a coherent whole: out of that which links them from a religious and literary-historical point of view one can trace the development of our young devotee's evangelical ideal. ❧ Beecher Stowe, who declared that her pen was guided by none other than God himself, has gone down in literary history as the author of the 1852 bestseller *Uncle Tom's cabin*. The intelligible manner in which she managed to convey her ideas made a deep impression on Van Gogh: 'In the Negro's hut *par excellence* the artist has set things in a new light, and thus through this book – even if it is already starting to become somewhat outdated, written as it was many years ago – everything becomes new. It is so finely felt, so thought through, so masterly. It is written with so much love, so much gravity and so much realism and knowledge of its subject. It is so modest and simple, but at the same time so truly sublime, so noble and so distinguished' [151/130]. The book's novelty, its tone of consola-

53. Alphonse Legros, *Thomas Carlyle*, Paris, Bibliothèque Nationale de France, Cabinet des Estampes tion, its simplicity and authenticity clearly made it relevant to Van Gogh's own daily life, and he did not hesitate to label Beecher Stowe a modern apostle and her work a continuation of the gospel. ⁂ The simplicity Van Gogh so admired in Beecher Stowe is certainly not a characteristic of the writings of Thomas Carlyle (fig. 53), one of the most important English thinkers of his time. Influenced by Enlightenment philosophy, Carlyle had come to abandon religion; simultaneously, however, he rejected atheism because, in his opinion, it rendered human existence meaningless. Carlyle found a reflection of the Christian values he continued to maintain in the work of various German authors, among them Johann Wolfgang von Goethe, whom he discovered through the work of Mme de Staël, notably *De l'Allemagne* 1813). Hereafter Carlyle proclaimed – for example in *On heroes, hero-worship and the heroic in history* (1841), with which Van Gogh was well acquainted – that art and labour were better able to encourage morality than blind faith in supernatural powers. Even after having discovered Carlyle's background and motivations, Van Gogh continued to view his ideas as compatible with his own ongoing faith. As he wrote to his friend Anthon van Rappard in 1883: 'He – Carlyle – has learned much from Goethe, but to my mind much more from a certain man who has written no books, but whose words – although not written down by himself – have remained valid, i.e., Jesus' [327/R30]. ⁂ George Eliot – who Van Gogh, like so many others, long believed to be a man – defended in her books a form of atheistic rationalism that stood in marked opposition to her upbringing and earliest literary efforts, which were still essentially evangelical in nature. Like Carlyle, she, too, eventually rejected the dogmas of faith and began writing didactic and moralising stories. The acuity of her observations and the care with which she created the most complete picture possible of her characters' social situation made her a forerunner of realism. This approach to writing appealed to Van Gogh, as indicated by his admiration for the scrupulous descriptions found in *Scenes of clerical life* (1857), and by his comparison of Eliot's work with that of two of his favourite French authors: 'Eliot analyses like Balzac or Zola, but from an English point of view and with English feeling' [69/55]. Despite her professed atheism, he recognised an evangelical message in her books. Eliot regarded Christian values as morally correct, but saw nothing godly in them. She sought to disassociate what she found ethically defensible from all forms of organised reli-

gion, and regretted the corruption these ideals had undergone at the hands of the Christian world. Van Gogh appears to have been entirely unaware of this backdrop to Eliot's novels, as one may infer from his plan to give his father *Felix Holt, the radical* (1866) for his birthday in 1876.[9] ⁂ Charles Dickens's vast oeuvre denounces the extreme social inequalities and injustices of his time. This champion of the poor derived many of his ideas about art and social idealism from Carlyle, translating them into a form that made them readily accessible to a broad reading public. Dickens's work is above all a eulogy to modesty, virtue and human dignity – precisely the same values Van Gogh had earlier sought and found in the Christian authors mentioned above. The majority of Dickens's novels are set in London, where Van Gogh lived from June 1873 to May 1875, and where he sought work as a preacher in 1876 with the idea of giving succour to the destitute so aptly described by the English writer. ⁂ Van Gogh regarded the work of the radical anticleric Jules Michelet – whom he several times refers to as 'Father Michelet' – as a kind of sequel to the Bible. He wrote the following passage in Etten, in 1881: 'The Bible is of course eternal and everlasting, but Michelet provides such surprisingly practical and clear signals, which are so applicable to the fast-paced, agitated modern life you and I find ourselves living, that he quickly helps us make progress and we soon can't do without him. The difference between Moses and Noah on the one hand, for example, and Jesus and Paul on the other. In my opinion Beecher Stowe and Michelet are a *continuation* of the gospel, not *a repetition*. Look at [them], they don't say the gospel has become invalid but instead try to show us how it may be relevant to our own time, to our own lives, to you and me, just to take an example. Michelet even says things perfectly and out loud the germs of which are only whispered in the gospel, and Stowe in fact goes just as far as Michelet' [187/161]. ⁂ Van Gogh regarded the French author as a modern apostle, who preached the gospel in a clear, pragmatic and contemporary manner. And, indeed, Michelet in no way repudiated the moral values defended by Christ; like Eliot, however, he could not reconcile these with the Church and its authorities. He believed that the liberation of the people, which was to come about through an historical process that was as natural as it was inevitable, would eventually lead to a society not incompatible with the majority of Christian norms. Van Gogh's letters, however, fail to reveal the exact extent of his understand-

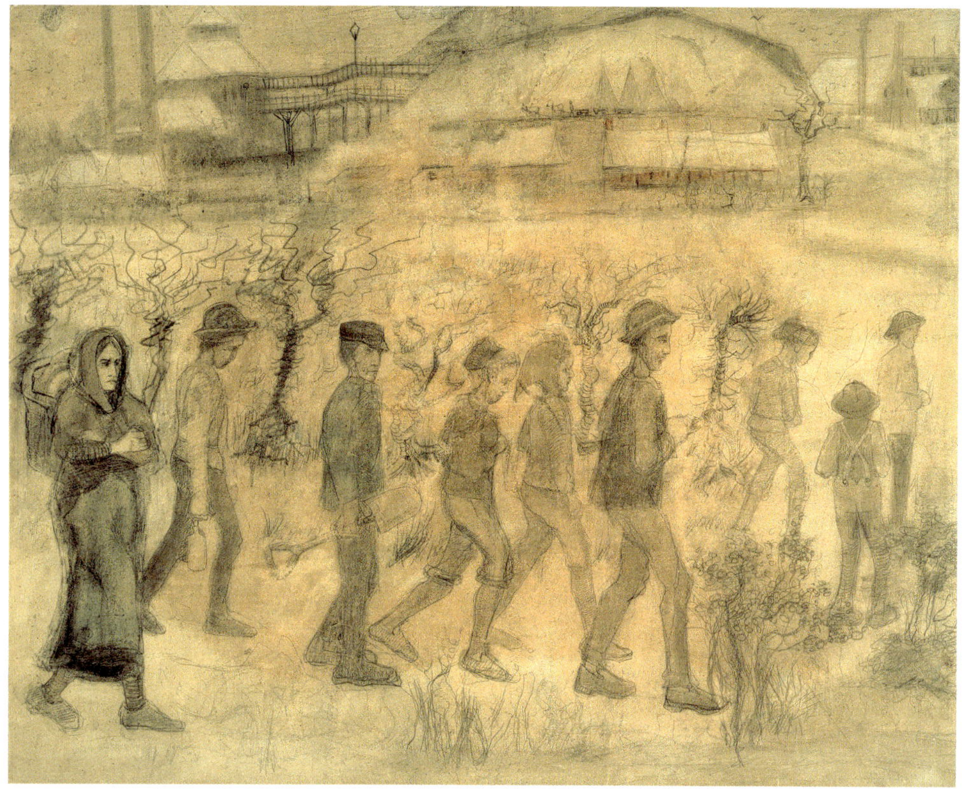

ing of the historian's ideas on religion. Michelet was the writer who accompanied Van Gogh the longest, in times of blind faith but also of extreme doubt and anticlericalism; he found support and justification in the Frenchman's work in just about every spiritual or intellectual plight. ❧ As noted above, seen from the perspective of the development of his ideas, the young Vincent van Gogh's literary preferences can be said to form a coherent whole. This development runs parallel to the long historical evolution of notions regarding religion that began with the doubt sown by Fénelon within the established order of the French Catholic Church and ended with the anticlericalism of Eliot, Michelet and Dickens.[10] It does, however, remain difficult to determine whether Van Gogh was influenced by what he read or if he simply read the things that confirmed his beliefs. There was undoubtedly interplay between his concepts and his readings, in which he recognised almost as much of himself as he learned. He was especially fond of stylistic simplicity, of clear standpoints on the issues of the day and of the proclamation of Christian values, provided they could be separated from the centuries-old

ecclesiastical traditions and dogmas. ❧ Van Gogh was in search of the so-called 'living Christ', whom, he believed, was to be found beyond the walls of the church, among the common people. In the Borinage he suited action to word, and from 1878-81 sought to bring the gospel of the 'living Christ' to the Walloon miners. It was an effort without much success, as once his contract was over his employers suggested he seek his fortunes elsewhere. Van Gogh's conclusion was that the imitation of Christ was incompatible with institutions of any kind. These experiences may well have influenced his choice to lead the life of an artist: if it was impossible to imitate Christ as a preacher than perhaps he could bring consolation to humanity through art. This was in any case a conviction he shared with the much-admired Carlyle, although he was probably as yet unacquainted with the Englishman's thoughts on the subject. As is demonstrated by his interpretation of the non-religious authors he read, the idea of imitating Christ continued to inspire him: he chose, however, to do this in a contemporary and highly individual manner (fig. 54).

54. **Vincent van Gogh,** *Miners* (F 831 JH -), 1880, Otterlo, Kröller-Müller Museum

In December 1881 Van Gogh settled in The Hague, where he intended to continue training as a draughtsman and painter. As far as his intellectual development was concerned, he now began moving further away from the religious and often dogmatic texts he had previously consumed with such passion. His new taste tended towards French authors, and he even read Dickens and the Dutch writer Hendrik Conscience in French translation – although of course we have no real way of knowing whether this was out of a conscious preference for the French language or for some other, at present obscure, reason. ❧ While in The Hague Van Gogh not only began to acquire more feeling for the specifically literary aspects – descriptions, above all – of the books he read, he also came to the conclusion that reading modern literature was a duty for someone in his position. Of the recent publications he could easily obtain in The Hague in 1881, the writings of Zola – the founder of French naturalism – were probably the most 'modern'. In the early 1880s 'modern' by no means meant avantgarde, and Van Gogh's pleasure in the popular novels of Emile Zola was thus hardly to be called unique. Zola's aim in his work was to depict reality as it really was (fig. 55). He was convinced that human beings were determined by heredity, milieu and education. For him a novel was a social experiment, something to be executed in a scientific manner, beyond all forms of idealism or established morals.[11] In Van Gogh's literary pantheon the atheist Zola, too, was quickly given the status of modern apostle, a term he had already applied to both Beecher Stowe and Michelet. Van Gogh read many of Zola's novels in quick succession during 1882 – *Le ventre de Paris* (1873), *Nana* (1880), *La curée* (1871), *La faute de l'abbé Mouret* (1875), *Son excellence Eugène Rougon* (1876) and *Une page d'amour* (1878). Regarding the latter he wrote to Theo: 'some of the descriptions of the city [are] masterly, masterfully painted or drawn [...]. Did you know that *drawing* with words is also a form of art and that it sometimes reveals a kind of hidden power – just like a puff of blue or grey smoke betrays a hearthfire' [244/212]. ❧ While in The Hague Van Gogh also read the work of Hugo, Balzac and Flaubert, but his favourite remained Zola, who was considered as controversial as he was modern. Fyodor Dostoevsky and Friedrich Nietzsche, for example, thought little of him. Conservative critics deplored his 'pornographic' descriptions and could not imagine (let alone appreciate) the beauty he found

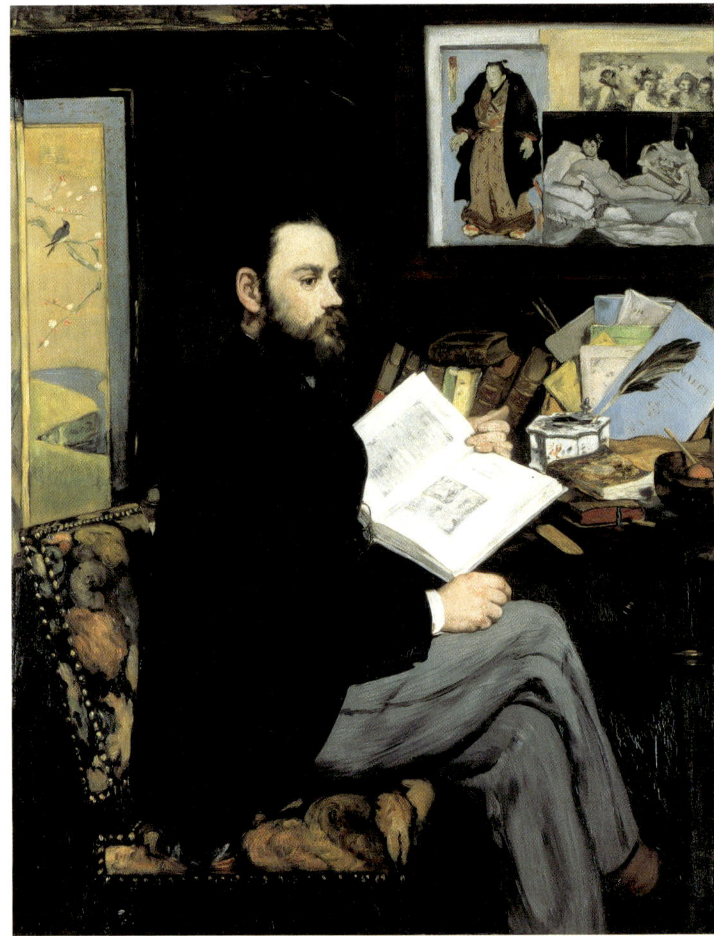

in the poorer quarters, garrets, market stalls or kitchens.[12] Van Gogh, however, could, and like Zola believed that there was beauty to be found even in a third-class waiting room. ❧ For Van Gogh, truth and beauty were intimately linked. Only when an artwork was 'true' could it also be beautiful. This did not mean, however, that the goal of art was to reproduce reality exactly – one of the initial aims of Zola and other naturalist authors. Instead, it was to provide as good and rounded a picture of it as possible. For Van Gogh, a work of art should create a plausible illusion of reality, one that would give the spectator the feeling that it was genuine. ❧ Zola, too, had eventually come to the same conclusion. According to him, art could never reproduce reality objectively, as the personality of the artist always interfered in the complex relationship between the viewer, the work and the outside world. At the same time, however, he also believed that the distorted pic-

55. Edouard Manet, *Portrait of Emile Zola,* 1868, Paris, Musée d'Orsay ture of reality the author inevitably created was not necessarily in conflict with objectivity. ⚜ Van Gogh found in Zola a deeply rooted sympathy for the people and the popular, quite similar to that he had earlier discovered in Dickens. And it was very likely this sense of compassion that enabled him to make a link between Christianity and naturalism. For someone of this period in search of traditional Christian values and norms in literature, Victor Hugo would have been a more logical choice. Hugo was a romantic poet, a man of vision, who saw the sublime in revolution and the soul of France revealed on the barricades, and who more than once proclaimed his belief in supernatural powers. Van Gogh certainly read Hugo with pleasure, but Zola and the naturalists captured and retained his special admiration, probably because their works offered him the possibility of identification with the realities of his own life. Hugo was more the representative of a bygone era that had little to do with Van Gogh's daily existence. ⚜ Van Gogh's Hague period was one of both literary discoveries and the confirmation of old loves. For although he acquired a taste for the modern he did not entirely forget his adolescent passions – Eliot, Carlyle, Dickens and Longfellow. Only the purely ecclesiastical writers such as Bunyan and Bossuet disappeared forever from his literary pantheon. In these years Van Gogh's religious frame of reference was replaced by a nostalgic fancy for another past time he much admired: the French Revolution and the early 19th century. He came to know this epoch above all through the writings of the author-duo Emile Erckmann and Charles-Alexandre Chatrian (better known as Erckmann-Chatrian), Michelet, Balzac, Hugo, Carlyle and Dickens, many of the writers he had previously turned to for their religious views. Now he discovered in them power, renewal and daring – characteristics he felt his own age lacked.

IRONY AND FANTASY

Little is known about Van Gogh's reading habits and taste during his Paris period (1886-88). Only from February 1888 onwards, when he had settled in Arles, does he again begin to write about the things he was reading, and probably had already read while in the French capital. As before, these were mainly the works of modern French authors (fig. 56). His interests seem to have changed somewhat, however, and he tended less towards the contemporary, socially engaged novels of naturalists like Edmond and Jules de Goncourt and the realistic tales of peasant life by Antoine-Louis-Camille Lemonnier, preferring instead more ironic works, such as *Candide* (1759), by the French Enlightenment philosopher Voltaire, or *Tartarin de Tarascon* (1872) by Alphonse Daudet. ⚜ *Candide* caricatures the gravity of its petty-minded characters, systematically placing this in opposition to the innocence of the story's hero, who is entirely unaware of any form of evil. Helplessness is his only weapon of defence against the unscrupulous people he encounters on his journey through life. ⚜ Daudet uses a similar ironic trope in *Tartarin*, although in a somewhat more subtle fashion. His main figure, Tartarin from Tarascon, is a caricature of a southern Frenchman. In the stories he loves to tell, his wild imagination regularly leads him to forget the difference between reality and fantasy. Van Gogh was quite keen on *Tartarin*, and tasted in Arles something of the spirit of this brilliantly written farce. The simplicity of its plot and style, the precision of its imagery and its humour made a lasting impression on him. He came to feel that his own time had little cheer or comfort in it, and he became increasingly convinced that only art was capable of offering humanity any form of consolation. The realistic literature he had previously so admired could provide little along these lines. ⚜ While in the south Van Gogh developed a taste for literary works in which the focus was not so much day-to-day existence but rather a more fictionalised reality. This allowed him in 1888 to appreciate Flaubert's *Bouvard et Pécuchet* (1880),[13] the highly entertaining tale of two clerks whose inheritance allows them to give up their jobs and devote themselves to the pursuit of knowledge and the enjoyment of art. In Saint-Rémy he began rereading Shakespeare; earlier, while still in Arles, he had discovered the work of the French naval officer Pierre Loti (fig. 57). ⚜ Loti was certainly no literary genius, and his novels failed to garner him a permanent place in the literary canon. Van Gogh, however, was a great admirer, and in his letters he mentions having read *Le Mariage de Loti* (1880), *Madame Chrysanthème* (1888) (fig. 58), *Pêcheur d'Islande* (1886) and *Mon frère Yves* (1883).[14] These are all stories in which sea voyages play an important role, and exotic scenes and distant lands are described in a simplified and idealised manner. Reading Loti, for example, strengthened Van Gogh's belief that Japan was a pure paradise of light and colour. And Brittany – where Gauguin had stayed

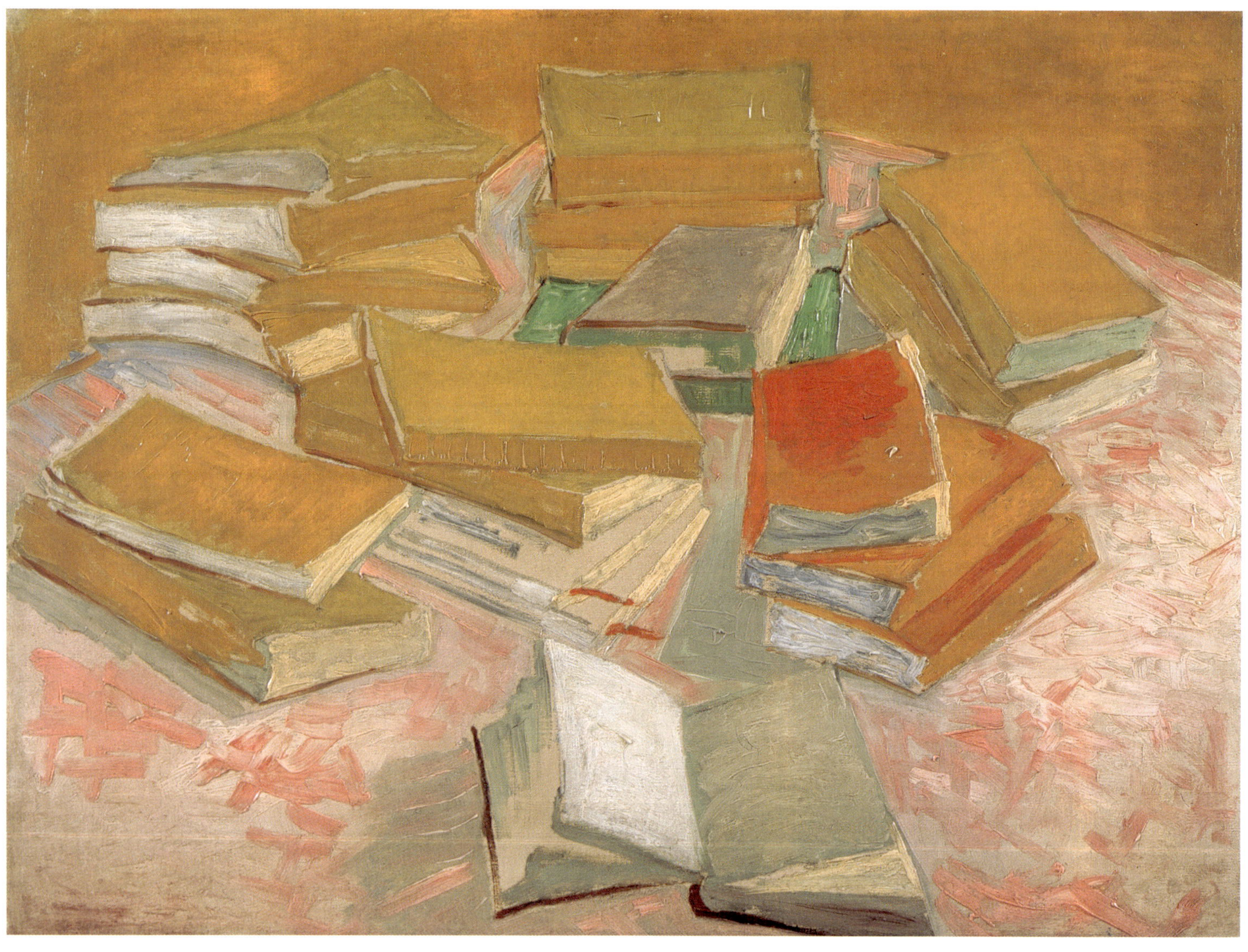

56. **Vincent van Gogh,** *Study for 'Romans parisiens'* (F 358 JH 1612), 1888, Amsterdam, Van Gogh Museum (Vincent van Gogh Foundation)

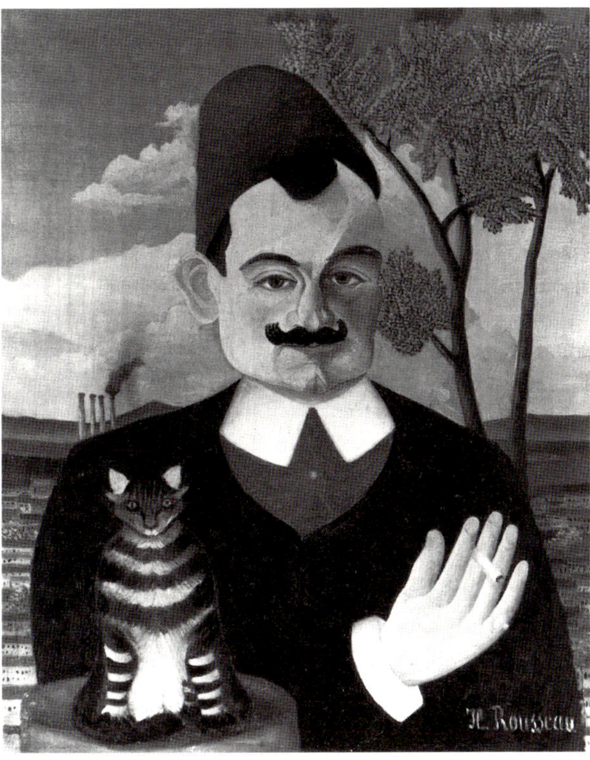

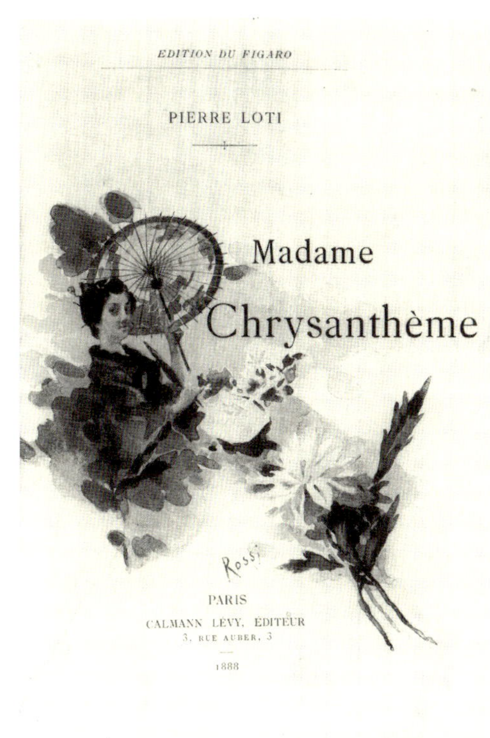

before joining Van Gogh in Arles in October 1888 – was presented by Loti as a precious collection of remote harbours, where
women mourned their drowned husbands and boys grew up to
die at sea. ❧ From Maupassant's *Bel-Ami* (1885), *Les lettres de
mon moulin* (1869) by Daudet and Zola's *L'oeuvre* (1886), Van
Gogh learned how wonderful and innocent the south of France
was, particularly in comparison with its antipode, the dreaded
Paris. In these works the city is shown to be quite capable of
destroying all those human values whose expression Van Gogh
so treasured in the work of Eliot, Dickens and Michelet: simplicity, humility and dignity. ❧ During the penultimate year of his life
Van Gogh mainly mentions purely fictional, 'fantastic' or, on the
contrary, entirely non-fictional, historical works in his letters.
Maupassant, with his intriguing short stories in which the supernatural (or the suspicion of it) plays a small but essential role,
came to occupy an important place in Van Gogh's literary world.
As already noted, he reread Shakespeare's historical plays, and
Jules Verne, author of *Le tour du monde en quatre-vingt jours*
(1872), also suddenly makes an appearance. And he planned, as
mentioned above, to reread all of Balzac. Zola remained one of

his favourites, but no longer because his books represented
modernity but because in the future they would be important
documents of the past.[15] ❧ Van Gogh was apparently unable to
find among the writers of the moment one who could eventually
replace Zola as his modern apostle. Loti was, in fact, his last literary discovery: simultaneously an end and a starting point,
as his reading of this author must be regarded as a form of
escapism. As such it stood in sharp contrast to Van Gogh's literary taste during his Hague period, when he was fascinated by
the objective, 'truthful' description of reality, particularly in combination with a clearly socially engaged message. In the work of
Loti there is no trace whatsoever of the Christian values that for
so long had determined Van Gogh's choice of reading material
and drawn him to the work of, among others, Zola and Maupassant. Van Gogh appears to have resigned himself to the notion
that all efforts to improve humanity's lot were futile. Characteristic of this new attitude is a citation from Voltaire's *Zadig, ou la
destinée* (1747) in one of his letters from Arles: 'We finally came
to the conclusion that the things of this world do not always go
according to the wishes of the most wise' [596/474].

LITERATURE AS EXPLORATION

It is difficult to determine Van Gogh's reading behaviour and taste with any exactitude, as he rarely says anything negative and makes no mention of books he rejected or simply passed over. For example, he must have had the opportunity to read Jean-Jacques Rousseau, the poems of the symbolist Charles Baudelaire and the 'decadent' works of Joris-Karl Huysmans. But whether he did read them and, if so, whether he liked them or not, will always remain a mystery. ✤ Van Gogh appears to have used literature as a reconnaissance instrument: he read the *Imitatione Christi* by Thomas à Kempis before he became an evangelist; *Le ventre de Paris* by Zola before he moved to the French capital; and *Tartarin de Tarascon* by Daudet before he left Paris for Arles. Having arrived in the south he now turned to fantasy, the exotic and the ironic, rejecting the disquieting tone and 'here and now' of naturalism. His enthusiasm for Loti, then, may be linked to his plan to travel overseas or to settle for a time in Brittany. The onset of his illness at the close of 1888 put a halt to these schemes. His first mental crisis also brought an abrupt – and for a passionate reader like Van Gogh, certainly involuntary – end to this literary voyage of discovery: Van Gogh refers for the last time to a work of literature in September 1889, an article by Loti. ✤ Van Gogh himself provided a summary of his literary preferences while in Paris in 1887, in a letter to his sister Wil: 'So I, for instance, who can count so many years of my life during which I lost any inclination to laugh – leaving aside whether or not this was my own fault – I, for one, feel the need for a really good laugh above all else. I've found it in *Guy de Maupassant* and there are others – Rabelais among the older writers, Henri Rochefort among those of today – who provide it as well – and *Voltaire* in *Candide*. If, on the other hand, one wants truth, life as it is, then there are, for example, the Goncourts in *Germinie Lacerteux* and *La fille Elisa*; Zola in *La joie de vivre* and *L'assommoir*, and so many other masterpieces, all portraying life as we feel it ourselves, thus satisfying our need for being told the truth. [...] Is the Bible enough for us? These days I think Jesus would say again to those who sit down in melancholy: "It is not here, it is risen. Why seek ye the living among the dead"' [576/W1] ✤ For Van Gogh literature had to be simple, powerful and useful; it had to provide direction and consolation in times of trouble. Romantic literature, avant-garde writing – symbolist poetry in particular – and any other form of non-ethical work could never hold his attention. Van Gogh admired in books and authors those things that make his own art so special: enthusiasm, tenacity, passion, discipline, belief in self-determined values and, finally, the possibility they offered of escaping from all the difficulties of the contemporary world by revealing the eternal. From Bunyan to Loti, Van Gogh maintained and applied these criteria, thus creating a literary panorama in which we may recognise the essence of his personality.

'CHRIST, THIS GREAT ARTIST' – VAN GOGH'S SOCIO-RELIGIOUS CANON OF ART

JOAN GREER

Among the works most admired by Vincent van Gogh are a large number of texts and images that may be broadly classified as religious and socio-religious in nature. He turned to these works early in life when he was learning the trade of art dealer, later when he was preparing himself for the ministry and working as a lay preacher, and continued to consult them as sources of inspiration and as study tools in his largely autodidactic quest to train himself and formulate a theoretical position on the role of the modern artist. Religious works usually afforded Van Gogh great comfort, but at times they drove him into a frenzy of anxiety.[1] This ambivalence came to the fore particularly in themes dealing with Jesus Christ – arguably the subject that preoccupied Van Gogh most profoundly throughout his life, and one that resonated closely with his own identification with Christ and his christocentric approach to life and to artistic production.[2] ❦ In June of 1888 Van Gogh wrote a letter to Emile Bernard linking the task of the artist to Christ. In it he articulated clearly his preoccupation with Christ and christocentric imagery, stating that Christ was 'a greater artist than all other artists' and that he alone 'took as his principal theme the certainty of eternal life, the endlessness of time, the nothingness of death, the need for and the justification of calmness and devotion' [635/B8]. With these words Van Gogh identified what he felt art should be about. He then went on to discuss the form of Christ's communication, saying that 'Christ, this great artist' had turned his back on literature as a means of expressing ideas, 'but was much less disdainful of the spoken word – especially of the parable. (What a sower, what a harvest, what a fig-tree! etc.).' Here, too, Van Gogh underlined an essential aspect of his own theoretical views concerning art – namely, that it should communicate widely and on a non-elitist level – and pointed to the biblical origins of some of his own favourite artistic motifs. ❦ In the same letter Van Gogh identified those artists whom he felt had been successful in representing Christ in their pictures: 'The figure of Christ has only been painted as I perceive him by Rembrandt and Delacroix [...] and further [by] Millet [...], who has painted the teaching of Christ' [635/B8]. Two kinds of representations are identified here. The first is religious imagery in a direct or literal sense, as seen in works like Rembrandt's *Christ at Emmaus* (fig. 59) and Delacroix's *Christ asleep during the tempest* (plate 124), while the second represents a more oblique or metaphoric approach to religious content, as in Millet's *Sower* (fig. 60, plate 45). Although all three paintings were the objects of an admiration on Van Gogh's part that verged on veneration, they form only a small part of his religious canon of art. Of the two approaches to conveying religious ideation, it was to the non-supernaturalist approach of Millet and other naturalists that he would turn most consistently. ❦ As indicated in his letter to Bernard, Van Gogh saw Christ as an artist. The converse was also true: he constructed the artist as Christ. Indeed, during the late 19th century one increasingly finds the figure of the artist encoded in the person of Christ – a parallel endorsed by the art-critical construction of the artist as someone with a mission to communicate higher truths to the people. Other characteristics of this construct were a lack of recognition within one's own lifetime and the inevitability of self-sacrifice in fulfilling one's vocation. The legacy of the romantic concept of genius here intersects with that of both Christ and artist.

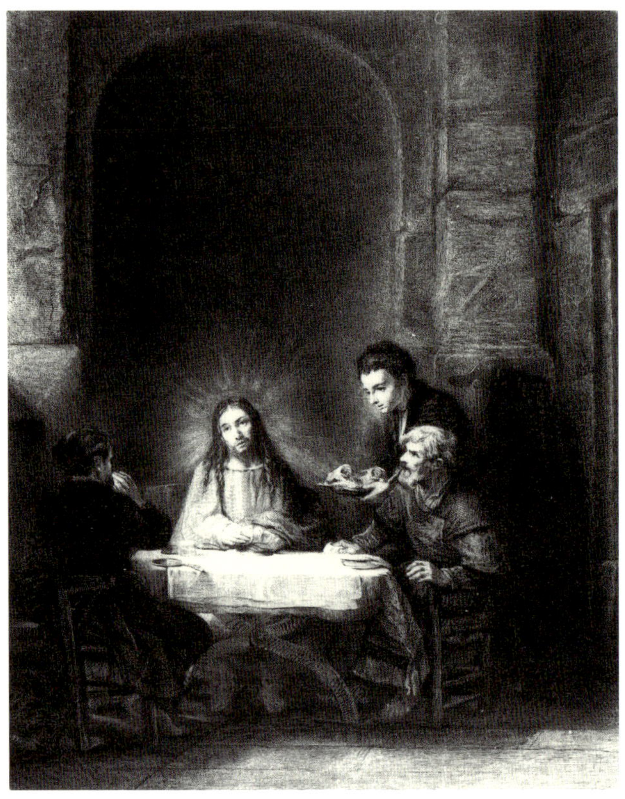

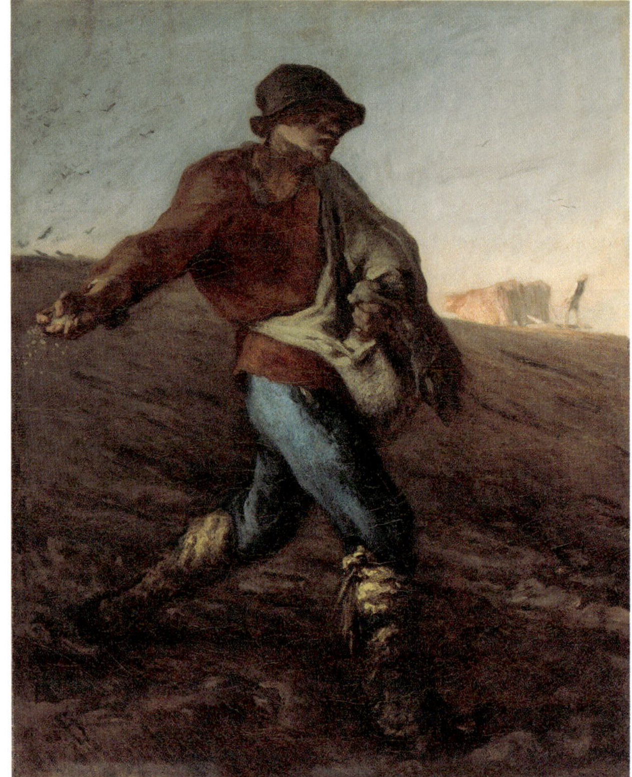

This essay will address how the religious art and literature favoured by Van Gogh before moving to France were of relevance
throughout his life vis-à-vis his christocentric approach to art,
and how they functioned in relation to the dominant discourses
that shaped his ideation: those of the culture of 19th-century
Dutch theologians. How these in turn intersected with modern
art-critical and biographical discourses on the one hand and
those of social politics on the other will form an important sub-
theme. The focus, then, will be on the fundamental underpinnings of this pervasive and dominant Dutch religious culture or
'dominocratie', as it has been called, in the formation of Van
Gogh's theories concerning cultural production, including those
subsequently articulated to Bernard.³ ✎ One of the contributions
this essay intends to make to the current art-historical literature
on Van Gogh is to consider the two religious streams in which
the artist grew up as lenses through which he experienced – to
varying degrees – all the art and literature he encountered. Van
Gogh's direct knowledge through his uncle Stricker of the Modern School of religious thought in particular has still not been

fully investigated by art historians, and never in the specific context of Van Gogh's reception of art. In considering this subject,
This essay emphasises the relationship between constructions of
religious figures such as Christ and those of the artist and how
these affected Van Gogh's attraction to and reception of certain
texts, including the writings of Théophile Thoré and Alfred Sensier. A final component is Van Gogh's tentative endorsement,
albeit at arm's length, of a radical social stance.

THE BIBLE

In any consideration of the works that were important to Van
Gogh, a logical point of departure is the Bible (fig. 61), as it served
as a touchstone for much else he encountered. Here, again, the
letter to Bernard quoted above is revealing, showing how, at this
late point in Van Gogh's life, he saw the reading of the Bible as
essential and yet problematic. Applauding Bernard for turning to
the Bible for artistic inspiration, he wrote: 'The Bible, that is

---

59. After **Rembrandt van Rijn,** *Christ at Emmaus,* 1875, Bordeaux,
Musée Goupil

60. Jean-François Millet, *The sower,* 1850, Boston, Museum of Fine Arts,
Gift of Quincy Adams Shaw through Quincy Adams Shaw, Jr., and Mrs.
Marian Shaw Haughton

Christ.' He added, however, that the study of Christ inevitably leads to 'an artistic neurosis'. Further developing a kind of contradiction often found in his writings on religious matters, he proposes Christ as the solution or, as he puts it, the 'consolation' to the problems he finds inherent in the examination of biblical scripture: 'But the consolation of the so melancholic Bible [...] is Christ' [655/B8]. ☙ The Bible chosen for reproduction in figure 61 belonged to Van Gogh's father, serving as a reminder that this text or, better said, collection of texts, was central to the religious environment of his paternal home. Van Gogh's knowledge of and attitudes toward the Bible (and all other works that referred to it) had their most basic foundations in the religious context of his upbringing and subsequent religious studies. Indeed, the Bible signifies in two distinct ways in Van Gogh's conception. First, it provided a source to which one could turn in order to contemplate and understand Christ – or the more abstract religious concept he termed 'quelque chose là-haut' [402/337] – and thus oneself and one's role in life. This use of scripture remained relatively constant throughout Van Gogh's life, although he increasingly supplemented it with other writings and imagery, especially those he felt could transmit the truths he found in the Bible in a form more relevant to contemporary humanity. Modern literature and art, he believed, could both fulfil this role.[4] Van Gogh's favourite biblical passages focused on those parts of Christ's life (or Old Testament prefigurations) with which he identified most strongly, including those dealing with Christ's human qualities: his sufferings and feelings of doubt, and his mission of selflessly ministering to the less fortunate in society. Two of Van Gogh's best-loved quotations, appearing repeatedly in his correspondence, were Isaiah's 'man of sorrows and acquainted with grief' (Isaiah 53:3) and the words of Paul, 'sorrowful yet always rejoicing' (II Corinthians 6:10).[5] ☙ However, the Bible could also be a referent to Van Gogh's own father and a symbol of the latter's approach to religion – which Van Gogh originally embraced but later came to reject. As discussed elsewhere, this rejection had to do with Van Gogh's falling out with his father at the end of 1879, and marked the point at which he decided to become an artist.[6] From a more theoretical point of view, it also had to do with Van Gogh's perception of his father as hypocritical and intolerant vis-à-vis the fundamental tenets of the Groningen School, the form of Dutch Protestant thought to which he subscribed.[7] Van Gogh did not turn his back on the basic ideas underpinning this theolo-

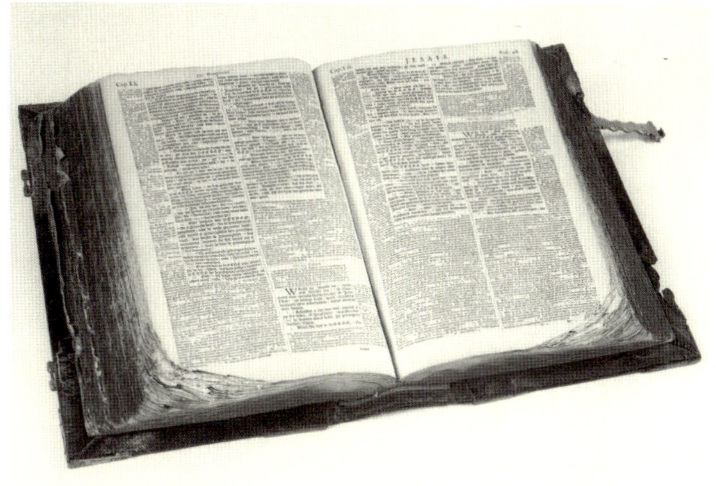

gy, but only on the corruption he felt it had undergone at the hands of individual members of the clergy, something he came to feel was inevitable with the institutionalisation of religious thought. The same sentiments governed Van Gogh's feelings toward the ideas found in the type of Protestant theology espoused by his uncle J.P. Stricker – that of the Modern School.[8] In fact, these schools of thought, as will be seen, provided Van Gogh with the fundamental intellectual basis upon which his own attitudes towards cultural production were formed.

'DOMINOCRATIE'

If one considers Van Gogh's background – that is, his family life, studies, professional aspirations and work experience – even prior to the point at which he definitively turned to painting, one encounters religion and art as dominant themes, with books and print culture fulfilling an important secondary role. In his attempt to make a career in the art trade, from 1869-76, he followed in the footsteps of three of his uncles. In his endeavours to become a minister in the Dutch Reformed Church, for which he did preparatory studies in Amsterdam in 1877-78, followed by a period working as a lay preacher among the Belgian miners in the Borinage district, he had his grandfather, father, and uncle Stricker as

61. Theodorus van Gogh's Bible, Leiden, Doopsgezinde Gemeente (on loan to the Van Gogh Museum, Amsterdam)

role models. ❦ The Groningen School, which, as stated, was the form of Protestantism to which Van Gogh's father adhered, was named after the circle formed around Petrus Hofstede de Groot, who had become professor of theology at the university of Groningen in 1829. Its members focused on service to others and taught that God could be found in all peoples and within nature, and that individuals could become more god-like through the revelation embodied in the person of Jesus Christ. Moderate and non-dogmatic in approach, Groningers held that religious enlightenment could be achieved through numerous channels, including the study of the Bible but also of non-biblical texts and images. The notion that art – both literary and visual – could communicate religious meaning was widespread among the members of this school, and it was this aspect, along with the emphasis on faith being rooted in a personal experiencing of Christ and the emulation of him in his humility and service to others, that had the most profound effect on Van Gogh. ❦ Van Gogh's most basic understanding of the tenets of the Groningen School was formed in his childhood. Growing up as the son of a minister in the small village of Zundert in the predominantly Catholic province of Brabant (fig. 62), he heard many sermons in which his father brought together textual and visual imagery as a means of communicating religious ideas to a community of agricultural labourers. He was aware of the difficult social conditions in which these people lived, and of the fact that his father's task as a preacher was to address not only their spiritual needs but, more pressingly, the elemental questions concerning their basic livelihood.[9] Van Gogh sought to emulate his father in his work with this class of people. Addressing their oppressed social circumstances from a material and spiritual point of view became part of his life project, both in the early years when he attempted to follow in his father's footsteps by becoming a minister, and later when he turned to art as his profession. His preoccupation with the lower classes and rural labour profoundly affected both his reception and creation of art, which he felt should be able to speak to the people. ❦ Another aspect of the Groningen School was its nationalist tendency, which led to an interest in Netherlandish literary and intellectual sources predating – and thus pre-empting – the doctrines of Calvin. One of these was the popular 15th-century work of Thomas à Kempis, *De imitatione Christi* (fig. 52), which Van Gogh read in a number of languages and referred to repeatedly in his early correspondence.

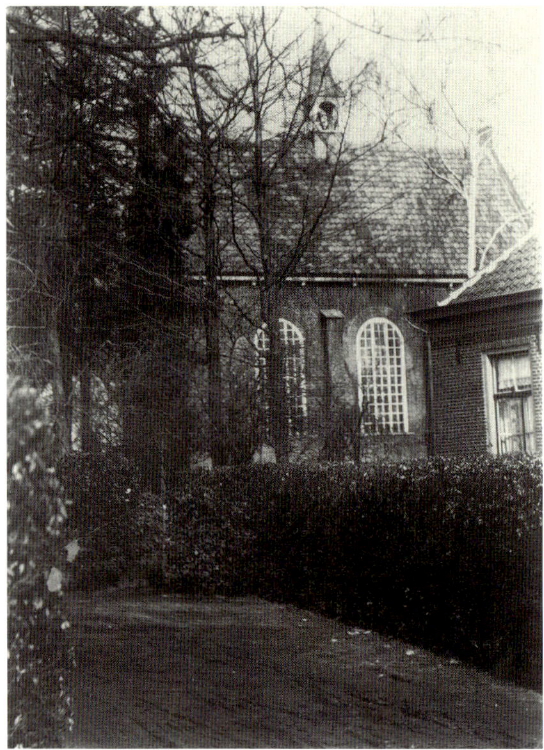

This piece of devotional literature was of central importance to Van Gogh and the Van Gogh family.[10] Just as later he would copy visual works by his preferred artists, Van Gogh reported in a letter to Theo from Amsterdam in September of 1877 that he was copying out a French translation of the treatise in its entirety [128/108]. The book provided a model of Christ that was accessible and personal and, in Van Gogh's eyes, one that transcended differences of belief, nationality, class and gender.[11] Like the biblical verses from Isaiah and Corinthians referred to earlier, it also emphasised self-denial and suffering in the service of others. Furthermore, it described Christian life in terms of a pilgrimage leading to ultimate union with Christ.[12] ❦ As was the case with biblical scripture, Van Gogh cited *De imitatione Christi* frequently and often in conjunction with his favourite visual images. From Amsterdam, for example, he wrote to Theo that he had asked to borrow a copy of this 'sublime' work and had begun copying it out as a result of an irresistible longing. This longing, he suggests, may have resulted from his frequent viewing of a lithograph of the same title he had hanging in his room.[13] The work, Luis Ruyperez's *The imitation of Christ*, depicts a monk – perhaps

62. The church at Zundert

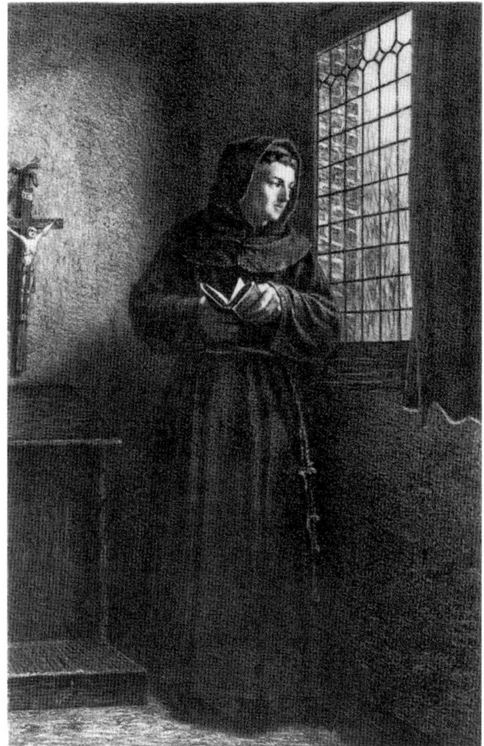

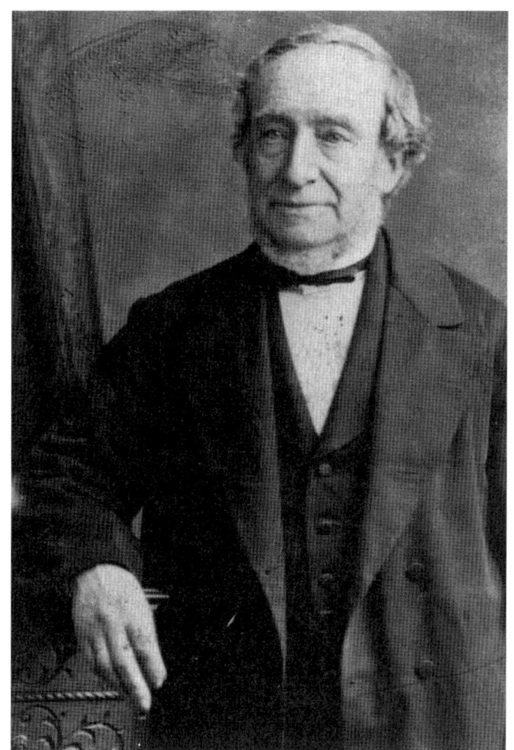

a reference to Thomas à Kempis himself – holding an open book while gazing pensively out of a window (fig. 63). At the left hangs a wooden crucifix. Van Gogh mentions the print in a number of letters during this early period, and relates that he had written under it the words he and Theo had so often heard their father say: 'Lord, I so want to be earnest' [112/93]. For Van Gogh the lithograph functioned as an object of devotion and meditation, reminding him of Thomas à Kempis and his book.[14]

Van Gogh's christocentric approach to cultural production, then, was fundamentally rooted in Groningen theology. By mid-century, however, the Modern movement had taken over the role of bringing renewal and reform to Dutch Protestantism. It was a far more radical tendency, indeed leading some Moderns, including notable figures such as Ferdinand Domela Nieuwenhuis and Allard Pierson, to leave the Church altogether, turning instead to anarchist politics and an academic career in art history, respectively. The Modern School insisted on Christ's human nature, rejecting the supernatural events of his life and emphasising the need for thoroughgoing historical Bible criticism. Religion, it was

felt, had to be in step with modern science in order to be of relevance to society. It was here that Van Gogh would find the ideas that encouraged him the most in conflating the roles of artist and theologian and, ultimately, artist and Christ. ❦ While in Amsterdam in 1877-78 Van Gogh came under the direct influence of his uncle J. P. Stricker (fig. 64), who supervised his Bible studies in preparation for his (ultimately unsuccessful) attempt to write university entry exams in theology. Van Gogh studied under Stricker, discussed his ideas with him and attended his sermons. He also knew and admired Stricker's writings. The close relationship he enjoyed with his uncle came to an end, however, when Van Gogh's unwelcome attentions to Stricker's daughter, the widow Kee Vos, resulted in her rejection of him. Nonetheless, his uncle's ideas, and those of the Modern School he had come to know so intimately through him, had a profound and lasting effect on Van Gogh's own ideation. There were three aspects of Stricker's belief system that were particularly important in shaping and reinforcing his views. First, Stricker's approach to conveying religious ideas was populist: his sermons and writings were popular in tone, and he saw his position as one of a *volks-*

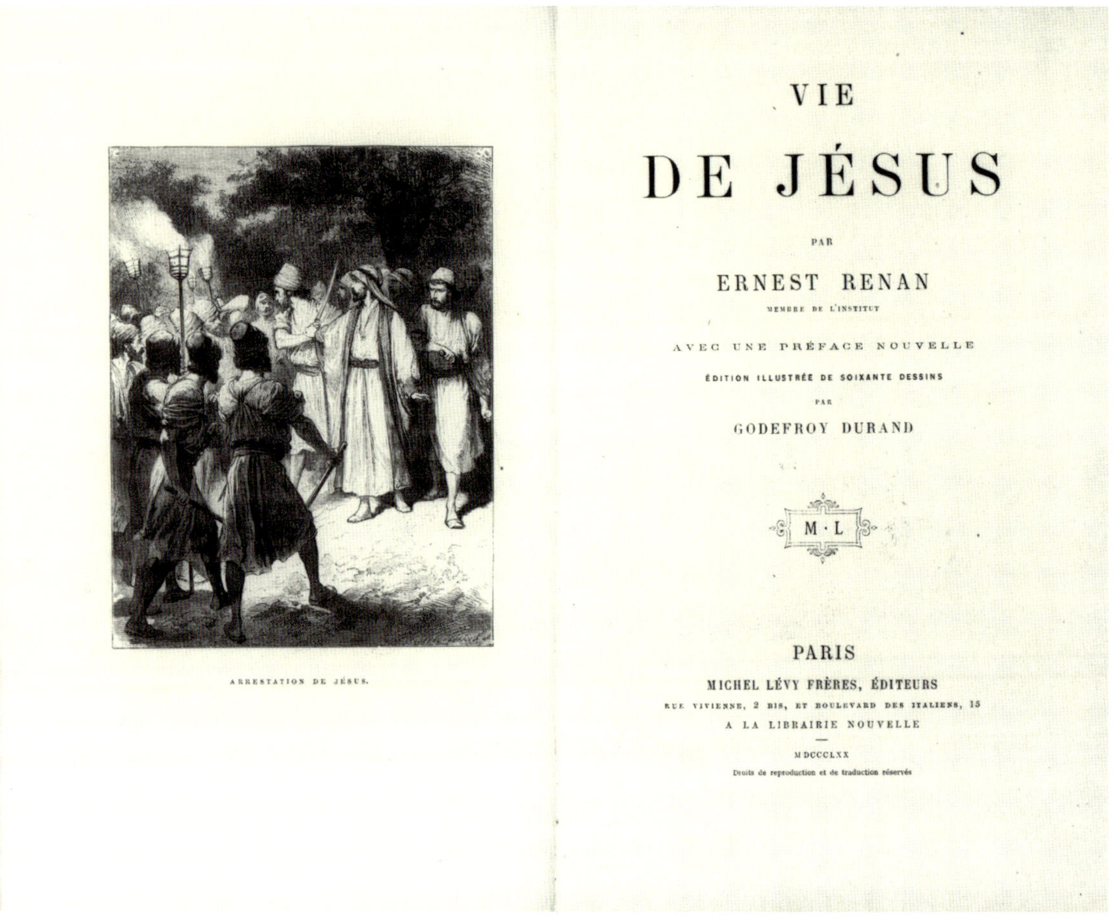

leraar or teacher of the people.[15] Furthermore, he brought together the notions of religious and artistic communication. Finally, Stricker was an anti-supernaturalist, considering Christ's miracles and other similar events in the Bible to be allegorical as opposed to literal, a view he espoused in his most important publication, *Jezus van Nazareth, volgens de historie geschetst* of 1868.[16] ❧ That Van Gogh knew of *Jezus van Nazareth*, whether through conversations with his uncle or through a direct reading of the text, seems certain, although he does not specifically refer to it in his correspondence. This book would have reinforced many of Van Gogh's ideas concerning Christ as a human rather than supernatural being, a suffering servant and man of the people. Taking part in the wider tendencies of historical Bible criticism, it reiterated many ideas that were already known to Van Gogh through his readings of Ernest Renan's *La vie de Jésus*, a work he greatly admired (fig. 65).[17] Stricker hoped with his study to address some of the general confusion that he felt had accompanied this feature of Modern School biblical critique and that had left the ordinary person wondering what was left in the study of the Bible and Christ.[18] He outlined those aspects of Christ's life he felt were proven historical facts and relegated all else to the mythology that had grown up around Christ's person. In Stricker's mind, however, this 'non-historical' side of the Christ story was not without literary and allegorical merit, and it became the subject of an unpublished sequel to *Jezus van Nazareth* entitled *De Christus der legende*.[19] ❧ Another of Stricker's publications that had a decided impact on Van Gogh was *De schriftelijke nalatenschap der oud-Israelitische profeten, wijzen en dichters* of 1880. Stricker hoped with this work to make accessible the Old Testament, which, as he wrote, contained 'greater treasures' than many realised, and which all those interested in 'beauty or in good' would agree had incomparable value.[20] Van Gogh's re-

65. **Ernest Renan,** *La vie de Jésus*, ed. Godefroy Durand, Paris 1863

sponse to this book, when he read it in the summer of 1881, reveals how closely he related the work of his uncle to the task of the artist. Even though the two men continued to be estranged, there can be no doubt he felt a deep affinity with Stricker's writings and ideas. In November he wrote to Theo: 'Do you know that J.P.S[tricker] is really a very clever man, in fact, an artist?' [187/161] Stricker's characterisation of Isaiah in particular would have echoed Van Gogh's own interest in the prophet, emphasising as it does the convergence of aesthetic beauty and religious mission. Not only does Isaiah – especially in the suffering servant passage of 'the man of sorrows' – prefigure the coming of Christ for both men, in Stricker's book he is even construed as a poet: 'He is in the fullest sense of the word a poet [...]. In him is seen most clearly what a prophet actually is, preacher and consoler as well.'[21]

This background is essential to understanding Van Gogh's taste in art and literature but needs, in turn, to be situated within the larger context of Protestant Holland, so that the full extent of the theologians' cultural domination can be understood. Until the end of the 19th century, clergymen held an extremely powerful position in Dutch society,[22] not just as religious leaders, but also as politicians, educators, poets and writers of literary and art criticism.[23] During Van Gogh's youth and early adulthood, cultural production and reception was largely governed by the strong voices of the Reformed Church, and until very late in the century the cultural elite in the Netherlands was largely made up of those educated to enter the clergy. In 1830, for example, this group represented more than half of all Dutch university students, and from the 1850s through the 1870s the number of doctorates granted in theology rose to an all time high.[24] There is yet another reason for considering university theological studies in relation to the discussion at hand. Early in the 19th century a restructuring had taken place in Dutch higher education that would significantly affect the generation of theologians most influential in Van Gogh's life. One of the notable results was to encourage a closer relationship between theology and other university disciplines. This was part of an effort to push the university towards producing graduates with an understanding of their own field but also with a wide enough general knowledge and education to enable them to contribute to society as a whole. It is relevant to note in this respect that the sermon was studied as one component of letterkunde (literary studies), alongside other

literary forms such as poetry, drama and the novel.[25] In this way universities hoped to stimulate theologians to take part in the cultural formation of the nation,[26] widening the parameters of their area of study and encouraging the cross-disciplinal.

RELIGIOUS TEXT-IMAGE COMBINATIONS

Protestant clergymen employed works of visual art to signify religious meaning in a number of ways. The use of *bijschriften poëzie*, i.e. a combination of image and poem, to convey religious ideas is a case in point. Its importance in 19th-century Dutch theological culture has now been recognised,[27] but its significance within the reception of art in the Netherlands has yet to be fully investigated. Images in *bijschriften poëzie* were sometimes explicitly religious in nature but more often depicted humble everyday scenes that invited contemplation on some aspect of devotion or encouraged the viewer to lead a morally worthy life. In other words, they represented an indirect rather than literal approach to the subject, similar to the distinction Van Gogh would make to Bernard in relation to christological works that represented 'the teaching of Christ' as opposed to those depicting Christ himself. [635/B8] 'After the storm', a poem by the popular poet-preacher J.J.L. ten Kate, accompanied by a reproduction of a work by the Hague School artist Jozef Israëls (fig. 66) is an example of *bijschriften poëzie* designed to communicate religious meaning by association. This kind of work had strong ties to the Dutch emblematic tradition of the 16th and 17th centuries, in which text and image were brought together to illustrate religious concepts and moral lessons, locating the universal within the everyday and the transcendent within the natural world.[28] It can also be related to Dutch 17th-century genre paintings of lowly interiors. Although there is no way of knowing whether Van Gogh saw the exact book of *bijschriften poëzie* in which this poem-image was reproduced, he was certainly familiar with this kind of publication,[29] and admired both Ten Kate, whom he heard preach on a number of occasions in Amsterdam, and Jozef Israëls, whose pictures he often praised in his correspondence. Israëls's image is representative of the kind of naturalist work that was among the most consistently privileged in Van Gogh's view of what constituted successful religious art. In particular, the device of light pouring onto a domestic scene as the only signification of religious

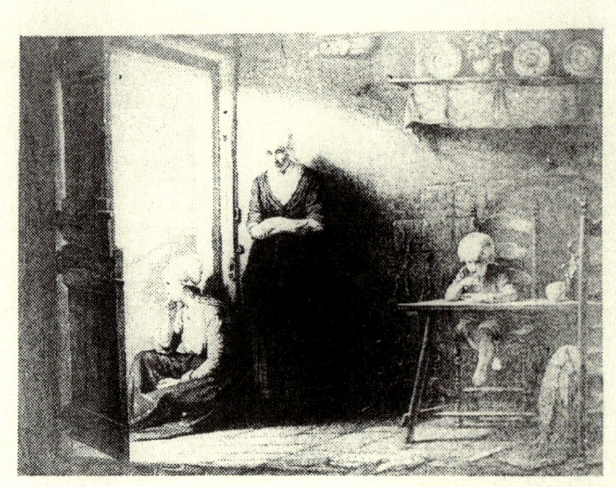

meaning held strong resonance for him, as did the working-class subject matter (plate 65).[30]

A naturalist artwork that Van Gogh did know was *Funeral procession through a wheatfield* of 1862 by Jacobus Jan van der Maaten (fig. 67). A print of it hung in his room [37/30] as well as in his father's study [36/29]. Van Gogh wrote that the Reverend had referred to it in a funeral sermon, alongside biblical passages from the books of Mark, John, Corinthians and Thessalonians – passages dealing with the themes of Christ's resurrection and second coming and the promise of eternal life, and which also include a number of agricultural metaphors [127/107].[31] ☙ *Funeral procession*

through a wheatfield was popular in the Dutch Protestant community, and at least two other ministers, Bernard ter Haar and Eliza Laurillard, made reference to it in their sermons.[32] In Amsterdam, Van Gogh gave a copy of the print to Maurits Benjamin Mendes da Costa, his teacher of Latin and Greek, after having filled the borders and reverse side with quotations from the gospel in Latin and added, on either side of the image, a passage of written verse. The one on the left, taken from the hymnal of the Dutch Reformed Church, alludes to death through references to agricultural labour,[33] while the one on the right, a passage in English from Longfellow's poem 'Afternoon in February' – like Van der Maaten's work itself – makes use of landscape to approach the theme. The scripture cited by Van Gogh centres on the promise of resurrection and eternal life and on agricultural themes, including two of the excerpts cited in the sermon by his father on 'the grain of wheat' and the parable of the sower.[34] ☙ The image itself is of a flat Dutch landscape with a church, centrally placed, silhouetted against the sky and surrounded by a few other simple buildings and trees. In the foreground is a field of wheat with a procession of diminutive figures filing through it. To the right, an equally small figure of a labourer with a scythe continues his work. The human element is insignificant in comparison to the wide expanse of the field and vastness of the sky – broken only slightly by the church spire thrusting upward. ☙ The only indications other than the title that *Funeral procession through a wheatfield* actually depicts a funeral, or that it may have a religious significance, is the central position of the church, with the members of the procession trudging through the field towards it, and the lonely figure of the reaper toiling to the right. There is no allusion to a supernatural presence or to the afterlife. It is thus an eminently naturalist representation of death. To the 19th-century Dutch eye, however, conditioned as it was by the use of visual imagery to convey religious messages, the work functioned metaphorically. ☙ Not only did Van Gogh situate this image within a religious framework; here, at this early period in his life, he transformed it into his own form of *bijschriften poëzie*, adding biblical and poetic texts to it. Soon, however, the words conveying religious meaning would be deemed unnecessary, as they became embedded in the image itself. His treatment of *Funeral procession through a wheatfield*, then, reveals the extent to which Van Gogh viewed art as a potentially integral part of religious communication, with naturalist scenes of rural labour be-

66. Jan Jacob Lodewijk ten Kate, 'Na den storm,' with an illustration by Jozef Israëls, from J.J.L. ten Kate, *Nieuwe Photographiën met dichterlijke bijschriften*, Amsterdam 1870

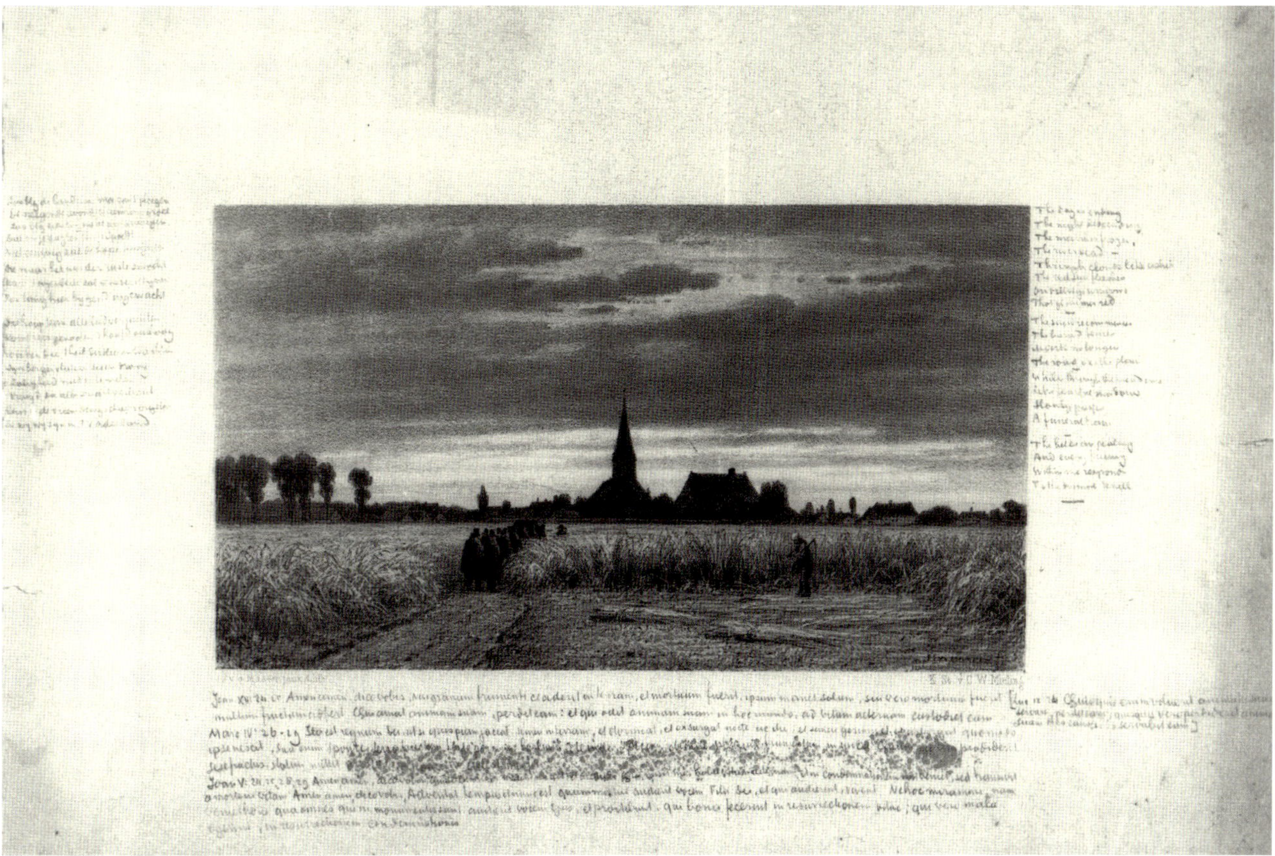

ing among the themes he considered most successful in achieving this. Van der Maaten's image also, of course, contains much that Van Gogh would incorporate into his own future artistic production: the landscape with its expansive sky and wheatfield, the church, and the field labourer with scythe would become some of the most compelling motifs in his own iconography.

The ability of artworks like *Funeral procession* to function on a religious level was shaped by the public's general expectations concerning religion. These had undergone major shifts during the 19th century and were continuing to encounter what in some cases would prove to be insurmountable challenges. German philosophical writings such as those of Friedrich Schleiermacher and Friedrich Schelling, for example, encouraged a subjective experiencing of religion, which to some implied the redundancy of the Church. Added to this were the questions being raised by contemporary scientific discoveries, in particular Darwin's theory of evolution, and historical Bible criticism. Works investigating the historical Jesus (already encountered in Stricker's writings), such as David Friedrich Strauss's *Leben Jesu* (1835) and, later, Ernest Renan's *La vie de Jésus* (1863), were read widely and had a profound effect on the way the person of Jesus Christ and the personal and social role of religion were viewed, and contributed to a growing contingency of liberal theologians, Protestant and Catholic alike. This occurred not only in the Netherlands but in the Christian world as a whole. As a result, by mid-century many forms of Christianity had moved away from traditional ideas and were defining belief systems based on a christocentric humanitarianism that went hand in hand with calls for social reform. Here the religious, social and political discourses of the 19th century began to converge, and one could sometimes find in the person of Christ the religious leader and radical social reformer in one.[35] One artist who contributed to this new tendency was Ary Scheffer.

67. After **Jacobus Jan van der Maaten,** *Funeral procession through a wheat field,* 1862, Amsterdam, Universiteitsbibliotheek

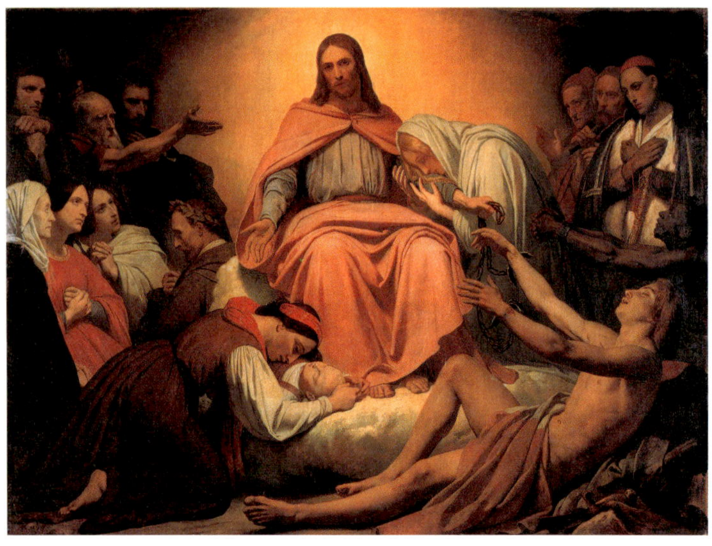

ARY SCHEFFER'S *Christus consolator*

In the early days, Scheffer was one of the most notable artists included in Van Gogh's list of luminaries of religious painting. His *Christus consolator* of 1837 was a work Van Gogh venerated throughout most of his life, but rejected by the end of it (fig. 68, plate 9). ❦ Scheffer, an expatriate Dutchman who spent most of his career in France, was extremely popular among clergymen, and his work featured prominently in *bijschriften poëzie*. In the Christus consolator, a recognisable figure of Christ, bearded and robed according to convention, is the focus of the composition. The work was disseminated widely in print form and became one of the most celebrated religious images of the 19th century. In Dutch Protestant circles the *Christus consolator*, and indeed Ary Scheffer's works in general, were highly esteemed. They had a particular significance for the Van Gogh family as well.[36] Not only did Van Gogh's father own a drawing by Scheffer, but the founding member of the Groningen School, Petrus Hofstede de Groot, wrote one of his first biographies.[37] The *Christus consolator* was also one of Van Gogh's personal favourites. He saw and admired the painting – as well as others by Scheffer – during his Dordrecht period and had a print of it that decorated his rooms in London, Dordrecht, Amsterdam and The Hague. In fact, in Dordrecht there were two reproductions of the work on the wall, both sent to him by his brother Theo.[38]

The notion of 'consolation' expressed by the *Christus consolator* had deep resonance for Van Gogh. Referred to earlier in this essay in Van Gogh's statement that 'the consolation of the so melancholic Bible [...] is Christ' |635/B8|, and encountered in Stricker's writings as belonging to the role of prophet, it was a recurring theme in both Van Gogh's writings and art. It was inextricably intertwined with his ideas concerning artistic representation and religion and their functions within society,[39] which themselves invariably involved the provision of comfort and solace – that is, of consolation. Scheffer's painting, with the stigmata clearly visible on Christ's right hand, emphasises his suffering and compassion toward those in need. The work is based on the biblical passage Luke 4:18 in which Christ reads from the prophet Isaiah: 'The spirit of the Lord is upon me, because he hath anointed me to preach the gospel to the poor; he hath sent me to heal the brokenhearted, to preach deliverance to the captives, and recovering of sight to the blind, to set at liberty them that are bruised.' However, while the style and the appearance of the Christ figure in the painting conform to tradition, the iconography as a whole does not. ❦ The diversity of figures in need of Christ's ministrations make this painting a compendium of age-old and modern-day oppression and social hardship. The focus is on enslavement – both actual and metaphoric.[40] Christ reaches out with his left hand to break the handcuffs of a dying Pole wrapped in the national flag. Behind him are four men representing slavery from the ancient, medieval and modern worlds, including a chained black man – an allusion to the ongoing slave trade – a figure that was politically charged enough to warrant its being omitted in prints of the work destined for the United States.[41] Mary Magdalene kneels on this side of the composition, kissing the outstretched arm of Christ. To the right of Christ is a group of three females, representing the sufferings of the three ages of woman. Behind them are three men: one, knife poised, is about to take his own life; another, a seaman, has his hand outstretched to the one who can calm the waters; and, beside him, an exile leans on his walking staff. In the foreground, bent over what appears to be her dead child, is a mourning mother. This collection of suffering humanity is made complete by the inclusion on the same side of the symbol of tormented artistic suffering, the misunderstood poet Torquato Tasso. ❦ Bringing together socio-political and religious themes, the *Christus consolator* makes use of the modern religious iconographic language that

68. Ary Scheffer, *Christus consolator*, 1837, Amsterdams Historisch Museum (on loan to the Van Gogh Museum, Amsterdam)

began to take hold among a number of painters around mid-century.[42] This development in the visual arts paralleled and indeed had its roots in the liberal theologies of the day.[43] In Catholic France, where Scheffer's work was conceived and first exhibited, the ideas of Johan Adam Möhler encouraged the development of a new humanitarian Catholic stream. Möhler's writings were popularised by the liberal priest Félicité de Lamennais, who, in turn, had a profound influence on many of his compatriots. Lamennais's radical concern for addressing social injustices helped promote a religious iconography in which Christ was constructed in ways that could be understood by and would be of direct relevance to the lower classes. This included a vision of Christ as a labourer and man of the people, friend of the poor and liberator of the oppressed.[44] Others whose work exhibit Mennaisian and Möhlerist ideas include the theorist Pierre-Joseph Proud'hon, the writer George Sand and the artists Hippolyte Flandrin, Emile Signol and, of particular relevance in the case of Van Gogh's artistic canon, Eugène Delacroix.[45] ❦ By the time Van Gogh moved permanently to France in 1886 the *Christus consolator* no longer held the exalted position for him it had had for so many years. At least until 1883, while living in The Hague, however, he revered the work and had regarded it as a source of personal inspiration and, indeed, of consolation.[46] Its importance to him lay in the fact that it combined the two familiar themes of suffering and the provision of solace to the less fortunate in society – the working classes, foreigners, social outcasts. The role he saw Christ fulfilling here confirmed what he had found in the religious schools of thought of his father and of Stricker – and this role he increasingly ascribed not to the clergy but to the modern artist.[47] The socio-political character of the part did not escape him.

ART-CRITICAL AND BIOGRAPHICAL INTERVENTIONS

By 1886 Van Gogh's most basic ideas concerning religious art had not changed. What had changed, however, was the form he felt these works could best take. Increasingly, Van Gogh came to associate Scheffer's polished, academic style with elitism. In other words, a work like Scheffer's was not sufficiently divorced from the world of the upper-class salon-goer to be able to function in a truly democratic fashion. Van Gogh continued to adhere

to populist notions he had long held, only now applying them to the formal aspects of art. In this he conformed rather closely to the kind of theories propagated by writers such as Théophile Thoré, an art critic and historian who was instrumental in developing a critical framework into which Van Gogh could place and further evolve his own christocentric ideals of art, without compromising the basic premises formed by the Dutch theological culture from which he was now emerging. ❦ Thoré, writing under the pseudonym William Bürger, was the first French art historian to attribute the rise of 17th-century Dutch naturalist painting to the political and religious freedom associated with the Dutch Republic. He would subsequently be echoed in this by other writers on Dutch art, such as Charles Blanc, who continued to emphasise the significance of the political and religious situation for creativity in the Golden Age. Van Gogh knew the work of both authors and, in particular, had considered Thoré's *Musées de la Hollande* (1858-60) essential reading since his early years when he was training as an art dealer.[48] Thoré identified contemporary naturalist painting as the legitimate heir of the art of the Dutch Republic, and felt it heralded a truly democratic form of art for the future.[49] Influenced by Saint-Simonian thought and his radical affiliations during the Revolution of 1848, Thoré brought together notions of religion, art and revolutionary politics in his writings. Praising 17th-century Dutch naturalism, he established Johannes Vermeer's reputation, wrote extensively on Frans Hals and admired Rembrandt, stating that even in his religious works the latter focused on the natural world and ordinary people.[50] As far as the works of his own time were concerned, Thoré eschewed academic art he felt to be conservative, and championed those artists he saw as the most progressive – including Delacroix, Millet and other artists of the Barbizon School. Here, then, was a kind of art criticism to which Van Gogh could completely relate, and although he had always been conversant with it, by his French period such criticism was supplanting more specifically religious writings, while at the same time endorsing many of the same ideas. Van Gogh's admiration for works like Rembrandt's *Christ at Emmaus* (fig. 59), Delacroix's *Christ asleep during the tempest* (plate 124) and Millet's *Sower* (fig. 60, plate 45), mentioned at the beginning of this essay, all fit logically into the theoretical framework provided by Thoré. The primary importance given to Dutch art by Thoré also held further personal significance for Van Gogh at this point in his life, trying, as he was, as a Dutchman to make his way in the French art world. ❦ Other forms of art discourse, such as the artist's biography, also had an increasing impact on Van Gogh's ideation, and again it was those writings that confirmed ideas long cherished that had the most resonance. Alfred Sensier's biography of Jean-François Millet, which Van Gogh read soon after it was published in 1881, for example, conflated the role of the artist with that of religious figure.[51] Van Gogh's admiration for Millet, whom he already regarded as both an artistic and spiritual mentor, increased even further upon reading Sensier's biography. ❦ Sensier's image of Millet brings to mind Isaiah's suffering servant and combines this with the agricultural metaphors of rural labour so beloved by Van Gogh. According to Sensier, Millet was a melancholic and suffering figure, but one who was, above all, strong in his convictions: 'faithful and proud in his religion and in his art'; Sensier then goes on to call Millet a labourer, and the field his art.[52] This construction of the artist as deeply religious, living humbly among the farm workers, labouring at his own task of art, speaking of the miserable plight of the worker,[53] could hardly have failed to appeal to Van Gogh. He saw in Millet a kindred spirit and took a part in sanctifying him through his own writings, referring to him as 'Father Millet'. One need look no further than Millet's *Sower* to find a christological image that fulfilled all that Van Gogh saw as essential in religious art, and that harked back to the earliest of venerated motifs found in his personal canon. The fact that Sensier added a revolutionary note to his description of Millet's *Sower*, stating that his gesture had been interpreted as threatening – like throwing 'handfuls of bullets heavenwards, as though protesting the misery of the worker'[54] – would have made its appeal to Van Gogh all the stronger. Not only was this an image dealing with the teaching of Christ in the form of a parable, it did so in a naturalist style and using an agricultural metaphor that made it of direct relevance to and easily understood by the people, at the same time subtly implying revolutionary change.

CONCLUSION

The textual and visual works addressed in this essay, while making up only a small part of Van Gogh's religious canon of art, illustrate the most basic determinants of his taste in this kind of work. The convergence of religious, artistic and social ideas within them functions logically in the context of the 19th-century Dutch 'dominocratie'. As we have seen, however, this became more complicated once Van Gogh left his homeland to begin working in France, which lacked the same religious or cultural backdrop against which his works and ideas could be understood. Nonetheless, there were a number of tendencies in French art discourses that endorsed Van Gogh's own christological image of the artist and reinforced his belief that the function of art was to serve and be understood by the people, providing them with spiritual consolation and hope for change in ways that were modern and relevant. His reception of art, then, continued on the most fundamental level to be informed by the directions in Dutch theology he knew best. While this relationship with his Dutch religious past was not unproblematic, its very turbulence mirrors that of these religious circles themselves as they struggled to meet the challenges presented by modern society.

❦

VAN GOGH'S TASTE FOR REALITY, ON EARTH AS IT IS IN HEAVEN

EVERT VAN UITERT

VAN GOGH THE REALIST

Vincent van Gogh, an avid reader of Honoré de Balzac, Emile Zola and other realist and naturalist authors, and inspired his whole life long by Jean-François Millet, can safely be called a realist or naturalist. With a few exceptions he always painted from life, and he declared that he wanted to excel in portraiture, a supremely realistic genre.[1] ❧ His preference for certain painters and schools is also indicative of this.[2] Like so many 19th-century painters, he was a great admirer of the 17th-century Dutch masters. He saw them through the eyes of Théophile Thoré, a critic who also lauded painters of the Barbizon School like Millet and Théodore Rousseau.[3] Thoré defended a naturalist art which, in his opinion, was in step with the development of the human spirit, beneficial science, society and politics, and as such was an expression of modern times.[4] ❧ Van Gogh preferred to read Thoré himself rather than Dutch authors like Johannes van Vloten who derived their ideas from him. The same applied to the work of other Frenchmen like Charles Blanc and Eugène Fromentin, for they simply wrote better about the old Dutch school of painting than the Dutch themselves did.[5] It was these authors who helped shape his ideas about art. Thoré and Jules Michelet, another guiding spirit for the young Dutchman, belonged to the generation that had shown its allegiance in the revolutions of 1830 and 1848.[6] The work of the artists and writers who emerged then provided a guideline for the young Van Gogh.[7] In 1873 he read the first volume of Thoré's *Musées de la Hollande* (1858)

with approval, and derived many of his insights and preferences from it. As a result, he always retained a certain nostalgia for the past, specifically for the 17th and, broadly speaking, the mid-19th centuries. He also felt a political and social kinship with the revolutionary generation of 1848.[8] ❧ Van Gogh's mentality is also revealed by his reaction to the diaries of Gerard Bilders (1838-1865), a Dutch landscape painter who died young, which were published in a small edition in 1865.[9] Bilders was a very promising painter with an eye for the developments taking place in modern French art, which is what may have caught Van Gogh's attention. However, he felt that Bilders's view of life was too 'romantic' and, although he found him appealing, he preferred to read 'the life of father Millet or of Th. Rousseau or of Daubigny' [260/227]. ❧ In particular, Van Gogh associated the socially engaged and long-neglected artist Honoré Daumier (fig. 69) with the revolutionary generation of 1848,[10] and not Gustave Courbet (plates 119-120), who had launched realism with his one-man show at the 1855 World's Fair. Daumier became increasingly important to Van Gogh after 1882, and he regularly mentioned him in the same breath as Millet: 'People like Daumier – one must respect them, for they are among the pioneers' [522/418]. He continued to honour him even after he had become better acquainted with the very latest movements, not least because he regarded Daumier, who was born in Marseilles, as a man of the south, as he himself wanted to be. He wrote to Bernard, saying that Daumier was 'a very great genius', lending force to the realism underlying his own art, which had been criticised by Gauguin and Bernard [653/B13].[11] ❧ The painters of the Hague School also confirmed Van Gogh's view of realism, but their opinions were soon outdated by the developments taking place in France.

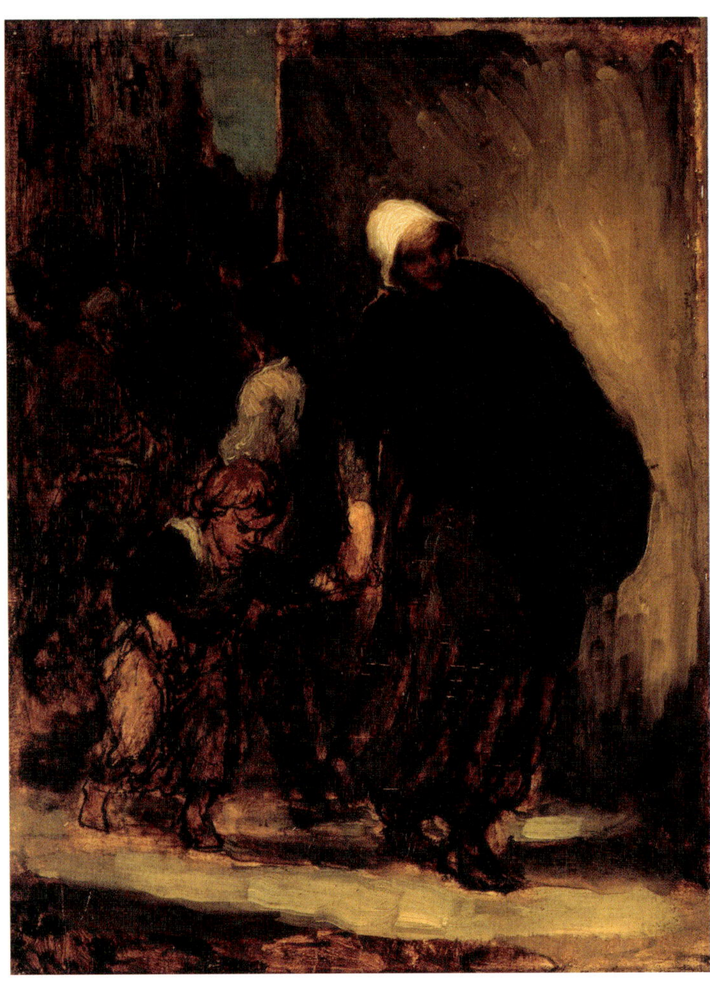

When Van Gogh set out to establish himself in Paris in 1886 he had to make up for lost ground. He succeeded in doing so, but the next step, which entailed a rejection of the old principles of art, was one he found impossible to take. He clung to old, realist ideas, although that does not alter the fact that he made revolutionary paintings.

So Van Gogh's fundamentally realist approach to art was not without its problems. The critic Albert Aurier summed them up in his article of 1890, 'Les isolés: Vincent van Gogh'. He described him as an heir to the realist Dutch painters and burghers of the Golden Age, before presenting him as an idealist who had risen far above banal reality. This was a plausible analysis. For posterity, however, the realist gradually disappeared behind the iconic

overstrung artist, the seeker after God, the unsung genius. His art was seen as reflecting this mythic image.[12] ❧ This essay deals with the tensions between idealist and realist views of art. The question of why Van Gogh clung so firmly to the 'principle of reality' will not be discussed however. Leaving aside the fact that he came to painting fairly late in life, this must have been due to the mental illness that manifested itself in Arles at the end of 1888. Only by holding fast to the reality that he saw before him could he fight off the hallucinations that plagued him during his attacks, and that ultimately led him to take his own life.

REALISM, IMPRESSIONISM, AND THE NATURALISM OF ZOLA

At first sight it appears that Van Gogh chose the path of revolutionary realism in art, but initially he was poorly informed about the most recent advances in painting. In 1884, when he was still living in Brabant, he knew only that Manet had taken up Courbet's mantle, but had seen few of his works and was totally ignorant of impressionism. ❧ Courbet and Manet had organised alternative exhibitions at the 1867 World's Fair, and were often mentioned in the same breath – by Zola, among others. Van Gogh's reaction in July 1883 to Zola's collected literary and Salon criticism, *Mon salon and Mes haines* (both of 1866), was typical in this regard. He said that mainly they had shown him Zola's weak points. He considered the criticism 'enormously mistaken, his ideas entirely wrong, except partly his appreciation of Manet – I find Manet clever too – but it is very interesting' [361/R38]. *Mes haines* continued to fascinate him, and he returned to it in January 1884. He was developing into a painter at the time, so was looking at painting in a different way. He now wrote that he had always found Manet's work 'very original', although he had seen 'very few of his pictures' [429/355] (fig. 70). His ambivalence towards Zola and the latter's defence of Manet's new art also emerges in the same letter. 'I do not think it exaggerated that some people, Zola for instance, *rave* about him, though I, for one, do not think he can be reckoned among the very first of this century. But his is a talent which *most certainly* has its *raison d'être*, and that is a great thing in itself. [...] For my part, I cannot agree with Zola's *conclusion*, as if Manet were a man who opens a new future to modern ideas of art. I consider Millet, not Manet, to be that essentially modern painter who opened a new horizon to

69. Honoré Daumier, *Beggar woman with two children,* Rotterdam, Museum Boijmans Van Beuningen

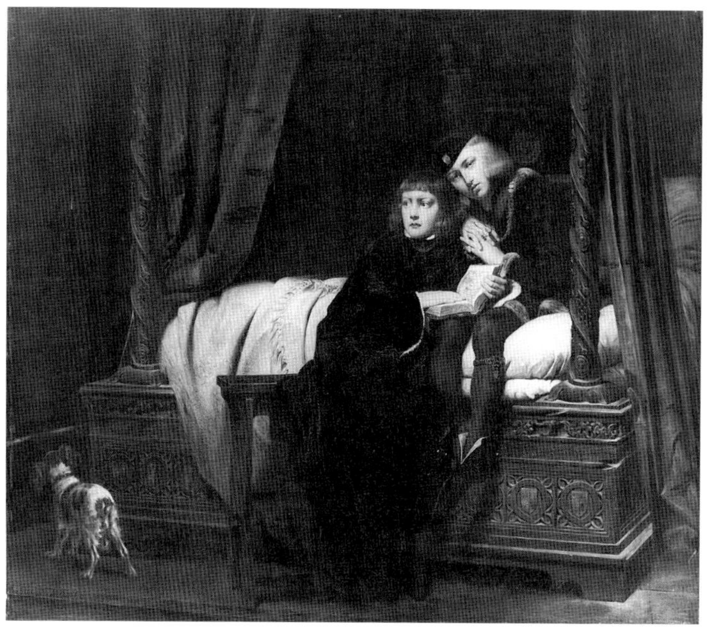

many.' Here Van Gogh was adopting a conservative modernist standpoint, which he would never entirely abandon. He took it amiss of Zola that he had not even mentioned Millet. ෆ The choice between Manet and Millet continued to preoccupy him. In the autumn of 1884 he observed that it was rather difficult in Holland to discover precisely what impressionism amounted to. As an artistic provincial he did realise that undoubtedly 'new, unexpected conceptions are beginning to arise. That pictures are starting to be painted in a very different tone than some years ago' [469/385]. The problem became pressing in 1885, when he finished his first major painting, the Millet-like *Potato eaters* (plate 44). His brother Theo and his colleague Anthon van Rappard criticised it for its lack of colour and for the deformation of the forms. Van Gogh bridled at these accusations, and defended his supposed errors, *'which a realist would not lightly commit'*, by drawing attention to their function, which was to strengthen the characteristic elements. Moreover, he was counting on viewers who would appreciate 'the spiritual conception of things' [529/R57]. ෆ As a novice painter, Van Gogh was becoming increasingly interested in the laws of colour, and here he found support in the

views of Delacroix, in Blanc's *Grammaire des art du dessin*, and in the works of art that he studied. In October 1885 he visited the newly opened Rijksmuseum and the Fodor Collection in Amsterdam, where he saw work by many of the painters he admired (Decamps, Diaz), but also by Meissonier.[13] ෆ When he moved to Antwerp in November 1885, Van Gogh was branching out in a new direction, as shown by his criticism of masters he had previously admired, and by his growing appreciation of Manet and Courbet. There, too, he saw many paintings, including work by Henri de Braekeleer, which he found 'like Manet, or at least as *original* as Manet' [550/459]. On the other hand, 'Delaroche-esqueness, *mediocrity*' angered him [554/445]. Delaroche was the main representative of the so-called *juste milieu*, which produced work of an historical and anecdotal nature painted in a photographic style (fig. 71). In a single breath Van Gogh spoke of 'Scheffer and Delaroche and Dubufe and Gérôme, who have so little of the *painter in them*' [554/445]. His guiding light was now not so much Millet as Delacroix. 'And once again Delacroix has tried to make people believe in the symphonies of the colours, and one would say in vain, if one remembers that what almost everybody understands by "good colour" is the *correctness* of the local colour, the narrow minded exactness – which neither Rembrandt nor Millet nor Delacroix nor whoever else, not even Manet or Courbet, has

70. Edouard Manet, *Peonies,* 1864, Paris, Musée d'Orsay.

71. Paul Delaroche, *Edward V and the Duke of York in the Tower,* 1830, Paris, Musée du Louvre aimed at, as little as Rubens or Veronese' [555/444]. Van Gogh's preference for colour and brushstroke, for painterliness, was unshakable.

FOR AND AGAINST IMPRESSIONISM

It was only in Paris in 1886 that Van Gogh first set eyes on colourful, impressionist paintings. At that time impressionism was establishing itself as an avant-garde movement. In addition, he saw that Seurat had taken yet another stride forward with his neo-impressionism. Impressionism was still renewing itself, but the next artistic generation felt the need for a more fundamental change of course. ⁊ Together with Gauguin, Bernard and others, Van Gogh tried to give shape to Richard Wagner's 'artwork of the future'. Although they initially retained the term impressionism, it soon became clear that making faithful depictions could no longer be the primary aim of modern art. The three artists had an interesting exchange of views, with Van Gogh being put on the theoretical defensive. He wrote to Bernard in August 1888 to clarify his position. 'Now we see that the Dutch paint things just as they are, apparently without reasoning, just as Courbet painted his beautiful nude women. They painted portraits, landscapes, still lifes. Well, one can be stupider than that, and commit greater follies' [659/B14]. The implication was that Bernard and Gauguin were perhaps committing a folly by deviating too far from this healthy 'Dutch' realism. ⁊ The upshot was that, after heated discussions with Gauguin in Arles, Van Gogh returned to his old views, to Rembrandt and to Millet, to Daumier for his distinctive handling of line, and to Delacroix for colour. He stuck to the study of nature as the point of departure for making a painting with style, which he believed sprang from a personal vision of nature, not from abandoning it. When he and Gauguin visited the museum in Montpellier, Van Gogh was greatly impressed by Delacroix's portrait of Alfred Bruyas (plate 117). He associated it with an unhappy man dressed in black from a poem by Alfred de Musset, and was deeply touched by this consoling portrait. That museum visit helped shift his focus from bright colour effects to halftones, which he found above all in the work of Delacroix.[14] In Arles he thought that all the new things he had seen in Paris had vanished, and that he had returned to the views he had developed in Nuenen, that is to say before he had discovered the impres-sionists. Once again relying on Delacroix he wrote: 'Because instead of trying to reproduce exactly what I have before my eyes, I use colour more arbitrarily, in order to express myself forcefully' [663/520]. ⁊ In May 1890, on his way to Auvers-sur-Oise, he saw the work of Pierre Puvis de Chavannes in Paris, and came to the conclusion that here was someone who could regenerate art. He had already written approvingly of him in 1884,[15] and later shared that admiration with his copains Bernard and Gauguin and the painters of the younger generation.[16] In May 1888, speaking of Puvis's *Hope* (fig. 11), he predicted: 'There is an art in the future, and it should be so beautiful and so young that, in truth, if we lose our youth to it we can only gain in serenity by it' [613/489]. Puvis had found a stylistic compromise between realism and idealism that greatly appealed to Van Gogh. He found Puvis's *Beheading of John the Baptist* as 'staggeringly beautiful and as magical as the one by Eugène Delacroix' [635/B8]. He gave a glowing account of Puvis's *Inter artes et naturam* (plate 94), accompanying it with a sketch (fig. 12). 'When you see the painting and look at it for a long time, you get the feeling of being present at a rebirth, irrevocable but benevolent, of everything you have believed in, have wished for, a strange and happy meeting between distant antiquity and raw modernity.' In addition to the sketch he drew his own *Arlésienne*, saying: 'What impassions me the most [...] is the portrait, the modern portrait' [883/W22]. Not surprisingly, then, Van Gogh was also struck by several portraits by Puvis.

MEISSONIER, A STRANGE BUT LASTING ATTACHMENT

Although Van Gogh appears at first sight to have been in tune with the realism sanctioned by modernism, it turns out on closer examination that the painters he admired included several popular, high-priced, academic, smooth-finish realists. Their reputations waned rapidly, as they did with Van Gogh after his initial enthusiasm. ⁊ He had a habit of listing the names of his favourite painters, and in January 1874 he mentioned no fewer than 61, mainly artists of the *juste milieu*, painters of peasant life and members of the Barbizon School.[17] The lists also contain popular masters of the day like Scheffer, Delaroche, Gérôme and Henri de Braekeleer. Numerous reproductions of their works were in circulation, and had been sold by Van Gogh when he was working as an art dealer.[18] ⁊ In 1872 he had seen De Braekeleer's

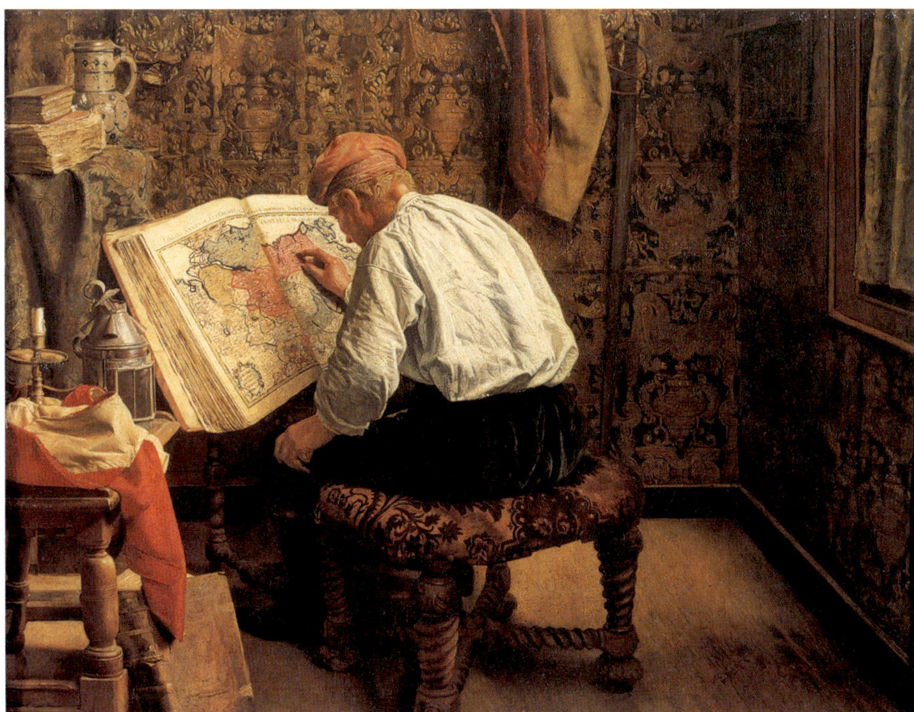

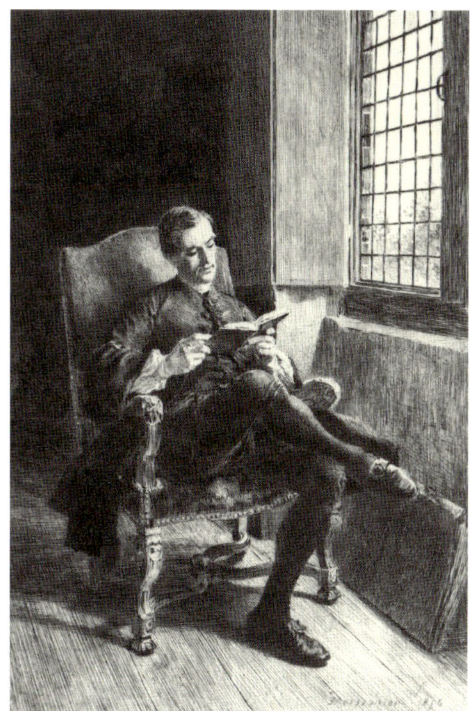

The geographer (fig. 72), and he was fulsome in its praise. When he began to paint seriously, this appreciation took on greater significance. He did not rank De Braekeleer among those 'who everywhere look for the mother-of-pearl effect', but praised him for his 'very interesting endeavour to be literally true', for the fact that 'he stands quite apart', and for his 'intelligent simplicity which is not afraid of honest technique' [550/439]. Van Gogh must have been well aware that De Braekeleer drew his inspiration from 17th-century Dutch models. Both his subject matter and his technique betrayed this, and in that respect he was not in step with the more contemporary realism of Courbet, with the landscape painters of Barbizon, or with the Hague School. ଓ The same applies to the popular genre painter Ernest Meissonier.[19] Van Gogh must have appreciated the early Meissonier as an illustrator because he had the same ambition himself. For instance, he had always found Jacquemart's etching after Meissonier's *The reader* (fig. 73) 'splendid' [690/542]. He had acquired his 'boundless admiration for Meissonier' from his teacher Anton Mauve [854/626a]. According to Van Gogh, Meissonier belonged with Daumier, Delacroix, Millet and Géricault.[20] He considered painters like Meissonier (and Rousseau) 'very interesting for

those who love them and try to understand what the artist felt.' According to him, one could look at a good Meissonier for more than a year. The old Dutch masters would have had no quarrel with his essentially French workmanship, and 'yet it is different from them, and modern' [799/602 and 602a]. ଓ Unlike the avant-garde, Van Gogh made no fundamental distinction between good, progressive realism and conservative, detailed, smoothly painted, photographic realism, although he certainly knew the difference between the two.[21] To him, Millet, Delacroix and Meissonier were unsurpassable.[22] ଓ What did Van Gogh see in Meissonier and painters of his ilk? In Meissonier's case it was above all the expressive figures. He had painted 'men', as in his *Smoker by the window* (fig. 74) and *Young man having lunch*, he wrote in 1875 [38/31], and in 1882 he admired *The draughtsman* (plate 92) for 'the action of intense attention', which reminded him of 'a certain figure by Rembrandt' [290/248]. Unlike other painters of the *juste milieu* with their mother-of-pearl effects, Van Gogh had no objection to Meissonier's technique, any more than he had to the illusionistic technique of the Belgian Henri de Braekeleer. He even quoted an undogmatic saying of Meissonier's with approval: 'la science – nul ne l'a' – no one has the only correct technique

72. Henri de Braekeleer, *The geographer,* 1871, Brussels, Musées royaux des Beaux-Arts de Belgique

73. After **Ernest Meissonier,** *The reader,* 1856, Paris, Bibliothèque Nationale de France, Cabinet des Estampes

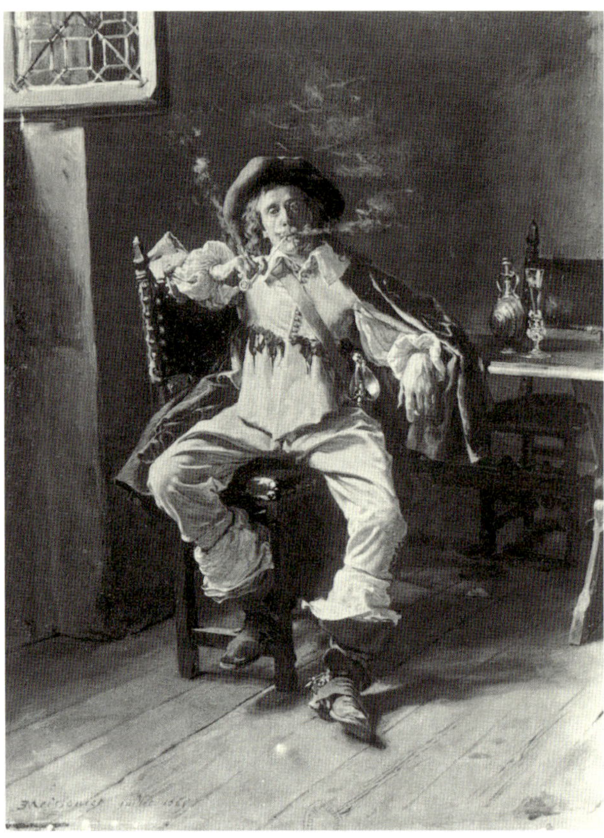

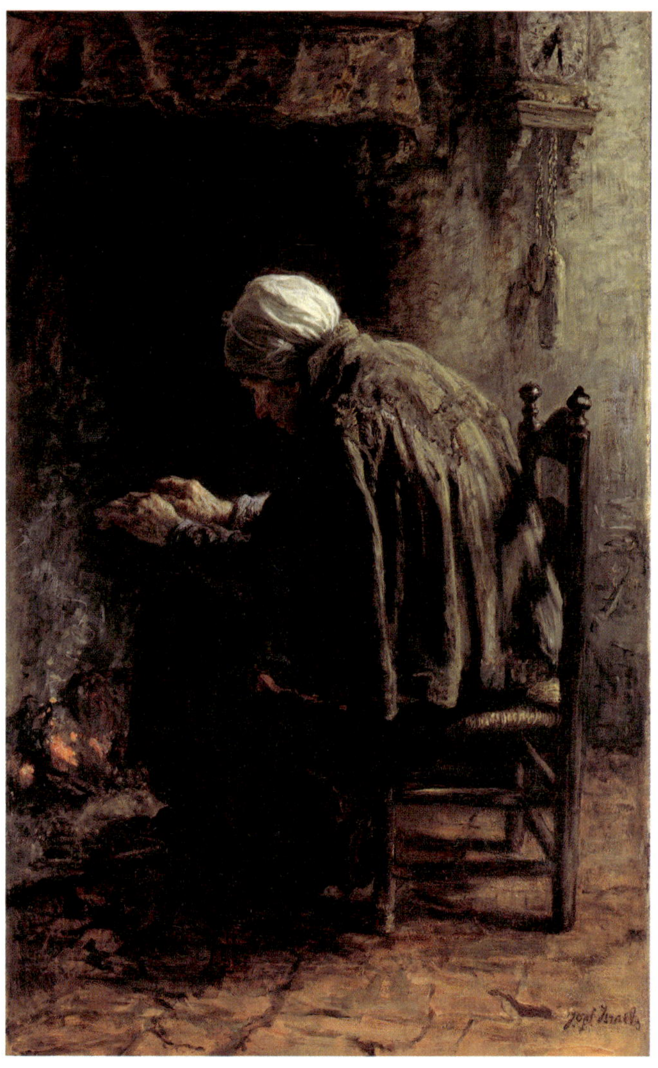

[513/R52].[23] ❧ In expressing his admiration for Meissonier, Van Gogh also referred to the 17th-century Dutch painters Brouwer, Van Ostade and Terborch. 'Well, Meissonier does it like they did – a very well-considered, very well-calculated touch, but done with a single stroke, and if possible correct the first time' [538/427]. At the back of his mind he may have been thinking of passages from *Musées de la Hollande* in which Thoré drew attention to the French imitation of the Dutch masters in subject matter and execution, and to the expressiveness of Jan Steen and Rembrandt.[24] The expressiveness of a figure was something Van Gogh always prized, in the work of draughtsmen like Daumier and Gavarni as well. In addition, he followed Mauve in admiring Meissonier's workmanship, his virtuoso technical skill. That Meissonier's subjects were not contemporary evidently did not matter. ❧ However, Van Gogh did not consider the subjects in this anecdotal form of painting entirely unimportant. In 1878, for example, he said that he 'would much rather see an ugly woman by Israëls (fig. 75) or Millet, or an old woman by Eduard Frère'

than Gérôme's beautiful Phryne (fig. 76), 'for what's the use of a beautiful body like Phryne's; animals have it too, perhaps even more so than humans, but animals do not have a soul as it lives in the people painted by Israëls or Millet or Frère' [138/117]. Van Gogh, echoing the romantic cliché, found beauty in ugliness because it was commoner and more moving.

THEORETICAL PRONOUNCEMENTS ABOUT ART

Van Gogh usually coupled his pronouncements about his taste and ideas with specific artists and works. From the very outset,

74. After **Ernest Meissonier,** *The smoker by the window,* Paris, Bibliothèque Nationale de France, Cabinet des Estampes

75. **Jozef Israëls,** *When we grow old,* 1883, The Hague, Gemeentemuseum

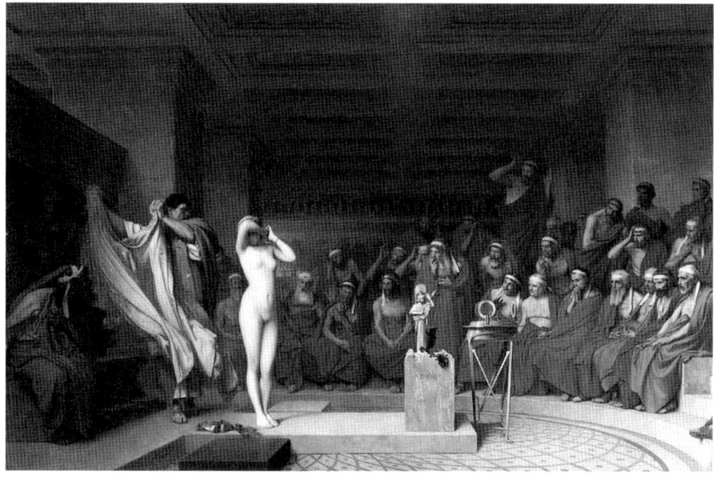

though, he also philosophised in general about the relationship between artist, nature and work of art. In June 1879 he wrote from the village of Wasmes in the Borinage mining region: 'I still have no better definition of the word art than this: L'art c'est l'homme ajouté à la nature [Art is man added to nature], nature, reality, truth, but with a significance, a conception, a character, which the artist brings out in it, and to which he gives expression, "qu'il dégage," which he disentangles, sets free, clarifies. A painting by Mauve or Maris or Israëls says more, and says it more clearly, than nature itself' [151/130].[25] ଔ That art should imitate nature and strive for truth was a time-honoured commonplace in the 19th century. The question had always been which truth the artist should seek. It is clear that Zola's definition of art as a part of nature seen through a temperament is a variant of the definition by Francis Bacon cited by Van Gogh in the above letter and quoted by Charles Blanc: 'Homo additus naturae, l'homme ajoutant son âme à la nature.'[26] ଔ The quotation shows that Van Gogh elected early on for a personal assimilation of what the painter observed in nature. He dismissed the realism of photographs. 'The real thing is not an absolute copy of nature, but to know nature so well that what one makes is fresh and true – that is what so many lack' [293/251]. ଔ One also finds echoes of Zola's definition of art in Van Gogh's letters. In 1882 he defended his own toiling over model drawing with the argument that it matched his character, and that he wanted to render and express in accordance with his own temperament.[27] Paraphrasing Zola, he wrote from Nuenen, when he was beginning to make

progress with his painting: 'At the point I am now, however, I see a chance of giving a truly experienced impression of what I see. Not always literally exact, or rather never exact, for one sees nature through one's own temperament' (emphasis added) [495/399].

VAN GOGH'S PRACTICE: WRESTLING WITH NATURE

At first Van Gogh concentrated on making studies from life, like the heads of peasants in Nuenen. 'There is something of life itself in true studies,' he wrote [299/257]. But studies from life had to lead to a painting, in this case The potato eaters mentioned earlier. He painted this composition from memory in his studio, with the intermediate stage of a painted composition sketch to help him. That was standard practice, 'for in the picture the painter gives more of a personal idea, and in a study his aim is simply to analyse a bit of nature, either to get his idea or conception correct, or to find an idea' [268/233]. He described studies from life as food for the imagination. A painting, then, had to express an idea; the painting had to be 'premeditated', as he also put it. The poetic thoughts could be inspired by the intensive study of nature, but in addition were equally often associated with the books Van Gogh had read. 'And I am daily more convinced,' he wrote in 1885, 'that people who do not in the first place wrestle with nature never succeed' [483/393]. ଔ In his eyes, that drudgery, that wrestling with nature, was an almost sacred duty. This was connected with his views about nature, to which he attached the name of Millet as a result of Alfred Sensier's monograph. When the painting was the result of many studies, 'that is the highest thing in art,' he said, 'and there art sometimes rises above nature – in Millet's sower, for instance, there is more soul than in an ordinary sower in the field' [299/257] (plate 45). He also borrowed a phrase from Sensier's La vie et l'œuvre de J.-F. Millet, a book that he had devoured, when speaking about nature with 'quelque chose là-haut', 'something up above'. It is 'a painter's duty [...] to try to put an idea into his work' in order to reveal that 'quelque chose là-haut in which Millet believed, namely the existence of a God and an eternity' [290/248]. In a rather melancholy letter from Drenthe he defined this further as something that was 'incomprehensible, awfully unnameable, for no name can be found for it loftier than that nature'. He was not ashamed to say that 'it exists, that white light – and [...] I seek it, and

76. Jean-Léon Gérôme, Phryne before the Areopagus, 1861, Hamburg, Kunsthalle

only this do I consider simplicity' [405/339a]. Van Gogh soon abandoned this mystical approach to nature, or at least he never again spoke of it in such terms.[28] It is impossible, by the way, to overlook the romantic component in Van Gogh's views about nature and art. ❧ One crucial element in the criticism of realist and naturalist art was the preference for banal, and sometimes vulgar and coarse, subjects depicted in a style that was far from lofty. The requirement of observing a certain decorum was ages old, and was fiercely defended by most official bodies, including the academies. The realist transgressors of that decorum had to justify themselves, and Van Gogh's favourite authors, the Goncourt brothers, Zola, Guy de Maupassant, the early J.-K. Huysmans and others, did so.[29] Van Gogh praised them because they voiced 'life as we ourselves feel it'. They spoke the truth, and anyone who failed to become acquainted with their work did not belong 'to one's own time' [576/W1]. As far as his own work was concerned, he likened some of his own deliberately coarser canvases to the cheap, colourful prints sold in bazaars, and to barrel-organ music, although he believed that his own works did have more style.[30] Although artists did describe and paint raw reality, they did not identify with the outcasts, labourers and peasants they depicted.

THE GODLIKE RENDERED VISIBLE

Very much in the romantic tradition, Van Gogh sought for the secret, the enigma, of nature. 'Life in the abstract is already an enigma; reality makes it an enigma within an enigma. And who are we to solve it?' [282/242]. Van Gogh the realist, who studied and analysed nature so assiduously and seriously, was also a romantic: 'In the work of Millet, of Lhermitte, all reality is also symbolic at the same time' [536/425]. This sounds like an echo of Thomas Carlyle's *Sartor resartus* (1834), which parodies the art theory of the German romantics. Van Gogh read the book in 1883. Carlyle said that all true works of art were symbols which had the power to render 'the Godlike visible'.[31] Man, and thus the artist too, could in this way participate in 'the infinite deeps of the Invisible'. According to Carlyle, nature was infinite, and here he used the metaphor of the immeasurable ocean, which Van Gogh also cited,[32] and spoke about all the illusionary apparitions that conceal the wonder of nature. In Carlyle's inimitable words, nature is

'the Time-vesture of God, and reveals Him to the wise, hides Him from the foolish.'[33] Van Gogh, as a wise artist, undoubtedly wanted to get closer to God through the study of this divine vesture. ❧ The relationship between artist and nature was also captured in the metaphor of the mirror and the lamp, with the mirror reflecting reality and the lamp standing for the artist.[34] It is the artist, Carlyle asserted, who as a 'poet' or 'seer' colours the mirror image, provides it with meanings and thus, as a lamp, casts light on the world. Artists teach us how to see because they are seers, and that was Van Gogh's opinion too.[35] He lamented that he could not do it as strikingly and beautifully as reality itself, of which his work of art 'is but a weak reflection in a dark mirror' [290/248]. The ambition was there, but he realised that he still had a long way to go before his mirror shone clearly. ❧ Van Gogh had also come across the mirror metaphor in the novel *Adam Bede* (1859), in which George Eliot included a manifesto-like passage about the realist wellsprings of art. She did not wish to put her own words into the mouths of her characters, but wanted to give a reliable picture of people and affairs as they were reflected in her mind. 'The mirror is doubtless defective; the outlines will sometimes be disturbed, the reflection faint or confused; but I feel as much bound to tell you as precisely as I can what that reflection is, as if I were in the witness-box narrating my experience on oath.'[36] Her mirror was imperfect, as Van Gogh said his was. However, he also understood that a witness, or eyewitness, could never be objective.

LITERARY THEORY AND THE LEGITIMISATION OF VAN GOGH'S REALISM

Van Gogh had read *Adam Bede* and other books by George Eliot back in the 1870s. In addition to her realism – he compared a description of a landscape with a painting by 'the leader' Georges Michel (fig. 77) – he admired her religiosity.[37] He owed his first acquaintance with realism as an art theory partly to Eliot, but also to Dickens. In 1882 he wrote that 'English writers like Dickens and Eliot and Currer Bell [the pseudonym of Charlotte Brontë] and [...] the Frenchmen Balzac are so astonishingly "plastic", if I may use the expression, that it is as powerful as, for instance, a drawing by Herkomer or Fildes or Israëls. And Dickens sometimes used the expression "I have sketched"'

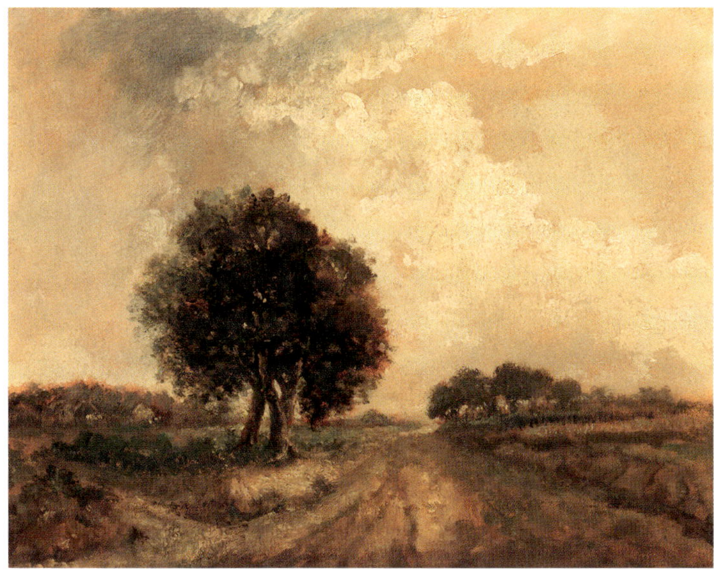

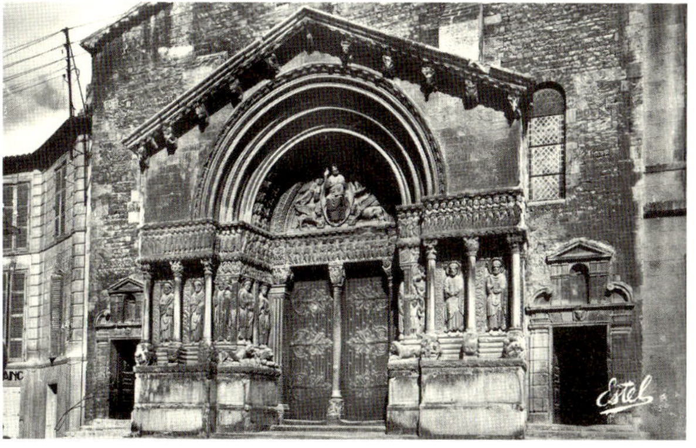

[251/R8]. ⧉ When it came down to theoretical justifications for realism and naturalism in literature, Van Gogh could also turn to his beloved French authors, who often provided their novels with a theoretical apologia in an introduction. For example, he referred to the introduction to *Chérie* (1884) by the Goncourt brothers, and to Guy de Maupassant's 'Etude sur le roman' (1887), which he used as the foreword to his novella *Pierre et Jean* (1888).[38] Van Gogh read the book in March 1888, and spoke about the foreword in a letter. It made it clear 'that the artist has the liberty to exaggerate, to create in his novel a nature more beautiful, more simple, more consoling than ours', and goes on to explain what Flaubert may have meant when he said that 'Talent is long patience, and originality an effort of will and of intense observation' [589/470]. As he did on other occasions, Van Gogh pasted different phrases together to make the author's ideas his own. ⧉ In his 'Etude', Maupassant discussed several questions of a general, theoretical nature, such as the role of the temperament, the truth and credibility of a work of art, talent and originality. He also rejected the image of the realist or naturalist artist as someone with the credo: 'The whole truth and nothing but the truth'. The artist had to go in search of the unexplored, the unknown. It was for that reason that Maupassant preferred to call 'the talented realists' 'illusionists'. Finally, he argued for simplicity and the avoidance of a bizarre, complex, prolix, Chinese vocabulary, and praised the French language as pure water that could not be

ruined by mannered writers.[39] ⧉ All these notions can be found in Van Gogh's letters. Having paraphrased Maupassant, he wrote: 'There is a Gothic porch here [in Arles] which I am beginning to find admirable, the porch of St-Trophime [fig. 78]. But it is as cruel, as monstrous, as a Chinese nightmare, that even the most beautiful monument in so grand a style seems to me to be another world, and I am as glad not to belong to it as to that other glorious world of the Roman Nero' [589/470]. And indeed, Van Gogh painted neither the Romanesque porch of Saint-Trophime nor any of the many Roman monuments in and around Arles. He did not share the romantic taste for the grotesque, the cruel and the peculiar, although in other respects he did support romantic doctrines, including the role of the imagination. ⧉ For him, imagination came into play when he made a 'willed' painting. In it, the line and above all colour – the style – had a meaning of their own, which did not coincide with faithfulness to nature. These were not new ideas; he could find them in Blanc's *Grammaire*, which he studied assiduously in 1885. After a discussion of the use of colour, 'of his knowledge of the beautiful effect of colours, [...] which is rather different from copying nature mechanically and obsequiously,' he rather rhetorically anticipated Theo's reaction. 'Do you call this a dangerous inclination towards romanticism, an infidelity to "realism", a "peindre de chic" [painting without a model], a caring more for the palette of the colourist than for nature? Well, so be it. Delacroix, Millet, Corot, Dupré, Daubigny, Breton, thirty names more, do they not form the heart of this century [...] *though they surpassed romanticism?* Fiction and romanticism are the imaginative force of our time, and painters must have imagination and sentiment. *Luckily*, realism and naturalism *are not free of it*. Zola *creates*, but *does not hold up a mirror* to

---

77. Georges Michel, *Group of three trees,* The Hague, Museum Mesdag

78. The porch of Saint-Trophime in Arles

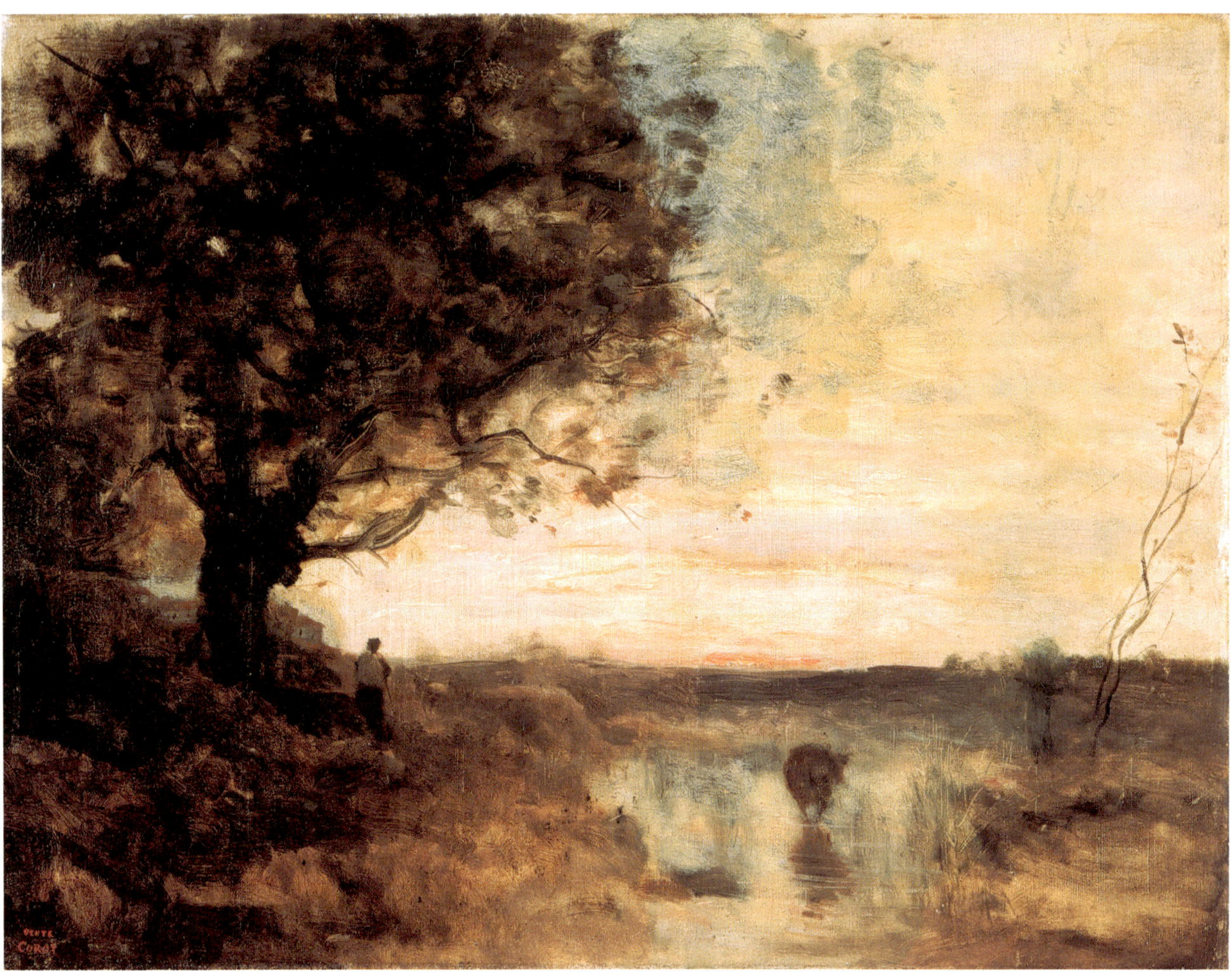

things, creates them *amazingly*, but *creates, poeticises*, that is why it is so beautiful. So much for naturalism and realism, which are *nonetheless* connected to romanticism. And I repeat that I am touched when I see a picture from the days of '30-'48, a Paul Huet, an old Israëls like the Fisherman of Zandvoort (plate 64), a Cabat, an Isabey' [540/429]. ∞ It was not only impressionism that Van Gogh got to know in Paris. He must also have taken part in discussions about old and new ideas, such as the artist's own contribution and the liberties he could permit himself by relying on his fantasy, his imagination. In the earlier theory of art, the power of the imagination was both valued and feared. It could bring forth monsters, as Goya had demonstrated in his famous etching.

WORKING FROM THE IMAGINATION RATHER THAN FROM NATURE

The esteem in which the imagination was held increased greatly in the 18th century. The romantics rated it above everything else as a formidable creative force. The following, realistically in-clined generation provided a corrective to these overly fantastic, romantic excesses, which were too far removed from reality, but without rejecting the romantic theory of art out of hand. The poet and critic Charles Baudelaire showed in his review of the Salon of 1855 that he was a warm advocate of the imagination, which he called 'the queen of the faculties'. He praised Delacroix as the most imaginative painter, and eloquently dismissed photography.

79. Camille Corot, *Sunrise,* c. 1870-72, The Hague, Museum Mesdag

Delacroix himself had once embarked on a 'dictionnaire des beaux arts', in which he wrote: 'Imagination. Elle est la première qualité de l'artiste' (Imagination. It is the first quality of the artist).[40] ∝ In his essay, 'Le peintre de la vie moderne' of 1863, Baudelaire devoted a section to 'L'art mnémonique', an art which relied on the faculty of memory. As an example he took the landscapist Corot, who was also a favourite of Van Gogh's (fig. 79). It is a synthetic art that abbreviates things, summarises them, presents the broad outlines and emphasises the distribution of light and shade. Van Gogh knew little of Baudelaire's work and, unlike Bernard, did not care for it very much. That does not alter the fact that in Arles he did consider another way of working. 'I sometimes regret,' he wrote to Bernard, 'that I cannot make up my mind to work more at home and from fantasy. The imagination is of course a capacity which we must develop, one which alone can lead us to the creation of a more exalting and consoling nature than that which we can observe with a single glance at reality – which we see constantly changing and passing as swiftly as a flash of lightning' [597/B3]. The latter was a problem that had also faced the impressionists, which is why some of them took lessons from the academy teacher Horace Lecoq de Boisbaudran, who had published a method under the title *Education de la mémoire pittoresque*.[41] Van Gogh must have heard of it. He had worked from the imagination or from memory even before his *Potato eaters*. He had read about it in books about his cherished Delacroix, who had stated 'that the best paintings are made from memory. "Par coeur," he said' [500/403]. ∝ Gauguin, too, propagated the romantic principle that images observed in nature had to be reworked by the artist in a personal way. The actual creation took place from the imagination or, as it was also said, from the memory. One had to dream in the presence of nature, Gauguin advised his colleague Schuffenecker: 'One piece of advice, do not copy from nature too much. Art is an abstraction; extract it from nature while dreaming before it, and think more about the creation than the result. That is the only way of rising up to God – by doing as our divine master did.'[42] Gauguin described the self-portrait he painted for Van Gogh as a successful abstraction (plate 172). ∝ Van Gogh, who called that portrait a 'symbol', became a little confused by Gauguin's ideas. He wrote to him about three weeks before the latter arrived in Arles on 23 October 1888: 'I consider my views of art excessively ordinary compared with yours. I have always had the coarse tastes of an animal. I neglect everything for the external beauty of things, *which I cannot reproduce* because I render it so ugly and coarse in my picture, whereas nature seems so perfect to me' [699/553a]. Van Gogh did, incidentally, believe that ugliness and coarseness had 'a degree of sincerity, perhaps original at times, about what I feel'. Banality and animality, the coarse and the ugly, were reprehensible qualities for the opponents of realism and naturalist literature, but Van Gogh embraced them. ∝ However, as stated above, he must have agreed with Gauguin's statement that he wanted to rise up to God through his abstractions. Gauguin, too, had caught sight of 'quelque chose là-haut', although in his case it was not the study from life that was most important but the free, creative imagination. Originally that had belonged to God alone, because God had created something from nothing. Man had to rely on God's creation for his art. Van Gogh could only adapt hesitantly. 'I cannot work without a model', he confessed to Bernard shortly before Gauguin came to live and work with him. 'I won't say that I don't turn my back on nature ruthlessly in order to turn a study into a painting, arranging the colours, enlarging and simplifying, but in the matter of form I am too afraid of departing from the possible and the true' [702/B19]. He was, and remained, 'so fixed on what is possible and really exists'. He hardly had 'the desire or the courage' to surrender himself to abstractions as Bernard and Gauguin did. In the depths of his heart he probably felt, as an artist, that he was no God. He said that ultimately he had not thought up the entire painting himself, but had found it ready-made in nature.

VAN GOGH'S ATTEMPTS AT ABSTRACTION

Van Gogh wrote to Bernard from Saint-Rémy in November 1889 to tell him about his own experiences with abstraction, in other words creating from the imagination. He now set out his own position more clearly: 'When Gauguin was in Arles, I once or twice allowed myself to be led astray into abstraction, as you know, for instance in the Berceuse, in the *Woman reading a novel*, black in a yellow library. At the time, I considered abstraction an attractive method.' Then comes his criticism of it: 'But, that was delusion, dear friend, and one soon comes up against a brick wall. I don't say one might not try one's hand at it after a whole life long of experimentation, of hand-to-hand struggle

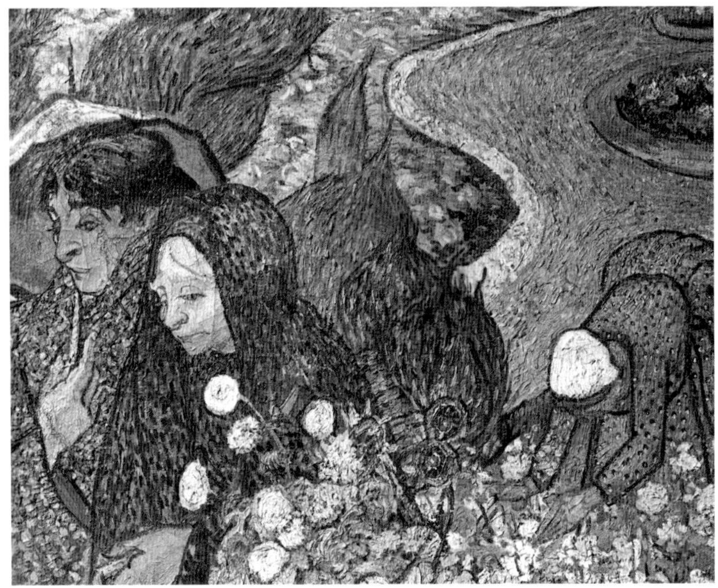

with nature, but personally I don't want to trouble my head with such things. All year I was doing little things after nature, without giving a thought to impressionism or whatever else' [824/B21]. ⊗ Oddly enough, Van Gogh failed to mention his *Memory of the garden at Etten* (fig. 80), with its portraits of his mother and his sister Wil. 'I know this is hardly what one might call a likeness, but for me it renders the poetic character and the style of the garden as I feel it' [725/W9]. He achieved that effect primarily through his use of colour. Style, in this 'abstraction', was more important than faithfulness to life, and the word 'memory' in the title makes that abundantly clear. The images had been processed by the memory. Elsewhere, incidentally, Van Gogh speaks of a reminiscence of the garden at Nuenen. That may have been a slip of the pen, but all the same, in a positive sense these instances do point to the ability of the imagination to fuse different impressions into a single image. ⊗ It was also possible to use one's imagination to paint biblical figures one could never encounter in life. Van Gogh had major objections to this, the objections of a realist. He quoted Courbet, who had said that he could not paint angels because he had never seen one.[43] Van Gogh was dejected and irritated by the religious art of Bernard and Gauguin, particularly by their scenes of Christ in the Garden of Olives (figs. 31, 40). They infuriated him. He had no idea how to deal with this new development. According to him, Rembrandt and Delacroix had painted biblical

subjects in an admirable way, and in Saint-Rémy he made coloured copies after them using black-and-white prints (plates 74, 125). For his part he did not want to try 'to paint a Christ in the Garden of Olives, but the picking of the olives as you still see it, giving the exact proportions of the human figure in it, perhaps that would make people think' [822/614]. And he did indeed paint a series of olive groves with women picking the fruit (fig. 81). 'What I have done is a rather hard and coarse realism beside their abstractions, but it will have a rustic quality, and will smell of the soil of the locality' [825/615]. Basically, all Van Gogh wanted to do was work steadily from nature, as he had announced so many times when he was living in the Netherlands. ⊗ He knew very well why he rejected the painting of biblical subjects, because he had himself painted a Christ in the Garden of Olives, but had scraped the paint off because the figure had not been done from a model, 'which is necessary in such cases' [702/B19]. He later described, as an alternative, his own canvas of the garden of the asylum in Saint-Rémy (fig. 82), in which he had expressed 'a feeling of anguish without making direct reference to the actual Gethsemane' [824/B21].

CONCLUSION: PORTRAITS AS 'APPARITIONS'

Of all artists, Van Gogh was the one who remained most faithful to Millet, and even more so to his 'semi-religious doctrine', which Van Gogh had learned of from Alfred Sensier's book on the artist rather than from Millet's work itself, which he barely knew in the original. In Saint-Rémy in 1889-90 he made colour translations after prints of the work of, among others, Rembrandt (plate 74), Delacroix (plate 125), Doré, Daumier, and above all Millet (plates 51, 52). 'I feel that I am increasingly returning to the ideas I already had before I came to Paris,' he wrote [771/590]. He now believed more than ever 'in the eternal youth of the school of Delacroix, Millet, Rousseau, Dupré and Daubigny, as much as in that of the present, or even in that of the artists to come' [780/593], and concluded: 'I hardly think that impressionism will ever do more than, say, the romantics.' ⊗ The work of Pierre Puvis de Chavannes gave him hope, particularly the portraits (plate 90). Portraiture had also become a speciality for Van Gogh, because essentially it is a realistic genre. 'What impassions me the most – much, much more than all the rest of my métier – is the por-

80. Vincent van Gogh, *Memory of the garden at Etten* (F 496 JH 1630), 1888, St Petersburg, Hermitage

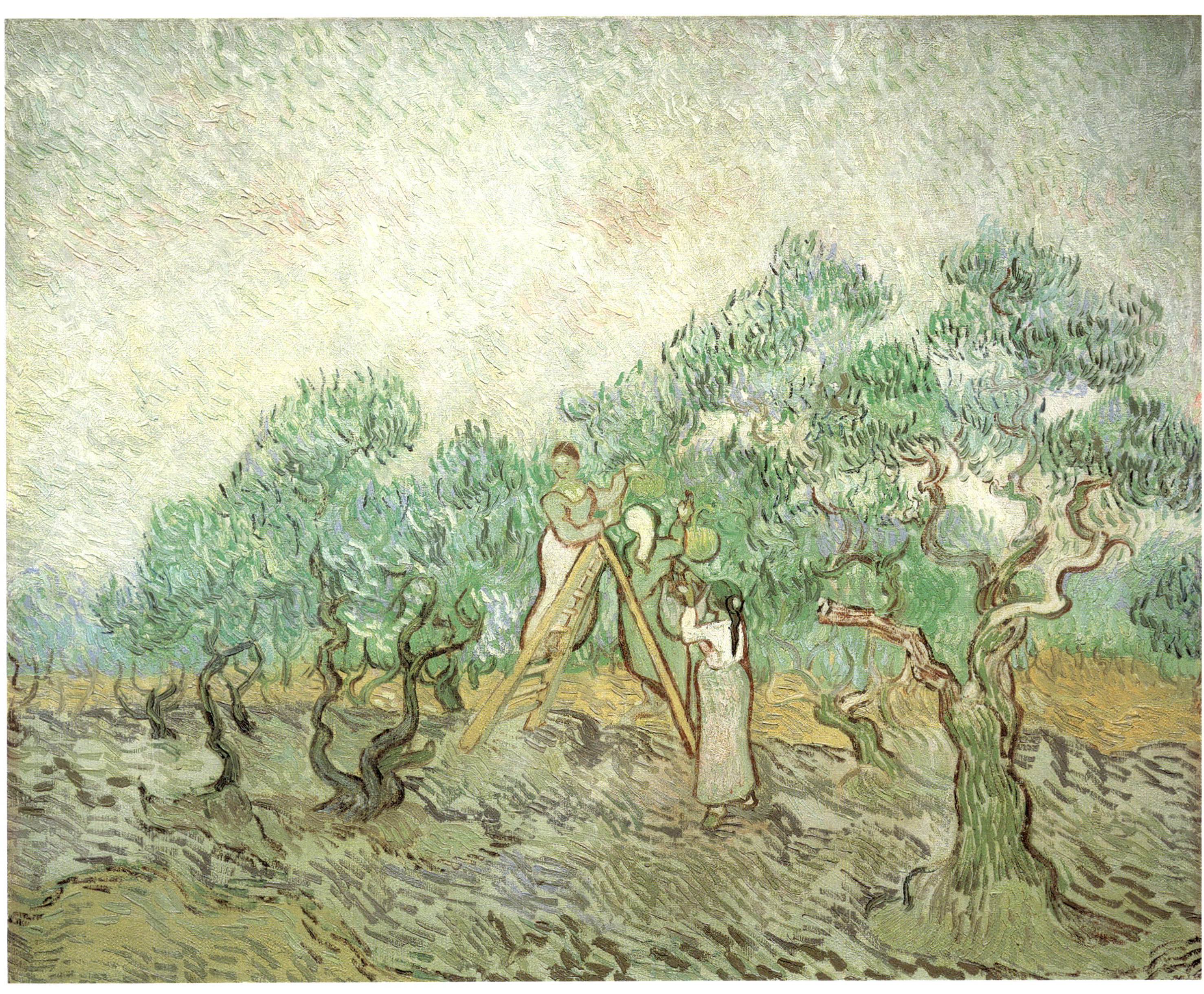

81. Vincent van Gogh, *Women picking olives* (F 656 JH 1870), 1889,
Washington, National Gallery of Art, Chester Dale Collection

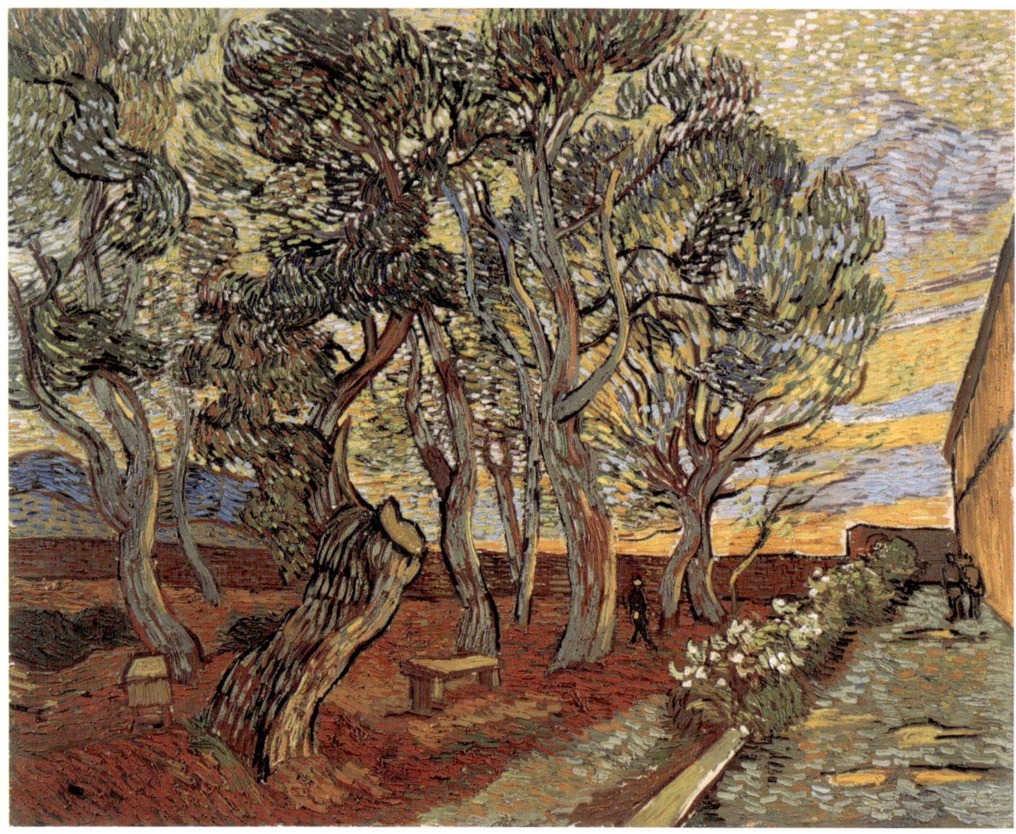

trait, the modern portrait. I seek it in colour, and surely I am not the only one to seek it in that direction' [883/W22]. To his way of thinking, a portrait had to be more than just a faithful likeness. It should record history for future generations, not in the form of history paintings, but as 'apparitions', individuals with a significance that transcended the individual. 'I should like to paint portraits which would appear after a century to people living then as apparitions' [883/W22]. Vincent van Gogh championed an art of realist vision. His gaze was directed not only at nature, but on high and towards the future.

ଷ

82. Vincent van Gogh, *The garden of Saint Paul's Hospital* (F 659 JH 1850), 1889, Amsterdam, Van Gogh Museum (Vincent van Gogh Foundation)

ON RUSTICS AND LABOURERS: VAN GOGH AND 'THE PEOPLE'

NIENKE BAKKER

One of the most striking aspects of Vincent van Gogh's taste was his life-long interest in the subjects of work and peasant life in art and literature. In his own paintings and drawings, too, working men and women play a seminal role, particularly in his Dutch period (1880-85).[1] In his first large-scale figure painting, *The potato eaters* (plate 44), he sought to express the very essence of rural existence through the image of the primitive farm labourer who earns his living by the sweat of his brow.[2] ❧ Van Gogh was convinced that an artist who drew his motifs from 'the heart of the people' [529/R57] had, in fact, to live among peasants and workers himself, if he hoped to be able to capture them with appropriate feeling. His vision of 'the people' was coloured by ideas about their 'nature' derived from his upbringing and strongly influenced by art and literature.[3] He considered labourers to be simple, kind-hearted and courageous, and in general regarded them more highly than 'those who call themselves civilised' [529/R57]. During his years in Holland he viewed peasants and artisans as pious, nobly toiling men and women like those found in the paintings of Jean-François Millet and Jules Breton. Later, under the influence of the naturalist novels of Emile Zola and the Goncourts, he became interested in their coarser and more primitive aspects. This new trope became mixed with his idealised image à la Millet.

For Van Gogh, the concepts of 'work' and 'the people' were inextricably linked. His decidedly ethical notion of labour meant that it was virtually only the working classes that interested him. His sympathy for the lower strata of society was dictated not by pity, but rather by esteem for the characteristics he ascribed to these segments of the population, such as fortitude, sincerity and zest for work. As an artist, too, he focused on labourers of different kinds, a choice closely related to his preference for figures in action. ❧ Van Gogh admired workers and peasants for what he saw as their ingenuous, rudimentary nature and their intimate connection with the land, and he continually endeavoured to identify with them as a community. Nonetheless, he was well aware of class difference and the fact that the regular workingman's world had little to do with his own. In a letter of 1885 he wrote: 'I often think peasants form a world apart, better in many ways than the civilised world. Not in all ways, though, for what do they know about art and other such things?' [501/404]. ❧ Art historians have both overestimated the degree of Van Gogh's commitment to social causes and denied its existence all together.[4] Although his vision of 'the people' was clearly highly idealised and, moreover, determined by his own class, there can be no doubt that he felt a true sympathy for the poor – perhaps less so during his years as an artist than in his youth, when religious enthusiasm had motivated much of his thought. A deeply felt need to be useful to his fellow man took him as a preacher to the Belgian Borinage at the age of 25, where he experienced the hardships of the miners' lives at first hand. In the same period (1878-80) he spent time nursing the sick and injured, again indicating a concern for those less fortunate than himself. This applies equally to his decision in 1882 to set up house with the prostitute Sien Hoornik and her children – although here other factors certainly played a role as well, such as a desire for a stable family life. In The Hague he invited residents of the men's old-age home to visit

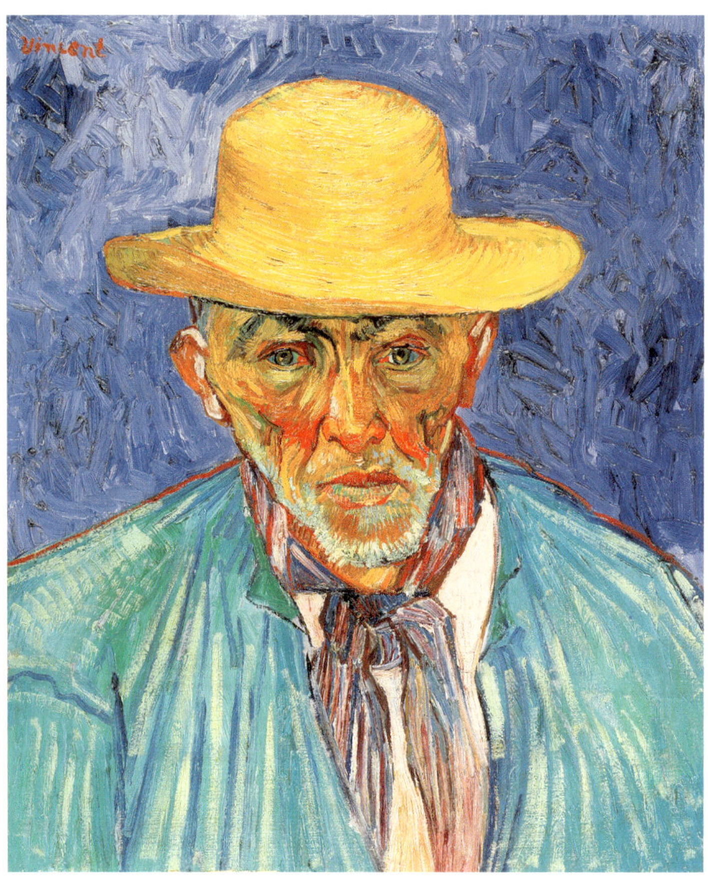

him in his studio, where he had them pose for his drawings. Naturally, this was an inexpensive means of acquiring models, but he also cherished the idea that his workplace might one day become a refuge for the destitute.[5] ❧ If in the beginning Van Gogh sought to bring relief and consolation to labourers and the impoverished through religion, later it was art that was to take over this function. In 1882 – he was then living in The Hague – he devised a project to create 'drawings of working-men and to publish them in a popular edition, from the people for the people, the whole conceived as a kind of mission and a charitable affair' [295/251]. For practical reasons, however, he eventually abandoned this noble plan; if he hoped to sell his work, he realised, he had to direct his efforts towards a wealthier clientele. Still, he always maintained a belief in reproduction techniques as a means of bringing art to the masses. As he wrote in 1889: 'How I wish there were more good reproductions after Millet; that way some would end up in the hands of the people' [792/600].

In his letters, Van Gogh regularly compared the urban population to the inhabitants of rural areas, claiming that there was more chance of 'meeting a reasonable person in the country than in the city' [400/334]. He often explored this opposition in painting as well. The brilliant colours and battered countenance of the old peasant in his *Portrait of Patience Escalier* of 1888 (fig. 83, plate 140), for example, were meant to symbolise rustic life and the hard labour of the fields. The likeness, he wrote, would make an interesting contrast with Toulouse-Lautrec's *Young woman at a table 'Poudre de riz'*, a portrait of a mondaine Parisian that Theo owned [663/520] (plate 139). ❧ Van Gogh's idealised vision of country life originated in his youth. He grew up in a region where farming was highly respected and farmers were regarded as hardworking and honest. In Van Gogh's time, Zundert, a small Protestant community in the province of North Brabant comprising mainly rural labourers and craftsmen, suffered from endemic poverty and unemployment. His father, Reverend Theodorus van Gogh, was an advisor to the Maatschappij van Welstand (Society for Prosperity), a clerical organisation that sought to improve the lives of the poor through relief works in the agricultural sector.[6] Van Gogh admired his father's good relationship with the locals. In 1877, for example, he wrote to Theo on the death of the peasant Jan Aerssen and the special link their father had had with the man and his family.[7] ❧ As far as Van Gogh's religious upbringing was concerned, simplicity, benevolence and hard work were considered of paramount importance. His father was a follower of the so-called Groningen School, a moderate movement within the Reformed Church. Its adherents took Thomas à Kempis's 1441 treatise *De imitatione Christi* as their starting point for the propagation of faith. The imitation of Christ in humility, the practice of charity and support for the poor represented the road to salvation.[8] Van Gogh first read this book at a very young age and would later reread it many times (and in various languages), putting its principles into literal practice during his time in the Borinage, when he abandoned all his worldly possessions and took up residence in a miserable hut.[9] Although his parents had always stressed the necessity of leading a humble life, they were less than pleased with his rather extreme interpretation of the doctrine. In the years to come, too, they would often criticise their son's shabby appearance and his associations with members of the lower classes.[10] ❧ Van Gogh's parents set the peace and quiet of the countryside above the demanding and unhealthy life of the

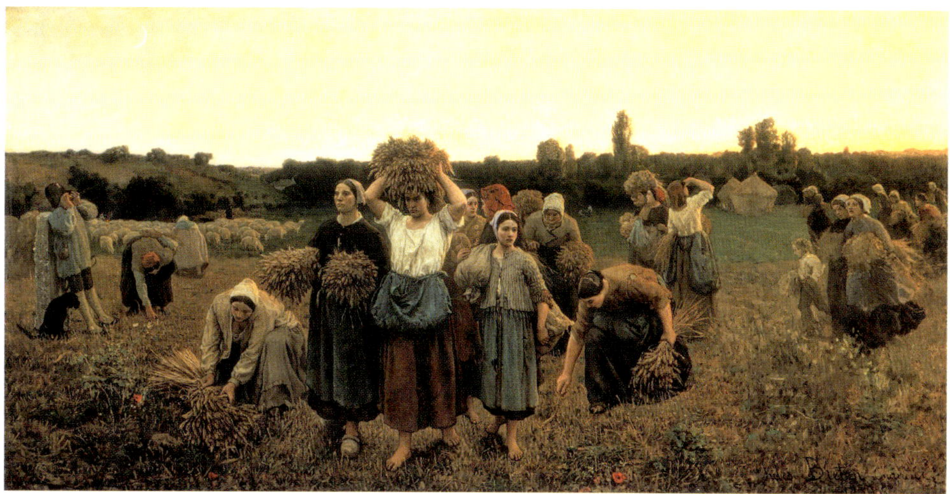

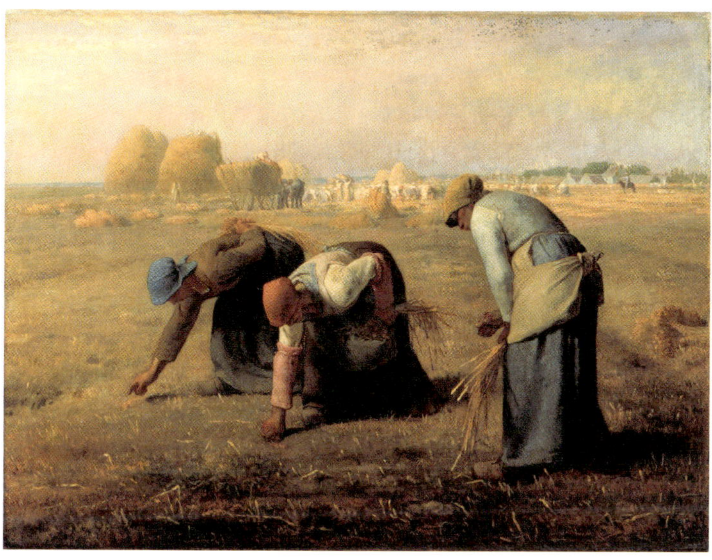

metropolis. In a letter to Theo, his father described the village of Etten as a 'simple, pretty place of simple people',[11] and he often warned his sons against the temptations and dangers of the urban environment. Although Vincent considered himself a rustic who felt most at home in the country, he was continually drawn to the city by a desire for what he called 'the land of pictures' [154/133]. He was also dependent on it for selling his work and for contact with other artists. In The Hague it was the ready availability of periodicals and reproduction techniques that bound him to the place.[12] In the end, however, he gave preference to the

repose of rural life; as he wrote to his sister Willemien in 1890: 'It's better for a painter to work in the country, everything there speaks a different language, everything is firm, everything explains itself; if you're tired in the big city you cease to understand a thing and you feel lost' [843/W19]. ❧ This vision of the countryside as a place of tranquillity and ease, inhabited by gentle people, was widespread among the middle classes in the 19th century. Both the literature and art of the period exhibit a new interest in the peasant, who was regarded as a primitive being living in harmony with nature. Many writers contrasted the unspoilt farm labourer with the decadent city-dweller, while the innumerable paintings of rustics and fishermen exhibited at the Paris Salon from the 1820s onwards glorified country life.[13] In the wake of the Revolution of 1848, the worker and his toils became a major theme in French art, worthy of being depicted on the scale of history painting. In contrast to Gustave Courbet, however, whose *Stonebreakers* of 1849 shocked the public at large with its directness and realism, artists like Millet and Breton provided a more romantic, quasi-religious vision of labour.[14] Their monumental paintings of pious peasants at work or resting in the fields created an idealised picture of agrarian society that conformed completely to the 19th-century bourgeoisie's nostalgic conceptions of the countryside and its inhabitants (figs. 84, 85). ❧ In his preference for art focusing on the themes of work and rural life, then, Van Gogh was a man of his time. The paintings of Millet and Breton perfectly reflected his own ideas about 'the people' and labour in general. He would always regard these artists as

84. **Jean-François Millet,** *The gleaners*, 1857, Paris, Musée d'Orsay

85. **Jules Breton,** *The return of the gleaners*, 1859, Paris, Musée d'Orsay

the unsurpassed masters of the peasant figure, as 'the voice of the wheat' [878/614a].

LITERARY INFLUENCES

While in the Borinage Van Gogh read *Uncle Tom's cabin* (1852) by Harriet Beecher Stowe and *Hard times* (1854) by Charles Dickens, novels that reinforced his image of the labourer as hardworking and courageous. These authors were highly critical of the exploitation of the poor and oppressed, and preached a Christian message of charity that greatly appealed to Van Gogh at a time when he was experiencing the misery of the working-man's life at first hand. As his dissatisfaction with the Church as an institution grew, the writings of authors like Jules Michelet, Harriet Beecher Stowe, Thomas Carlyle and George Eliot became increasingly important to him.[15] If initially Van Gogh appreciated the novels of the English author George Eliot primarily for their religious themes, he later came to admire them mainly for the scenes from working-class life and the personalities of the main characters, often themselves of low birth. The hero of Eliot's *Felix Holt, the radical* (1866) was a particular favourite. This fictional persona, who chose a frugal existence among the workers above a career in the family business, had the kind of humility Van Gogh believed was necessary for artists as well. In 1889 he wrote regarding the painting of his bedroom at Arles that his intention had been to achieve an effect of simplicity 'such as one finds described in Felix Holt' [814/W15]. It was in 1882 that Van Gogh first became acquainted with the French naturalists, and his admiration for Zola, the Goncourts, Flaubert and Maupassant further nourished his taste for everyday, popular types. Emile Zola in particular had a profound influence on his image of 'the people'. Van Gogh referred to him as 'the painter of society' and praised the 'Monday-morning sobriety and studied self-restraint' of his figures [274/237]. He began reading Zola during his affair with Sien Hoornik, and he associated this 'woman of the people' with the women in Zola's books. He recognised himself in the character of Madame François in *Le ventre de Paris* (1873), a market woman who befriends a political refugee. Van Gogh lauds her generosity and compares her good deeds to what he himself had done for Sien.[16] This image was designed to justify his actions to Theo, who, like the rest of the family, condemned his relationship with

the ex-prostitute. The extraordinarily candid and often harsh manner in which Zola portrays the lower classes changed Van Gogh's conception of them as well. While studying the peasants at Nuenen he read *Germinal* (1885), a social-critical novel about a miners' uprising in France. The book reminded him of his time in the Borinage, and he wrote that he would someday like to paint miners as well.[17] Although this plan was never carried out, the motif continued to have special significance for him. In 1889 he wrote with great admiration about the Belgian painter and sculptor Constantin Meunier, who had painted the workers in the Borinage (plate 43), a subject he had always wanted to tackle himself.[18] Upon finishing *Germinal* he sent Theo a sketch of a peasant woman's head that he described as 'the head of a "herscheuse" or "sclôneuse" [female miner] with something of a lowing cow about it' [509/410]. To illustrate the point, he cited a passage from Zola's novel in which the workers are described as 'a black, vengeful army lying ripening in the furrows'. Incidentally, Van Gogh himself felt he had captured this image still better in another study of the same subject made even before he had read the book. In this way he sought to make clear that his vision was comparable to Zola's, without having been directly influenced by it. In fact, however, the depictions in novels such as *L'assommoir* (1877) and *Le ventre de Paris*, which Van Gogh had read before coming to Nuenen, had already coloured his ideas. Zola describes many of his characters as ugly and rude, their appearance strongly marked by their debilitating lives. His labourers are essentially good, but their origins make them ignorant and primitive. They attempt to extricate themselves from their hopeless situations, but are finally ruined by alcohol and violence.

EXAMPLES FROM PAINTING

Thanks to his work at the art dealers Goupil & Cie in The Hague, London and Paris (1869-76), Van Gogh came into contact with international art early on. At the age of 22 he was deeply impressed by the Millet pastels and drawings he saw at a sale-exhibition from the collection of Emile Gavet in Paris, among them *Vineyard labourer resting* (plate 53) and *Woodcutter and his wife preparing faggots* (plate 50).[19] Visiting the Musée du Luxembourg, too, his attention was drawn to depictions of rural life. Included in his list of favourite works – in addition to three monumental paintings by

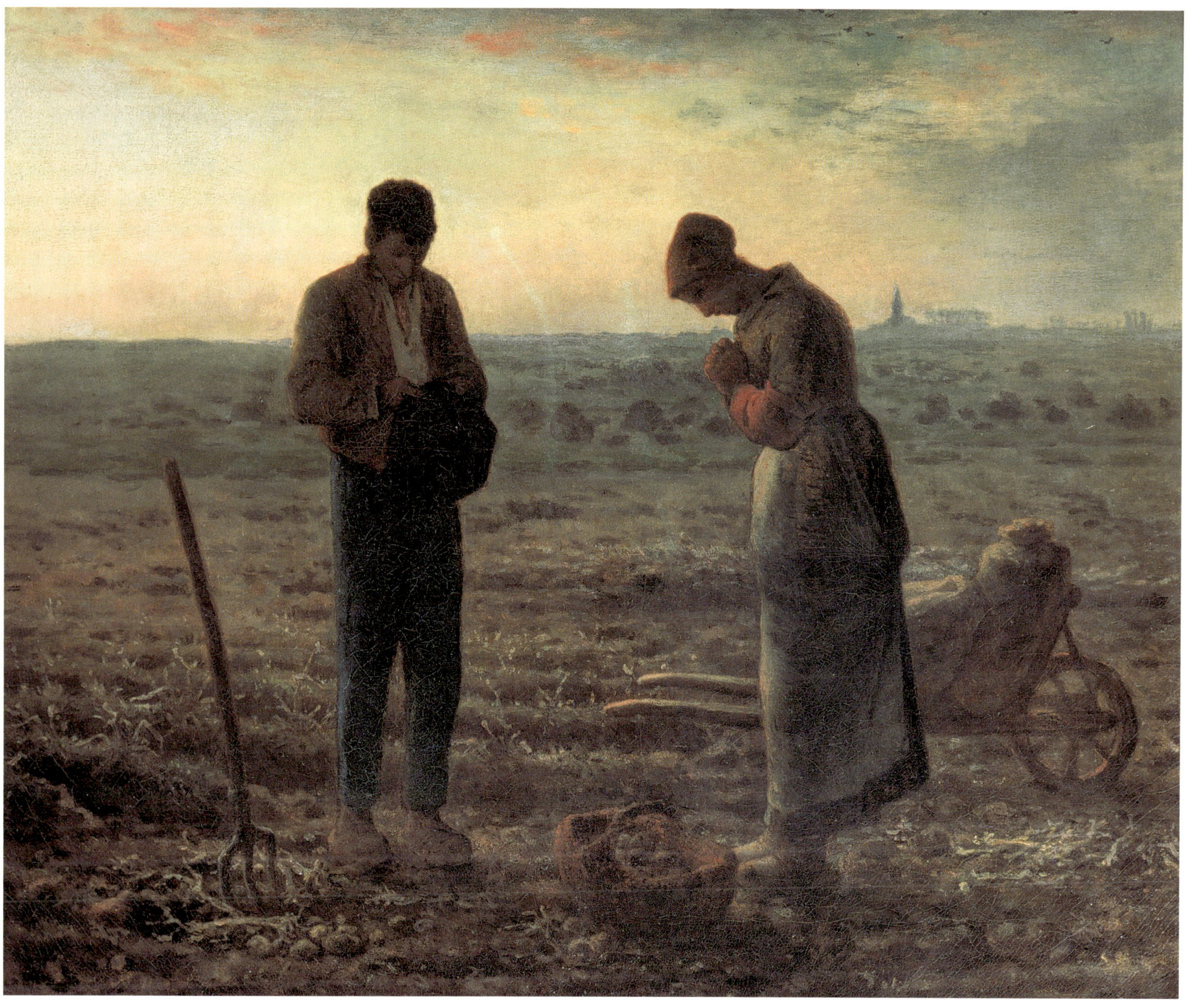

86. **Jean-François Millet,** *The angelus,* 1857-59, Paris, Musée d'Orsay

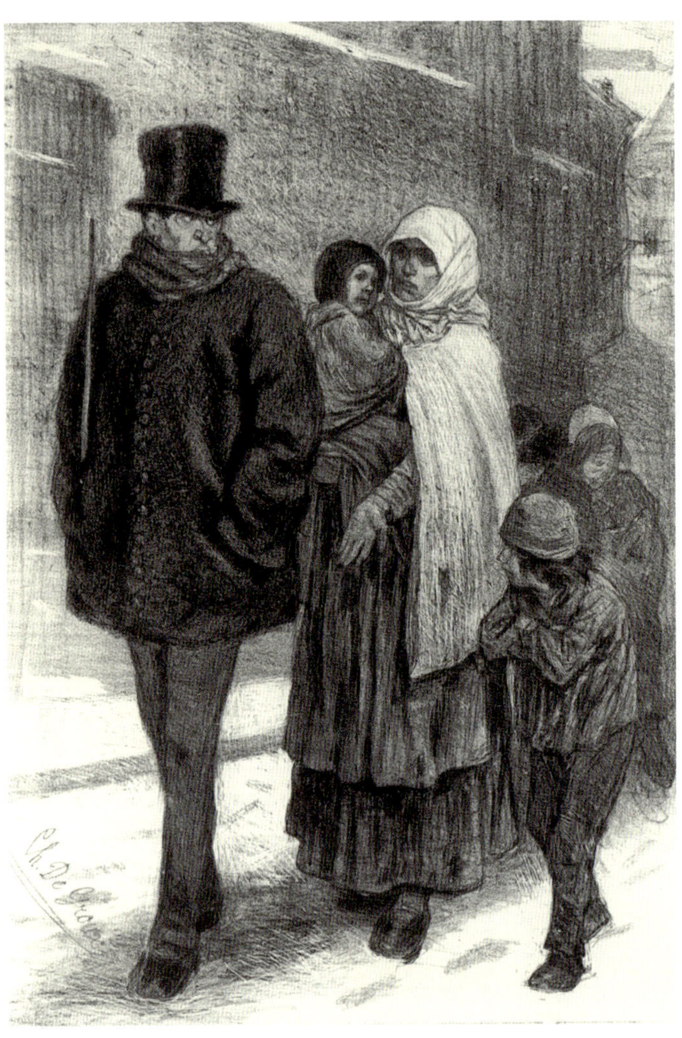

lism and immediacy thanks to the precise depiction of the clothing and the peasants' poses.[22] Van Gogh admired Brion and referred to this as one of his best works.[23] Although he would later conclude that the artist's paintings were nothing more than folkloristic genre pieces, he continued to regard Brion's illustrations to Victor Hugo's *Les misérables* (1865) as unrivalled: 'Is it then so little to know the people, the humanity of the period, so well that one never makes a mistake in either expression or type?' [799/602]. ❧ Van Gogh also praised Charles De Groux for his excellent 'types'. His studies and drawings had the same 'white-hot' passion that Vincent recognised in the heads of Frans Hals and Honoré Daumier, and in the novels of Zola and Honoré de Balzac [312/265]. De Groux was one of the first Belgian artists to treat the difficult social circumstances of the rural population and the working classes. His social-realist paintings were harshly criticised, not only for their subject matter, but also and above all because his figures were ugly. Although stylistically De Groux was undoubtedly influenced by the realism of Courbet, in terms of content his work is far more closely related to the romantic naturalism of Millet and Breton.[24] ❧ De Groux's work shows a Christian vision of poverty: the viewer is incited to pity and to empathise with the common man. While he was working as an evangelist in Belgium it was this aspect of De Groux's art in particular that appealed to Van Gogh. He owned a print after *The paupers' pew* (plate 10), which depicts the poor as pious, honest people resigned to their fate and seeking consolation in faith. The scene, which he described as a group of indigents 'sunk and rooted still deeper in poverty' [147/126], clearly spoke to Van Gogh's desire to bring religion to the masses. ❧ As an artist, Van Gogh would come to admire the truthfulness of De Groux's types, his elevated subject matter and sturdy, powerful draughtsmanship. In a letter of 1882 to Anthon van Rappard, he wrote that the De Groux lithographs published in the magazine *Uylenspiegel* were 'as beautiful as Israëls' [277/R15]. *On the street* (fig. 87), which depicts a mother with three children on a snowy street begging from a passer-by, is indeed comparable to the work of Jozef Israëls in both style and content. The shabbily dressed woman, her youngest child on her arm and her little son beside her, recalls Israëls's *At the churchyard* (plate 64), in which a fisherman is shown carrying his daughter while his son walks along beside him. De Groux's lithograph, however, is a far stronger social indictment, with the man – elegantly dressed in black and wearing a top hat – completely ignoring the suffering family. ❧ Even in

Breton – was a landscape with a ploughman by Camille Bernier, *January – Brittany*.[20] Seven years later, in 1882, he still thought of this work as 'a model' [293/251]. Breton's *Evening* (plate 38) – which Van Gogh calls 'Seule' ('Alone')[21] and later describes as 'that single figure of Breton's in the Luxembourg' [467/378] – was for him as sublime as Millet's *Angelus* (fig 86): it had 'that same twilight, that same eternal emotion' [467/378]. ❧ Gustave Brion's *Vosges peasants fleeing before the invasion* (plate 40) is another excellent example of Van Gogh's early taste, which was formed by the traditional art he saw in museums and at Goupil's. In this scene from contemporary history the heroes are peasants forced to flee their village in Alsace following an invasion by the Prussian army. Although the work was painted in Brion's Paris studio, it is given a sense of rea-

87. Charles De Groux, *On the street,* c. 1857, Brussels, Bibliothèque royale de Belgique

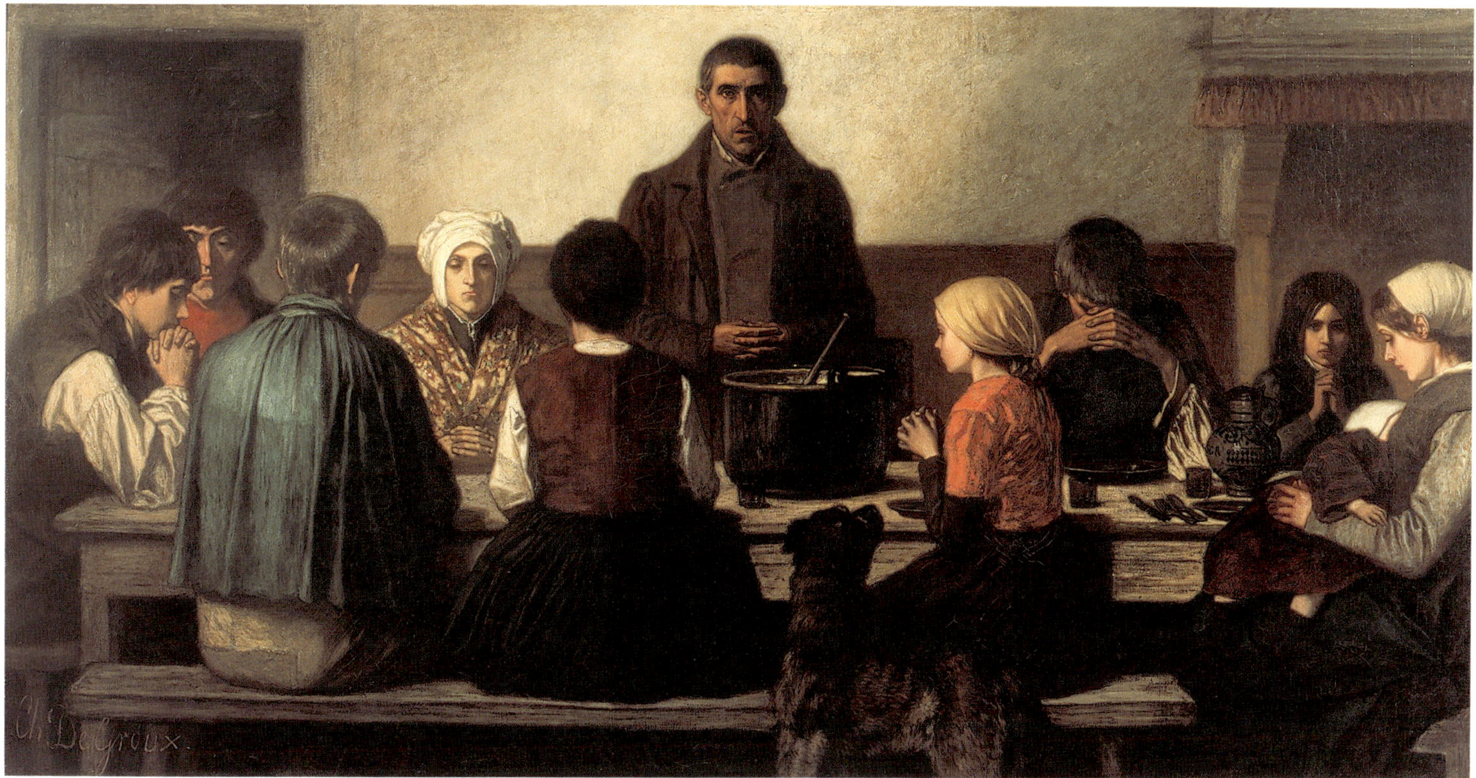

1885, while working on his studies of peasants for *The potato eaters*, Van Gogh still had De Groux's 'simple Brabant types' at the back of his mind [478/390]. In justifying his decision to become a peasant painter to Theo and Van Rappard he used not only Millet but also De Groux as an example. He stressed the fact that, although the latter had received little recognition, he had nonetheless remained faithful to his goal of painting 'the people' as they really were.[25] De Groux's *Grace* (fig. 88) has often been cited as a source of inspiration for Van Gogh's *Potato eaters*, as has a similar scene by Jozef Israëls depicting a peasant family at table, which Van Gogh had seen in 1882 at Goupil's in The Hague.[26] Van Gogh regarded De Groux as the Belgian equivalent of Israëls, who 'will never be surpassed here in Holland […] and will always, in my opinion, remain the master' [505/408]. Israëls was one of the most successful Dutch painters of his time. His heroic representations of fishermen and farm labourers helped raise the status of genre painting and marked the beginnings of realism in the Netherlands.[27] Van Gogh, who became well acquainted with Israëls's art while working at Goupil's, was a great admirer of his choice of

subject matter, technique and use of colour. ❧ Israëls's scenes of pious, simple fishermen and peasants dovetailed perfectly with Van Gogh's idealised vision of 'the people'. Already in 1878 he wrote that he would rather look at an ugly woman by Israëls than one of Gérôme's classical nudes, as Israëls painted the human soul.[28] During his Dutch period Van Gogh regarded Israëls as highly as he did Millet and Breton. He included him among those 'in search of the truly simple' and whose modest lifestyle made them a model for other artists. He returned to this latter aspect in Nuenen, remarking, however, that in contrast to Millet both Israëls and Mauve lived too opulently to be good examples for a young painter.[29]

What Van Gogh particularly admired in the depictions of peasants and labourers by Millet, Breton, De Groux and Jozef Israëls was their high-mindedness and 'grave sentiment' [279/240]. And it was above all the warm and respectful representation of working men and women that attracted him to the numerous prints he collected from English and French periodicals while in The Hague. Van

88. Charles De Groux, *Grace,* 1861, Brussels, Musées royaux des Beaux-Arts de Belgique

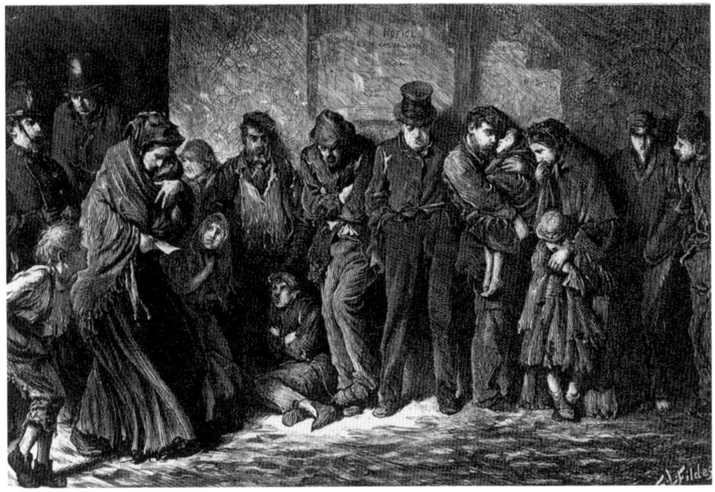

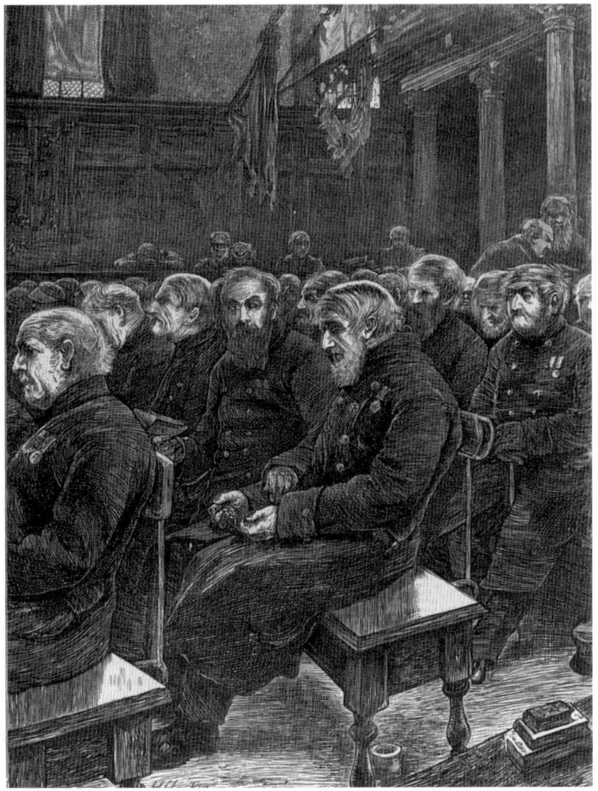

Gogh believed artists should show compassion for the plight of humankind, and he praised the way in which those working for *The Graphic* were able to arouse sympathy for the poor. Luke Fildes's *Houseless and hungry* (fig. 89) and Hubert von Herkomer's *Sunday at Chelsea Hospital* (fig. 90) were among his favourite works in this vein. ❧ Van Gogh's collection of magazine illustrations not only provided him with an insight into the methods and techniques of printmaking, but also supplied him with an arsenal of examples for the depiction of city life, figures at work and social-realist scenes of the lower classes. In imitation of 'the great draughtsmen of the people' [264/R12], he drew men and women on the street, in the third-class waiting room at the railway station and in hospitals, and made plans for a series of sheets that would help bring art to the masses.[30] Following the model of the series 'The heads of the people' published in *The Graphic* (figs. 91, 129), Van Gogh drew large portraits of orphan men and fishermen – popular 'types' – while in The Hague [299/257] (fig. 92). ❧ Although he was interested in prints of more socially engaged subjects, like strikes or factory workers, in his own art he limited himself to more traditional forms of labour. While in The Hague he drew pictures of diggers in the dunes and paviours, and in Nuenen of weavers and peasants. Unlike some of the printmakers whose work was included in his collection, Van Gogh never regarded his drawings as a form of social critique. He saw 'the people' with an artist's eye and sought out subjects that were 'typical' and 'picturesque'.[31] ❧ Initially, Van Gogh's preferences tended towards the English draughtsmen, but as time went on he gradually became more interested in the French artist Honoré Daumier. He became increasingly concerned with the depiction of types and characters in his own drawings, and he regarded Daumier as one of the greatest masters in this genre (fig. 93).[32] Unlike the English prints, the work of Daumier continued to inspire him even after he had left the Netherlands forever. He referred to the Arles postman, Joseph Roulin, as a kind of Daumier figure and wrote that he had painted his portrait in the style of that artist.[33] Just as Millet represented the rustic countryside of the north with its hardworking peasants, Van Gogh associated the inhabitants of Provence – who in his opinion were much lazier than 'the real workmen of the north' [781/594] – with the coarse popular types found in Daumier and Zola.[34]

BRETON AND MILLET: MASTERS OF THE PEASANT GENRE

'In my opinion, there was still progress up to *Millet and Jules Breton*, but to surpass them – don't even think of it. In the past, pres-

89. After **Luke Fildes,** *Houseless and hungry,* 1869, Amsterdam, Van Gogh Museum (Vincent van Gogh Foundation)

90. After **Hubert von Herkomer,** *Sunday at Chelsea Hospital,* 1875, Amsterdam, Van Gogh Museum (Vincent van Gogh Foundation)

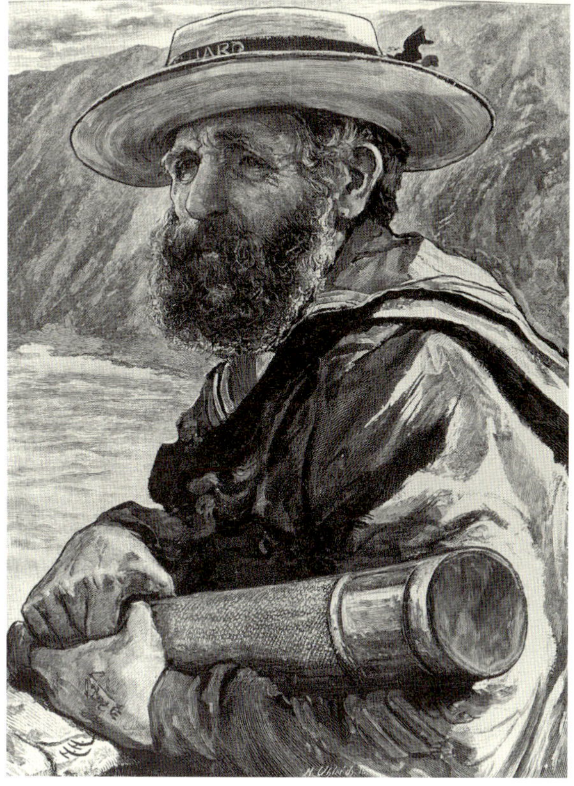

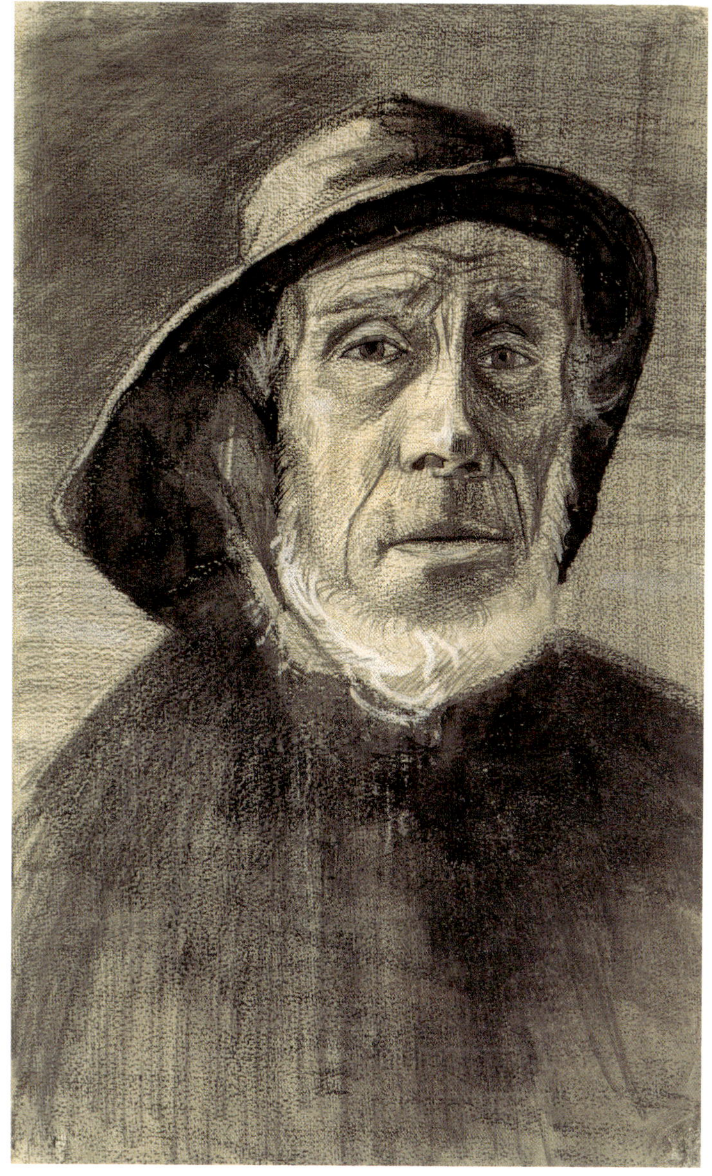

colour' [841/623] of Millet's *Rural labours, The sower, Men digging* and *The four times of the day*, combining the older artist's figures with the bright palette of Eugène Delacroix and the impressionists (plates 49, 51). With these copies, Van Gogh returned to his earliest models: as a novice painter he had copied the same prints over and over again in order to master the technique of depicting the figure. Breton, too, had played an important role in this period: Van Gogh himself described his visit in 1880 to Courrières, where Breton lived, as a kind of turning-point, the moment when he

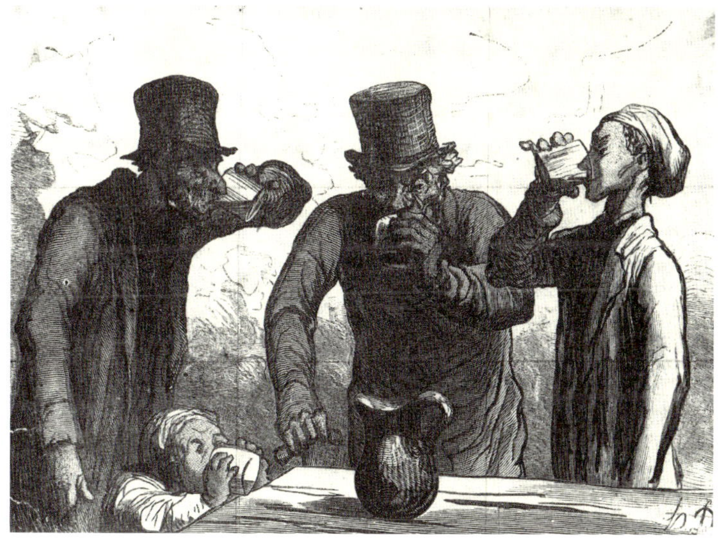

ent or future their genius may be equalled, but it will never be eclipsed', wrote Van Gogh in 1882 [281/241]. He remained true to his convictions even after becoming acquainted with the art of the Paris avant-garde. In Saint-Rémy he made 'interpretations in

91. After **Hubert von Herkomer,** *Heads of the people – the coastguardsman,* 1879, Amsterdam, Van Gogh Museum (Vincent van Gogh Foundation)
93. After **Honoré Daumier,** *The four ages of a drinker,* 1862, Amsterdam, Van Gogh Museum (Vincent van Gogh Foundation)

92. **Vincent van Gogh,** *Head of a fisherman with a fringe of beard and a sou'wester* (F 1017 JH 302), 1882-83, Amsterdam, Van Gogh Museum (Vincent van Gogh Foundation)

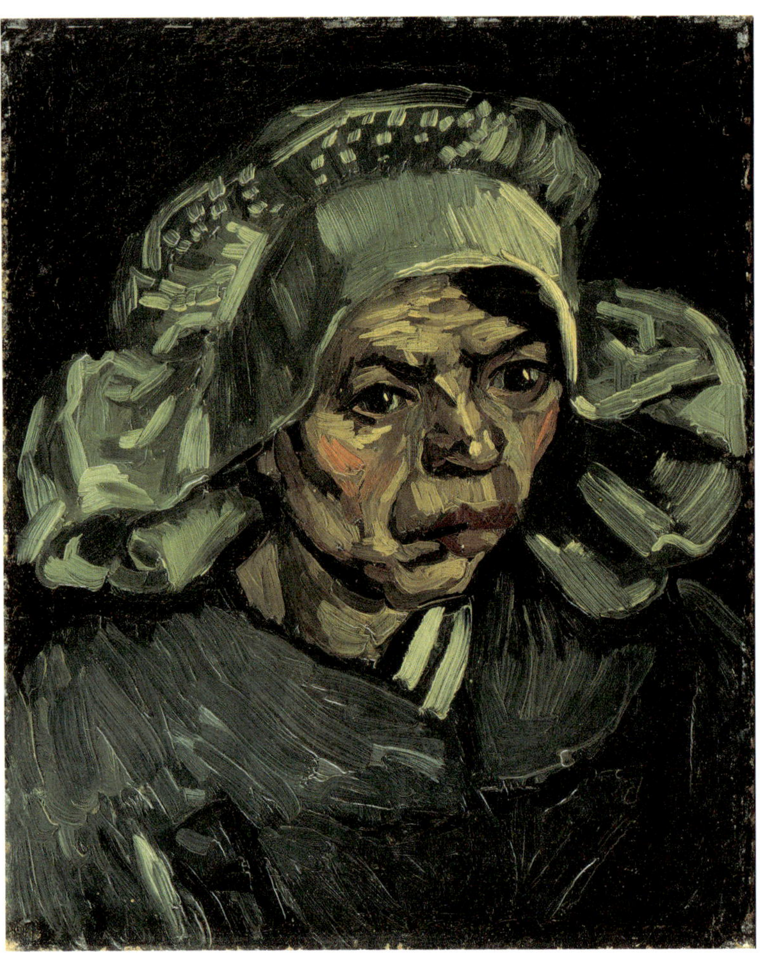

decided to devote himself entirely to drawing.[35] ✍ In his letters Van Gogh often mentions Millet and Breton at one stroke; for him they represented the same thing: not only 'the very heart of modern art' [522/418], but also mankind's oneness with the earth, as symbolised by the peasant working in the fields. In the work of these two artists, he saw a deeply religious feeling for nature, a belief in 'quelque chose là-haut'. This 'something up above', described by Van Gogh as 'the existence of a God and an eternity' [290/248], was expressed in the continual cycle of the seasons and the various rural labours associated with it. Like Millet and Breton, he depicted seasonal farm work in his paintings: ploughing, sowing, harvesting and reaping. He regarded the sower and the corn sheaf as symbols of the infinite[36] and Millet's *Sower* (plate 45) – in which 'there is more soul than in an ordinary sower in the field' [299/257] – as the apex of art. This masterpiece continued to fascinate him throughout his life, and he made innumerable drawings and paintings of the same motif (plates 46-47).[37] ✍ As a '*type* distilled from many *individuals*', Millet's *Sower* had a kind of eternal value, and Van Gogh regarded it as 'above nature' [299/257]. He sought to achieve the same thing in his own series of 'popular types', among them his Nuenen peasant heads and his Provençal portraits. In imitation of Millet, who had captured 'mankind and that something above' in his work [857/W20], Van Gogh sought to depict common people as if they were 'holy men and women' [802/605].[38] He strove to express the eternal and universal in his figures.

Van Gogh's admiration for Millet grew enormously following his reading of Alfred Sensier's *La vie et l'oeuvre de J.-F. Millet* (1881) in 1882. It characterises the artist as a deeply religious man who

94. Vincent van Gogh, *Head of a woman* (F 388r JH 782), 1885, Amsterdam, Van Gogh Museum (Vincent van Gogh Foundation)

himself lived the life of a poor peasant and never achieved the recognition he deserved – a picture that only partially conformed to the truth.[39] For Van Gogh, however, it was reason enough to declare the Frenchman his great mentor in both life and art. He recognised in Millet a kindred spirit and through him saw himself justified in his choice to make 'the people' the focus of his art. A short time later he decided to return to Brabant in order to follow in the footsteps of Millet, Breton and Léon Lhermitte, and to devote himself to depicting rural life. ✍ Van Gogh's conception of what an artist's life should be was confirmed by his reading of Sensier. Vincent believed that an artist who sought his motifs among 'the people' had to live modestly and among the subjects he chose to paint. Earlier he had praised the English draughtsmen, who 'by living among the masses and paying attention to things other people simply ignore, by remembering what most others forget,' were able to see and depict the poor as they really were [219/190]. This was equally true of the Frenchman Jean-François Raffaëlli, who painted pictures 'from the very heart of the urban work force' [522/418], using his neighbourhood ragpickers as models. ✍ Millet was the embodiment of Van Gogh's ideal of the artist as worker. Sensier stressed Millet's humble origins as the son of a peasant family, and the sober, rural life the artist led throughout his career. Van Gogh himself was content to live in virtual poverty, always assuming that an existence among the rustics would be enough to make one happy. He imputed the same lifestyle to other artists he admired. He was convinced, for example, that as painters of the lower classes Breton and Herkomer, too, must have always remained unaffected, and the same was undoubtedly true of Lhermitte and Delacroix. The Japanese artists whose prints he collected were also worthy of imitation for the peaceful and brotherly lives they were presumed to have led.[40] ✍ Van Gogh was particularly impressed by Millet's statement, cited by Sensier, that the critique of his paintings would perhaps bother him if he were a wearer of elegant shoes, 'mais avec des sabots, je crois que je m'en tirerai' – 'in my clogs, however, I think I can manage.' He quoted this sentence in a letter to Theo in order to prove that an artist – like Millet – should be satisfied 'with that which satisfies the peasants' [496/400]. The image of clogs as a symbol of rural life appealed to the Van Gogh brothers: Vincent referred to paintings of peasants as 'paintings in clogs' [663/520], and Theo related Millet's *bon mot* to their friend Camille Pissarro, 'who feels more comfortable in a pair of clogs than in patent-

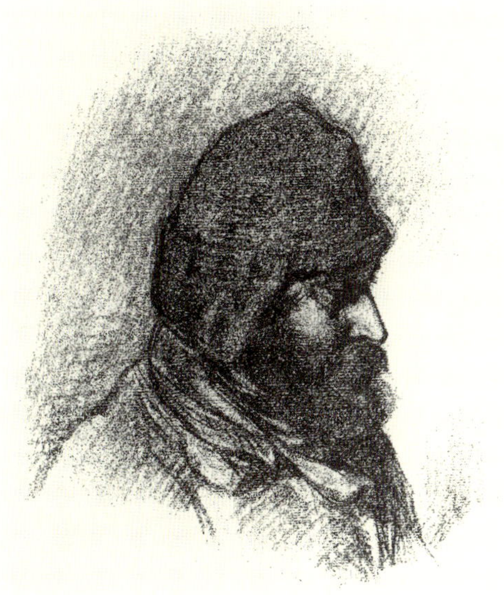

leather boots' [800/T16]. Pissarro, like Van Gogh a great admirer of Millet, was the only impressionist painter to devote himself almost exclusively to country life and labour.[41]

Sensier's biography formed not only Van Gogh's image of Millet but also influenced his painting technique and use of colour. Inspired by Sensier's reference to Théophile Gautier's pronouncement that Millet's *Sower* 'appeared to be painted with the earth being sown,' Van Gogh depicted his Nuenen peasants using thickly applied earthen tones (fig. 94).[42] ✍ For Van Gogh, coarse brushwork and exaggerated facial features were one means of emphasising the rough nature of his subjects. His goal was to depict the archetypal peasant, a primitive, brutish creature, and to this end he sought models 'with coarse, flat faces, low foreheads and thick lips, not sharp ones but full and Millet-like' [454/372]. Earlier he had described one of his Hague sitters as 'a kind of cockerel type', while another was 'rather thick-set, somewhat like an ox' [293/251].[43] Van Gogh was familiar with this analogy of rural labourers and animals from Sensier, who notes that by investigating various types and exaggerating his figures' physiognomy, Millet intended to give visual expression to the idea that human beings were not always superior to animals.[44] This characterisation of man as but a species of animal apparently appealed to Van Gogh, as he often used it himself and not only in reference to peasants.[45] Even Millet was not spared the comparison: what Van Gogh most

95. Jean-François Millet, *Self-portrait with a woollen cap,* from Alfred Sensier, *La vie et l'oeuvre de J.-F. Millet,* Paris 1881

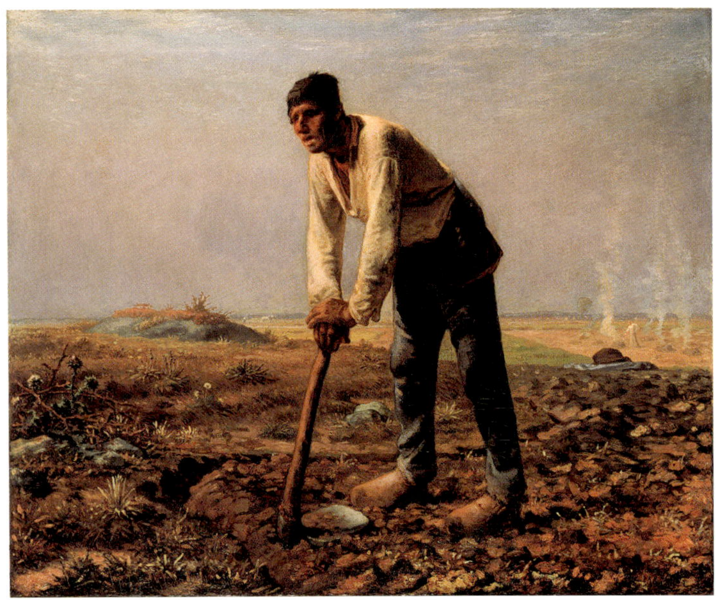

admired in the self-portrait reproduced in Sensier's biography was the artist's 'cockerel-like gaze' [290/248] (fig. 95). ✍ While in Arles Van Gogh twice painted portraits of Patience Escalier (fig. 83, plate 140), which he referred to as 'painting[s] in clogs' and compared with his peasant studies and *The potato eaters*.[46] He was quite satisfied with his likeness of this primitive 'man of nature', writing to Bernard: 'One of course knows what that is, a peasant, how he smells like a wild animal, if you find a really authentic one' [669/B15]. In a telling letter to Theo, Van Gogh linked the painting to both Zola and Millet. Because it was so exaggerated, he wrote, the work would probably be regarded as a mere caricature, but 'we've read *La terre* and *Germinal* and when we set out to paint a peasant we want to show that these books have finally become a part of ourselves' [663/520]. In *La terre* (1887) a farmer and his wife, driven by the desire for land and money, are transformed into unscrupulous murderers. In this work Zola places particular emphasis on the brute, bestial nature of his characters. By explicitly stating that these novels had served him as a model, Van Gogh acknowledged that they had profoundly changed his view of the rural labourer. He calls Escalier 'a "man with the hoe"-type' [663/520] – an allusion to *Man with a hoe*, one of Millet's 'rough' paintings without any religious overtones, in which the

figure is given almost inhuman features (fig. 96). In his *Portrait of Patience Escalier*, Van Gogh gave visual expression to this new vision of the peasant: Millet with a touch of Zola.

CONCLUSION

The primitive, beastlike nature of man was a recurring theme in Van Gogh's correspondence with Emile Bernard and Paul Gauguin, both of whom were also searching for man in his natural state. Van Gogh wrote to Bernard regarding Gauguin: 'I have long been convinced that those of us who have chosen the miserable profession of painter have great need of someone with the hands and stomach of a worker. […] Well, now we undoubtedly find ourselves in the company of an unspoiled creature with the instincts of a savage' [721/B19a]. That Gauguin also regarded himself in much the same manner becomes clear in his letter to Van Gogh on his paintings of Breton peasants: 'I'm trying to put into these sad figures something of the wildness that I see in them and that I also have in myself' [812/GAC 36]. ✍ In Provence, on the other hand, Van Gogh once again sought to realise his ideal of a life as a labourer in harmony with nature. At the same time, he was well aware that he was no peasant, and even less a savage, writing that 'it is perhaps our duty to love our (so-called) civilisation' [775/591]. He recognised that he was not a simple rustic and never would be: as an artist he worked too much with his head. Despite his efforts to become – like Millet – a true member of the rural community, he had allowed himself, as he wrote, to become distracted by pride and eccentricity.[47] ✍ As an artist, Van Gogh failed to be assimilated into 'the heart of the people'. In his effort to bring art to the masses, however, he would prove extraordinarily successful: the long queues at the entrance to the Van Gogh Museum are made up of a huge cross-section of the population, and reproductions of his work hang in living rooms all over the world – entirely in accordance with his pronouncement in 1885: 'it would be even better if these peasant pictures would end up *in homes*, through illustrations and other reproductions, in direct contact with the people' [511/412].

✍

96. Jean-François Millet, *Man with a hoe,* 1860-62, Los Angeles, The J. Paul Getty Museum

'RUMMAGING AMONG MY WOODCUTS' – VAN GOGH AND THE GRAPHIC ARTS

HANS LUIJTEN

Artists never work in a vacuum. Those privileged with a glimpse into the artist's studio will frequently find reproductions scattered about or hanging on the walls, sometimes seemingly carelessly stuck up with pins. Such images can serve as inspiration, motivation or even a form of consolation. There are numerous examples of artworks in which other paintings or prints have left their trace. ❧ It is almost impossible to overestimate the importance of the graphic arts for Vincent van Gogh. He wrote repeatedly about the engravings he had seen, collected, hung, traded or copied. His preference for certain works and the appreciative comments he made on them tell us much about the tasks he set himself as an artist. Prints inspired him to think of a career as an illustrator, and to try his hand at giving these black and white images his own colourful interpretation. For Van Gogh, prints were useful in several ways: they not only answered to his aesthetic sense but also provided him with information of a formal nature, for example on the power of contour lines or how to set up a composition and create mood. They were thus an important stimulus to his own work.[1] ❧ Most reproduction engravings – and these are mainly what we are dealing with here – were very affordable, even for Van Gogh. Rather than buying the more expensive sheets, he simply committed them to memory instead. The Van Gogh family estate comprises some 1,700 prints, mostly magazine illustrations. Around one fifth are Japanese in origin. The subject matter clearly reflects Vincent's taste for the socially engaged. At the same time, such themes were generally popular at the end of the 19th century and dominated the illustrated

press. His choice was therefore in some sense limited.[2] ❧ In the early years Van Gogh was particularly attracted to the graphic works of the Barbizon and Hague schools and reproductions of religious paintings by artists such as Paul Delaroche and Ary Scheffer – all well represented in Goupil's stocks. He must have begun collecting almost immediately upon taking up his post. While in The Hague he concentrated mainly on recent magazine illustrations, and from 1886 he started acquiring Japanese woodcuts. It is interesting to note that Van Gogh rarely writes about old master prints or printmakers in his letters, focusing instead on contemporary works – and then only of a certain kind, namely illustrations from the weeklies. Prints by Manet or Degas, for example – which he must have seen in Paris – are never mentioned.

EARLY ACQUAINTANCE WITH THE GRAPHIC ARTS

The Van Gogh brothers' interest in the graphic arts developed while they were working for Goupil & Cie – Vincent from 1869, Theo from 1873. Here they were surrounded by enormous numbers of photographs, photo-engravings, engravings and etchings. Goupil's already large stock was augmented twice a year by the so-called *nouveautés*, among them prints after works shown at the annual Salon.[3] ❧ Prints were a familiar item within the family as well. Uncles Vincent and Cor van Gogh, renowned dealers who introduced their nephews Vincent and Theo to the art business, had an extensive collection. And at home in Brabant, too, the boys often showered them on their kinsmen. Exactly what type of works these were is revealed by the following request

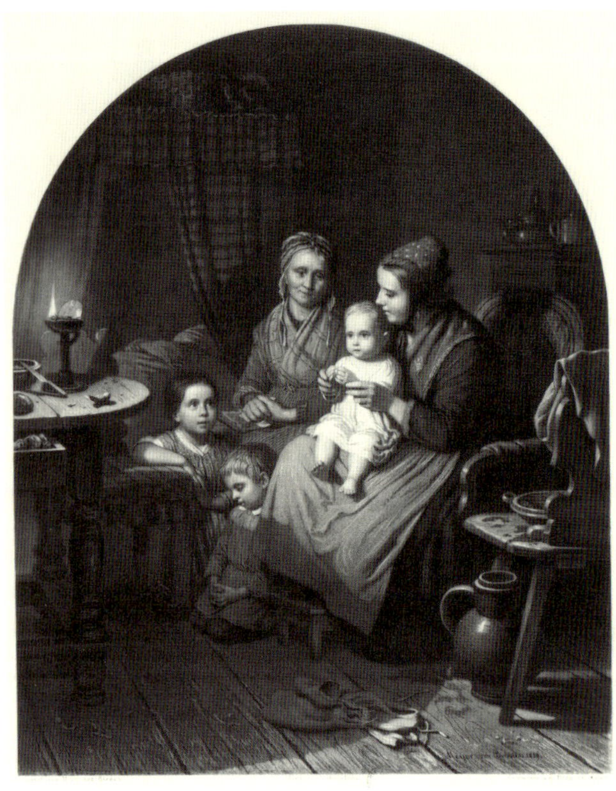

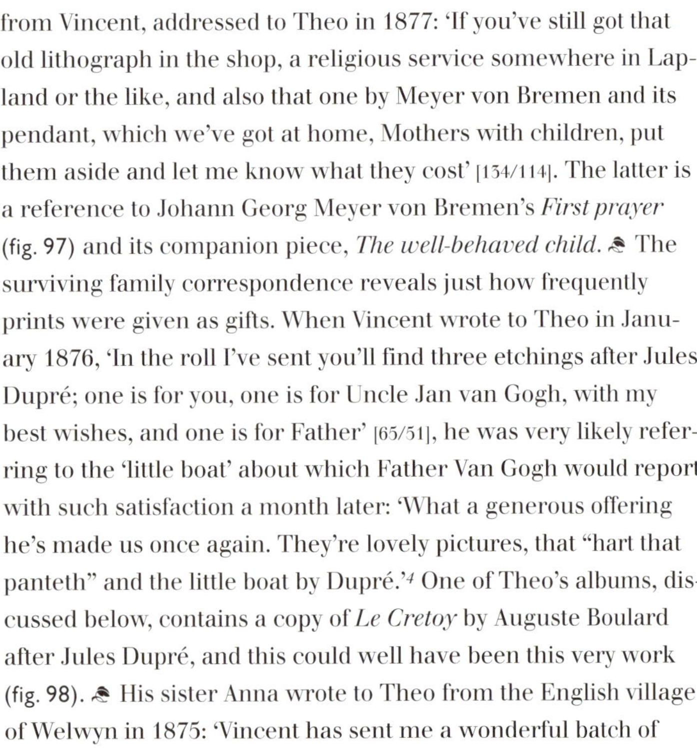

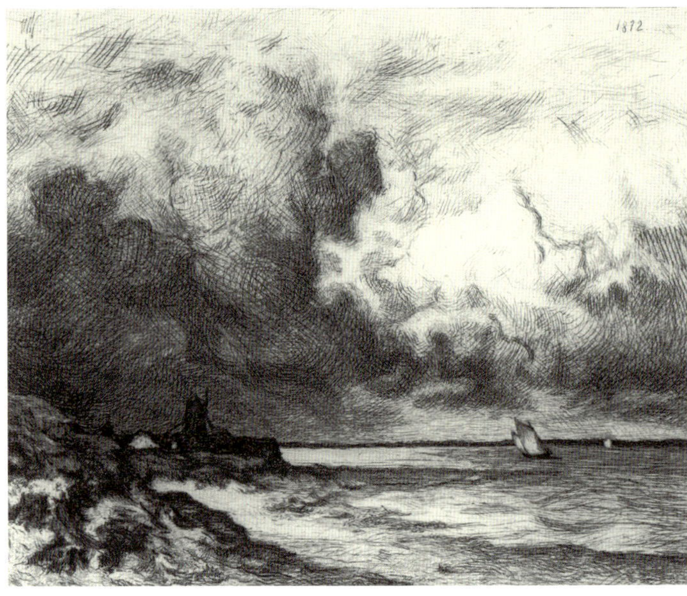

from Vincent, addressed to Theo in 1877: 'If you've still got that old lithograph in the shop, a religious service somewhere in Lapland or the like, and also that one by Meyer von Bremen and its pendant, which we've got at home, Mothers with children, put them aside and let me know what they cost' [134/114]. The latter is a reference to Johann Georg Meyer von Bremen's *First prayer* (fig. 97) and its companion piece, *The well-behaved child.* ≈ The surviving family correspondence reveals just how frequently prints were given as gifts. When Vincent wrote to Theo in January 1876, 'In the roll I've sent you'll find three etchings after Jules Dupré; one is for you, one is for Uncle Jan van Gogh, with my best wishes, and one is for Father' [65/51], he was very likely referring to the 'little boat' about which Father Van Gogh would report with such satisfaction a month later: 'What a generous offering he's made us once again. They're lovely pictures, that "hart that panteth" and the little boat by Dupré.'⁴ One of Theo's albums, discussed below, contains a copy of *Le Cretoy* by Auguste Boulard after Jules Dupré, and this could well have been this very work (fig. 98). ≈ His sister Anna wrote to Theo from the English village of Welwyn in 1875: 'Vincent has sent me a wonderful batch of

prints, the nicest of which I've hung up. Do you know Pasini's "Le soir"? It's lovely.'⁵ This was undoubtedly the same scene as in the lithograph *Evening* by Alberto Pasini, which was also part of Theo's album.⁶ ≈ Father Van Gogh reported to Theo: 'Last night a box full of magnificent prints arrived. My dear fellow! What a wonderful and so very precious gift. What you've done to help decorate our new vicarage [in Etten]! And even if we still feel a bit like strangers in the house, thanks to these exquisite engravings from you and Vincent it will be like having you to talk to. But really, it's too much, simply too much!'⁷ In 1883 Theo presented his sister Willemien with a group of Japanese prints, and shortly before their father's death, in 1885, there was yet another 'beautiful plate' – as he put it – for his birthday. Following his emigration to South Africa in August 1889, the youngest brother, Cor, thanked Theo and his wife Jo, whom he had visited in Paris before his departure, for 'the prints of the exhibition, which I've hung up; they give the room a cheerful aspect'.⁸ ≈ Vincent's current state of mind was reflected in the walls of the rooms where he lived and worked. Their 'decoration' was clearly more than simple adornment. He became preoccupied with different types

---

97. After **Johann Georg Meyer von Bremen,** *The first prayer,* 1859, Paris, Bibliothèque Nationale de France, Cabinet des Estampes

98. After **Jules Dupré,** *Le Cretoy,* Amsterdam, Van Gogh Museum (Vincent van Gogh Foundation)

of prints depending on his phase in life. During his religious period, for example, he surrounded himself with an abundance of Christian images, as appears from an eyewitness account. His Dordrecht roommate Paulus Coenraad Görlitz recorded that in early 1877 Van Gogh had asked him if it would be all right to 'hang up a few biblical pictures'. He had agreed, and 'Within half an hour the whole room was decorated with biblical scenes and depictions of the Ecce Homo, and under each head of Christ Van Gogh had written: "as sorrowful, yet always rejoicing."'[9]

An investigation into the ways in which Van Gogh came into contact with prints other than through his work at Goupil's indicates that chance played a large role. He often mentions things he has seen on the street or in shops, such as in Amsterdam at his uncle Cor's gallery or in his collection – which comprised, for example, the 1852 volume of *L'Illustration*, the year Adrien Lavieille's engravings after Emile Jacque's *The twelve months of the year* were published.[10] Five years later Van Gogh recalled the series, remembering that the drawing had 'something concise about it, reminiscent of Millet' [281/241]. He also writes enthusiastically about *De Katholieke Illustratie*, having seen a prospectus for it while working in the bookshop of the publishers Blussé & Van Braam in Dordrecht: 'If you can afford it – and if I can, I'll do it too – sign up for this year's *Katholieke Illustratie*; it contains Doré's prints from London, depicting the wharves on the Thames, Westminster, Whitechapel, the Underground railway, etc., etc.' [101/84]. His eagerness is palpable. ☙ During his London years (1873-75) Van Gogh saw engravings and other kinds of reproductions in the show windows of the printers of *The Graphic* and *The Illustrated London News*; and later, in The Hague, large etchings at Goupil's, for example *The dead Kabyle* by Mariano Fortuny y Carbó (plate 96). He knew the graphic work of Hans Holbein, Albrecht Dürer and Alfred Rethel. He found Rethel's *Death as a friend* (plate 26) extremely moving: 'When I was in London one could see it in the windows of almost every print shop' [120/101]. ☙ He became acquainted with the works exhibited at the annual Salon through the illustrated catalogues, among them that of Ernest Boetzel and François-Guillaume Dumas, and from special editions of the art journals: 'Saw the harvest by Lhermitte in the illustrated catalogue; it looks good – there's so much truth about work and the peasant in it' [345/285].[11] ☙ Van Gogh often discussed prints with fellow artists such as

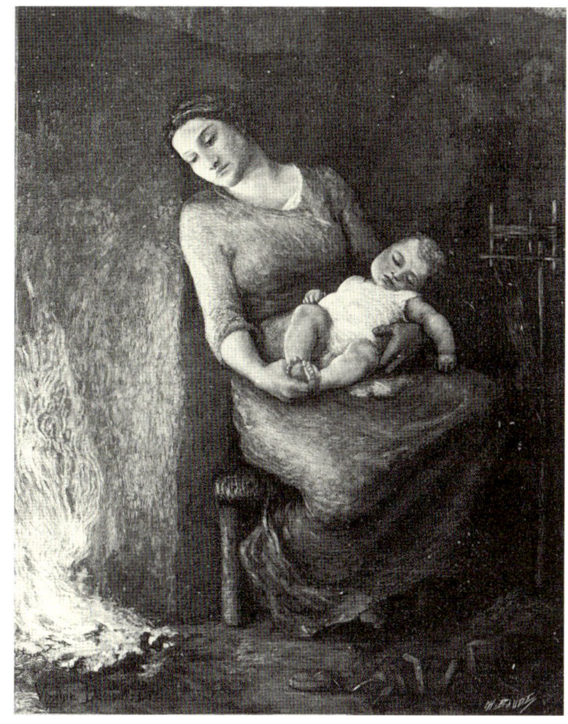

Anthon van Rappard and Herman van der Weele, and leafed through and read the periodicals he borrowed, was sent or bought. He could be quite insistent when it came to asking Theo to send him the latest issue of certain magazines, and the reviews of the *Black & White* exhibitions always piqued his curiosity. It is obvious he was extremely keen to absorb as much as he could, and in this he succeeded. He recognised a print he had seen in *L'Univers Illustré* in a copy of William Black's novel *That beautiful wretch* sent to him by Van Rappard. The journal reproduced an engraving that had appeared, oddly cropped, in Black's book. ☙ Through the years the brothers continued to keep each other informed about the interesting graphic works they came across. In the last years of his life Van Gogh also began to develop an interest in contemporary prints. In July 1888, for example, he reports: 'The Lautrecs have just come, I think they are beautiful' [641/505]. The reference is to the illustrations created by Henri de Toulouse-Lautrec for Emile Michelet's article 'L'été à Paris'.[12] Even after he had entered the hospital at Saint-Rémy, Van Gogh continued to follow the illustrated weeklies. 'There's also a guard here whom I've promised a copy of Le Monde illustré, no. 1684, dated 6 July 1889, which contains a lovely engraving after

99. After **Virginie Elodie Demont-Breton,** *Man is at sea,* 1889, Amsterdam, Van Gogh Museum (Vincent van Gogh Foundation)

Demont-Breton' [801/604]. He would eventually make a copy of this *Man is at sea*, engraved by Charles Baude (fig. 99).[13]

TARGETED COLLECTING

It has been suggested that Van Gogh built up his collection of prints 'systematically'.[14] There does not, however, seem to have been much system in his accumulation as such, although there certainly was in the future organisation of the material. Van Gogh was always on the lookout for reproductions, and he must have acquired many works on mere impulse. Moreover, his means were rather limited. His purchases were at least partly determined by what was available at the local booksellers, who often bought up auction remainders or dealt in second-hand books, among them copies from lending libraries.[15] ☙ One of his major reasons for collecting was already set out in February 1881: 'If I can put together a good group [of prints], I might get some use out of them, since it may well turn out that I'll eventually go to work for a wood engraver' [162/141]. In addition to inexpensive, loose sheets – in early June 1882 Van Gogh claims already to have assembled as many as 1,000 [233/204] – the estate included two scrapbooks, each containing dozens of prints and reproductions. The exact circumstances of their creation are difficult to reconstruct, as some of the prints were added later, while others were removed or transferred from one album to the other.[16] ☙ Both albums include engravings, etchings, lithographs and photographs mentioned in the correspondence, among them Théodore Rousseau's *A kiln in Les Landes*; Jules Dupré's *Stormy day* of 1872; and Johannes Bosboom's *Service in a village church*. Compared to the first, the second album is more of a hotchpotch. Only 59 of the 264 pages are filled. We find illustrations from French, Dutch and German publications, and, particularly at the end, reproductions from 20th-century magazines. This indicates that the book continued to be used even long after Theo's death – perhaps by his son Vincent Willem. Prints cited in the correspondence found here include Jacob Maris's *Return from the cemetery*, lithographed by F.H. Weissenbruch, and a photograph of Gustave-Jean Jacquet's *Little girl with a sword*. Sometimes the reproductions are arranged thematically – landscapes, animals, interiors. At other times the lithographer or engraver appears to have been the determining factor.[17] The choices give insight into Van Gogh's

taste in the 1870s, as it was he who sent most of the prints to Theo.

During the 1880s the periodicals Van Gogh most often plundered were *The Graphic*, *The Illustrated London News*, *Harpers* (both *Weekly* and *Monthly*), *L'Illustration*, *Le Monde Illustré*, *L'Univers Illustré* and *La Vie Moderne*. In the past, little attention has been paid to several other publications that can be considered equally important in this context, namely *De Hollandsche Illustratie* and the *Illustrirte Zeitung*. The former, for example, was the source of Auguste-André Lançon's *Gathering of ragpickers*, beneath which Van Gogh even pencilled the French title – 'Rendez-vous des chiffoniers'. He did the same with *The poor of Paris: distribution of soup*, writing below it 'Distribution de soupe'.[18] His copy of Honoré Daumier's *The four ages of a drinker*, which he squared up to make it easier to copy, also came from *De Hollandsche Illustratie* (plate 149). In 1890 the sheet would become the starting point for *Men drinking* (F 667 JH 1884); he gave the image colour and filled in the background. In a letter to Van Rappard of 1883 he mentions the discovery of two Daumiers, 'Rencontre de ceux qui ont vu un drame et de ceux qui ont vu une vaudeville' and 'Amateurs de tableaux' [311/R21], literally: 'Those who have seen a drama meeting those who have seen a vaudeville' and 'Lovers of paintings'. Once again, the French is misleading for those in search of Van Gogh's source. The works he refers to are *Leaving the theatres* (plate 99), with the caption 'Those having seen a drama. Those having seen a comedy', and *Art lovers at an exhibition*, both engraved by C. Maurand for *De Hollandsche Illustratie*.[19] ☙ Until now, the *Illustrirte Zeitung* has been completely ignored. The anonymous *New Year's Eve* (fig. 100); Ludwig Knaus's *Piglet*; Carl Koch's *Rowing regatta* and *Police raid on a robbers' lair*; Paul Meyerheim's *The monkey academy*; and Benjamin Vautier's *An arrest* are all mentioned in the letters and were known to Van Gogh from issues of this German periodical published in the years 1879-81.[20] ☙ The brothers sometimes acquired prints through trading. These exchanges took place at various times, meaning that Vincent may never have seen some of the works that entered the collection in this way. It is certain, however, that he knew the woodcuts of Lucien Pissarro, who wrote: 'I own Van Gogh's apples and the picture is dedicated to me – we made an exchange: I gave him a collection of my wood engravings.'[21]

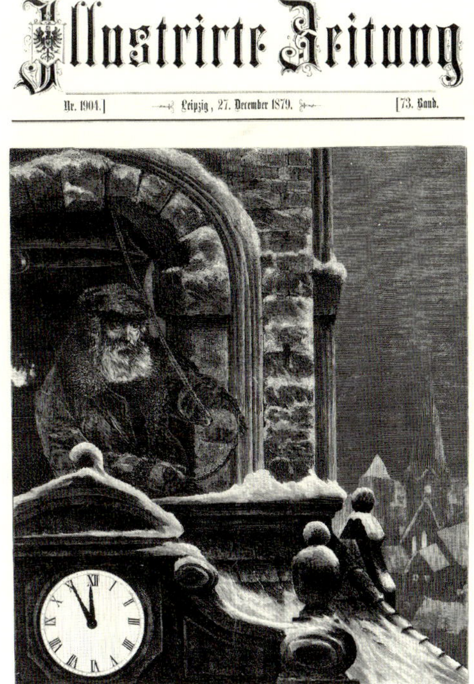

THE COLLECTOR FINDS HIS FORM

Van Gogh's interest in magazine illustration began to develop in the early 1880s. He bought hundreds of prints, mainly wood engravings – which he often mistakenly refers to as 'woodcuts' – from *The Graphic* and *The Illustrated London News*, even acquiring whole volumes. He was fascinated by the realism and candour of these works, and they inspired him to hone his own technical skills. For some time he toyed with the idea of becoming an illustrator, hoping to make monthly drawings that could then be used for double-page engravings: 'Do you know what I often think about? Getting in touch with the Graphic or London News in England. I was hoping, now that things are going better, to do some large compositions that might be suitable for illustrated magazines' [350/288].[22] Van Gogh was a great admirer of this art of black and white, not only engravings but also chalk and charcoal drawings as well. And although, as he writes, some might disparage 'such things as one might find in The South-Holland Coffeehouse' [213/184], in his opinion these artists were actually creating a kind of painting and their work had a right to be recognised. When it snows, he remarked, the whole world is transformed into a *Black & White* exhibition [334/276]. Later, arriving in Arles in February of 1888, he found it had just snowed. By this time, however, his points of reference were elsewhere, and he could think of nothing but colourful Japanese prints: 'And the landscape in the snow, with those white mountain tops standing out against a sky as bright as the snow itself, were just like those winter landscapes done by the Japanese' [579/463]. Van Gogh's largest purchase of prints was made in The Hague. In September 1882 he found himself in negotiation 'with a fellow who has for sale a large number of periodicals from a reading circle. I'm determined to get hold of them' [269/R14]. He bought not only individual issues for specific prints – such as *The Illustrated London News* for *The workman's train* by Edward R. King – but finally, at the end of January 1883, ten bound years of *The Graphic*.[23] These heavy volumes, 21 in all, dating from 1870 to 1880, cost him 'only' 21 guilders, disgracefully cheap in his opinion [306/R24]. Still, the acquisition was a huge financial strain for someone whose pockets were chronically empty and who also had to pay over 12 guilders a month in rent. (His only income was the circa 75 guilders a month sent to him by Theo.) It seems likely that it was Van Rappard's recent procurement of a batch of periodicals from the period 1870-76 that encouraged Van Gogh to make this enormous expenditure.[24] Among the prints was George Pinwell's *The sisters*, which aroused the poet in him: 'a composition, as simple as possible, into which he has put such grave sentiment that I find nothing to compare it with except the nightingale's song on a spring night' [306/R24]. Having taken the decision – after much hesitation – to cut the prints from their bindings, Van Gogh began arranging them, making them easier to search. He affixed them to pieces of rough brown, green or grey paper, where they have remained to this day. We can therefore be fairly certain that such sheets were actually once in Vincent's own collection. Something of the way in which he arranged them can also be garnered from the list he sent to Theo in June 1882. It indicates that he spent many hours cutting and pasting before classifying the works according to subject matter, artist and format (fig. 101). Van Gogh informed Van Rappard in detail not only about this purchase but about many others as well. They also exchanged duplicates and discussed particularities of technique and which prints were their favourites. Street life, popular

100. **Anonymous,** *New Year's Eve,* 1879, The Hague,
Koninklijke Bibliotheek

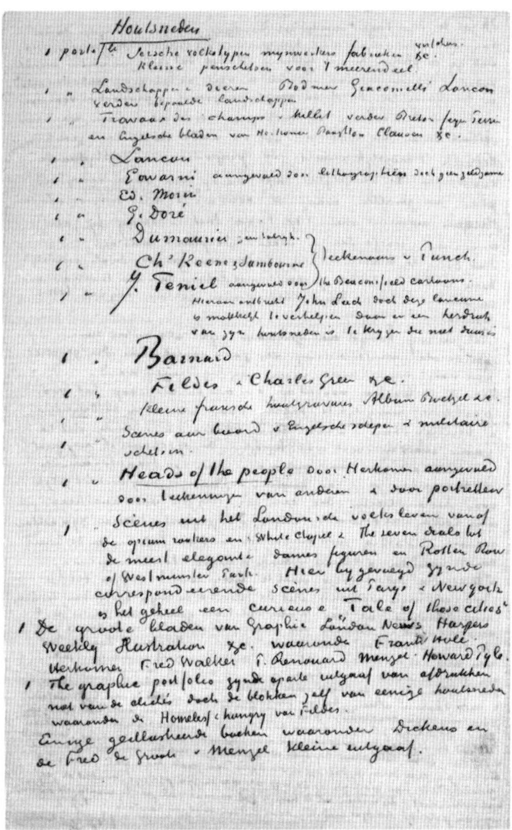

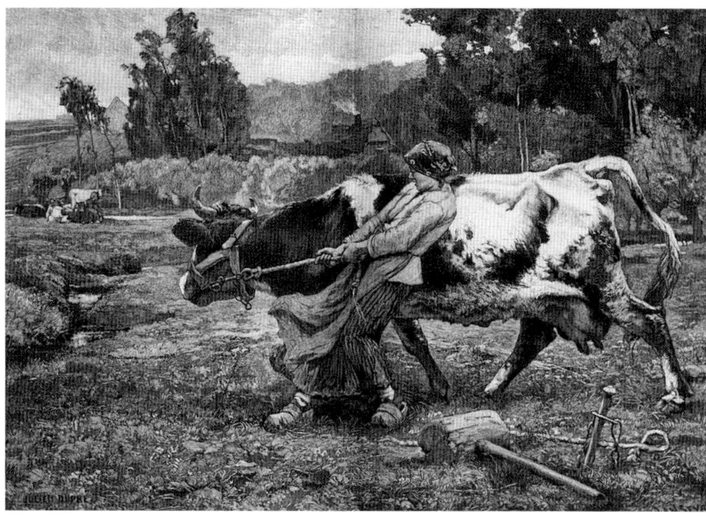

the degree to which the social or Christian message came across (in reference to the sense of compassion with his fellow human beings he speaks of 'grave sentiment' [279/240])[26] to the mood of a landscape; from the refinement of the drawing to the technical skill of the engraver. These are the categories that determined his taste, and they provide us with a key as to why it was often so unexpectedly heterogeneous and changed over time: the phase in Van Gogh's career and the questions with which he saw himself confronted determined which aspects of a print he admired. ☙ Van Gogh's evaluation is positive when the work in question has what he calls 'body', 'soul' and 'character'. Other favourable attributes include 'realistic', containing 'noble sentiment', 'energetic' and 'sincere'. He found the work of Hubert von Herkomer 'heartfelt'.[27] That his own ambition was to create something along these same lines becomes clear when he writes to Theo that his 'enthusiasm for these draughtsmen isn't simply frivolous but arises from a desire and yearning to make something myself that is realistic but nonetheless done with feeling' [198/169]. He relies heavily in his judgments on the assertions made by Herkomer in his article 'Drawing and engraving on wood',[28] for example when he declares himself in favour of a well thought-out but nonetheless unaffected drawing style: 'The old way of engraving, the well-considered, honest, unpretentious drawing is far and away the best' [280/R17]. ☙ While in The Hague Van Gogh sought to master the technique of lithography, directing his attention to early examples in the medium. 'The lithographs by Emile Vernier after Millet and Corot and Daubigny have qual-

images, labourers, travellers; according to Van Gogh the artist should draw his motifs 'from the heart of the people' [335/277]. He was thus particularly inspired by the series 'Heads of the people' published in *The Graphic* (figs. 91, 129), and decided to attempt something similar himself. This led to his group of fishermen's heads and orphan men (fig. 92). The illustrations to the articles 'Artist strolls in Holland' and 'Sketches from London', about which he wrote with such enthusiasm, find their analogy in the drawings of Hague city life that he made for his uncle Cor, a kind of 'Sketches from The Hague'.[25]

VAN GOGH'S TASTE

The criteria by which Van Gogh judged prints appear to vary and are difficult to reduce to a common denominator: they ranged from the way in which something was done (its expressivity) to the realism of the image (that which made it 'touching'); from

101. Letter 235/205, Vincent van Gogh to Theo van Gogh, The Hague, 3 June 1882, Amsterdam, Van Gogh Museum (Vincent van Gogh Foundation)

102. After **Julien Dupré**, *In the meadow*, 1882, Amsterdam, Van Gogh Museum (Vincent van Gogh Foundation)

103. Vincent van Gogh, sketch in letter 359/296 to Theo van Gogh, The Hague, between c. 23 and 28 June 1883, Amsterdam, Van Gogh Museum (Vincent van Gogh Foundation)

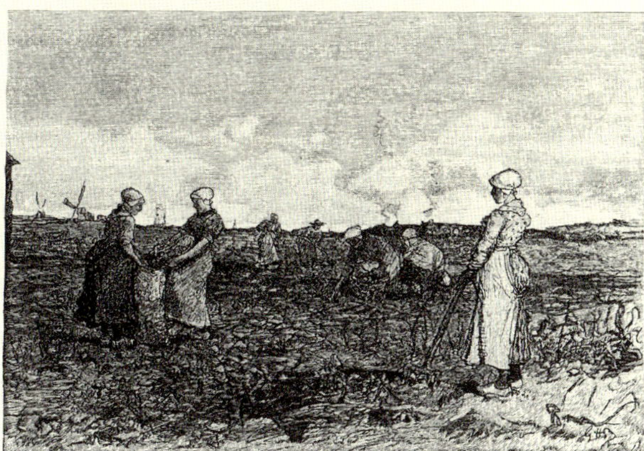

174 HARPER'S NEW MONTHLY MAGAZINE.

IN THE POTATO FIELD.

There are still in Haarlem a goodly number of charming old houses of the seventeenth century. Some of their gables lean rather forward toward the street or sideways toward their next-door neighbor in a way suggestive of fundamental debility. At first sight it seems safer to walk in the middle of the road, and look out for falling bricks. But one soon gets over the tottery character; in fact, some one told us that they were built originally at that angle forward. When they lean sideways, they admit the mouldering pile beneath, and own to the sinkage. The fine old city walls and ramparts that withstood the famous siege have been pulled down, all but one fine old gateway, a splendid specimen of its kind, picturesque to the last degree. That is all there is left to illustrate one of the greatest chapters in the history of Haarlem. The boulevard and the tram car have risen over the dust of all the rest. I should like to say something more worthy of this memorable siege, there is such a splendid opportunity; but on second thought perhaps it is as well to refer the reader to Motley, and not seek to supersede that admirable history.

If any reader should feel inclined to notice the lack of Serious Purpose in this article, let me hasten to say that we scarcely had a serious moment there; we enjoyed it so much that we found no time to get serious. There is no use whatever in lamenting the sad fact that the Dutchman of to-day will, whenever he gets a chance, pull down remorselessly his most lovely old ramparts and town walls or halls, or, in fact, any relic of the past, to make way for a boulevard or a railway station. To tell the truth, we found the pick-axe and shovel being wielded on one or two old city gates in a way to make the antiquarian's heart bleed. The demon of improvement seems to be let loose at the present moment all over the land. Perhaps there may be some good healthful purpose served, after all, now and again. Wiser heads must settle these matters; as I said before, let us take things as we find them.

The cathedral at Haarlem is not so fine in form or so picturesquely situated as that at Dort, but it seems better cared for and preserved. The restorer has not enjoyed himself over it from time to time. The great organ is its show piece. It did not happen to play while we were visiting the church, and as we did not happen to want it to play seriously enough to pay the fee for the far-famed special perform-

ities I truly admire. How I would love to talk to someone who is so good at his metier! Not because I want to make reproductions of paintings, but just to get a better understanding of what lithography can do. Just imagine original drawings with those odd greys and that peculiar rendering of textures' [335/277]. Van Gogh continually sought to discover the secrets of the craft and to understand how to express certain tones or motion in a print. 'Do you know whose work has really affected me? I saw some reproductions after Julien Dupré [...] a wonderful woodcut from *Le Monde Illustré*, a peasant woman driving her cow to a field. It seemed to me so outstanding, so very energetic and sincere'

[282/242]. This energy and truth to nature must have been linked to the opposing movements of the woman and the animal so convincingly suggested in Dupré's *In the meadow* (fig. 102). In early July 1883 Van Gogh paid a visit to Van Rappard's studio, where he was given a number of books and magazines on loan; he wrote to his friend almost immediately thereafter: 'I'm so happy to be able to look at the Boughtons and Abbeys at leisure. "In the potato field" is the nicest of them all, and the "Bell-ringers" by Abbey' [561/R38]. Not only the subject matter of George Henry Boughton's *In the potato field* – which, after all, was so in keeping with his own efforts of a week earlier to depict four

104. After **George Henry Boughton**, *In the potato field*, 1883, Amsterdam, Universiteitsbibliotheek

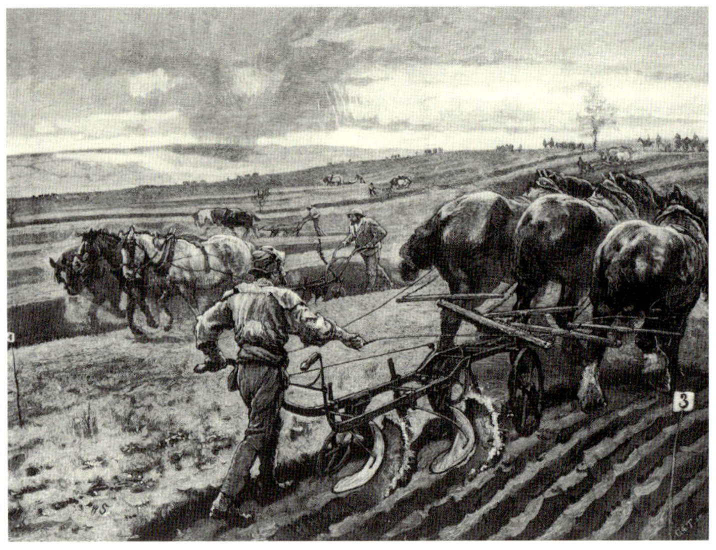

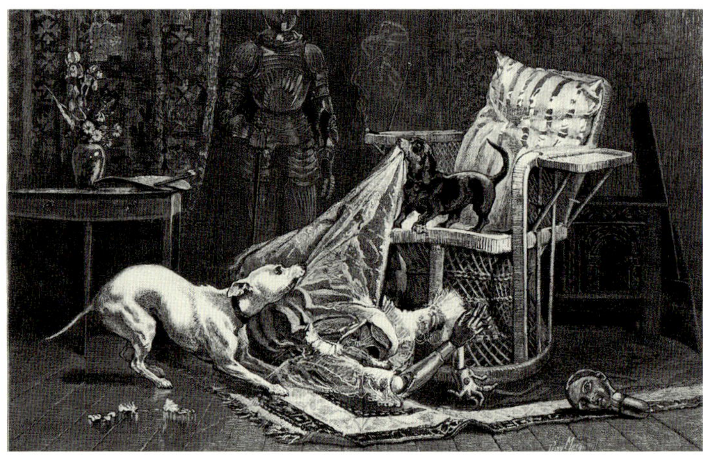

potato diggers convincingly (fig. 103) – but also its sketchiness and composition must have appealed to him (fig. 104). Besides being 'beautiful' and 'wonderful', it is also 'outstanding' and 'important' – all words that do little really to characterise the work. ☙ What exactly the designation 'superb' meant is difficult to judge, but there are several prints by Francis Holl to which he more than once applies the term, among them *The foundling*. He also uses it in reference to a large wood engraving after William Small's *An English ploughing match* (fig. 105). In these two cases it was probably the broadly conceived composition and the precision of the execution that Van Gogh admired.[29] He seems to allude to this kind of refinement once again when at the end of his life, in 1890, he saw Félix Bracquemond's etched *Portrait of Auguste Comte* at Paul Gachet's in Auvers-sur-Oise. Van Gogh, who by this time had painted dozens of portraits himself, referred to the meditative head with its large eyes as a 'masterpiece' [881/638]. ☙ But there are negative assessments as well. '*The British Workman* and *The Cottager & Artisan*, both penny papers published by the London pamphlet society, sometimes contain things that are rather tame' [277/R15]. He owned 'a large sheet' by Percy T. Macquoid, 'the corner of a studio – a mannequin that has fallen over, two dogs playing with a piece of drapery. It's exquisite, but it gives me little satisfaction, it's a bit priggish and fastidious.' His rejection of this *Disarrangement in blue* was undoubtedly partially based on his dislike of the subject

matter. The sophistication of the execution was no match for an uninteresting and unimaginative motif (fig. 106). ☙ Van Gogh developed an excellent eye for the way in which certain prints had been carried out. Doré's *Falling leaves* was 'roughly done, but excellent in sentiment' [311/R21];[30] Abbey's *Christmas in Old Virginia* astonished him and he wondered if perhaps the drawing 'hadn't been done entirely in pen' [306/R24];[31] while *A city church congregation* by Green was 'so beautifully drawn, so exquisitely done' [361/R38].[32] For Van Gogh, himself always in search of 'feeling', it was the sense of compassion that emanated from the English wood engravings that made them so special. They were genuine and captured the very essence of the motif. 'What you've said about French woodcuts in general is my feeling as well; the English have found the *soul* of the woodcut, its essential character, which is just as particular as the character of etchings. For example, Buckmann's "A London dustyard", and "Harbour of refuge" by Walker.[33] Still, Boetzel and Lavieille have achieved the same thing, although Swain is the boss. I think the *Lançons*, engraved by Moller, also has something of this authenticity as well. There's soul in Boetzel's Feyen Perrins and Lavieille's Millets, for example. But it's different somehow; they sometimes degenerate into the mechanical and unfeeling' [327/R30]. The artist's hand, the illustrator's individuality, was what counted, but then only if in Van Gogh's mind his work had feeling and spirit. ☙ According to Van Gogh, Alfred-Philippe Roll's *Miners' strike* (fig. 107) perfectly combined bold character drawing – both literally and figuratively – with poses that expressed a mood and sentiment

---

105. After **William Small**, *An English ploughing match*, 1875, The Hague, Koninklijke Bibliotheek

106. After **Percy T. Macquoid**, *A disarrangement in blue*, 1880, Amsterdam, Van Gogh Museum (Vincent van Gogh Foundation)

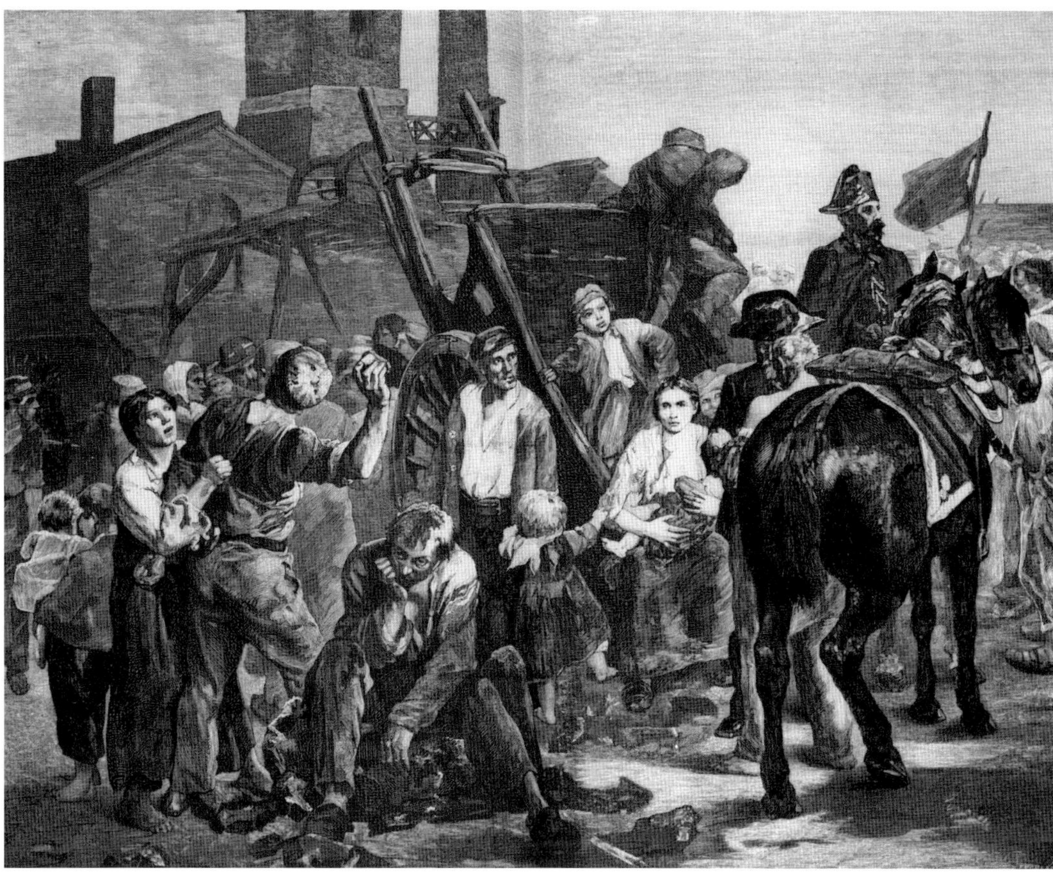

appropriate to the subject. He sent Theo a strikingly detailed and thorough commentary on it: 'I recently had a look at a large woodcut I own after a painting by Roll called "Une grève de charbonniers". [...] The figures are excellent and the whole thing is roughly and freely drawn (and certainly also painted), entirely suitable to the nature of the motif. It's nothing like Knaus or Vautier, but done with true passion – there are almost no details, just masses,[34] and everything is simplified – and still there's great style to it. It's very expressive and there's so much mood and feeling in the figures' poses; their various actions are masterfully depicted. It really moved me' [273/238]. This appreciative characterisation reveals what was important to Van Gogh: a print should be frank, spontaneous, unpolished, elementary, true to life and full of life. Only then was it truly convincing.[35] ≋ Every once in a while Van Gogh expressed his admiration through comparison. This was also a means of showing off his knowledge of art history: 'I knew nothing of

Gordon Thompson, he did that piece showing derby spectators called "Clapham road" [...]. This is an unbelievably clever sheet, it looks like a Dürer or Quinten Masys, for example' [306/R24].[36] And he wrote to Van Rappard: 'Do you know "The wayfarers" by Fred Walker? It is a large etching of a blind old man led by a boy along a frozen road, with a ditch with copsewood covered with glazed frost, and osiers, on a winter evening. It is certainly one of the most sublime creations in that genre, with a peculiar, modern sentiment, perhaps less powerful than Dürer in his "Knight, Death and devil", but perhaps even more intimate, and certainly as original and sincere' [251/R8]. Such positive associations of a different kind spanning the centuries are typical for Van Gogh, who shows himself quite capable of linking Fred Walker's more or less empty *Wayfarers* (plate 108) with Dürer's masterpiece (plate 105). It was probably the natural settings that led him to this association.

107. After **Alfred Philippe Roll,** *Miners' strike,* 1881, Amsterdam,
Van Gogh Museum (Vincent van Gogh Foundation)

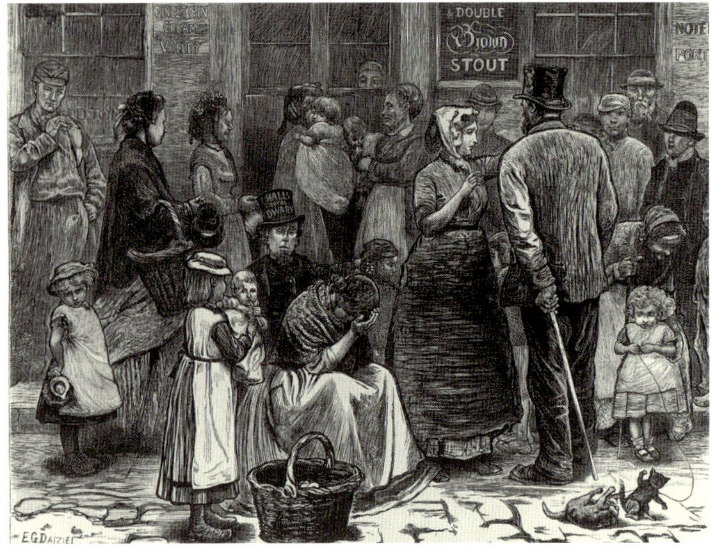

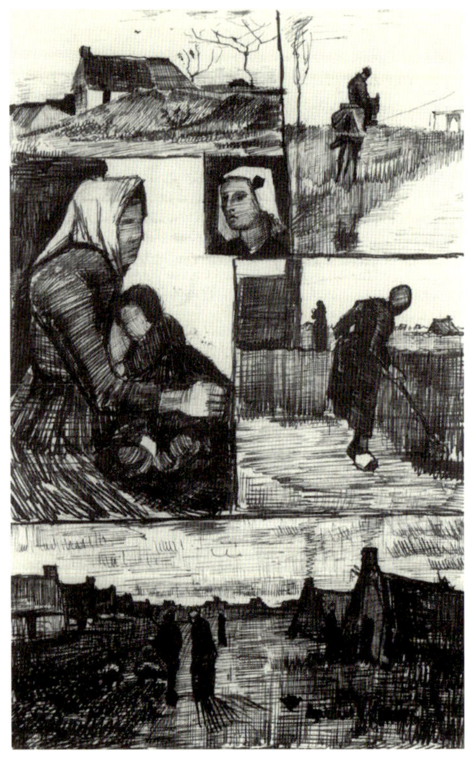

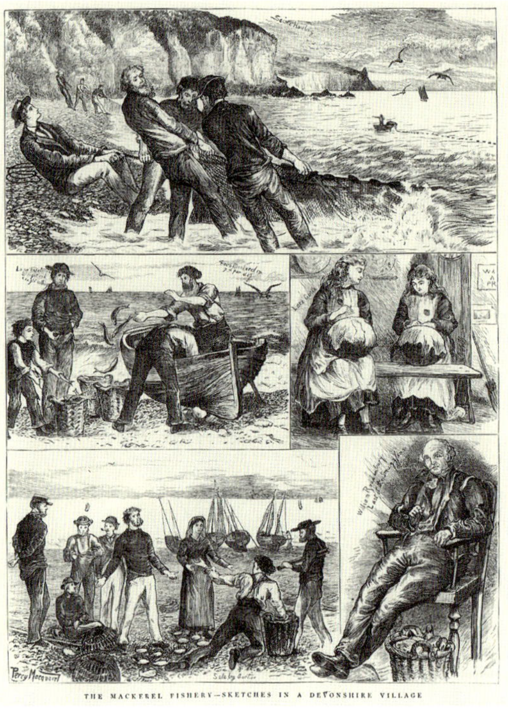

PURVEYORS OF POSES, COMPOSITIONS AND MOTIFS

Although Van Gogh often worked with sitters, his prints also
furnished him with models for his drawings and helped him

develop his understanding of proportion, anatomy and composition. They thus saved him money and provided him with a
permanent source of inspiration. Still, the source of his enthusiasm for a specific print is not always clear. When in February
1883 he characterised the anonymous *Labourer's home at Whit-
nash* as 'first-rate' this probably had less to do with the quality
of the print than with the fact that in this period he himself was
searching for an appropriate way of depicting people in interiors.[37] 🖝 That leafing through his collection gave him ideas,
and that he then borrowed from his prints directly, is more
likely in some cases than in others. The pose of the seated
woman at the centre of *London sketches – Sunday afternoon,
1 pm – Waiting for the public house to open*, from the studio of
the brothers Edward and George Dalziel (fig. 108), for example,
may have been used for the chalk drawing *Woman sitting on
a basket, with head in hands* (F 1060 JH 326); while the pose
of the figure at the right in *Soup distribution in a public soup
kitchen* (F 1020a JH 330) resembles the woman to the left of the
'Stout' billboard. Van Gogh's drawings were executed in March
1883, and the print is mentioned in a letter from the end of
February [323/R29]. The handling of a number of Drenthe scenes

108. After **Edward** and **George Dalziel,** *London sketches – Sunday
afternoon, 1 pm – Waiting for the public house to open,* 1874, Amsterdam,
Van Gogh Museum (Vincent van Gogh Foundation)
109. Letter 395/330, Vincent van Gogh to Theo van Gogh,
Nieuw-Amsterdam, probably 2 October 1883, Amsterdam,
Van Gogh Museum (Vincent van Gogh Foundation)

110. After **Percy T. Macquoid,** *The mackerel fishery – sketches in
a Devonshire village,* 1874, Amsterdam, Van Gogh Museum
(Vincent van Gogh Foundation)

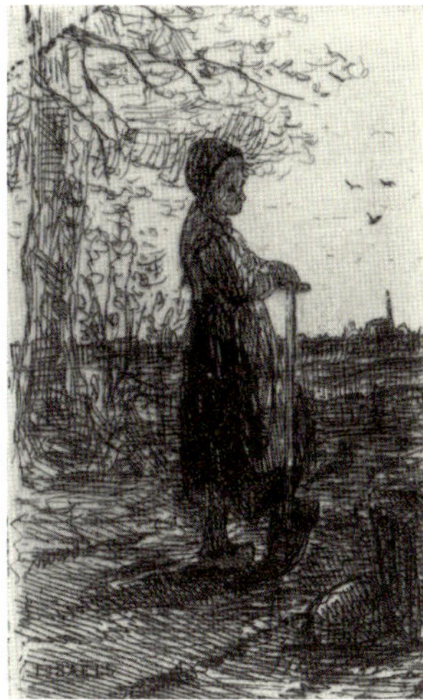
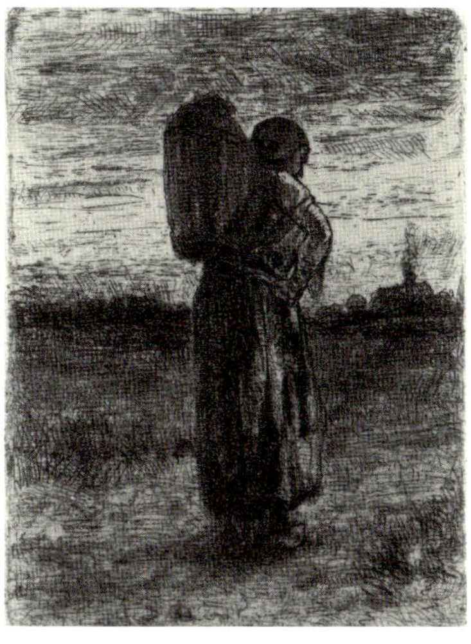
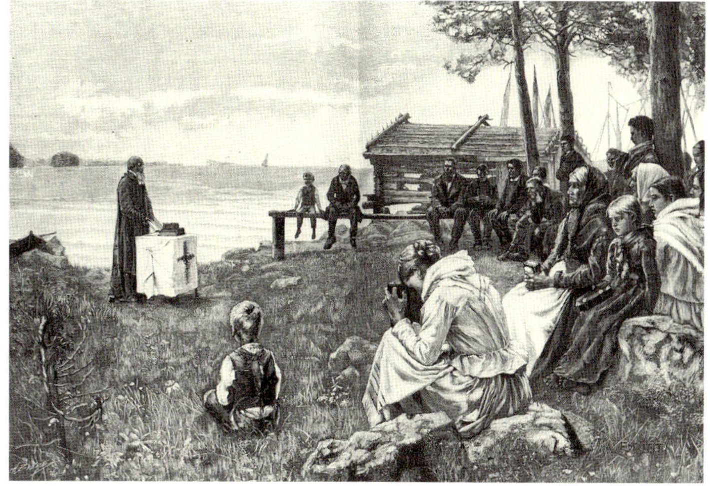

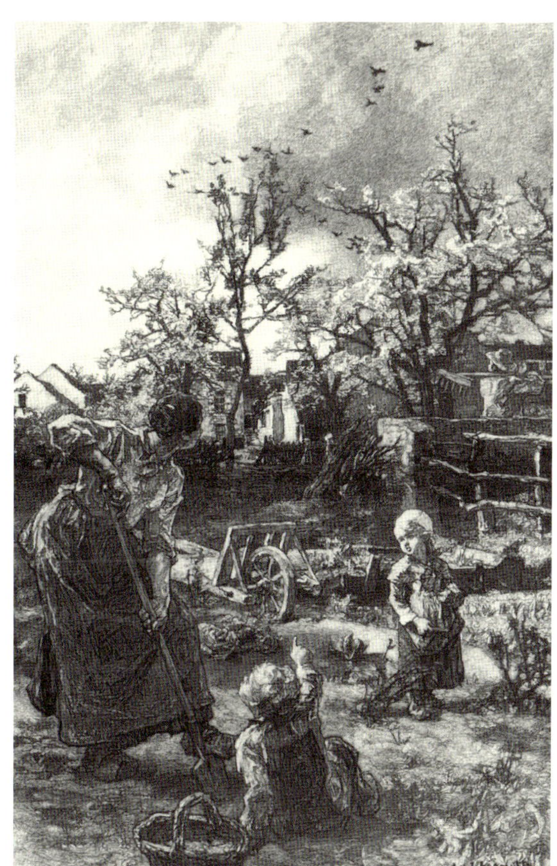

sketched during his barge trip from Hoogeveen to Nieuw-Amsterdam, which he grouped together to form an almost kaleidoscopic whole in a letter-sketch (fig. 109), recalls Percy T. Macquoid's *Mackerel fishery – sketches in a Devonshire village*, a wood engraving Van Gogh owned (fig. 110). ☙ Van Gogh's own search for suitable poses may explain the purchase of certain original prints. 'I have two little etchings by Israels, perhaps his very best, a girl with a shovel in a garden and a woman with a basket on her back. Do you know them?' |328/273| (fig. 111). On the one hand, Van Gogh recognised his own aims in the work of his predecessors; on the other, he sought to adopt and adapt pre-existing solutions. As he was working on the figures of a peat collector and a kneeling man and became aware that he needed to grasp their physical structure before he could work on their expression, he refers to Edelfelt's *Religious service on the beach, Finland*: 'Edelfeldt is good at expression – but even he seeks it not only in the faces, but in the poses as well' |340/281| (fig. 112). Further, the pose of the woman with a child on her lap in the foreground right of Hubert von Herkomer's *Low lodging house St Giles's* may have had an influence on Van Gogh's own *Woman with a child on her lap* (F 1067 JH 356). ☙ Van Gogh's ideal of the artist becoming one with his subject is articulated in a letter from Nuenen of May 1885 – he had by now read Sensier's biography of Jean-François Millet, in which the latter is characterised as a peasant who paints. Van Gogh here responds to Léon Lhermitte's *Rural labours, April: swallows (gardening)* (fig. 113), which had appeared the month

111. **Jozef Israëls,** *Girl leaning on a spade* and *Woman with a basket on her back (On the way home)*, 1875, Amsterdam, Rijksprentenkabinet

112. After **Albert Gustaf Aristide Edelfelt,** *Religious service on the beach, Finland,* 1882, Amsterdam, Van Gogh Museum (Vincent van Gogh Foundation)

113. After **Léon Lhermitte,** *Rural labours. April: swallows (gardening),* 1885, Amsterdam, Van Gogh Museum (Vincent van Gogh Foundation)

before: 'The small woman with a shovel in Lhermitte is so full of life and truth: *as if done by a peasant who can paint*, it's masterly. If I were you, I would go out and buy these Lhermittes and keep them for ten years. They're masterworks for the price of 50 *centimes*' [505/406].

THE 'FEELING' COPY

Van Gogh began making drawn copies after prints in 1880, in the Borinage. Having received a package of engravings and reproductions, he went to work almost immediately.[38] Despite the fact that he was then living on a mere pittance, he nonetheless spent 2,50 francs on two volumes of *Le Musée Universel* that contained a number of wood engravings that interested him, including three by Millet.[39] ✎ Towards the end of his life, Van Gogh made a number of painted copies after biblical and religious prints by Rembrandt (plate 74) and Delacroix (plate 125), works by Doré and Daumier, and peasant scenes by Millet (plates 49, 51, 52, 54). He used them to explore form and colour, aspiring to create a personal interpretation of the motif and thus a new, independent work of art.[40] ✎ Writing from Saint-Rémy in September 1889, he gave a detailed account of his aims: 'I now have seven copies out of the ten of Millet's "Travaux des Champs". I can assure you that making copies interests me enormously, and it means that I shall not lose sight of the figure, even though I have no models at the moment. [...] This is exercise I need, because I want to *learn*. Although copying may be the *old* system, that makes absolutely no difference to me. [...] You will be surprised at the effect "Les travaux des champs" takes on in colour, it is a very intimate series of his. I am going to try to tell you what I am seeking in it and why it seems good to me to copy them. We painters are always asked to *compose* ourselves and be nothing but *composers*. [...] I put the black and white by Delacroix or Millet or something made after their work in front of me as a subject. And then I improvise colour on it, not, you understand, altogether being myself, but searching for memories of *their* pictures – but the memory, the vague consonance of colours which are at least right in feeling – that is my own interpretation. [...] And then my brush goes between my fingers as a bow would on the violin, and absolutely for my own pleasure. Today I tried the "Woman Shearing Sheep" in a colour scheme ranging from lilac to yellow' [806/607]. ✎ Van Gogh referred to his copies after Delacroix's *Pietà*, lithographed by Célestin-François Nanteuil-Leboeuf, as 'feeling' [802/605].[41] Conveyance of sentiment had always been his aim; works of art were capable of evoking emotional experiences, and it thus made no difference whether they were self-invented compositions or copies: 'Whether in the figure or in landscape what I want to express is not some kind of mawkish melancholy but rather real pain. What I want, finally, is for people to say of my work: that man feels deeply, that man feels acutely. Despite my so-called coarseness – do you see? – or perhaps just because of it' [250/218].

JAPANESE PRINTS

It was during his sojourn in Antwerp (1885-86) that Van Gogh began collecting Japanese prints.[42] 'My studio is fairly tolerable, particularly now I've pinned up a group of Japanese prints that give me great pleasure. You know, those women in gardens or on the beach, riders, flowers, knotty branches' [548/437]. A short time later, in Paris, he started to expand the collection and to buy with more discernment. The brothers owned a total of around 350 sheets, among them many so-called *ukiyo-e* prints, 'visions of the floating world'. Kunisada is well represented, and there are a number of works by Kuniyoshi and Hiroshige. The majority are of Japanese nightlife, courtesans, bordellos and theatre performances. Among the '*Japanoiseries*' Theo sent him in September 1888 was a café-concert scene 'in two sheets, with the line of violet girl musicians against the yellow illuminated wall, [it] is very beautiful' [689/540]. Van Gogh admires the works, which, he says, he had not seen before. Having received a whole package of prints, it seems he did not immediately realise that a third sheet was also part of the work, forming a triptych depicting *The Matsumotorō theatre in the Tokyo entertainment district*, executed in 1870 by Utagawa Kunisada II (plate 164). ✎ One of the brothers' main suppliers of Japanese prints was the Paris art dealer Siegfried Bing. Vincent encouraged Theo to visit his storerooms, where he would find 'a pile of 10,000 Japanese prints, landscapes, figures and even older works. If you go on Sunday he'll let you look through them and choose for yourself; get as many as you can of the

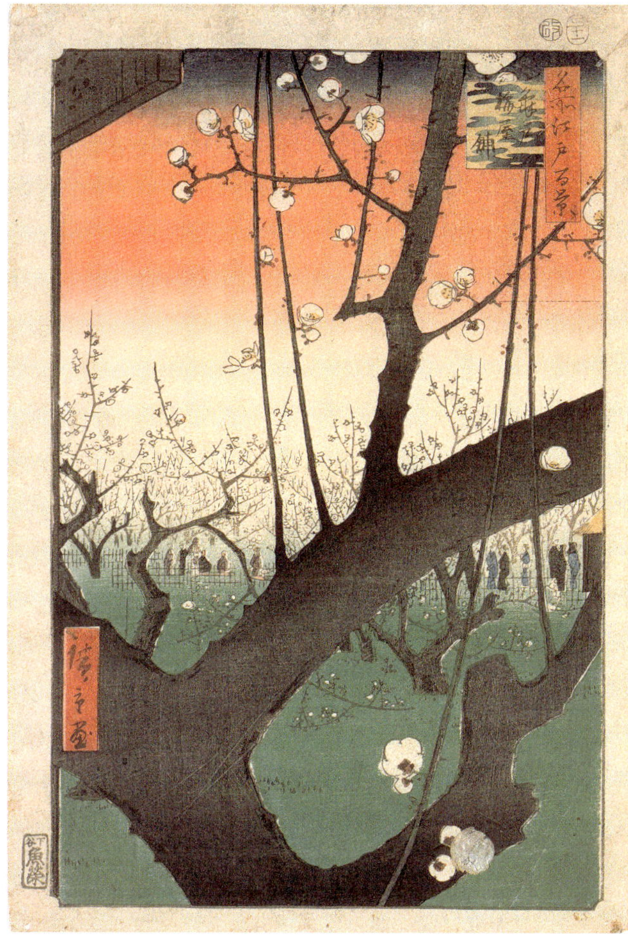

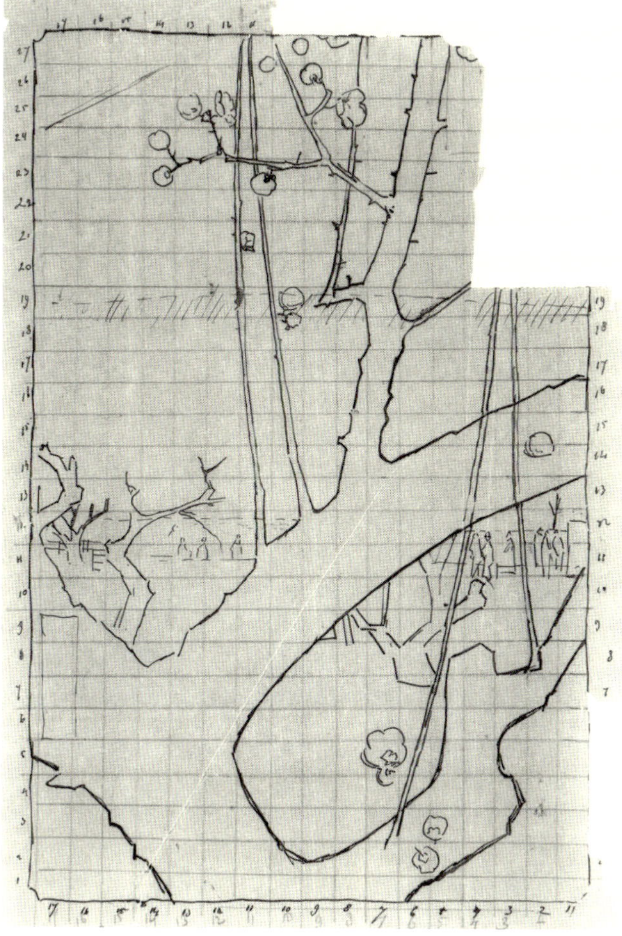

older things' [644/510]. As is the case with the non-Japanese prints, it is almost impossible to tell which of the two men was responsible for which part of the collection. ❧ In 1887 Van Gogh put together a small exhibition of Japanese prints at the Café du Tambourin, and he would later do the same at the Grand Bouillon-Restaurant du Chalet. He was convinced that other artists would be interested in them as well.[43] What appealed to him were the bright (often primary) colours, the daring compositions with their unexpected croppings and aerial perspective, the powerful contours, the decorative patterns and novel, non-western motifs. To Bernard he wrote: 'The Japanese pay no attention to reflection and put non-gradated tones next to one another, while the movements and forms are captured with characteristic lines' [625/B6]. ❧ As time went on, the influence of these works on Van Gogh's development became ever greater. This was not simply because he found the 'uniform tones of coloured Japanese prints' [690/542] so beautiful.[44] He also projected onto them an idealised, utopian vision of Japan, formed by his readings, with which he strongly identified.[45] For him, Japan was intimately linked with certain ideas about the artistic calling, in which notions such as simplicity, tranquillity, a life in harmony with nature, and the search for light and colour played an important role. It was this ideal he hoped to achieve in his 'Studio of the south', with the help of other artists, living as monks in fellowship and with a common artistic, social and philosophical goal. ❧ It was this that led him to copy several of his Japanese prints in oil, resulting in *The courtesan* (after Keisai Eisen's *Oiran*),[46] *The bridge in the rain*[47] (plates 160-161) and *The flowering plum tree* (F 371 JH 1296) (both after Utagawa Hiroshige). The latter was modelled on

---

114. Utagawa Hiroshige, *The plum tree teahouse at Kameido,* 1857. Amsterdam, Van Gogh Museum (Vincent van Gogh Foundation)

115. Vincent van Gogh, *Tracing of Hiroshige, The plum tree teahouse at Kameido,* 1887, Amsterdam, Van Gogh Museum (Vincent van Gogh Foundation)

The plum tree teahouse at Kameido, with its striking suggestion
of distance between the tree in the foreground and the visitors
in the background (fig. 114, plate 163). It is not a copy in the
strict sense. The Japanese characters along the borders were
borrowed from other sources, and Van Gogh intensified the
reds and greens. The tracing he made in preparation for the
painting has survived; the grid allowed him to enlarge the
image to scale (fig. 115). A few months later he began his own
series of blossoming orchards. ✎ Van Gogh's enthusiasm for
these *Japanoiseries* left other traces in his work as well: he
sometimes sought to imitate the texture of the works, which
were printed on crepe paper (*crépons*), as in his *Still life with
quinces and lemons* (plate 145) or the *Portrait of a woman with
carnations* (F 381 JH 1355). He even looked at the Rhône with
Japanese prints at the back of his mind: 'I witnessed a very
beautiful and strange effect this evening: an enormous barge
on the Rhône, loaded with coal and moored at the quay. Seen
from above, it was all shiny and wet from a rain shower. The
water was yellow-white and murky pearl grey, the air was lilac
with an orange stripe to the west, and the town was lilac, too.
Running about were tiny blue and dirty-white figures, unload-
ing the boat. It was pure Hokusai' [656/516].[48] Finally, it seems
possible that *Almond blossom* (F 671 JH 1891) was influenced
by a Kunisada *Portrait of a woman* that is also part of the Van
Gogh estate and in which flowering branches are a prominent
motif.[49] Van Gogh's increased interest in other natural details
(for example, butterflies and poppies), in irises, panoramic
landscapes and in unexpected bisections of the composition,
is undoubtedly related to his predilection for such motifs in
Japanese prints.[50] Kōdera has quite correctly referred to these
works as 'catalytic'.[51]

THE 'MUSÉE IMAGINAIRE'

What reading the Bible had been for Van Gogh in his youth,
leafing through his collection of prints became during his
career as an artist: his very own 'imaginary museum'.[52] As he
wrote to Van Rappard in reference to his illustrations from *The
Graphic*: 'In my opinion, sheets like these are a kind of Bible
for the artist, which he can consult at will in order to tune himself – it is not only a good idea to know them, but to have them
always about the studio' [513/R25]. Years later, when he painted
pictures with the aim of inducing a certain emotion in the
viewer, he compares the print style with that of his own work:
La berceuse, for example, is like 'a chromolithograph from a
cheap shop' [747/574], in other words, like a cheap colour print.
✎ Prints were not only models, but also a stimulus. As Van
Gogh put it, they gave him 'energy' and offered him a means
of distancing himself from certain traditional notions [307/262].
Anton Kerssemakers remembered how in Van Gogh's Nuenen
studio there were 'drawings, studies, illustrations everywhere
– especially from *The Graphic* – to the left and right on the
floor, on chairs – a real mess.'[53] ✎ Both the black-and-white
and Japanese prints coloured Van Gogh's vision. In September
1882 he confessed: 'When I can't sleep at night, which is quite
often the case, I like to pass the time rummaging among my
woodcuts' [262/229].[54] Anyone who can claim that, rather than
raiding the medicine or drinks cabinet in the middle of the
night, he can instead pass the hours happily leafing through
an album of prints, knows that he lives for art and art alone.

VINCENT VAN GOGH AND THE AVANT-GARDE: COLLEAGUES, COMPETITORS, FRIENDS

CORNELIA HOMBURG

Vincent van Gogh decided to move from Antwerp to Paris when he felt that he had established himself as a modern painter and could participate in the international art scene. Arriving in the art capital of Europe in 1886, Van Gogh hoped to further his career and to find like-minded artists to share his ideas and ambitions. He did not know that he was far behind in terms of the more contemporary developments in painting. By the mid-1880s the impressionists were well recognised as modern artists, but Van Gogh could not have known their ideas from his isolated position in the Netherlands. He could not have known that his heroes Millet and Delacroix had long become respected as masters of a past era, and that they did not represent modern thought. With shock, Van Gogh realised that his *Potato eaters* (plate 44), which he considered his modern masterpiece, did not seem particularly modern in Paris. If he wanted to be part of the avant-garde, he would have to learn quickly about contemporary ideas. He also needed to study the new art and learn a new brushstroke and colour palette. Van Gogh had two opportunities to achieve this goal. His brother Theo, the art dealer, could introduce him to members of the impressionist generation, whose work he was showing in his gallery; and Vincent himself could make contact with artists who, like himself, were trying to establish themselves on the art scene. Determined, he pursued both.

MONET, DEGAS, CAMILLE AND LUCIEN PISSARRO

Theo, who ran the Montmartre branch of the well-known art gallery Boussod, Valadon & Cie in Paris was interested in the work of several of the impressionist painters who were increasingly sought after by leading galleries. Theo had followed Claude Monet's work for quite a while, and by the mid-1880s was trading his paintings.[1] When Vincent arrived in Paris, Theo was working hard to establish closer ties with Monet, efforts that eventually culminated in a contract and an exhibition in 1888. ❋ As early as 1885, on a visit to the Netherlands, Theo had described to Vincent the new kind of painting that Monet was exploring. Vincent mentioned this conversation in a letter to his friend Van Rappard in which he gave him the news from Paris. He referred to Monet as 'a landscape painter and colourist' [529/R57]. Such a description resonated with Van Gogh, as he himself was working on landscape and was becoming increasingly concerned with colour. However, in 1885 he could not imagine the type of colour Monet was using. He was studying the writings of Charles Blanc and Théophile Silvestre about Delacroix's use of colour at the time [2] and, when he attempted to make still lifes with complementary colour contrast, the results were exceedingly dark and did not reflect Delacroix's palette, let alone Monet's. ❋ Encountering Monet's work soon after his arrival in Paris in 1886 must have been an immense surprise for Van Gogh. He began to develop a deep admiration for the painter, and respected him as a leading member of the impressionists. Monet was the modern master who had achieved the type of recognition that Van Gogh was eager to attain for himself,

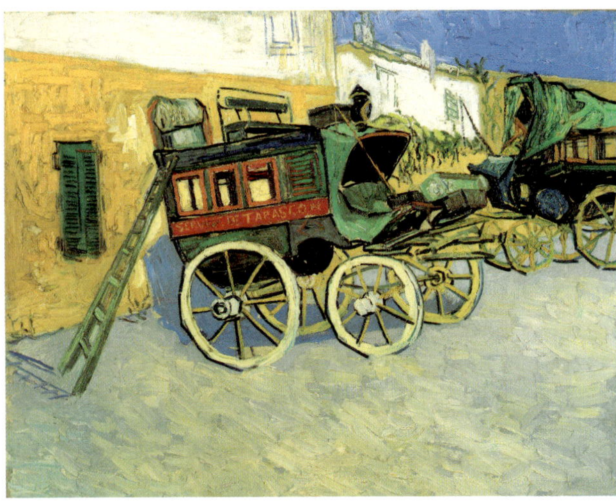

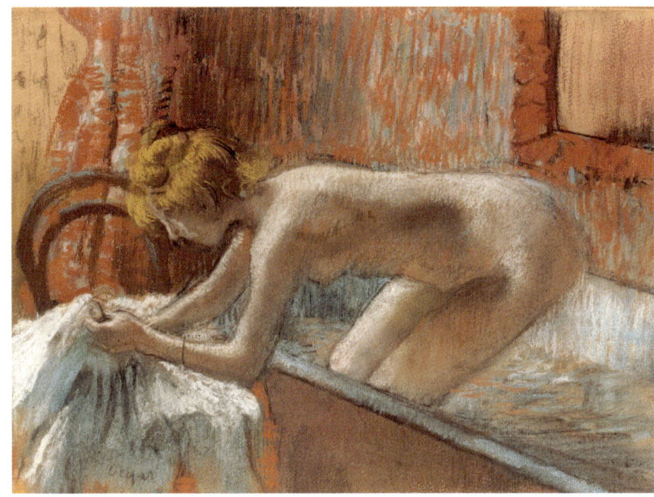

while Monet's paintings became a yardstick by which to measure his own achievements. In the beginning, Monet's work inspired Van Gogh to brighten his palette and to use a lighter, more spontaneous brushstroke. In Arles, for example, when he painted the intensely coloured, sunny picture, *The Tarascon stagecoach* (fig. 116), Van Gogh compared the colour and simplicity of his design with Monet's painting *Boats on the beach* (plate 129), which he had seen in Paris some time before.[3]
⚜ Several months later Gauguin compared Van Gogh's still life of sunflowers favourably with Monet's painting of the same subject. In the letter to Theo in which Vincent happily reported this, he continued: 'if by the time I am forty I have done a picture of figures like the flowers Gauguin was speaking of, I shall have a position in art equal to that of anyone' [726/563]. This ambition became a kind of *leitmotiv* whenever Van Gogh mentioned Monet. Not only was it his personal goal to paint great portraits and figures, but he wanted to excel in this area as Monet had excelled in landscape painting.[4] Until the end of Van Gogh's life, Monet played an important part in his efforts to achieve recognition. When Van Gogh presented work at the Salon des Indépendants in 1890, Theo could not have reported higher praise than from Monet who had found Vincent's works 'the best in the exhibition' [862/T32]. ⚜ After Monet, Degas was a role model for Van Gogh. He could study Degas's work in Theo's gallery, as Theo had begun working with the painter in 1886. In early 1888 Theo had an exhibition of pastel nudes (fig. 117), which Vincent saw before he left for the south of France.

In Van Gogh's eyes Degas was one of the important leaders of impressionism, whose main contribution was the introduction of the modern figure. In the fall of 1886 he had written to his friend H.M. Livens in Antwerp: 'In Antwerp I did not even know what the impressionists were, now I have seen them and though *not* being one of the club yet I have much admired certain impressionists' pictures – *Degas* nude figure – *Claude Monet* landscape' [572/459a]. While Van Gogh liked Degas's nudes, he did not refer to his work in the same way as he did to Monet's. He rarely painted the nude figure himself, and focused instead increasingly on portraiture. ⚜ Van Gogh admired Degas for his absolute dedication to his work. Degas supposedly disdained nightlife and women, and lived a secluded life dedicated to art. Van Gogh was both amused and amazed, even envious of this stance, which he could not imagine for himself. The great impressionist was a master to be admired and studied from a distance, but impossible to emulate. ⚜ By the time Vincent came to Paris, Theo van Gogh had known Camille Pissarro and dealt in his work for several years. Pissarro was approachable and always open to questions from the younger generation. He lived with his family in the countryside in Eragny, and focused his work primarily on the rural scenery surrounding him. His depiction of peasants and their labours in the fields resonated with Van Gogh's own passionate interest in this topic. If his *Potato eaters* was not acceptable from a stylistic point of view, at least the subject matter could be appreciated and shared with Pissarro. The

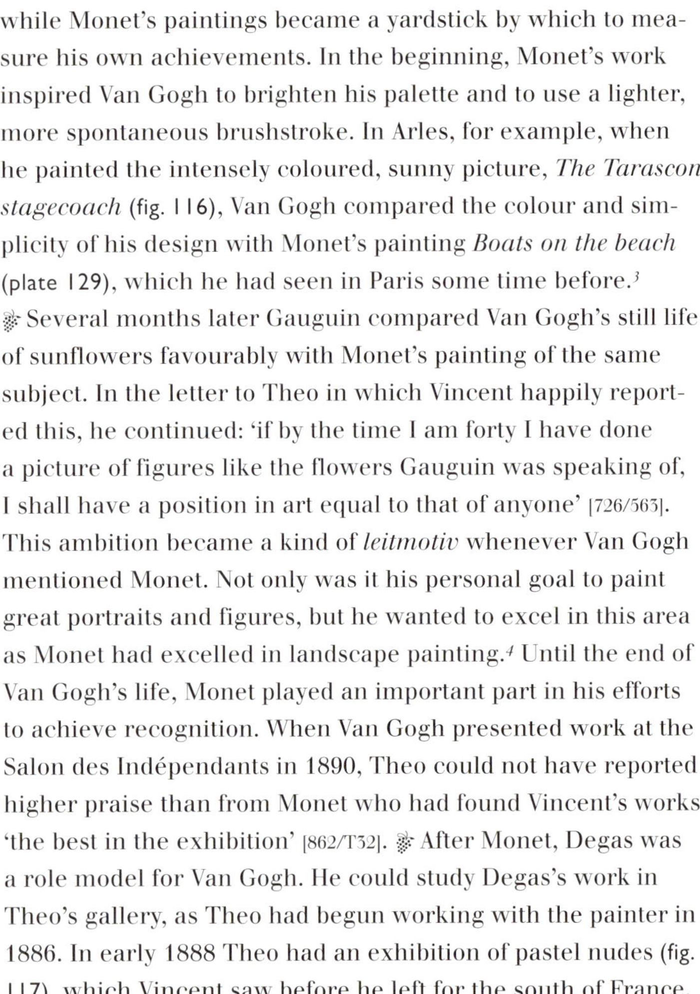

116. Vincent van Gogh, *The Tarascon stagecoach* (F 478a JH 1605), 1888, Princeton, The Art Museum, The Henry and Rose Pearlman Foundation, Inc.

117. Edgar Degas, *Woman leaving her bath,* 1886-88, private collection

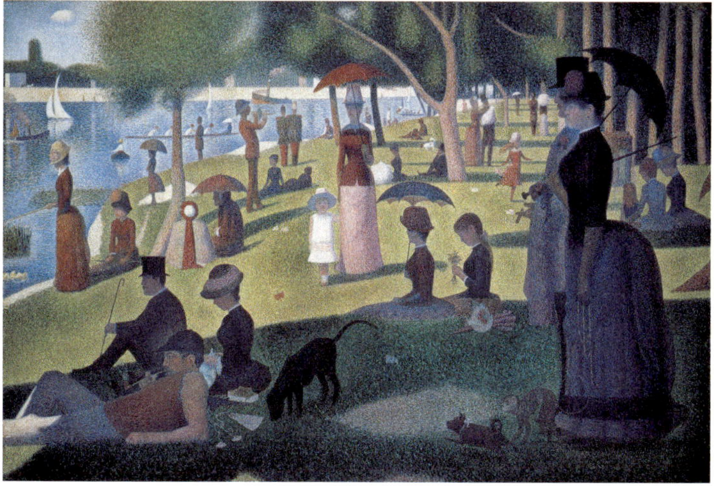

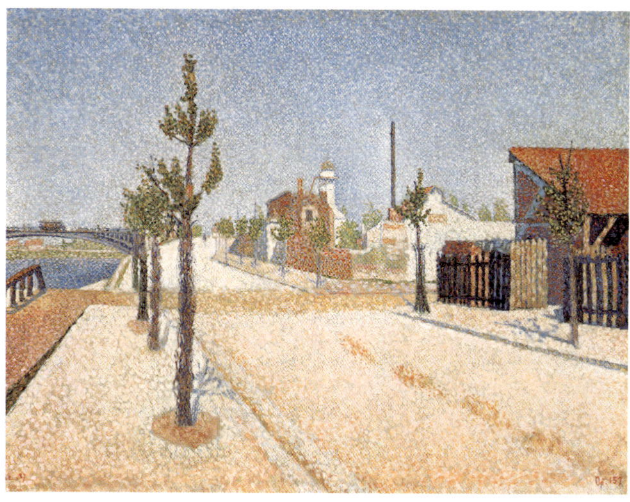

artist's personality and his work must have offered Van Gogh a level of comfort that was otherwise hard to find in the urban metropolis of Paris. ❧ Van Gogh also met Pissarro's son Lucien, who like him was aspiring to enter the contemporary art scene. The two men shared an interest in graphic arts and illustration. Van Gogh had been an avid collector of illustrations from journals such as *The Illustrated London News*, while Lucien was a printmaker and tried to publish his prints in French and English journals. They were both committed to social issues, and found cheap prints an appropriate way of disseminating knowledge about art. Their acquaintance is documented in an exchange of works. When Lucien presented Vincent with a group of wood engravings, the Dutchman reciprocated with a *Basket with apples* (F 378 JH 1340) inscribed 'à l'ami Lucien Pissarro'.

NEO-IMPRESSIONISM

The Pissarros surely would have played a role in Van Gogh's encounter with neo-impressionism. Camille was particularly taken with the new style and changed his own painting accordingly. His work *View from my window in cloudy weather* (plate 137) illustrates this beautifully. The composition is organised with obvious deliberation, and the painting is executed with pointillist brushwork. The result is a dramatic departure from the more spontaneous scenes of earlier years.

❧ Pissarro might also have helped Van Gogh gain access to the circle of the neo-impressionists. In the spring of 1886 at the Salon des Indépendants, Seurat presented his enormous canvas *A Sunday afternoon on the island of La Grande Jatte* (fig. 118). His new style of painting, which differed dramatically from impressionism in both theory and technique, received immediate critical acclaim.[5] It had an excellent promoter in Seurat's close friend Paul Signac, and had an immense following among artists in the next few years, so much so that Seurat began to worry in 1888 that the movement would lose its standing in the avant-garde.[6] By the mid-1880s impressionism had already been well established as a modern form of painting, and younger artists could no longer participate in its development. Neo-impressionism, on the other hand, offered all the novelty and notoriety of an avant-garde movement, and relative newcomers could participate enthusiastically. ❧ Van Gogh probably went to the Salon des Indépendants of 1886 shortly after his arrival in Paris, but it took him at least until the last months of that year to recognise the importance of neo-impressionism. He met Signac during the winter of 1886/87, and went out painting with him in the suburbs of Paris the following spring. Signac helped him understand the principles of neo-impressionism so that he could apply this knowledge to his own work.[7] Their excursions together into the northern suburbs are reflected in paintings such as Signac's *Quai de Clichy* (fig. 119) and Van Gogh's *Factories at Asnières seen from the Quai de Clichy* (fig. 120). These parts of the city were char-

118. Georges Seurat, *A Sunday afternoon on the island of La Grande Jatte,* 1886, The Art Institute of Chicago, Helen Birch Bartlett Memorial Collection

119. Paul Signac, *Quai de Clichy,* 1887, The Baltimore Museum of Art, Gift of Frederick H. Gottlieb

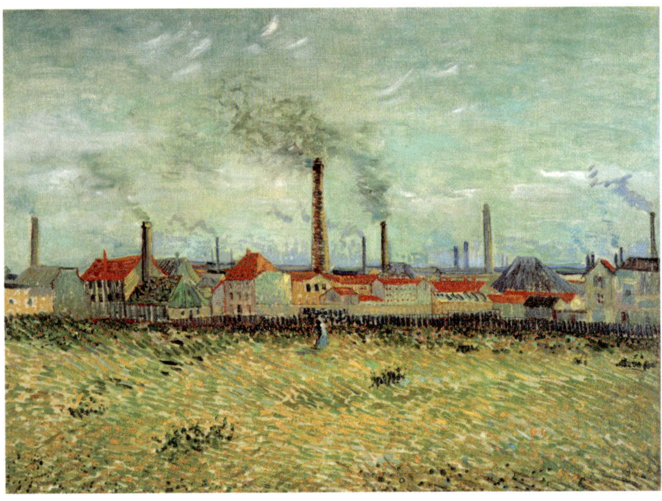

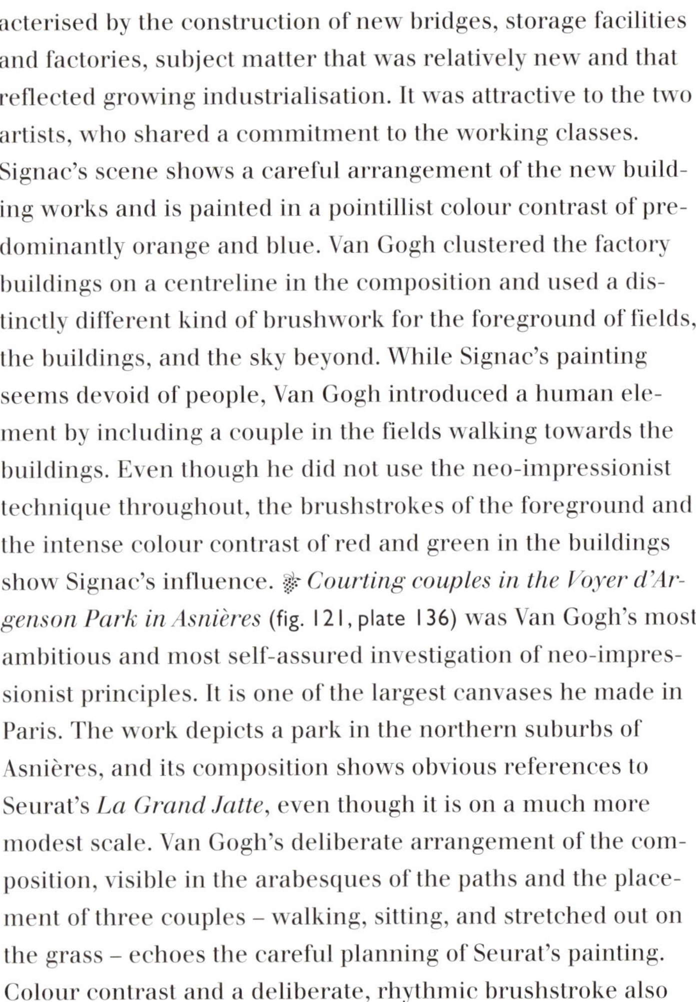

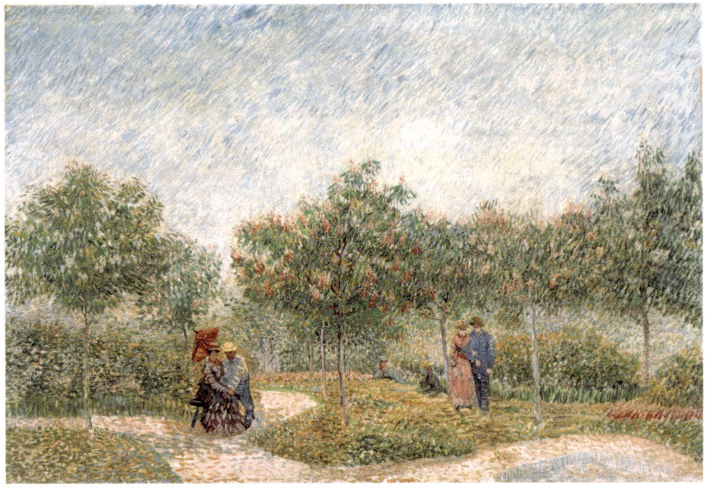

acterised by the construction of new bridges, storage facilities and factories, subject matter that was relatively new and that reflected growing industrialisation. It was attractive to the two artists, who shared a commitment to the working classes. Signac's scene shows a careful arrangement of the new building works and is painted in a pointillist colour contrast of predominantly orange and blue. Van Gogh clustered the factory buildings on a centreline in the composition and used a distinctly different kind of brushwork for the foreground of fields, the buildings, and the sky beyond. While Signac's painting seems devoid of people, Van Gogh introduced a human element by including a couple in the fields walking towards the buildings. Even though he did not use the neo-impressionist technique throughout, the brushstrokes of the foreground and the intense colour contrast of red and green in the buildings show Signac's influence. ❈ *Courting couples in the Voyer d'Argenson Park in Asnières* (fig. 121, plate 136) was Van Gogh's most ambitious and most self-assured investigation of neo-impressionist principles. It is one of the largest canvases he made in Paris. The work depicts a park in the northern suburbs of Asnières, and its composition shows obvious references to Seurat's *La Grand Jatte*, even though it is on a much more modest scale. Van Gogh's deliberate arrangement of the composition, visible in the arabesques of the paths and the placement of three couples – walking, sitting, and stretched out on the grass – echoes the careful planning of Seurat's painting. Colour contrast and a deliberate, rhythmic brushstroke also

reflect the neo-impressionist influence, even if Van Gogh did not imitate the *pointillé*. Distinctly different from the work of his colleagues, this painting shows an emotional investment typical of Van Gogh. He referred to it as the 'jardin aux amoureux' ('Park with lovers'), and the title suggests his yearning for romantic love.[8] Such a sentimental note contrasts dramatic-ally with the ironic distance with which Seurat treated his figures in *La Grande Jatte*. ❈ Van Gogh's friendship with Signac, as well as his investigation of neo-impressionism, helped him attain a certain level of acceptance by the group. He visited the reclusive Seurat in his studio before he left Paris in the spring of 1888, and in the preceding months his *Courting couples in the Voyer d'Argenson Park in Asnières* had been included with canvases by Seurat and Signac in the small show at the Théâtre Libre. The foyer of this theatre was a modest venue for the avant-garde, but people interested in the latest developments in art went there. ❈ While Signac was the more accessible, Seurat held, in Van Gogh's eyes, the undisputed leadership role among the neo-impressionists. His admiration of Seurat's achievements was immense. Even though Van Gogh did not imitate Seurat's ideas in any detail, the latter's deliberate use of his brush and his lessons about colour contrasts were of vital importance to Van Gogh's own artistic evolution. In Arles especially, he repeatedly referred admiringly to Seurat, and his own use of intense colour and colour contrasts was certainly influenced by this appreciation.[9]

---

120. **Vincent van Gogh,** *Factories at Asnières seen from the Quai de Clichy* (F 317 JH 1287), 1887, The Saint Louis Art Museum, Funds given by Mrs. Mark C. Steinberg, by exhange

121. **Vincent van Gogh,** *Courting couples in the Voyer d'Argenson Park in Asnières* (F 314 JH 1258), 1887, Amsterdam, Van Gogh Museum (Vincent van Gogh Foundation)

A MODERN IDENTITY

Neo-impressionism gave Van Gogh new insights into the use
of pictorial means and served as a useful example of how to
establish a modern identity, but he also joined forces with
other aspiring artists. Seurat and Signac were recognised as
leaders of the avant-garde. Van Gogh's friendships with artists
like Emile Bernard, Henri de Toulouse-Lautrec and Louis
Anquetin were based more on an equal footing. All of them
were struggling to create their personal artistic identity.
❦ They all met at the private studio of Fernand Cormon, a professor at the Ecole des Beaux-Arts, which they had entered at
various times to study drawing. Also, Van Gogh, being largely
self-taught, felt the need for direction, which was one of the
reasons he came to Paris. At Cormon's studio in 1886 he met
a whole group of enterprising artists from a variety of coun-
tries. Emile Bernard, young and adventurous, was always open
to new ideas. His enthusiasm and irreverence seem to have
inspired the older Van Gogh. The ease with which Bernard
struck up friendships will also have facilitated contacts for Van
Gogh. Like him, Bernard explored neo-impressionism, but he
rejected its principles relatively quickly. He was more fascinated by the use of pure colour and simplified forms. Bernard's
ambitions to define new territory with regard to style must
have helped Van Gogh in the early stages of their friendship.
The two artists discussed new ideas and went painting together, making landscapes, and in at least one instance they chose
the same model for their portraits: Julien Tanguy, the dealer in
artists' supplies who loved new art and who occasionally accepted paintings in exchange for materials. His little shop in
the Rue Clauzel was a hangout for artists, a place to meet new
people and to see new work. Bernard and Van Gogh were regular visitors. Van Gogh had his earliest opportunities to show-
case his work in Tanguy's shop window, and he continued to
buy paints and canvases from him after he had moved to Arles.
❦ The portraits Bernard and Van Gogh painted of Tanguy, most
probably in Bernard's studio in Asnières, show their different
stages of development. Bernard's portrait focuses on the head
of his sitter, revealing very little of the man's dark suit and tie
(plate 88). He used distinctive brushwork in a daring combination of green and pink, and gave the paint an almost tactile
quality. This modern effect was supported by the decorative

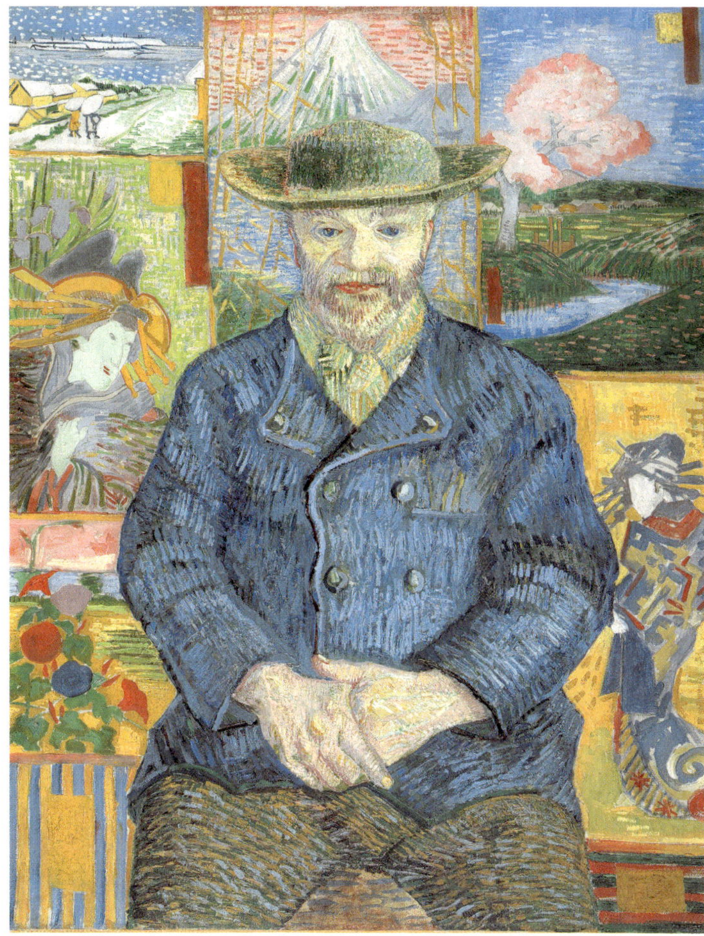

arabesque of the background in white and blue. Bernard provided an image that associated both himself and his sitter with
the newest tendencies in painting. It was not only the portrait
of a specific person, but also a statement about Bernard's position as an artist. Van Gogh, who at that time was not as adventurous stylistically, decided on a completely different approach
(fig. 122). He used bright colours and a new brushstroke, but he
focused on interpretation and content. In his three-quarter-
length portrait he presented Tanguy in workman's clothes and
a straw hat – not Bernard's gentleman. Van Gogh chose a front-
al "Buddha-like" pose, and surrounded Tanguy with Japanese
prints, images that he considered essential elements of modernity. The arrangement of images also indicates an interest in
decoration, but it is expressed in much more literal terms than
in Bernard's portrait. ❦ Bernard's experiments were important

122. Vincent van Gogh, *Portrait of Père Tanguy, half-length*
(F 363 JH 1351), 1887, Paris, Musée Rodin

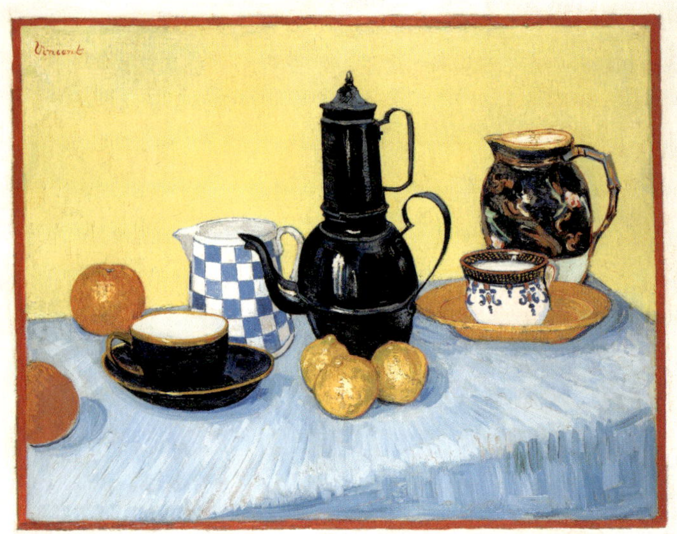

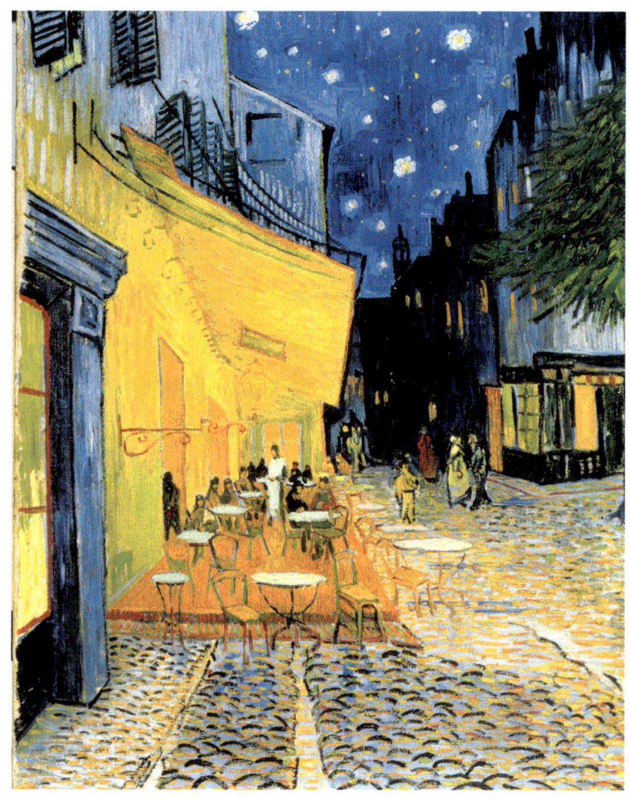

for Van Gogh's long-term development. In Arles he used a stylised background for his portraits of *La berceuse* (plate 84) that recalls Bernard's *Portrait of Père Tanguy*. In other instances Bernard's paintings influenced Van Gogh's work even more directly. He greatly admired Bernard's *The blue coffeepot* (plate 143), which he would have seen in an early stage before his departure to the south of France in February 1888.[10] In response, he painted his own *Still life with coffeepot* (fig. 123, plate 144), which echoed Bernard's approach of clearly outlined objects in intense colour. Van Gogh used a slightly more pronounced brushstroke but achieved a similar density in brushwork and hues. Van Gogh heaped praise on Bernard for still lifes such as this one as well as the portraits of his grandmother that he painted around the same time. These works were for Van Gogh signs that Bernard needed to be taken seriously as an artist and as a man. He went so far as to draw on Rembrandt in his praise for Bernard's portrait of his grandmother (plate 86), a powerful image that dramatically placed the dark figure in a shallow space of intensely coloured patterns.[11] ❋ Louis Anquetin, also a student at Cormon's, shared Bernard's and Van Gogh's fascination with pure colour. Like Bernard, he had rejected neo-impressionism early on, but the three men shared a passion for Japanese woodblock prints. It appears that Van Gogh stimulated this interest. He took his friends to the Café du Tambourin, where he had arranged an exhibition of Japanese prints from his own collection. He also introduced them to the dealer Siegfried Bing, who was a major supplier of such prints to Van Gogh and his brother. ❋ Anquetin combined the lessons he had learned from Japanese prints and his and Bernard's exercises with coloured glass to create a style of painting with intense colours and strong outlines. Deriving his imagery from scenes observed in real life, he transformed them into highly stylised, dramatic compositions that were the admiration (and envy) of his colleagues. In early 1888 he was hailed as the inventor of cloisonism by the avant-garde critic Edouard Dujardin,[12] which displeased Bernard, who felt he had also deserved such recognition. For Van Gogh some compositions by Anquetin took on such importance that they inspired his own paintings. When he created his *Café terrace at night* (fig. 124) in Arles, he based its compositional structure on Anquetin's *Avenue de Clichy* (plate 146) from the year before.[14] Both works depict a nocturnal scene, but Van Gogh did not go so far as to imitate Anquetin's cloisonist style. Instead he relied primarily on the blue and yellow colour contrast for the

123. Vincent van Gogh, *Still life with coffeepot* (F 410 JH 1426), 1888, private collection

124. Vincent van Gogh, *Café terrace at night* (F 467 JH 1580), 1888, Otterlo, Kröller-Müller Museum expressive impact of his work. ❋ Anquetin was a close friend of Henri de Toulouse-Lautrec. Also a student at Cormon's, Toulouse-Lautrec began to develop a greater interest in new ideas around 1886. He found most of his subject matter in the milieu of cabarets and nightlife, an environment to which he introduced Bernard and Van Gogh. While Bernard was enthralled by such surroundings and began to depict them in his work, Van Gogh did not find them appropriate for his paintings. Apart from a number of café and restaurant scenes, he obviously preferred to stick to the outdoors for his subject matter. Toulouse-Lautrec organised weekly soirées in his studio, and this provided Van Gogh with another opportunity to meet people, even though his awkward social skills did not make him particularly popular.[14] ❋ The two artists shared not only an interest in Japanese prints, but also found common ground in their passion for illustration and caricature. Toulouse-Lautrec published drawings and prints in various journals, while Van Gogh had long been an avid collector of mass-produced prints. Both artists admired Daumier for his caricatures, which so powerfully exposed social problems and human weakness. If Van Gogh was committed to social responsibility, Toulouse-Lautrec preferred satirical commentary. But they were united in their fascination with Daumier's ability to capture and characterise modern life. Like Bernard and Anquetin, Toulouse-Lautrec flirted only briefly with neo-impressionism. His most closely related work was *Young woman at a table 'Poudre de riz'* (plate 139), in which he employed a fine, feathery brushstroke to depict a seated woman with a container of rice powder in front of her. Van Gogh admired this work intensely, and Theo bought it for the brothers' personal collection. Vincent referred to it repeatedly when discussing his own work.[15]

PROMOTION OF THE AVANT-GARDE

The exploration of new ideas and the exchange of new insights were all part of Van Gogh's friendship with artists such as these. They were ambitious, tried to define their own position, worked together to advance their cause, and associated with others to make contacts and to discuss the latest artistic developments. One major challenge that all artists of the younger generation faced was to find places where they could exhibit

their work. None of them was represented by a gallery. Naturally, any friendship with Vincent van Gogh brought with it the knowledge that his brother Theo was an art dealer with a prominent firm who was open to new ideas. Theo did show interest in his brother's activities and friends, and Vincent often encouraged him to buy work for their own collection, as in the case of Toulouse-Lautrec and Seurat, or to look more closely at a painter's work, as with Signac.[16] Vincent was aware of Theo's impact and used it for his own purposes when needed. When he was trying to convince Charles Angrand to exchange pictures, he attempted to impress him by inviting him to his brother's gallery, where works by Degas and Pissarro were on view.[17] ❋ However, as Theo was not yet prepared to mount an exhibition of the work of Van Gogh and his colleagues, other venues had to be found. The Salon des Indépendants was an obvious one, but as a stronghold of the neo-impressionists it did not readily permit the establishment of a new identity. Places such as Père Tanguy's shop window offered a much more modest venue, but it was definitely frequented by other avant-garde artists. Van Gogh organised a number of exhibitions in various restaurants in Montmartre, where he and his colleagues lived and worked. In addition to that show of Japanese prints that he took his friends to see, and presentations of his own work at the Café du Tambourin, Van Gogh also put together a group show. It took place at the Grand Bouillon-Restaurant du Chalet on the Avenue de Clichy, where Van Gogh, Bernard, Anquetin, Toulouse-Lautrec, and the young Dutchman Koning displayed a large group of works. While there was no catalogue, it was noticed by other members of the avant-garde, among them Seurat, Signac, Gauguin and Guillaumin, who went to visit. It even brought some financial success, as both Bernard and Anquetin made sales there.[18] ❋ Van Gogh's efforts to launch himself and his colleagues as the new avant-garde are also reflected in the fact that he coined the term 'painters of the Petit Boulevard'. Even though there was no cohesive group as such, and various factions of the avant-garde did not like to deal with each other, Van Gogh tried to highlight that there was indeed a new group of artists that had to be distinguished from the older, established impressionists, whom he called the 'painters of the Grand Boulevard'. The terminology was both descriptive and figurative: the impressionists did live in the grander boulevards and streets of

Paris, while the younger generation gathered and lived in the smaller, less chic streets of Montmartre in the north of the city. At the same time, the impressionists had arguably achieved a level of recognition that brought exhibition opportunities in prestigious venues as well as financial success, which distinguished them from their more junior colleagues.[19] Van Gogh was tireless when it came to marketing the new avant-garde. From Arles he wrote about hopes to organise exhibitions in the south, and he tried to gain access to the Netherlands via his old acquaintance H. G. Tersteeg, who was a representative of Boussod, Valadon & Cie in The Hague. He also attempted to convince Theo to strike out and break new ground in England, where he envisioned a lively market for the art of the Petit Boulevard.[20] Most of these efforts show a less than realistic assessment of the chances of success, but they underline Van Gogh's commitment to this new movement.

Apart from promoting the avant-garde as a whole, Van Gogh continued to develop his own ideas and career. He realised that it was important to keep his contacts with Paris even after he had moved to the south of France in 1888. Paris was after all the centre of the art market. Not only was Theo a faithful informant, Van Gogh also exchanged letters with Toulouse-Lautrec, Bernard, and Gauguin, among others. He continued to make new acquaintances and nurtured them, especially if they could help him further his cause. Having met the painter Eugène Boch in Arles, Vincent intensified his contacts when he learned that Eugène was the brother of Anna Boch, one of the founders of the prestigious avant-garde group Les XX in Brussels.[21] The annual exhibitions of Les XX were well known to Van Gogh, and both Signac and Toulouse-Lautrec had exhibited there the year before. Van Gogh's decision to paint the *Portrait of Eugène Boch* (F 462 JH 1574) receives added significance, as his new friend not only provided an interesting model but connections as well. Van Gogh's detailed comments about this particular portrait and his views about the significance of modern portraiture have to be seen as an attempt to establish himself as an avant-garde painter in the eyes of his peers. ❧ Portraiture became a key component in Van Gogh's

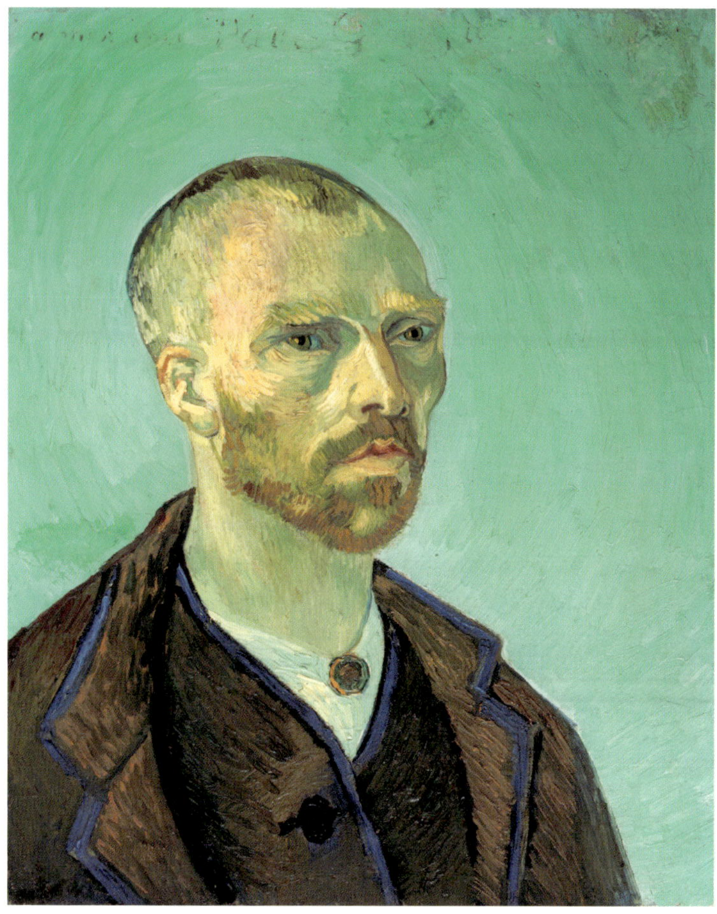

efforts to craft an avant-garde identity. It also led to important discussions with some of his colleagues. Van Gogh was convinced that portraiture offered the potential for contributions as influential as those which Monet had made to landscape painting. A major opportunity presented itself in that portrait of Eugène Boch. Not only did the sitter have an interesting face, he was also someone who could be dazzled by new ideas. Vincent wrote to Theo: 'I at last have a first sketch of that picture which I have dreamed of for so long – the poet' [677/531]. ❧ Intent on emphasising his modern stance, Van Gogh explained that he wanted to go beyond the straightforward representation of the sitter and hoped to express 'portraiture with the thoughts, with the soul of the model in it' [677/531]. He used exaggerated colour to intensify his model's natural appearance and to present his interpretation of the sitter. Instead of the narrative elements in his picture of Tanguy, Van Gogh now

125. **Vincent van Gogh,** *Self-portrait dedicated to Paul Gauguin (Bonze)* (F 476 JH 1581), 1888, Cambridge MA, Courtesy The Fogg Art Museum Harvard University Art Museums, Bequest – Collection of Maurice Wertheim, Class of 1906

used vibrant colour to create the emotive content of his portrait. ❧ These ideas were presented at a time when Van Gogh
had the opportunity to paint all the members of the Roulin family in Arles. Among the most important of this group of pictures
Van Gogh counted the portraits of the postman and his wife. He
associated the postman with republican ideals similar to Tanguy's,[22] and recalled Daumier's immediacy in portraying life.
Van Gogh's portrait turned Mme Roulin into a secular Madon-
na, who was consoling and comforting.[23] The extent to which
Van Gogh was willing to project his personal associations onto
his sitter became apparent when he painted *The raising of
Lazarus* (plate 74) in 1890. He used the images of Mme Roulin
and another of his sitters, Mme Ginoux, to represent the two
sisters of the dead man. At a time when he was planning to
leave the south, hoping for a healthier beginning in the north,
he cast himself as Lazarus, thus turning a biblical scene into
a very personal interpretation.[24] ❧ Portraiture played a signifi-
cant role in the discussions Van Gogh had with his colleagues,
in particular with Paul Gauguin and Emile Bernard. Van Gogh
had met Gauguin, like most of his other acquaintances, in
Paris. He was older and more seasoned than the rest of his
friends, and attempted to assert himself in a leadership role.
Closer contacts between the two men developed by letter in
advance of Gauguin's visit to Arles in the autumn of 1888 and
during their two months of collaboration.[25] Their competition
began in earnest during the summer of 1888 when Van Gogh
suggested that he, Gauguin and Bernard should each paint
a self-portrait for exchange among themselves. Van Gogh was
intent on using this opportunity to assert his identity as a modern artist. Using intense colour contrast and a dramatically
simplified composition, he styled himself as a Japanese bonze
(fig. 125), a monk who had banned all worldly pleasures from
his life to dedicate all his powers to his work as an artist.[26]
Worried that his portrait might not be able to stand up to
Gauguin's effort, Van Gogh was greatly relieved when he saw
his colleagues' paintings. 'My portrait, which I am sending to
Gauguin in exchange, holds its own, I am sure of that'[701/545].
Gauguin had also assumed a pose for his portrait, casting himself in the figure of Victor Hugo's Jean Valjean.[27] He must have
been deeply impressed by Van Gogh's powerful image and
must have realised that his friend had created something
extraordinary. Gauguin's response came a year later, when he

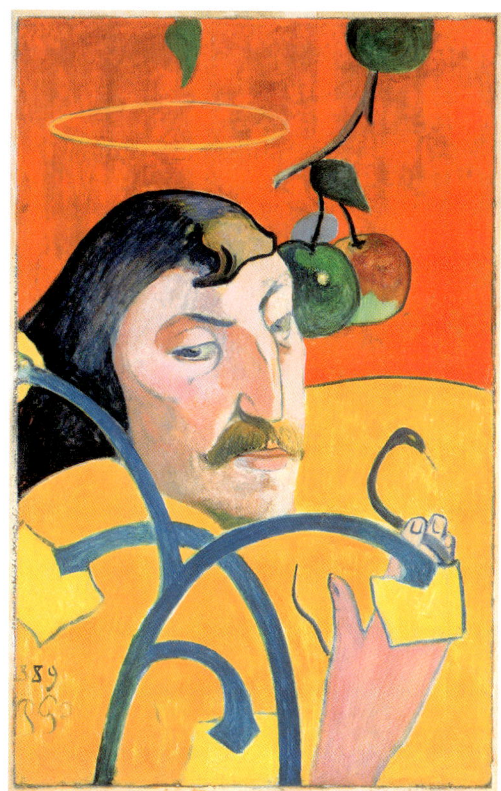

painted his striking *Self-portrait with halo* (fig. 126). The daring
flatness of this composition, in which Gauguin's head seems
to float in fields of red and yellow, ironically suggested an assumption of power that was intended to assert his position as
an avant-garde artist.

PAINTING OF BIBLICAL SCENES

Van Gogh admired Gauguin greatly for his adventurous spirit
and travels to exotic places. Gauguin's paintings from Martinique, which he had visited in 1887, were of great importance
to Van Gogh. He praised Gauguin's representation of exotic
subject matter. Theo had bought Gauguin's *Under the mangoes
at Martinique* (fig. 127) for their personal collection, and Vincent
compared many of Gauguin's later paintings to the standard of
this canvas. ❧ An area in which the artists did not agree was
the painting of religious themes. In 1880 Gauguin and Bernard
sent sketches and photographs of their paintings of biblical

126. Paul Gauguin, *Self-portrait with halo,* 1889, Washington, National
Gallery of Art, Chester Dale Collection

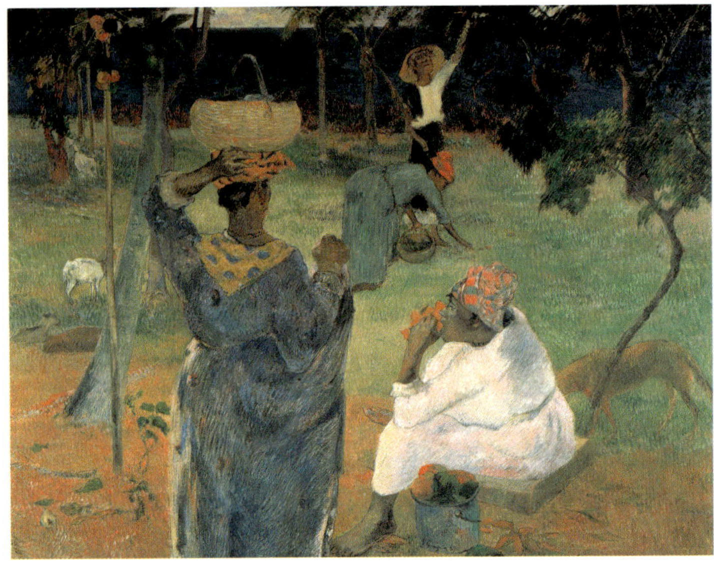

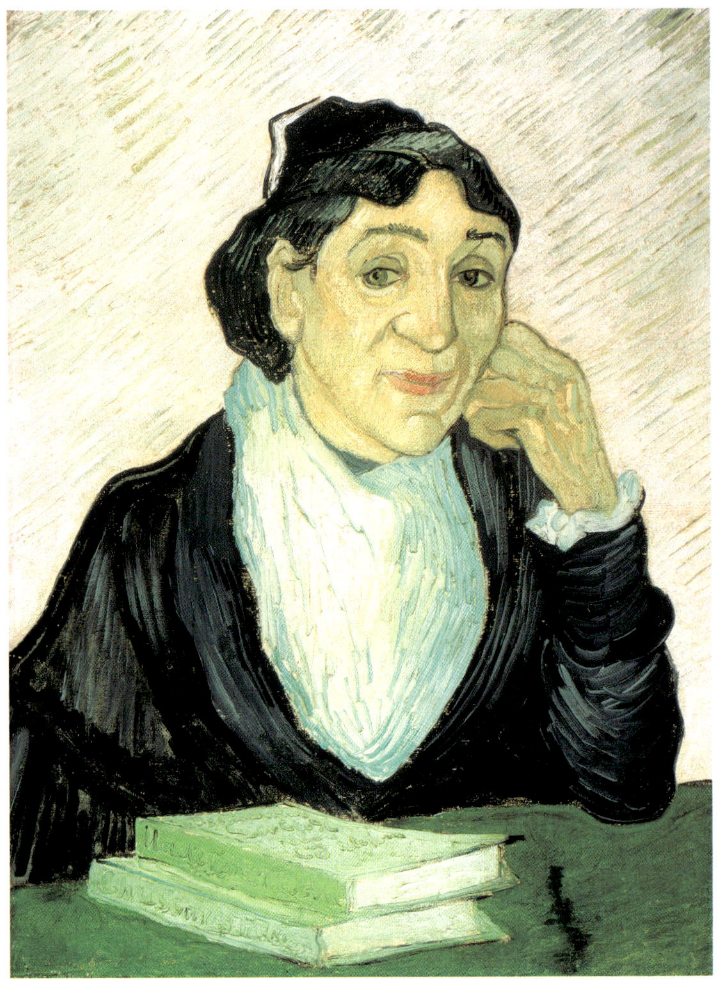

scenes to Van Gogh, who responded with severe criticism. Frustrated in his own attempts to deal with this subject matter,[28] partly because of his ambivalent attitude towards Christianity, partly because of the lack of models, Van Gogh was furious that his friends had succeeded where he had not. He painted olive orchards instead (plate 15, fig. 81).[29] ❧ Van Gogh's admiration for Gauguin, however, did not stop with this disagreement. In early 1890, for example, he used a drawing of an *Arlésienne*, which Gauguin had executed in Arles, to make a series of portraits in a variety of colour combinations (fig. 128). Van Gogh was extremely pleased when Gauguin wrote in admiration: 'I have seen the canvas of Madame Ginoux. Very beautiful and very remarkable, I like it better than my drawing' [890/GAC 41]. In a letter to Gauguin, Van Gogh called his painting 'a synthesis of the Arlésiennes' [893/643], and 'a summary of our months of work together' [894/642], thus acknowledging the influence Gauguin had on his work. ❧ Despite their different approaches to art, Gauguin regarded many of Van Gogh's works as extremely important in the history of modern art. He keenly felt his friend's vying for a leading place among the

avant-garde. During the last year of his life, in particular, Van Gogh's fame increased considerably, and it took a leap after his sudden death.[30] Gauguin decided to travel to the South Seas to found a studio of the tropics, much along the lines of Van Gogh's studio of the south,[31] and struggled for the rest of his life to carve out his own position in the art world, especially vis-à-vis Van Gogh.

❧

127. Paul Gauguin, *Under the mangoes at Martinique,* 1887, Amsterdam, Van Gogh Museum (Vincent van Gogh Foundation)

128. Vincent van Gogh, *The Arlésienne (Madame Ginoux)* (F 541 JH 1893), 1890, Otterlo, Kröller-Müller Museum

WORKING IN BLACK-AND-WHITE AND COLOUR: VAN GOGH'S REGARD FOR TONALITY AND TECHNIQUE

SJRAAR VAN HEUGTEN

The course of Van Gogh's career is almost invariably portrayed as a succession of radical innovations. However, it is also a story of remarkable constants, for he always remained faithful to some of his basic tenets regarding content and technique. His weakness for the palette of certain artists and its incorporation in his own paintings and drawings is one of those constants. ❧ Van Gogh is one of the greatest colourists in the history of art, and needless to say colour also played an important part in his appreciation of other artists. A good, expressive use of colour could send him into raptures. His love of it is reflected in his own work in his sombre Nuenen pictures as well as in the bold modern scenes he painted in the south of France. In both cases there was little difference in the basic theoretical principles he was applying. ❧ Colour, and by extension the monochrome work from his early period, is the most important technical *leitmotiv* running through Van Gogh's oeuvre. Technical questions regarding colour occupy a central position in this essay, but first a few other issues will be examined in order to put the lessons Van Gogh received from Anton Mauve, a leading master of the Hague School, into their proper perspective. ❧ This essay, more than any of the others in this catalogue, focuses on Van Gogh the *artist*, for his technical preferences only become apparent from the moment he decided to pursue an artistic career.[1] As a painter, he is unequivocal in his praise of a particular palette, and it turns out that it played a great role in shaping his artistic taste. His love of Delacroix, for example, can mainly be attributed to this, while Delacroix's

subjects did not affect his admiration one way or the other. An indication of his approval of a particular artist's tonality is, of course, the fact that he used it in his own work.

A YOUNG ARTIST'S ROLE MODELS

Van Gogh had acquired a thorough knowledge of old master and contemporary art between 1869 and 1876, when he worked as a young art dealer in The Hague, Paris and London, and again in 1877-78, when he was training to be a preacher in Amsterdam. His departure for the Borinage mining region of Belgium in December 1878 ushered in a long period of artistic celibacy, and one of the reasons for his ultimate decision to become a painter was his longing for the imaginary 'land of pictures' [154/133]. ❧ When examining the colouristic and technical influences on Van Gogh, it is important to remember particularly as regards the early oeuvre that, although he had already seen many paintings in his life, his study of them had taken place years before he embarked on his artistic career, at a time when he was not yet looking at paintings with an artist's eye. The content and aesthetics of a work were always important to him, but he only began making technical analyses when he started out as a draughtsman in The Hague in 1882-83. ❧ His conversion to the artist's life took place in 1880, and in the early spring of 1881 he visited the Koninklijk Museum voor Schilder- en Beeldhouwkunst (Royal Museum of Painting and Sculpture) in Brussels, where he had moved in the autumn of the previous year. There, among other things, he admired the work of Charles De Groux. In April he left to live with his parents in the North Brabant village of Etten. ✍ Artistic models were not exactly plentiful there, so Van Gogh sought refuge elsewhere, with his cousin by marriage Anton Mauve in The Hague. A visit of several days in August 1881 was followed by a move to The Hague in December that year, where he remained until September 1883. He had the opportunity to study both old and new art in The Hague. The Royal Cabinet of Paintings, better known as the Mauritshuis, had a superb collection of 17th-century Dutch masters, which he had already gazed at in admiration back in 1869, when he was working in the art trade in The Hague. The city was also home to masters of the Hague School like Anton Mauve, Jozef Israëls and Johan Hendrik Weissenbruch. Van Gogh got to know their work in dealers' galleries, at exhibitions, and occasionally in their studios. ✍ There is nothing to indicate that Van Gogh visited the Mauritshuis again during the 20 months he spent in The Hague in the early 1880s. It is not mentioned in his letters, and his name does not appear in the museum's visitors' book (although it should be added that there was no obligation to sign it).[2] It is hard to accept that he did not take the opportunity to renew his acquaintance with it but, if he had, he would undoubtedly have informed Theo with great enthusiasm, referring to it over several letters. It is possible, of course, that he and Theo went there together, for the latter visited him in The Hague several times, and if that was the case he would have had no need to write about it, although even then one might expect a reference to the outing. That, though, is pure speculation, and without any evidence of a visit an investigation into the influence on the novice artist of the 17th-century masters on show in the Mauritshuis would have no solid basis in fact. ✍ Van Gogh evidently sought his examples for a working method primarily among contemporary artists, whose work he could see at art dealers, in the Hague artists' society Pulchri, and in the painters' own studios (see Chronology: 1882). There were also manuals he could read. The medium he concentrated on in his early years as an artist was drawing, so it was works in black-and-white that preoccupied him.

EARLY TRIALS IN BLACK-AND-WHITE

The drawings and prints from Van Gogh's Hague period are probably the most experimental works he ever made. His tech-

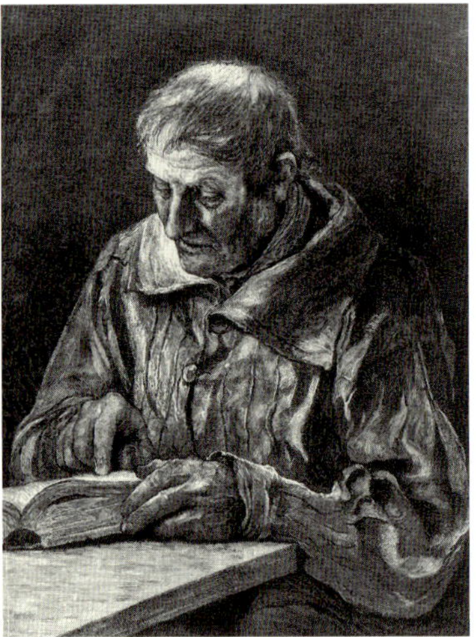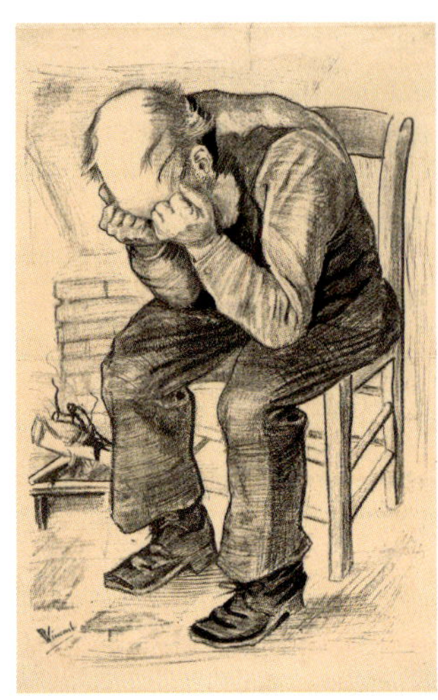

niques are often decidedly unorthodox, and one searches in vain for comparable working methods among his contemporaries. That, however, is not to say that his experiments were arbitrary.[3] ✍ In his early years he had an immense admiration for the graphic art he found in English and French illustrated magazines, much of which was imbued with a spirit of social realism (fig. 129). Those black-and-white prints, most of them wood engravings, were drawn by very experienced artists and were usually cut in the wood by expert craftsmen. Almost all of them have a certain robustness, and owe much of their expressive force to effects of light and shade. ✍ Van Gogh set out to bring a similar power of expression to the drawings and six lithographs that he made in The Hague in 1882. Technically, a wood engraving has so little in common with a drawing that it offered Van Gogh no artistic solutions for his need for expression. In his drawings he did develop a heavy, angular handling of line that was indebted to those illustrations, but he achieved his black-and-white effects in several ways of his own devising. For example, he soon discovered that a sturdy carpenter's pencil was the drawing implement that suited him best. He combined it with a preference for a coarse sort of watercolour paper called *torchon*, which was so strong that he could safely draw lines with great force, while the surface relief of the paper enabled him to render subtle grey effects by using the pencil lightly, covering only the peaks of the relief with graphite (fig. 130). ✍ Van Gogh made one very welcome discovery by pure chance. He had probably read in a manual by

129. After **Hubert von Herkomer,** *Heads of the people drawn from life, II: The agricultural labourer – Sunday,* Amsterdam, Van Gogh Museum (Vincent van Gogh Foundation)

130. Vincent van Gogh, *Worn out* (F 997 JH 267), 1882, Amsterdam, Van Gogh Museum (Vincent van Gogh Foundation)

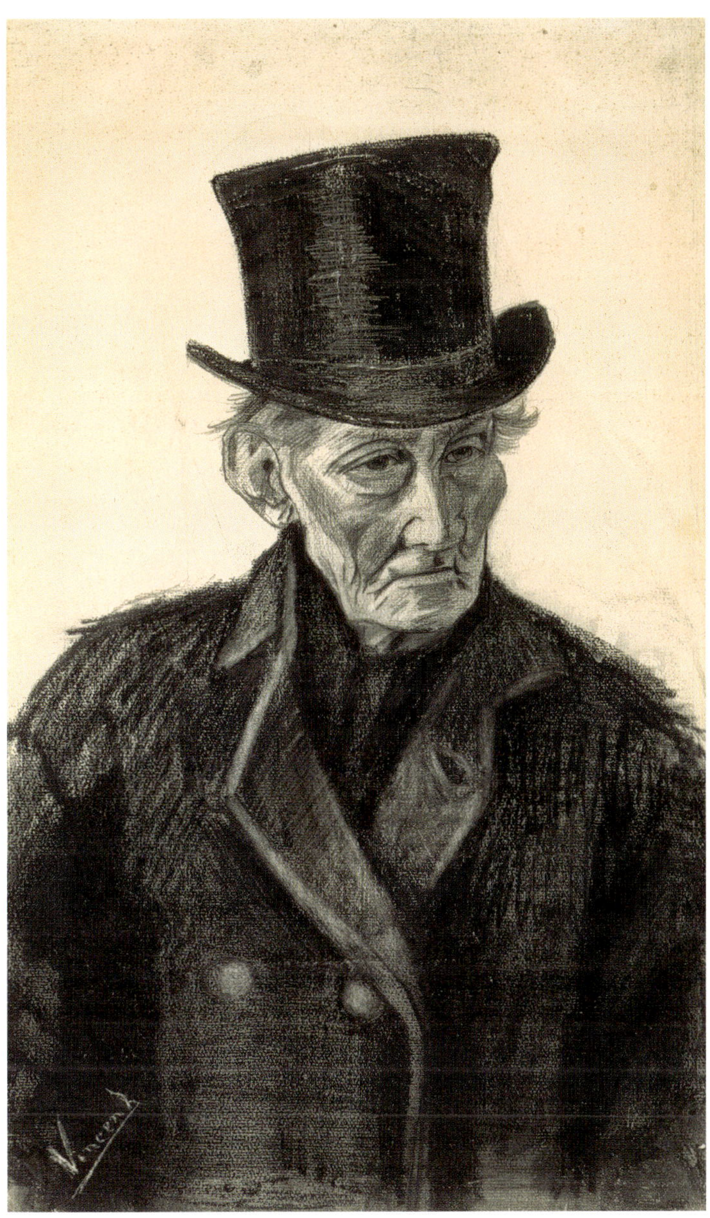

the magazine illustration but not in accordance with its technique. Some of these pencil drawings, however, contain clues that might well point to a direct influence of the prints. For example, he would scrape off drawing material with sharp implements – a process that he may have derived from graphic models. The process of making wood engravings is the reverse of that for a drawing. In the latter, black lines are drawn to create an image, whereas the lines cut into a block of wood remain white, giving the image its very distinctive appearance. This may have prompted Van Gogh's scraping technique, which is rather unusual for a draughtsman. He found an ideal way of applying this in a method that he developed in the course of 1882. He first made a drawing with the pencil and then drew on top of that with lithographic crayon. The greasy crayon lines could easily be scraped off the smooth graphite to create lighter and darker passages (fig. 131). ✑ There are very few traces of the technical influence of other artists in his early work; he appears to have acquired his draughtsman's skills mainly from manuals. He must have learned some things from Mauve, but technically there are few striking similarities between the latter's drawings and Van Gogh's. He had taken a few lessons in watercolour from the older master in 1881, but from the technical point of view they left no mark on his own watercolours worth speaking of. Once again, he picked up his working method from manuals.[4]

EARLY PAINTERLY INFLUENCES

The earth tints in the handful of paintings that Van Gogh made in his Hague period clearly show a debt to the painters of the Hague and Barbizon schools, whom Van Gogh had known and admired from an early age. Most of those paintings, however, have one feature that was to run through his entire oeuvre: this is the highly impasted brushstrokes, which appear spontaneous but are at the same time very cohesive. It is not easy to work with such a heavy impasto, and it is all the more remarkable that there are no obvious examples either in Van Gogh's immediate circle or among the earlier masters whom he admired that he could have taken as his models. Many aspects of a work of art are governed by the personal nature of the artist, and it seems that this way of working came naturally to

Armand Cassagne that a mixture of water and milk could be used as a fixative for pencil. It had to be sprayed over the graphite. However, Van Gogh found in practice that the use of undiluted milk over graphite gave an attractive, velvety black effect, and from then on he applied it liberally to his figure drawings. ✑ By using such techniques derived from standard practice or the literature on art, but applying them in an idiosyncratic way, Van Gogh was indeed working in the manner of

131. **Vincent van Gogh,** *Orphan man with top hat* (F 985 JH 286), 1882, Amsterdam, Van Gogh Museum (Vincent van Gogh Foundation)

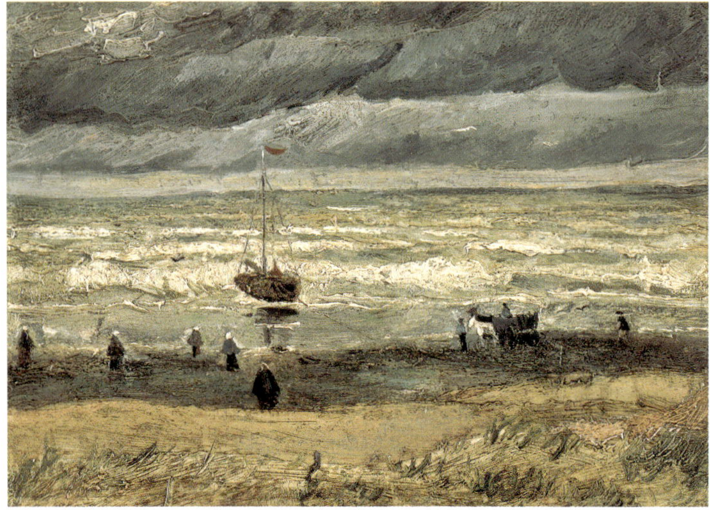

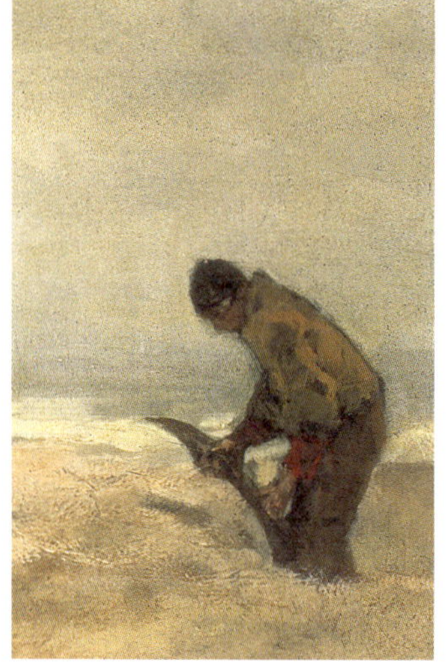

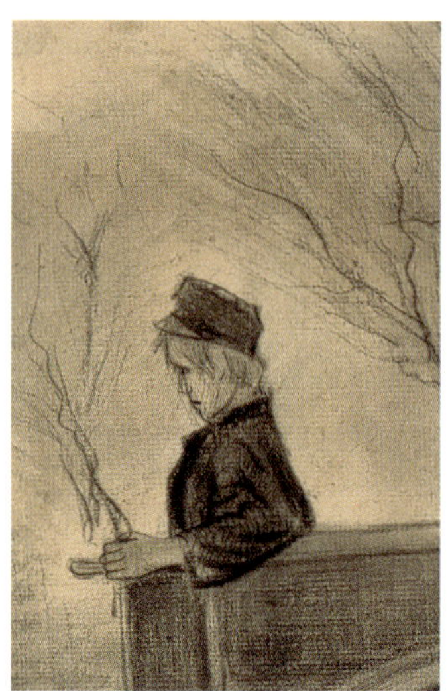

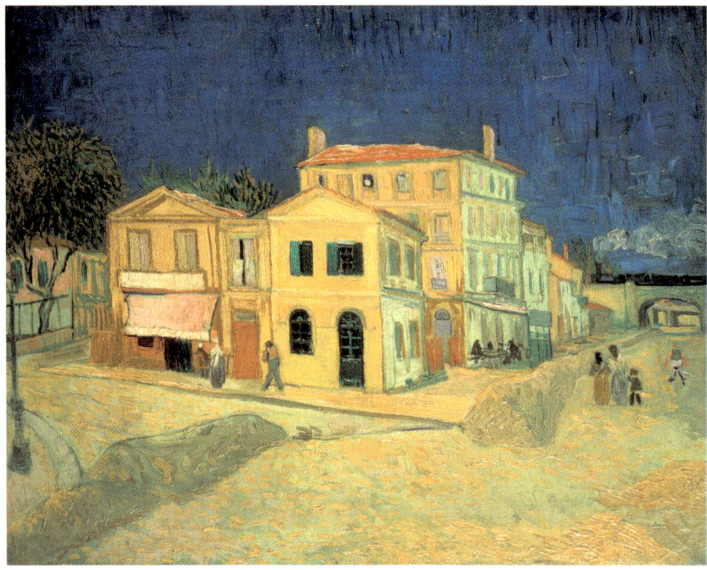

way in which Mauve rendered the weary expression of the exhausted horses, which have paused to rest for a moment. ❧ Leaving aside this narrative element, Van Gogh would also have learned something about technique from Mauve. As this painting shows, his teacher had a very skilful control of the way in which the foreground in a canvas of this kind should be painted. He did so with a broad, loose touch, in a way that looks virtuoso close up, and which at a distance leads the viewer's eye straight to the main subject, without the distraction of unnecessary details. The apparent simplicity is very deceptive. Van Gogh tried to imitate this device, albeit in his own heavy impasto. Even in his very earliest work one finds rapidly painted foregrounds, which may have a structure but which do not lead the gaze away from the main subject, such as a ship at sea (fig. 132). The knowledge he had acquired early on in his career continued to play a role in his late work as well, although that is not to say that he was still consciously thinking of Mauve (fig. 133). ❧ Van Gogh undoubtedly learned more from Mauve, but one aspect stands out in both his paintings and his drawings. In December 1881 Mauve set him to work making watercolours of women sewing, and would also have given him other tips about depicting the human figure. In Mauve's large fishing picture and other works, Van Gogh was able to study how the older painter handled the figure (fig. 134). Up until then, Van Gogh's own figures were very laboured, and mainly show how he conscientiously tried to reproduce every

Van Gogh, who had no academic training. ❧ It can now be seen that Mauve's importance to Van Gogh as a painter was greater than is commonly thought. He is regarded as the young artist's only teacher in his early career, but usually nothing is said about his technical influence. His studio, however, was the place where Van Gogh could observe the finer points of the artist's craft. For instance, he saw Mauve at work on his large painting *Fishing boat on the beach* (plate 68). Van Gogh was very impressed with this work, and in particular by the clever

---

132. Vincent van Gogh, *View of the sea at Scheveningen* (F 4 JH 187), 1882, Amsterdam, Van Gogh Museum (Vincent van Gogh Foundation)

133. Vincent van Gogh, *The yellow house ('The street')* (F 464 JH 1589), 1888, Amsterdam, Van Gogh Museum (Vincent van Gogh Foundation)

134. Detail of **Anton Mauve,** *Fishing boat on the beach,* 1882, The Hague, Gemeentemuseum

135. Detail of **Vincent van Gogh,** *Donkey and cart* (SD 1677 JH 52), 1881, Amsterdam, Van Gogh Museum (Vincent van Gogh Foundation)

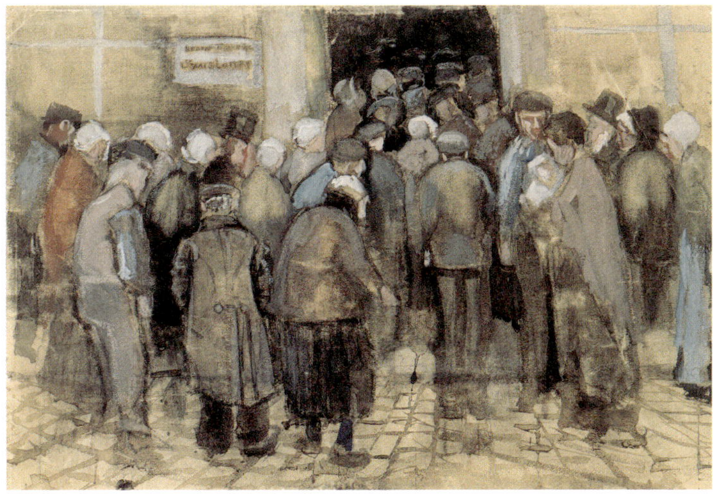

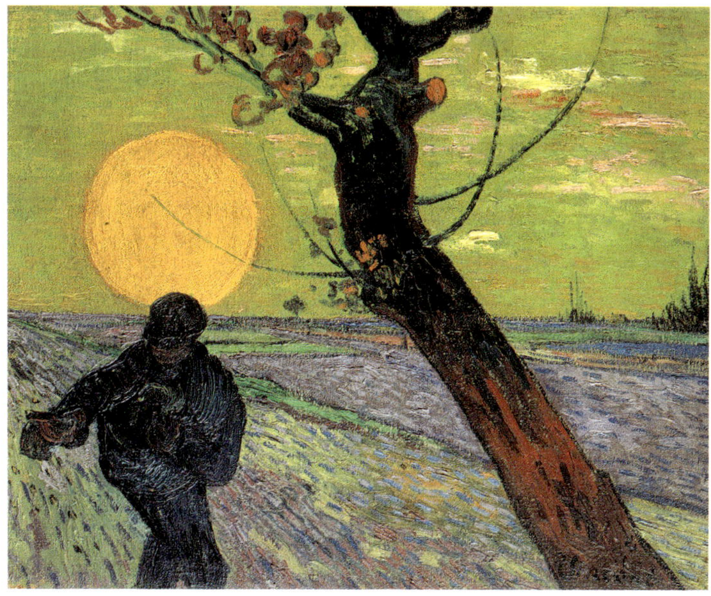

facet. The figures are generally large, wear appropriate clothing, in which every crease is lovingly depicted, and the faces
are like portraits. Even a small figure on a cart, no more than a
minor detail, has a face and hands rendered minutely (fig. 135).
❧ From the time he began studying with Mauve, he took a
broader approach, as in *The waiting room* (F 909 JH 94). The
figures are indicated with loose strokes, and there is absolutely
no detail; nothing must detract from the mood of the scene as
a whole. This, once again, is a classic painterly technique, and
was certainly not exclusive to Mauve, although he did apply it
with remarkable skill. Van Gogh adopted it, and sometimes
took it to quite extreme lengths in his early work. The foreground figures in the watercolour *The poor and money* are so
prominent that one would have expected them to have been
rather more detailed. Although the overall composition is convincing, the head of the third man from the left, for example, is
not very successful (fig. 136). The similarities to Mauve's *Fishing boat on the beach* are striking: broad in conception, no
elaboration of any of the constituent parts, with the eye firmly
on the composition as a whole. A look at Van Gogh's late work
shows that this was another lesson he never forgot (fig. 137).

COLOUR

Van Gogh's models as far as subject matter was concerned
were Jean-François Millet and Jules Breton. But for his tech-

nique, and above all his palette, there is no painter who had a
greater influence on him than Eugène Delacroix. ❧ In The
Hague, Van Gogh had deliberately avoided spending too much
time studying colour or the artistic and scientific theories about
it. That did not fit into his strict regime, in which he concentrated on acquiring a skilled drawing hand, a mastery of
human anatomy, and a grasp of perspective. ❧ In Nuenen,
where painting predominated, colour became a central issue.
This gave rise to a remarkable phenomenon. Van Gogh assiduously studied the colour theories set out in Charles Blanc's
Grammaire des arts du dessin and *Les artistes de mon temps*,
and other books. He greatly admired the principles formulated
by Delacroix, which he found in the books by Blanc, Jean
Gigoux and Théophile Silvestre.[5] However, it was all book
learning, for Van Gogh had not seen a painting by Delacroix in
years, and he would not see another until he arrived in Paris in
March 1886. His memory of works by the Frenchman that he
had seen as an art dealer in Paris in 1875 may have been quite
strong but, as noted above, he was not yet seeing with an
artist's eye. In addition, back then, he had been more interested in subject matter than he was later, and it was that which
guided him in his admiration for the great masters. ❧ The lack
of a teacher and of the right paintings from which he could
assess the lessons in the manuals lay at the heart of the dark

136. **Vincent van Gogh,** *The poor and money* (F 970 JH 222), 1882,
Amsterdam, Van Gogh Museum (Vincent van Gogh Foundation)

137. **Vincent van Gogh,** *The sower with setting sun* (F 450 JH 1627),
1888, Zürich, Foundation Collection E.G. Bührle

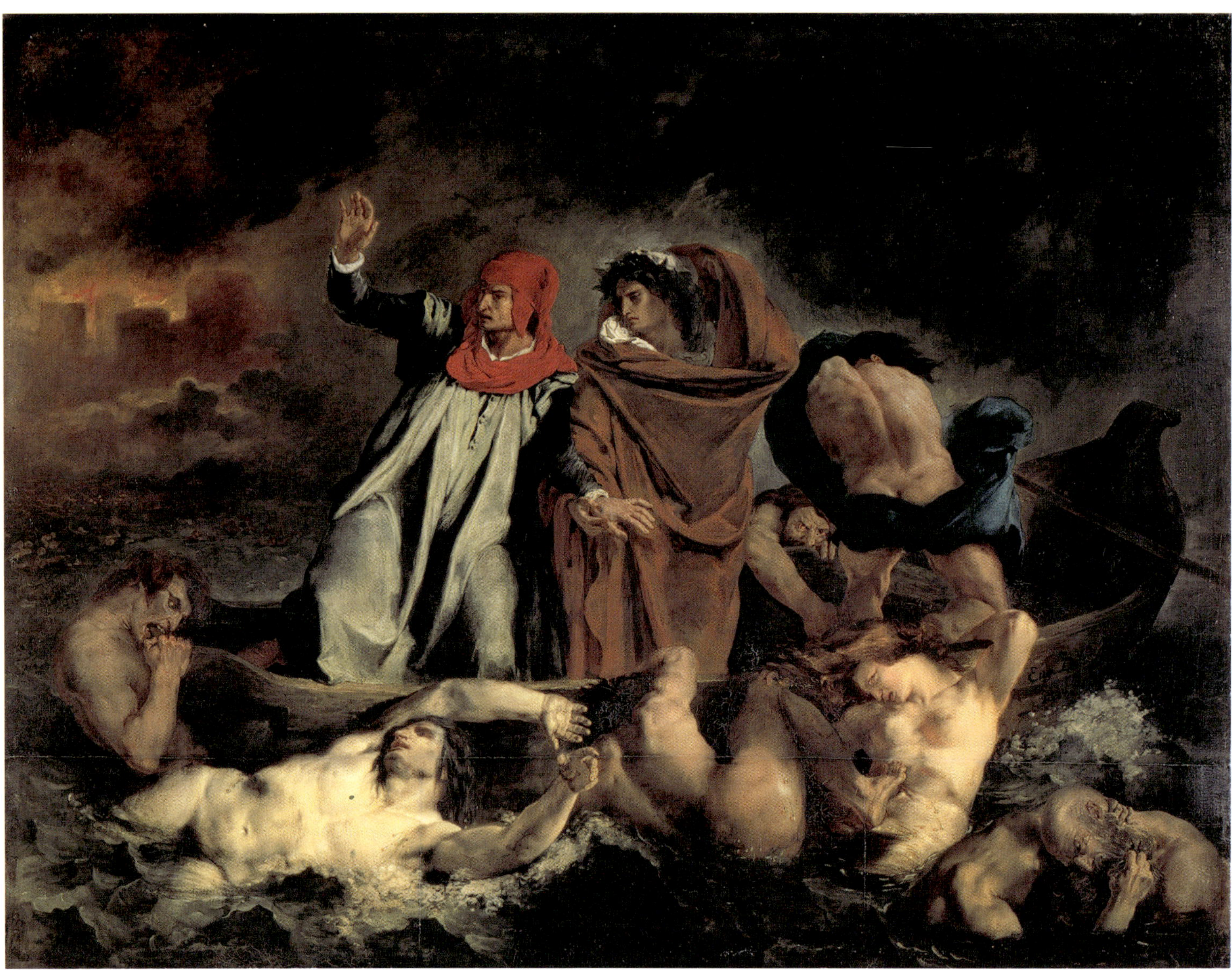

appearance of his paintings from Nuenen. For instance, he learned from Delacroix that the light or dark effect of a colour was governed by the entirety of the surrounding colours, and that one should not therefore automatically use the colour that an object has in reality. One of the lessons that Van Gogh drew from this was that one could make a colour very dark and yet have it appear light by making the others darker. That seems logical, but has disastrous consequences in practice, because many colours, such as yellow and orange, lose their force in a spectrum that is too dark. One quick look at works by skilled colourists would have set Van Gogh straight, but having no alternative he continued experimenting in isolation.[6] In the process he carried on even further down a false trail. Lacking the relevant canvases by Delacroix, he turned to paintings that he could study closely – works by masters of the Hague School, chiefly Jozef Israëls and Anton Mauve. Typical of the error of judgement he now made is the comparison of Jozef Israëls with Delacroix that he made in a letter to Theo. 'Just listen, the

138. **Eugène Delacroix,** *The barque of Dante (Dante and Virgil in hell),* 1822, Paris, Musée du Louvre

technique, the mixing of colours, the modelling of the fisherman of Zandvoort (plate 64), for instance, is in my opinion Delacroix-like and superb, and today's cold, flat greys are technically not worth much, become *paint*, and Israëls is above the paint' [537/426]. And in his next letter: 'But I repeat – speaking of technique – there is a very much healthier and sounder technique in Israëls, for instance in that very old canvas, the fisherman of Zandvoort, with its splendid chiaroscuro, than the technique of those who are always equally smooth everywhere, flat and distingué through their iron-cold colour. The fisherman of Zandvoort, well you can safely hang it beside an old Delacroix – "the barque of Dante" (fig. 138), and it is the same family. *Those are the things I believe in*, but each time I detest more and more those pictures which are light all over' [538/427]. ☙ The dark palette that Van Gogh evolved in Nuenen had little to do with the fact, as is so often asserted, that he was ignorant of impressionism, the modern art of his day. The essential point is that he was unable to study the work of Delacroix and other renowned colourists. The theories he applied were based on a very different, brighter use of colour than that of the painters of the Hague and Barbizon schools, with their far more tonal palettes. Van Gogh understood Delacroix's theories in principle, but he was unable to get them to work by unleashing them on the very greyed range of an artist like Israëls, which was governed by earth tints. Moreover, he lacked the more extensive theoretical or practical knowledge that could have enabled him to correct himself. It was as if he were unthinkingly playing music on a double bass that had been written for the violin. Taking the wrong kind of work as a guide for the application of his new knowledge, he set off down a path that did not lead to a bright use of colour full of contrasts, but to the dark palette with few nuances that we know from his Dutch period. ☙ In the two years he spent in Paris he was able to study the work of Delacroix closely, and he came to a very different conclusion concerning the correspondence between his palette and that of the painters of the Hague School. This emerges in a letter of April 1888, in which it turns out that Delacroix and Israëls have little in common, after all. 'So, of all the colours I ordered, the three chromes (orange, yellow, citron yellow), the Prussian blue, the emerald, the madder lakes, the Veronese green, or the orange lead, hardly one of them is to be found on the Dutch palette, in Jacob Maris, Mauve or Israëls. They are only to be found in Delacroix, who had a passion for the two colours that are most condemned, and with very good reason, citron yellow and Prussian blue. And yet, I think he did superb things with them, blues and citron yellows' [598/476]. In June 1888 he lamented to Bernard: 'My God, if only I had known this country at 25 instead of coming here at 35! At that time I was fascinated by grey, or rather by lack of colour. I kept dreaming of Millet, and then I also had such acquaintances among the Dutch painters as Mauve, Israëls, etc.' [630/B7]. A little later he wrote to his sister Wil: 'You will understand that Israëls and Mauve, who did not use whole colours, who were forever working in grey, with all due respect and love, do not satisfy the present-day desire for colour' [633/W4].

LOOKING AT OLD MASTERS

In October 1885, Van Gogh and his friend Anton Kerssemakers visited the Rijksmuseum, the Museum Van der Hoop and the Fodor Collection in Amsterdam. In the Rijksmuseum it was Frans Hals and Rembrandt who excited him the most, and in the Fodor Collection he was able to study a favourite work, Jozef Israëls's *At the churchyard* (plate 64). Theo soon received an elated report. 'Just listen, Frans Hals's flesh colours are also earthy, used here in the sense that you know. Often at least. Sometimes, I would dare say always, there is also a relation of contrast between the tone of the costume and the tone of the face. Red and green are opposites; the singer (Dupper Collection) (plate 109), who has carmine tones in the flesh colour, has green tones in his black sleeves, and ribbons on those sleeves *of a red OTHER* than that carmine. The orange-white-blue fellow I wrote about has a *relatively* neutral complexion, earthy, pink, violetish, due to the contrast with his Frans-Hals-yellow leather suit. The *yellow* fellow, citron amorti, has decidedly dull violet in his mug. Well – the darker the costume the lighter the face, *sometimes* anyway (*not* accidentally) – his portrait and that of his wife in the garden contain *two* black violets (blue violet and reddish violet) and a plain *black* (yellow-black?) – I repeat – reddish violet – and blue-violet – black and – black, in other words the three gloomiest things – well – the faces are VERY fair, *extremely* fair, even for Hals. Well. Frans Hals is the colourist *among the colourists*, a colourist like

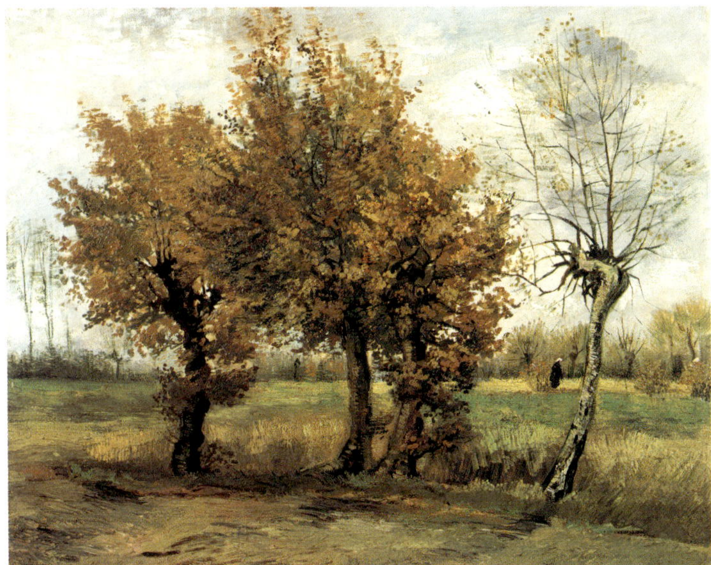

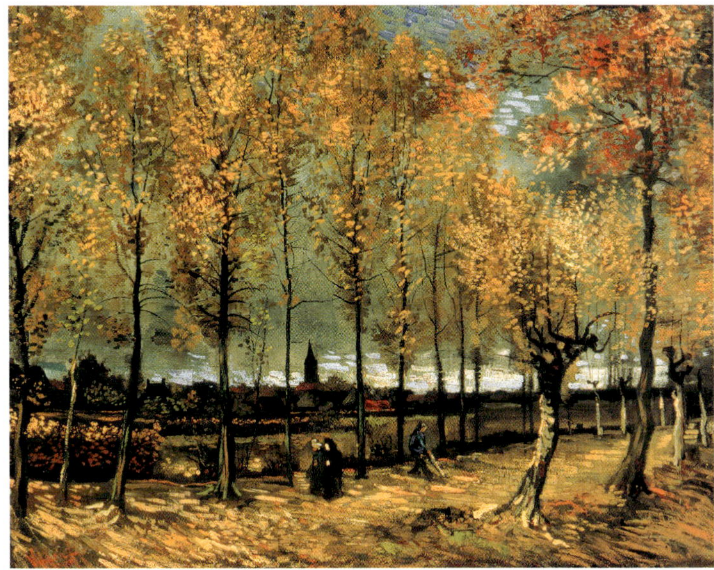

Veronese, like Rubens, like Delacroix, like Velázquez. It has very rightly been said of Millet, Rembrandt and, for instance, Israëls, that they are more – harmonists than colourists. But – tell me – *black* and *white*, may they be used or not? Are they forbidden fruit? I don't think so; Frans Hals has no less than twenty-seven blacks' [539/428]. ❧ The main thing that Van Gogh was seeking from the old masters was confirmation of his ideas about colour, and by labelling Frans Hals 'the colourist *among the colourists*' (and that while emphasising his use of black) he succeeded without much difficulty. Hals makes a delicate use of touches of colour in his paintings, but it is not exactly customary to regard him as one of the great colour innovators, any more, for that matter, than it is for Velázquez, whom Van Gogh bluntly mentions in the same breath as Veronese, Rubens and Delacroix. This is further evidence of Van Gogh's fallibility in matters of colour. ❧ All the same, the visit to Amsterdam did lead to a brightening of his palette. Whether he understood it properly or not, he could not have failed to realise during his three days of looking at old masters that by far the majority of the works he saw were considerably lighter in tone than his own canvases, despite the yellowed layers of varnish with which 17th-century paintings were covered at the time. On his return to Nuenen, where he concentrated on painting landscapes before leaving for Antwerp at

the end of November, it was reason enough for him to try using colour less heavy-handedly. The results included two autumn landscapes (figs. 139, 140). Broadly speaking, though, the importance of the visit to Amsterdam was not for its impact on Van Gogh's use of colour. Rather, it provided him with new insights into aspects of portraiture and figure painting, and into technical issue like brushstroke and a spontaneous touch. ❧ At the end of November Van Gogh moved to Antwerp, where he eagerly visited museums and churches. Although he produced only a handful of paintings in the Belgian city, it is clear that he had now abandoned the very dark colours of his Nuenen period. His portraits contain light flesh tones of the kind he could study in the work of Rubens and others like him.

COLOUR AND MODERNITY

The impressionists and the younger artists in Paris had an enormous influence on Van Gogh, and it was decisive in making him adopt the light palette and varied brushstroke that dominated his work from 1886-87 on. Delacroix, however, remained his principal colouristic guide, as François Gauzi, a fellow student, testified: 'Colour drove him mad. Delacroix

139. Vincent van Gogh, *Autumn landscape with four trees* (F 44 JH 962), 1885, Otterlo, Kröller-Müller Museum

140. Vincent van Gogh, *Lane with poplars* (F 45 JH 959), 1885, Rotterdam, Museum Boijmans Van Beuningen was his god, and when he spoke of this painter his lips trembled with emotion.'[7] Equally revealing is the letter Van Gogh wrote to the Englishman Horace Livens, probably in the late summer of 1887.[8] He said that there was a lot to see in Paris, such as Delacroix. He went on to describe himself as an admirer of the impressionists, but not a follower, and said that his ambition was to paint in intense colour instead of a grey harmony. Modern art played an important part in the realisation of this goal, which involved him distancing himself from his earlier work, but above all he fell back on Delacroix. ❧ The widespread belief that the modern art he saw in Paris forced Van Gogh to adopt his new palette therefore requires considerable refinement, although not total revision. However, far more prominence should probably be given to his study of the older masters than is usually done. He was undoubtedly shocked when he saw the very latest in modern art in Paris, but it is highly unlikely that he immediately took that as his lodestone and began brightening up his palette accordingly. He was not the kind of person to do that. His ideas may not always have been correct, but they did form a well thought-out, coherent whole, which could not be tossed overboard just like that. And, as so many of the discussions in his letters make clear, it always took an effort to persuade him to abandon a standpoint he had taken. In June 1888 he wrote from Arles to tell his sister Wil that he could understand that people could dislike impressionist art at first, because he had done so himself: 'One has heard about the impressionists, one expects a lot of them, and... when one sees them for the first time one is bitterly, bitterly disappointed and finds it slovenly, ugly, badly painted, badly drawn, with bad colour, everything that's miserable. That was my first impression, too, when I arrived in Paris with the ideas of Mauve and Israëls' [633/W4]. Although this passage has never been overlooked, nor has it led to the conclusion that Van Gogh's passion for innovation was lit with a slow fuse. ❧ Not only did he initially have his reservations about modernism, but now that he was in Paris he finally had the opportunity to test his ideas about colour in the presence of the masters whom he had been invoking for years but whose work he had been unable to see. Delacroix made a shattering impression on him. His *Christ asleep during the tempest* (plate 124), which he saw at an exhibition in 1886, a few months after arriving in Paris, was to set the tone for his later

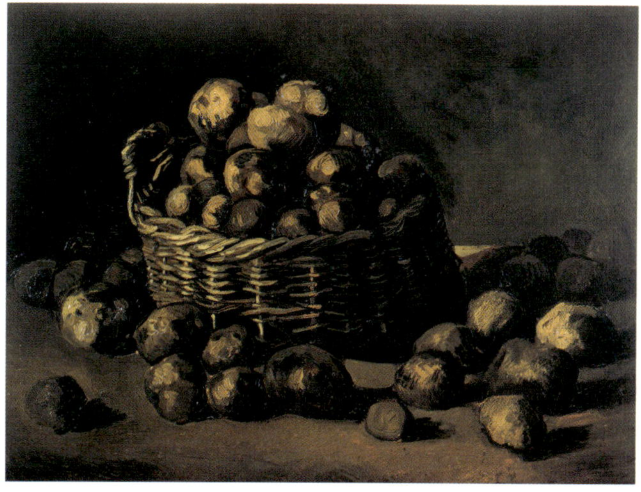

experiments with colour, when, in Arles, he set out to translate his adored icon of peasant life by Millet, *The sower* (plate 45), into a modern idiom. ❧ It can certainly be assumed that Van Gogh did not spend his first few months in Paris studying the impressionists and their followers, but that he seized the chance to visit the Louvre, the Musée du Luxembourg and other places where he could admire the models that he had loved for years. The study of those works, too, must have forced him to conclude that he needed to revise his ideas about colour, which he had already started doing to some extent after Amsterdam and Antwerp. This is what prompted the many flower still lifes that he painted in his first months in Paris to enliven his palette, not the work of the impressionists, let alone the contemporary avant-garde. He could only be receptive to new ideas after he had finally come to a complete understanding of the significance of Delacroix's ideas about colour. ❧ Apart from correcting the erroneous ideas of his Dutch period, there was very little change in his theoretical notions of colour. Complementary contrasts, simultaneous contrasts, and the experiments with tone and colour in Nuenen, can basically be traced back to the same theories as in his French period. A study like *Basket of potatoes* (fig. 141) has the same theoretical underpinnings as the *Still life with quinces and lemons* (plate 145): both are studies in closely related tints in approximately the same tone, but the latter work displays a

141. **Vincent van Gogh,** *Basket of potatoes* (F 100 JH 931), 1885, Amsterdam, Van Gogh Museum (Vincent van Gogh Foundation)

fundamental understanding of the properties of the colours used that is lacking in the first still life. ❧ He never wavered in his loyalty to Delacroix, and even gave him an apostle in the unsuspecting figure of Adolphe Monticelli, to whom he attributed a comparable colouristic talent, and of whose work he and Theo were putting together a small collection. 'As far as I know, there is no colourist who stems so directly from Delacroix, and yet it is probable, in my opinion, that Monticelli knew of Delacroix's colour theories at second hand only; he had them in particular from Diaz and from Ziem', as he wrote to the critic Albert Aurier from Saint-Rémy in February 1890 [854/626a]. In Monticelli he not only found many of the colour contrasts he was looking for, but the lush impasto of this painter from the south of France also appealed to him greatly and encouraged him to develop his own heavy brushwork even further. ❧ The range of influences that Van Gogh underwent in Paris was staggering. Claude Monet, whom he acknowledged as a great renewer of landscape, clearly set his stamp on several of the colourful landscapes that Van Gogh made in Asnières in the summer of 1887 (plate 130). Camille Pissarro and young members of the avant-garde like Bernard, Gauguin, Angrand, Signac, Seurat and Anquetin, all left their traces in his work, as did the powerful, highly contrasted areas of colour in Japanese prints. Taken as a whole, these influences led to the new, colourful palette that Van Gogh evolved in Paris. It is not possible to give a detailed account of it here. On the one hand it is a long, reasonably familiar range of influences, but very close technical study of the Paris paintings reveals that many surprises still await us.[9] ❧ One note in passing about Van Gogh and the impressionists – a term that he employed very loosely, even applying it to the younger artists. As he wrote to Livens, he did not consider himself to be one of them. After leaving for the south of France, he often said that he considered the achievements of impressionism to be of paramount importance, but that he also had his reservations.

PAINTING IN ARLES: THE MODERN COLOURIST

From the time of his departure for Arles, Van Gogh only sporadically underwent colouristic influences of any importance. When Paul Gauguin came to visit him in Arles in the last nine weeks of 1888, they both experimented with each other's style and use of colour – Van Gogh more intensively and eagerly than Gauguin. Those influences, however, were short-lived. Van Gogh continued to re-examine and revitalise his use of colour, his brushstroke and other technical aspects of his work, but he did so within the range of options that he had investigated in previous years and that, as an experienced artist, he now had firmly under his control. ❧ Delacroix was and remained his guiding light and, despite all the outward changes in his work, Van Gogh's philosophy from his Dutch years still applied, as he told Wil in the letter cited above: 'In my own technique I have the same ideas about colour, even thought about them when I was in Holland' [635/W4]. In a letter to Theo of August 1888 he put it a little more strongly: 'And I shall not be very surprised if the impressionists soon find fault with my way of working, for it has been fertilised by Delacroix's ideas rather than theirs. Because instead of trying to reproduce exactly what I have before my eyes, I use colour more arbitrarily, in order to express myself forcefully' [663/520]. ❧ Delacroix provided Van Gogh with the ideal use of colour for the expressiveness he wanted in his paintings. The impressionists had never been interested in this sort of power of expression, almost symbolist in conception, so their work naturally offered Van Gogh no point of reference. The older master, by contrast, supplied him with the means to advance modern art one step further, just as he had provided him with material for his experiments in Nuenen. It was precisely this kind of unwavering partiality that enabled him to absorb new influences of every kind during his very brief career, and fuse them into a startling new style.

❧

Leo Jansen – Vincent van Gogh's belief in art as consolation

[1] According to Du Quesne-Van Gogh 1923, p. 69.

[2] See Maupassant 1982, p. 51.

[3] Ibid., p. 47.

[4] Van Gogh's interest in the work went no further than this. He says nothing about the significance of the figures in the background – a carefully chosen ensemble of historical and symbolic personages. Here, too, he contented himself with a highly selective interpretation.

[5] See Sjraar van Heugten's contribution to this volume.

[6] See also 'It is consoling for artists to realise that real people have a feeling for paintings. But there aren't many of them' [805/W14]. For a (pastoral) confirmation that Van Gogh succeeded in this respect see Nouwen 1976.

[7] See Kôdera 1990, pp. 9-26. See also Verkade-Bruining 1989, esp. pp. 13-24 and 180-82.

[8] This is also confirmed by the fact that there is little mention of religion in the correspondence with the other children, except, of course, for the usual parental admonitions and advice.

[9] 'Sad and lonely I have climbed the sad and naked dune, / where the sea quenches its eternal sighs, / the dune where the wave dies in great hollows, / a monotone path to tormented hiding places.' The passage is from Edmond Roche's 'Les dunes'; see Roche 1863, pp. 48-50. The poetry albums are published in Pabst 1988.

[10] See Van Uitert 1987-II, p. 24.

[11] Verkade-Bruining 1989 has characterised Van Gogh's conception of religion following the break with the official Church as 'pantheistic' and 'monistic'; see pp. 133, 114 and 185, respectively.

[12] See letter 291/249.

[13] It is often assumed that in this letter Van Gogh explicitly states that with *La Berceuse* he was striving for a consoling effect. Strictly speaking, however, the painting functions more as the occasion for a more general lament about art. (See, for example, Van Uitert 1987-II, p. 24; Amsterdam 1990, nos. 82-83, p. 195; and Chicago & Amsterdam 2001-02, p. 271.)

[14] The quote also shows that for Van Gogh portraiture could have an important consoling effect; see below.

[15] Van Gogh was unacquainted with the music of Berlioz, as he confesses in the same letter to Gauguin. And it is for precisely this reason, he explains, that he expresses himself with colour, for example in *La Berceuse*. Once again Van Gogh discusses matters he knows nothing about but with which he linked certain expectations that were enough for him to base his ideas and judgments on.

[16] In a letter of 22 May 1889, Van Gogh writes to Theo that he sees it as his duty to work for his bread and to prove himself worthy of the funds he received from his brother; he couldn't allow himself the luxury of art for art's sake: 'If I were a man of means I would feel freer in my mind to create art for art's sake; now I simply content myself with the thought that if you work hard you do in fact make some progress' [778/592].

[17] In the last chapter of the novel Martin suggests: 'Let us work without speculating; it's the only way of rendering life bearable.' See Voltaire 1867, p. 62. With thanks to Rachel Esner, who pointed out the similarity between Van Gogh's and Voltaire's statements.

[18] See letter 747/574. The link between consolation and hope can also be found – in addition to the passage from letter 615/490 cited in the beginning – in letter 698/544, and in the letter to Bernard of June 1888, in which the patron saint of painters, St Luke, is described as a consoling figure [635/B8]. Joined with numerous other passages in which Van Gogh claims to find comfort in true friendship, the heart of his concept of consolation appears to come close to the famous quotation in Paul's first epistle to the Corinthians (I Cor. 13:13), only in Van Gogh's case it would of course read 'faith (in art), hope and love/friendship'.

[19] See also letters 635/B8, 878/614a and 883/W22.

[20] For further discussion of this issue see Van Lindert 1990, esp. pp. 80-100, 'Het portret als troost'.

[21] The complex problem of Van Gogh's identification with Christ is, of course, linked with this material, but the issue has not been taken into account here. For a discussion of this aspect see, for example, Greer 2000, pp. 7-21, and Greer 2001. For the notion of the portrait as consoling see the literature cited in note 20.

Chris Stolwijk – Van Gogh's nature

[1] See Schouten 2001, p. 11.

[2] See letter 282/242.

[3] See Van Uitert 1999.

[4] See, in particular, Green 1990, and also the essay by Nienke Bakker in this catalogue.

[5] See, for example, Chicago & Amsterdam 2001-02, pp. 11-21; Kôdera 1988; Murray 1978; Verkade-Bruining 1989; and the essay by Joan Greer in this catalogue.

[6] Laurillard 1882, p. 1-2: '[...] veel en velerlei. [...] de Heere God door den hof horen wandelen, [...] de door God geteekende symboliek der natuur te verstaan.' For a detailed discussion of Laurillard's ideas and writings in relation to Van Gogh's views on art and nature see Kôdera 1988, pp. 34-38.

[7] The phrase is taken from Micah 6:8, which actually reads: '[...] walking humbly with thy God'.

[8] See, for example, letter 151/130.

[9] On this see the essay by Evert van Uitert in this catalogue.

[10] See letter 290/248.

[11] See also letter 801/604.

[12] Kôdera 1988; Silverman 2000; Silverman 2001; and Chicago & Amsterdam 2001-02.

[13] See also the essay by Joan Greer in this catalogue.

[14] Streng 1997, p. 296.

[15] See letter 34/27.

[16] Lemaire 2002, p. 41. Schama regards the entire landscape tradition as a product of cultural developments, and as being composed of myths, obsessions and memories; see Schama 1995, p. 14.

[17] The theme of the pilgrim, which is well known from religious writings, can be detected very early on in Van Gogh's correspondence and was at the heart of a sermon he delivered in Richmond, near London.

[18] See letter 11/10.

[19] See letter 91/75.

[20] On this see especially Pollock 1998; Chicago & Amsterdam 2001-02, pp. 97-111; and Silverman 2001.

[21] The hero of Daudet's *Tartarin de Tarascon (Aventures prodigieuses de Tartarin de Tarascon)* of 1872. On this see the essay by Wouter van der Veen in this catalogue.

[22] Lemaire 2002, p. 43.

[23] Alain de Botton gives a good example of this in *The art of travel*. He found little to appreciate in Provence when he first went there, but learned to discover its beauty through Van Gogh's work; see Botton 2002, pp. 185-213.

[24] See letter 101/84.

[25] See letter 384/319.

[26] See letter 627/497.

[27] See letter 274/237.

[28] See letter 363/299. For Van Gogh's views on the difficulties of figure painting see the essays by Nienke Bakker and Evert van Uitert in this catalogue.

[29] Stolwijk 1998, pp. 51-52.

[30] Streng 1007, p. 276.

[31] For a detailed analysis of this debate see Streng 1995, pp. 71ff.

[32] See letter 19/14.

[33] Streng 1997, pp. 291-93.

[34] Van Gogh had a very high opinion indeed of Thoré (whose pseudonym was William Bürger) and had already read the first volume of his *Musées de la Hollande* in 1874. In 1884 he cited Charles Blanc's *Les artistes de mon temps* of 1876, and that same year he read Eugène Fromentin's *Les maîtres d'autrefois: Belgique - Hollande*

(1876) with great pleasure. See letter 15/12 (on Thoré), letter 452/370 (Blanc) and letter 453/371 (Fromentin).

[35] On Thoré-Bürger see, for example, Suzman Jowell 1977; Hecht 1998; and the essay by Evert van Uitert in this catalogue.

[36] Van Santen Kolff 1877, p. 231: '[...] waarheid van karakterteekening en voorstelling, soberheid van compositie en harmonie, [...] geest van eenvoud en waarheid, [...] gezond realisme.'

[37] Hecht 1998, p. 169.

[38] See letter 646/511.

[39] See, for example, Stechow 1966; Amsterdam, Boston & Philadelphia 1987-88; Falkenburg 1989.

[40] For the metaphor of the mirror see the essay by Evert van Uitert in this catalogue.

[41] Giltaij 2001-02.

[42] See letter 327/R30.

[43] Van Gogh had a small etching by Daubigny after this work on the wall of his attic room in Montmartre (1875-76). In 1880 he was delighted to acquire a new and larger one, which he put in a prominent position in his room in The Hague. He also planned to make a drawing of it but never did so, or at least no such drawing is known.

[44] See letter 188/R6.

[45] This blurred the boundaries, once so rigid, between studies from nature and a finished painting.

[46] Zimmerman 1999, pp. 18-39.

[47] Streng 1997, p. 301.

[48] House 1998, p. 23.

[49] See especially Pil 1993 for the 'picturesque' in 19th-century landscape painting and art criticism.

[50] See, for example, Moffet 1983.

[51] See letter 661/519.

[52] Tempel 1999. On Van Gogh and his ideas about colour see the essay by Sjraar van Heugten in this catalogue.

[53] House 2001, pp. 161-64. See also the essay by Cornelia Homburg in this catalogue.

[54] See London, Amsterdam & Williamstown 2000-01.

[55] See, for instance, Bretell 1984-85.

[56] See letter 822/614.

[57] See letter 876/636.

[58] See letter 889/W23.

Roelie Zwikker – Van Gogh's teachers

[1] See Fens 1994, p. 7: 'Ook de autodidact heeft zijn leermeesters. Hij heeft ze echter waarschijnlijk nooit ontmoet; hun gestalte en stem heeft hij geschapen uit het beste wat zij, in zijn veronderstelling, nalieten: hun werk, en waarschijnlijk vooral uit de schijnbare moeiteloosheid ervan, naar de stijl en de erin verwerkte eruditie.'

[2] See letter 159/138, and Van Heugten 1996, pp. 16-17.

[3] The painter in question was probably Adriaan Johannes (Jan) Madiol of Groningen, who had settled in Brussels in 1870. See letter 163/142; Hulsker 1985, p. 152; and De Bodt 1995, p. 144.

[4] They were Cassagne's *Guide de l'alphabet du dessin ou l'art d'apprendre et d'enseigner les principes rationnels du dessin d'après nature* (1880) and *Traité d'aquarelle* (1874), and Bargue's *Cours de dessin* (1868-70) and *Exercices au fusain pour préparer à l'étude de l'académie d'après nature* (1871). For Cassagne see, for example, letters 167/146 and 213/184, and Van Heugten 1996, pp. 18-22. For Bargue: letters 155/115 and 156/155, and Van Heugten 1996, p. 15.

[5] Such as his uncle Cor, an art dealer, or through Tobias Victor Schmidt, a dealer with Goupil & Cie. Van Gogh asked his brother to put in a good word for him with these people. See letters 158/137 and 163/142, and Hulsker 1985, p. 149.

[6] See letter 163/142.

[7] For the relationship between Van Gogh and Mauve see also Moffet 1983, and Pollock 1980-81.

[8] Van Heugten 1996, pp. 22. The painter Johannes Bosboom also made suggestions when he saw some studies by Van Gogh at the end of August or early September. Although Van Gogh was eager to have more corrections from him, it happened only this once. See letter 170/149.

[9] See Van Tilborgh and Vellekoop 1999, p. 32.

[10] See letters 198/169 and 199/170.

[11] See, for example, letters 201/172, 343/R34, 467/378 and 854/626a.

[12] See letter 198/169.

[13] See letters 592/472, 593/W3, 594/473 and 596/474. In February 1882, when he was no longer able to study with Mauve, he was delighted to receive some advice about drawing from Johan Hendrik Weissenbruch. See letter 204/175.

[14] See Hulsker 1985, pp. 226, 234; Van Heugten 1996, pp. 27-29; and the essays by Sjraar van Heugten and Hans Luijten in this catalogue.

[15] See letter 545/434.

[16] See letter 558/447.

[17] This makes it all the odder that Van Gogh mistook a work by Verlat in the city's church of St Andrew for a Rubens or a Van Dyck. See letter 554/443.

[18] For Herkomer's influence on Van Gogh see the essay by Hans Luijten in this catalogue.

[19] See Destremau 1996.

[20] This is suggested by an eyewitness account by Van Gogh's fellow student François Gauzi. When Cormon instructed his pupils to concentrate solely on the study of a female model, Van Gogh was the only one to disregard him, enthusiastically immersing himself in the colour composition. There was a hush in the studio as Cormon inspected the finished painting, but he totally ignored the colour and corrected the drawing alone. See Gauzi 1954, pp. 28-30.

[21] See letter 572/459a.

[22] 'Everything his hands make has a gentle, pitiful, astonishing character,' Van Gogh continued. Here he was referring to works Gauguin had made on Martinique in 1887, two of which he and Theo had in their collection.

[23] Gauguin had sent him a sketch of it. See letter 822/614, and Van Lindert 1990, pp. 97-100.

[24] See Van Uitert 1983, pp. 93-94; and for a detailed account of the influence the one had on the other Chicago & Amsterdam 2001-02.

[25] See letter 522/418.

[26] See letter 380/315.

[27] See letter 313/R25.

[28] On this see the essay by Hans Luijten in this catalogue.

[29] See, for instance, letters 503/406, 522/418 and 532/423. See Van Uitert 1993, pp. 129-45, for artists with whom Van Gogh identified.

[30] See Van Lindert 1990, pp. 27-45.

[31] See letter 550/439, and Homburg 1996, p. 57.

[32] See letter 559/448.

[33] The reference is to a preliminary study for the work that Van Gogh had seen in the church of Saint-Sulpice in Paris.

[34] See letter 806/607.

[35] See Homburg 1996, pp. 46-53. For the influence of Delacroix's use of colour on Van Gogh see also the essay by Sjraar van Heugten in this catalogue. Van Gogh also admired Delacroix because he had succeeded in investing Christian subjects with a contemporary air. See Van Lindert 1990, p. 97.

[36] See letter 686/538.

[37] See letters 522/418 and 802/605.

[38] On Van Gogh and Millet see especially Amsterdam 1989; Paris 1998-99; and the essays by Nienke Bakker and Evert van Uitert in this catalogue.

[39] See letter 501/404, and Van Tilborgh 1993, pp. 13-15.

[40] They were the first figure studies he made after leaving Paris. See Amsterdam 1989, and Homburg 1996, pp. 85-92.

[41] See letter 210/181.

[42] See Amsterdam 1989, pp. 12-13, and letter 250/218.

[43] See letter 646/511.

[44] See also the essay by Sjraar van Heugten in this catalogue.

[45] See Arnold 1997, pp. 155-66; Van Uitert 1990, pp. 116-20; and letter 700/B18.

[46] In 1883 Van Gogh gave lessons to the surveyor Antoine-Philippe Furnée (see letter 372/307); and a year later to the tanner Anton Kerssemakers, the goldsmith Toon Hermans, and the telegraphist Willem van de Wakker. He also gave advice to the draughtsman Dimmen Gestel and to Johannes van der Harten. See Van Tilborgh and Vellekoop 1999, cat. 9, cat. 38 and cat. 39, note 9. In Arles he taught Lieutenant Paul-Eugène Milliet to draw.

[47] See Essen & Amsterdam 1990-91.

Wouter van der Veen – An avid reader

[1] Gauguin 1923, p. 15.

[2] Pabst 1988.

[3] In the short space of this essay it is of course impossible to provide a complete overview of everything Van Gogh read, what he thought about it, and how exactly his literary taste developed and changed over time. My research into Van Gogh's literary preferences is largely based on the findings of Leo Jansen and Hans Luijten, editors of the Van Gogh letters project sponsored by the Van Gogh Museum and the Constantijn Huygens Instituut. For previous investigations of Van Gogh's taste in literature and its implications see, among others, Chicago & Amsterdam 2001-02; Nordenfalk 1947; Pabst and Van Uitert 1987; and Sund 1992.

[4] See letter 639/508.

[5] For this reason I have here left aside the Dutch literature Van Gogh read.

[6] In letter 874/655, having expressed his hope that Jo van Gogh-Bonger, Theo's wife, would not mind him writing to her in French, Van Gogh crossed out the phrase 'le son de notre hollandais me', replacing it with 'je crois, ainsi faisant, mieux vous dire ce que j'ai à dire'.

[7] The family correspondence is kept in the archives of the Van Gogh Museum.

[8] See letter 128/108.

[9] See letter 65/51.

[10] Fénelon's questioning of ecclesiatical tradition had a strong influence on Jean-Jacques Rousseau, one of the most important thinkers of the French Enlightenment. Enlightenment ideas caused Carlyle to lose his faith, and Dickens in turn found in Carlyle the theoretical framework for his own novels.

[11] In practice this goal, promoted by Zola in particular, was followed in only moderate measure by authors like Alphonse Daudet, Guy de Maupassant and Joris-Karl Huysmans, and was later rejected all together. In the writings of these 'dissidents', poetic value was clearly in conflict with the intended literary objectivity.

[12] Fréville 1952.

[13] See letter 673/528.

[14] In letters 593/W3, 630/B7, 719/558b and 805/W14, respectively.

[15] The last book by Zola Van Gogh read was *Le rêve* (1888), his least realistic novel. Vincent did not like it and jokingly compared it to the work of the romantic poet Lamartine [784/593].

Joan Greer – 'Christ, this great artist'

[1] See Greer 2001.

[2] See Greer 2000, pp. 7-40.

[3] See Kodera 1990; Greer 1997; and Greer 2000.

[4] This subject was addressed by Van Gogh in his painting *Still life with Bible* (F 117 JH 946) via the juxtaposition of the Bible with a modern French novel. See Greer 1997.

[5] See Greer 1997, p. 10.

[6] Ibid., pp. 10-14.

[7] Ibid., pp. 16-17.

[8] See Berlage 1887, p. 46.

[9] See Kools 1990, and Silverman 2000, p. 145.

[10] For Thomas à Kempis's *De imitatione Christi*, see Erickson 1998, pp. 43-53.

[11] See letter 136/116.

[12] The theme of Christian pilgrimage is also found in John Bunyan's *Pilgrim's progress*, a work that became particularly important to Van Gogh while he was in England, where he also became acquainted with Methodism. See Bailey 1992 and Silverman 1992 respectively, and Erickson 1998, esp. pp. 47-53.

[13] See letter 128/108.

[14] Both Kempis's and Ruyperez's works would also have appealed to Van Gogh for their evocation of a simpler, non-corrupt life, as propagated by Primitivist discourses in which he took part and most notably expressed in his ideas about Provence and Japan.

[15] Berlage 1887, p. 45.

[16] See Greer 1997, p. 39.

[17] See for an early example of this interest letter 33/26, or letter 768/W11.

[18] Berlage 1887, pp. 46-48.

[19] See Greer 1997, p. 39.

[20] Stricker 1880, pp. 3-4.

[21] Ibid., pp. 26-27.

[22] See Kodera 1990, pp. 15-39.

[23] See Greer 1997, p. 37.

[24] Bos 2002, pp. 84-85.

[25] Ibid., p. 88. Literary criticism and scientific discussion were also included here.

[26] Ibid., p. 85.

[27] Kodera 1990.

[28] See Chicago & Amsterdam 2001-02, pp. 11-15.

[29] Kodera 1990, pp. 15-18.

[30] For Van Gogh's tendency to convey holiness through nature and, in particular, his use of a symbolic sun, see Kodera 1990.

[31] The Reverend Van Gogh spoke on I Thessalonians 4:13-18, 5:1-10; Mark 4:26-29; John 12:24; and I Corinthians 15:35-38, 40-58 [127/107].

[32] Kodera 1990, p. 15.

[33] Number 189 from the hymnal of the Dutch Reformed Church; see Kodera 1990, pp. 13-14.

[34] The citations below the image are from John 5:24, 25, 28, 29 and 12:24-25; Mark 4:26-29; and Luke 9:24. On the reverse side is a long, incomplete quotation from John 20:1-17; see Kodera 1990, pp. 13-14.

[35] See Bowman 1987.

[36] See Dordrecht 1990, p. 8. For a list of publications by clergymen on Scheffer's work see Kodera 1990, p. 102, note 31.

[37] Hofstede de Groot 1872.

[38] See letter 101/84. For Van Gogh's interest in works by Ary Scheffer, see Dordrecht 1990.

[39] For a discussion of 'consolation' as a leitmotiv in Van Gogh's thought see Leo Jansen's contribution to this volume. For 'consolation' in relation to Van Gogh's Saint-Rémy period, see Greer 2001, esp. pp. 111-12.

[40] The explanation of the iconographic programme given here is based on a contemporary account, related in Dordrecht 1990, p. 21.

[41] Ibid.

[42] See Polistena 2001.

[43] Ibid.

[44] Ibid., p. 128. Van Gogh's correspondence indicates that he may have known of Lamennais. See letter 129/109.

[45] Polistena 2001, esp. pp. 128-32.

[46] Van Gogh's last mention of the *Christus consolator* is in February 1885 [318/267] and was a statement of praise. By 1886, however, his correspondence makes clear that he had rejected the art of Ary Scheffer. See letter 554/445.

[47] Polistena 2001, esp. pp. 152-53.

[48] Van Gogh mentions the treatise to Theo as early as 1873. See letter 15/12.

49 Suzman Jowell 1977.

50 Ibid., p. 246.

51 See Amsterdam 1989, esp. pp. 11-12.

52 Sensier 1881, pp. viii, x.

53 Ibid., p. ix.

54 Ibid., p. 126.

Evert van Uitert – Van Gogh's taste for reality

1 See Van Lindert and Van Uitert 1990.

2 See Pabst and Van Uitert 1987.

3 See Grijzenhout and Van Veen 1992, and Suzman Jowell 1977.

4 See letter 651/B12. For a survey of the period see Sloane 1973.

5 See Van der Grinten 1947 for the Dutch authors, and particularly for the all-important view of the 17th century.

6 See Thoré-Bürger 1900; Petroz 1884; Suzman Jowell 1977.

7 See letter 143/122.

8 See letter 465/380.

9 Bilders 1876, vol. 2, *Dagboek* (second edition).

10 It was not until 1878, a year before his death, that Daumier gained recognition not just as a caricaturist, but also as a painter and sculptor, and was hailed as a forerunner in the context of the recent realist and impressionist movements. See Loyrette 1999-2000, and Clark 1982.

11 See also letter 659/B14.

12 See Van Uitert 1987-I.

13 See Reichwein, Bergvelt and Wieringa 1995.

14 See letters 801/604 and 802/605.

15 Van Gogh first spoke of Puvis in 1884. See letter 449/368.

16 See also letter 877/648 (never posted); Amsterdam 1994; Prather and Stuckey 1987.

17 See letter 17/13.

18 Works by many of the painters whom Van Gogh admired were exhibited in 1973 in the Musée des Arts Décoratifs in Paris. The catalogue of that show, *'Equivoques'–Peintures françaises du XIXe siècle*, is very informative in that it includes contemporary criticism. See also Rosen and Zerner 1984, and Harding 1977.

19 See Rosenthal 1914, pp. 380-81.

20 See letter 690/542.

21 See letter 854/626a.

22 Aurier 1890. For an English translation see Stein 1986, pp. 181-93.

23 See Rosen and Zerner 1984, esp. chs. 6 and 7.

24 Bürger 1858-60.

25 It is unclear where Van Gogh picked up the saying that was so famous in the 19th century: 'l'art c'est l'homme ajouté à la nature'.The best-known sources are the *Grammaire des art du dessin* by Charles Blanc and *Manette Salomon* (1867), a novel about artists by Edmond and Jules de Goncourt. Blanc's *Grammaire* first appeared in instalments in the *Gazette des Beaux-Arts* before being published as a book in 1867, and was reprinted many times thereafter. Van Gogh got to know the *Gazette des Beaux-Arts* at an early date, when he was working in the art trade, but did not buy the book until 1885. The Goncourts attribute the quotation to the 17th-century writer and politician Francis Bacon. It is not clear when Van Gogh read *Manette Salomon*. His first reference to it is in 1890, when he included it in his portrait of Dr Gachet, and he mentions it in a letter from Auvers. This is much later, in other words, than the definition in the letter of 1879. There is a huge gap between the learned text of Charles Blanc and the artists' musings on beauty sketched by the Goncourts. The latter give a fascinating picture of the aesthetic confusion of artists of the 1850s and 1860s, the period in which Van Gogh was so interested. The Goncourts refer to *Über das Kunstschöne* (1797) by Ludwig Hirt, who had launched this aesthetic concept. Hirt was cited by Goethe and Schlegel and thus entered the art theory of the romantics.

26 Blanc 1870, pp. 10 and 17.

27 See letter 206/177.

28 This metaphor of light turned up again in abstract art. Kandinsky spoke of the 'white, fertilising ray': 'Dieser weisze Strahl führt zur Evolution, zur Erhöhung. So ist hinter der Materie, in der Materie der schaffende Geist verborgen' ('This white ray leads to evolution, to elevation. However, the creative spirit is not only hidden behind matter but concealed within matter'). See Kandinsky und Marc 1965, p.132.

29 See also the essay by Wouter van der Veen in this catalogue.

30 See letters 777/T9 and 778/592.

31 Carlyle 1908, p. 168. I do not know which edition Van Gogh read.

32 Van Gogh once wrote that he wanted to be a fisherman in the 'Ocean of reality' [188/R6].

33 Carlyle 1908, p. 198.

34 See Abrams 1960, and Abrams 1973.

35 See letter 17/13.

36 Becker 1967, pp. 112-13.

37 In Arles he compared her with Tolstoy, who was also 'enormously interested in the religion of his people' [690/542].

38 Gershman and Whitworth 1972, pp. 362-80.

39 Gershman and Whitworth 1972, pp. 363-80.

40 Delacroix 1996, pp. 113-14. The article 'Réalisme' opens with the words: 'Le *réalisme* devrait être défini l'antipode de l'*art*,' p. 165.

41 The three brochures published by Lecoq were reissued in book form after his death, together with a letter by Auguste Rodin dated 1913, notes, a foreword and a 'Notice sur la vie de l'auteur' by L.-D. Luard. A photographic reprint was published in 1953. See Rewald 1973 for Lecoq's reputation among artists.

42 Gauguin 1984, p. 210, letter 159, Quimperlé, 14 August 1888.

43 See letter 522/418.

Nienke Bakker – On rustics and labourers

1 For Van Gogh and the themes of work and the people see, among others: Ködera 1990; Pollock 1980-81; 's-Hertogenbosch 1987-88; and Zemel 1985.

2 See letter 501/404. Van Gogh always regarded this painting as his best work; see letter 576/W1.

3 The word 'people' is used here to denote a social concept: 'the mass of inhabitants of a country (a state), in contrast to persons of rank and higher civilisation, the lowest classes of a nation' (Van Dale). The Winkler Prins encyclopaedia of 1881 gives a similar definition. The word can, of course, have negative connotations, as a means of marking a particular type of person, but Van Gogh does not use it in this way.

4 See Pollock 1980-81, pp. 62 and 120. As an example of the 'common myths about Van Gogh's social commitment' Pollock gives a quotation from Meyer Shapiro's *Van Gogh* of 1950. Pollock, however, insists that Van Gogh's interest in 'the people' had nothing to do with 'sympathy' for the poor, but was rather merely a symptom of notions that were all class-based.

5 See letter 336/278.

6 In this capacity Theodorus van Gogh was actively engaged in agricultural issues and he set up a variety of relief works. Based on the Reverend's advice, the Maatschappij purchased farms and land for lease, and gave loans to farmers. See Kools 1990, ch. 4.

7 See letter 111/91-91a.

8 Silverman 1994, p. 147.

9 Van Gogh-Bonger 1913, p. 12.

10 Van Gogh's parents often complained about his 'togs' and regularly sent him new clothes. See, for example, b 2492, Mother Van Gogh to Theo van Gogh, August 1880: 'He looked quite alright, except for his get-up'. They also disapproved of his relationship with Sien Hoornik; see, among others, letter 350/288, in which Vincent reports to Theo on a discussion he had had with their father during the latter's visit to The Hague.

[11] b 2348, Father Van Gogh to Theo van Gogh, 14 July 1875.

[12] 'I wouldn't mind never having seen a locomotive, but never being able to look at a printing press again, that would be difficult' [360/297].

[13] See 's-Hertogenbosch 1987-88, pp. 14-26.

[14] Nochlin 1971, pp. 112, 117-18.

[15] Van Gogh regarded these writers as 'at the head of modern civilisation' [185/160]. See also the contribution by Wouter van der Veen in this volume.

[16] See letter 251/219.

[17] See letter 506/409.

[18] See letter 810/610.

[19] See Paris 1875, nos. 15 and 54.

[20] See letter 54/42. Camille Bernier, *January – Brittany*, Paris, Musée d'Orsay. Van Gogh calls the painting 'Les champs en hiver' ('The fields in winter'), a variation on the original title, *Labour en hiver*.

[21] See letter 54/42.

[22] See Cleveland 1980-81, p. 136.

[23] See letter 134/114.

[24] See Ypres 1995, p. 46.

[25] See letter 496/400.

[26] Van Tilborgh 1993, p. 19. Van Gogh described the Israëls painting in letter 210/181.

[27] Dekkers 1989, p. 7.

[28] See letter 138/117.

[29] See letters 401/336 and 496/400, respectively.

[30] See, among others, letters 279/240 and 291/249.

[31] See letters 262/229 and 251/R8, respectively.

[32] See letter 363/299.

[33] In letters 663/520 and 667/525, respectively.

[34] See letter 686/538.

[35] See letter 157/136.

[36] See letter 630/B7.

[37] Paris 1998-99, pp. 90-105.

[38] Ibid., p. 65.

[39] See Parsons 1983.

[40] Van Gogh praises these artists for their simple lifestyle in letters 401/336, 503/406, 767/588 and 700/B18.

[41] Van Gogh had got to know Pissarro quite well while in Paris, and undoubtedly discussed with him at length his vision of the countryside and the role of art. Although in contrast to Van Gogh the French artist was politically active and a radical socialist, he did share the Dutchman's abhorrence of industrialisation and his view of rural life and traditional craft as the ideal image of a harmonious society. Van Gogh regarded 'Père Pissarro' as a kind of mentor and placed great value on his opinion of his work.

[42] Sensier 1881, p. 127. In letter 502/405 Van Gogh himself states that was influenced by this quotation from Sensier.

[43] See also Van Heugten 1996, p. 174.

[44] Sensier 1881, p. 355. Van Gogh was also familiar with Ysabeau's *Lavater et Gall: physiognomonie et phrénologie rendues intelligibles pour tout le monde*, an examination of the theories of the 18th-century scholar Johannes Caspar Lavater, one chapter of which is devoted to the physiognomy of animals.

[45] Examples of this can be found in letters 397/332, 415/346 and 482/392, in which Van Gogh compares pastors with pigs, himself with a 'big shaggy dog' and the Nuenen weavers with horses on their way to the slaughterhouse.

[46] See letters 663/520 and 669/B15

[47] See letter 857/W20.

Hans Luijten – 'Rummaging among my woodcuts'

[1] The most important studies on this subject to date are Nottingham 1974-75; Amsterdam 1975; Chetham 1976; Stanislaus 1979; Engen 1985; Manchester, Amsterdam & New Haven 1987; Van Tilborgh 1987; Van Rappard-Boon, Van Gulik and Van Bre-men-Ito 1991; Bailey 1992; Melbourne & Brisbane 1993-94; Van Heugten and Pabst 1995; Homburg 1996; Arnold 1997; and Amsterdam & Paris 1999-2000.

[2] See Wolff and Fox 1973.

[3] See Goupil 1877. In this copy the *nouveautés* of 1878-1880 were bound in. See further: Boussod 1894. Both catalogues are in the library of the Van Gogh Museum. See Verhoogt 1999.

[4] b 2254, Father Van Gogh to Theo van Gogh, Etten, 17 February 1876.

[5] b 2371, Anna van Gogh to Theo van Gogh, Welwyn, 7 November 1875.

[6] t 1487-23.

[7] b 2361, Father Van Gogh to Theo van Gogh, Helvoirt, 14 September 1875.

[8] b 2952, b 2267 and b 836, respectively.

[9] Letter from Paulus Coenraad Görlitz to Frederik van Eeden, published in *De Nieuwe Gids* (December 1890), and in *Verzamelde brieven* 1974, vol. 4, p. 350. See also b 2404. The biblical quotation is from II Corinthians 6:10.

[10] See letter 133/113.

[11] Léon-Auguste Lhermitte, *La moisson*, in *Catalogue illustré du Salon, publié sous la direction de F.-G. Dumas*, Paris [n.d.], p. 189.

[12] *Paris Illustré* 6 (7 July 1888), 3rd series, no. 27, pp. 425-27.

[13] Vincent van Gogh, *Woman with baby, sitting by the fireside (after Virginie Demont-Breton)* (F 644 JH 1805).

[14] Boime 1996, p. 73.

[15] See letter 264/R12.

[16] Albums, t 1487 and t 1488. It has been suggested Vincent collected the prints in the first album in his early Paris period (May 1875-March 1876). Given their make-up, however, it seems more likely they both belonged to Theo. Vincent, who was four years older, must have supplied him with many of the works, however. The earliest mention of Theo keeping an album dates to the end of March 1877 (see letter 110/90). Vincent continued to encourage Theo in this activity over the years. Vincent must also have kept such albums himself, as he writes to his parent from Brussels in 1881: 'I've started collecting wood engravings again and putting them in an album, like the ones Theo and Willemien once had' [162/141].

[17] See Amsterdam & Paris 1999-2000, pp. 153-55 and p. 206, note 7.

[18] *De Hollandsche Illustratie* 9 (9 September 1872), p. 4, and idem (6 December 1872), p. 4; t 466 and t 465. Both prints were engraved by F. Moller.

[19] *De Hollandsche Illustratie* 1 (1864-65), no. 12, p. 96, and idem 5 (1868-69), p. 51; t 1055 and t 8.

[20] With thanks to Harold Konickx.

[21] b 886, Lucien Pissarro to Paul Gachet, 26 January 1928. The picture referred to, painted in Paris in 1887, is *Basket with apples (Dedicated to Lucien Pissarro)* (F 378 JH 1340). The estate includes 20 Pissarro prints. Although Van Gogh claims to have certain prints in his possession, many of these have since disappeared – the large format works in particular. Two reasons may be given for this: either they were lost or given away (see, among others, letter 276/239), or they were left behind in Nuenen when Van Gogh departed for Antwerp in November 1885 (b 909, Theo van Gogh to Mother Van Gogh, Paris, 22 March 1887). Years later, a portion of the print collection was still in Mother Van Gogh's attic in Breda. What then happened remains a mystery. Until 1904 many items from the estate were stored with a carpenter named Schrauwen, among them 'a large number of magazine illustrations'; b 1560, F.E. Pels Rijcken to Johan M. Jolles, Breda, 1 September 1904.

[22] Earlier Van Gogh had written: 'If you can find out, do please let me know what kind of drawings one can submit to the periodicals. It seems to me they might be interested in pen drawings of popular types and I would so like to begin working on something that might be suitable for reproduction. I don't think the drawings are all drawn directly on the wood block; there must be a method for transferring them. Although frankly I don't know anything about it' [205/174].

[23] See letter 303/R22.

[24] He wrote elatedly to Van Rappard: 'Congratulations! 70-76 is such a good period, particularly for the English things. In those days *Black & White* was at its best. I think there must be some great things among them' [289/R18].

25 The Hague 1990.

26 It thus comes as no surprise that someone who thought artists should encourage sympathy for the poor was a great admirer of Luke Fildes's social indictment *House-less and hungry*. See Nottingham 1974-75, and Manchester, Amsterdam & New Haven 1987.

27 The terms cited are found in letters 267/R13 and 308/263.

28 See letter 280/R17. Van Rappard had sent him an excerpt from this article, published in *The Art Journal* (1882), pp. 133-36 and pp. 165-68.

29 Van Gogh named a group of prints that for him formed the core of a collection: 'Think about [...] coming over to have a look at these particular Graphics; they're absolutely wonderful and, besides, I want to discuss with you what to do with the doubles. There are quite a lot of them and some of the *most beautiful*: the *Last muster* by Herkomer, and his old age home for women and low lodging house at St Giles; *Emigrants* and BOARD SCHOOL by Frank Hol; *Caxton printing* by Small, *Old gate* by Fred Walker and the like, which ought to form the *core* of any print collection' [309/R20]. Also striking is the extraordinary diversity of these prints.

30 Gustave Doré, *Falling leaves* in *De Hollandsche Illustratie* 5 (1868-69), no. 15, p. 120.

31 Edwin Austin Abbey, *Christmas in Old Virginia*, engraved by Joseph Swain, in *The Graphic* 22 (25 December 1880), pp. 660-61.

32 Henry Towneley Green, *A city church congregation*, engraved by Joseph Swain, in *The Illustrated London News* 61 (5 October 1872), p. 333.

33 Edwin Buckman, *A London dustyard*, in *The Illustrated London News* 62 (1 March 1873), p. 193; Fred Walker, *The harbour of refuge*, in *The Graphic* 15 (7 April 1877), p. 328.

34 i.e., composed as a whole ('masse'), without working up the details.

35 Elsewhere he also remarked that there was 'something manly' in black and white, 'something coarse that I find very attractive' [309/R20].

36 John Gordon Thomson, *The return from the Derby: a roadside sketch at Clapham*, in *The Graphic* 5 (1 June 1872), pp. 508-09.

37 See letter 316/R26. Apart from that, the family life he was then attempting to keep together may also have played a role. Van Gogh found the interior scene in Michael Fitzgerald's *The poor Irish scholar*, engraved by F. Wentworth, in *The Illustrated London News* 60 (27 January 1872), p. 93, 'incredibly beautiful' [316/R26].

38 See letter 157/136.

39 See letter 156/135. The 13 engravings from *Le Musée Universel* included in the estate are all from volumes 4-6 (1876-78). The only work by Millet still left is *The woodcutter* from *Le Musée Universel* 4 (1876), pp. 216-17.

40 See Homburg 1996, *passim*.

41 See F 630 JH 1775 and F 757 JH 1776.

42 This section is based on Tsukasa Kōdera's contribution to Van Rappard-Boon, Van Gulik and Van Bremen-Ito 1991, which describes the collection of Japanese prints in the Van Gogh Museum.

43 While in Paris Van Gogh undoubtedly observed that Monet and Degas incorporated Japanese elements into their work. John Russell, with whom the brothers were in contact, also had a large collection of Japanese prints, and Emile Bernard recalls their passion for these seemingly simple woodcuts; see Bernard 1911, p. 14.

44 In the same letter he also mentions that he has hung up all his Japanese prints in the studio.

45 Among the most important works in this context were the writings of the Goncourt brothers, the novel *Madame Chrysanthème* (1888) by Pierre Loti and the contributions to a special issue of *Paris Illustré* entitled 'Le Japon'. See Van Rappard-Boon, Van Gulik and Van Bremen-Ito 1991, pp. 23-38.

46 F 373 JH 1298. Based on the cover of *Paris Illustré* (May 1886), from which he made a tracing. The work combines elements and details from a number of different prints.

47 F 372 JH 1297. He also incorporated Japanese woodcuts into his two portraits of the socialist colour merchant Julien Tanguy (F 363 JH 1351 and F 364 JH 1352): in the background we find Hiroshige prints of Mount Fuji, among others. See Van Rappard-Boon, Van Gulik and Van Bremen-Ito 1991, p. 23-24.

48 See *Coal barges* (F 437 JH 1570), in which, like the Japanese, Van Gogh placed bright, simple colours next to each other.

49 Amsterdam 1990, p. 252, no. 114. Flowering fruit trees – particularly cherries – are often found in Japanese prints.

50 For example, the tree in two versions of *The sower with setting sun* (F 451 JH 1629 and F 450 JH 1627). The two women walking in *Memory of the garden at Etten* (F 496 JH 1630) also recall the Japanese women in gardens in a number of prints in the collection. See, for example, Van Rappard-Boon, Van Gulik and Van Bremen-Ito 1991, pp. 163, 180 and 192. Van Gogh writes that he here sought to express a kind of 'the poetic character'. [725/W9].

51 Van Rappard-Boon, Van Gulik and Van Bremen-Ito 1991, p. 17. Vincent confessed to Theo: 'I have no doubt that I will always love the nature here, it is just like with the Japanese prints, once you've grown to love them you'll never regret it' [607/483].

52 The concept of the prints as a 'musée imaginaire' was used by Ronald Pickvance in New York 1986, p. 174.

53 b 1423, letter from Anton Kerssemakers to Johan Briedé, Eindhoven, 23 June 1914.

54 He also wrote to Van Rappard that he often got up in the night to have a look at his prints – 'so strong was the impression they made on me' [264/R12]. To Theo he reported on his Japanese prints: 'I can't get enough of those figures and those landscapes' [646/511].

Cornelia Homburg – Vincent van Gogh and the avant-garde
Research for this essay was previously published in Cornelia Homburg, 'Vincent van Gogh's avant-garde strategies', in: Exhib.cat *Vincent van Gogh and the painters of the Petit Boulevard*, Cornelia Homburg (ed.), St. Louis (Saint Louis Art Museum) & Frankfurt am Main (Städelches Kunstinstitut) 2001, pp. 21-64. I would like to thank Lorin Cuoco for her thoughtful comments on this manuscript.

1 For information on Theo's commercial interaction with the impressionists see Thomson 1999-2000.

2 Van Gogh had read Théophile Silvestre, *Eugène Delacroix: documents nouveaux*, Paris 1864, and Charles Blanc, *Les artistes de mon temps*, Paris 1876, among other titles.

3 See letter 708/552.

4 See, for example, letters 667/525 and 771/590.

5 The art critic Félix Fénéon coined the term 'neo-impressionism'. For the role played by him other critics see, for example, Ward 1996, pp. 49-63.

6 See, for example, Rewald 1978, pp. 102-04.

7 Compare Paul Signac's reminiscences as published by Gustave Coquiot, translated in Stein 1986, p. 89.

8 See letter 594/473; see also Van Uitert 1983, p. 38.

9 See, for example, letters 591/471 or 623/500.

10 See letters 602/478, 613/489, 614/B5 and 659/B14.

11 See letter 659/542.

12 Edouard Dujardin, *Revue Indépendante* (1 March 1888).

13 For an early discussion of the relationship between the paintings see Toronto & Amsterdam 1981, pp. 239-40.

14 'I remember Van Gogh coming to our weekly gatherings at Lautrec's. He arrived carrying a heavy canvas under his arm, put it down in a corner but well in the light, and waited for us to pay some attention to it. No one took notice. He sat across from it, surveying the glances, seldom joining in the conversation. Then, tired, he would leave, carrying back his latest work. But the next week he would come back, commencing and recommencing with the same stratagem.' Suzanne Valadon interviewed by Florent Fels in 1928. The translation is from Stein 1986, p. 87.

15 See, for example, letter 663/520.

16 See letter 587/469.

17 See letter 573/-.

18 See letter 644/510.

19 See St Louis & Frankfurt 2001 for a detailed discussion of Van Gogh's concept of the Petit Boulevard.

[20] See, for example, letters 580/464, 581/465, 586/468, 591/471 and 594/473.

[21] See letter 641/505: 'After what you told me about him, I am going to see him this afternoon.'

[22] See letter 656/516.

[23] For this interpretation see, for example, Amsterdam 1990, pp. 195-99; Sund 1992, pp. 216-21; Zemel 1997, pp. 117-21; also letter 747/574.

[24] Homburg 1996, p. 76.

[25] For a detailed study of their relationship see Chicago & Amsterdam 2001-02.

[26] See also Jirat-Wasiutynski 1984, and Childs 2001.

[27] For an interpretation of the painting, see Hoyle & Van Uitert 1987, p. 110.

[28] See letters 641/505 and 689/540. For a more detailed discussion of Van Gogh's attitude towards religious subject matter see Homburg 1996, esp. pp. 62-69.

[29] See letter 825/615: 'The thing is that this month I have been working in the olive groves, because they made me mad with their Christs in the Garden, in which nothing is observed. [...] I have been knocking about in the groves, and the result is five size 30 canvases, which along with the three studies of olives that you have, at least constitute an attack on the difficulty.'

[30] See in particular Zemel 1980.

[31] For a discussion of this project see Childs 2001, note 31.

Sjraar van Heugten –Working in black-and-white and colour

[1] Publications dealing with Van Gogh and colour, some detailed, some more general, appear with great regularity. Only the most relevant will be cited in this essay. See Badt 1981 for an overview, and for the technical aspects Van Uitert 1966. See Hummelen and Peres 1993, pp. 49-52, for the Nuenen period, and Peres 1991, pp. 32-36, and Bang 1991 pp. 57-59, for Arles.

[2] *Register der bezoeken aan het Koninklijk Kabinet van schilderijen Augustus 1866-Juli 1884.*

[3] For Van Gogh's graphic work from the Hague period see Van Heugten and Pabst 1995, pp. 11-25 and cat. nos. 1-8. For Van Gogh's monochrome experiments in The Hague see Van Heugten 1996, pp. 26-30.

[4] Ibid., p. 26.

[5] Blanc 1870, pp. 601-17; Blanc 1876, pp. 25-88; Gigoux 1885, pp. 64-83; Silvestre 1864.

[6] See, for example, letters 497/401, 499/402, 500/403 and 502/405.

[7] Gauzi 1954, p. 28: 'La couleur le rendait fou. Delacroix était son dieu, et lorsqu'il parlait de ce peintre, ses lèvres tremblaient d'émotion.'

[8] See letter 572/459a. For the dating of this letter see Vellekoop and Van Heugten 2001, p. 21.

[9] One such study is currently taking place in the Van Gogh Museum. In the second volume of the museum's catalogue of the paintings, due for publication in late 2003 or early 2004, technical questions of this kind will be discussed in great detail. What is already clear is that Van Gogh experimented even more extensively than was already suspected. There is a growing understanding of his use of colour, and the issue of pigment discolouration is being investigated in the framework of the De Mayerne project financed by the Netherlands Organization for Scientific Research.

Exhibition catalogues

Paris 1875
Catalogue des 95 dessins de J.-F. Millet, composant la collection de M. Gavet, Paris (Hôtel Drouot) 1875
Nottingham 1974-75
English influences on Vincent van Gogh, Ronald Pickvance *et al.*, Nottingham (University Art Gallery) 1974-75
Amsterdam 1975
De verzameling Engelse prenten van Vincent van Gogh, Amsterdam (Rijksmuseum Vincent van Gogh) 1975
Stanislaus 1979
Van Gogh in black and white: a study of the influences of illustrated magazines on the art of Van Gogh, H.B. Werness *et al.*, Stanislaus (California State College) 1979
Cleveland 1980-81
The realist tradition: French painting and drawing 1830-1900, Gabriel Weisberg, Cleveland (Cleveland Museum of Art) 1980-81
Toronto & Amsterdam 1981
Vincent van Gogh and the birth of cloisonism, Bogomila Welsh-Ovcharov, Toronto (Art Gallery of Ontario) & Amsterdam (Rijksmuseum Vincent van Gogh) 1981
New York 1986
Van Gogh in Saint-Rémy and Auvers, Ronald Pickvance, New York (The Metropolitan Museum of Art) 1986
's-Hertogenbosch 1987-88
Van Gogh in Brabant: paintings and drawings from Etten and Nuenen, Evert van Uitert (ed.), 's-Hertogenbosch (Noordbrabants Museum) 1987-88
Manchester, Amsterdam & New Haven 1987
Hard times: social realism in Victorian art, Manchester (Manchester City Art Gallery), Amsterdam (Van Gogh Museum) & New Haven CT (Yale Center for British Art) 1987
Amsterdam, Boston & Philadelphia 1987-88
Masters of 17th-century Dutch landscape painting, Peter C. Sutton (ed.), Amsterdam (Rijksmuseum), Boston (Museum of Fine Arts) & Philadelphia (Philadelphia Museum of Art) 1987-88
Amsterdam 1989
Van Gogh & Millet, Louis van Tilborgh and Sjraar van Heugten, Amsterdam (Rijksmuseum Vincent van Gogh) 1989
Amsterdam 1990
Vincent van Gogh: paintings, Amsterdam (Van Gogh Museum) 1990
Essen & Amsterdam 1990-91
Vincent van Gogh en de moderne kunst, Essen (Museum Folkwang) & Amsterdam (Van Gogh Museum) 1990-91
The Hague 1990
Van Gogh en Den Haag, Michiel van der Mast and Charles Dumas (eds.), The Hague (Haags Historisch Museum) 1990
Dordrecht 1990
Ary Scheffer bewonderd door Vincent van Gogh, Dordrecht (Dordrechts Museum) 1990
Melbourne & Brisbane 1993-94
Van Gogh, his sources, genius and influence, Judith Ryan (ed.), Melbourne (National Gallery of Victoria) & Brisbane (Queensland Art Gallery) 1993-94
Amsterdam 1994
Pierre Puvis de Chavannes, Aimee Brown Price, Amsterdam (Van Gogh Museum) 1994
Ypres 1995
Charles Degroux en het realisme, 1825-1870, Jan Dewilde *et al.*, Ypres (Stedelijk Museum) 1995

Paris 1998-99
Millet-Van Gogh, Louis van Tilborgh and Marie-Pierre Salé, Paris (Musée d'Orsay) 1998-99
Amsterdam & Paris 1999-2000
Theo van Gogh: art dealer, collector and brother of Vincent, Chris Stolwijk and Richard Thomson, Amsterdam (Van Gogh Museum) & Paris (Musée d'Orsay) 1999-2000
St. Louis & Frankfurt 2001
Vincent van Gogh and the painters of the Petit Boulevard, Cornelia Homburg (ed.), St Louis (Saint Louis Art Museum) & Frankfurt-am-Main (Städelsches Kunstinstitut) 2001
London, Amsterdam & Williamstown 2000-01
Impressionism: painting quickly in France, 1860-1890, Richard Bretell, London (National Gallery), Amsterdam (Van Gogh Museum) & Williamstown MA (Sterling and Francine Clark Art Institute) 2000-01
Chicago & Amsterdam 2001-02
Van Gogh and Gauguin: the studio of the South, Douglas W. Druick and Peter Kort Zeegers, Chicago (The Art Institute of Chicago) & Amsterdam (Van Gogh Museum) 2001-02

Books/articles

Abrams 1960
M.H. Abrams, *The mirror and the lamp: romantic theory and the critical tradition*, London 1960 [1st ed. 1953]
Abrams 1973
M.H. Abrams, *Natural supernaturalism: tradition and revolution in romantic literature*, New York 1973
Arnold 1997
Matthias Arnold, *Van Gogh und seine Vorbilder: eine künstlerische Selbstfindung*, Munich & New York 1997
Arier 1890
G.-Albert Aurier, 'Les isolés: Vincent van Gogh', *Mercure de France* (1 January 1890)
Badt 1981
Kurt Badt, *Die Farbenlehre Van Goghs*, Cologne 1981
Bailey 1992
Martin Bailey, 'A pilgrim's progress', in: Exhib. cat. *Van Gogh in England: portrait of the artist as a young man*, Martin Bailey (ed.), London (Barbican Art Gallery) 1992, pp. 63-72
Bang 1991
Mette Marie Bang, 'Van Gogh's palette', in Cornelia Peres, Michael Hoyle and Louis van Tilborgh (eds.), *A closer look. Technical and art-historical studies on works by Van Gogh and Gauguin*, Zwolle 1991, pp. 57-60
Becker 1967
George J. Becker (ed.), *Documents of modern literary realism*, Princeton NJ 1967 [1st ed. 1963]
Berlage 1887
H.P. Berlage, 'Levensbericht van Dr. J.P. Stricker', *Levensberichten der afgestorvene medeleden van de Maatschappij der Nederlandsche Letterkunde: bijlage tot de handeling van 1887*, Leiden 1887, pp. 27-55
Bernard 1911
Emile Bernard, *Lettres de Vincent van Gogh*, Paris 1911
Bilders 1876
A.G. Bilders, *Brieven en dagboek van A.G. Bilders*, ed. J. Kneppelhout, 2 vols., Leiden 1876

Blanc 1870
Charles Blanc, *Grammaire des arts du dessin, architecture, sculpture, peinture*, Paris 1870 [1st ed. 1867]

Blanc 1876
Charles Blanc, *Les artistes de mon temps*, Paris 1876

De Bodt 1995
Saskia de Bodt, *Halverwege Parijs: Willem Roelofs en de Nederlandse schilderskolonie in Brussel 1840-1890*, Ghent 1995

Boime 1996
Albert Boime, 'Van Gogh, Thomas Nast and the social role of the artist', in: Joseph D. Masheck (ed.), *Van Gogh 100*, Westport CT & London 1996, pp. 72-111

Bos 2002
David Bos, '"De godgeleerde wetenschap is thans geene magt meer, die vreemd is aan het volk": verwetenschappelijking en vermaatschappelijking van theologie in negentiende-eeuws Nederland', in: *Geleerden en leken: de wereld van de Hollandsche Maatschappij der Wetenschappen 1840-1880*, Haarlem & Rotterdam 2002, pp. 82-96

Botton 2002
Alain de Botton, *The art of travel*, London 2002

Boussod 1894
Catalogue Général de la Maison Boussod, Valadon & Cie. Editeurs-imprimeurs, Successeurs de Goupil et Cie. Gravures, Photogravures, Lithographies & Photographies, Paris 1894

Bowman 1987
Frank Paul Bowman, *Le Christ des barricades 1789-1848*, Paris 1987

Bretell 1984-85
Richard Bretell, 'The impressionist landscape and the image of France', in: Exhib. cat. *A day in the country: impressionism and the French landscape*, Los Angeles (Los Angeles County Museum of Art), Chicago (The Art Institute of Chicago) & Paris (Grand Palais) 1984-85, pp. 27-49

Bürger 1858-60
William Bürger [pseudonym of Théophile Thoré], *Musées de la Hollande*, 2 vols., Paris 1858, 1860

Carlyle 1908
Thomas Carlyle, *Sartor resartus*, London 1908 [1st ed. 1834]

Chetham 1976
Charles Scott Chetham, *The role of Vincent van Gogh's copies in the development of his art* (diss.), New York 1976

Childs 2001
Elizabeth Childs, 'Seeking the studio of the south: Van Gogh, Gauguin, and avant-garde identity', in: Exhib. cat. *Vincent van Gogh and the painters of the Petit Boulevard*, Cornelia Homburg (ed.), StLouis (Saint Louis Art Museum) & Frankfurt-am-Main (Städelsches Kunstinstitut) 2001, pp. 113-52

Clark 1982
T.J. Clark, *The absolute bourgeois: artists and politics in France, 1848-1851*, London 1982 [1st ed. 1973]

Dekkers 1989
Dieuwertje Dekkers, *Een visserstragedie groot geschilderd — Jozef Israëls' Langs moeders graf*, Zwolle 1989

Delacroix 1996
Eugène Delacroix, *Dictionnaire des beaux-arts*, ed. Anne Larue, Paris 1996

Destremau 1996
Frédéric Destremau, 'L'atelier Cormon (1882-1887)', *Bulletin de la Société de l'Histoire de l'Art Français* (1996), pp. 171-84

Engen 1985
Rodney K. Engen, *Dictionary of Victorian wood engravers*, Cambridge 1985

Erickson 1998
Kathleen Powers Erickson, *At eternity's gate: the spiritual vision of Vincent van Gogh*, Grand Rapids & Cambridge 1998

Falkenburg 1989
Reindert L. Falkenburg, 'De betekenis van het geschilderde Hollandse landschap in de zeventiende eeuw. Een beschouwing naar aanleiding van enkele recente interpretaties', *Theoretische Geschiedenis* 16 (1989), pp. 131-53

Fens 1994
Kees Fens, *Leermeesters, een keuze uit de maandagstukken*, Amsterdam 1994

Fréville 1952
Jean Fréville, *Zola semeur d'orages*, Paris 1952

Gauguin 1923
Paul Gauguin, *Avant & après*, Paris 1923

Gauguin 1984
Correspondance de Paul Gauguin. Documents. Témoinages, Edition établi par Victor Merlhès, Paris 1984

Gauzi 1954
François Gauzi, *Lautrec et son temps*, ed. David Perret, Paris 1954

Gershman and Whitworth 1972
Herbert S. Gershman and Kerman B. Whitworth Jr., *Anthologie des préfaces de romans français du XIXe siècle*, Paris 1972

Gigoux 1885
Jean Gigoux, *Causeries sur les artistes de mon temps*, Paris 1885

Giltaij 2001-02
Jeroen Giltaij, 'Jacob van Ruisdael, het revolutionaire wonderkind', in: Exhib. cat. *Jacob van Ruisdael: de revolutie van het Hollandse landschap*, Martina Sitt and Pieter Biesboer (eds.), Hamburg (Hamburger Kunsthalle) & Haarlem (Frans Halsmuseum) 2001-02, pp. 29-35

Van Gogh-Bonger 1913
Johanna van Gogh-Bonger, 'Inleiding', in: *De brieven van Vincent van Gogh*, ed. Han van Crimpen and Monique Berends-Albert, The Hague 1990, 4 vols., vol. 1, pp. 1-42

Goupil 1877
Extrait du Catalogue Général de Goupil & Cie, Paris 1877

Green 1990
Nicholas Green, *The spectacle of nature: landscape and bourgeois culture in nineteenth-century France*, Manchester & New York 1990

Greer 1997
Joan Greer, '"Een man van smerten ende versocht in krankheyt": het christologische beeld van de kunstenaar in Van Goghs *Stilleven met open bijbel*', *Jong Holland* 13 (1997) 3, pp. 30-42, 62-63

Greer 2000
Joan E. Greer, *The artist as Christ: the image of the artist in The Netherlands, 1885-1902, with a focus on the christological imagery of Vincent van Gogh and Johan Thorn Prikker* (diss. Vrije Universiteit, Amsterdam 2000)

Greer 2001
Joan E. Greer, 'A modern Gethsemane: Vincent van Gogh's *Olive grove*', *Van Gogh Museum Journal 2001*, pp. 106-17

Grijzenhout and Van Veen 1992
Frans Grijzenhout and Henk van Veen, *De Gouden Eeuw in perspectief: het beeld van de Nederlandse zeventiende-eeuwse schilderkunst in later tijd*, Nijmegen 1992

Van der Grinten 1947
H. van der Grinten, *Nederlandsche Aesthetica in de negentiende eeuw*, Helmond 1947

Harding 1977
James Harding, *Artistes Pompiers: French academic art in the 19th Century*, New York 1977

Hecht 1998
Peter Hecht, 'Rembrandt and Raphael back to back: the contribution of Thoré', *Simiolus* 26 (1998) 3, pp. 162-78

Van Heugten and Pabst 1995
Sjraar van Heugten and Fieke Pabst, *The graphic work of Vincent van Gogh*, Zwolle 1995

Van Heugten 1996
Sjraar van Heugten, *Vincent van Gogh: drawings – the early years 1880-1883*, Amsterdam 1996

Hofstede de Groot 1872
Petrus Hofstede de Groot, *Ary Scheffer*, Groningen 1872

Homburg 1996
Cornelia Homburg, *The copy turns original: Vincent van Gogh and a new approach to traditional art practice*, Amsterdam & Philadelphia 1996

House 1998
John House, 'Authority versus independence: the position of French landscape in the 1870s', in: Richard Thomson (ed.), *Framing France. The representation of landscape in France, 1870-1914*, Manchester & New York 1998, pp. 15-34

House 2001
John House, 'Towards the modern landscape', in: Exhib. cat. *Vincent van Gogh and the painters of the Petit Boulevard*, Cornelia Homburg (ed.), St Louis (Saint Louis Art Museum) & Frankfurt-am-Main (Städelsches Kunstinstitut) 2001, pp. 159-98.

Hoyle and Van Uitert 1987
Michael Hoyle and Evert van Uitert (eds.), *The Rijksmuseum Vincent van Gogh*, Amsterdam 1987

Hulsker 1985
Jan Hulsker, *Vincent and Theo van Gogh: a dual biography*, Ann Arbor 1990

Hummelen and Peres 1993
IJsbrand Hummelen and Cornelia Peres, '"To paint *darkness* that is nevertheless *colour*": the painting technique of The Potato Eaters', in: Louis van Tilborgh *et al.*, *The potato eaters by Vincent van Gogh*, Zwolle 1993, pp. 58-69

Jirat-Wasiutynski 1984
Vojtech Jirat-Wasiutynski *et al.*, *Vincent van Gogh's self-portrait dedicated to Paul Gauguin: an historical and technical study*, Cambridge MA 1984

Kandinsky and Marc 1965
Wassily Kandinsky and Franz Marc, 'Über die Formfrage', *Der Blaue Reiter*, ed. Klaus Lankheit, Munich 1965 [1st ed. 1912]

Kōdera 1988
Tsukasa Kōdera, *Christianity versus nature: a study of the thematics in Van Gogh's oeuvre*, Amsterdam (diss. Universiteit van Amsterdam) 1988

Kōdera 1990
Tsukasa Kōdera, *Vincent van Gogh: Christianity versus nature*, Amsterdam & Philadelphia 1990

Kools 1990
Frank Kools, *Vincent van Gogh en zijn geboorteplaats: als een boer van Zundert*, Zutphen 1990

Laurillard 1882
Eliza Laurillard, *Met Jezus in de natuur*, Amsterdam 1882

Lemaire 2002
Ton Lemaire, *Met open zinnen: natuur, landschap, aarde*, Amsterdam 2002

Van Lindert and Van Uitert 1990
Juleke van Lindert and Evert van Uitert, *Een eigentijdse expressie: Vincent van Gogh en zijn portretten*, Amsterdam 1990

Van Lindert 1990
Juleke van Lindert, 'Vincent van Gogh en de verheffing van het portret', in: Juleke van Lindert and Evert van Uitert, *Een eigentijdse expressie: Vincent van Gogh en zijn portretten*, Amsterdam 1990, pp. 7-100

Loyrette 1999-2000
Henri Loyrette, 'Situating Daumier', in: Exhib. cat. *Daumier 1808-1879*, Ottawa (National Gallery of Canada), Paris (Grand Palais) & Washington (The Phillips Collection) 1999-2000, pp. 12-21

Maupassant 1982
Guy de Maupassant, *Pierre et Jean*, ed. Bernard Pingaud, Paris 1982

Moffet 1983
Charles Moffet, 'Vincent van Gogh and the Hague School', in: Exhib. cat. *The Hague School. Dutch masters of the 19th century*, Ronald de Leeuw, John Sillevis and Charles Dumas (eds.), Paris (Grand Palais), London (Royal Academy of Arts) & The Hague (Haags Gemeentemuseum) 1983, pp. 137-46

Murray 1978
Ann H. Murray, 'The religious background of Vincent van Gogh and its relation to his views on nature and art', *Journal of the American Academy of Religion*, 44 (1978) 1, pp. 68-96

Nochlin 1971
Linda Nochlin, *Realism*, London 1971

Nordenfalk 1947
Carl Nordenfalk, 'Van Gogh and literature', *Journal of the Warburg and Courtauld Institutes* 10 (1947), pp. 132-47

Nouwen 1976
Henri J.M. Nouwen, 'Compassion: solidarity, consolation and comfort', *America* (13 March 1976)

Pabst and Van Uitert 1987
Fieke Pabst and Evert van Uitert, 'A literary life, with a list of books and periodicals read by Van Gogh', in: Michael Hoyle and Evert van Uitert (eds.), *The Rijksmuseum Vincent van Gogh*, Amsterdam 1987, pp. 68-84

Pabst 1988
Fieke Pabst (ed.), *Vincent van Gogh's poetry albums*, Zwolle 1988

Parsons 1983
Christopher Parsons, Neil McWilliam, 'Le Paysan de Paris: Alfred Sensier and the myth of rural France', *The Oxford Art Journal* 6 (1983) 2, pp. 43-44

Peres 1991
Cornelia Peres, 'An impressionist concept of painting technique', in Cornelia Peres, Michael Hoyle and Louis van Tilborgh (eds.), *A closer look. Technical and art-historical studies on works by Van Gogh and Gauguin*, Zwolle 1991, pp. 24-38

Petroz 1884
Pierre Petroz, *La critique d'art au XIXe Siècle*, Paris 1884

Pil 1993
Lut Pil, *'Pour le plaisir des yeux': het pittoreske landschap in de Belgische kunst*, Louvain & Apeldoorn 1993

Polistena 2001
Joyce Polistena, '*The agony in the garden* by Eugène Delacroix', *Van Gogh Museum Journal 2001*, pp. 124-33

Pollock 1980-81
Griselda Pollock, *Vincent van Gogh in zijn Hollandse jaren: kijk op stad en land door Van Gogh en zijn tijdgenoten 1870-1890*, Amsterdam 1980-81

Pollock 1998
Griselda Pollock, 'On not seeing Provence: Van Gogh and the landscape of consolation, 1888-9', in: Richard Thomson (ed.), *Framing France. The representation of landscape in France*, Manchester & New York 1998, pp. 81-118

Prather and Stuckey 1987
Marla Prather and Charles F. Stuckey (eds.), *Paul Gauguin 1848-1903*, New York 1987

Du Quesne-Van Gogh 1923
E.H. Du Quesne-Van Gogh, *Vincent van Gogh: herinneringen aan haar broeder*, Baarn 1923

Van Rappard-Boon, Van Gulik and Van Bremen-Ito 1991
Charlotte van Rappard-Boon, Willem van Gulik and Keiko van Bremen-Ito, *Catalogue of the Van Gogh Museum's collection of Japanese prints*, Amsterdam & Zwolle 1991

Reichwein, Bergvelt and Wieringa 1995
Gusta Reichwein, Ellinoor Bergvelt and Frouke Wieringa, *Levende meesters: de schilderijenverzameling van C.J. Fodor (1801-1860)*, Amsterdam 1995

Rewald 1973
John Rewald, *The history of impressionism*, London 1973 [1st ed. 1946]
Rewald 1978
John Rewald, *Post-impressionism: from Van Gogh to Gauguin*, New York 1978
Roche 1863
Edmond Roche, *Poésies posthumes*, Paris 1863
Rosen and Zerner 1984
Charles Rosen and Henri Zerner, *Romanticism and realism: the mythology of nine-teenth-century art*, London & Boston 1984
Rosenthal 1914
Léon Rosenthal, *Du romantisme au réalisme: essais sur l'évolution de la peinture en France de 1830 à 1848*, Paris 1914, pp. 380-81
Van Santen Kolff 1877
J. van Santen Kolff, 'Over de nieuwe richting in onze schilderkunst, naar aanleiding van de jongste tentoonstelling te Amsterdam', *De Banier* 3 (1877), pp. 222-53, 349-99
Schama 1995
Simon Schama, *Landscape and memory*, London 1995
Schouten 2001
Matthijs G.C. Schouten, *De natuur als beeld in religie, filosofie en kunst*, Utrecht 2001
Sensier 1881
Alfred Sensier, *La vie et l'oeuvre de J.-F. Millet*, Paris 1881
Silverman 1992
Debora Silverman, 'Pilgrim's Progress and Vincent van Gogh's métier', in: Exhib. cat. *Van Gogh in England: portrait of the artist as a young man*, Martin Bailey (ed.), London (Barbican Art Gallery) 1992, pp. 95-115
Silverman 1994
Debora Silverman, 'Weaving paintings. Religious and social origins of Vincent van Gogh's pictorial labor', in: *Rediscovering history*, Stanford CA 1994, pp. 137-68
Silverman 2000
Debora Silverman, *Van Gogh and Gauguin: the search for sacred art*, New York 2000
Silverman 2001
Debora Silverman, 'Framing art and sacred realism: Van Gogh's ways of seeing Arles', *Van Gogh Museum Journal 2001*, pp. 45-61
Silvestre 1864
Théophile Silvestre, *Eugène Delacroix: documents nouveaux*, Paris 1864
Sloane 1973
Joseph C. Sloane, *French painting between the past and the present: artists, critics, and traditions from 1848 to 1870*, Princeton NJ 1973 [1st ed. 1951]
Stechow 1966
Wolfgang Stechow, *Dutch landscape painting of the seventeenth century*, London 1966
Stein 1986
Susan Alyson Stein (ed.), *Van Gogh: a retrospective*, New York 1986
Stolwijk 1998
Chris Stolwijk, *Uit de schilderswereld: Nederlandse kunstschilders in de tweede helft van de negentiende eeuw*, Leiden 1998
Streng 1995
Toos Streng, *'Realisme' in de kunst- en literatuurbeschouwing in Nederland tot 1875*, Amsterdam 1995
Streng 1997
Toos Streng, 'De waardering van het landschap in Nederland in de eerste helft van de negentiende eeuw', *Nederlands Kunsthistorisch Jaarboek* 48 (1007), pp. 259-317
Stricker 1880
J.P. Stricker, *De schriftelijke nalatenschap der oud-Israelitische profeten, wijzen en dichters*, Amsterdam 1880
Sund 1992
Judy Sund, *True to temperament: Van Gogh and French naturalist literature*, Cambridge MA 1992

Suzman Jowell 1977
Frances Suzman Jowell, *Thoré-Bürger and the art of the past*, New York & London 1977
Tempel 1999
Benno Tempel, '"Such absurdity can never deserve the name of Art": impressionism in the Netherlands', *Van Gogh Museum Journal 1999*, pp. 112-31
Thomson 1999-2000
Richard Thomson, 'Theo van Gogh: een oprecht handelaar', in: Exhib. cat. *Theo van Gogh: kunsthandelaar, verzamelaar en broer van Vincent*, Chris Stolwijk and Richard Thomson, Amsterdam (Van Gogh Museum) & Paris (Musée d'Orsay) 1999-2000, pp. 61-152
Thoré-Bürger 1900
Thoré-Bürger peint par lui-même: lettres et notes intimes, ed. Paul Cottin, Paris (1900)
Van Tilborgh 1987
Louis van Tilborgh, '"A kind of Bible": the collection of prints and illustrations', in: Michael Hoyle and Evert van Uitert (eds.), *The Rijksmuseum Vincent van Gogh*, Amsterdam 1987, pp. 38-44
Van Tilborgh 1993
Louis van Tilborgh et al., *The potato eaters by Vincent van Gogh*, Zwolle 1993
Van Tilborgh and Vellekoop 1999
Louis van Tilborgh and Marije Vellekoop, *Vincent van Gogh: paintings — Dutch period 1881-1885*, Amsterdam & Blaricum 1999
Van Uitert 1966
Evert van Uitert, 'De toon van Vincent van Gogh: opvattingen over kleur in zijn Hollandse periode', *Simiolus* 1 (1966/67) 2, pp. 106-15
Van Uitert 1983
Evert van Uitert, *Vincent van Gogh in creative competition: four essays from Simiolus*, Zutphen 1983
Van Uitert 1987-I
Evert van Uitert, 'An immortal name', in: Michael Hoyle and Evert van Uitert (eds.), *The Rijksmuseum Vincent van Gogh*, Amsterdam 1987, pp.19-29
Van Uitert 1987-II
Evert van Uitert, *Het geloof in de moderne kunst*, Amsterdam 1987
Van Uitert 1990
Evert van Uitert, 'De zelfportretten van Vincent van Gogh', in: Juleke van Lindert and Evert van Uitert, *Een eigentijdse expressie: Vincent van Gogh en zijn portretten*, Amsterdam 1990, pp. 101-29
Van Uitert 1993
Evert van Uitert, 'Some artists with whom Vincent van Gogh identified', in: Tsukasa Kōdera, *The mythology of Vincent van Gogh*, Tokyo & Amsterdam 1993, pp. 129-45
Van Uitert 1999
Evert van Uitert, '"De voorzienigheid die een tuin waarlijk is..." Tuinen en parken door de ogen van Van Gogh', in: Exhib. cat. *Aardse paradijzen. De tuin in de Nederlandse kunst 1770 tot 2000*, Erik de Jong (ed.), Haarlem (Frans Halsmuseum) & Enschede (Rijksmuseum Twenthe) 1999, pp. 143-74
Vellekoop and Van Heugten 2001
Marije Vellekoop and Sjraar van Heugten, *Vincent van Gogh: drawings — Antwerp and Paris 1885-1888*, Amsterdam & Blaricum 2001
Verhoogt 1999
Robert Verhoogt, 'Kunsthandel in prenten: over de negentiende-eeuwse kunsthandels van Goupil en Gambart', *Kunstlicht* 20 (1999) 1, pp. 22-29
Verkade-Bruining 1989
A. Verkade-Bruining, *De God van Vincent: beschouwingen over de mens Van Gogh*, Amsterdam 1989
Voltaire 1867
Voltaire, *Candide ou l'optimisme*, in: Voltaire, *Romans*, Paris 1867

Ward 1996
Martha Ward, *Pissarro, neo-impressionism, and the spaces of the avant-garde*, Chicago 1996

Wolff and Fox 1973
Michael Wolff and Celina Fox, 'Pictures from the Magazine', in: H.J. Dyos and Michael Wolff (eds.), *The Victorian city: images and realities*, 2 vols., London & Boston 1973, vol. 2, pp. 559-82

Zemel 1980
Carol M. Zemel, *The formation of a legend: Van Gogh criticism, 1890-1920*, Ann Arbor MI 1980

Zemel 1985
Carol Zemel, 'The "Spook" in the machine: Van Gogh's pictures of weavers in Brabant', *The Art Bulletin* 67 (1985) 1, pp. 123-37

Zemel 1997
Carol Zemel, *Van Gogh's progress: Utopia, modernity, and late-nineteenth-century art*, Berkeley & Los Angeles 1997

Zimmerman 1999
Michael F. Zimmerman, 'Painting of nature — nature of painting. An essay on landscape and the historical position of "Barbizon"', in: Andreas Burmeister, Christoph Heilmann and Michael F. Zimmerman, *Barbizon: Malerei der Natur — Natur der Malerei*, Munich 1999, pp. 18-55

elkaar maar dikwijls
over schrijven; vindt maar
mooi zooveel je kunt, de
meesten vinden niet ge-
noeg mooi. —
Ik schrijf hieronder enkele
namen van schilders van
wie ik bizonder veel houdt.
Scheffer, Delaroche, Hébert
Hamon
Leys, Tissot, Lagye Boughton
Millais, Thys Maris, de Groux
de Braekeleer Jr.
Millet, Jules Breton, Feyen-Perrin
Eugène Feyen. Brion Jundt
George Saal. Israëls Anker
Knaus, Vautier, Jourdan
Jalabert, Antigna, Compte-Calix
Rochussen, Meissonier, Zamacois
Madrazzo, Ziem, Boudin
Gerome, Fromentin, de Tournemine
Passini

This catalogue comprises all the paintings, drawings, prints and photographs included in the exhibition *Vincent's choice: the Musée imaginaire of Van Gogh*, organised by the Van Gogh Museum, Amsterdam (14 February 2003 – 15 June 2003), on the occasion of Vincent van Gogh's 150th birthday.

Books, magazines and other objects are not listed in the catalogue

Each catalogue entry is made up of the following:
· an illustration;
· the name of the artist;
· the title and date of the work of art;
· its current location;
· a relevant quotation from the letters of Vincent van Gogh.

The works have been grouped thematically. Within these groups we have differentiated between paintings and drawings, and prints and photographs. Van Gogh's own works have been integrated where they can be linked with those of other artists.

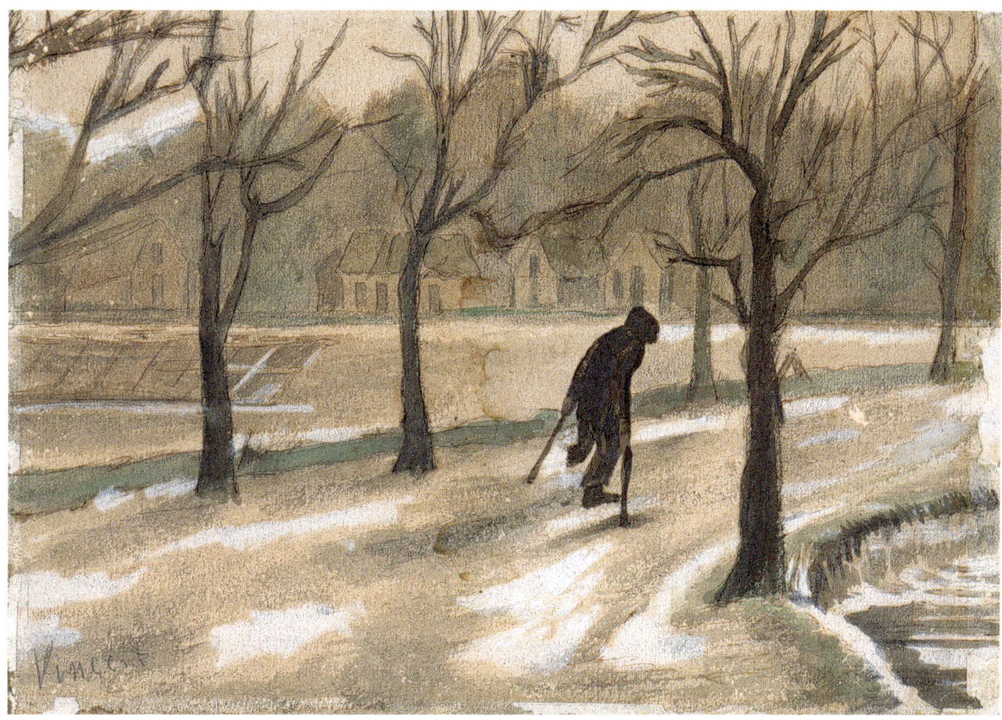

plate 1

Vincent van Gogh (1853-1890)
Winter, in life as well (after Jozef Israëls), c. 1877
Private collection

'I will tell you what they are, so that you will know what it looks like now
and what I have hanging up. [...] Israëls, a poor man on a snowy winter
road' [114/95].

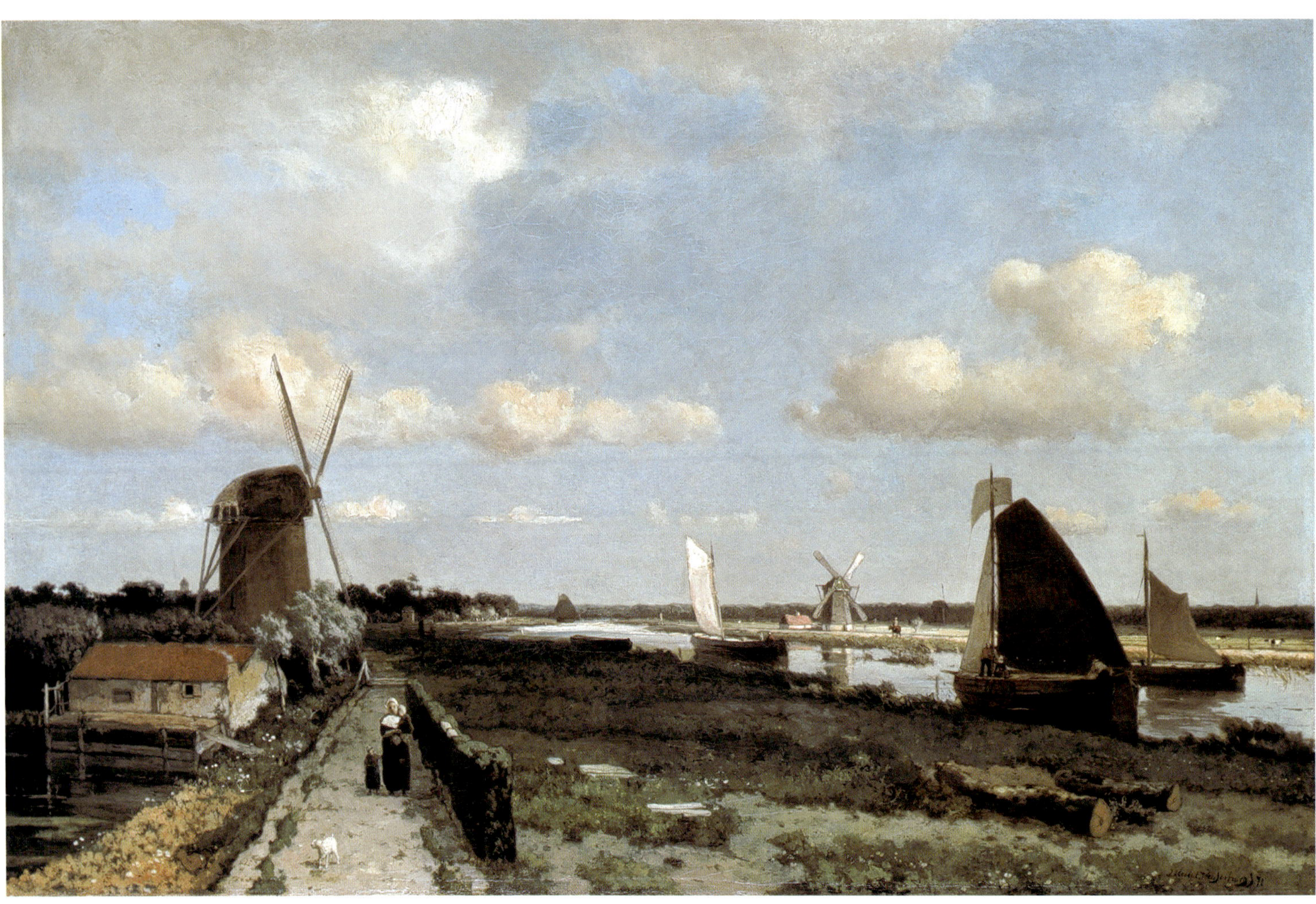

plate 2

Johan Hendrik Weissenbruch (1824-1903)
View of the Trekvliet, 1870
The Hague, Gemeentemuseum

'How much I should like to have you here, what pleasant days we spent together in The Hague. I still think so often of our walk on the Rijswijk road, where we drank milk at the mill after the rain. If those paintings we have from you are to be sent back, I'll send you a portrait of that mill by Weissenbruch. Perhaps you remember, the "merry and wise" is his nickname, "I say, superrrb." That Rijswijk road holds memories for me which are perhaps the most delightful I have' [11/10].

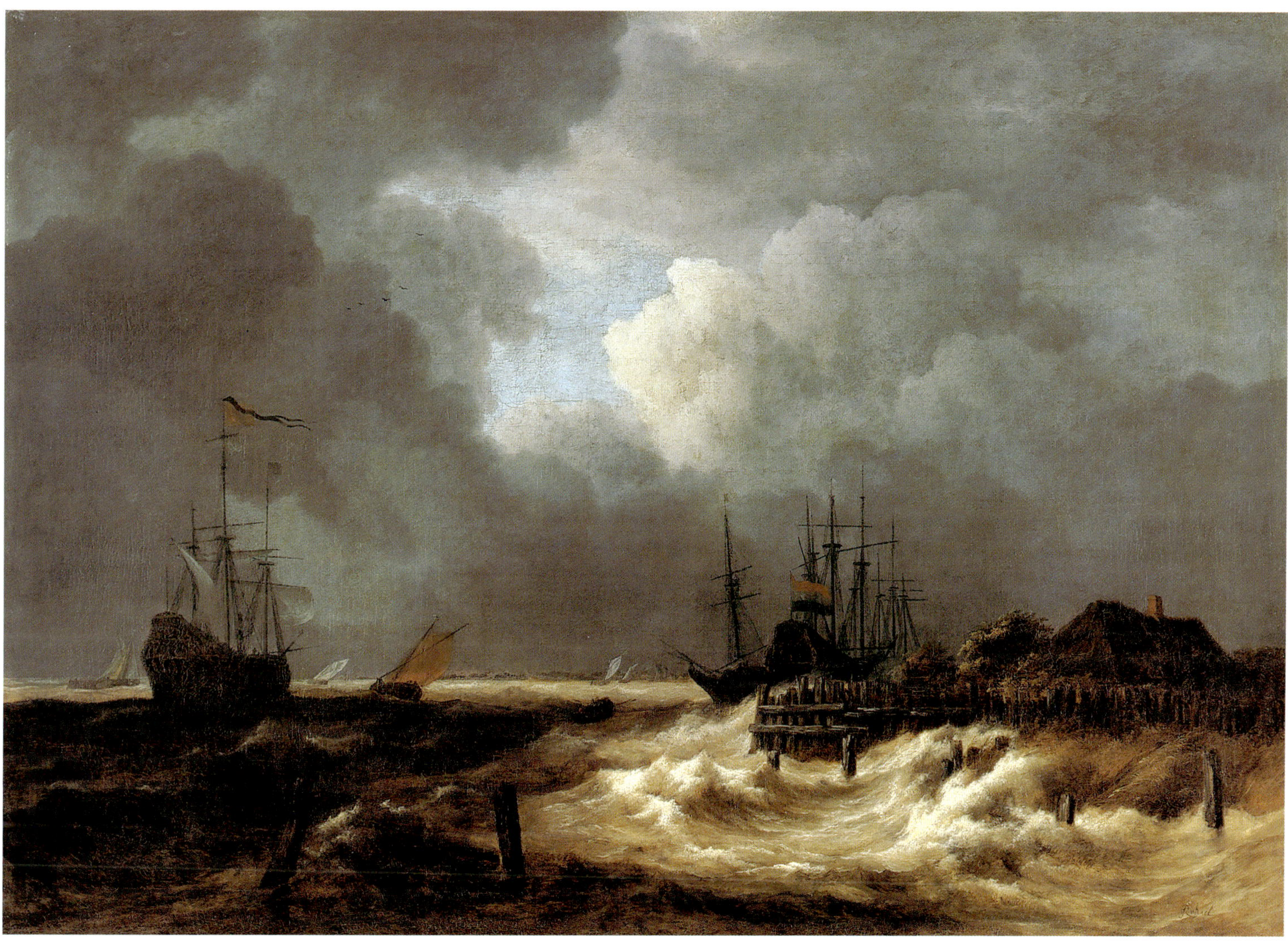

plate 3

Jacob van Ruisdael (1628/29-1682)
The storm, c. 1660
Paris, Musée du Louvre

'I know, Ruisdael himself has also had his metamorphoses, and perhaps his
most beautiful works are not the waterfalls and the grand forest views but
L'estacade aux eaux rousses and *Le buisson* in the Louvre, the Mills in the
Van der Hoop Collection, the bleacheries at Overveen in the Mauritshuis
here, and other more commonplace things which he turned to in later
years, probably under the influence of Rembrandt and Vermeer of Delft'
[327/R30].

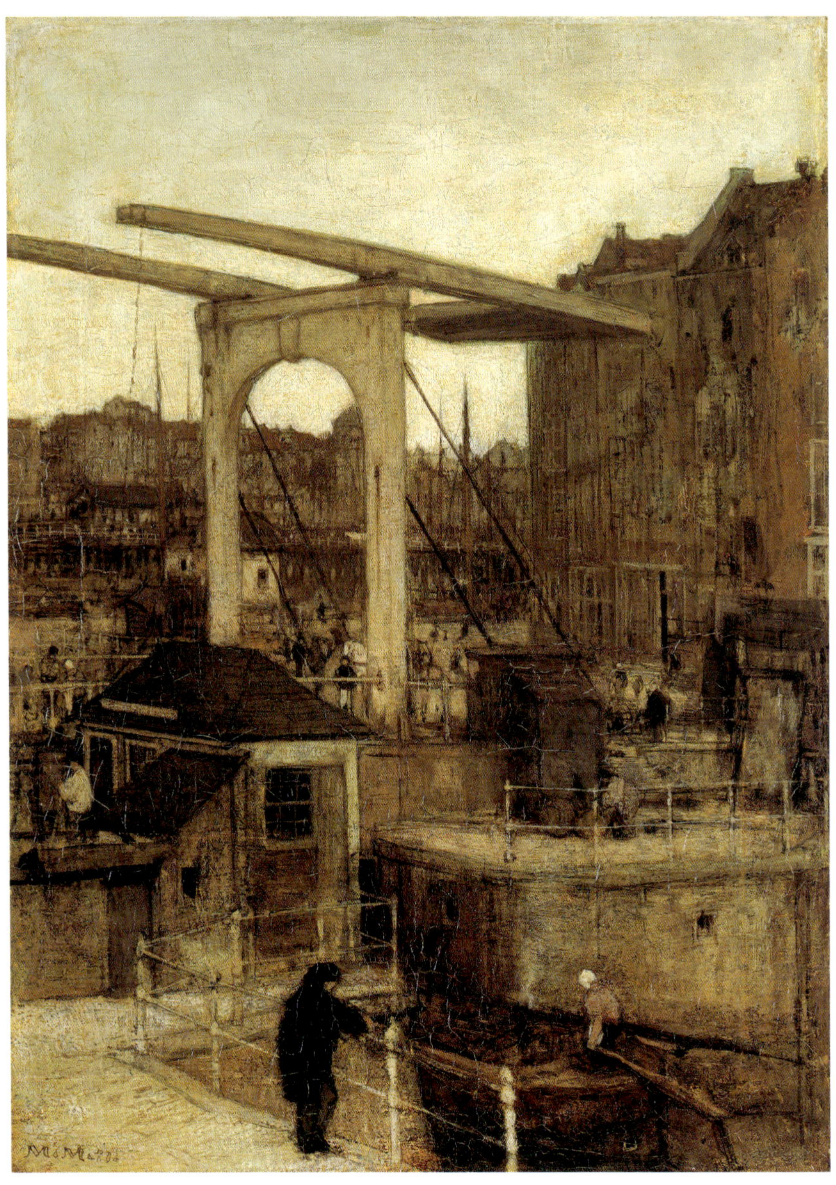

plate 4

Matthijs Maris (1839-1917)

The Nieuwe Haarlemse Sluis on the Singel, called 'Souvenir d'Amsterdam', 1871
Amsterdam, Rijksmuseum

'Some time ago I saw a painting by Thijs Maris, which reminded me of it. An
old Dutch town with rows of brownish red houses with step-gables and tall
flights of stairs, grey roofs, and white or yellow doors, window-frames and
cornices; canals with ships and a large white drawbridge, a barge with a man
at the tiller going under it. The little house of the bridge-keeper, whom one
sees through the window, sitting in his office. A way further on, a stone
bridge over the canal, with people and a cart with white horses crossing
it. And everywhere movement, a porter with his wheelbarrow, a man leaning against the railing, gazing into the water, women in black with white
caps. The foreground a quay with paving stones and a black railing. In the
distance a tower rises above the houses. A greyish white sky over everything. It is a small painting, upright. The subject is nearly the same as the
large J. Maris in Amsterdam, which you perhaps know, only this is talent
and the other is genius' [31/24].

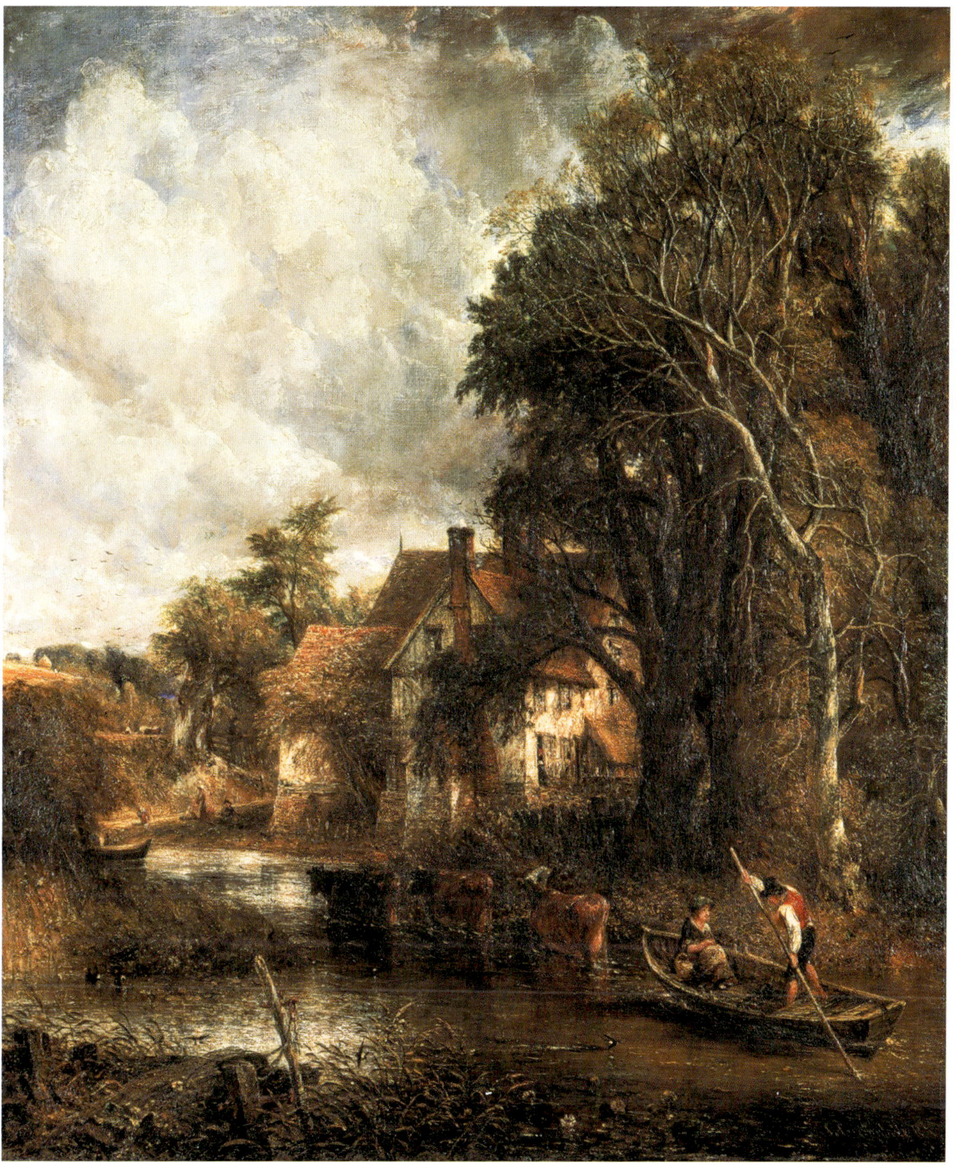

plate 5

John Constable (1776-1837)
The valley farm, 1835
London, Tate Gallery

'Look out for the *Hobbema* in the National Gallery. I am sure you will not
forget to look at a few very beautiful Constables there ("Cornfield"), and
in South Kensington (where that farm is, "Valley farm")' [456/374].

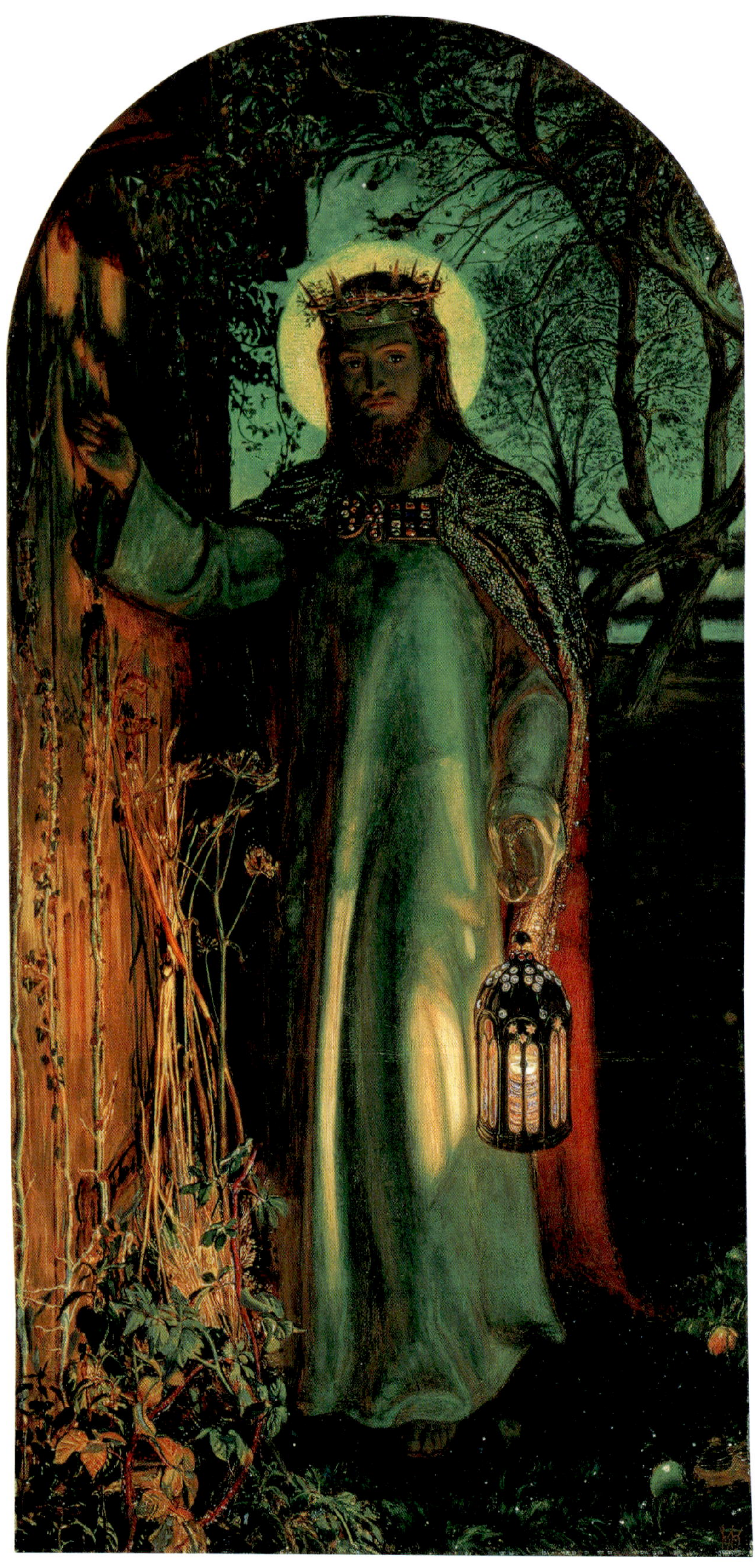

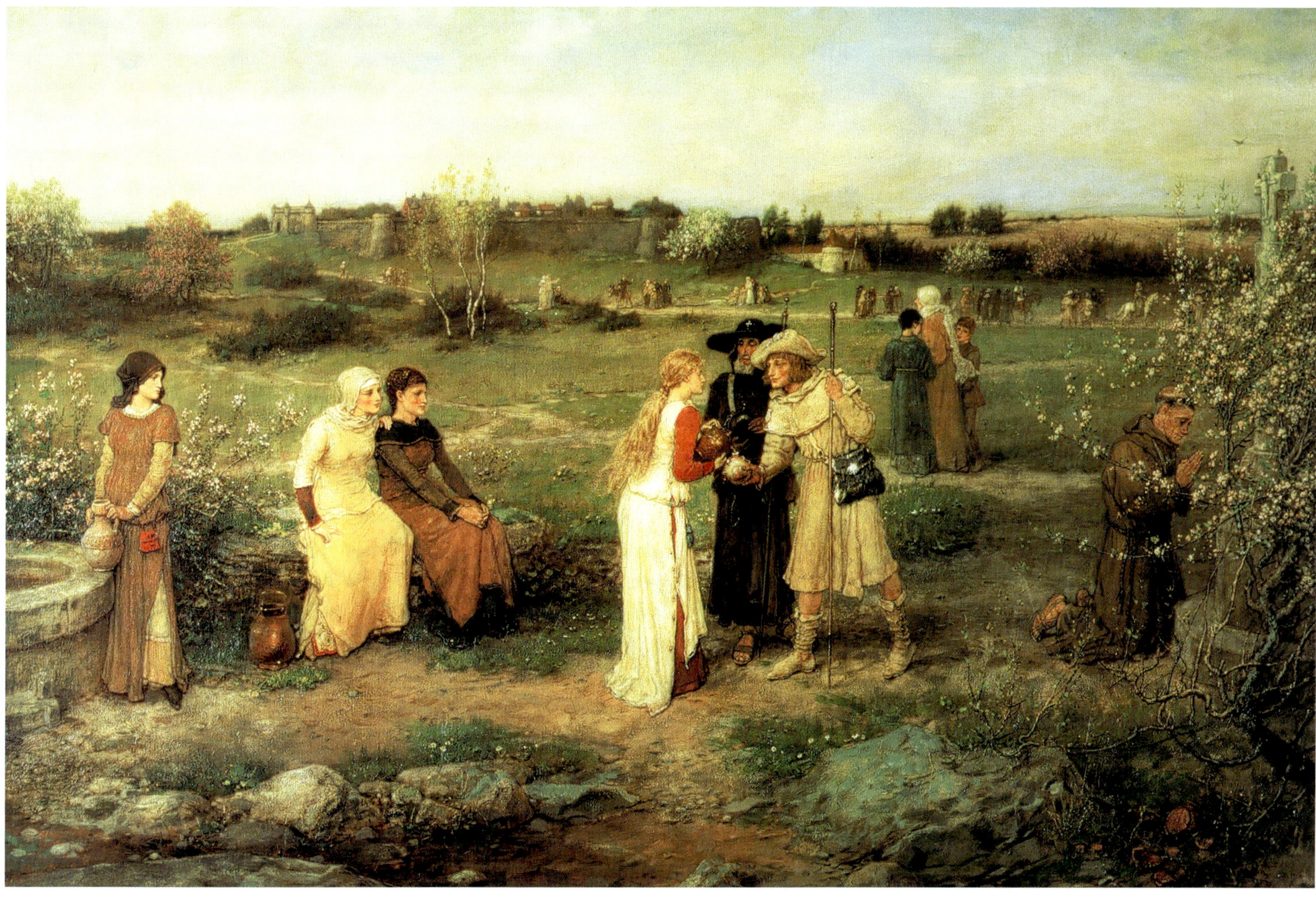

plate 6

William Holman Hunt (1827-1910)
The light of the world, 1851-56
Manchester, City Art Gallery

'What a difficult life the peasants in Brabant have, Aertsen's for instance. Where does their strength come from? And those poor women, what supports them in life? Is it not that image of Christ, the miraculous power of attraction of His name. Is it not what the artist painted in his "Light of the world"?' [108/88].

plate 7

George Henry Boughton (1833-1905)
God speed! Pilgrims setting out to Canterbury, 1874
Amsterdam, Van Gogh Museum

'Did I ever tell you about that painting by Boughton, "The pilgrim's progress"? It is towards evening. A sandy path leads over the hills to a mountain on which one can see the Holy City lit by the sun setting red behind the grey evening clouds. On the path, a pilgrim on his way to the city. He is already tired, and asks a woman in black, who is standing on the path and whose name is "Sorrowful, yet always rejoicing":
    Does the road go uphill then all the way?
    "Yes to the very end."
    And will the journey take all day long?
    "From morn till night, my friend"' [88/74].

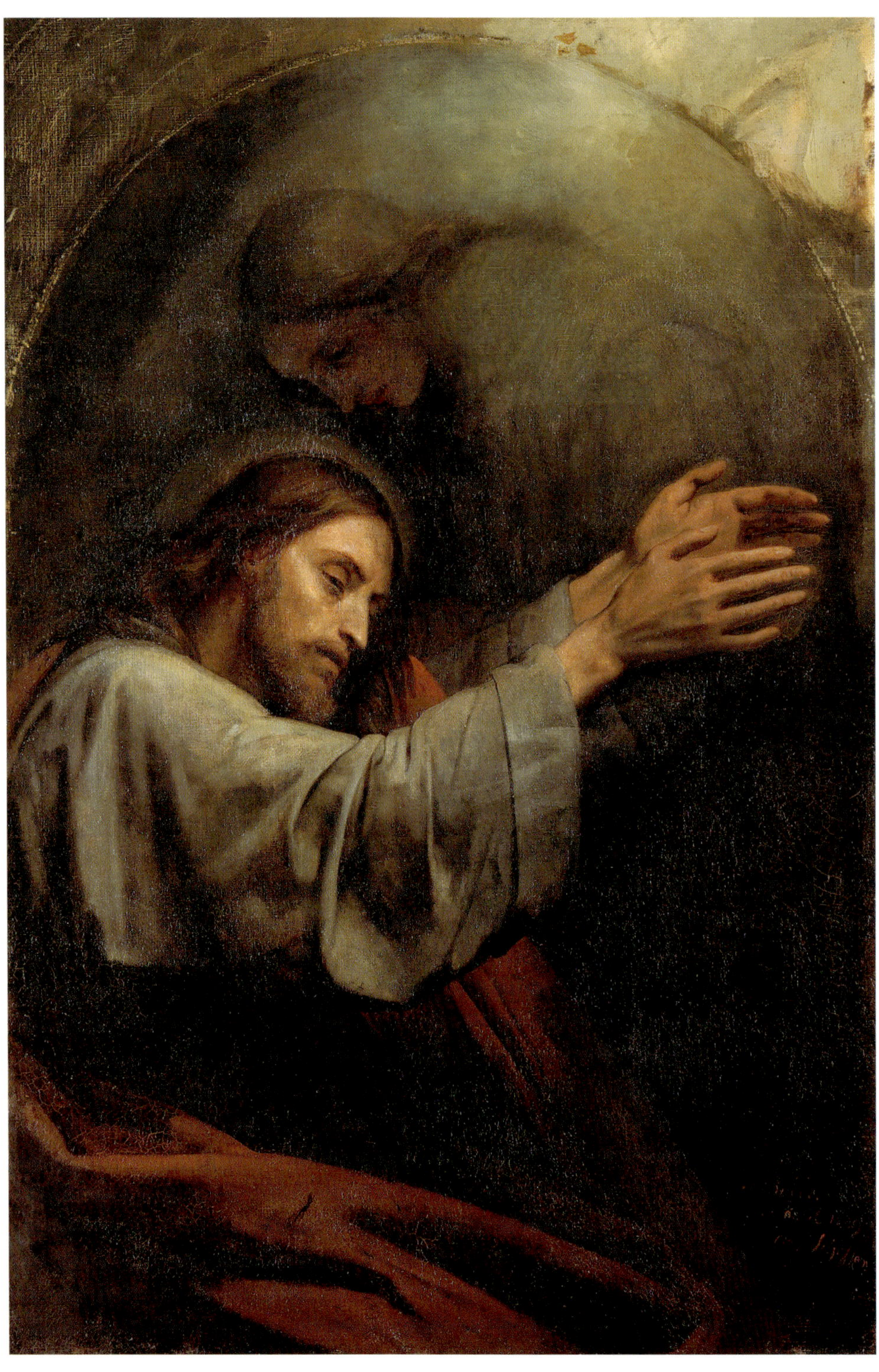

plate 8

Ary Scheffer (1795-1858)
The agony in the garden, 1839
Dordrechts Museum

'The two prints Christus Consolator that you gave me are hanging in my room. Saw the painting in the museum, as well as Scheffer's "Christ in Gethsemane", which is unforgettable. Long ago that painting struck Pa the same way' [101/84].

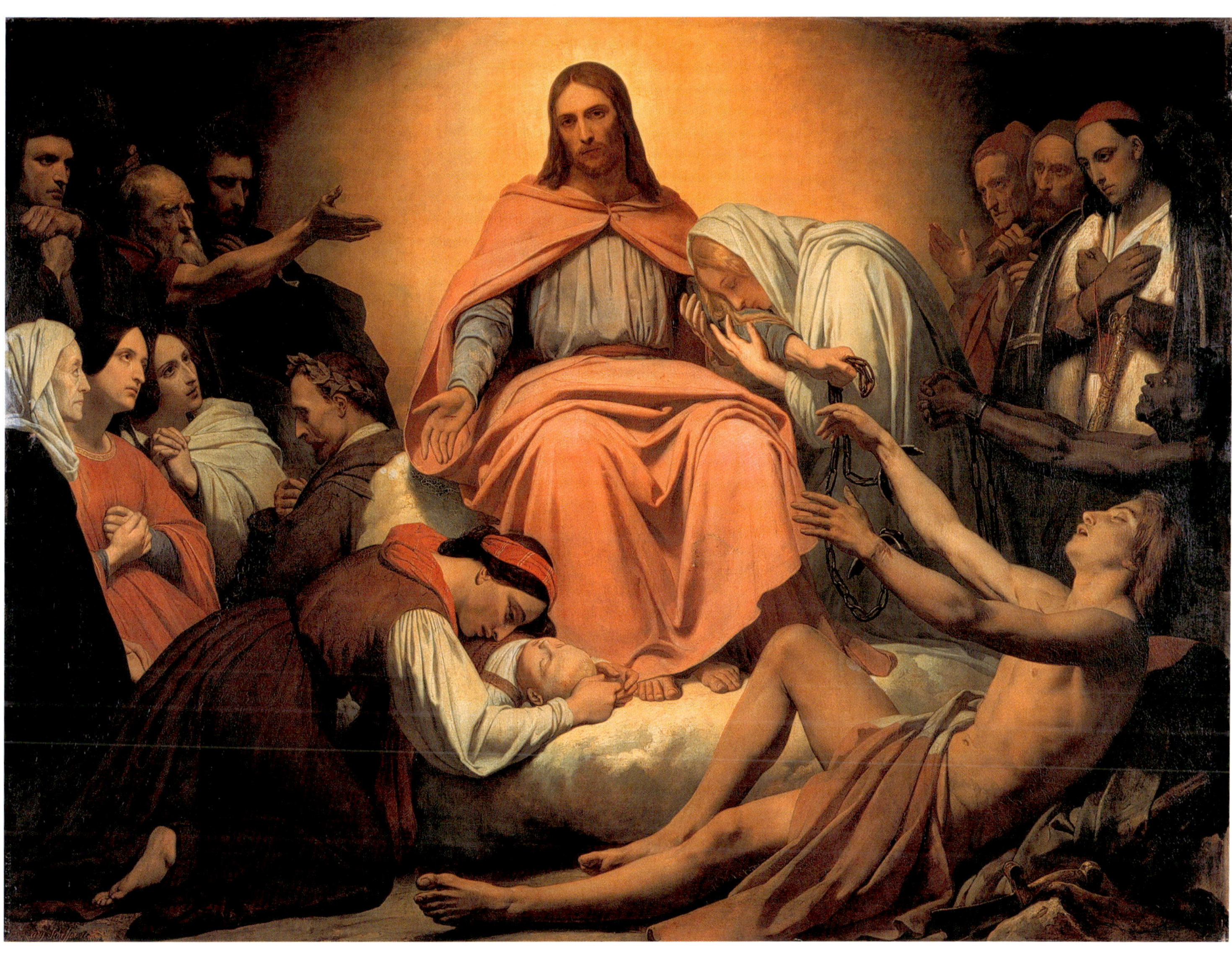

plate 9

Ary Scheffer (1795-1858)
Christus consolator, 1837
Amsterdams Historisch Museum (on loan to the Van Gogh Museum, Amsterdam)

'That book by Thomas a Kempis is as beautiful as, for instance, Ary Scheffer's "Consolator" – it can be compared to nothing else' [318/267].

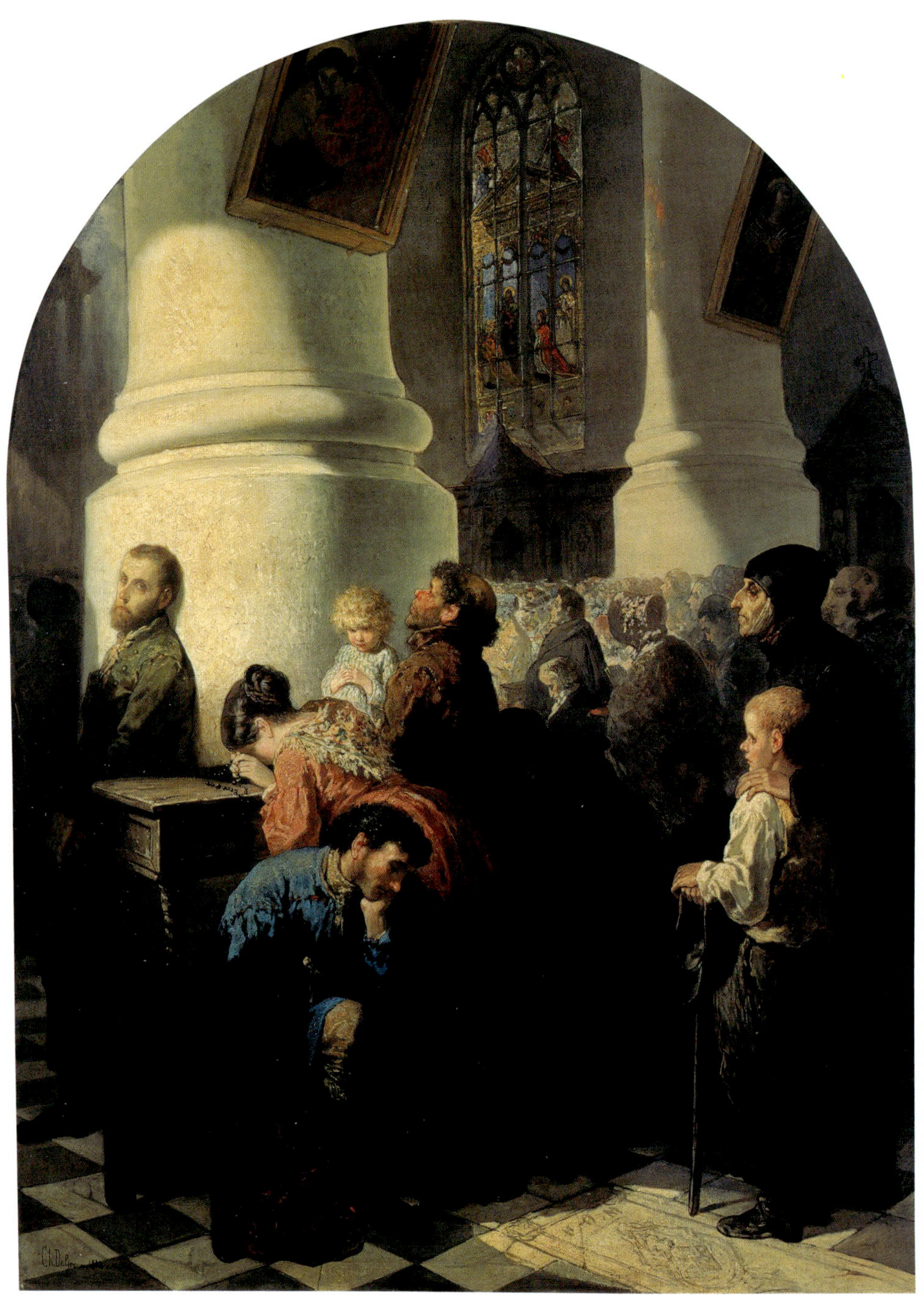

plate 10

Charles De Groux (1825-1870)
The paupers' pew, 1854
Brussels, Musées royaux des Beaux-Arts de Belgique

'As to the drivers themselves with their filthy dirty clothes, they seemed
sunk and rooted still deeper in poverty than that long row or rather that
group of paupers, that Master Degroux has drawn in his "Bench of the
poor". Write and tell me whether you know that print. Some time I would
really like to talk to the men of the rubbish carts, if they would just be
prepared to come and sit on the bench of the poor and felt it worth coming to hear about the Gospel, which is also the portion of the poor'
[147/126].

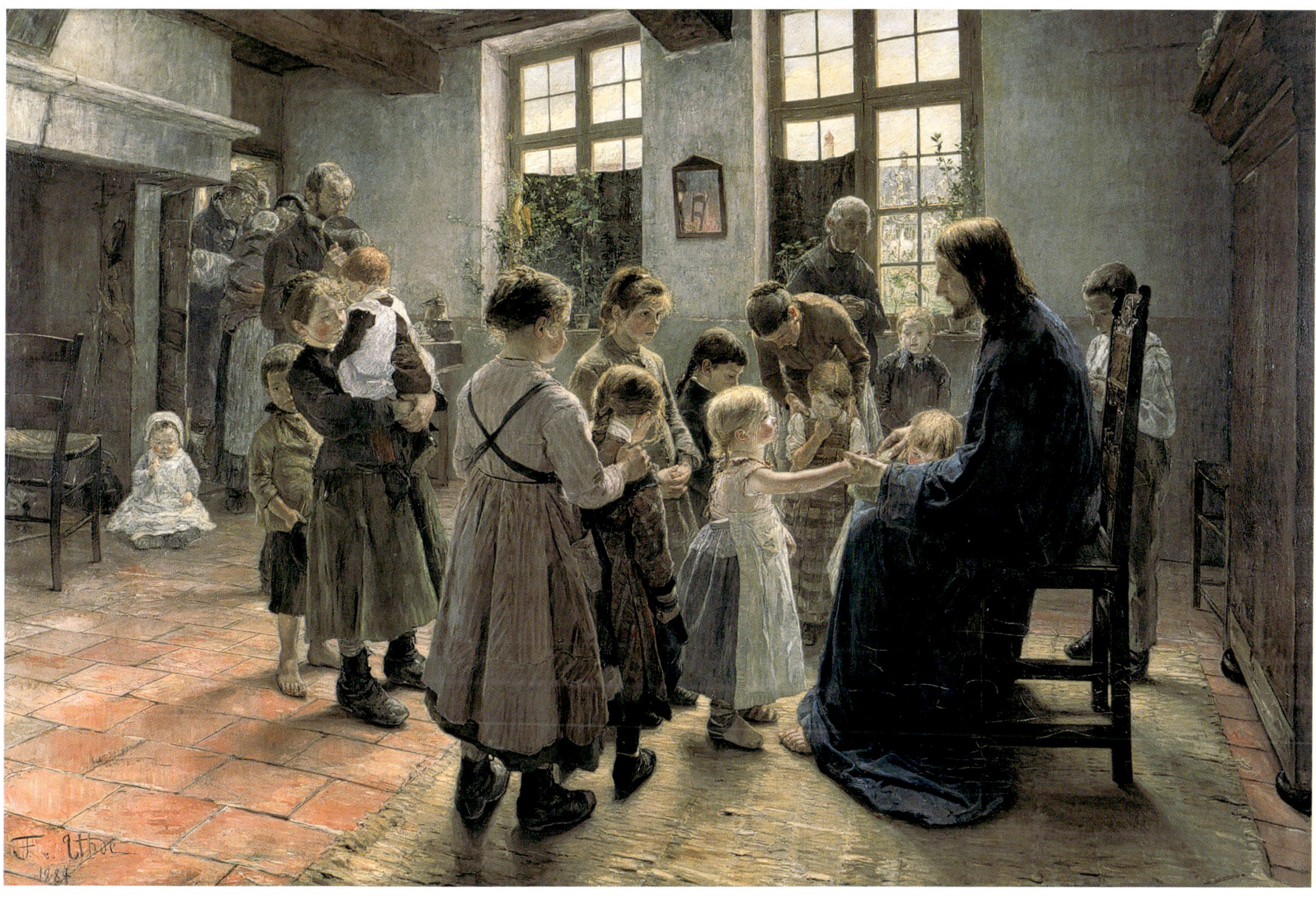

plate 11

Fritz von Uhde (1848-1911)
Suffer little children to come unto me, 1884
Leipzig, Museum der bildenden Künste

'Because I forgot to say something of *Uhde's* painting, "Suffer little children to come unto me." Yes, I do find it beautiful, but it isn't new. And I find interiors in a bright tone with peasant children, *without* a mystic figure of Christ, as with Israëls, as with Artz, more beautiful than this one, where one gets a mystic Christ into the bargain. The character of the children is very well done' [514/414].

plate 12

Camille Corot (1796-1875)
The agony in the garden, 1849
Langres, Musée d'art et d'histoire

'Corot did do a Mount of Olives, with Christ and the evening star, sublime.
In his work you can feel Homer, Aeschylus, Sophocles and sometimes the
Gospels as well, but so discreetly and always taking account of all the
modern feelings that all of us share' [824/B21].

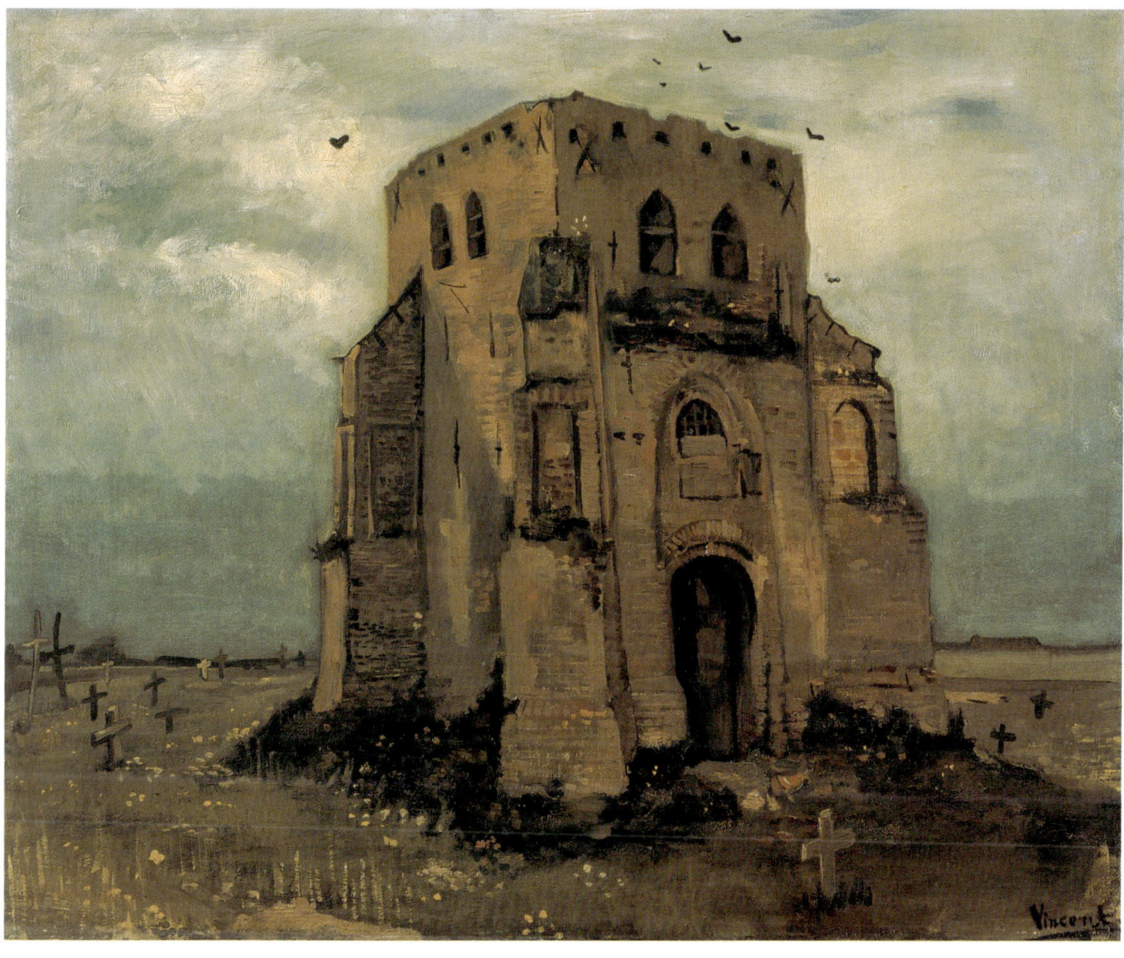

plate 13

Vincent van Gogh (1853-1890)
The old church tower at Nuenen, 'The peasants' churchyard' (F 84 JH 772), 1885
Amsterdam, Van Gogh Museum (Vincent van Gogh Foundation)

'Today I sent off the small box in question, containing, except what I have already mentioned, another picture, *Cimitière de paysans*. I have omitted some details – I wanted to express how that ruin shows that *for ages* the peasants have been laid to rest in the very fields which they dug up when alive – I wanted to express what a simple thing death and burial is, just as simple as the falling of an autumn leaf – just a bit of earth dug up – a small wooden cross. The fields around, where the grass of the churchyard ends, beyond the little wall, form a last line against the horizon – like the horizon of the sea. And now that ruin tells me how a faith and a religion mouldered away – strongly founded though they were – but how the life and the death of the peasants remain forever the same, budding and withering regularly, like the grass and the flowers growing there in that churchyard. "Les religions passent, Dieu demeure" [Religions pass away, God remains], is a saying of Victor Hugo's, whom they also laid to rest recently' [510/411].

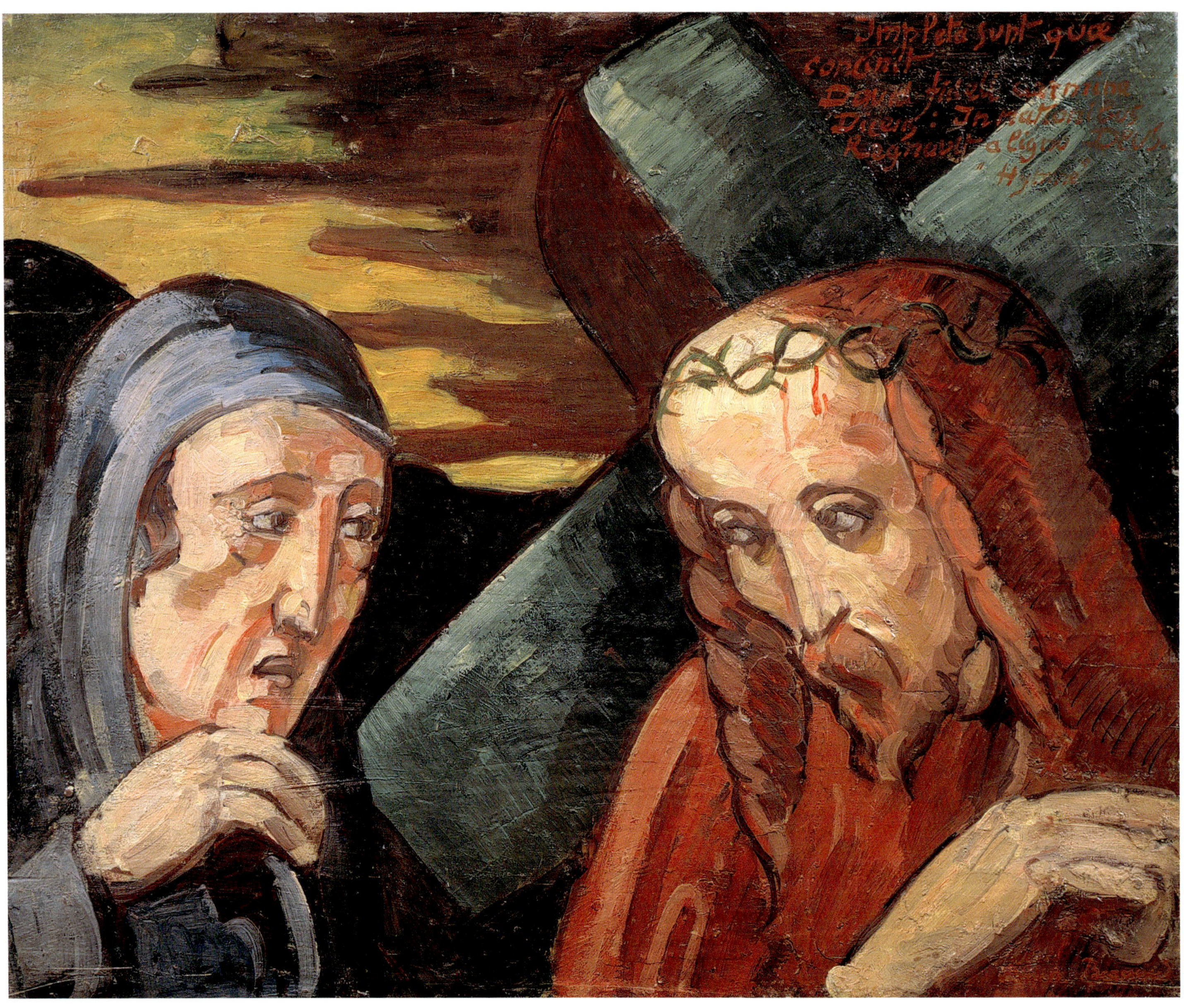

plate 14

Emile Bernard (1868-1941)
The road to Calvary, 1889
Private collection

'You ask me who Bernard is – he is a young painter – certainly no older
than twenty – very original. He is trying to do elegant modern figures in
the manner of the ancient Greek and Egyptian art. [...] He just sent me
6 photographs of paintings he has done this year, and by way of contrast
they are bizarre biblical subjects, and highly debatable – but by this you
see that he is an original, a seeker who tries everything. They are like
medieval tapestry, stiff and very coloured figures' [829/W16].

plate 15

Vincent van Gogh (1853-1890)
Olive grove (F 707 JH 1857), 1889
Amsterdam, Van Gogh Museum (Vincent van Gogh Foundation)

'The paints reached me at the right moment, because what I had brought
back from Arles was almost exhausted. The thing is that this month I have
been working in the olive groves, because they made me mad with their
Christs in the Garden, in which nothing is observed. Of course with me
there is no question of doing anything from the Bible – and I have written
to Bernard and Gauguin too that I considered that our duty is to think,
not to dream, so that when looking at their work I was astonished at their
letting themselves go like that. For Bernard has sent me photos of his can-

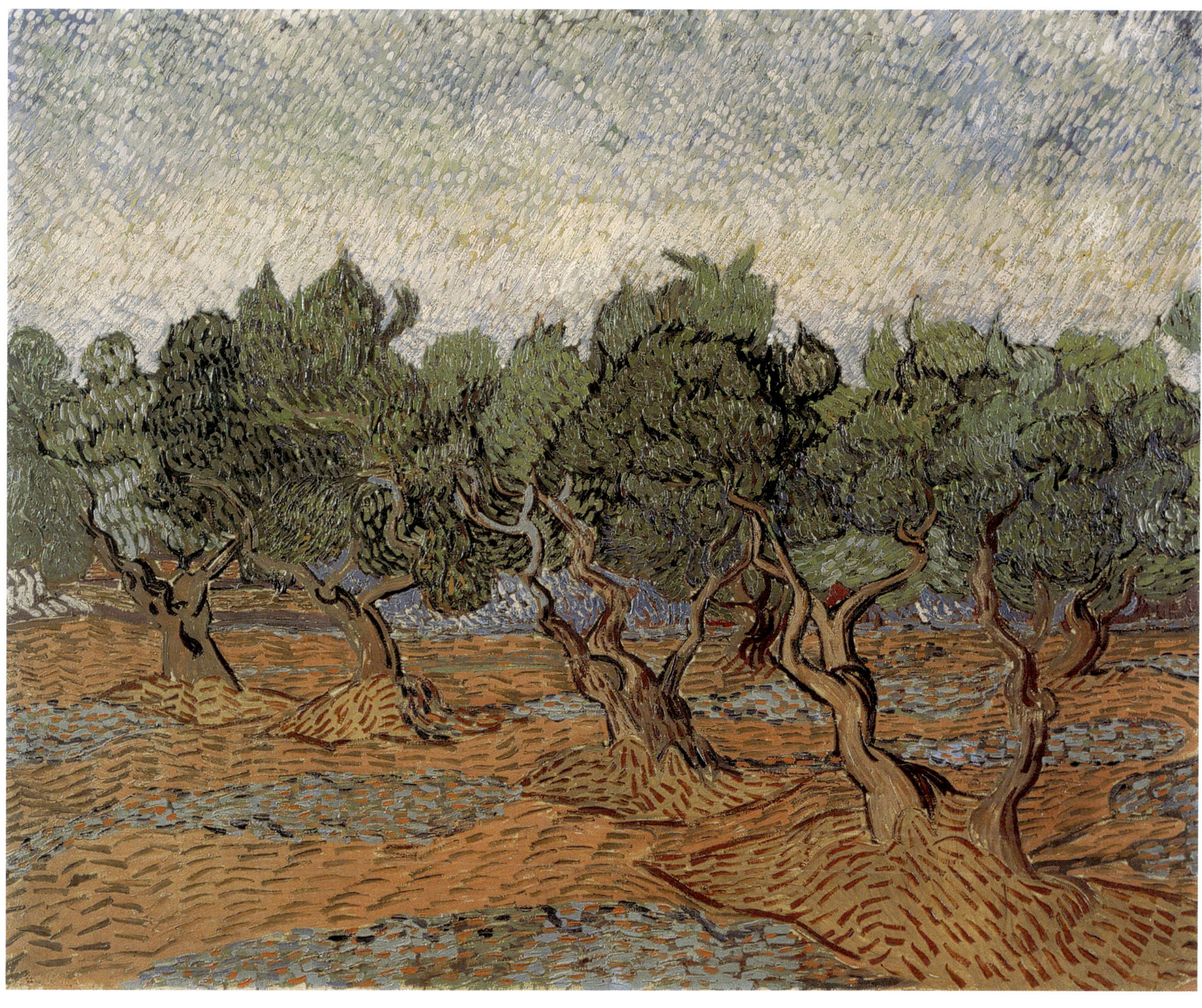

vases. The trouble is that what it has is that they are kinds of dreams or nightmares, that there is erudition – you can see that it is someone who is gone on the primitives – but frankly the English Pre-Raphaelites did it much better, and then Puvis and Delacroix are much healthier than the Pre-Raphaelites. So it is not that it leaves me cold, but it gives me a painful feeling of collapse instead of progress. Well, to shake that off, morning and evening these bright cold days, but with a very fine, clear sun, I have been knocking about in the groves, and the result is five size 30 canvases, which along with the three studies of olives that you have, at least constitute an attack on the difficulty. The olive is as variable as our willow or pollard willow in the north. You know the willows are very scenic, in spite of their seeming monotonous, they are the trees characteristic of the country.

Now the olive and the cypress have exactly the same importance here as the willow has at home. What I have done is a rather hard and coarse realism beside their abstractions, but it will have a rustic quality, and will smell of the soil of the locality' [825/615].

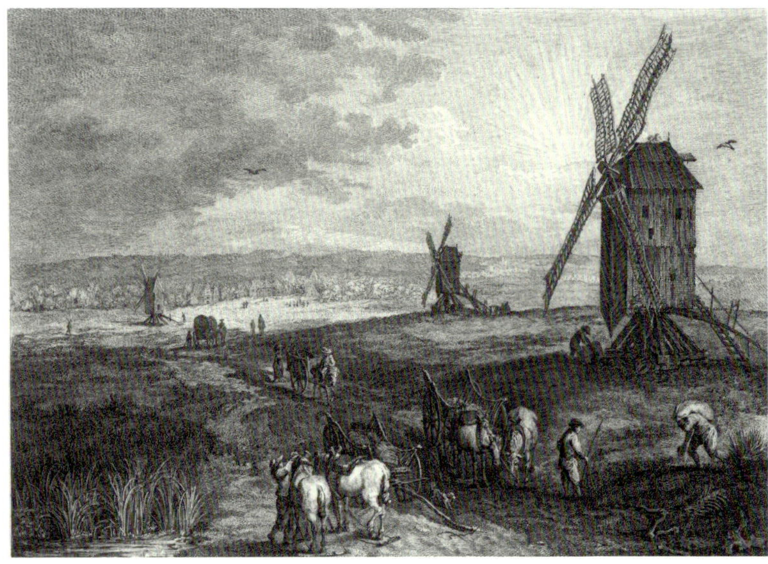

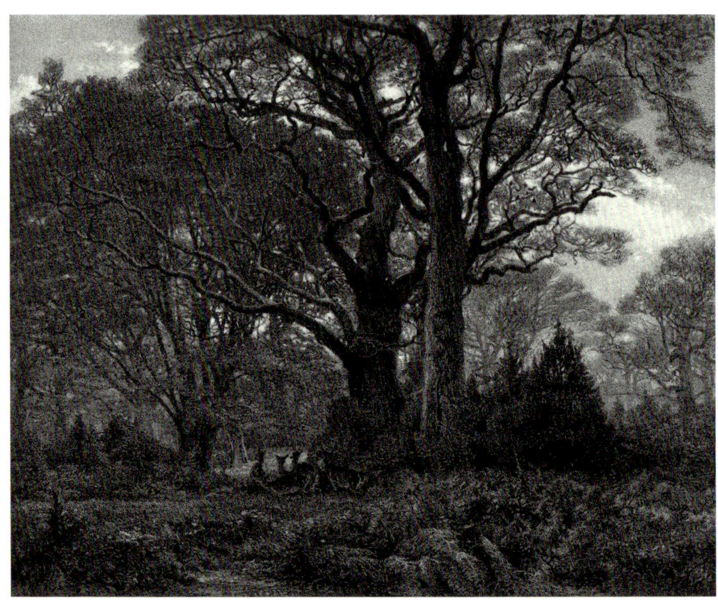

plate 16

After **Jan Brueghel the Elder** (1568-1625)
Three mills, 1772
Amsterdam, Rijksprentenkabinet

'I am very pleased with the two prints you gave me, but you ought to
have accepted that small etching, "The three mills", from me. Now you
have paid for it in full yourself, and not even allowed me to contribute
half as I wished to do. But you must keep it in your album, for it is remarkable, even though the execution is not so very good. In my ignorance,
I would attribute it to Peasant Bruegel rather than to Velvet Brueghel'
[147/126].

plate 17

After **Karl Bodmer** (1809-1893)
The Forest of Fontainebleau, 1859
Paris, Bibliothèque Nationale de France, Cabinet des Estampes

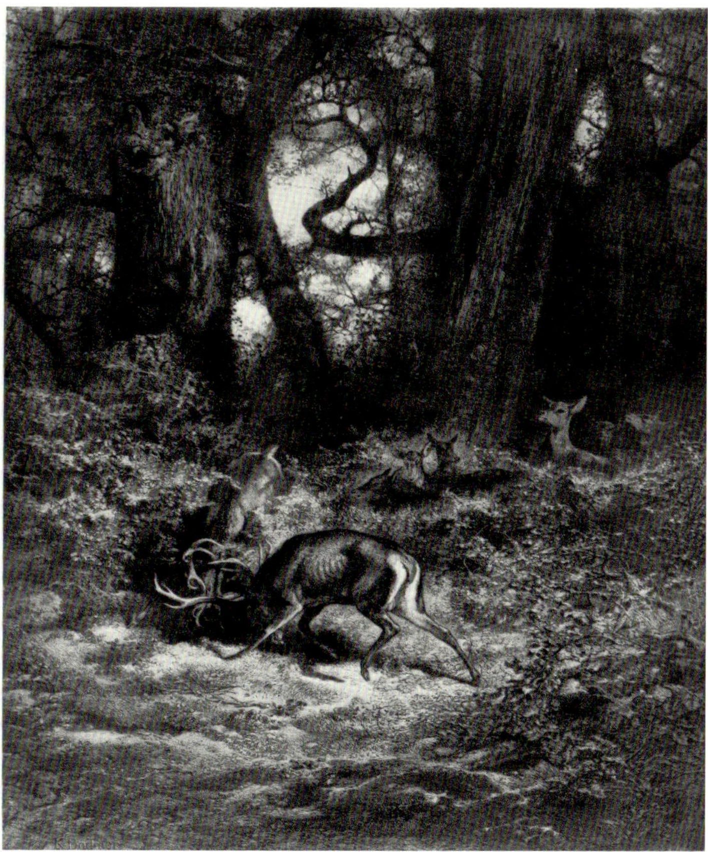

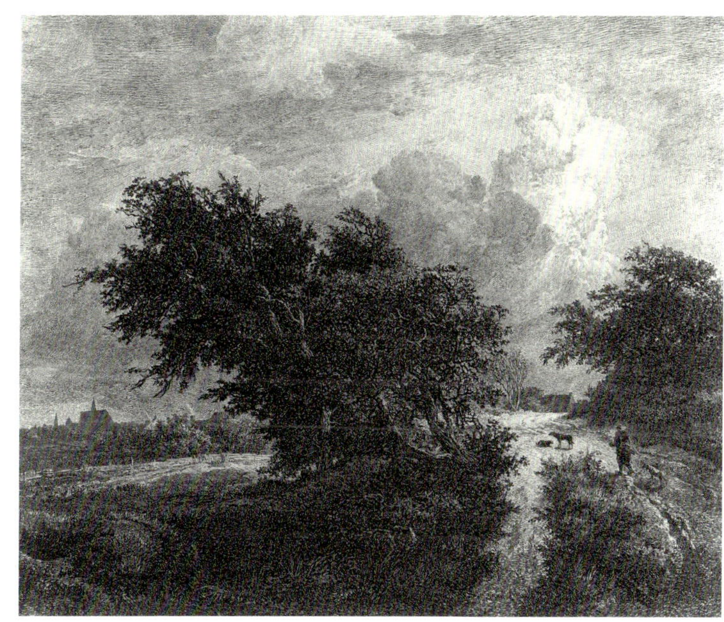

plate 18

After **Karl Bodmer** (1809-1893)
Stags fighting, Forest of Fontainebleau, 1861
Paris, Bibliothèque Nationale de France, Cabinet des Estampes

'Just imagine original drawings with those odd greys and that peculiar rendering of textures. Bodmer has found that, as an artist he is original, and at
the same time he has what one might call the lithographic tones, or rather
the grey colour scale. [...] Bodmer's sheets are prints finished like paintings' [335/277].

plate 19

Charles-François Daubigny (1817-1878) after **Jacob van Ruisdael**
Dune landscape near Haarlem (Le buisson), 1855
Paris, Bibliothèque Nationale de France, Cabinet des Estampes

'In the first crate we send to Holland you'll find [...] an etching by
Daubigny after Ruisdael's "Buisson"' [35/28].

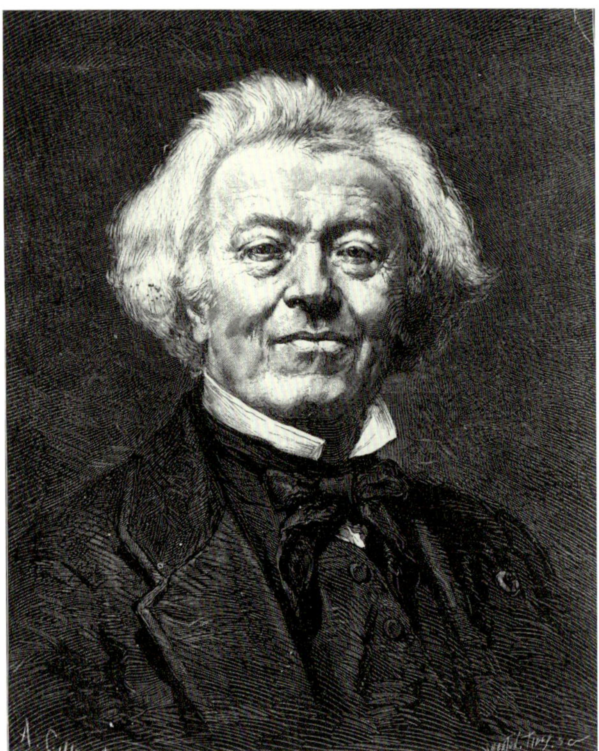

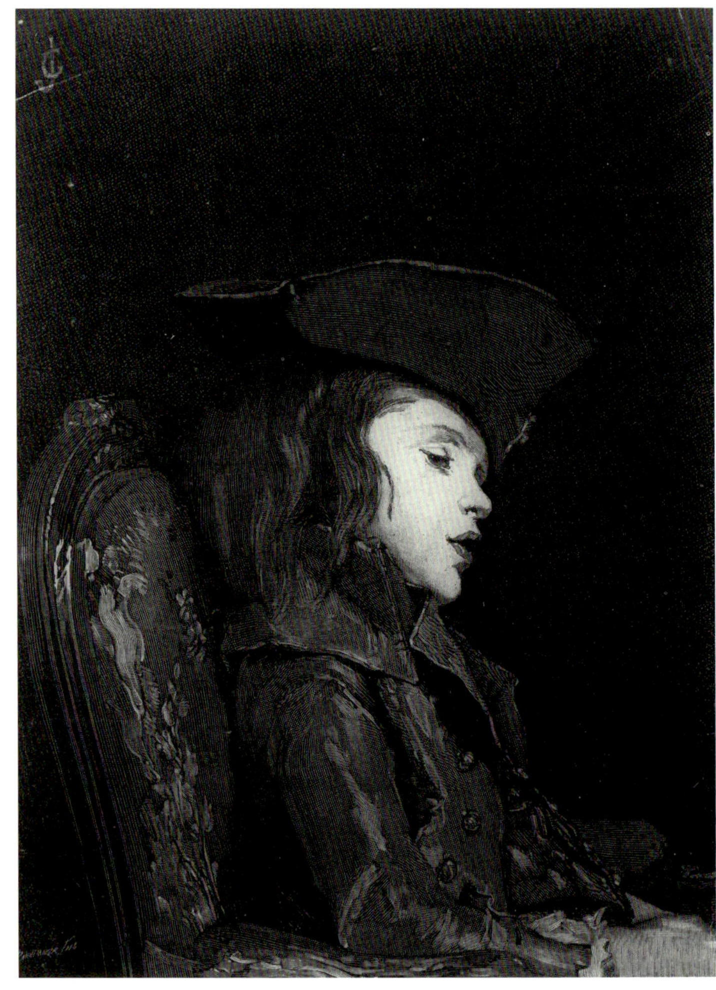

plate 20

After **Achille-Isidore Gilbert** (1828-1899)
The late M. Corot, French painter, 1875
Amsterdam, Van Gogh Museum (Vincent van Gogh Foundation)

'Today, in the crate we'll be sending, I'm enclosing for you [...] a portrait by Corot, from the *London News*, which I also have hanging in my room' [30/23].

plate 21

After **Jules-Adolphe Goupil** (1839-1883)
A young citizen of the Year v, 1878
Amsterdam, Van Gogh Museum (Vincent van Gogh Foundation)

'What a beautiful, excellent wood engraving there was in *L'Illustration* the other day of "A young citizen of the year V" by Jules Goupil – did you see it? I have got hold of it and it is hanging on the wall of the room which is my own now, namely the old schoolroom which looks out on the garden and where the ivy climbs up around the windows' [144/123].

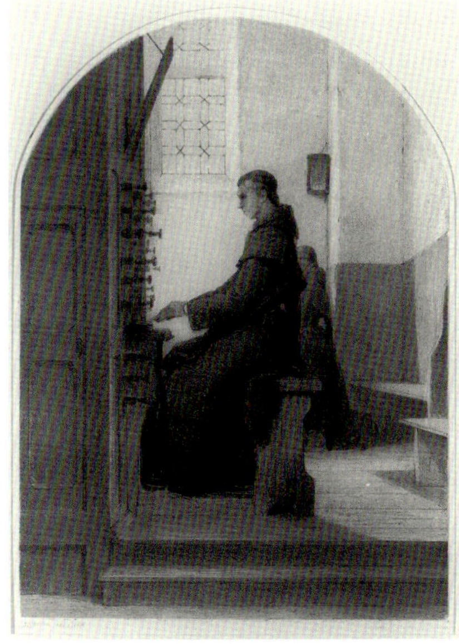

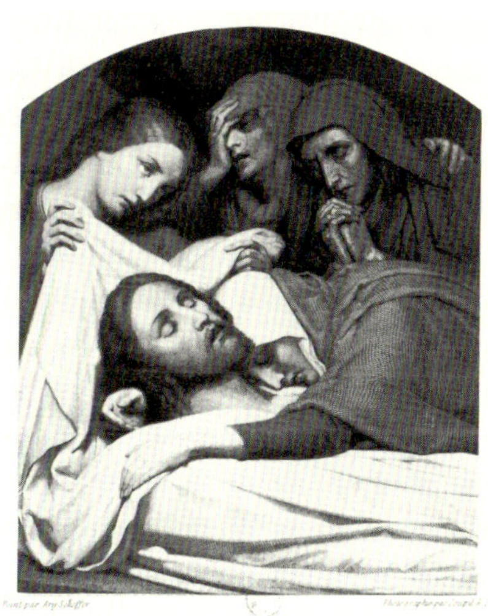

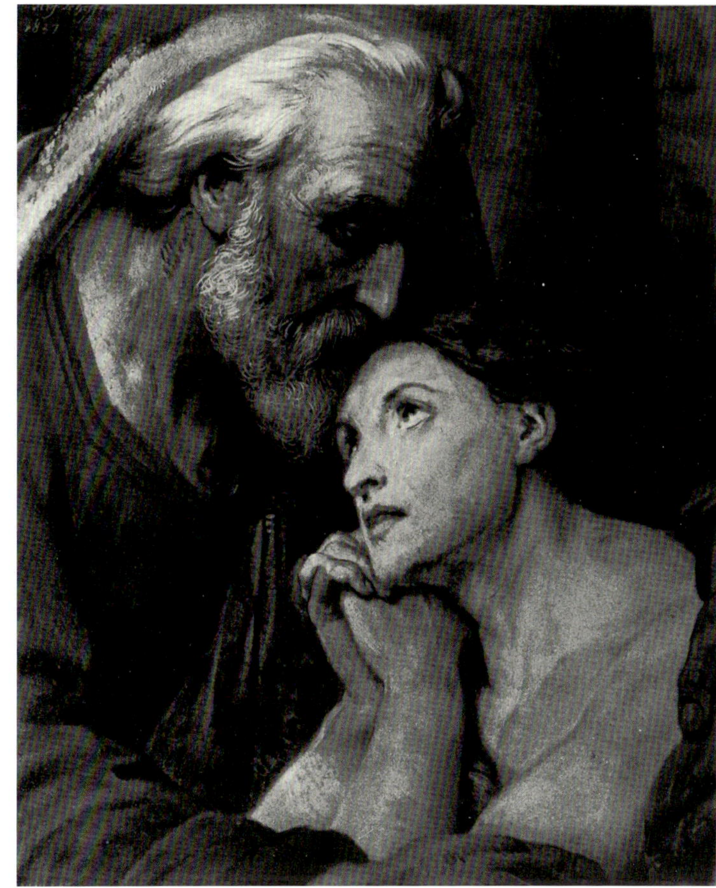

plate 22

Johannes Bosboom (1817-1891)
Carmelite playing the organ: cantabimus et psallemus, c. 1850
Amsterdam, Van Gogh Museum (Vincent van Gogh Foundation)

'In the list of what I have hanging in my room I forgot: [...] Bosboom,
Cantabimus et psallemus' [40/33].

plate 24

After **Ary Scheffer** (1795-1858)
The holy women at the tomb, 1845
Bordeaux, Musée Goupil

'How beautiful that engraving is after Ary Scheffer, "The holy women at
the tomb of Christ", I am so glad I have it, the old woman especially, she is
splendid' [131/111].

plate 23

After **Ary Scheffer** (1795-1858)
The prodigal son, 1857
Bordeaux, Musée Goupil

'If you can manage it, please send Ma a *carte de visite* for her birthday, No.
669 "The prodigal son" by Scheffer' [90/82a].

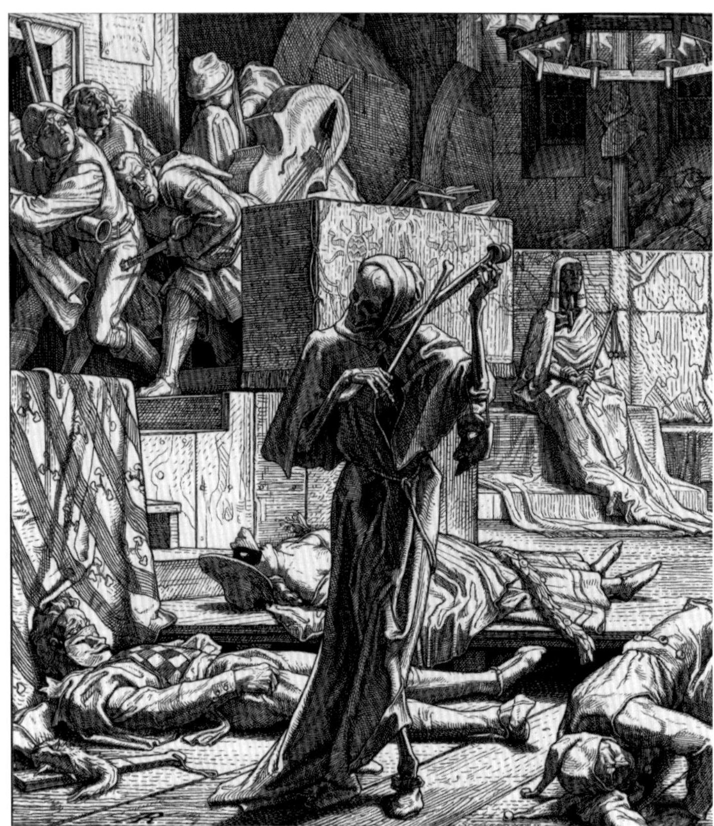

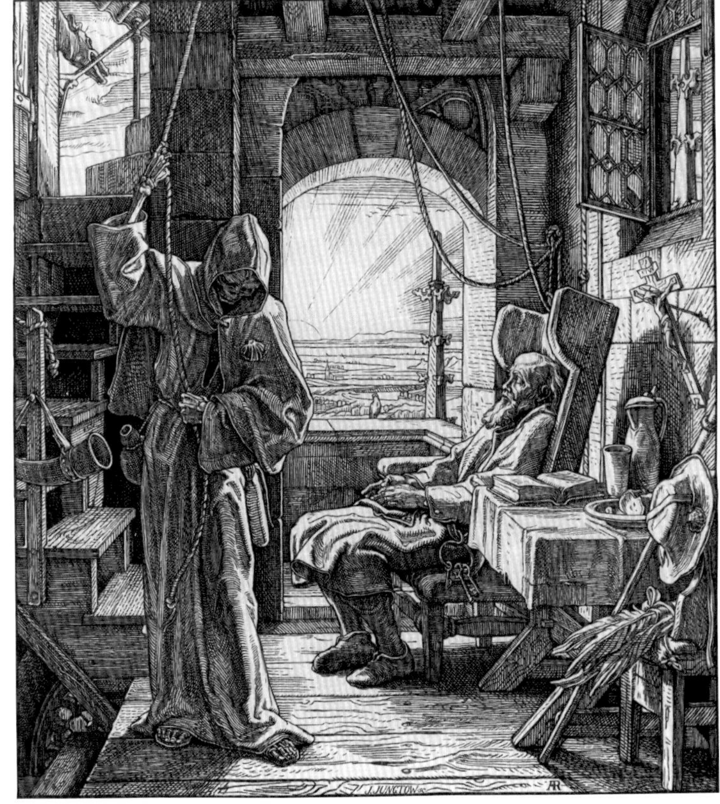

plate 25

After **Alfred Rethel** (1816-1859)
Cholera in Paris (Death as a foe), 1851
Amsterdam, Rijksprentenkabinet

plate 26

After **Alfred Rethel** (1816-1859)
Death as a friend, 1851
Amsterdam, Rijksprentenkabinet

'That sexton automatically reminded me of a woodcut, by Rethel I think, you will know it too – "Death as a friend". That scene has always struck me powerfully; when I was in London one could see it in the windows of almost every print shop. There is a companion piece, "Cholera in Paris", and the "Dance of Death" is also by Rethel' [120/101].

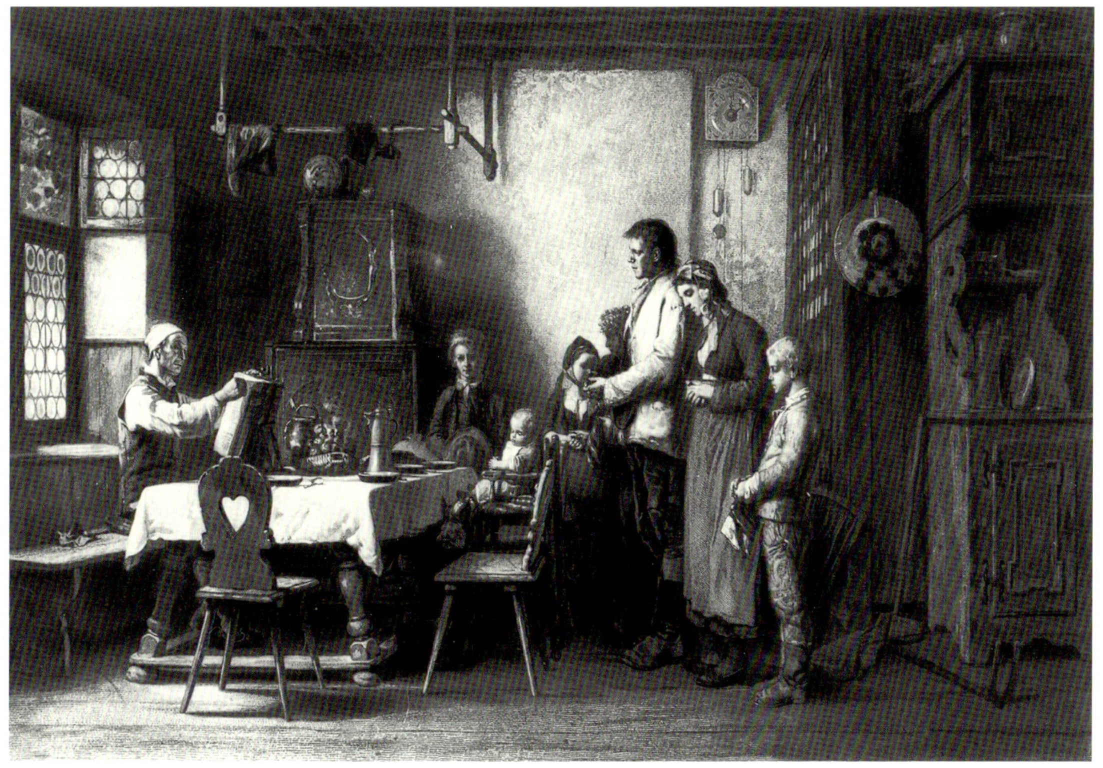

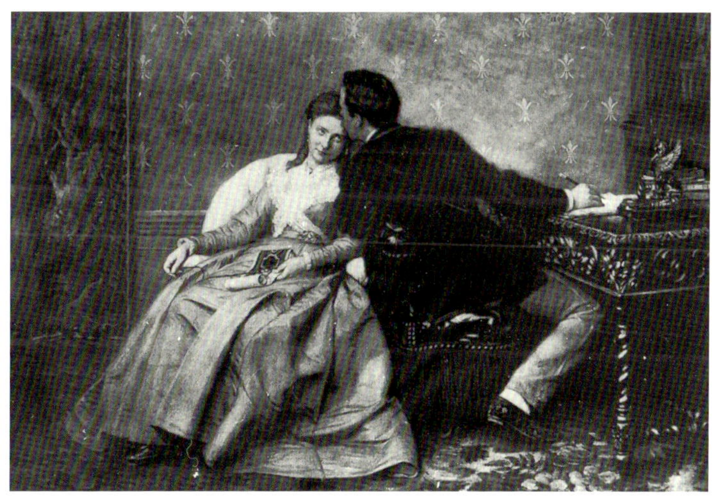

plate 27

After **Gustave Brion** (1824-1877)
Grace before the meal, 1862
Bordeaux, Musée Goupil

'Uncle told me that Daubigny had died. I freely confess that I was down-cast when I heard the news, just as I was when I heard that Brion had died (his Bénédicité hangs in my room), because the work of such men, if it is understood, touches us more deeply than one realises' [141/120].

plate 28

After **Eugène Feyen** (1815-1908)
The honeymoon, 1869
Bordeaux, Musée Goupil

'"The honeymoon" is by Eugène Feyen, one of the few painters who paint intimate modern life as it really is, and does not turn it into fashion plates' [14/11a].

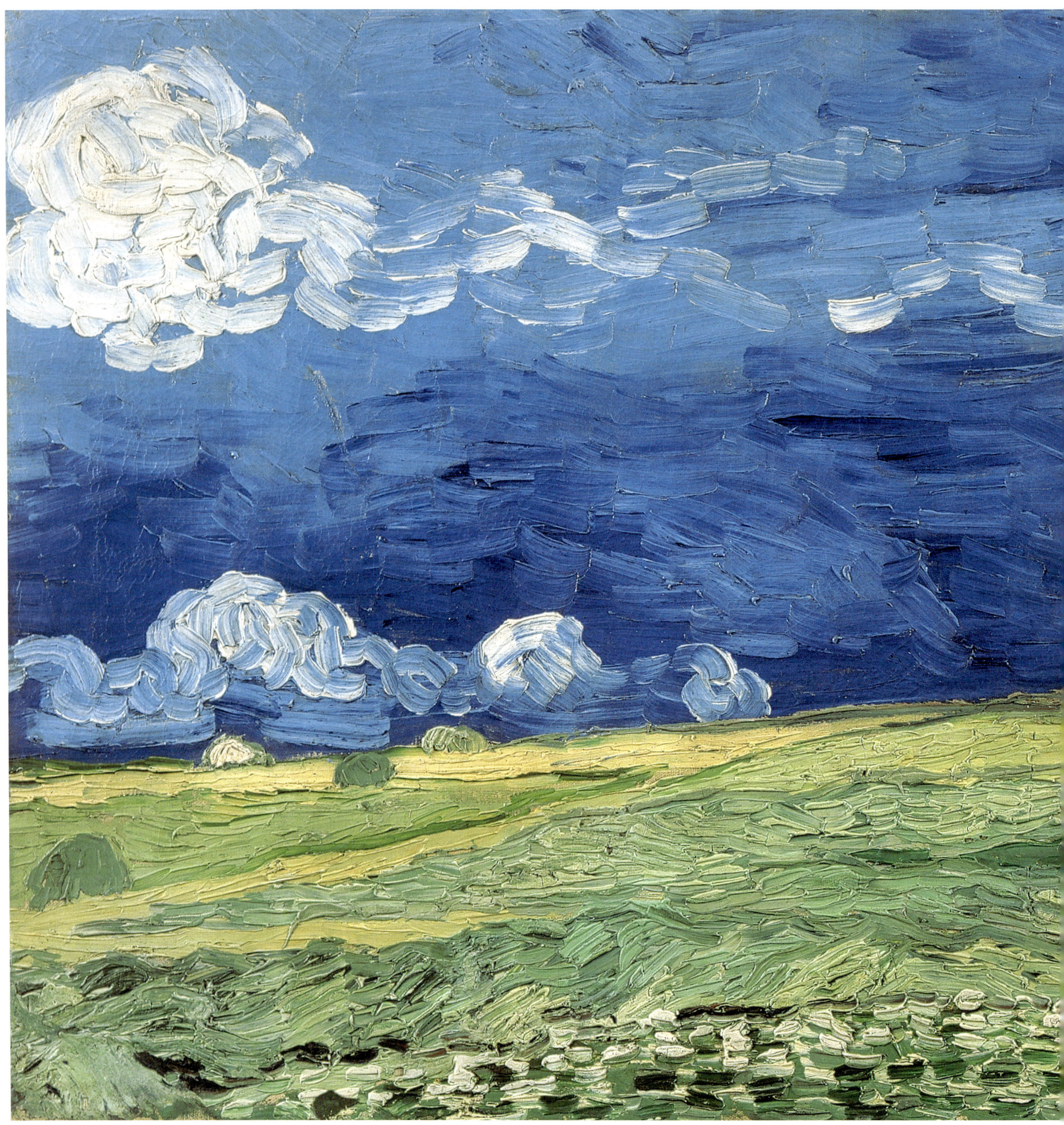

plate 29

Vincent van Gogh (1853-1890)
Wheat field under thunderclouds (F 778 JH 2097), 1890
Amsterdam, Van Gogh Museum (Vincent van Gogh Foundation)

'So – having arrived back here, I have set to work again – although the brush is almost falling from my fingers – and because I knew exactly what I wanted, I have painted three more large canvases. They are vast stretches of corn under troubled skies, and I did not have to go out of my way very

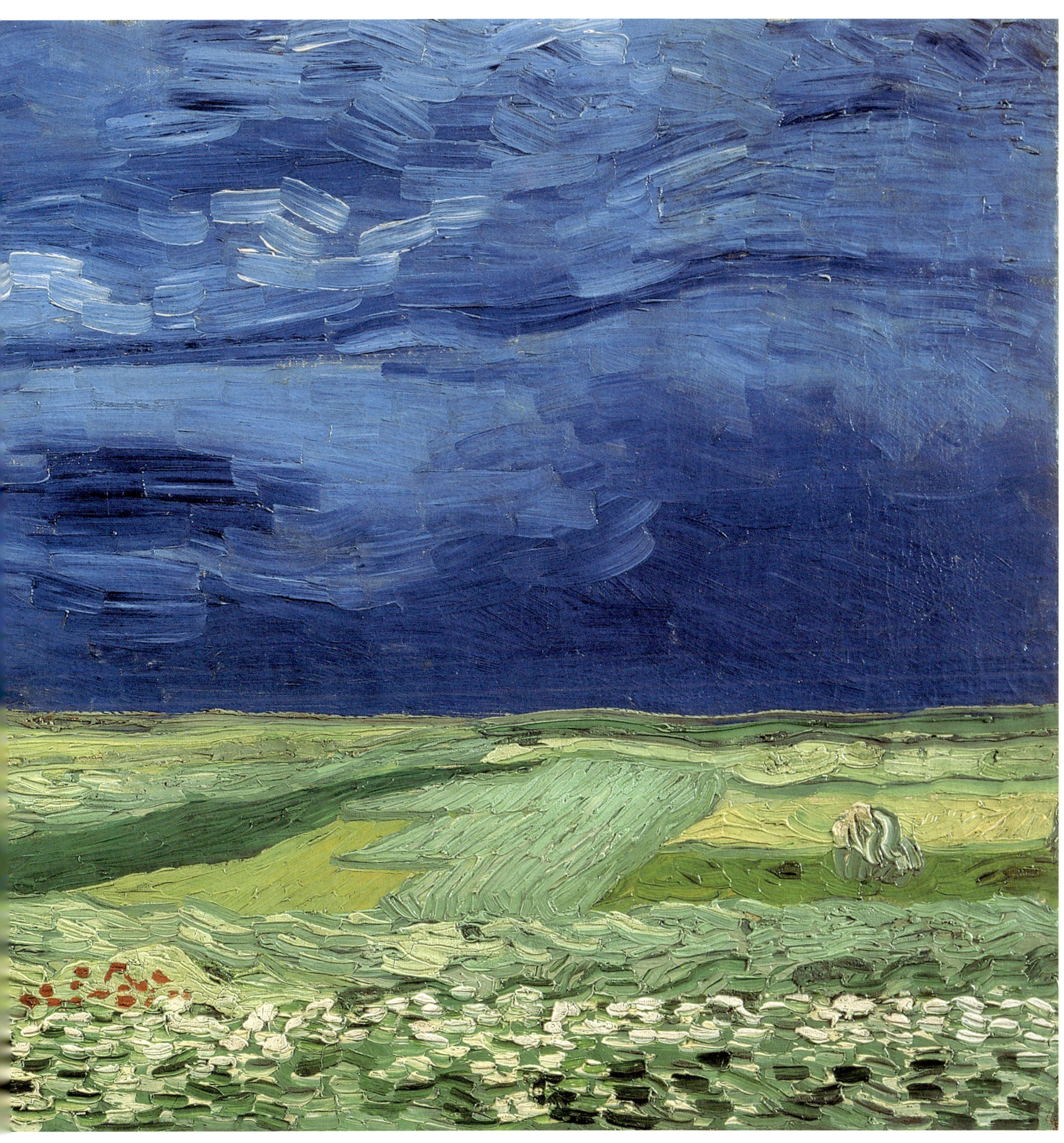

much in order to try to express sadness, extreme loneliness. I hope you
will be seeing them soon, since I hope to bring them to you in Paris as
soon as possible, because I'm fairly sure that these canvases will tell you
what I cannot say in words, that is, how healthy and invigorating I find the
countryside' [903/649].

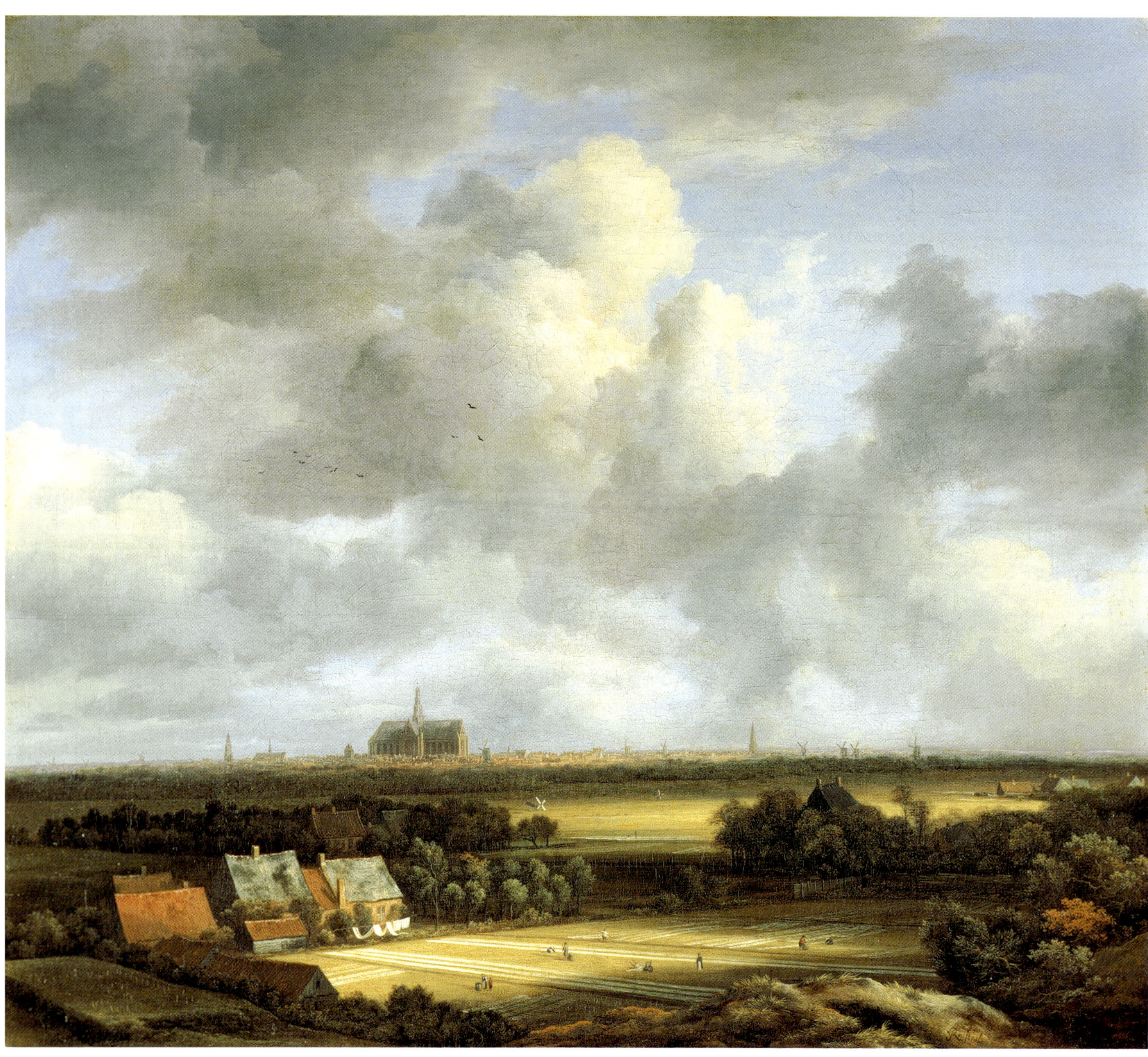

plate 30

Jacob van Ruisdael (1628/29-1682)
View of Haarlem with bleaching grounds
The Hague, Royal Cabinet of Paintings Mauritshuis

'I should so much like to take a few walks with you in this neighbourhood
some time. For undoubtedly you would find a lot of subject matter in
those fish-drying barns at Scheveningen for instance. They are enormously
Ruisdael-like (I mean that painting, the bleacheries at Overveen)' [231/R8].

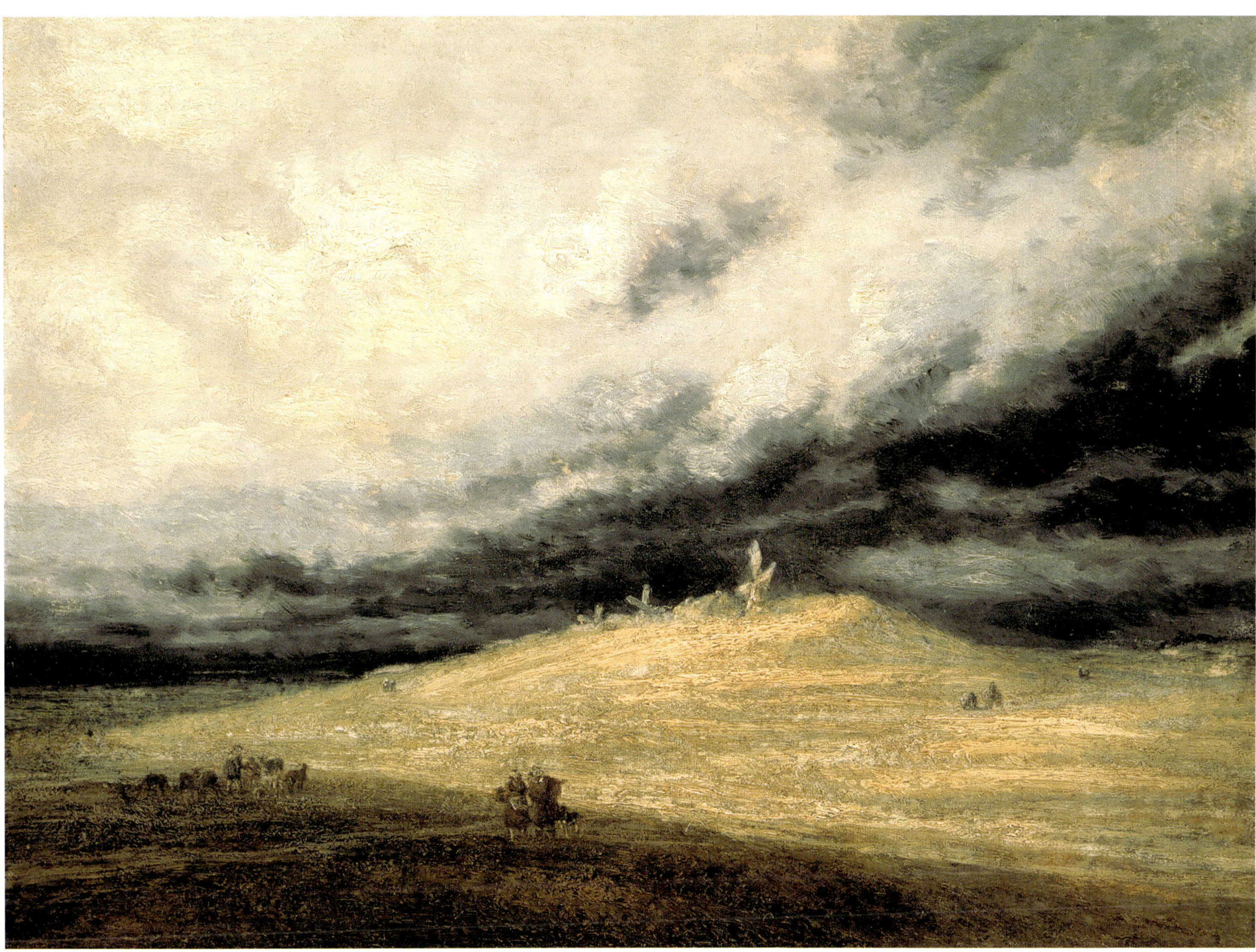

plate 31

Georges Michel (1763-1843)
Three windmills
The Hague, Museum Mesdag

'These days Montmartre will have those curious effects which Michel, for instance, has painted; that dry, withered grass and sand against the grey sky. At present, the colour in the meadows, at least, often reminds one of Michel, the soil yellow, brown, withered grass with a muddy road full of puddles, the tree-trunks black, the sky grey and white, the houses at a distance tonal, but with the red roofs, for instance, lending a little touch of colour' [314/266].

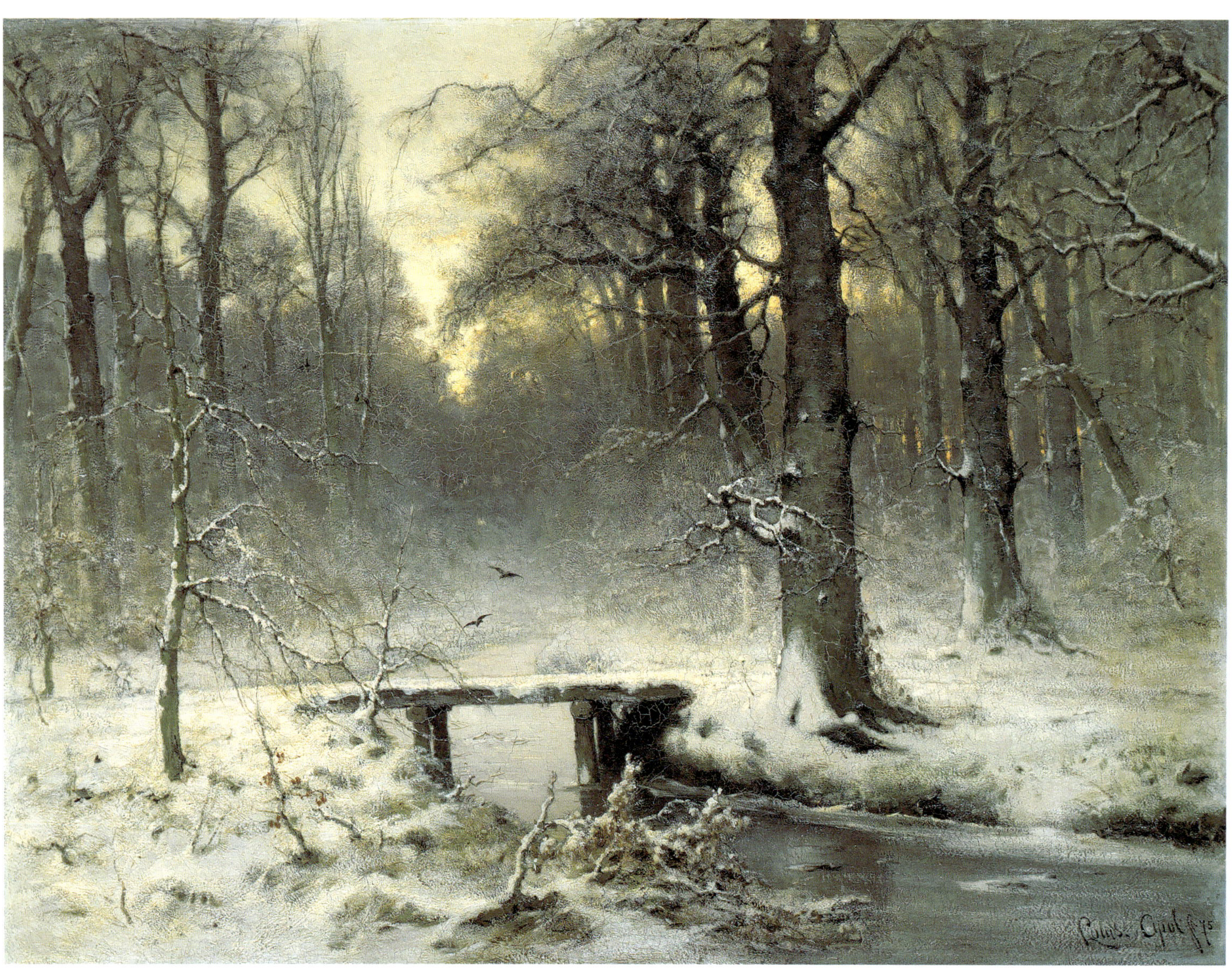

plate 32

Lodewijk Apol (1850-1936)
A January evening in the woods of The Hague, 1875
Amsterdam, Rijksmuseum

'Do you know that I often think the things by Apol, for instance, white on white, very well done. His sunset in the Hague Wood, for instance, which is in Amsterdam. That thing really is damned good' [539/428].

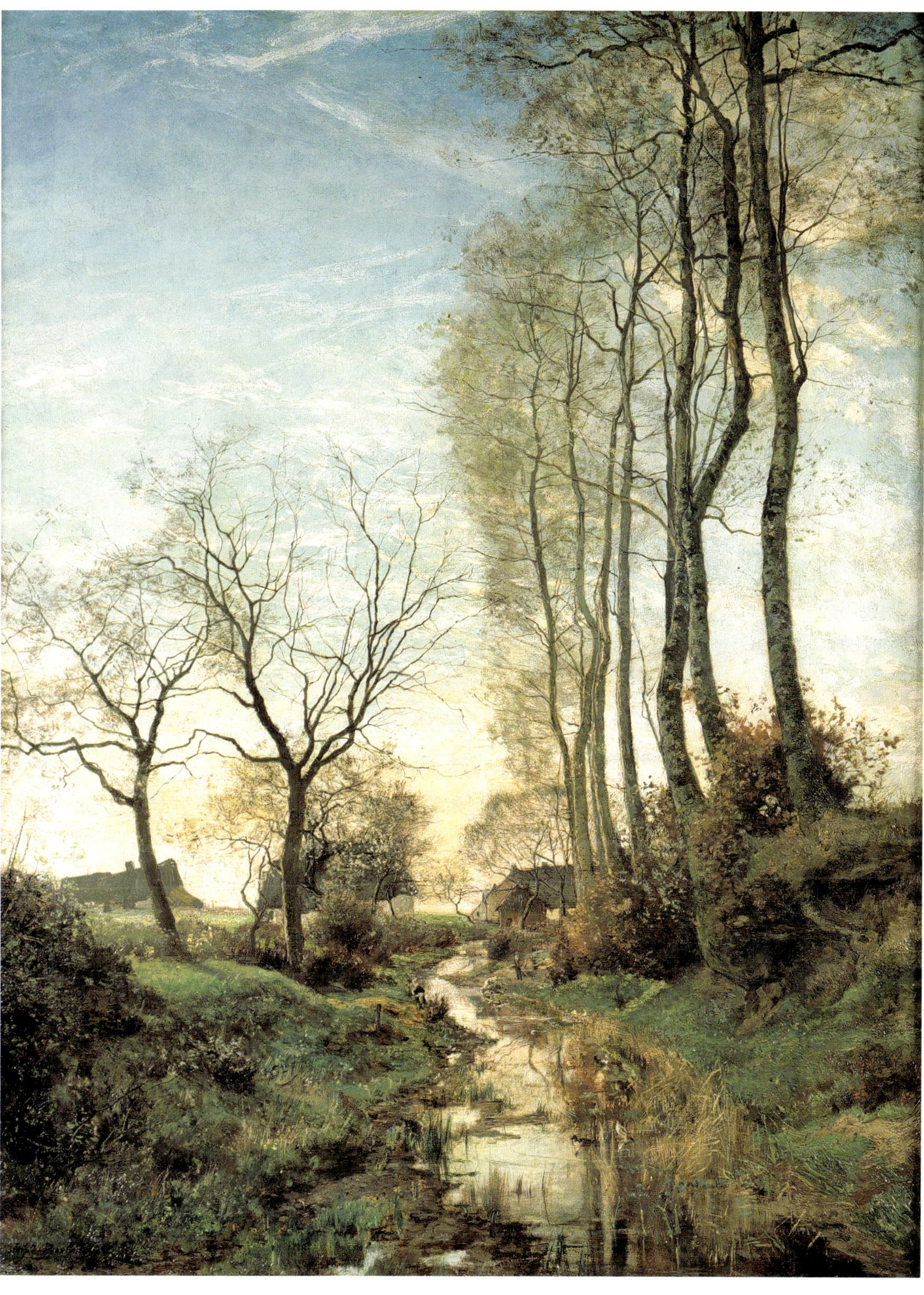

plate 33

Hippolyte Boulenger (1837-1874)
The Josapathwetering in Schaarbeek, 1868
Antwerp, Koninklijk Museum voor Schone Kunsten

'I often used to go for walks with Rappard where you said. Is the suburb
and the country beyond the Congress Column called Schaarbeek?
I remember a place called, I think, the valley of Jehosaphat, where there
were some poplars, and where Hippolyte Boulenger, the landscapist, did
some lovely things' [607/483].

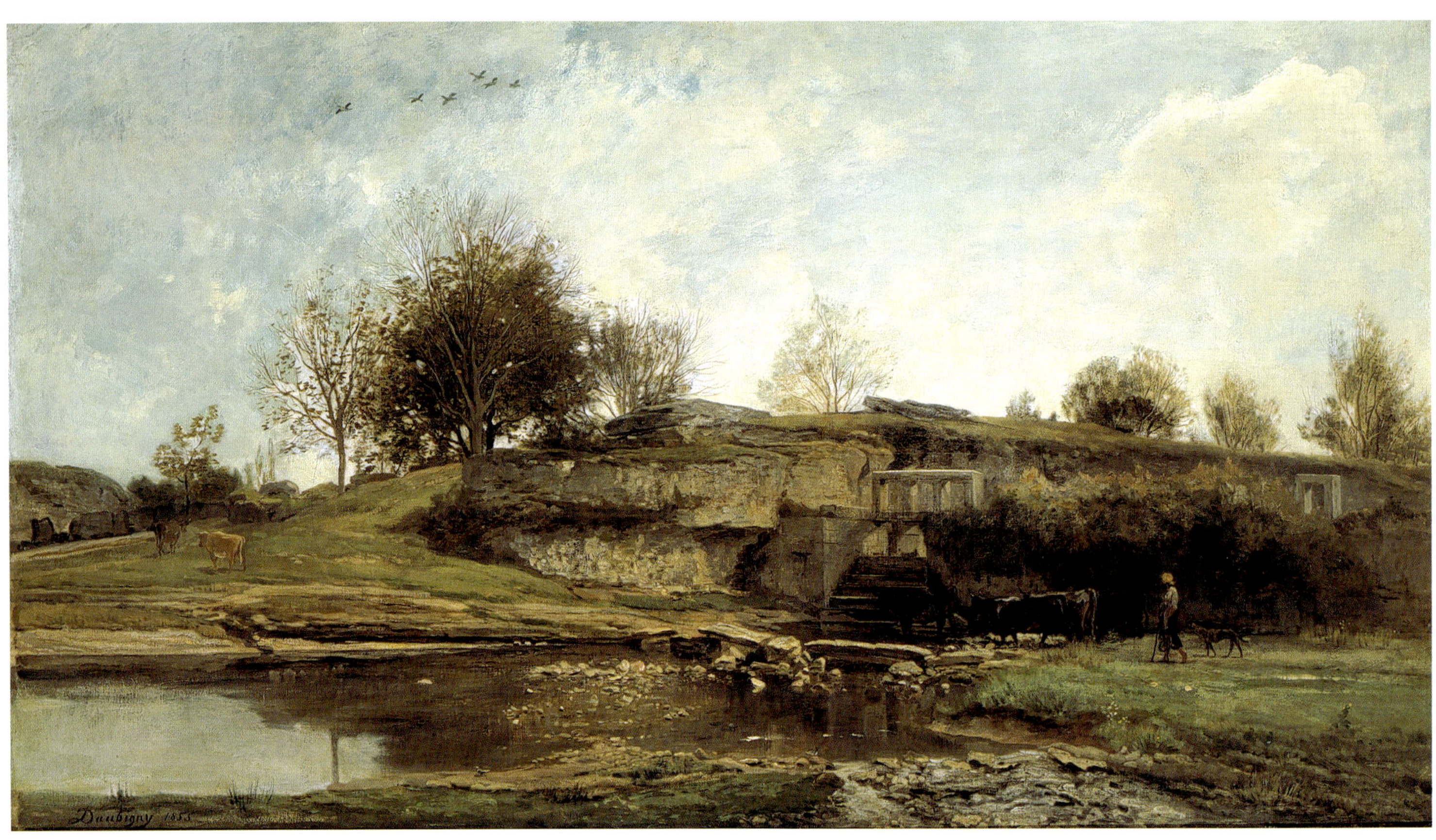

plate 34

Charles-François Daubigny (1817-1878)
The flood-gate at Optevoz, 1855
Paris, Musée du Louvre (on loan to the Musée des Beaux-Arts, Rouen)

plate 35

Charles-François Daubigny (1817-1878)
Spring, 1857
Paris, Musée du Louvre (on loan to the Musée des Beaux-Arts, Chartres)

'Yesterday we went to the Luxembourg together and I showed him the
paintings which I like the most. Daubigny, Spring and Autumn' [54/42].

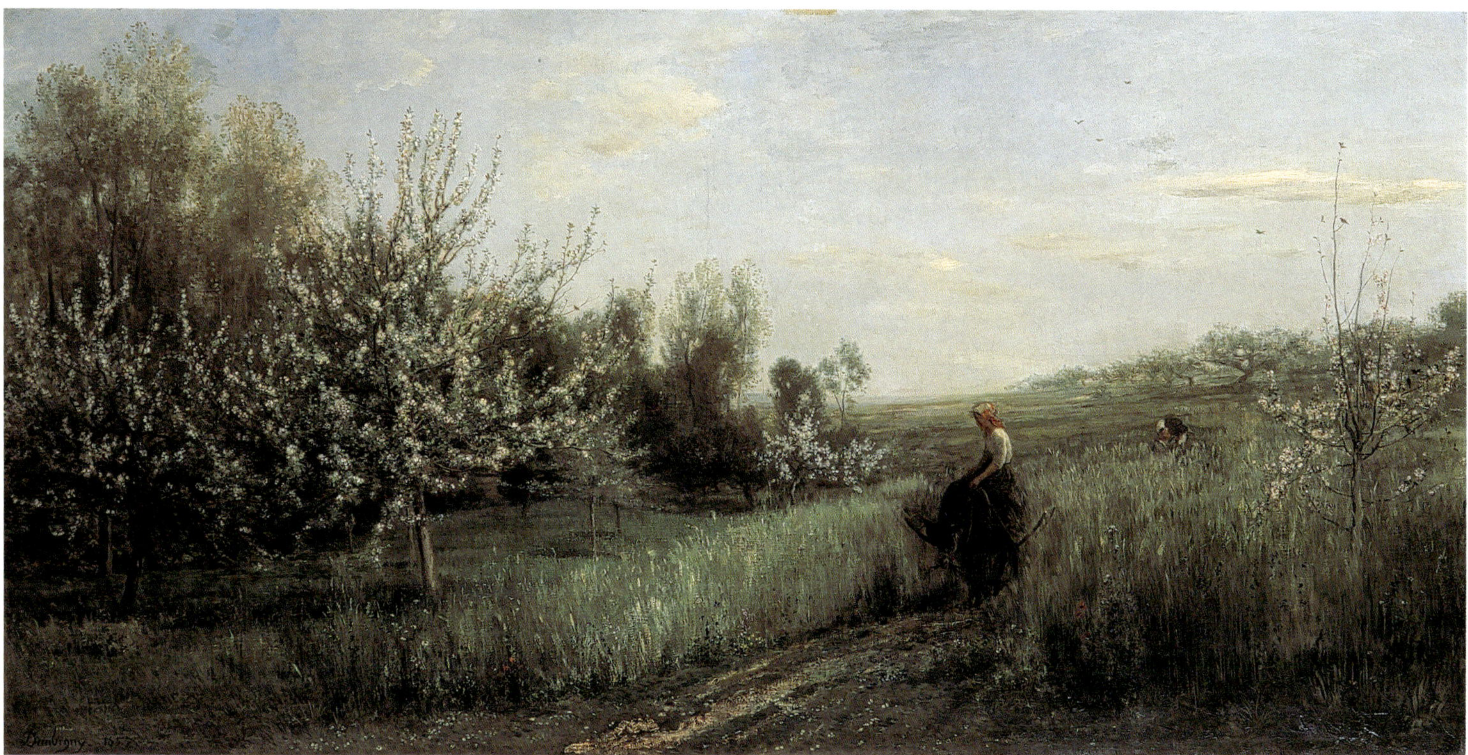

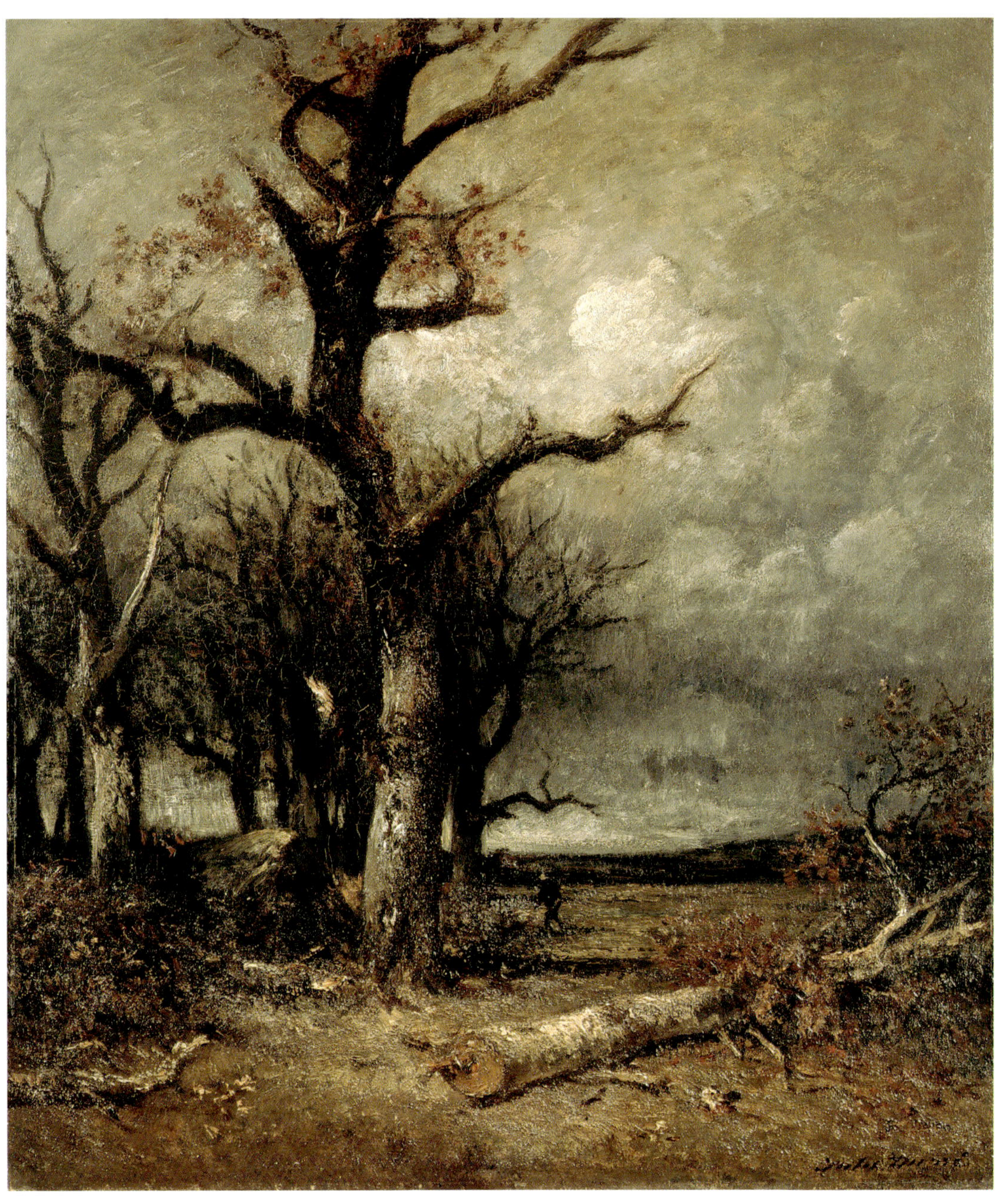

plate 36

Jules Dupré (1811-1889)
Autumn, c. 1865
The Hague, Museum Mesdag

'Israëls got it quite right when he said of a Jules Dupré (Mesdag's large one), "It is like a figure painting." It is that dramatic effect that gives it a je ne sais quoi which makes one feel what you say about it: "It conveys that moment and that place in nature to which one can repair alone, without company"' [363/299].

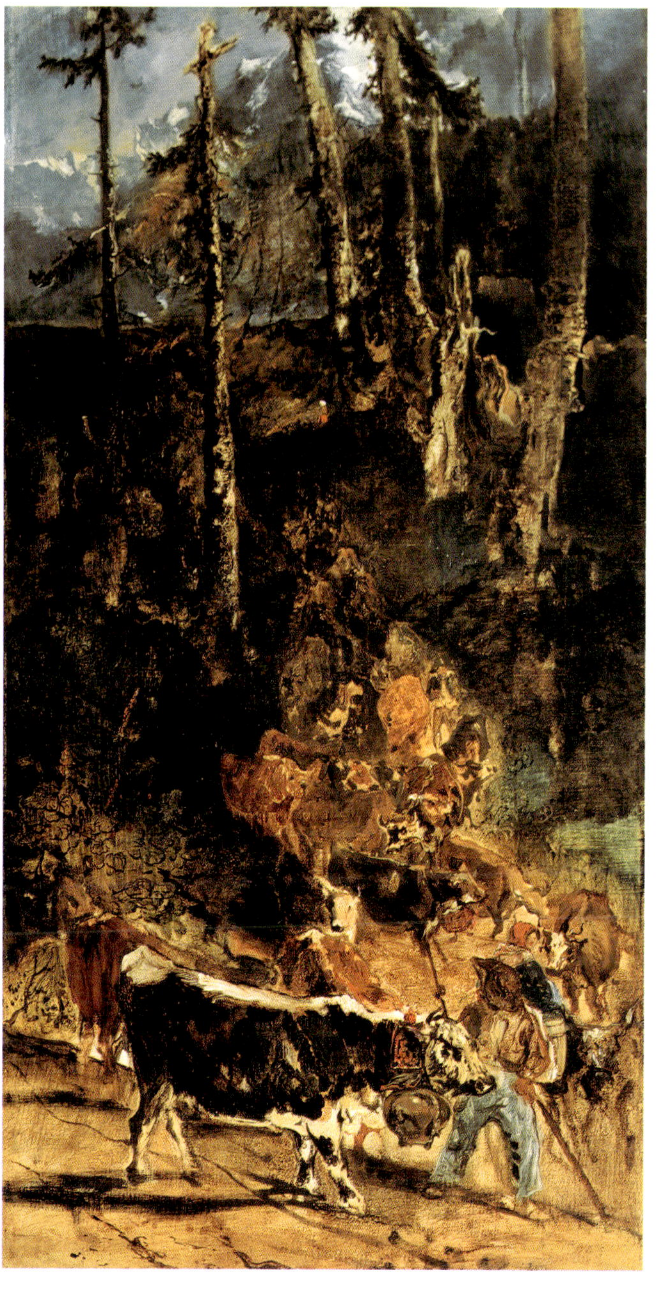

plate 37

Théodore Rousseau (1812-1867)
The descent of the cattle in the high Jura mountains, c. 1834-35
The Hague, Museum Mesdag

'The other day I saw the exhibition of French art (on the Boschkant) from the Mesdag, Post and other collections. [...] I also particularly admired the large sketch by Th. Rousseau from the Mesdag Collection – a herd of cows in the Alps' [247/215].

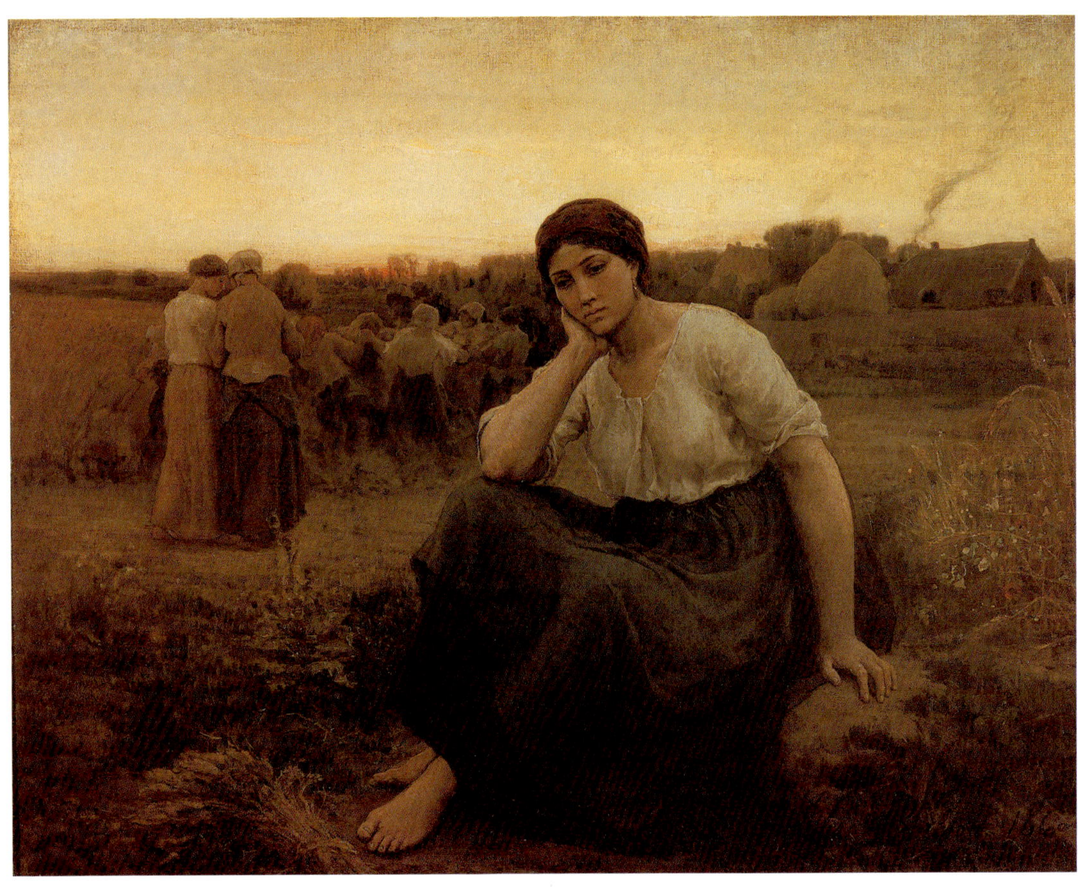

plate 38

Jules Breton (1827-1906)
Evening, 1860
Paris, Musée d'Orsay (on loan to the Hôtel de Ville, Cuisery)

'Read Zola's description of women in a room in the twilight – most of the
women aged between 30 and 50 – such a sombre, mysterious place.
I find it *splendid*, indeed *sublime*. But to me, Millet's Angelus is just as sublime, with that same twilight, that same infinite emotion – or that single
figure of Breton's in the Luxembourg' [467/378].

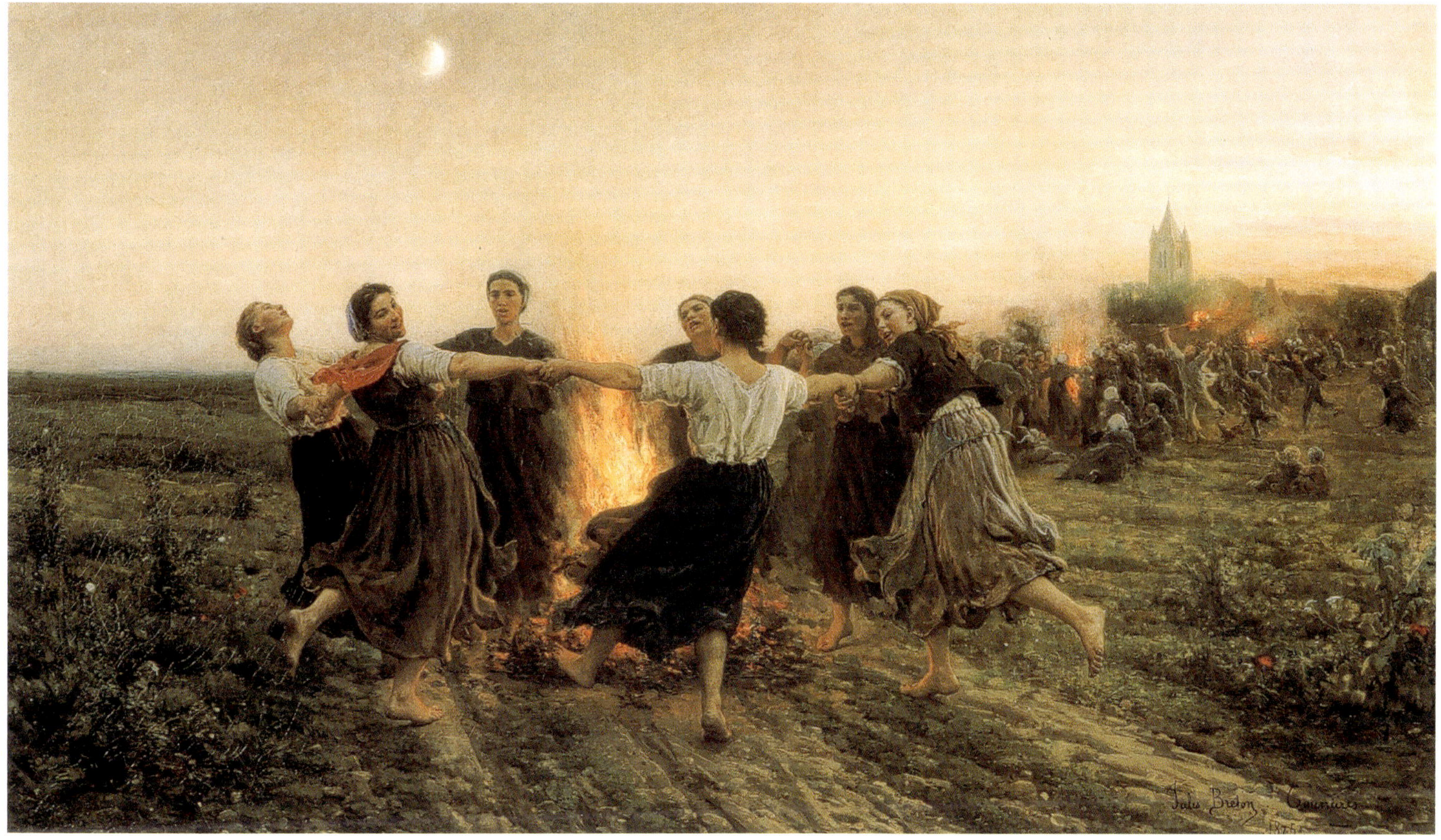

plate 39

Jules Breton (1827-1906)
The feast of St John, 1875
Private collection

'He has a beautiful painting at the Salon, "The feast of St John", peasant
girls dancing on a summer evening round the St John's bonfire, in the background the village with its church and the moon above it.
     "Dance, young maidens, dance,
     As you sing your songs of love!
     Tomorrow, at break of day,
     You'll go, hastening to ply your sickles"' [34/27].

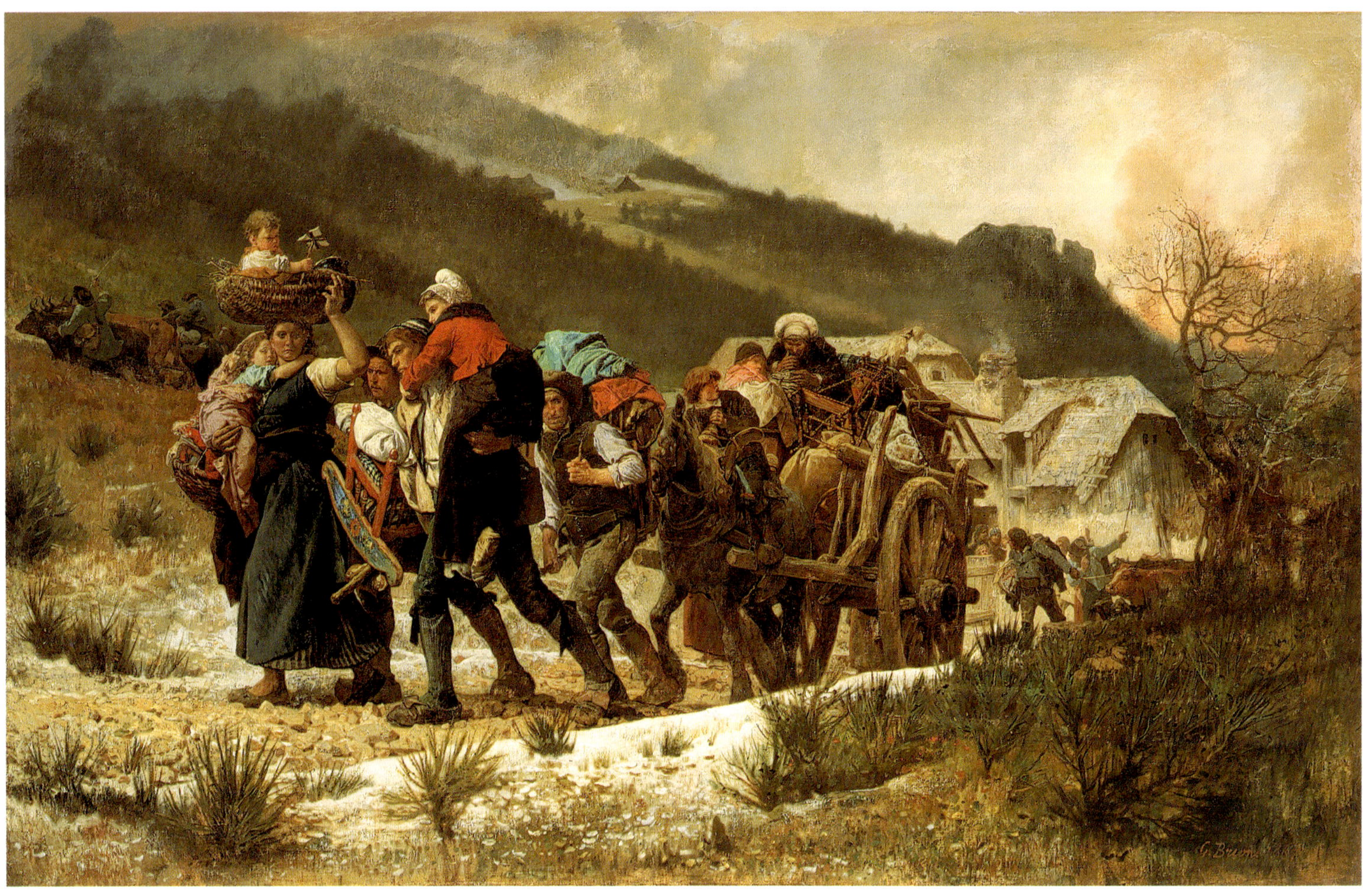

plate 40

Gustave Brion (1824-1877)
Vosges peasants fleeing before the invasion, 1867
St Louis, Washington University Gallery of Art, Bequest of Charles
Parsons, 1905

'And Brion has died too; well, he made beautiful work in his lifetime. [...]
How many things has he done! He had a great talent and has made the
most of it, and gained by it. There are many illustrations by him in the illustrated edition of Erckmann-Chatrian. "The invasion" is also one of his
most beautiful paintings' [134/114].

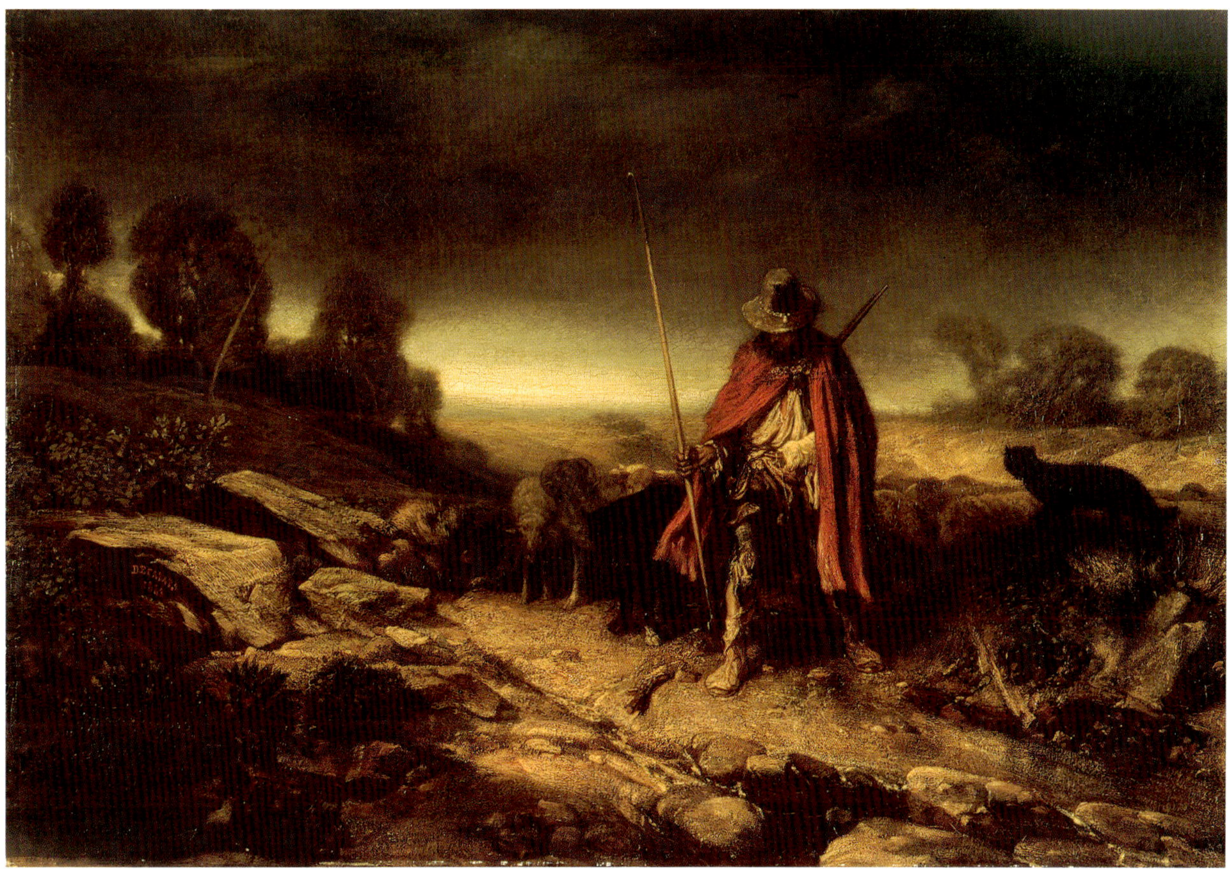

plate 41

Alexandre-Gabriel Decamps (1803-1860)
A shepherd with his flock, 1843
Amsterdams Historisch Museum (on loan to the Van Gogh Museum, Amsterdam)

'I have also seen the Fodor museum. "The shepherd" by Decamps is really a masterpiece' [537/426].

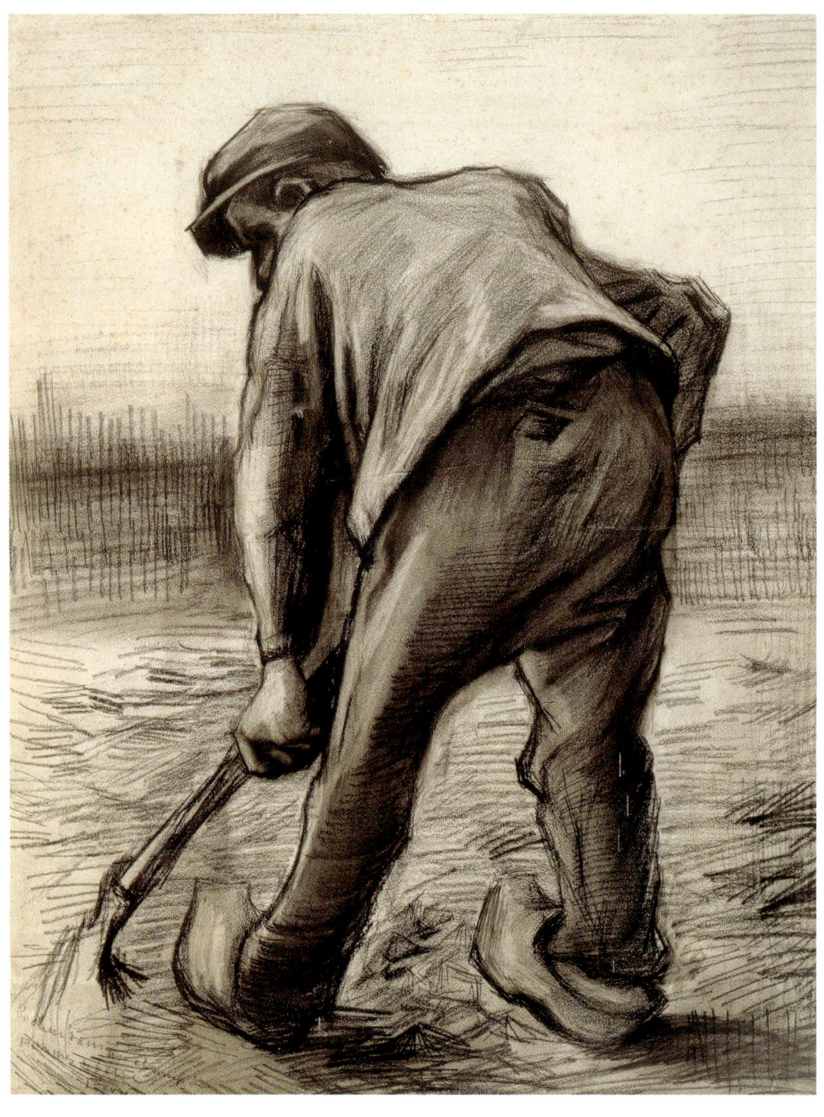

plate 42

Vincent van Gogh (1853-1890)
Digger in a potato field: February (F 1302 JH 859), 1885
Amsterdam, Van Gogh Museum (Vincent van Gogh Foundation)

'*Nothing seems simpler than painting peasants or ragpickers and other work-*
ers, but – there are no subjects in painting as difficult as those everyday figures!
As far as I know, there is not a single academy in which one can learn to
draw and paint a digger, a sower, a woman hanging a pot over the fire, or a
seamstress. But every city of any importance has an academy with a choice
of models for historical, Arabic Louis XV and, in a nutshell, EVERY SORT OF
FIGURE, PROVIDED THEY DO NOT EXIST IN REALITY' [522/418].

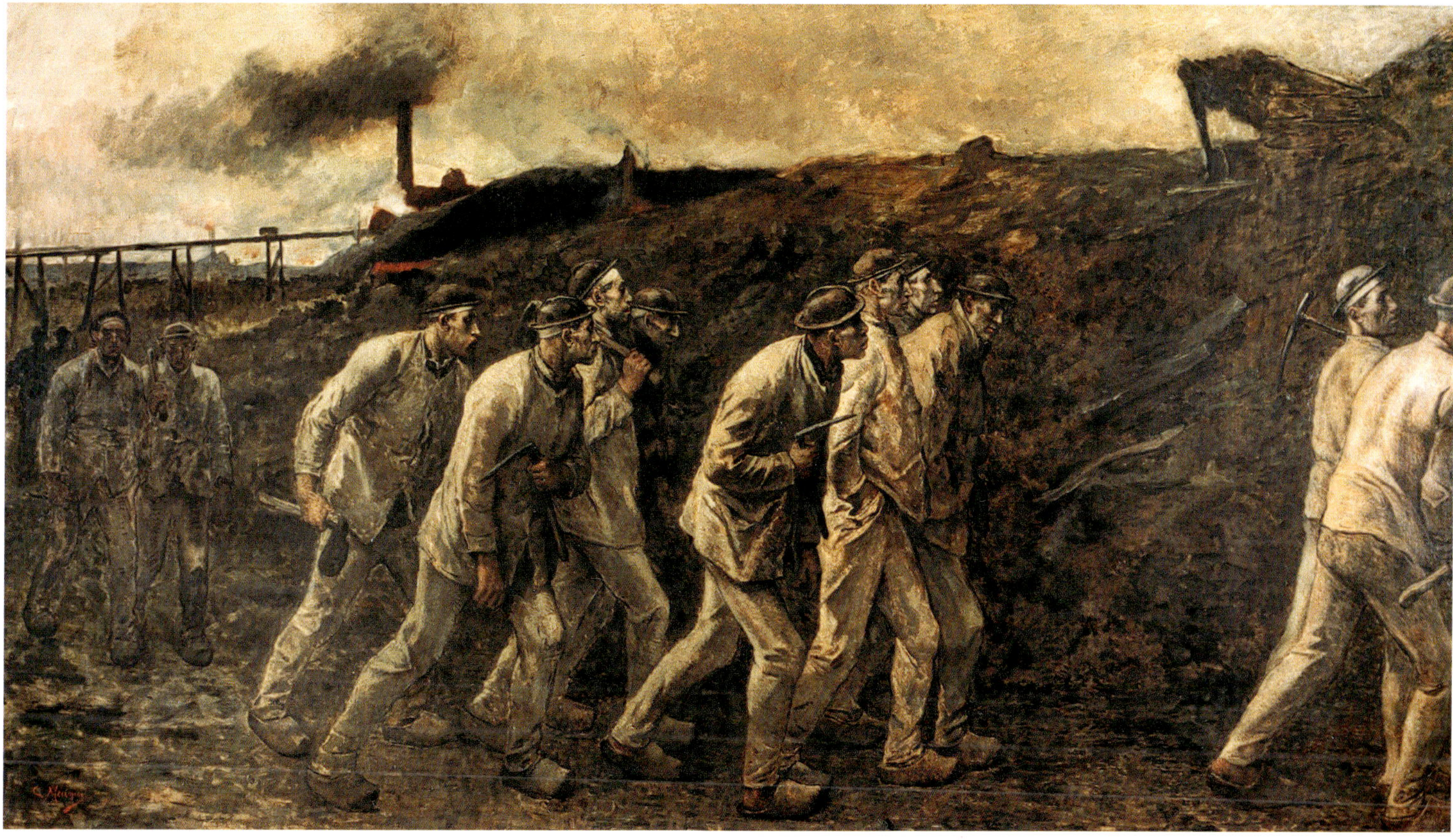

plate 43

Constantin Meunier (1831 1905)
The return of the miners, c. 1885
Private collection

'What I am not indifferent to is that a man who is very much my superior, Meunier, has painted the women coal hauliers of the Borinage and the shift going to the pits, and the factories, their red roofs and their black chimneys against a delicate grey sky – all things that I have dreamed of doing, feeling that it had not been done and that it ought to be painted' [810/610].

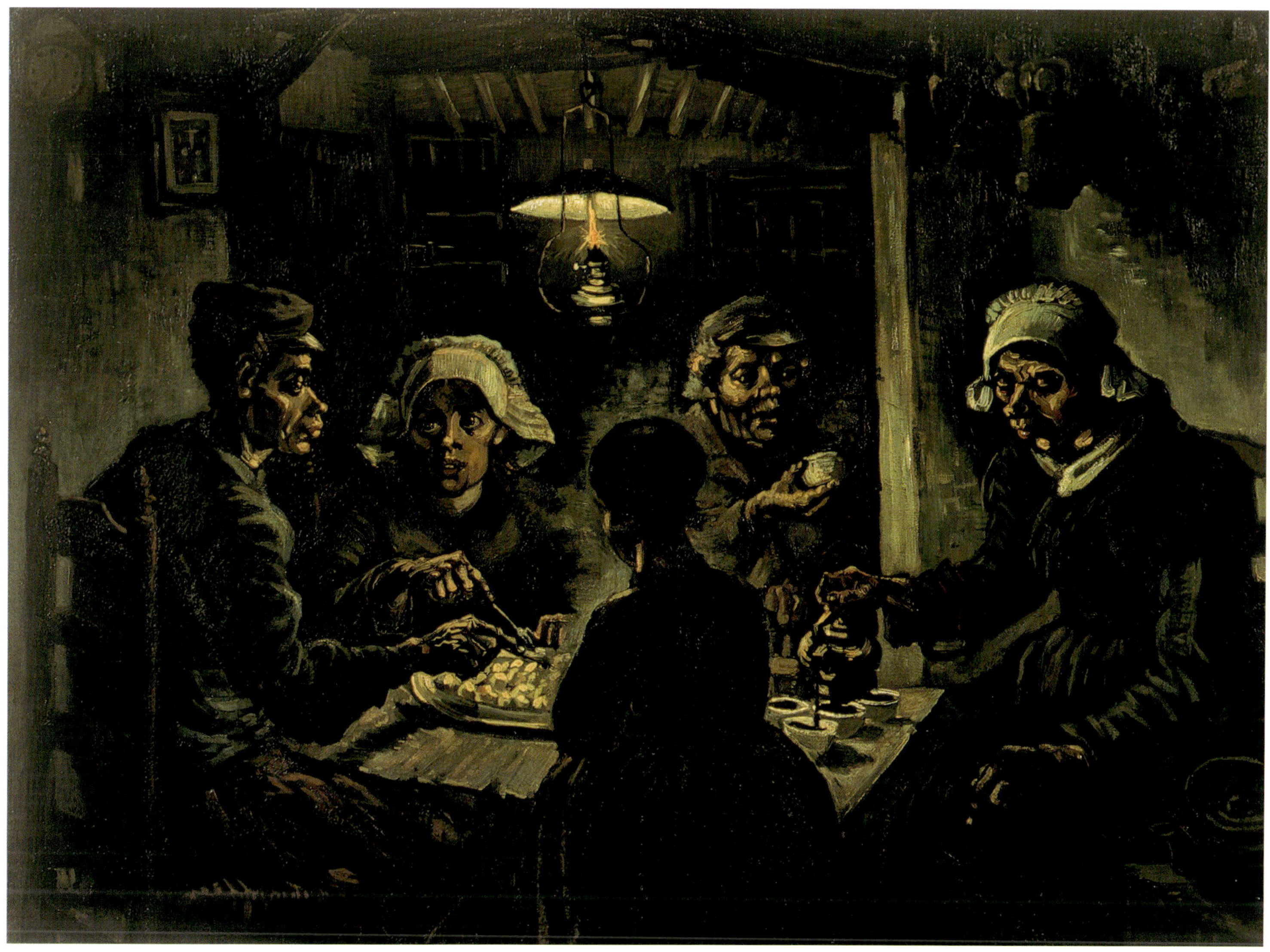

plate 44

Vincent van Gogh (1853-1890)
The potato eaters (F 82 JH 764), 1885
Amsterdam, Van Gogh Museum (Vincent van Gogh Foundation)

'Painting peasant life is a serious business, and I for one would blame
myself if I didn't try to make pictures that could give rise to serious reflection in those who think seriously about art and life. Millet, Degroux, so
many others, have set an example of character by turning a deaf ear to
such taunts as "sâle, grossier, boueux, puant" [nasty, crude, filthy, stinking]
etc. etc., so it would be a disgrace should one so much as waver. No, one
must paint peasants as if one were one of them, as if one felt and thought
as they do' [501/404].

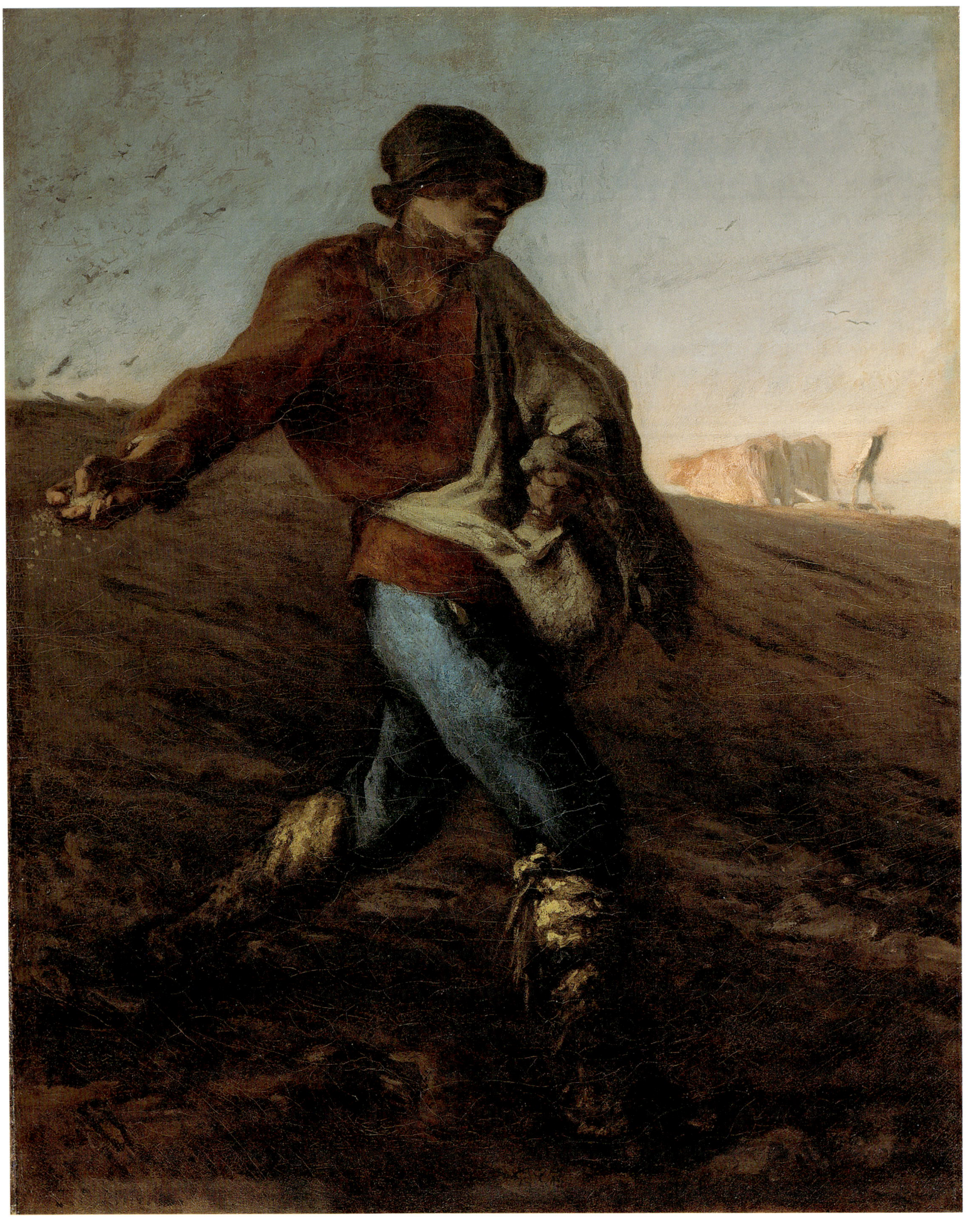

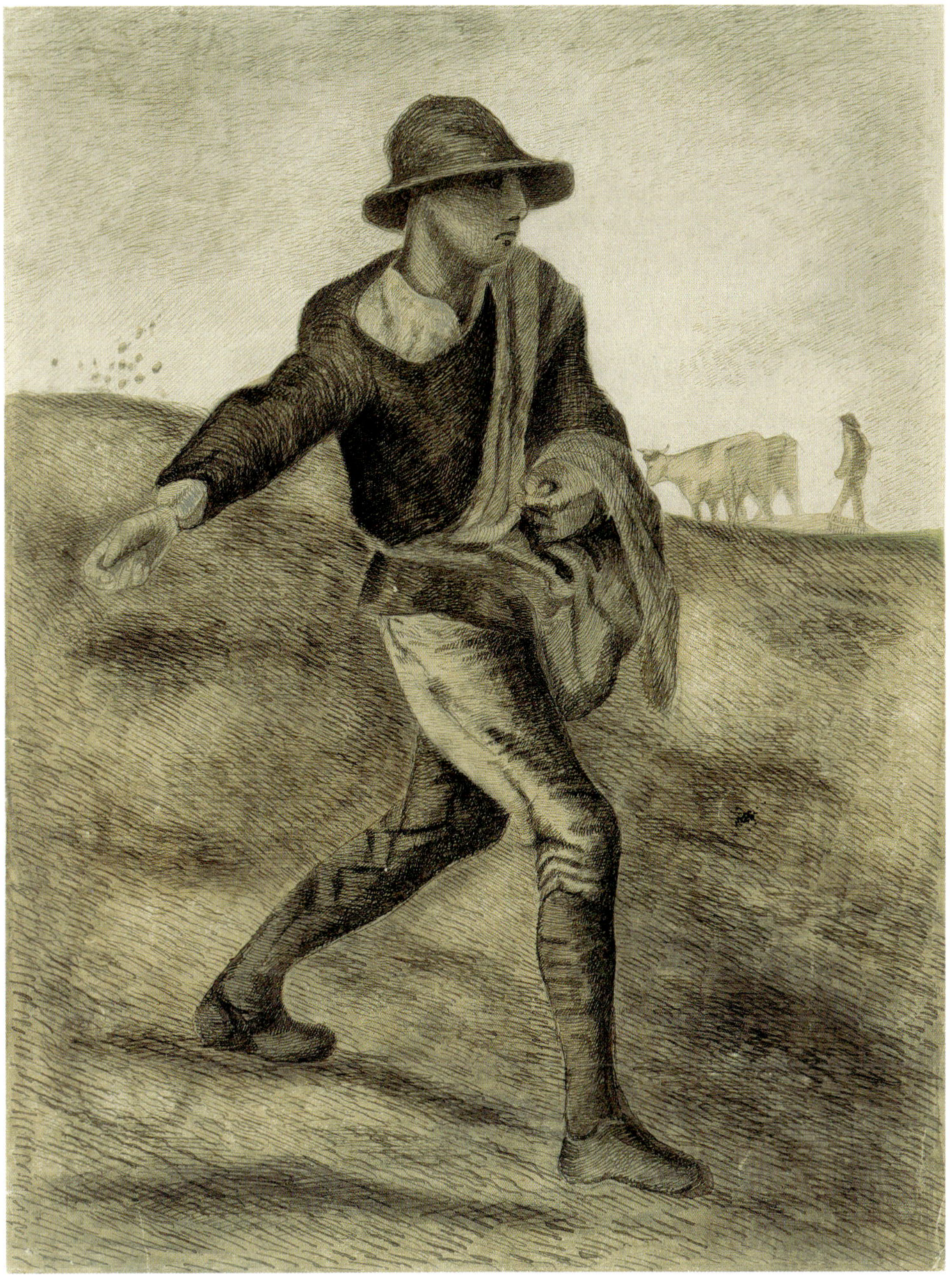

plate 45

Jean-François Millet (1814-1875)
The sower, 1850
Boston, Museum of Fine Arts, Gift of Quincy Adams Shaw through Quincy Adams Shaw, Jr., and Mrs. Marian Shaw Haughton

'There is something of life itself in true *studies*, and the person who makes one will respect nature in it, not himself, and so prefer the study to what he may perhaps make of it later – unless something quite different should finally result from many studies, namely the type distilled from many *individuals*. That is the highest thing in art, and there art sometimes rises above nature – in Millet's sower, for instance, there is more soul than in an ordinary sower in the field' [299/257].

plate 46

Vincent van Gogh (1853-1890)
The sower (after Millet) (F 830 JH 1), 1881
Amsterdam, Van Gogh Museum (Vincent van Gogh Foundation)

'Meanwhile, I have started on the Millets. The *Semeur* is finished, and I have sketched the Quatre heures de la journée. And now I still have to do Les travaux des champs' [165/144].

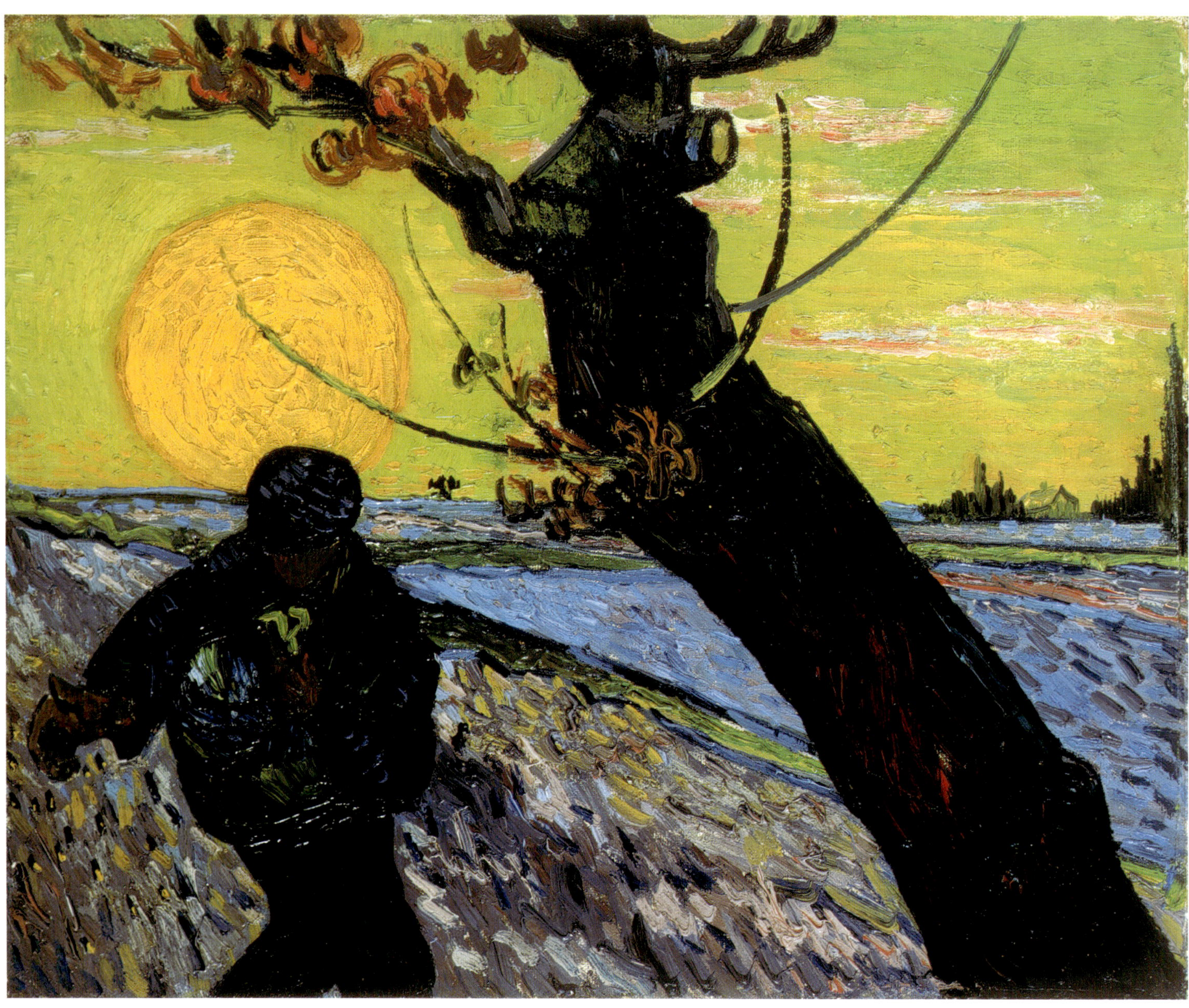

plate 47

Vincent van Gogh (1853-1890)
The sower with setting sun (F 451 JH 1629), 1888
Amsterdam, Van Gogh Museum (Vincent van Gogh Foundation)

'I will not conceal from you that I don't dislike the countryside, since
I grew up in it – I am still enchanted by snatches of the past, have a han-
kering after the infinite, of which the sower and the sheaf of corn are the
symbols' [630/B7].

plate 48

Jean-François Millet (1814-1875)
Shearing sheep, c. 1860
Private collection

'To show the PEASANT FIGURE IN ACTION, that – I repeat – is what a
figure is – essentially modern – the heart of modern art itself, something
that neither the Greeks nor the Renaissance nor the old Dutch school
have done. [...] Peasants' and workmen's figures began more as a "genre" –
but nowadays, with Millet, the perennial master, in the lead, that is the very
heart of modern art, and so it will remain' [522/418].

plate 49

Vincent van Gogh (1853-1890)
The sheep-shearer (after Millet) (F 634 JH 1787), 1889
Amsterdam, Van Gogh Museum (Vincent van Gogh Foundation)

'I now have seven copies out of the ten of Millet's "Travaux des Champs".
I can assure you that making copies interests me enormously, and it means
that I shall not lose sight of the figure, even though I have no models at
the moment. Besides, this will make a studio decoration for me or someone else. [...] Although copying may be the old system, that makes absolutely no difference to me. [...] You will be surprised at the effect "Les
travaux des champs" takes on in colour, it is a very intimate series of his.
I am going to try to tell you what I am seeking in it and why it seems good
to me to copy them. We painters are always asked to compose ourselves
and be nothing but composers. So be it – but it isn't like that in music –
and if some person or other plays Beethoven, he adds his personal interpretation – in music and more especially in singing – the interpretation of
a composer is something, and it is not a hard-and-fast rule that only the
composer should play his own composition. Very good – and I, mostly
because I am ill at present, I am trying to do something to console myself,
for my own pleasure. I put the black and white by Delacroix or Millet or
something made after their work in front of me as a subject. And then
I improvise colour on it, not, you understand, altogether being myself, but
searching for memories of their pictures – but the memory, the vague
consonance of colours which are at least right in feeling – that is my own
interpretation. Many people do not copy, many others do – I started on
it accidentally, and I find that it teaches things, and above all it sometimes
provides consolation. And then my brush goes between my fingers as a
bow would on the violin, and absolutely for my own pleasure. Today I tried
the "Woman Shearing Sheep" in a colour scheme ranging from lilac to
yellow' [806/607].

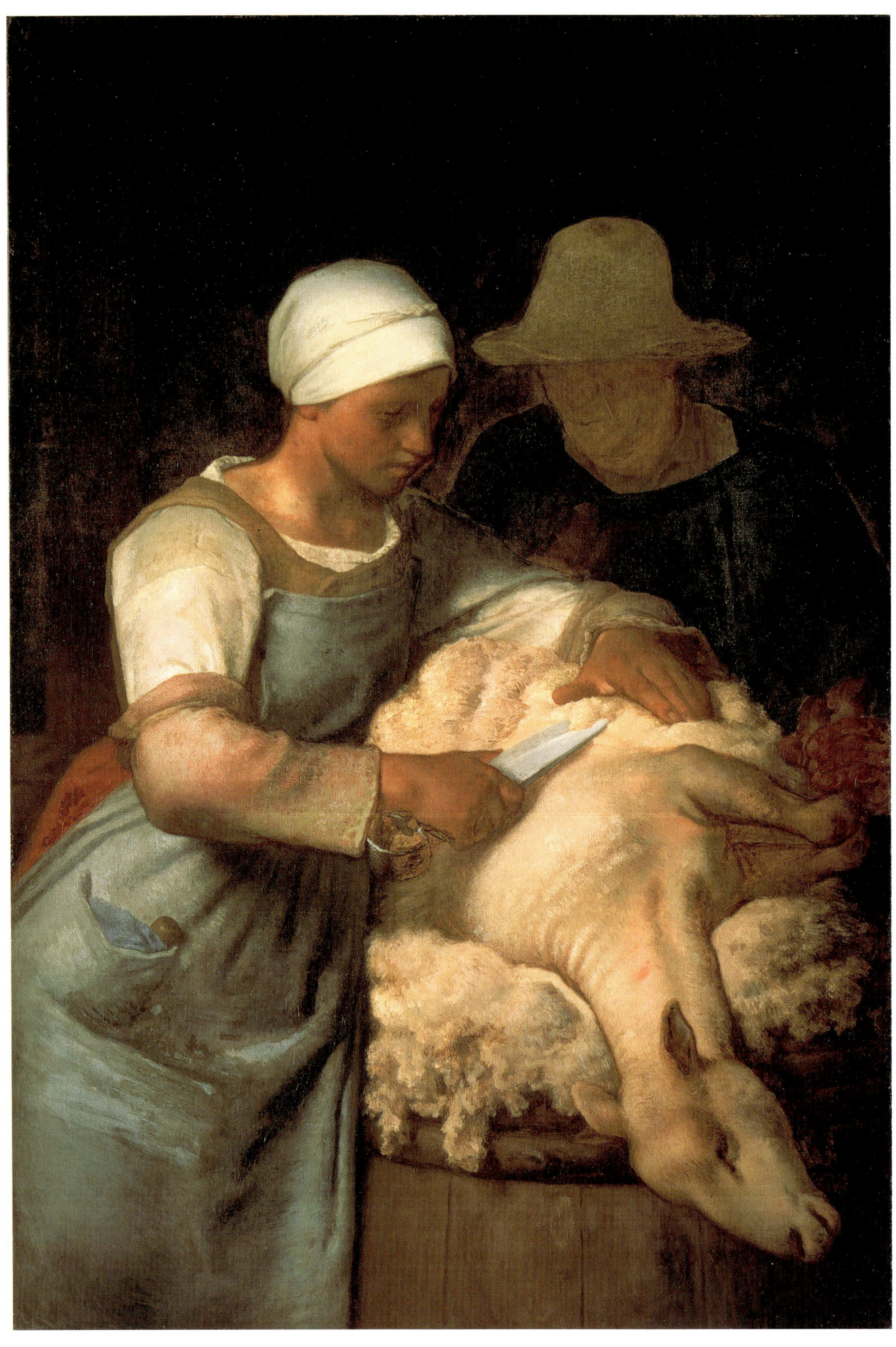

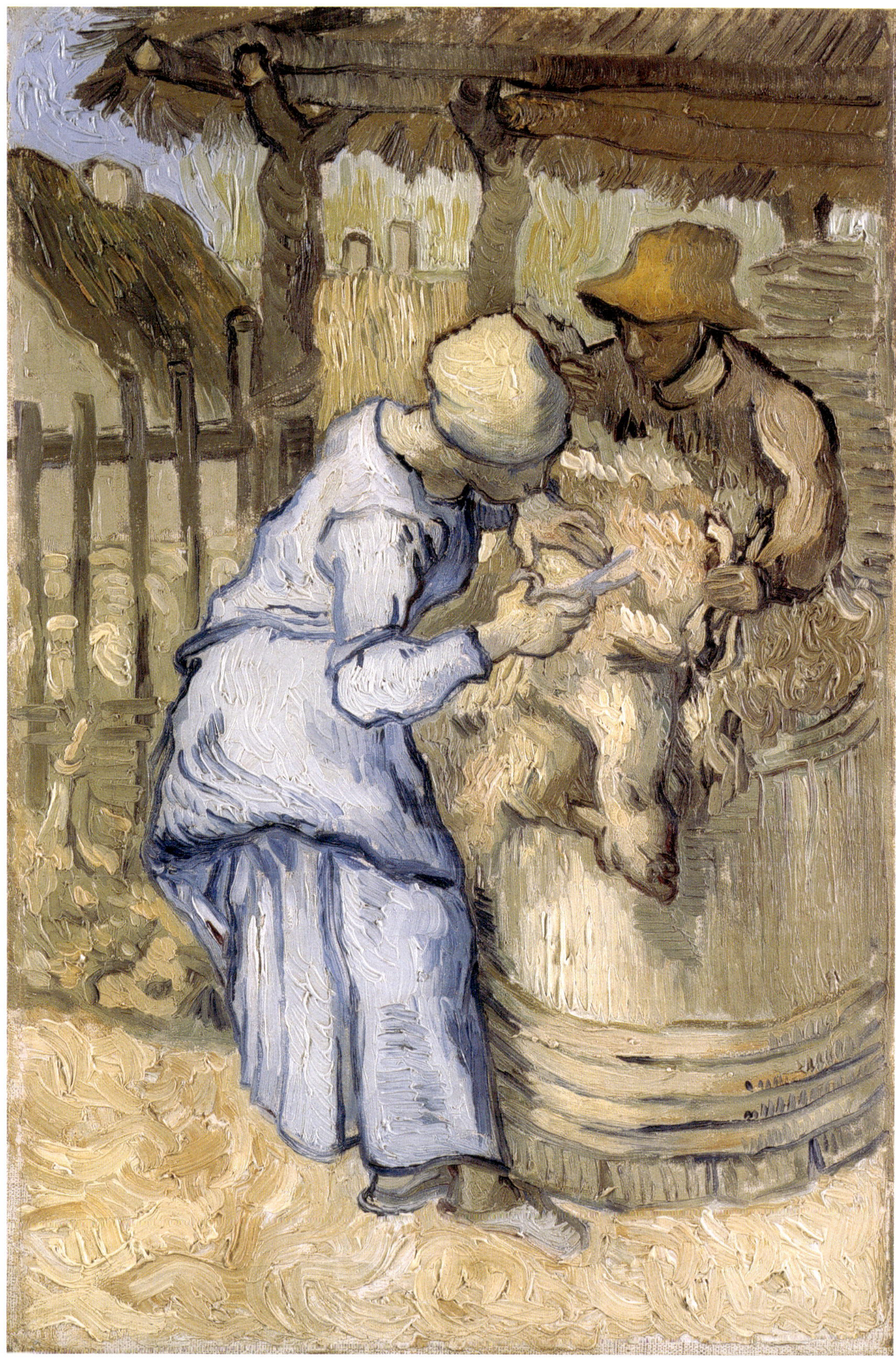

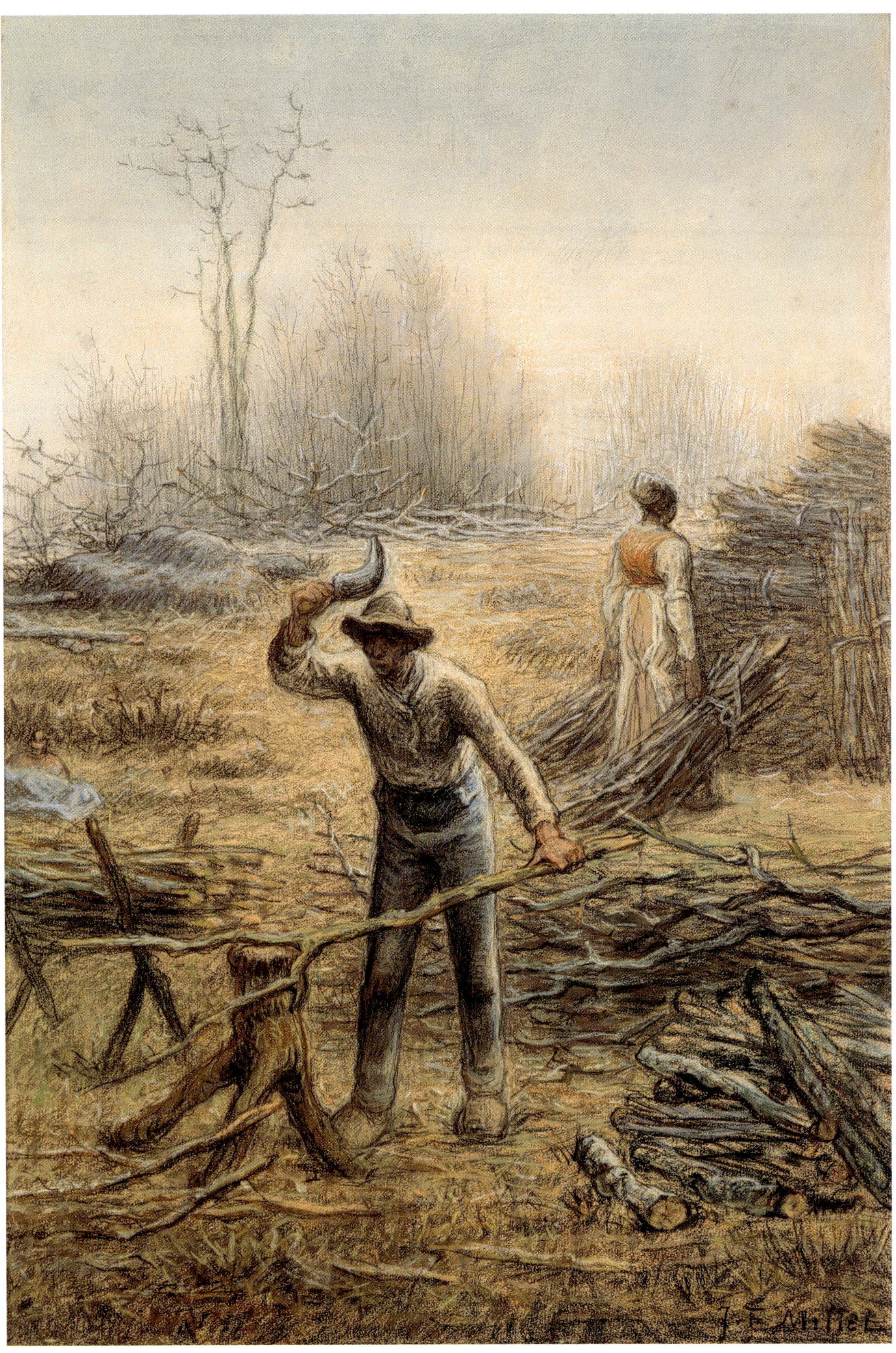

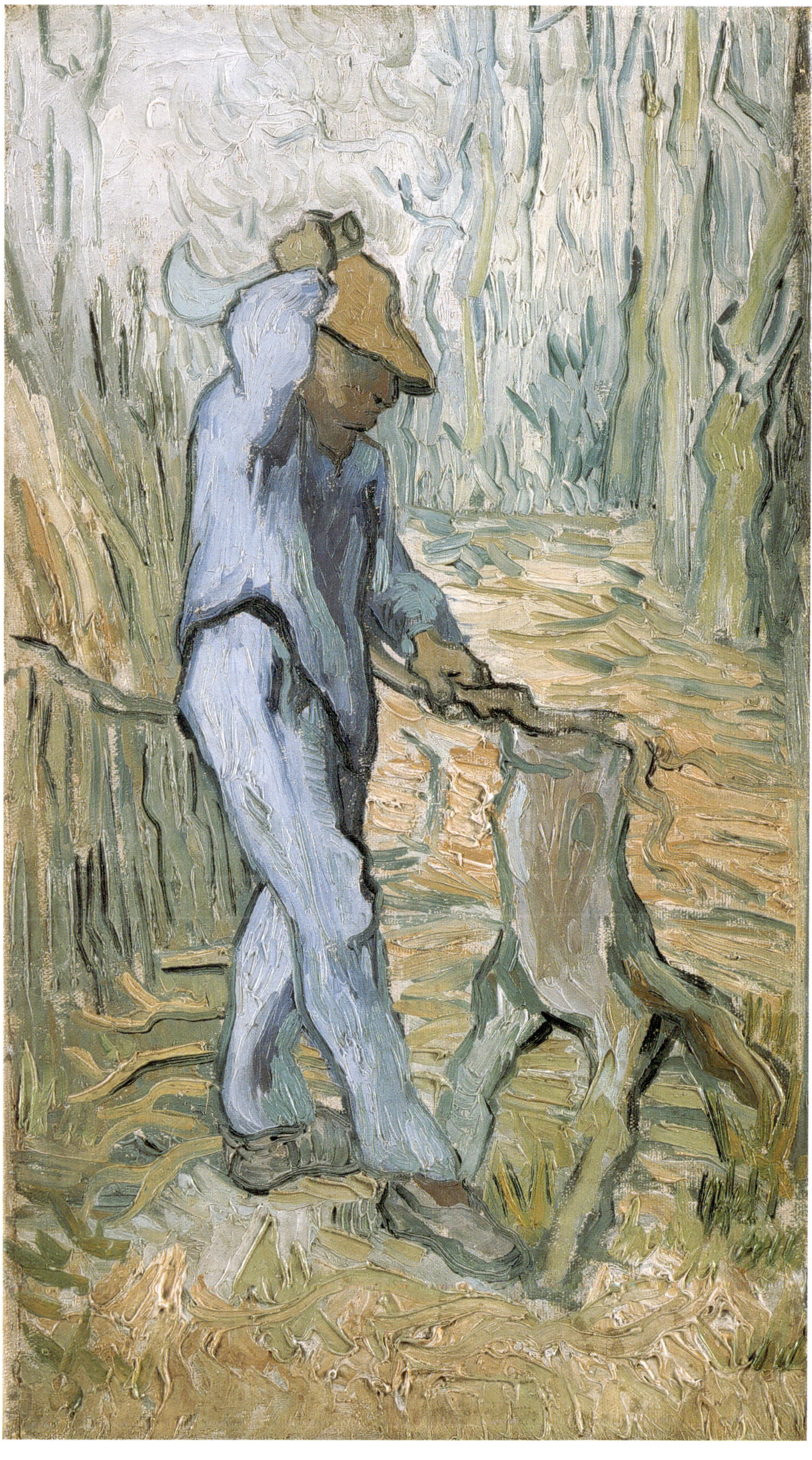

plate 50

Jean-François Millet (1814-1875)
Woodcutter and his wife preparing faggots, 1866-68
Private collection

'There was a sale here of drawings by Millet, I don't know whether I wrote
to you about it before. When I entered the room in Hôtel Drouot where
they were exhibited, I felt something akin to, "put off thy shoes from off
thy feet, for the place whereon thou standest is holy ground"' [36/29].

plate 51

Vincent van Gogh (1853-1890)
The woodcutter (after Millet) (F 670 JH 1886), 1890
Amsterdam, Van Gogh Museum (Vincent van Gogh Foundation)

'I now have seven copies out of the ten of Millet's "Travaux des Champs".
I can assure you that making copies interests me enormously, and it means
that I shall not lose sight of the figure, even though I have no models at
the moment. Besides, this will make a studio decoration for me or someone else. [...] Although copying may be the *old* system, that makes absolutely no difference to me. [...] You will be surprised at the effect "Les
travaux des champs" takes on in colour, it is a very intimate series of his.
I am going to try to tell you what I am seeking in it and why it seems good
to me to copy them. We painters are always asked to *compose* ourselves
and be *nothing but composers.* So be it – but it isn't like that in music – and
if some person or other plays Beethoven, he adds his personal interpretation – in music and more especially in singing – the interpretation of a
composer is something, and it is not a hard-and-fast rule that only the
composer should play his own composition. Very good – and I, mostly
because I am ill at present, I am trying to do something to console myself,
for my own pleasure. I put the black and white by Delacroix or Millet or
something made after their work in front of me as a subject. And then
I improvise colour on it, not, you understand, altogether being myself, but
searching for memories of *their* pictures – but the memory, the vague consonance of colours which are at least right in feeling – that is my own
interpretation. Many people do not copy, many others do – I started on it
accidentally, and I find that it teaches things, and above all it sometimes
provides consolation. And then my brush goes between my fingers as
a bow would on the violin, and absolutely for my own pleasure. Today
I tried the "Woman Shearing Sheep" in a colour scheme ranging from lilac
to yellow' [806/607].

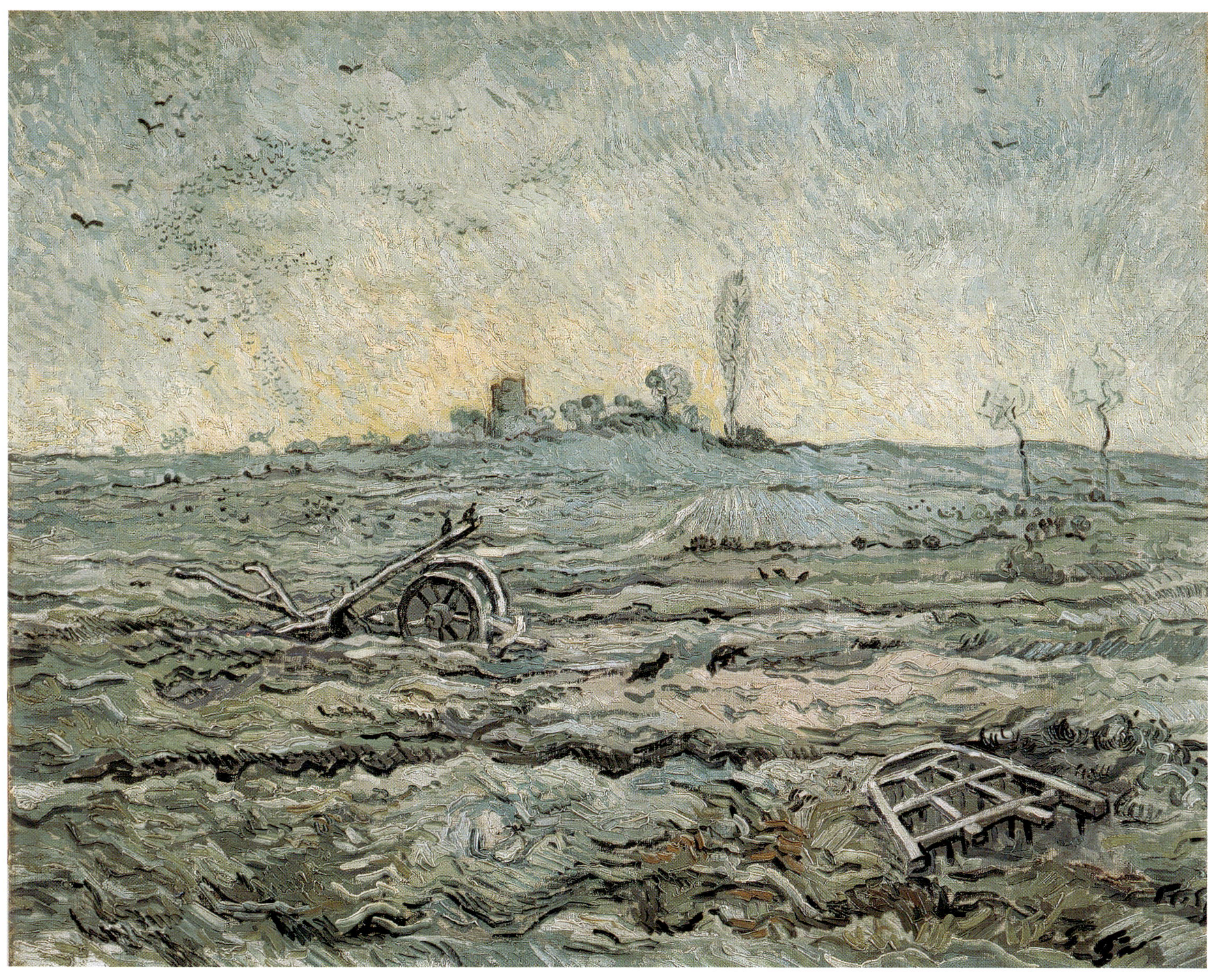

plate 52

Vincent van Gogh (1853-1890)
Snow-covered field with a harrow (after Millet) (F 632 JH 1882), 1890
Amsterdam, Van Gogh Museum (Vincent van Gogh Foundation)

'This week I am going to start on "The snow-covered field" and "The first
steps" by Millet, in the same size as the others. Then there will be six canvases in a series, and I can tell you, I have put much thought into the disposition of the colours while working on these last three of the "Hours of
the day"' [841/623].

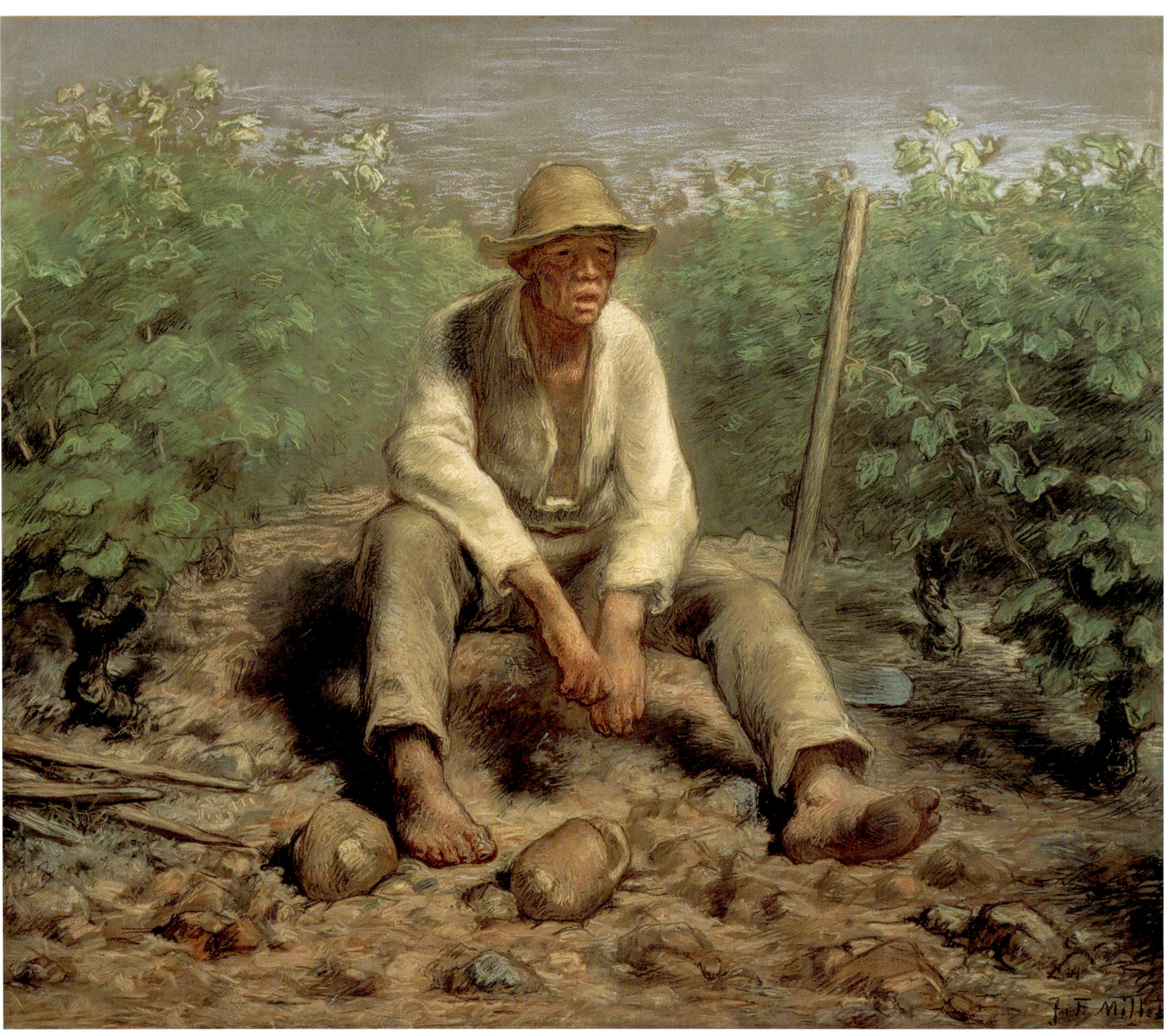

plate 53

Jean-François Millet (1814-1875)
Vineyard labourer resting, 1869-70
The Hague, Museum Mesdag

'There was a sale here of drawings by Millet, I don't know whether I wrote
to you about it before. When I entered the room in Hôtel Drouot where
they were exhibited, I felt something akin to, "put off thy shoes from off
thy feet, for the place whereon thou standest is holy ground"' [36/29].

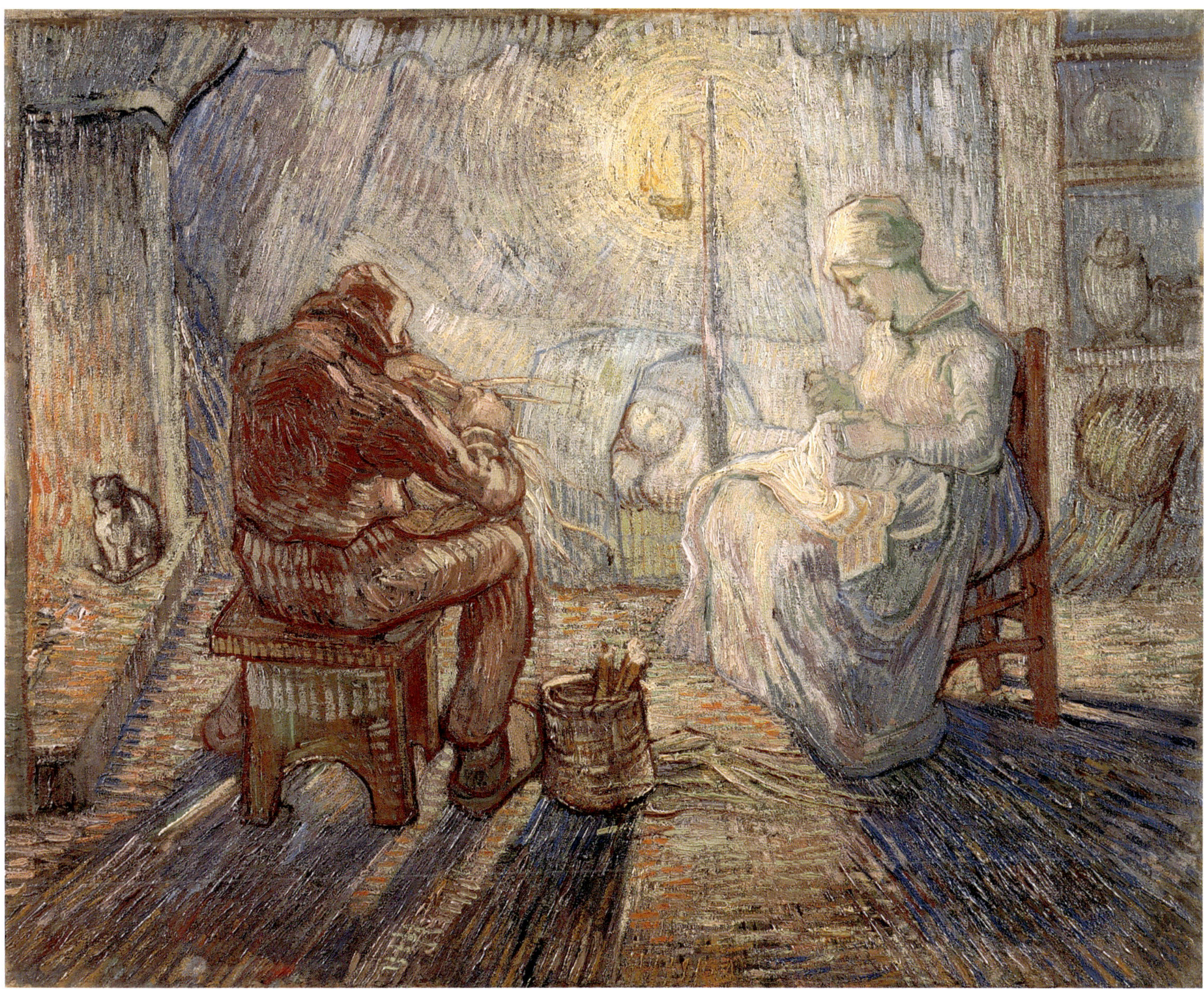

plate 54

Vincent van Gogh (1853-1890)
Night (after Millet) (F 647 JH 1834), 1889
Amsterdam, Van Gogh Museum (Vincent van Gogh Foundation)

'You gave me great pleasure by sending those Millets. I am working at them zealously. Because I haven't been seeing anything artistic, I was getting slack, and this has revived me. I have finished the "Veillée" and am working on the "Diggers" and the "Man putting on his jacket", size 30 canvases, and the "Sower", smaller. The "Veillée" is in a colour scheme of violets and tender lilacs with the light of the lamp pale lemon, then the orange glow of the fire and the man in red ochre. You will see it; it seems to me that painting from these drawings of Millet's is much more translating them into another tongue than copying them' [818/613].

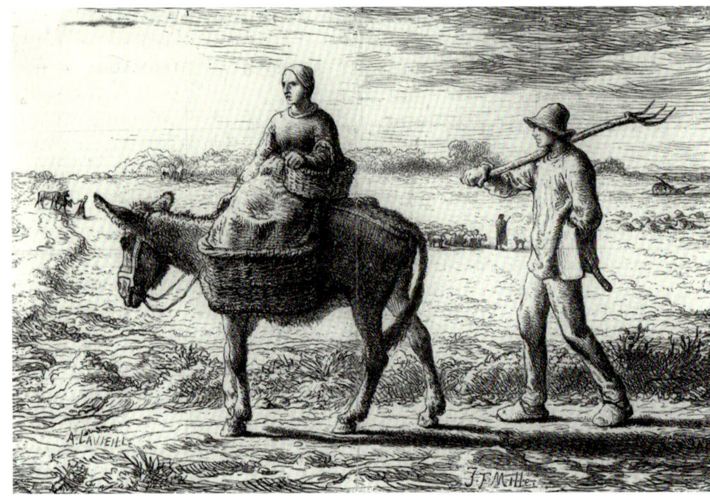

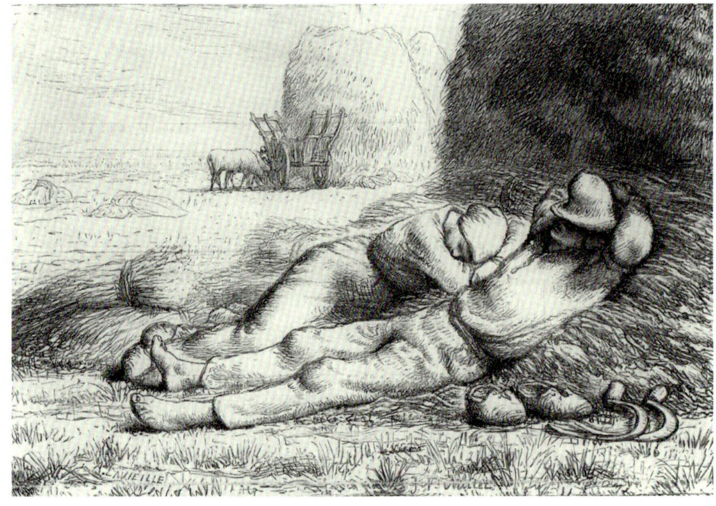

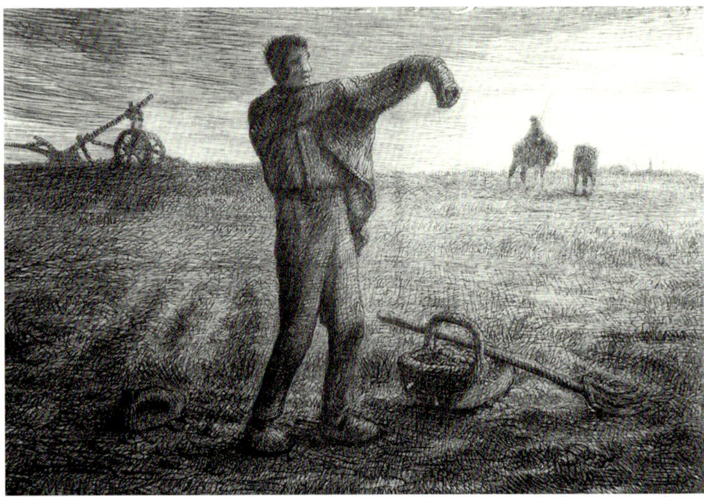

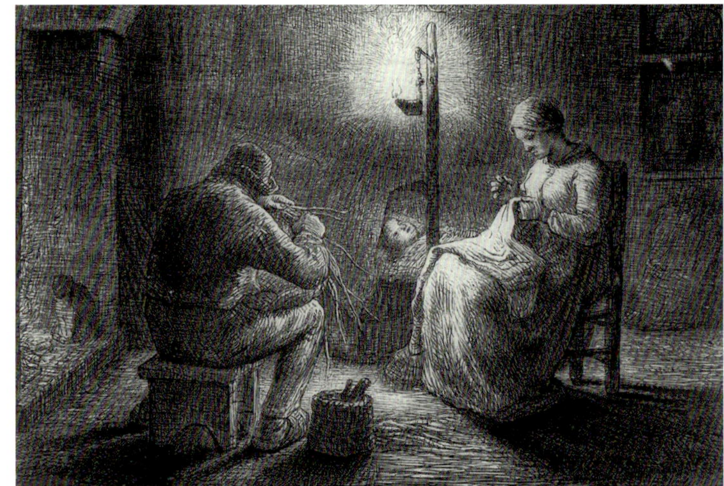

plate 55

After **Jean-François Millet** (1814-1875)

The four times of the day. Morning: going to work, 1873

Amsterdam, Van Gogh Museum (Vincent van Gogh Foundation)

plate 56

After **Jean-François Millet** (1814-1875)

The four times of the day. Noon: rest, 1873

Amsterdam, Van Gogh Museum (Vincent van Gogh Foundation)

plate 57

After **Jean-François Millet** (1814-1875)

The four times of the day. The end of the day, 1873

Amsterdam, Van Gogh Museum (Vincent van Gogh Foundation)

plate 58

After **Jean-François Millet** (1814-1875)

The four times of the day. Night: the watch, 1873

Amsterdam, Van Gogh Museum (Vincent van Gogh Foundation)

'I want to tell you which prints I have on the wall. [...] Millet, The hours of the day (woodcuts, 4 sheets)' [37/30].

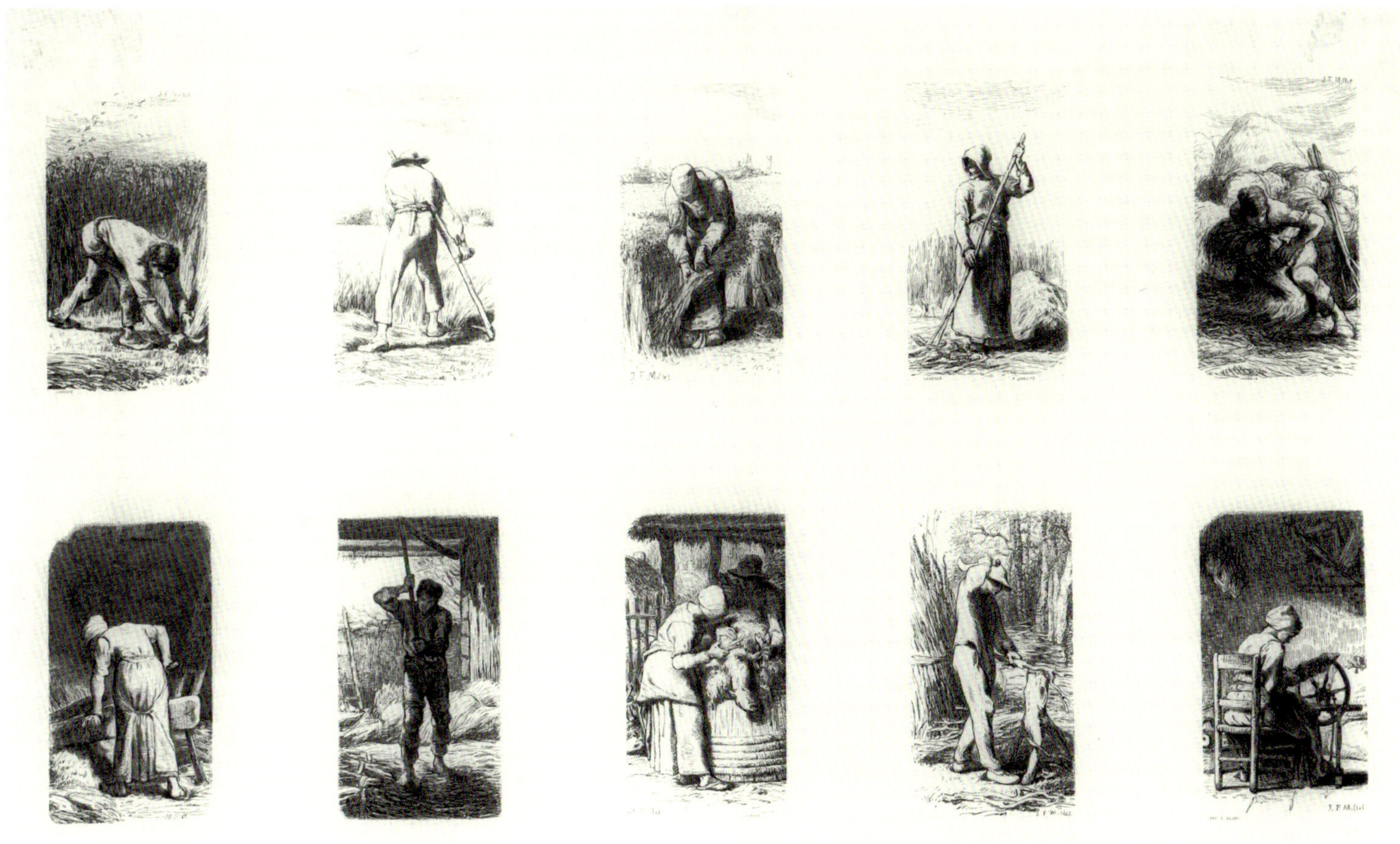

plate 59

After **Jean-François Millet** (1814-1875)
The labours of the fields, 1853 (series of ten prints)
Amsterdam, Van Gogh Museum (Vincent van Gogh Foundation)

'If I am not mistaken, you must still have "Labours of the fields" by Millet. Would you be so kind as to lend them to me for a while, and send them by mail? I must tell you that I am busy making large sketches after Millet, and that I have already finished "The hours of the day" and "The sower"' [155/134].

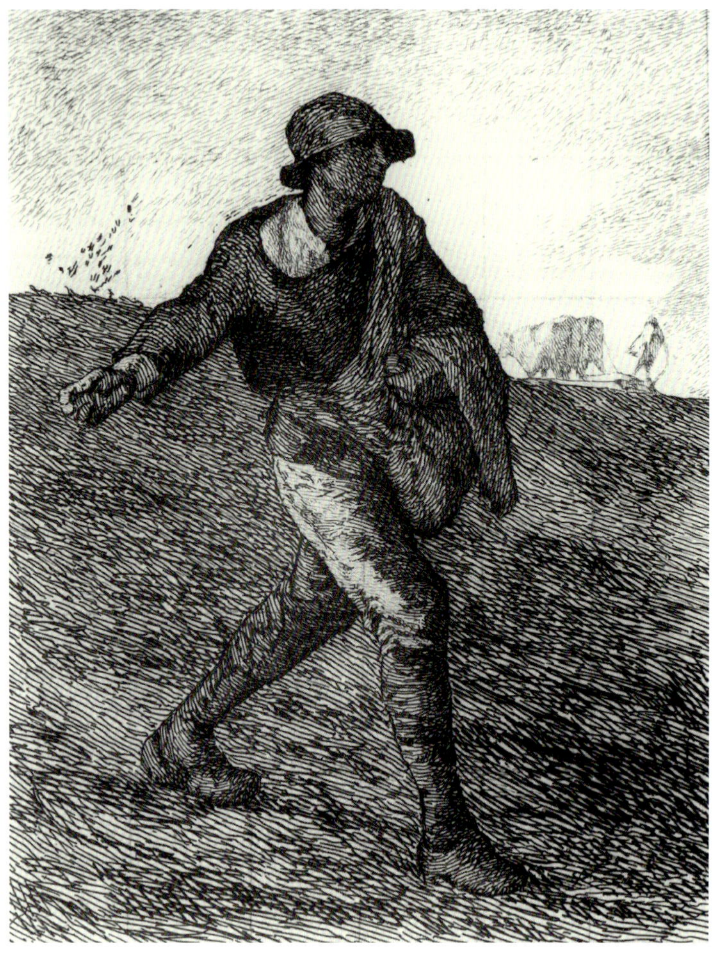

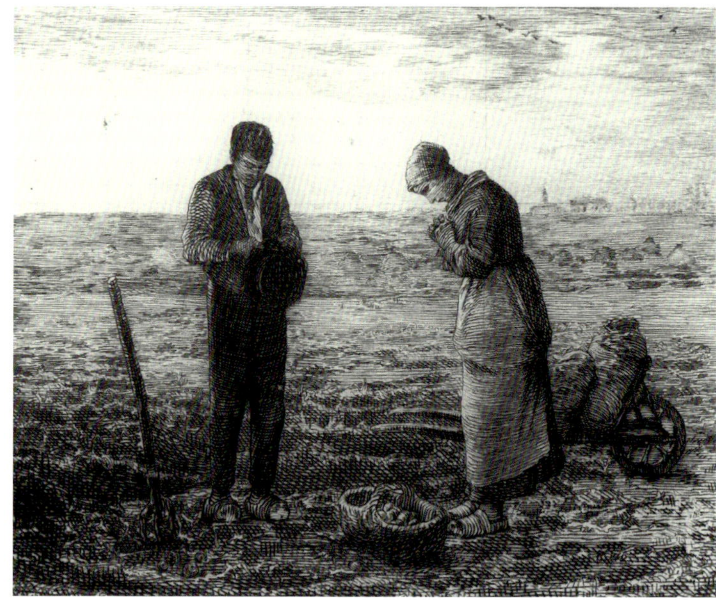

plate 60

After **Jean-François Millet** (1814-1875)
The sower, c. 1850
Amsterdam, Van Gogh Museum (Vincent van Gogh Foundation)

'If I am not mistaken, you must still have "Labours of the fields" by Millet. Would you be so kind as to lend them to me for a while, and send them by mail? I must tell you that I am busy making large sketches after Millet, and that I have already finished "The hours of the day" and "The sower"' [155/134].

plate 61

After **Jean-François Millet** (1814-1875)
The angelus, c. 1873
Amsterdam, Van Gogh Museum (Vincent van Gogh Foundation)

'Yes, that painting by Millet "The evening Angelus", "that is it." It's rich, it's poetry' [17/13].

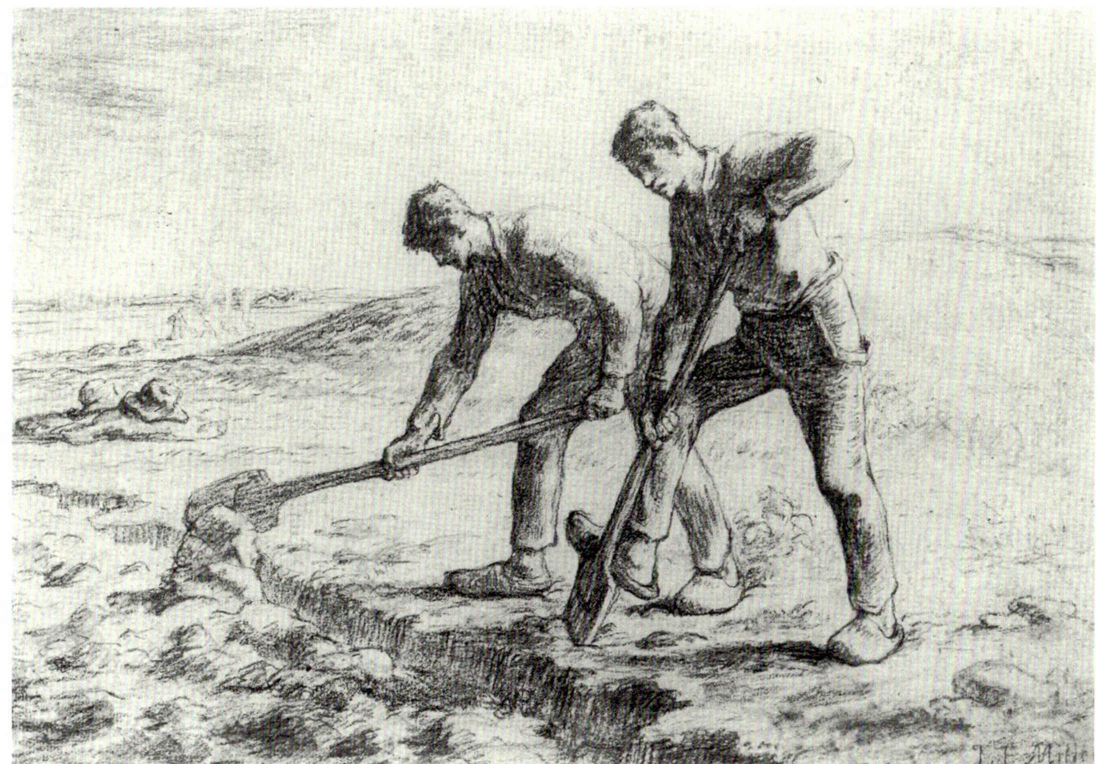

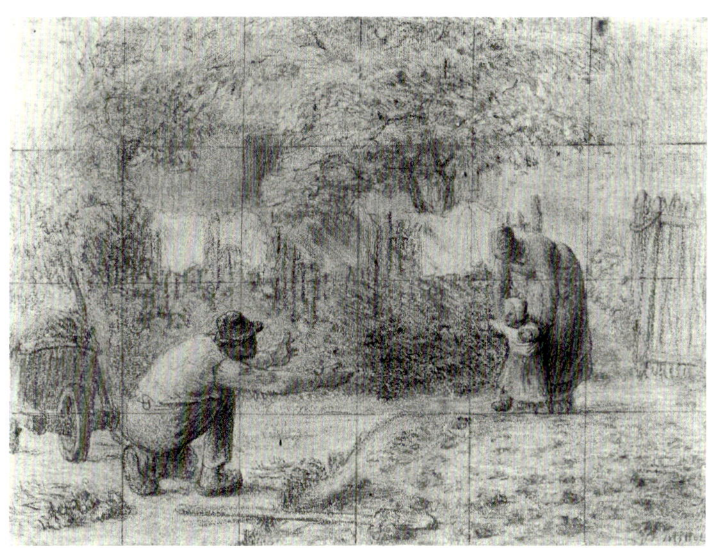

plate 62

After **Jean-François Millet** (1814-1875)
Men digging
Amsterdam, Van Gogh Museum (Vincent van Gogh Foundation)

'Did you ever see an original etching by Millet of a man wheeling a barrow full of manure into a garden on a day like today, in early spring? And remember, too, that he made an etching, "*Men digging*"; if you ever come across it you will not forget it in a hurry' [141/120].

plate 63

After **Jean-François Millet** (1814-1875)
The first steps, c. 1858
Amsterdam, Van Gogh Museum (Vincent van Gogh Foundation)

'How beautiful that Millet is, "A child's first steps"!' [817/611].

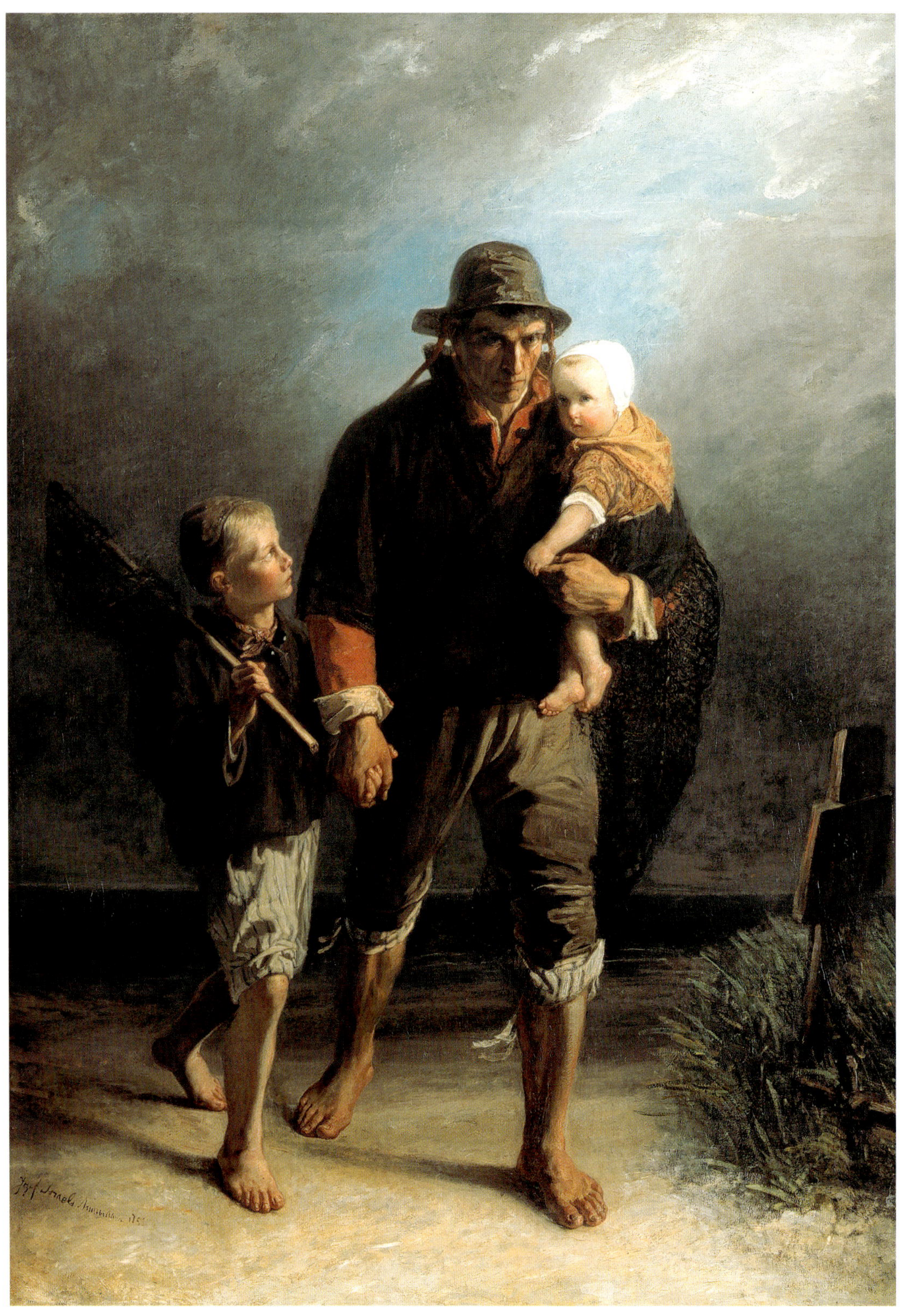

plate 64

Jozef Israëls (1824-1911)
At the churchyard, 1856
Amsterdam, Stedelijk Museum (on loan to the Groninger Museum)

'But I repeat – speaking of technique, there is a very much healthier and sounder technique in Israëls, for instance in that very old canvas, the fisherman of Zandvoort, with its splendid chiaroscuro, than the technique of those who are always equally smooth everywhere, flat and distingué through their iron-cold colour. The fisherman of Zandvoort, well you can safely hang it beside an old Delacroix – "The barque of Dante", and it is the same family' [538/427].

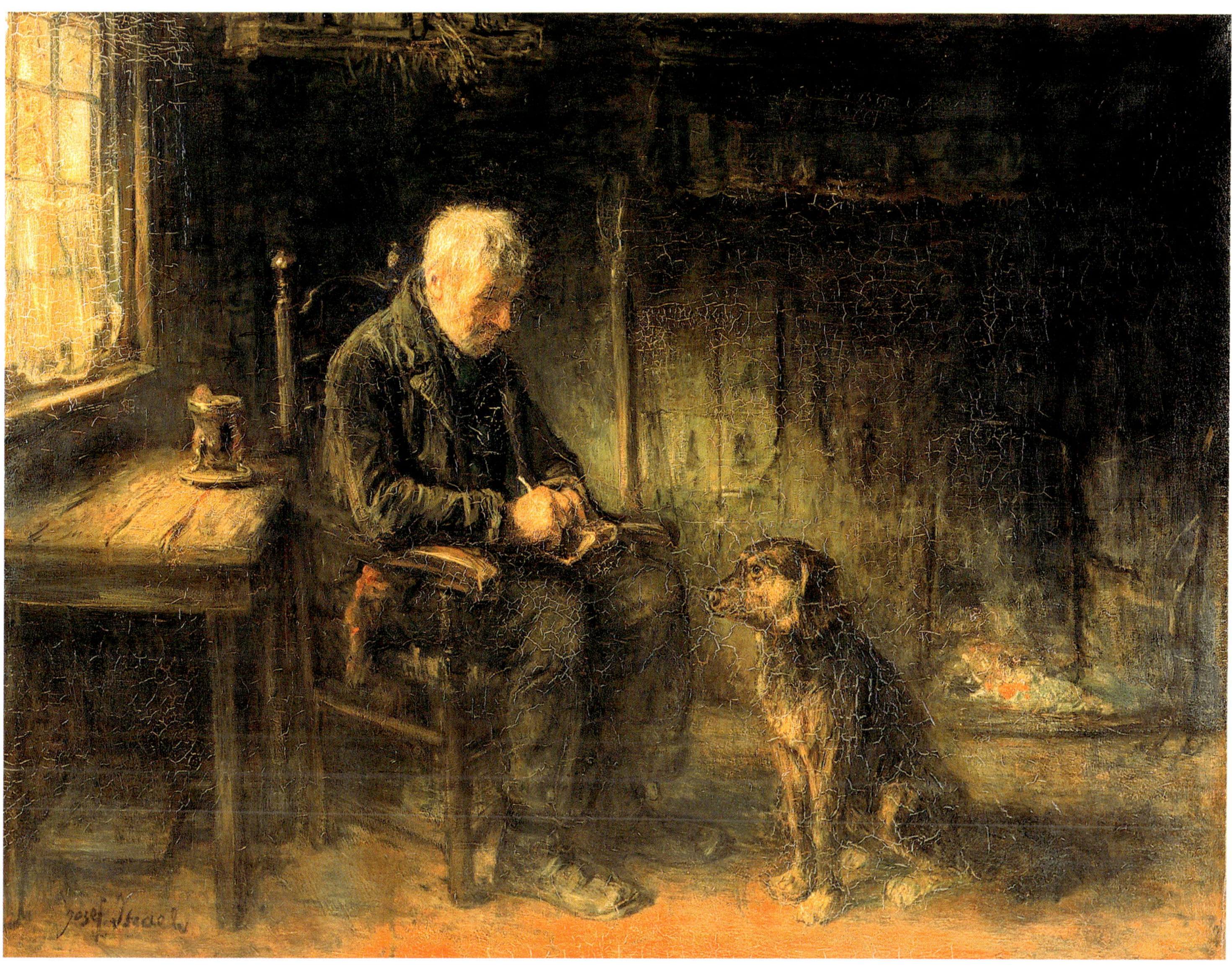

plate 65

Jozef Israëls (1824-1911)
Old friends, 1882
Philadelphia Museum of Art, The William L. Elkins Collection

'That is all – that twilight, that silence, that loneliness of those old two, the little man and the dog, the understanding between those two, that medita-tion of the old man – what he is thinking of I do not know, I cannot tell, but it must be a deep, a long thought, something, but I do not know what, that comes rising up from a past long gone – perhaps that is what gives the expression to his face, an expression melancholy, contented, submissive, something that reminds one of Longfellow's famous poem with the refrain: "But the thoughts of youth are long, long thoughts"' [210/181].

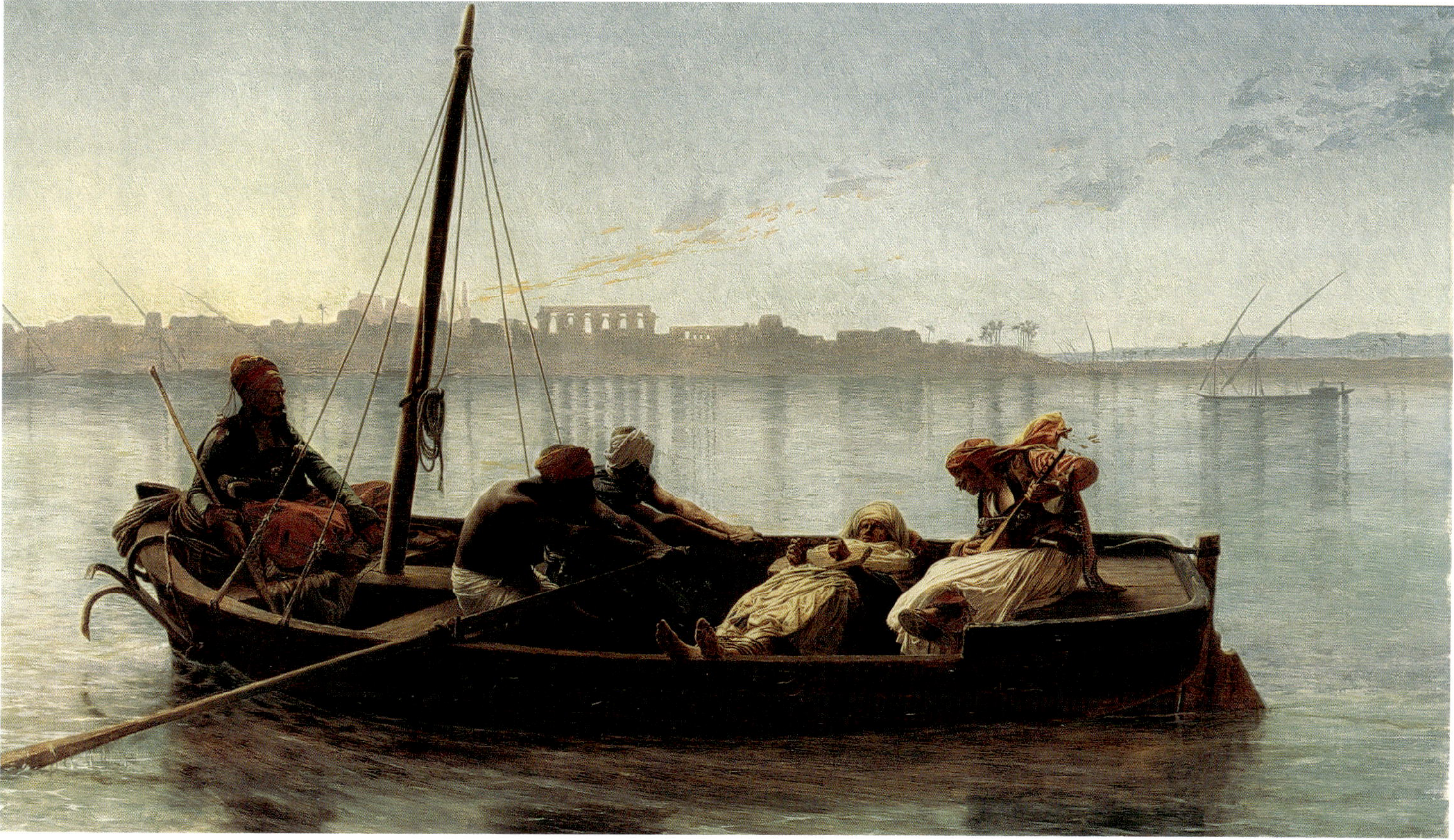

plate 66

Jean-Léon Gérôme (1824-1904)
The prisoner, 1861
Nantes, Musée des Beaux-Arts

'Take the *Prisoner* by Gérôme – the man lying fettered is most certainly in
an unpleasant situation, but to my way of thinking he is in a better condi-
tion than the fellow who has the upper hand and is harassing him. I tell
you this in order to point out the extremes of certain conditions. I am far
from confusing my own fate, for instance, with terribly aggravated misery
like the prisoner's. All the same, something of what I want to point out
can be seen in our society' [420/350a].

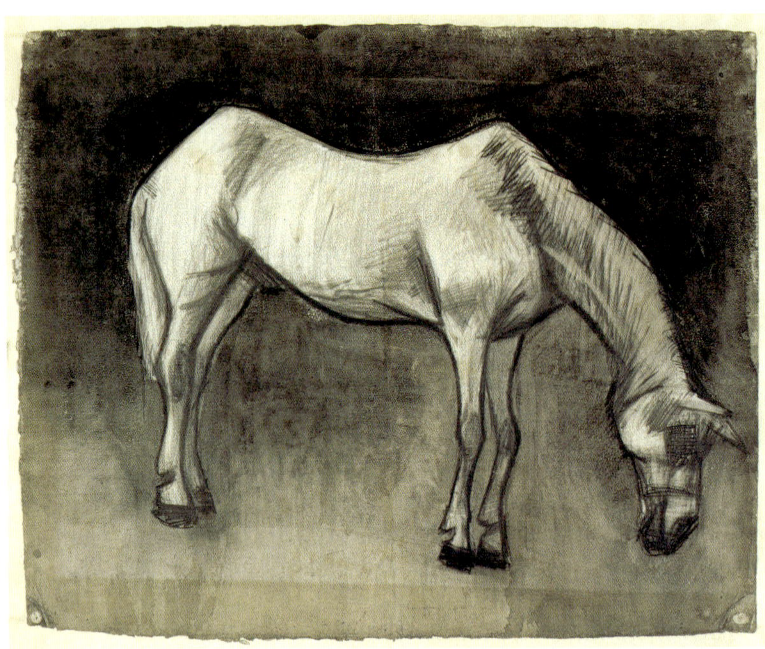

plate 67

Vincent van Gogh (1853-1890)
Old nag (F 1032 JH 368), 1883
Amsterdam, Van Gogh Museum (Vincent van Gogh Foundation)

'This drawing [an unknown drawing of a refuse dump] requires studies of
horses, and I made two of them today, in the stables of the Rhine railway
station, and I shall probably get an old horse at the refuse dump'
[352/289].

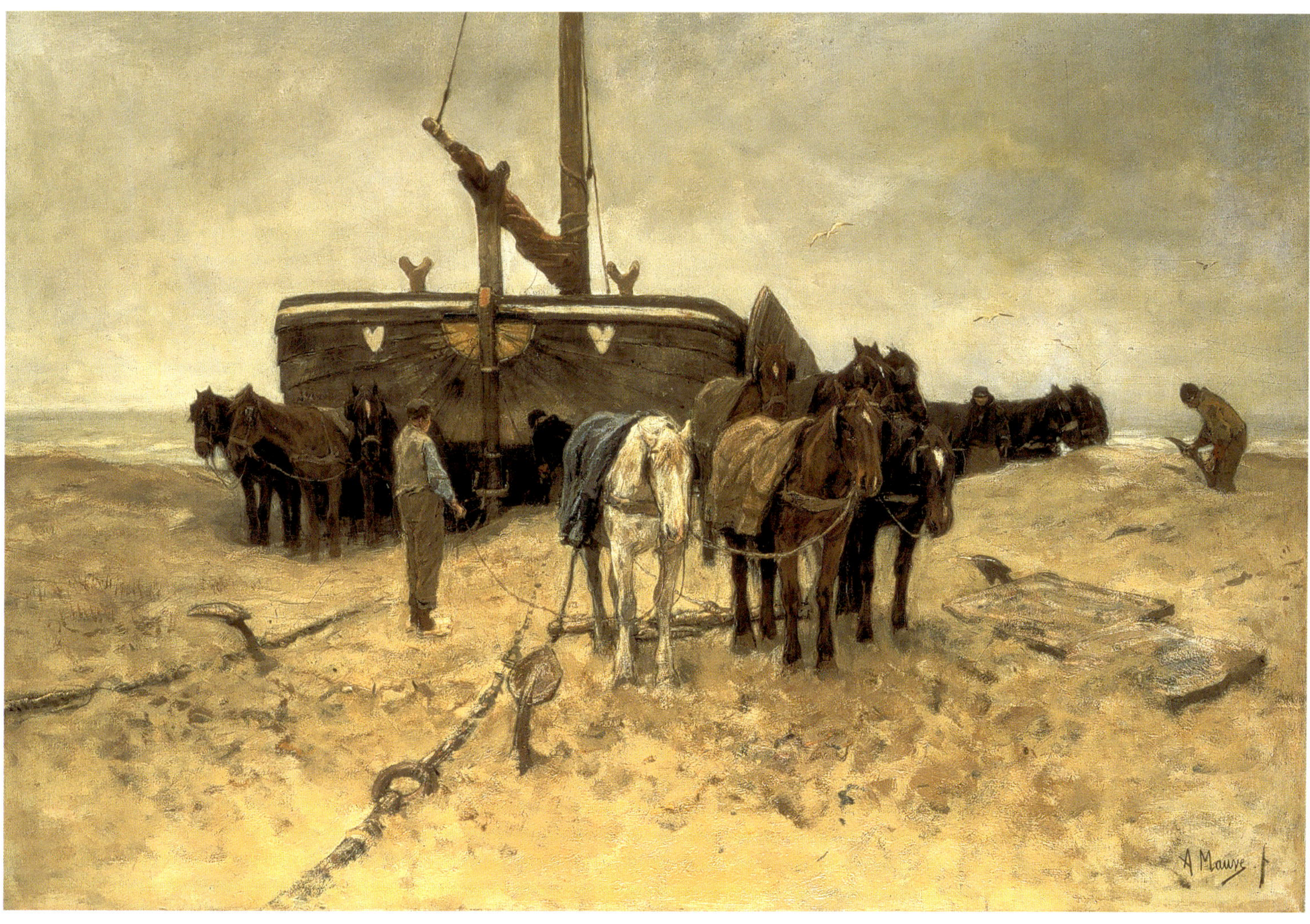

plate 68

Anton Mauve (1838-1888)
Fishing boat on the beach, 1882
The Hague, Gemeentemuseum

'There is a Mauve, the large painting of the fishing smack being drawn up the dunes; it is a masterpiece. I have never heard a good sermon on resignation, nor can I imagine a good one, except that painting by Mauve and the work of Millet. That is the resignation – but the real kind, not that of the clergymen. Those nags, those poor, broken-down old nags, black, white, brown; they stand there, patiently submissive, willing, resigned and quiet. They still have to draw the heavy boat up the last bit of the way – the job is almost done. Stop a moment, they pant, they are covered with sweat, but they do not murmur, they do not protest – they do not complain – about anything. They got over that long ago, years and years ago. They are resigned to living and working a little longer, but if they have to go to the knacker tomorrow, so be it, they are ready. I find such a mightily deep, practical, silent philosophy in this painting, it seems to say, "knowing how to suffer without complaining, that is the only practical thing, it is the great science, the lesson to learn, the solution to the problem of life." I think this painting by Mauve would be one of the rare paintings before which Millet would stand for a long time, and mutter to himself, "There is heart in that painter"' [210/181].

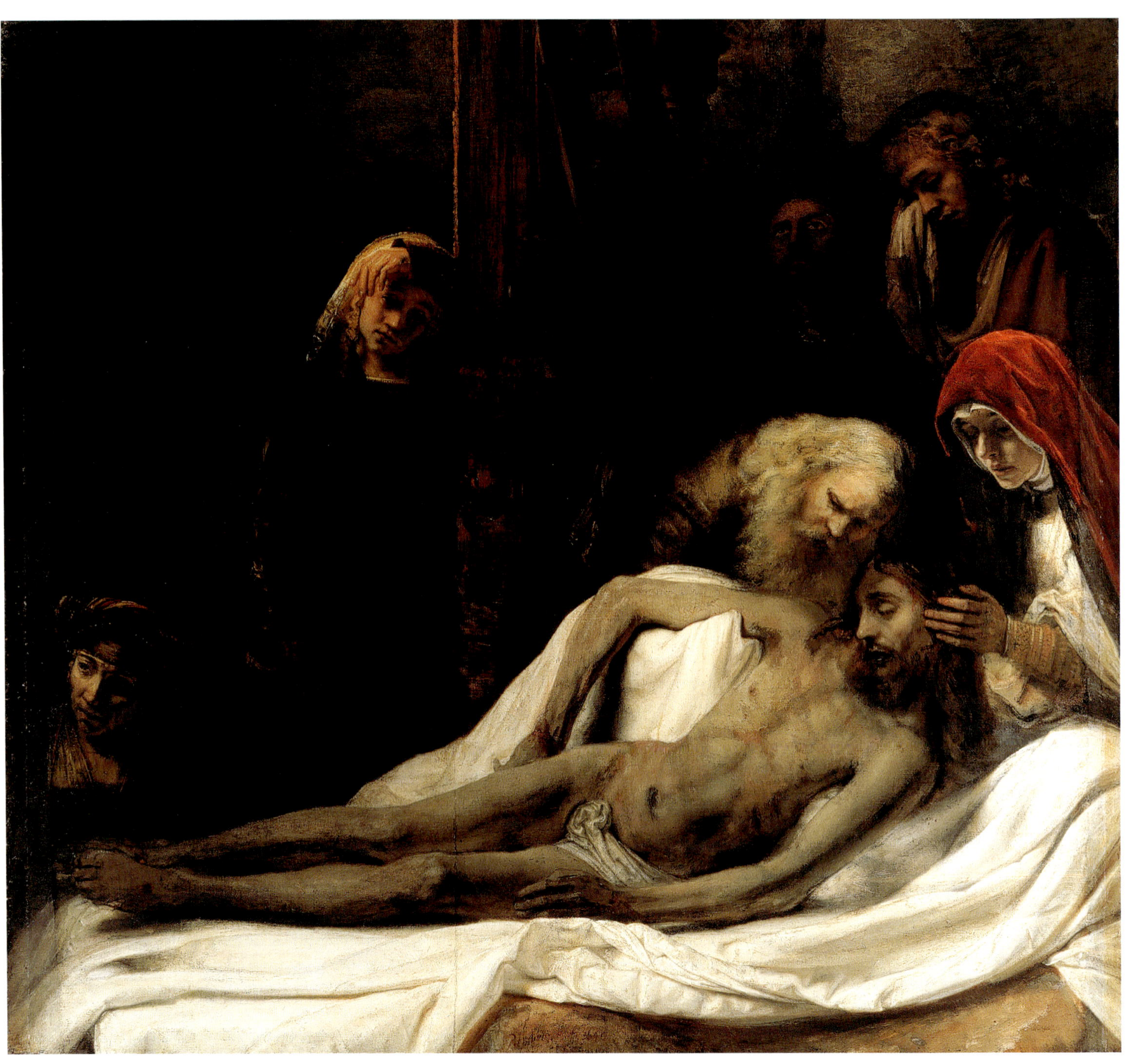

plate 69

Workshop of **Rembrandt van Rijn** (1606-1669)
The lamentation of Christ, c. 1650
Sarasota, The John and Mable Ringling Museum of Art, State Art Museum
of Florida, Bequest of John Ringling

'There's a nice exhibition of old art here, including a large "Descent from
the Cross" by Rembrandt, 5 large figures at twilight, you can imagine the
emotion' [29/22].

plate 70

Follower of **Rembrandt van Rijn** (1606-1669)
Christ in the house of Martha and Mary, c. 1650
London, British Museum

'Twilight is falling, "blessed twilight", Dickens called it, and indeed he was
right. Blessed twilight, especially when two or three are together in harmony of mind, and like scribes bring forth out of their treasure things old
and new, like a householder. Blessed twilight, when two or three are gathered together in His name and He is in the midst of them. And blessed is

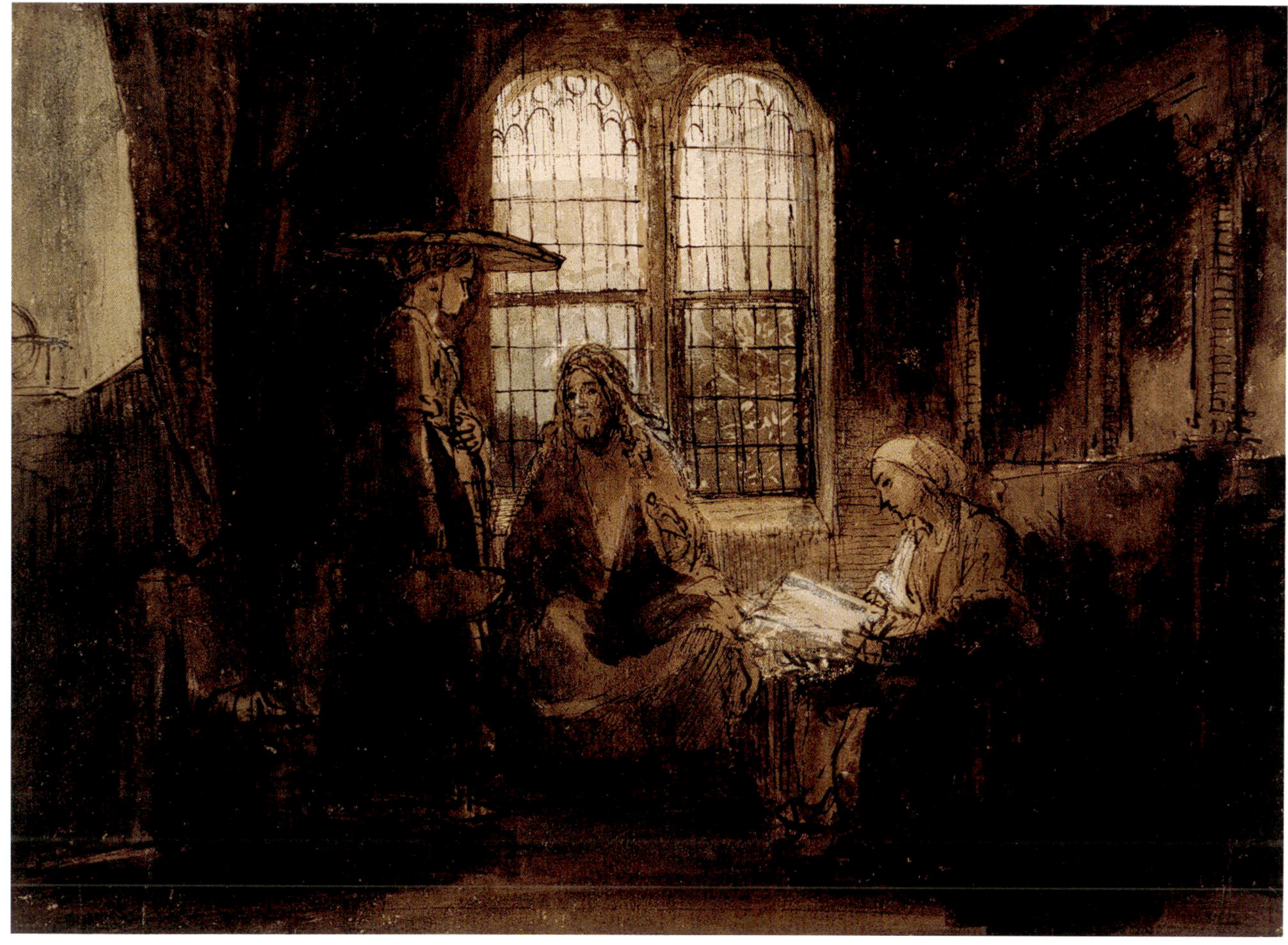

the man who knows these things and does them too. Rembrandt knew that, for from the rich treasure of his heart he brought forth among other things that drawing in sepia, charcoal, ink, etc. (the one in the British Museum), representing the house in Bethany. Twilight fills the room, the figure of Our Lord, noble and impressive, stands out gravely dark against the window through which the evening twilight falls. Like the figure of John Halifax, who said that he was a Christian, against a white-curtained window in a room at Rose Cottage, I think, on an evening like so many that are described with so much feeling in the book. At the feet of Jesus sits Mary, who has chosen the good part which shall not be taken away from her, and Martha is in the room busy with something or other, if I remember rightly she stirs the fire or something similar. That drawing I hope never to forget, nor what it seems to tell me: "I am the light of the world: he that followeth me shall not walk in darkness, but shall have the light of life, the light of the Gospel preached unto the poor in my Father's kingdom, shining like a candle on a candlestick upon all that are in the house"' [130/110].

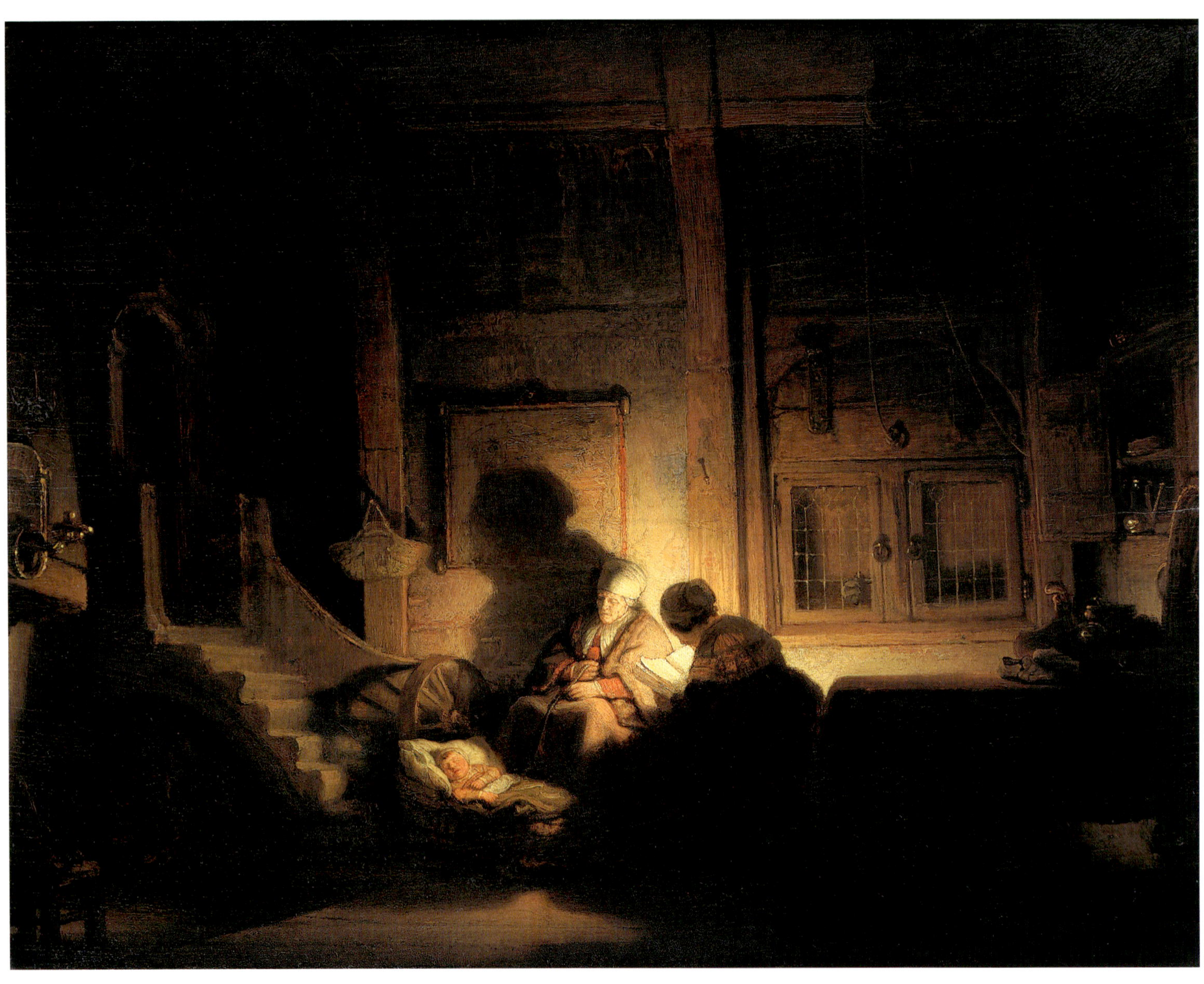

plate 71

Workshop of **Rembrandt van Rijn** (1606-1669)
The holy family at night, 1638-40
Amsterdam, Rijksmuseum

'A large, old Dutch room (in the evening, a candle on the table), in which
a young mother sits beside her child's cradle reading the Bible; an old
woman listens, [...] superb' [37/30].

plate 72

Rembrandt van Rijn (1606-1669)
Self-portrait, 1669
London, The National Gallery

'This is how Rembrandt painted angels. He does a self-portrait, old, tooth-less, wrinkled, wearing a cotton cap, a painting from life, in a mirror. He is dreaming, dreaming, and his brush takes up his self-portrait again, but this time from memory, and the expression on the face becomes sadder and more saddening, He dreams, dreams on, and why or how I cannot tell, but – as Socrates and Mohammed had their guardian spirits, so Rembrandt paints a supernatural angel with a da Vinci smile behind that old man who resembles himself' [651/B12].

plate 73

Vincent van Gogh (1853-1890)
Self-portrait as an artist (F 522 JH 1356), 1888
Amsterdam, Van Gogh Museum (Vincent van Gogh Foundation)

'Seeing that I am so busily occupied with myself just now, I want to see if I can paint my self-portrait in writing. In the first place I want to empha-sise the fact that in my opinion one and the same person may furnish motifs for very different portraits. Here I give a conception of mine, which is the result of a portrait I painted in the mirror, and which Theo now has. A pinkish-grey face with green eyes, ash-coloured hair, wrinkles on the forehead and around the mouth, stiff, wooden, a very red beard, consider-ably neglected and mournful, but the lips are full, a blue peasant's blouse of coarse linen, and a palette with lemon yellow, vermilion, Veronese green, cobalt blue, in short all the colours on the palette apart from the orange beard, but only whole colours. The figure against a greyish-white wall. You will say that this resembles somewhat, for instance, the face of – Death – in Van Eeden's book or some such thing – all right, but it is a figure like this – and it isn't easy to paint oneself – at any rate if it is to be *different* from a photograph. And you see – this, in my opinion, is the advantage that impressionism has over all the rest; it is not banal, and one seeks after a deeper resemblance than the photographer's' [633/W4].

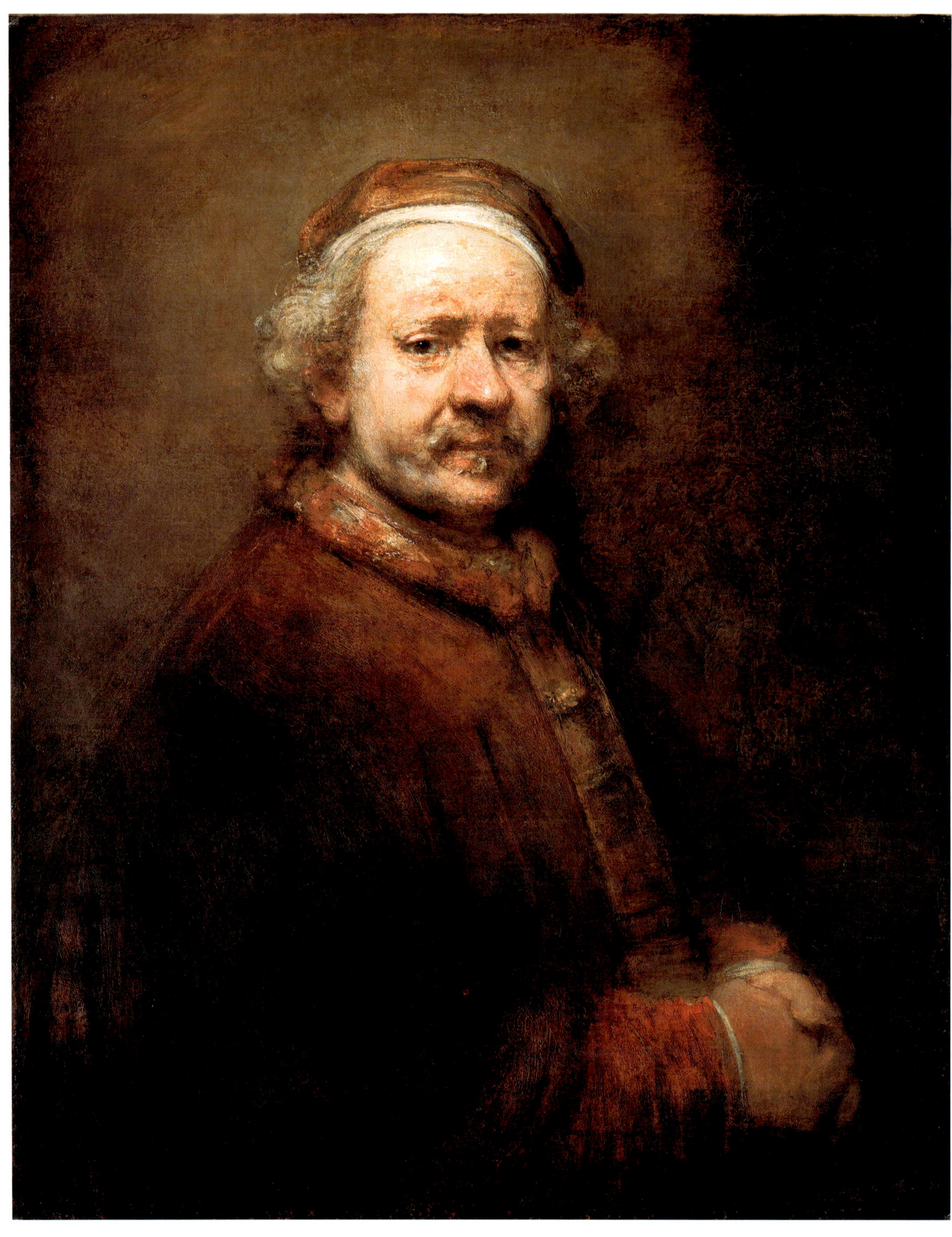

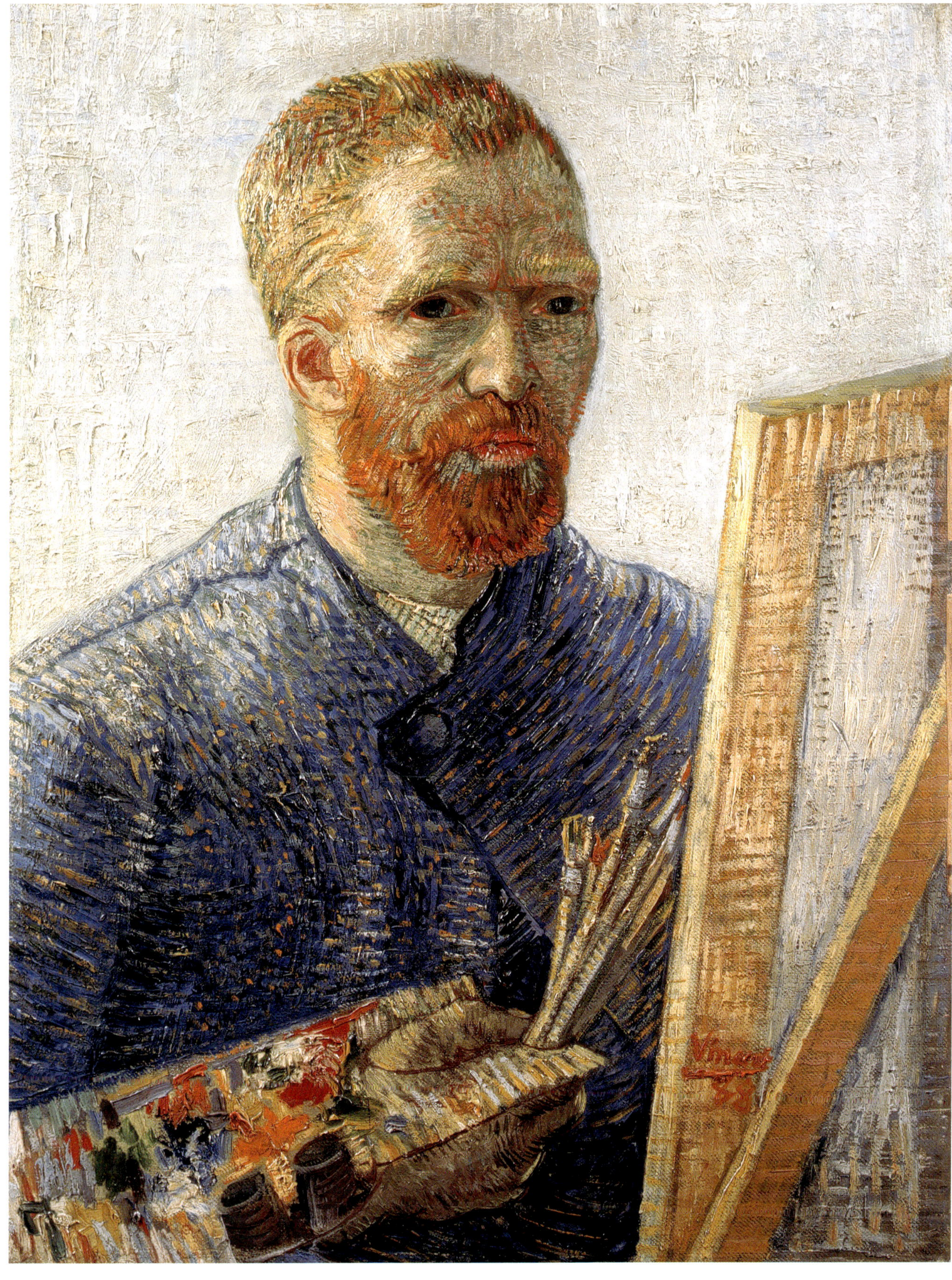

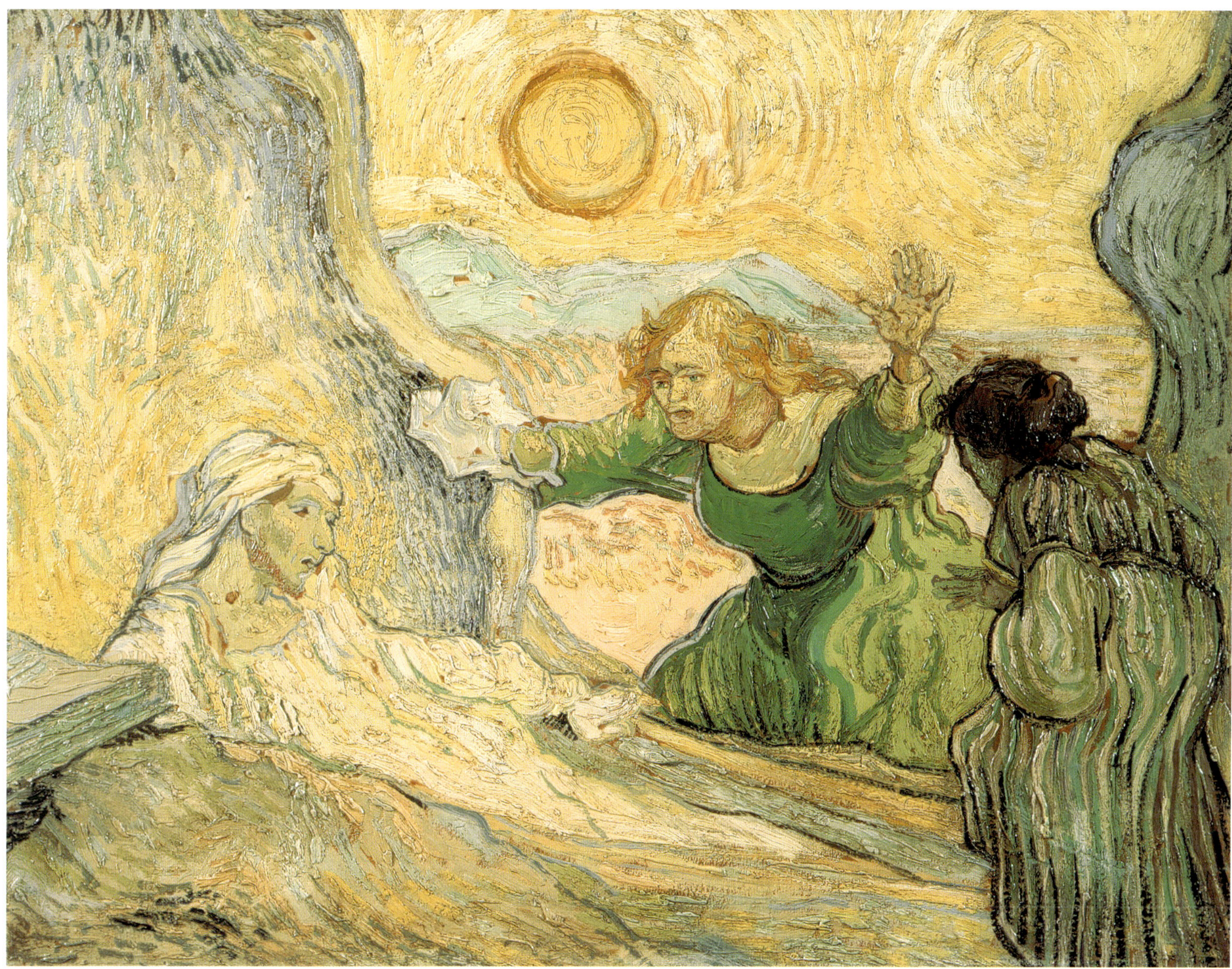

plate 74

Vincent van Gogh (1853-1890)
The raising of Lazarus (after Rembrandt) (F 677 |H 1972), 1890
Amsterdam, Van Gogh Museum (Vincent van Gogh Foundation)

'On the back of this page I have scribbled a sketch after a painting I have done of three figures which are in the background of the etching of Lazarus: the dead man and his two sisters. The cave and the corpse are white-yellow-violet. The woman who takes the handkerchief away from the face of the resurrected man has a green dress and orange hair. The other has black hair and a gown of striped green and pink. In the background a countryside, blue hills, a yellow sunrise. Thus the combination of colours would itself suggest the same thing that the chiaroscuro of the etching expresses' [867/632].

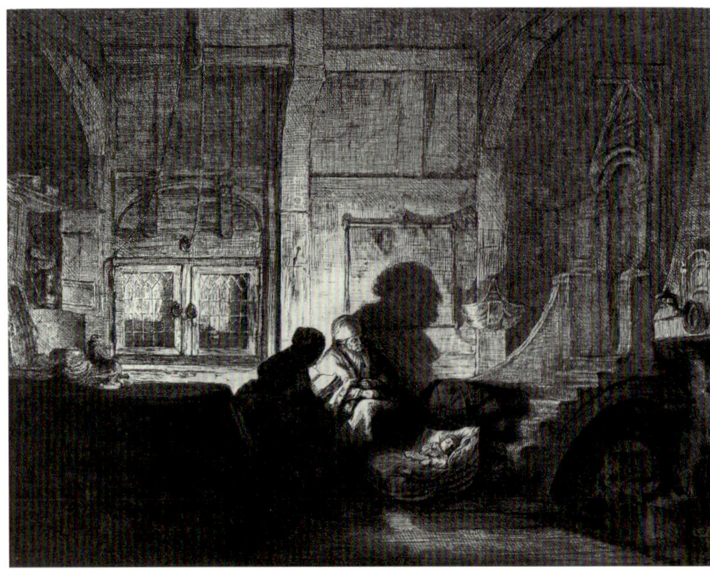

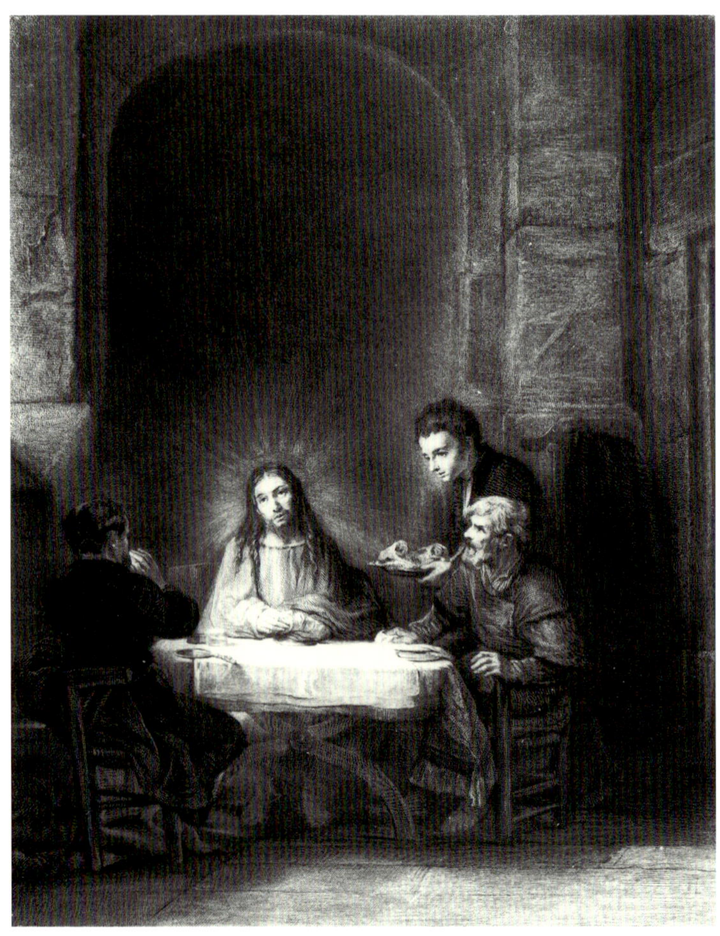

plate 75

After **Rembrandt van Rijn** (1606-1669)
The holy family at night, c. 1787
Paris, Bibliothèque Nationale de France, Cabinet des Estampes

'I want to tell you which prints I have on the wall. [...] Rembrandt, Reading the Bible (a large, old Dutch room (in the evening, a candle on the table), in which a young mother sits beside her child's cradle reading the Bible; an old woman listens, it is something that recalls: Verily I say unto you, "for where two or three are gathered together in my name, there am I in the midst of them," it is an old copper engraving, as large as "Le buisson", superb)' [37/30].

plate 76

After **Rembrandt van Rijn** (1606-1669)
Christ at Emmaus, 1875
Bordeaux, Musée Goupil

'Rembrandt's "Christ at Emmaus" of which I wrote has been engraved, Messrs G&Co [the art dealers Goupil & Cie] will publish the engraving in the autumn' [42/35].

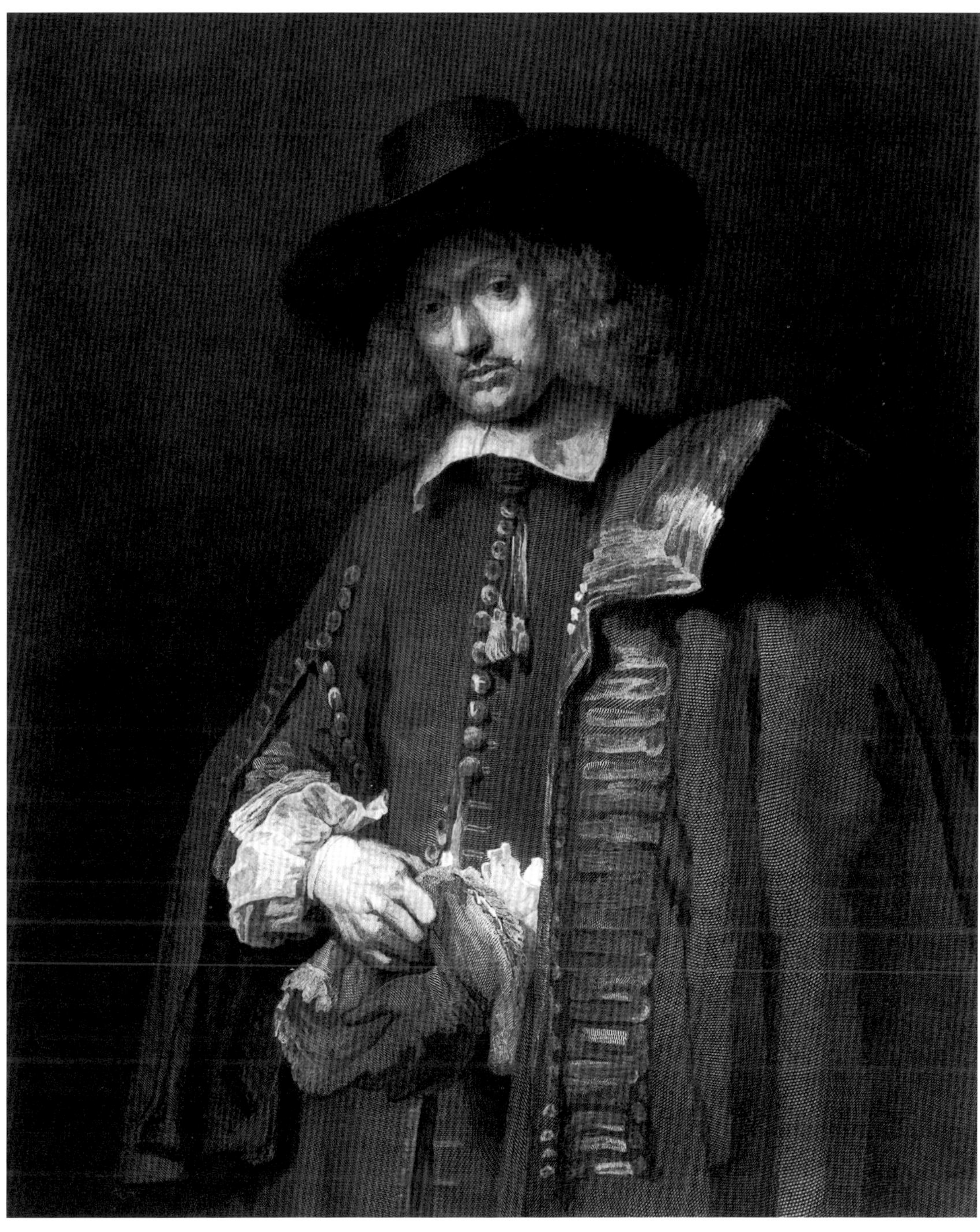

plate 77

After **Rembrandt van Rijn** (1606-1669)
Portrait of Jan Six, c. 1874-78
Amsterdam, Rijksprentenkabinet

'You know the etching by Rembrandt, Burgomaster Six standing in front of
the window, reading. I know that Uncle Vincent and Cor like it very much,
and I sometimes think that they must have looked like that when they
were younger. You also know the portrait of Six when he was older, I believe there is an engraving of it in your gallery. That life of his must have
been a fine and serious life' [46/37].

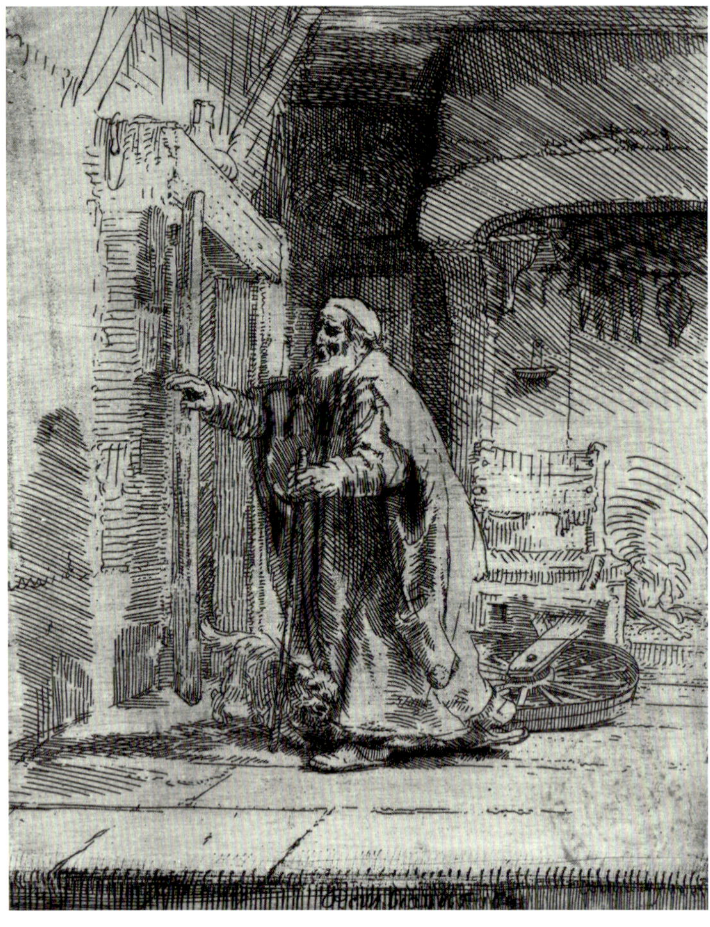

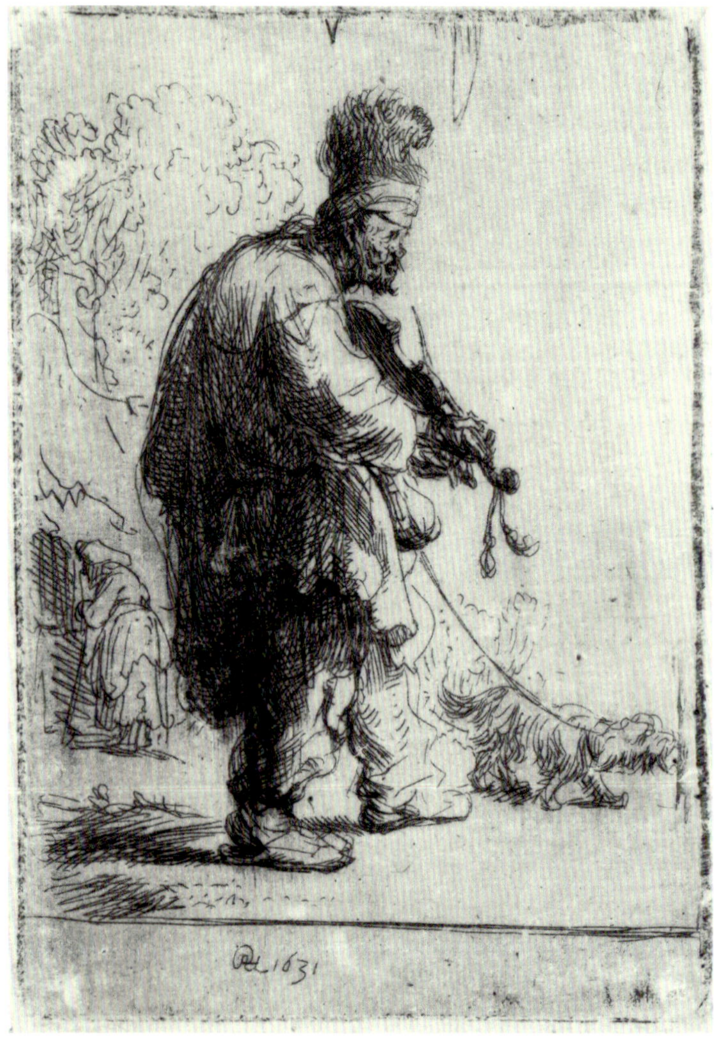

plate 78

Rembrandt van Rijn (1606-1669)
The blindness of Tobit, 1651
Amsterdam, Rijksprentenkabinet

'This morning I bought a small engraving, "Tobit" after Rembrandt, from a
Jew for 6 cents' [116/97].

plate 79

Rembrandt van Rijn (1606-1669)
The blind fiddler, 1631
Amsterdam, Rijksprentenkabinet

'Thank you very much for the etchings – you have chosen just the ones
I have liked for a long time now, [...] and you have added the "Blind man"'
[866/630].

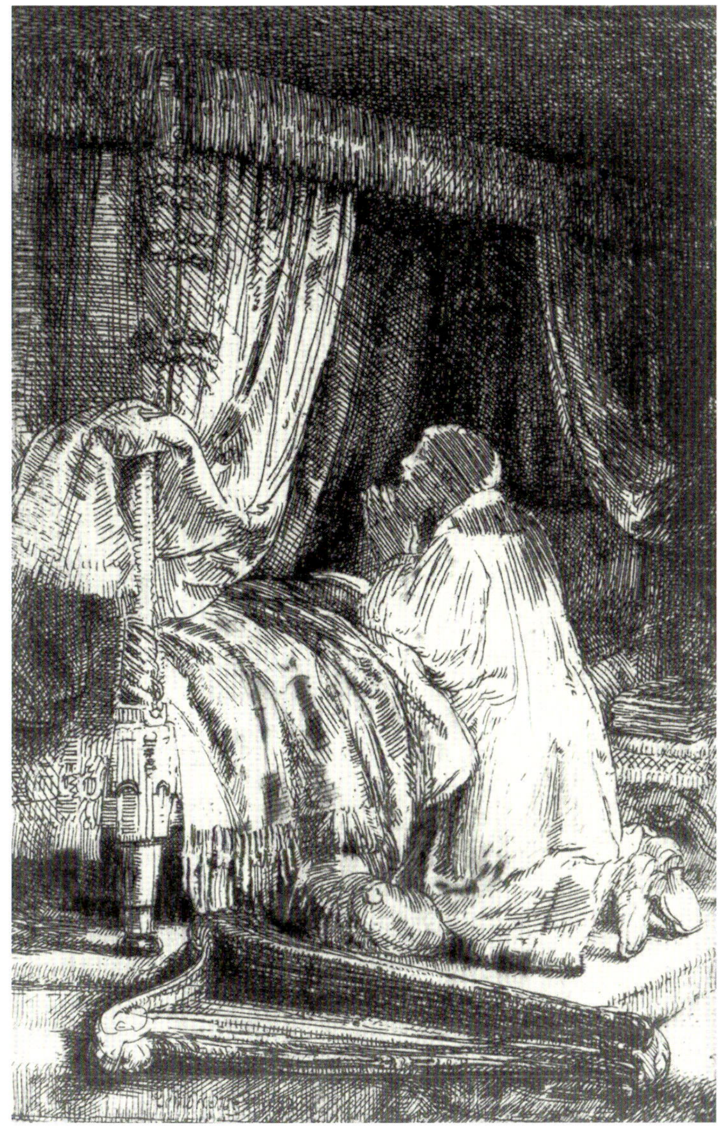

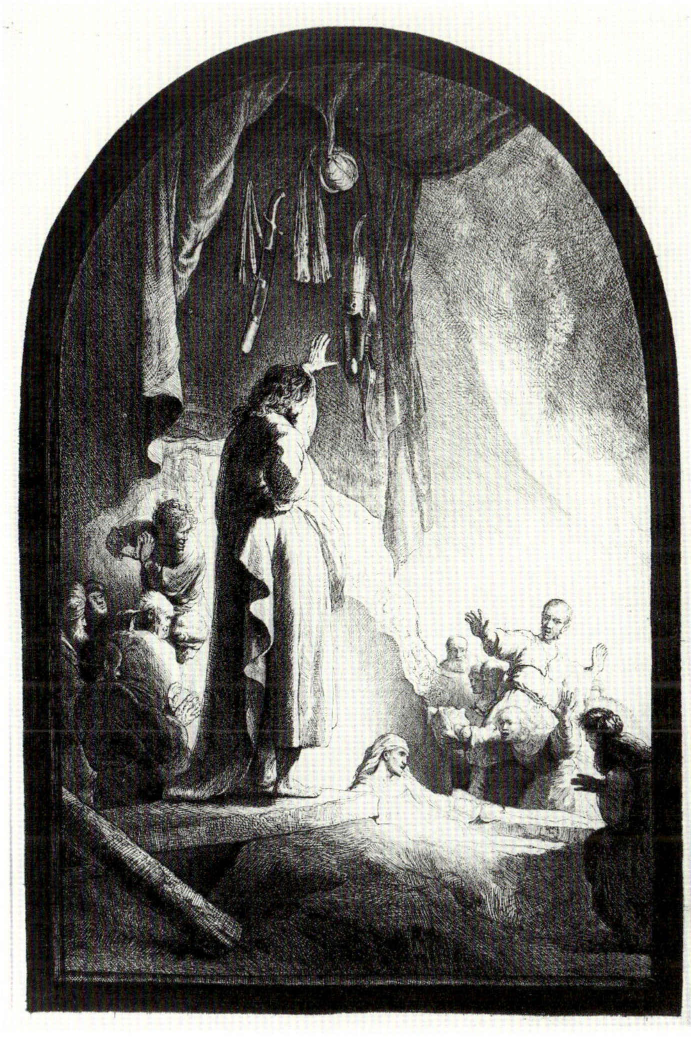

plate 80

Rembrandt van Rijn (1606-1669)
David in prayer, 1652
Amsterdam, Rijksprentenkabinet

'And in that picture by Ruipérez, the "Imitation of Jesus Christ", it is also twilight, and also in another etching by Rembrandt: *David in prayer to God.* Yes, it is to "blessed twilight" that we owe the words, "As the hart panteth after the water brooks, so panteth my soul after thee, O God. My soul thirsteth for God, for the living God"' [130/110].

plate 81

After **Rembrandt van Rijn** (1606-1669)
The raising of Lazarus
Amsterdam, Van Gogh Museum (Vincent van Gogh Foundation)

'Thank you very much for the etchings – you have chosen just the ones I have liked for a long time now, [...] the "Lazarus"' [866/630].

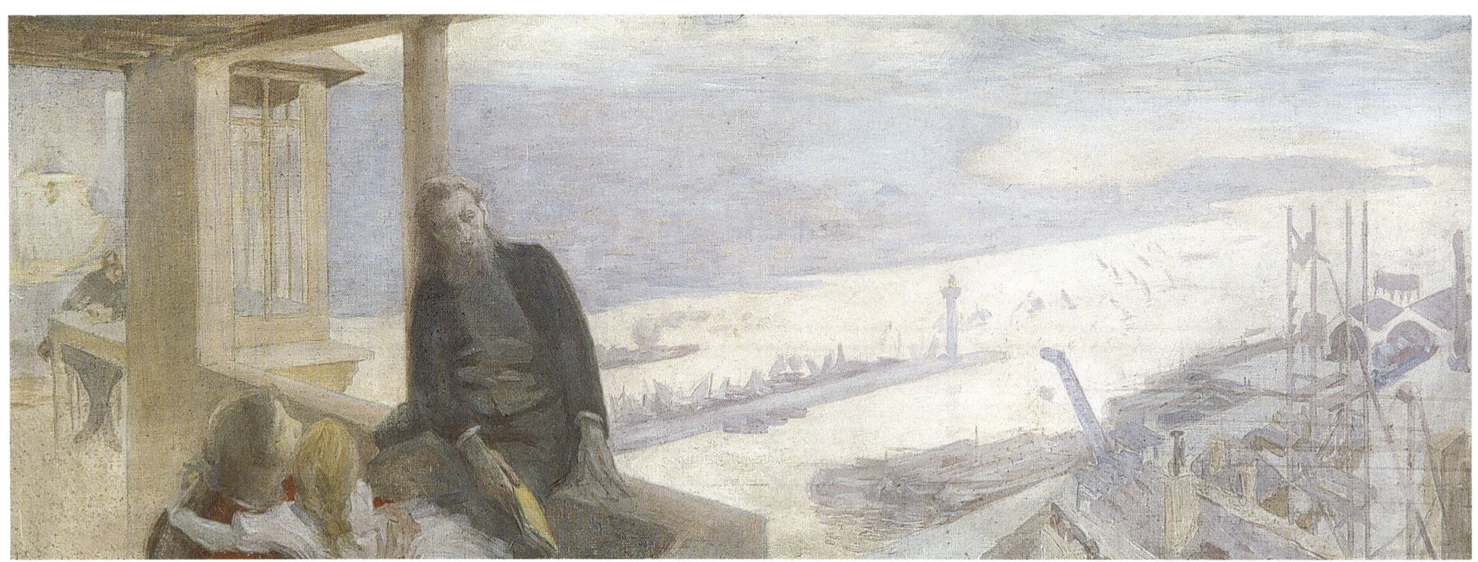

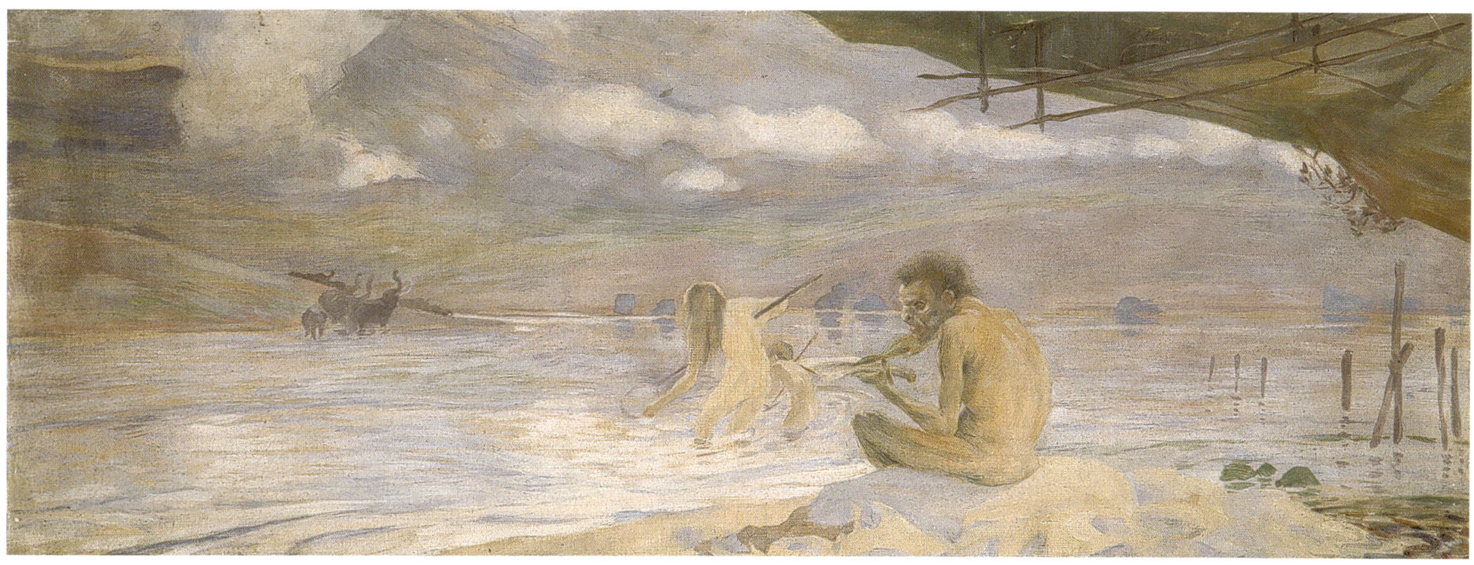

plate 82

Albert Besnard (1849-1934)
Modern man, c. 1884-86
Beauvais, Musée départemental de l'Oise

plate 83

Albert Besnard (1849-1934)
Prehistoric man, c. 1887
Private collection

'When Besnard did those two fine panels, primitive man and modern man, which we saw at Petit's, he expressed the same idea of making the modern man a reader' [799/602].

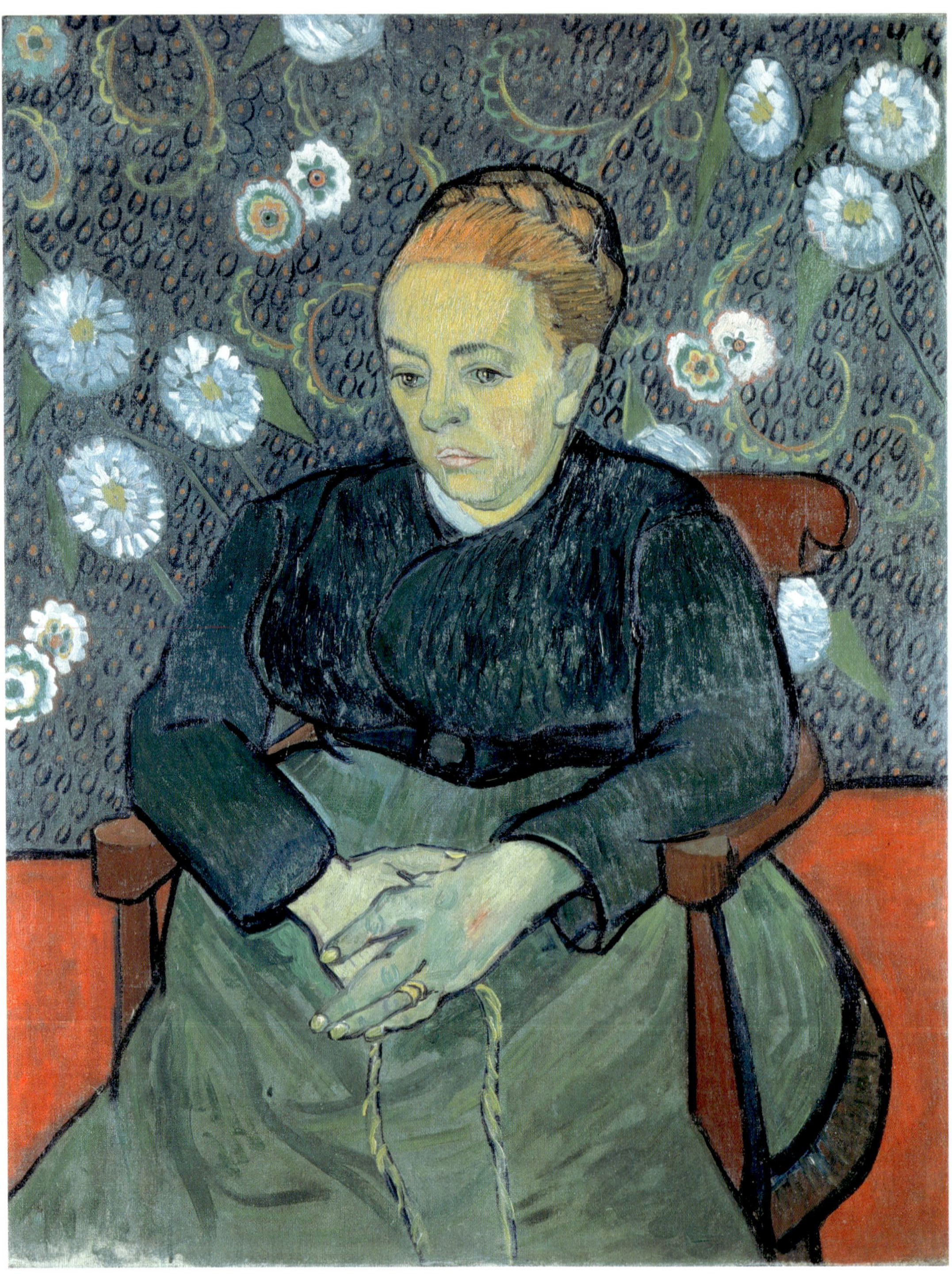

plate 84

Vincent van Gogh (1853-1890)

Augustine Roulin ('La berceuse') (F 507 JH 1672), 1888-89

Amsterdam, Stedelijk Museum (on loan to the Van Gogh Museum, Amsterdam)

'I have just said to Gauguin about this picture that when he and I were talking about the fishermen of Iceland and of their mournful isolation, exposed to all dangers, alone on the sad sea [...] the idea came to me to paint a picture in such a way that sailors, who are at once children and martyrs, [...] would feel the sense of being rocked come over them, reminding them of their own lullabies. Now, it may be said that it looks like a chromolithograph from a cheap shop' [747/574].

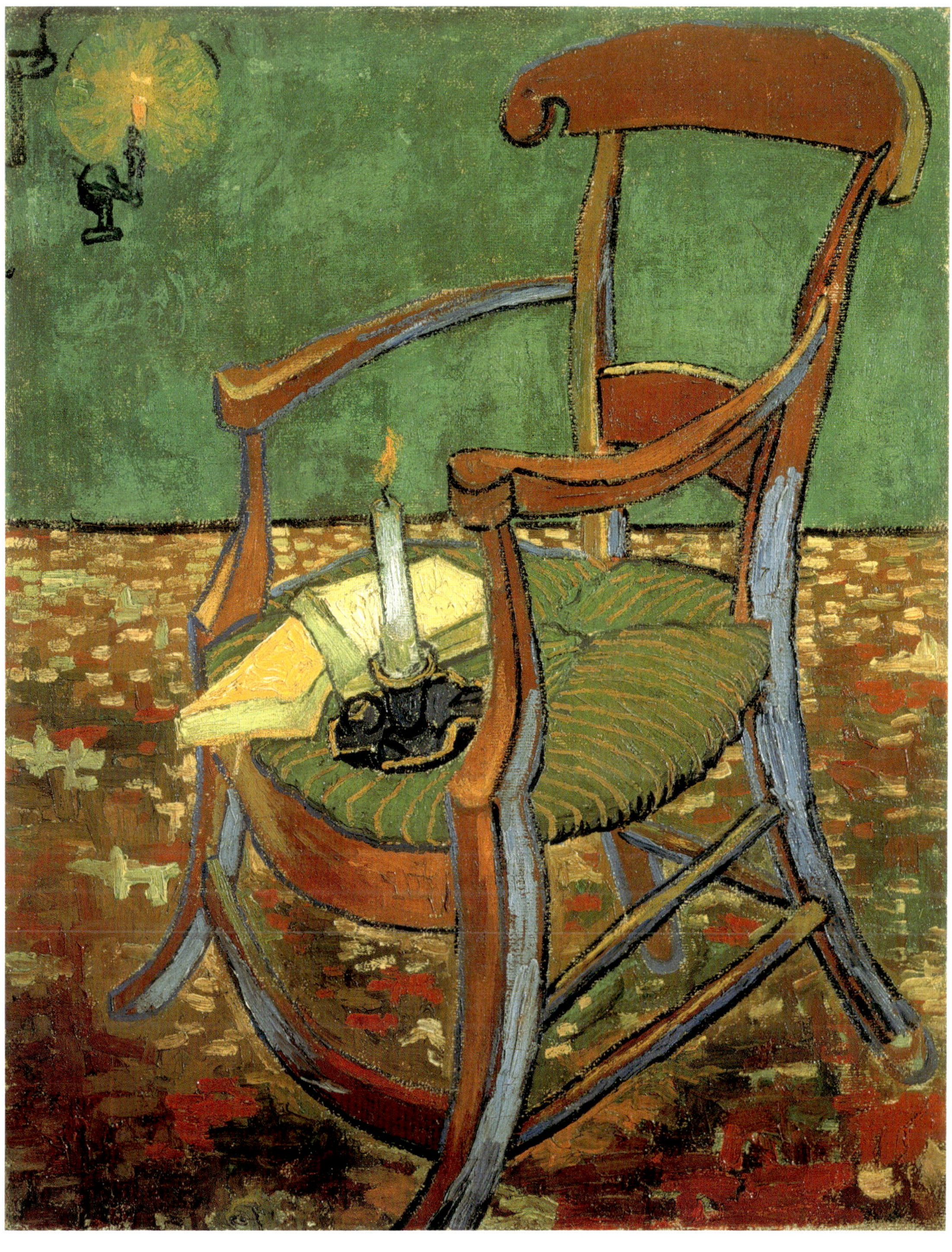

plate 85

Vincent van Gogh (1853-1890)
Gauguin's chair (F 499 JH 1636), 1888
Amsterdam, Van Gogh Museum (Vincent van Gogh Foundation)

'Then I owe a great deal to Paul Gauguin, with whom I worked for several months in Arles, and whom, moreover, I already knew in Paris. Gauguin, that curious artist, that strange individual, [...] that friend who likes to make one feel that a good picture should be equivalent to a good deed, not that he says so, but it is in fact difficult to be much in his company without being mindful of a certain moral responsibility. A few days before we parted company, when my illness forced me to go into a nursing home, I tried to paint "his empty place". It is a study of his wooden armchair, brown and dark red, the seat of greenish straw, and in place of the absent person, a lighted candle in a candlestick and some modern novels' [854/626a].

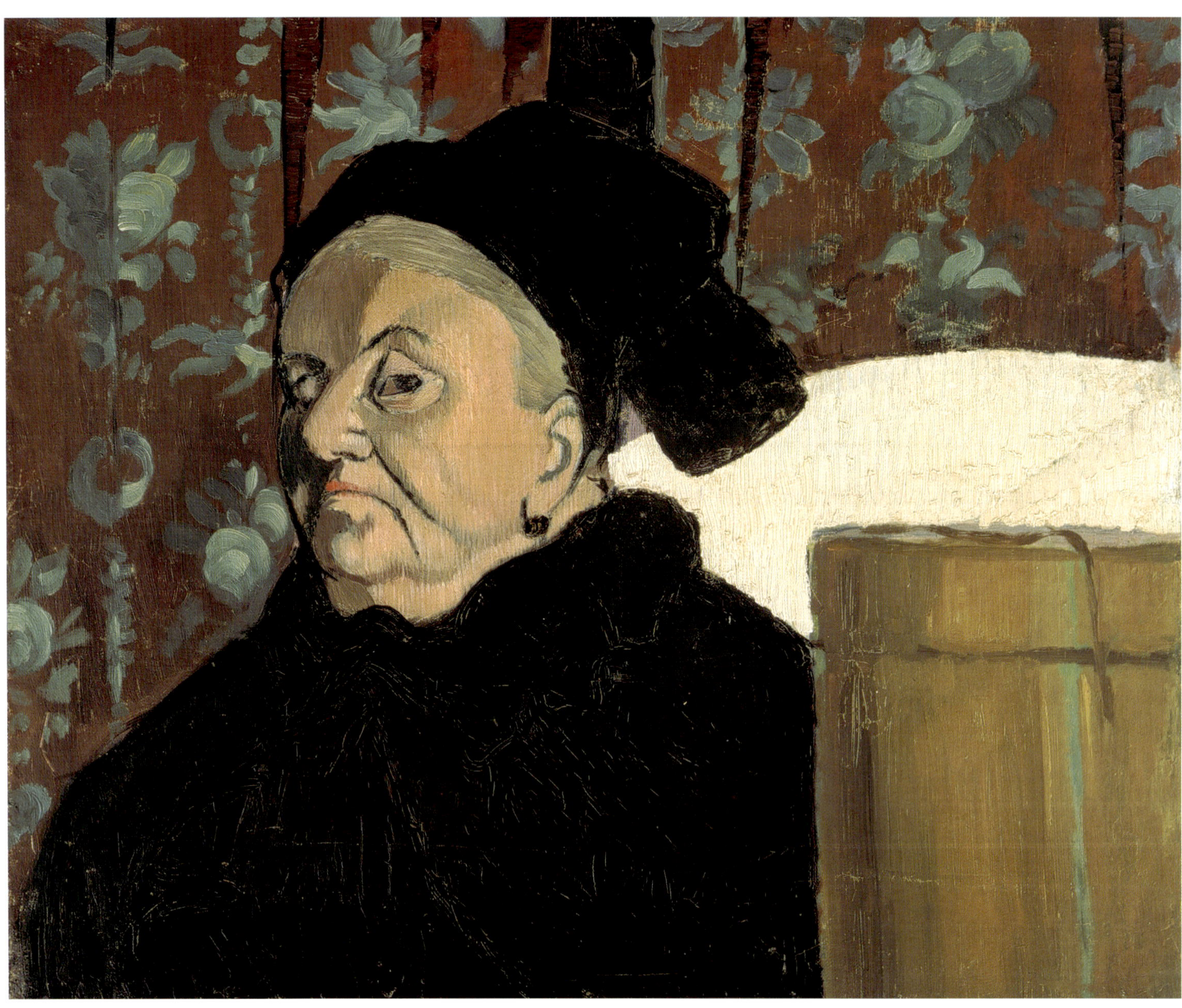

plate 86

Emile Bernard (1868-1941)
Portrait of Bernard's grandmother, 1887
Amsterdam, Van Gogh Museum (Vincent van Gogh Foundation)

'But I must speak to you again first of all about yourself, the two still lifes you have done and the two portraits of your grandmother. Have you ever done anything better than that, and have you ever been more *yourself* and a personality? I think not. [...] Do you know why I like these 3 or 4 studies so much? Because of that unknown quality of deliberateness, of great wisdom, that inexpressible quality of being steady and firm and self-assured of which they give evidence. You have never been closer to Rembrandt, old fellow, than in these studies' [659/B14].

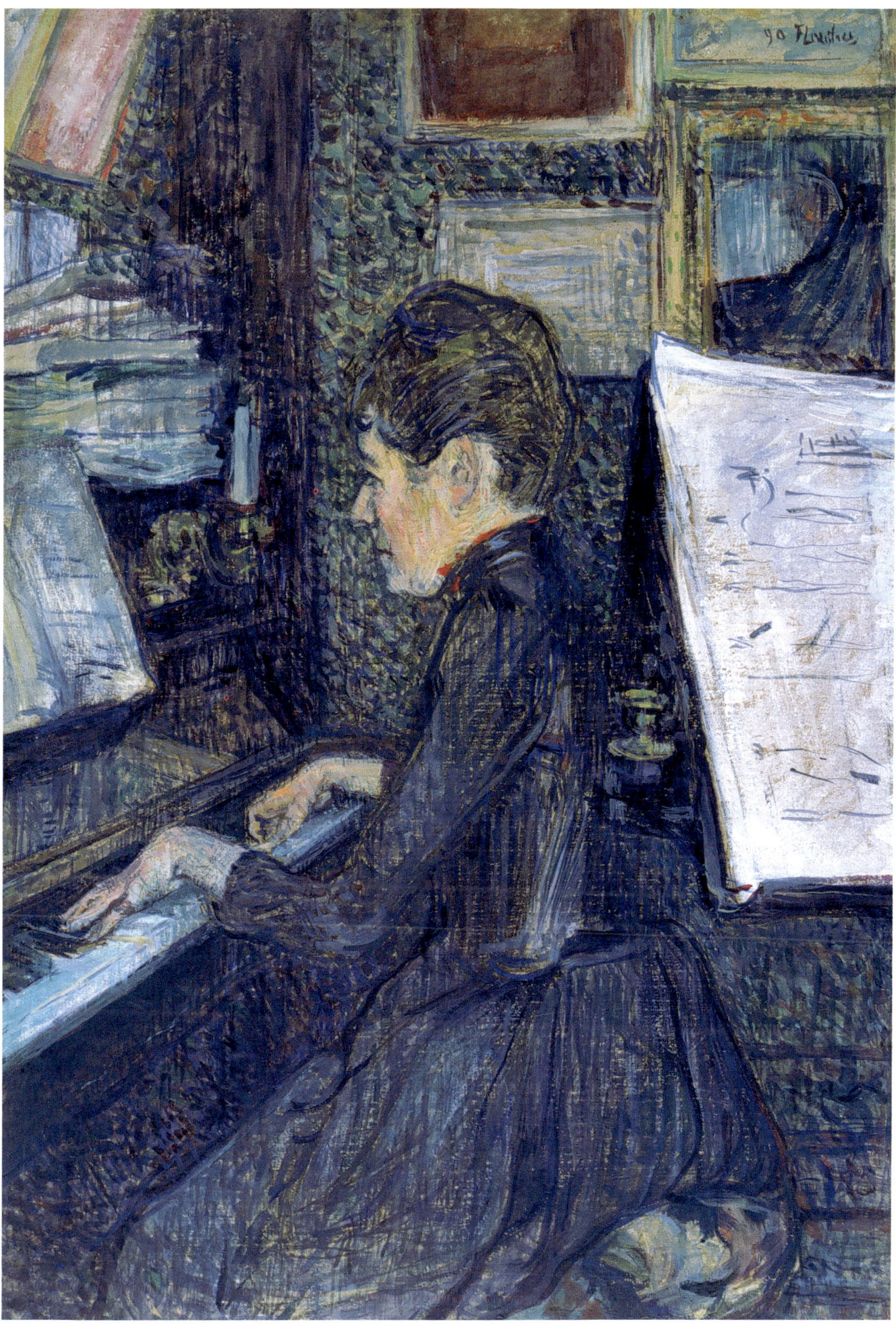

plate 87

Henri de Toulouse-Lautrec (1864-1901)
Mademoiselle Dihau playing the piano, 1890
Albi, Musée Toulouse-Lautrec

'Lautrec's painting, Portrait de musicienne, is quite wonderful, it moved me
when I saw it' [903/649].

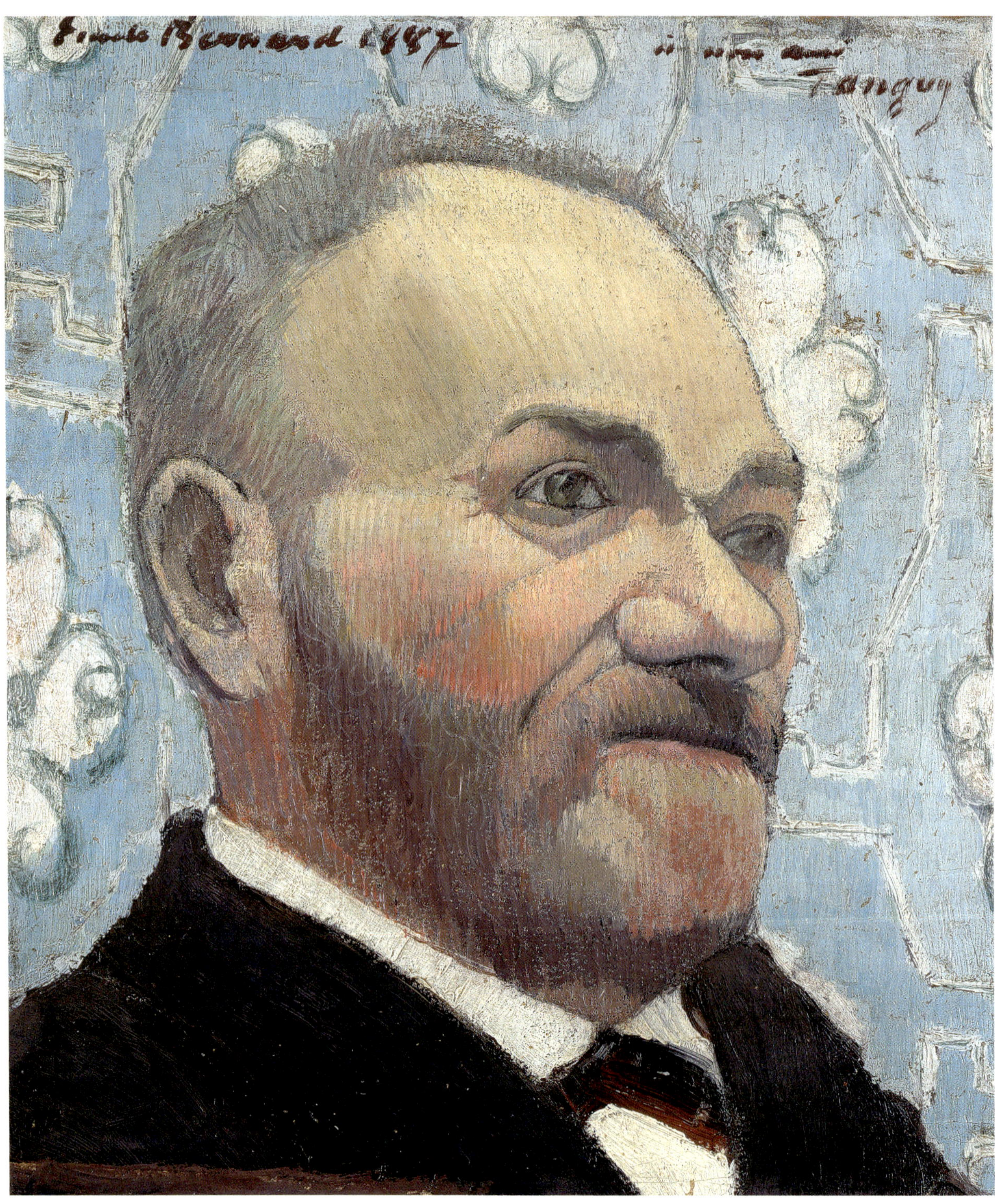

plate 88

Emile Bernard (1868-1941)
Portrait of Père Tanguy, 1887
Basel, Kunstmuseum, Öffentliche Kunstsammlung

'If I live long enough, I shall be something like old Tanguy' [689/540].

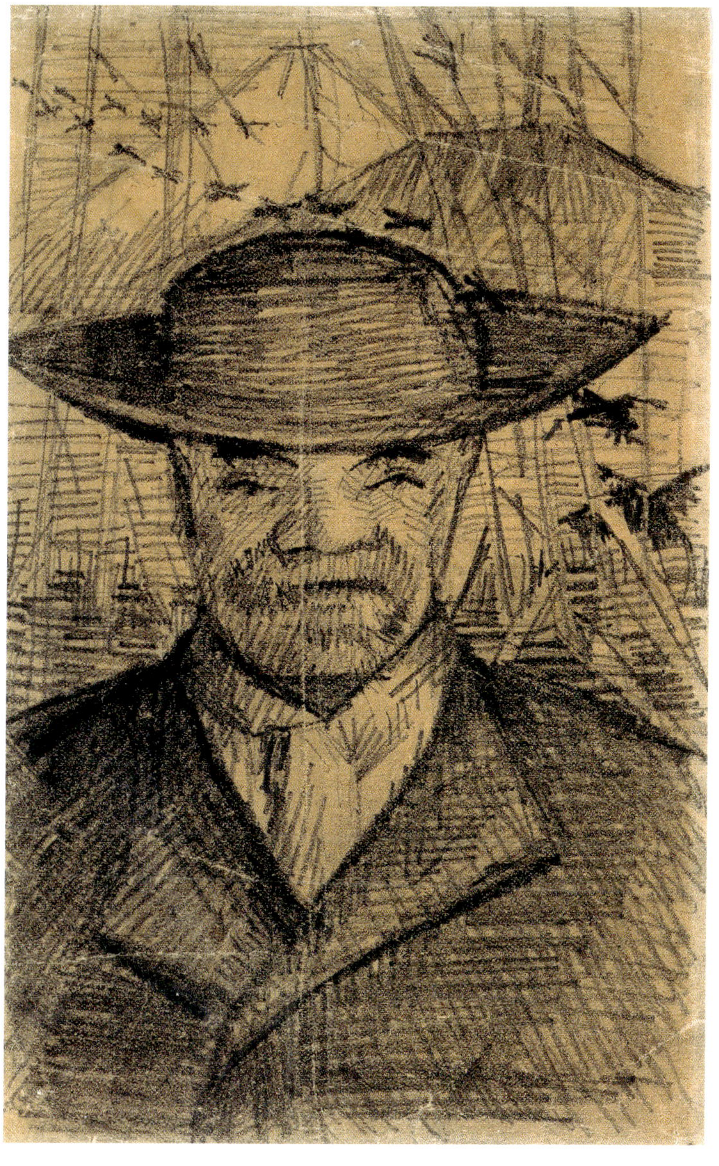

plate 89

Vincent van Gogh (1853-1890)
Portrait of Père Tanguy (F 1412 JH 1350), 1887-88
Amsterdam, Van Gogh Museum (Vincent van Gogh Foundation)

'I am as well as other men now, which I have never been except for
a short while in Nuenen for instance, and it is not unpleasant. By "other
men" I mean something like the navvies, old Tanguy, old Millet, the peasants. When you are well, you must be able to live on a piece of bread
while you are working all day, and have enough strength to smoke and to
drink your glass, that's necessary under the circumstances. And all the
same to feel the stars and the infinite high and clear above you. Then life is
almost enchanted after all' [663/520].

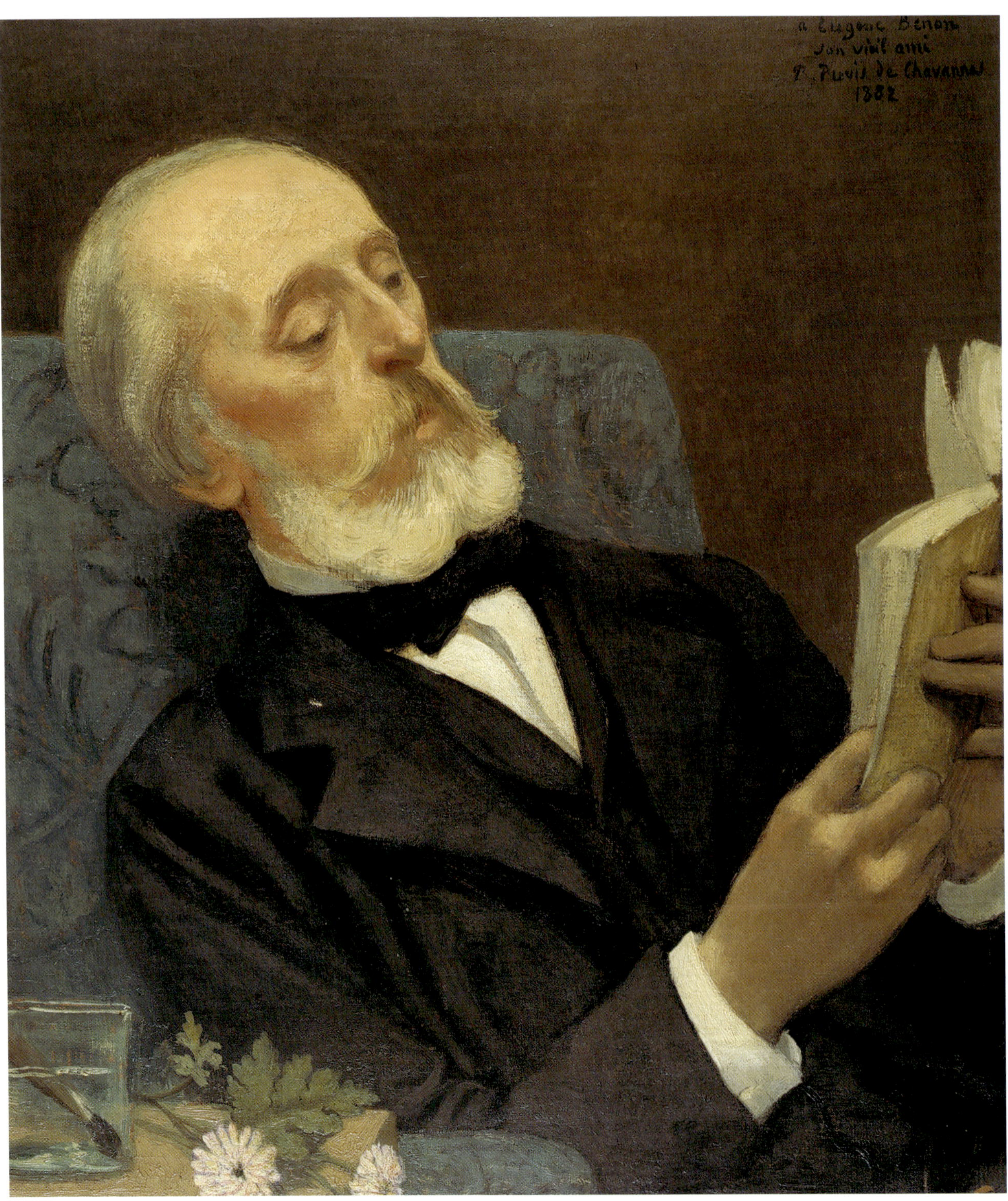

plate 90

Pierre Puvis de Chavannes (1824-1898)

Portrait of Eugène Benon, 1882

Private collection

'The "Portrait of a man" by Puvis de Chavannes has always remained an ideal figure for me, an old man reading a yellow novel, and beside him a rose and some watercolour brushes in a glass of water' [830/617].

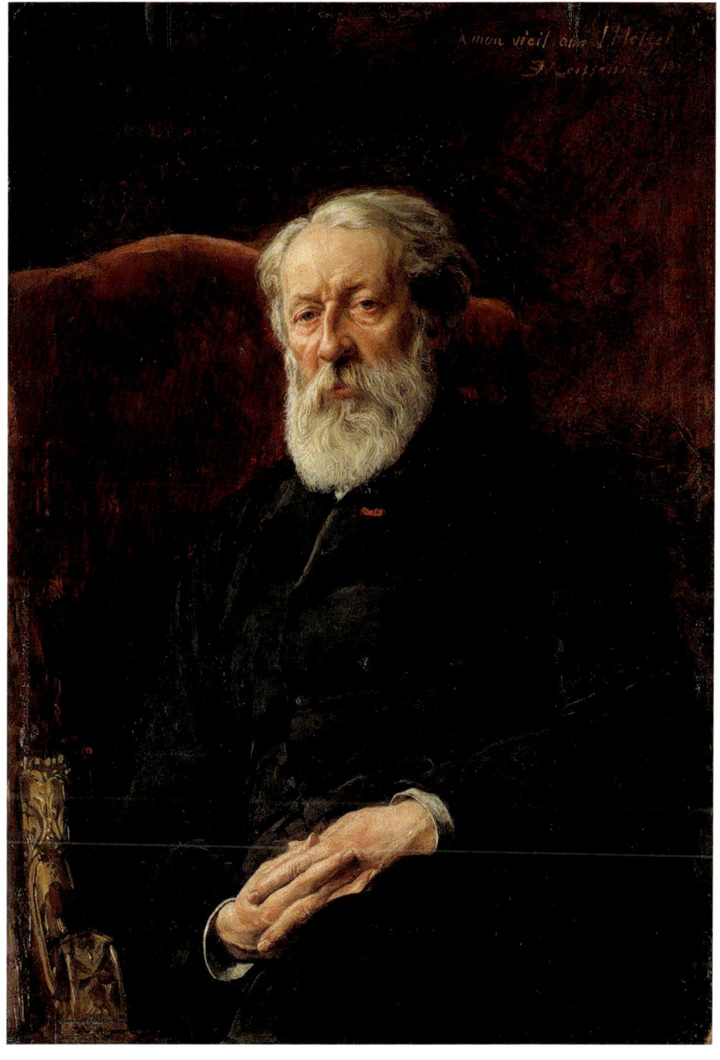

plate 91

Ernest Meissonier (1815-1871)
Portrait of Pierre-Jules Hetzel, 1879
Meudon, Musée d'art et d'histoire

'But Meissonier's workmanship, that something essentially French, above all when the old Dutchmen would have found nothing to quarrel with in it, and yet it is different from them, and modern; one must be blind to think that Meissonier is not an artist and – a first-rate one. Have many things been done which give the nineteenth-century note better than the portrait of Hetzel?' [799/602].

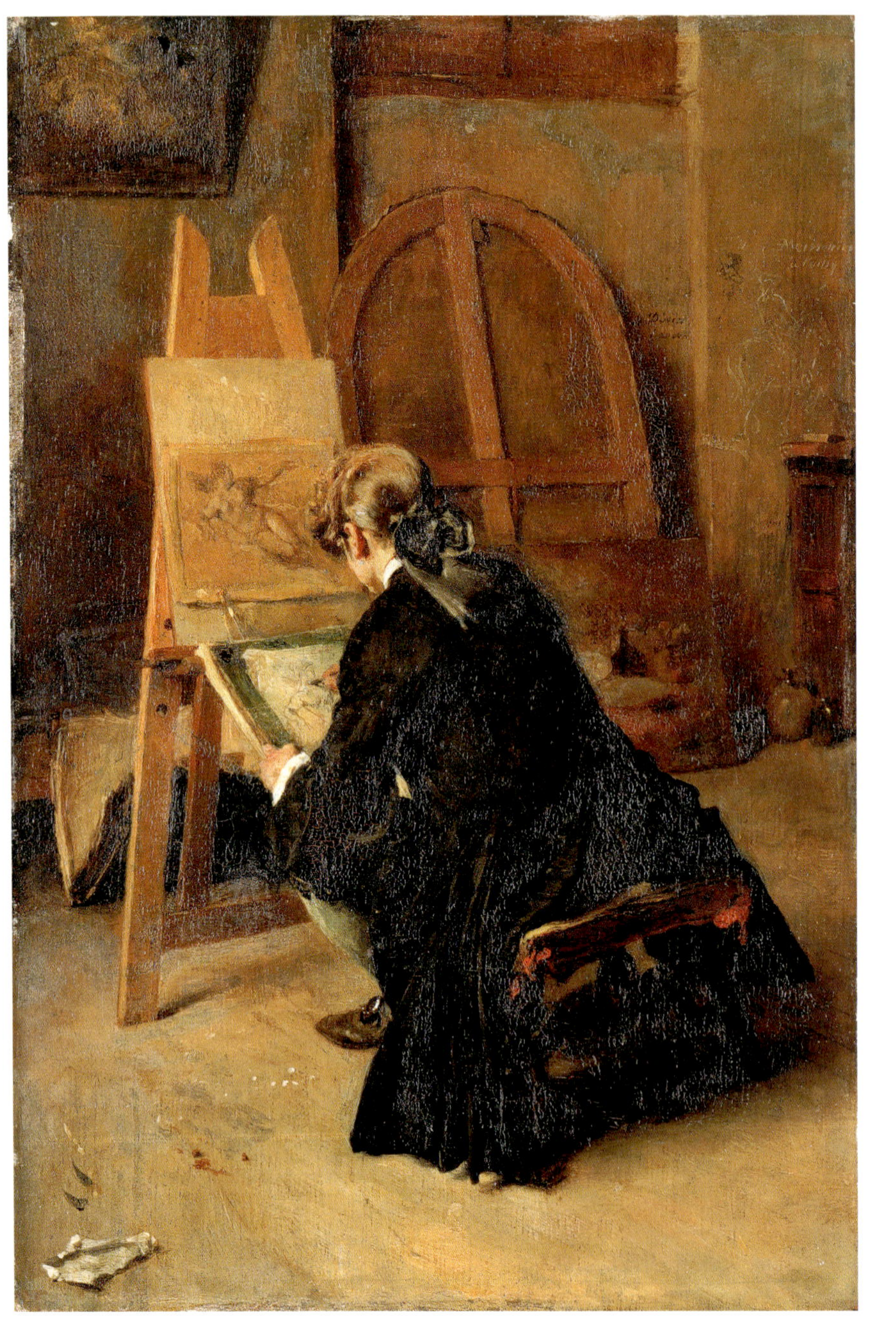

plate 92

Ernest Meissonier (1815-1871)
The draughtsman, 1855
Musée National du Château de Compiègne

'There is a painting by *Meissonier* which I think is beautiful, it is that figure
seen from behind, stooping over – with his feet, I think, on the rung of the
easel; one sees nothing but a pair of raised knees, a back, a neck, and the
back of a head, and just the glimpse of a fist holding a pencil or something
similar. But the fellow has been captured well, and one feels the action of
intense attention is there, as in a certain figure by Rembrandt, where a little fellow is sitting reading, also hunched up, with his head leaning on his
fist, and one instantly feels that he is absolutely lost in his book' [290/248].

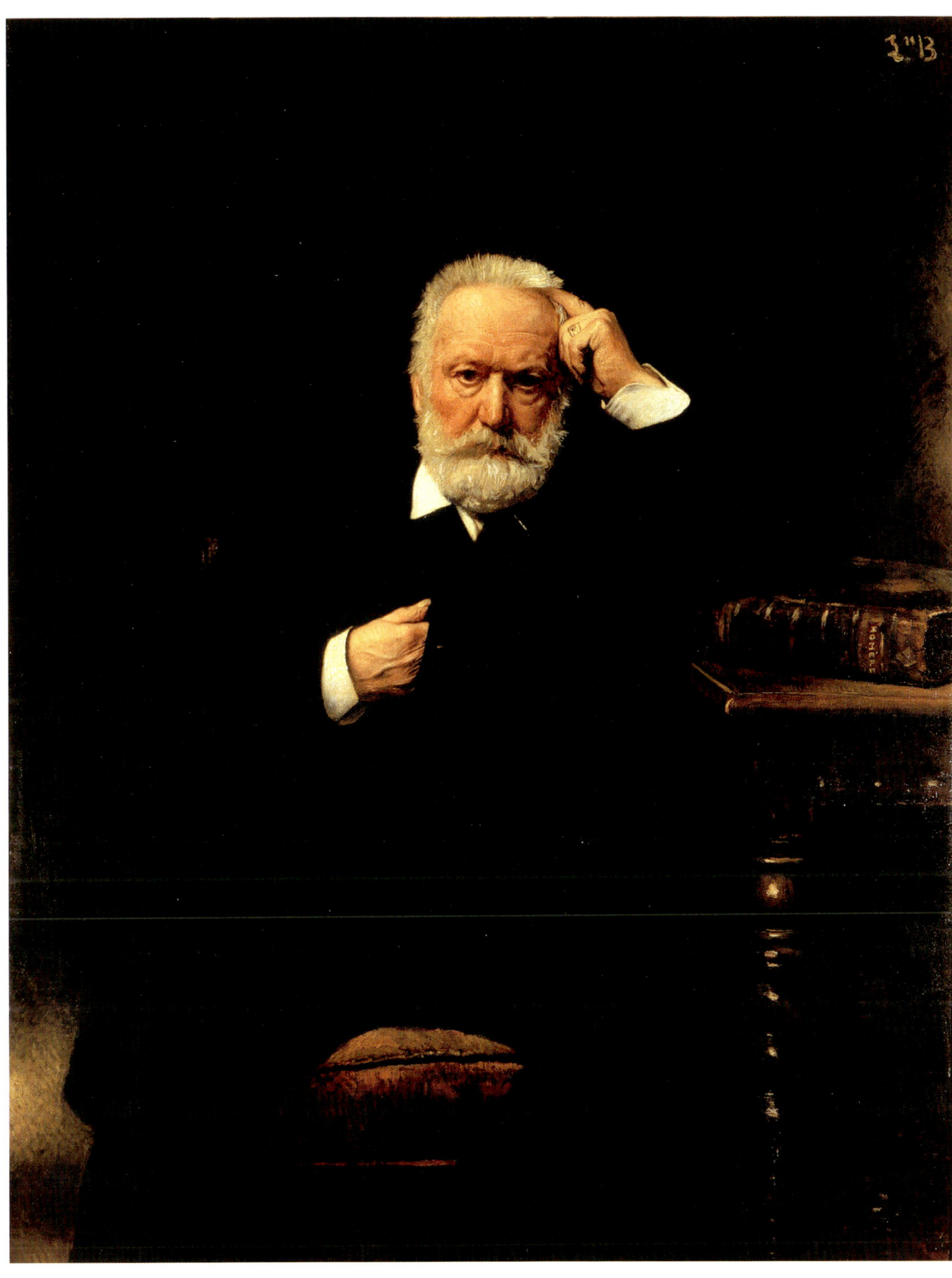

plate 93

Daniel Saubès (1855-1920) and **Léon Bonnat** (1833-1922)
Portrait of Victor Hugo in 1879, 1903
Paris, Maison de Victor Hugo

'Take Bonnat's Victor Hugo – fine, very fine – but even finer, to me, is the Victor Hugo described in words by Victor Hugo himself, nothing but this:
And as for me, I was silent,
Like a cock seen keeping silence
on the heath' [290/248].

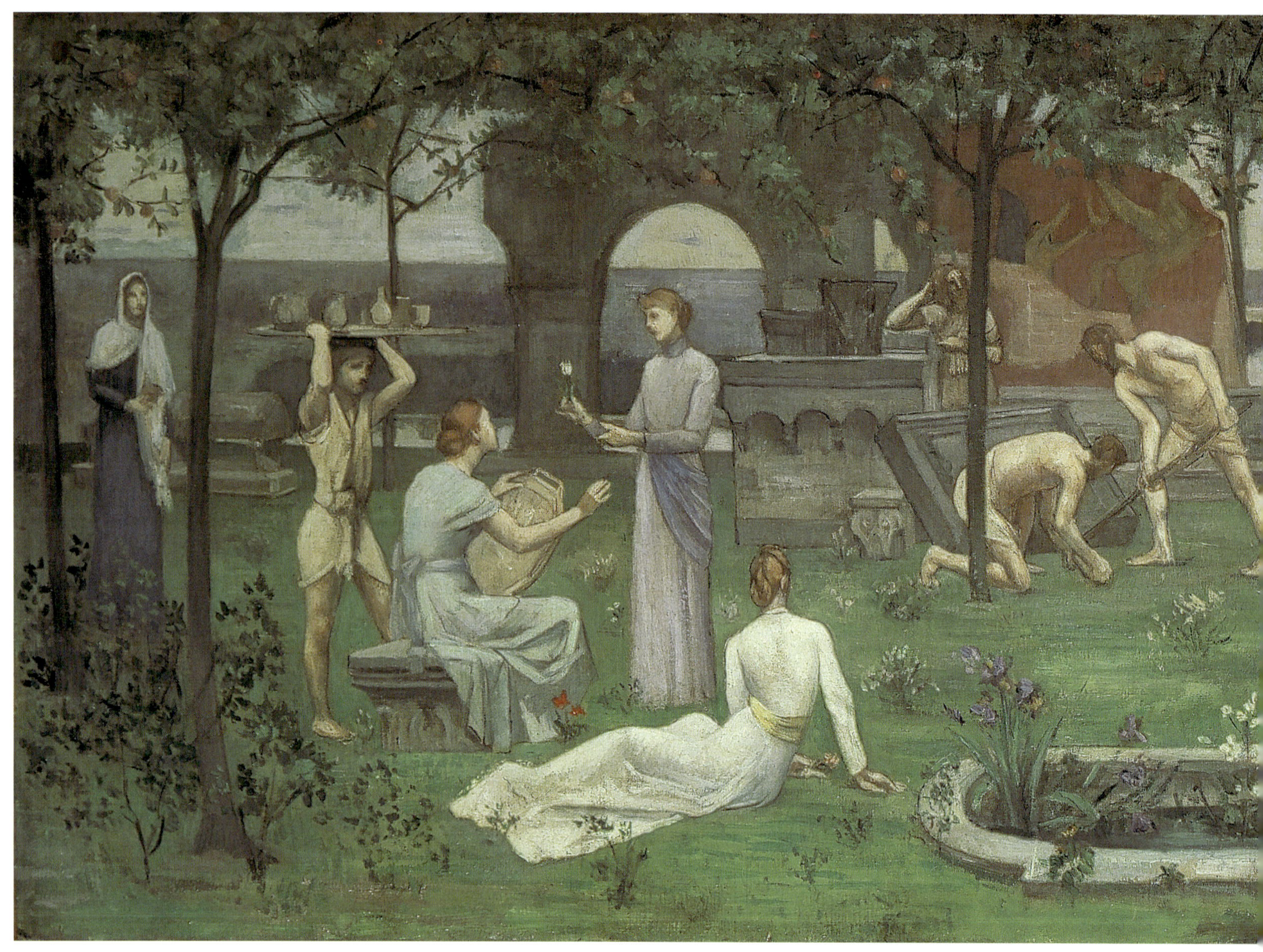

plate 94

Pierre Puvis de Chavannes (1824-1898)
Inter artes et naturam (Between art and nature), 1890
New York, The Metropolitan Museum of Art, Gift of Mrs Harry Payne
Bingham, 1958

'I begin to feel more and more that one may look upon Puvis de Chavannes as having the same importance as *Delacroix*, at least that he is on
a par with the fellows whose genius has attained a "thus far and no further", comforting for evermore. Among other paintings his canvas, now
at the Champ de Mars, seems to contain an allusion to an equivalence,
a strange and providential meeting of very far-off antiquities and crude
modernity. His canvases of the last few years are vaguer, more prophetic,
if possible, than even Delacroix, before them one feels an emotion as if
one were present at the continuation of all kinds of things, a benevolent
renaissance ordained by fate' [878/614a].

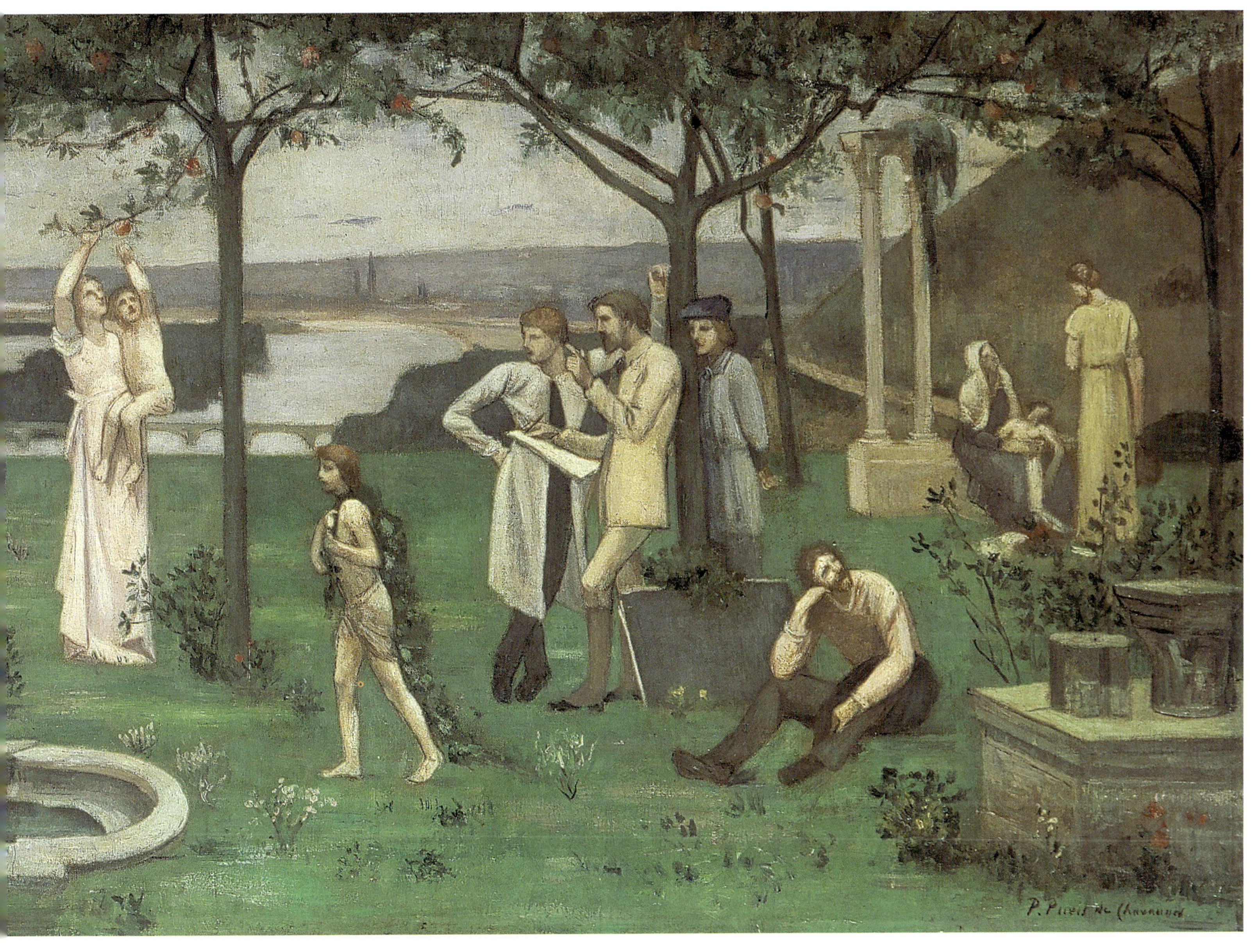

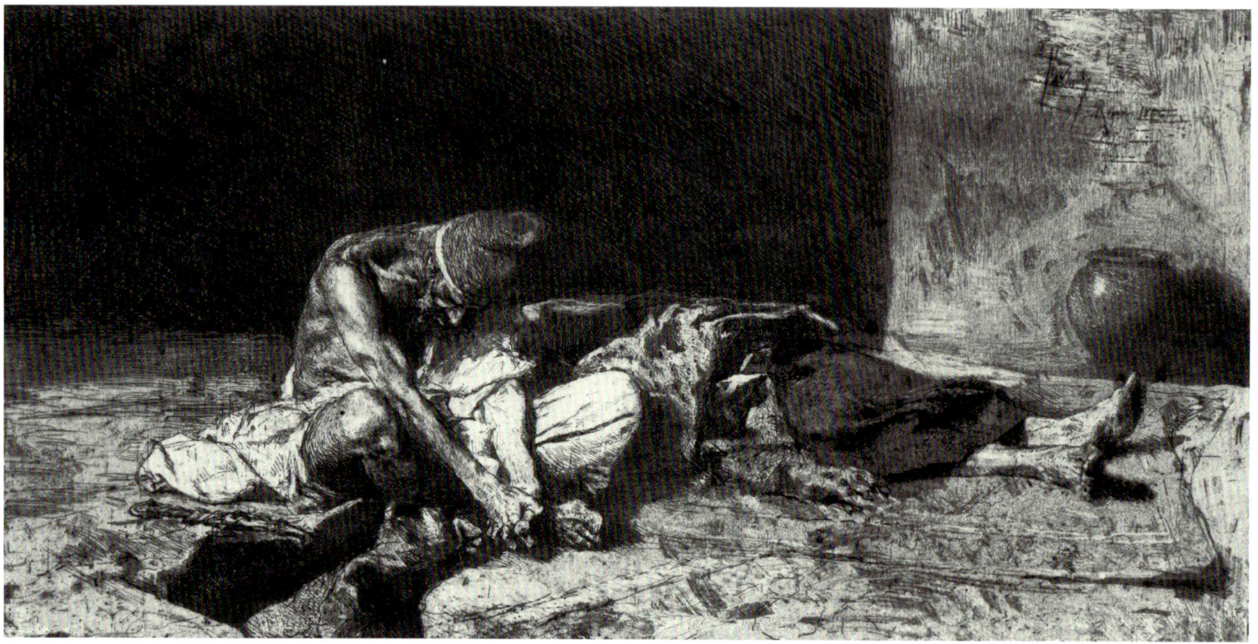

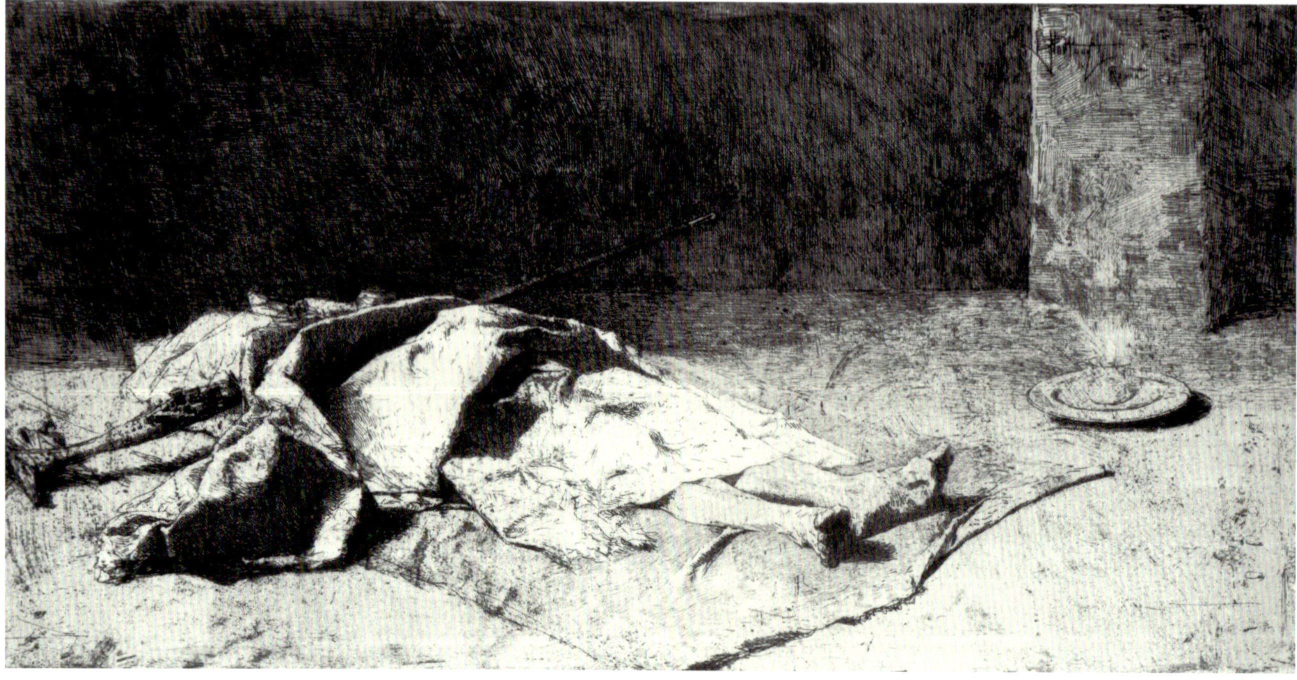

plate 95

Mariano Fortuny y Carbó (1838-1874)
An Arab watching over the body of his dead friend, 1866
Amsterdam, Rijksprentenkabinet

plate 96

Mariano Fortuny y Carbó (1838-1874)
The dead Kabyle, 1867
Amsterdam, Rijksprentenkabinet

'In Goupil & Co.'s show window I saw a large etching by Fortuny, "An anchorite", as well as his two beautiful "The dead Kabyle" and "The death-watch". I was very sorry then that I had recently told you that I didn't find Fortuny beautiful – I like this very much. But of course you understand this, too' [299/257].

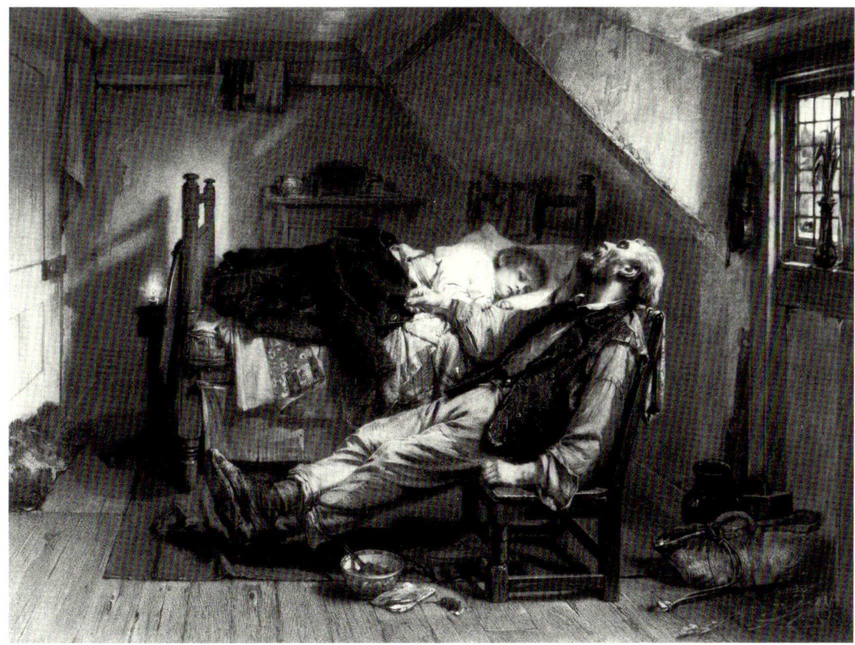

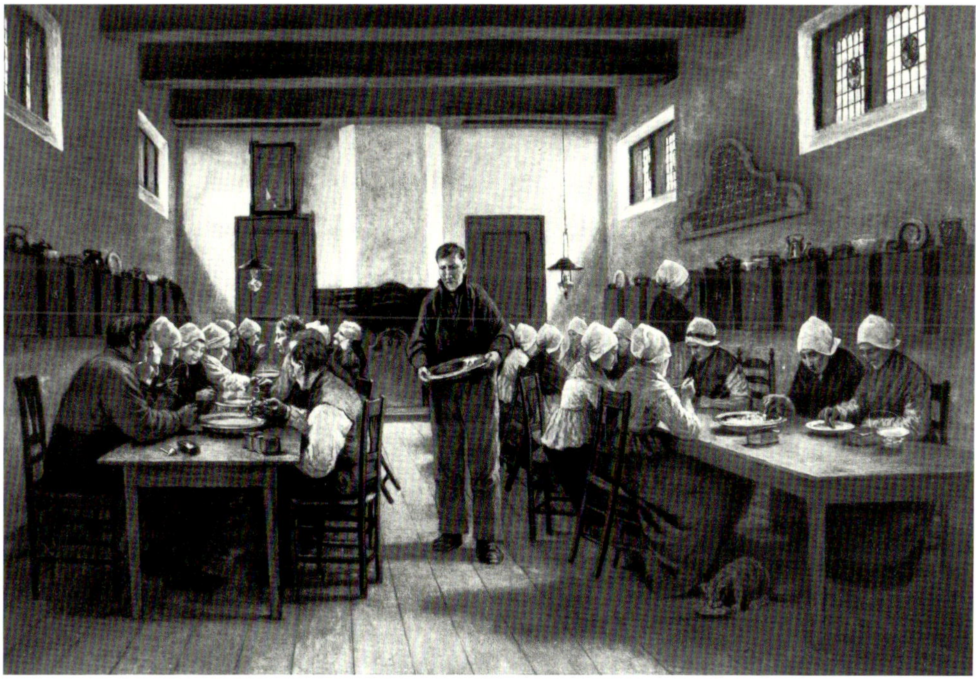

plate 97

After **Thomas Faed** (1826-1900)
Worn out, 1868
London, British Museum

'By the way, it took a long time before I found Thomas Faed's work beautiful, but now I do not hesitate about it any more; [...] "Worn out", for instance' [282/242].

plate 98

After **David Artz** (1837-1890)
Old people's home at Katwijk, 1882
Bordeaux, Musée Goupil

'The same can be said of engraving – the photogravure reproduction of the sewing class by Israëls, for instance, or of the picture by Blommers or Artz is superb – the way they are published by Goupil and Co.' [296/254].

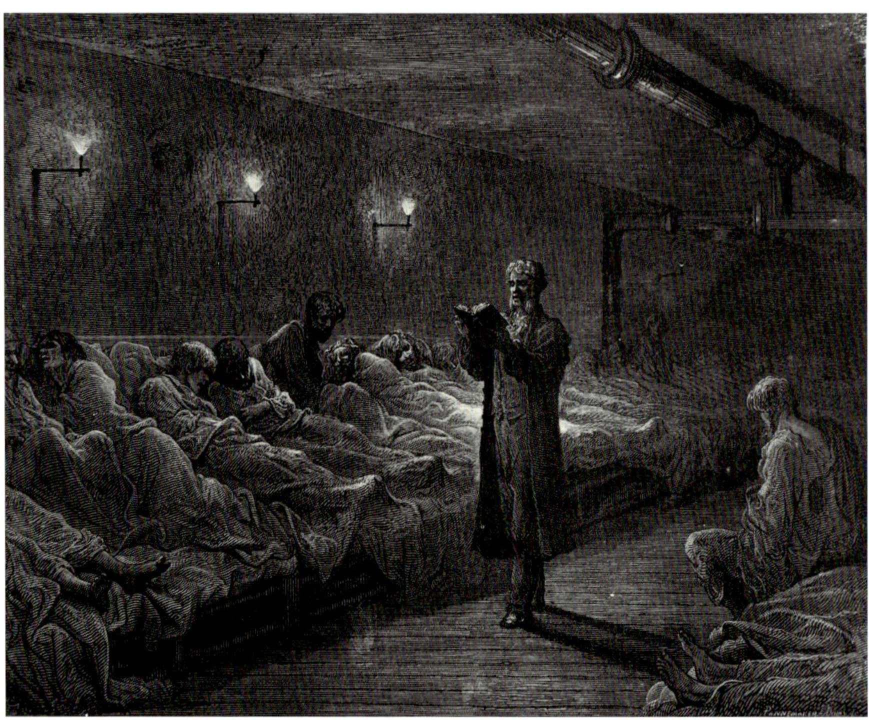

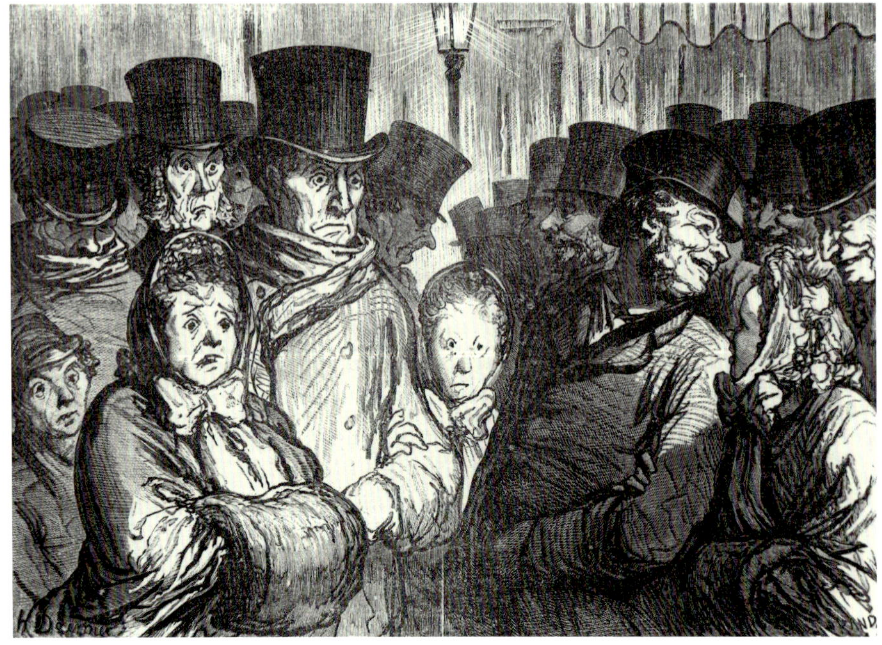

plate 99

After **Honoré Daumier** (1808-1879)
Leaving the theatres, 1864-65
Amsterdam, Van Gogh Museum (Vincent van Gogh Foundation)

'I have found [...] two Daumiers: "Those who have seen a drama meeting those who have seen a vaudeville" – and "Lovers of paintings"' [311/R21].

plate 100

After **Gustave Doré** (1832-1883)
Scripture reader in a night refuge, 1872-73
Amsterdam, Van Gogh Museum (Vincent van Gogh Foundation)

'The other day I saw all of Doré's work on London. I tell you it is superbly beautiful, and noble in sentiment – for instance that room in the "Night shelter for beggars"' [267/ R13].

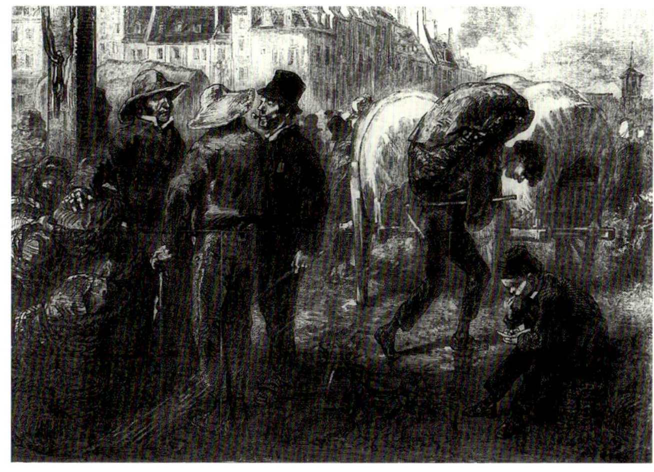

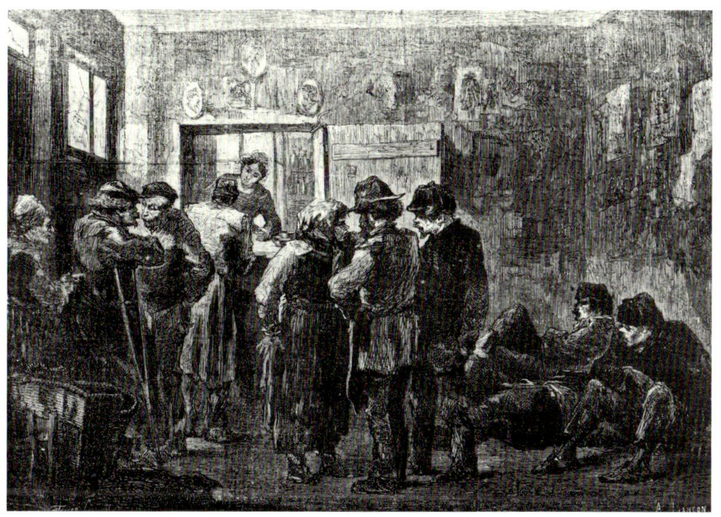

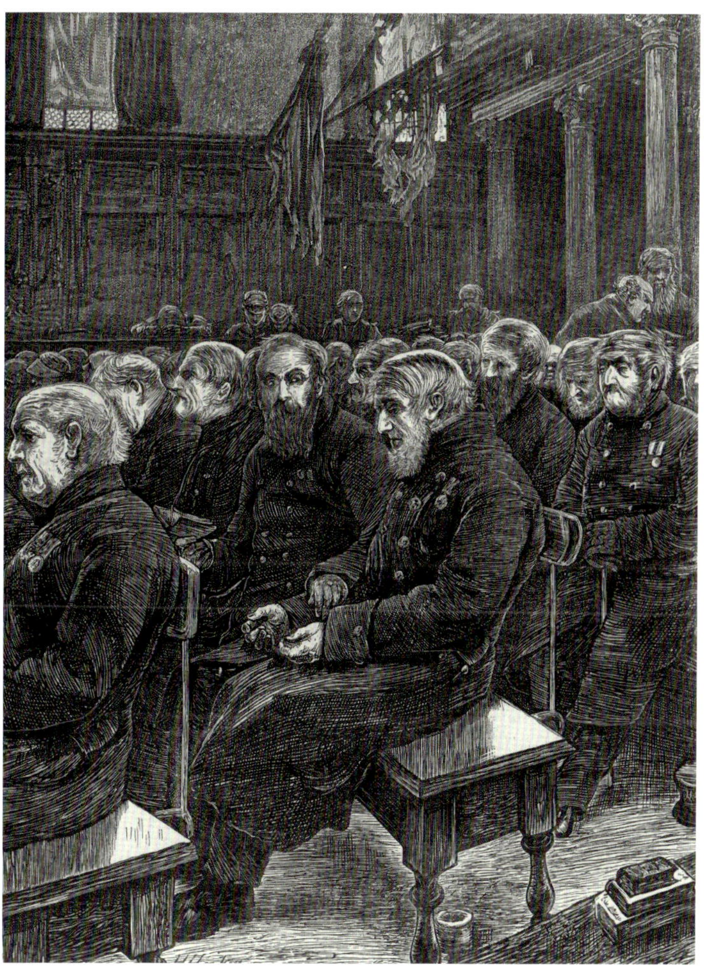

plate 101

After **Paul Gavarni** (1804-1866)
Porters of the vegetable market, 1855
Amsterdam, Van Gogh Museum (Vincent van Gogh Foundation)

'Two important Gavarnis, top quality, "Porters of the vegetable market",
"Women of the vegetable market"' [361/R38].

plate 102

After **Auguste-André Lançon** (1836-1885)
Gathering of ragpickers, 1872
Amsterdam, Van Gogh Museum (Vincent van Gogh Foundation)

'I mean A. Lançon. I looked over his wood engravings that I have – how
clever that man is. Among them I found a "Gathering of ragpickers",
a "Soup distribution", "Snow-clearing gang", which I think are splendid.
He is so very productive – it is as if he just tosses them off' [262/229].

plate 103

After **Hubert von Herkomer** (1849-1914)
Sunday at Chelsea Hospital, 1871
Amsterdam, Van Gogh Museum (Vincent van Gogh Foundation)

'The drawings by Herkomer, Frank Holl, Walker and others. I bought them
from Blok the Jewish bookseller, and picked out the best from an enormous pile of *Graphics* and *London News* for five guilders. There are some
superb things among them, for instance, [...] two large Herkomers and
many small ones, [...] and then another large Herkomer, "The invalids"'
[198/169].

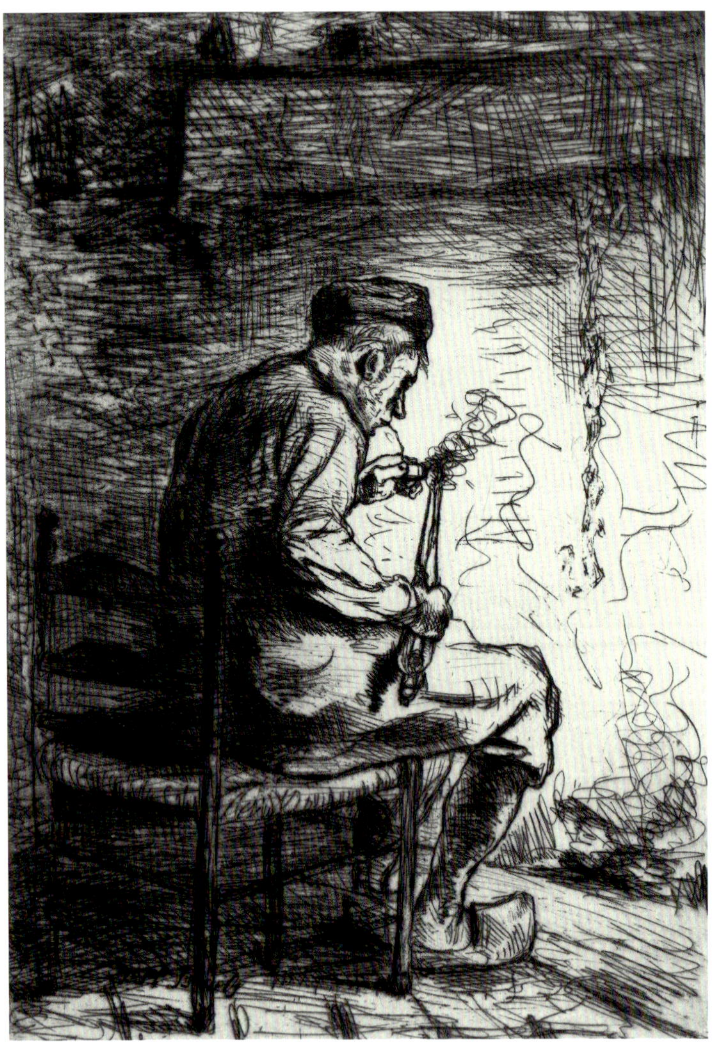

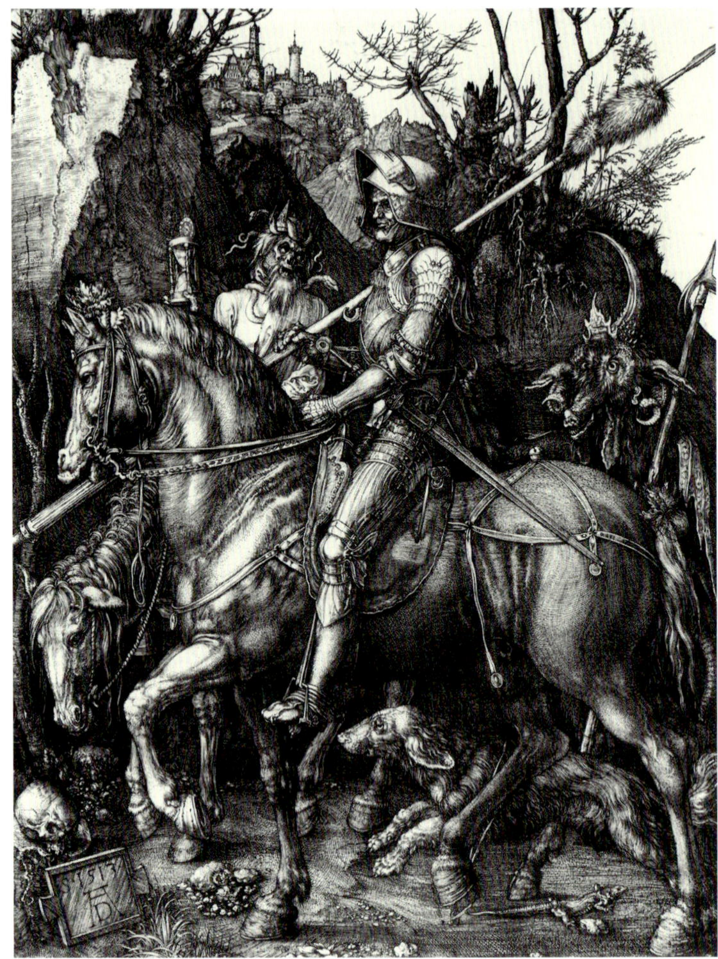

plate 104

Jozef Israëls (1824-1911)
Man lighting his pipe (The smoker)
Amsterdam, Rijksprentenkabinet

'Did I already write to you about those two large etchings by Israëls, a man lighting his pipe and the interior of a workman's home? How beautiful they are. I find it so splendid of Israëls that he carries on etching, the more so because all the others have given it up, so to speak, notwithstanding the enthusiasm with which the etching club was originally started' [328/273].

plate 105

After **Albrecht Dürer** (1471-1528)
Knight, death and devil, 1513
Amsterdam, Rijksprentenkabinet

'There are sunken roads here, overgrown with thornbushes and gnarled old trees with their freakish roots, which resemble perfectly that road on Dürer's etching, "Death and the knight"' [148/127].

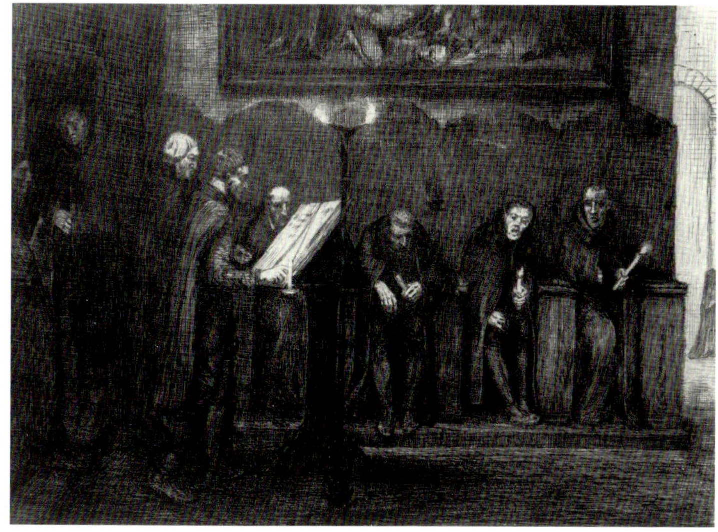

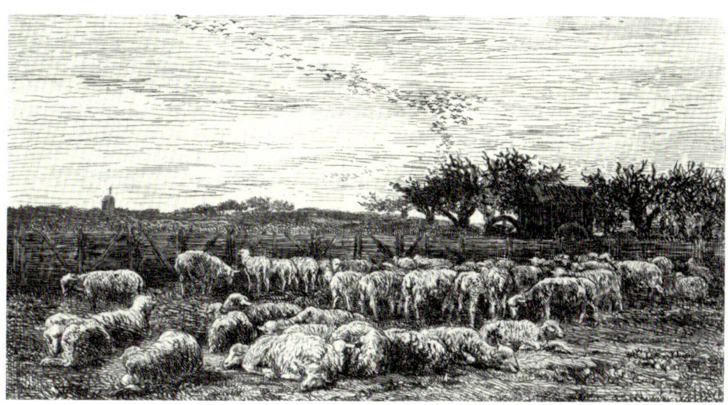

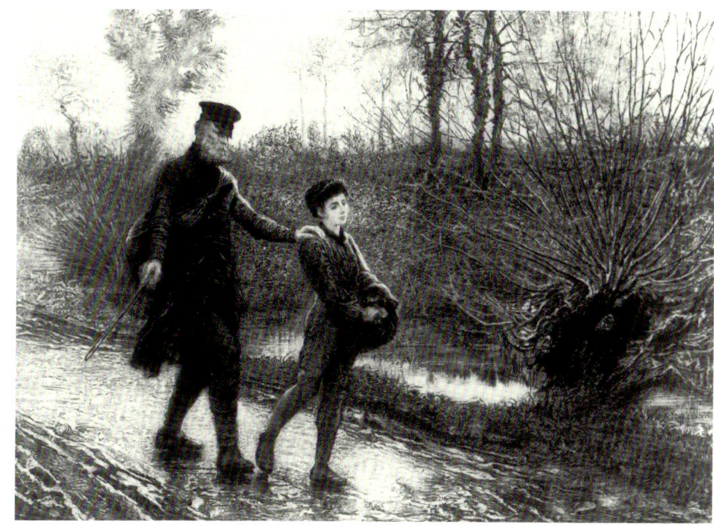

plate 106

Alphonse Legros (1837-1911)
The lectern (The Spanish choristers), 1865
Amsterdam, Rijksprentenkabinet

'[...] drawings or etchings by Legros, which are also very powerful and
broadly done, the pew, for instance' [310/264].

plate 107

Charles-François Daubigny (1817-1878)
The large sheepfold, 1861
Amsterdam, Rijksprentenkabinet

'I know that many beautiful etchings are published nowadays. But I mean
the old series, "Société des Aquafortistes" [Etchers' Club], containing "The
two brothers" by Feyen-Perrin and the "Sheepfold" by Daubigny and work
by Bracquemond and so many others — did they keep their full power or
did they become weaker?' [307/262].

plate 108

After **Frederick Walker** (1840-1875)
The wayfarers
London, British Museum

'Do you know "*The wayfarers*" by Fred Walker? It is a large etching of a
blind old man led by a boy along a frozen road, with a ditch with copsewood covered with glazed frost, and osiers, on a winter evening. It is certainly one of the most sublime creations in that genre, with a peculiar,
modern sentiment, perhaps less powerful than Dürer in his "Knight, Death
and devil", but perhaps even more intimate, and certainly as original and
sincere' [231/R8].

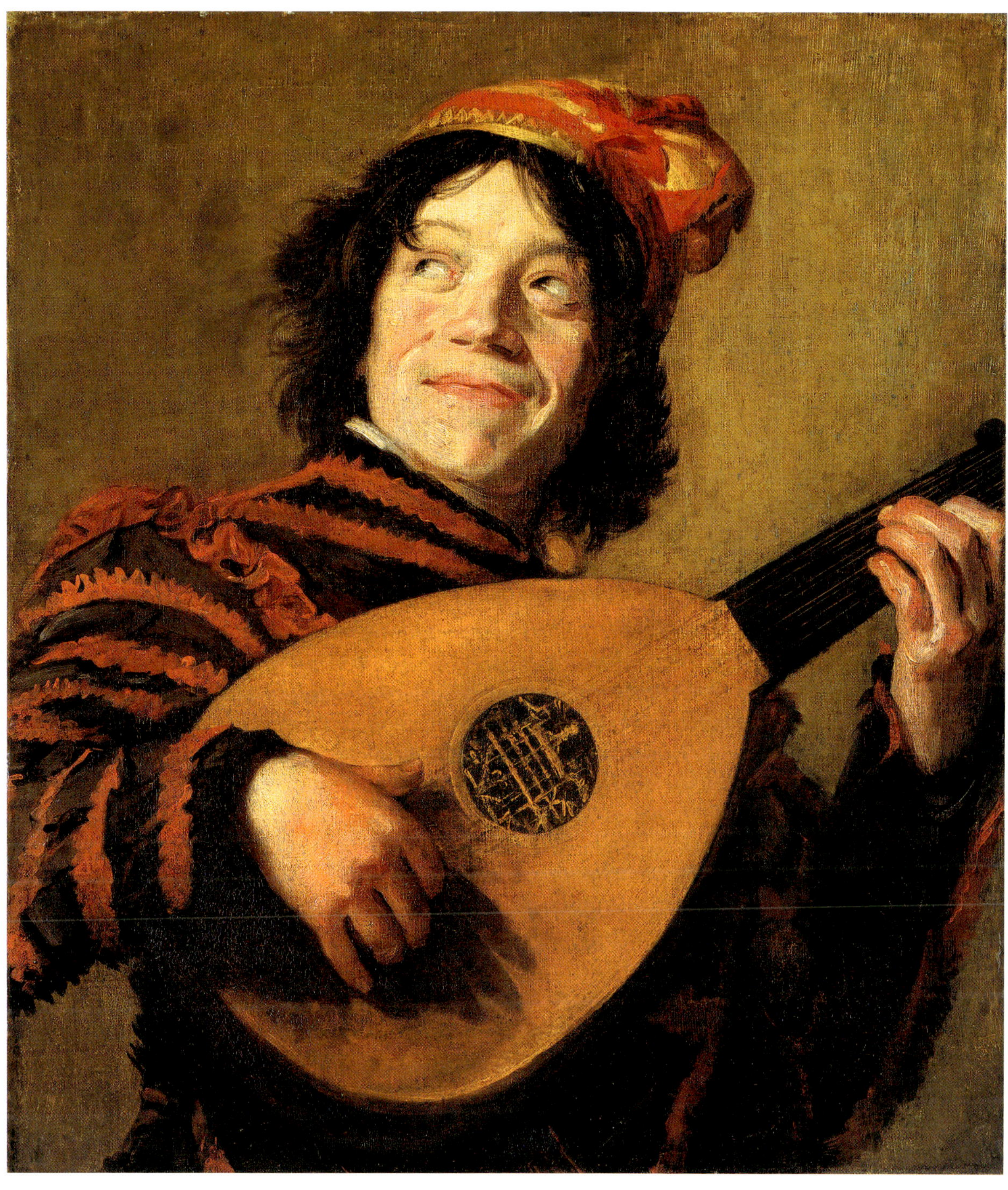

plate 109

Copy after **Frans Hals** (1581/5-1666)
The fool
Amsterdam, Rijksmuseum

'You know, Frans Hals's flesh colours are also earthy, used here in the sense that you know. Often at least. Sometimes, I would dare say always, there is also a relation of contrast between the tone of the costume and the tone of the face. Red and green are opposites; the singer (Dupper Collection), who has carmine tones in the flesh colour, has green tones in his black sleeves, and ribbons on those sleeves of a red OTHER than that carmine' [539/428].

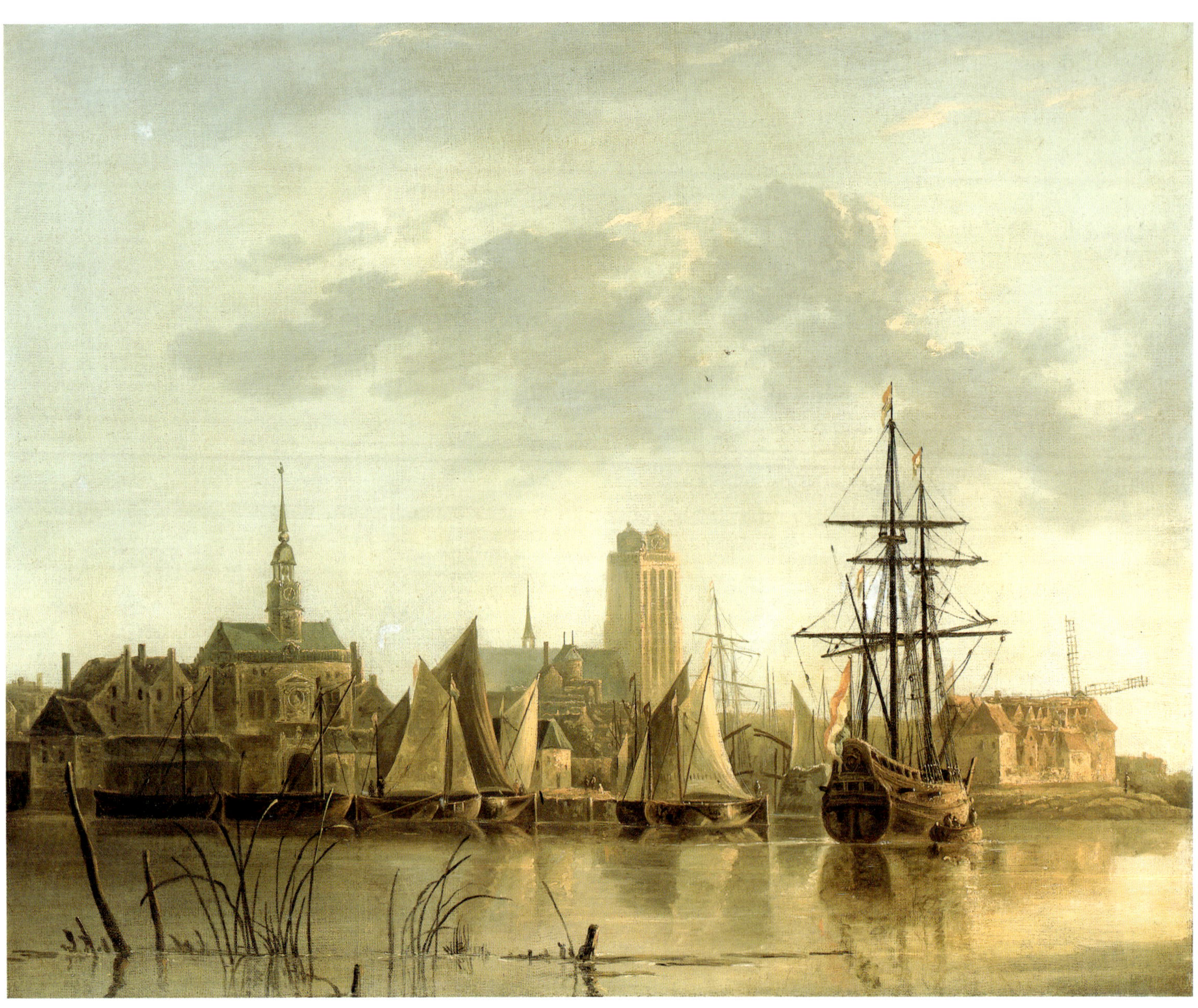

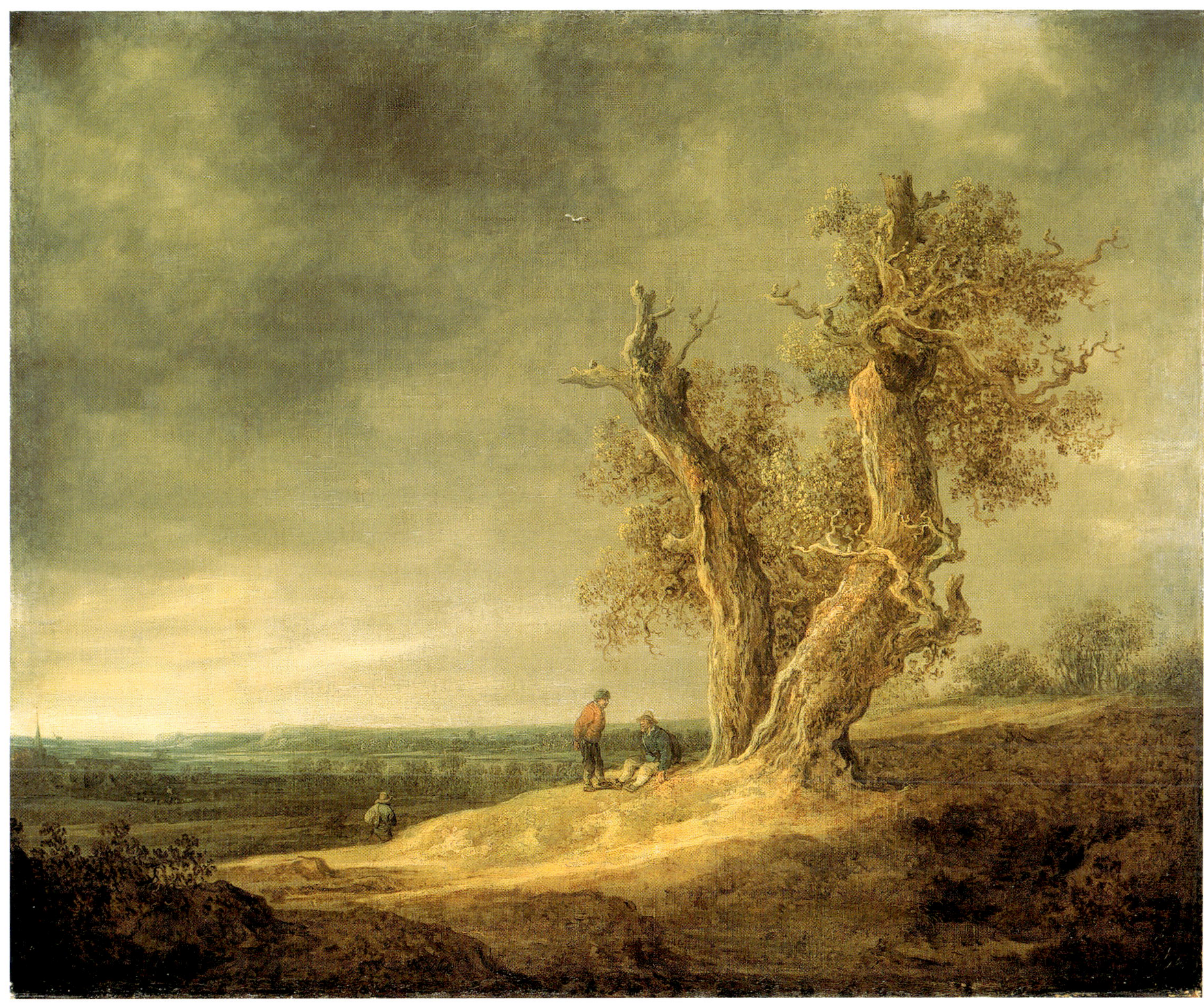

plate 110

Copy after **Aelbert Cuyp** (1620-1691)
View of Dordrecht at sunset, 18th century
Amsterdam, Rijksmuseum

plate 111

Jan van Goyen (1596-1656)
Landscape with two oaks, 1641
Amsterdam, Rijksmuseum

'A Van Goyen, for instance – I just saw that one of his in the Dupper
Collection, an oak tree on a dune in the storm; and the Cuyp, view of
Dordrecht. An astonishing technique, but done with nothing and quite
naturally – clear of paint, and – apparently – utterly simple. But either in
figure or in landscape, how the painters always tried to convince people
that a painting is something different from nature in a mirror, something
different from imitation, namely re-creation' [542/431].

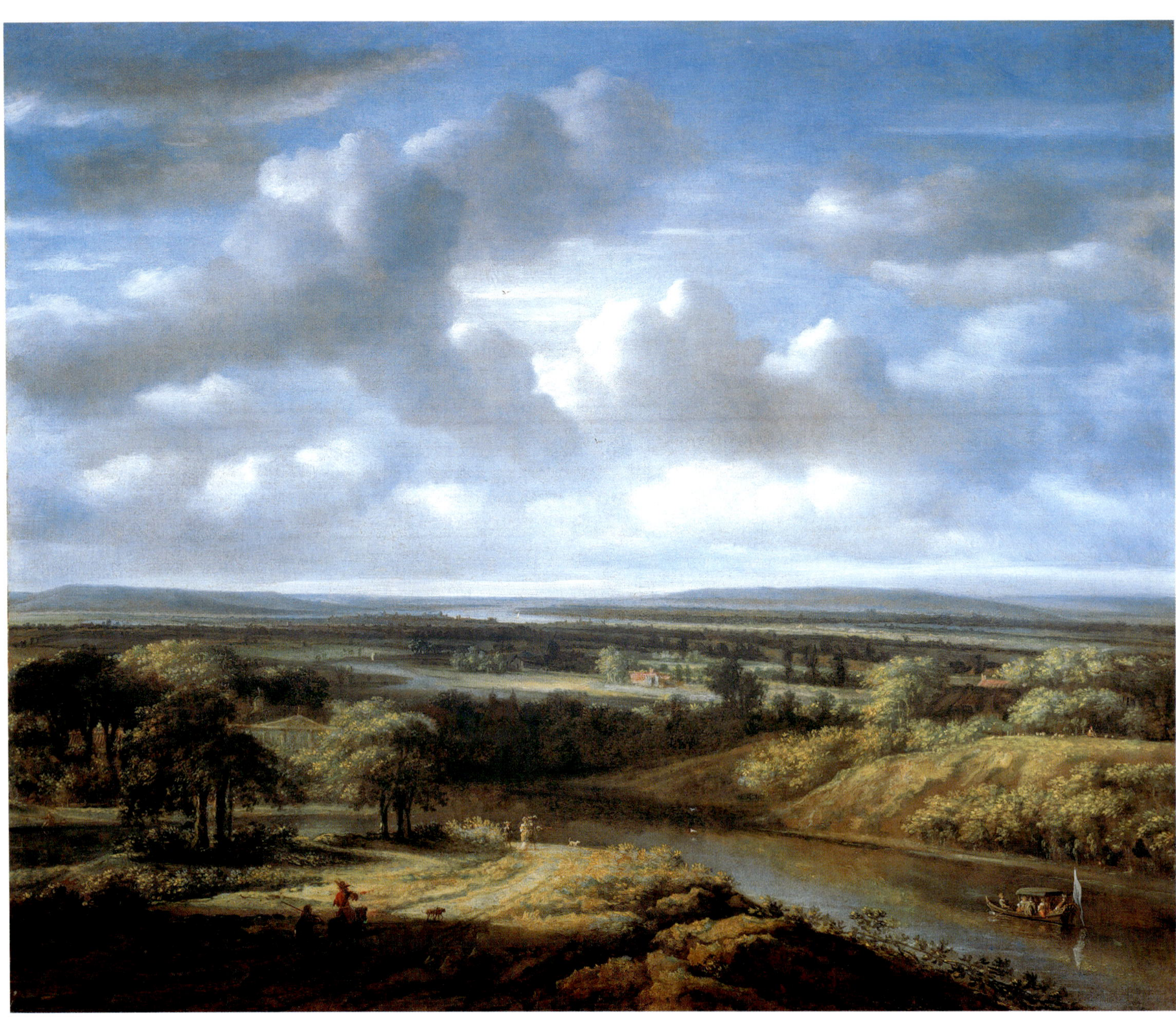

plate 112

Philips Koninck (1619-1688)
River landscape, 1676
Amsterdam, Rijksmuseum

'I am working on a new subject, fields green and yellow as far as the
eye can see. I have already drawn it twice, and I am starting it again as
a painting; it is exactly like a Salomon Koninck – you know, the pupil of
Rembrandt who painted vast level plains' [626/496].

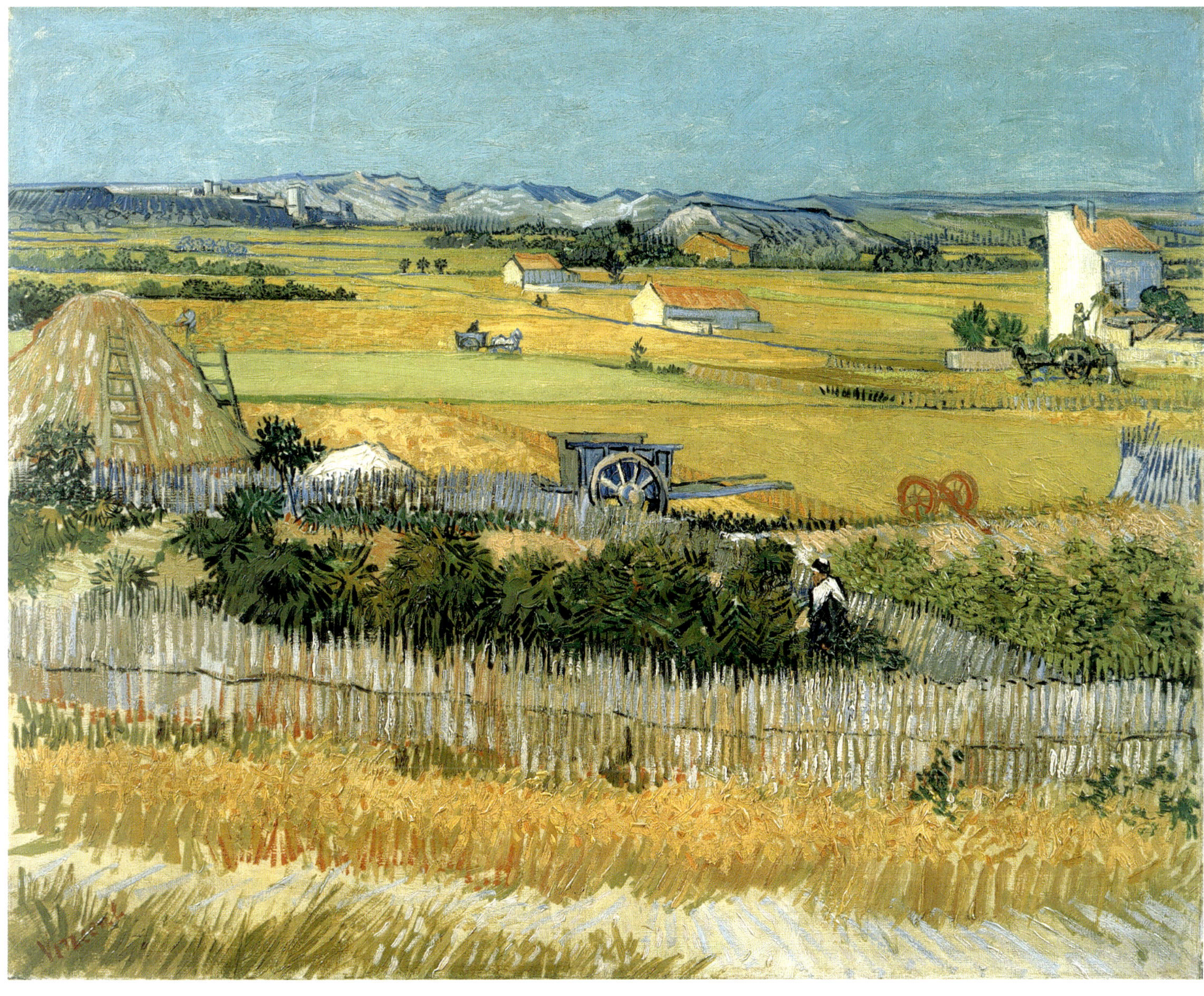

plate 113

Vincent van Gogh (1853-1890)
The harvest (F 412 JH 1440), 1888
Amsterdam, Van Gogh Museum (Vincent van Gogh Foundation)

'Today I sent you 3 drawings by post. You will think the one with the ricks in a farmyard too bizarre, but it was done in a great hurry as a cartoon for a picture, and it is to show you the idea. Now, the harvest is a little more serious. That is the subject I have worked on this week on a size 30 canvas; it isn't at all finished, but it kills everything else I have, apart from a still life which I patiently worked out. McKnight and one of his friends who has also been in Africa saw it today, this study, and said it was the best I had done. Like Anquetin and friend Thomas – you don't know what to think of yourself when you hear that said, but then I say to myself, the rest certainly must seem damned bad' [628/498].

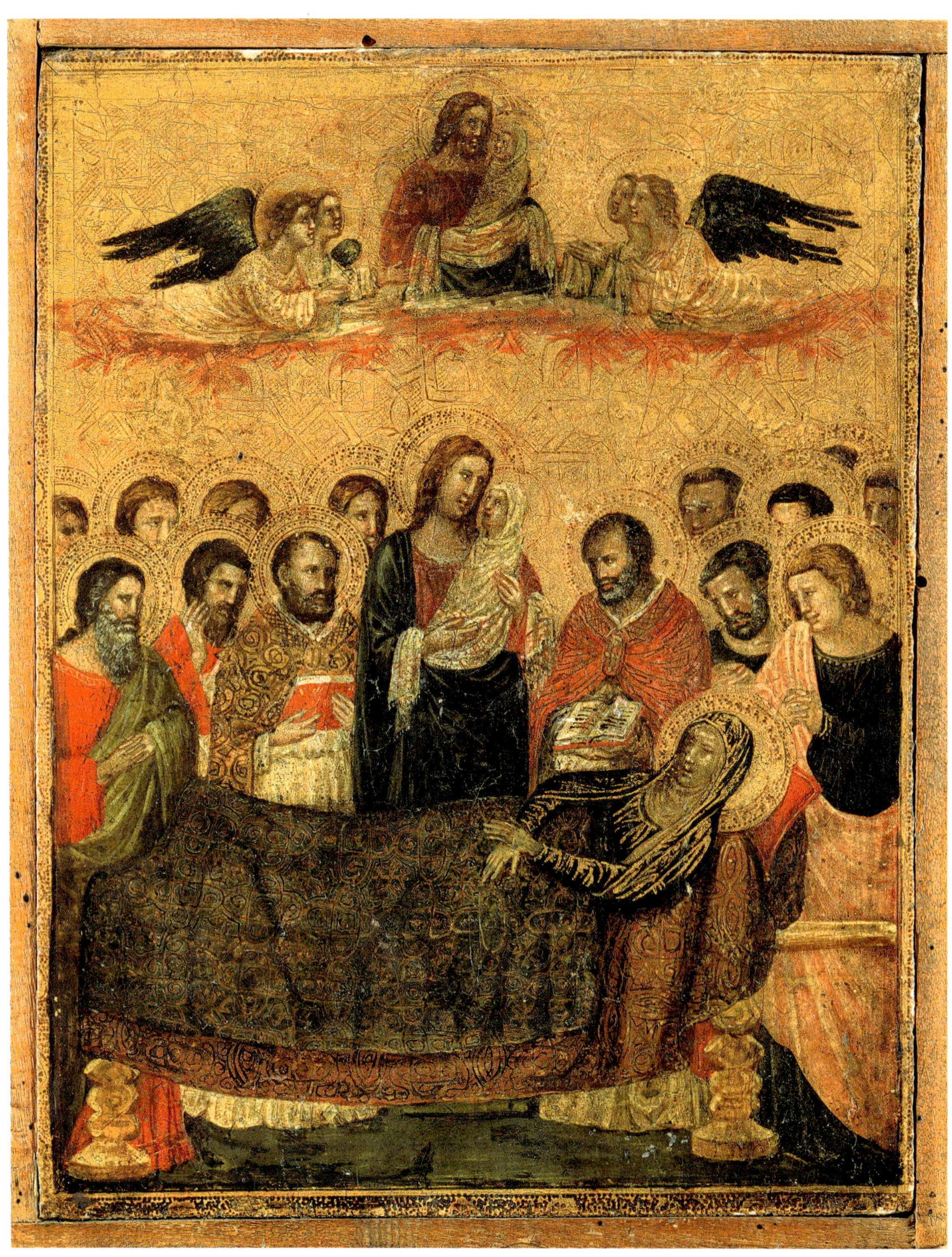

plate 114

Attributed to **Pietro da Rimini** (14th century)
The death and assumption of the Virgin
Montpellier, Musée Fabre

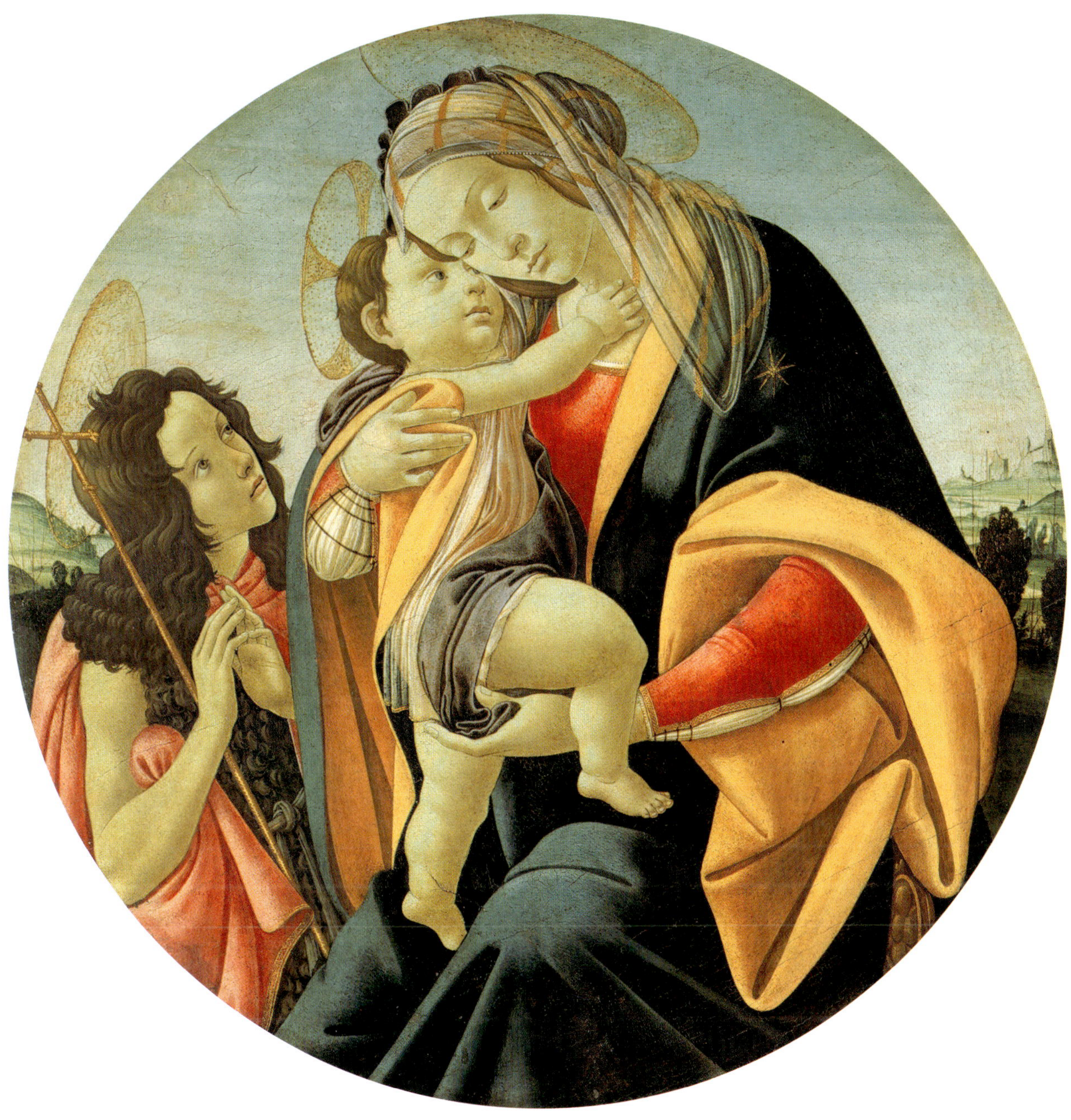

plate 115

School of **Sandro Botticelli** (1447-1510)
The Virgin and Child with John the Baptist
Paris, Musée du Louvre (on loan to the Musée du Petit Palais, Avignon)

'Gauguin and I went to Montpellier yesterday to see the museum there
and especially the Bruyas room. [...] Then there are paintings by Delacroix,
Courbet, Giotto, Paul Potter, Botticelli, Th. Rousseau, very fine' [730/564].

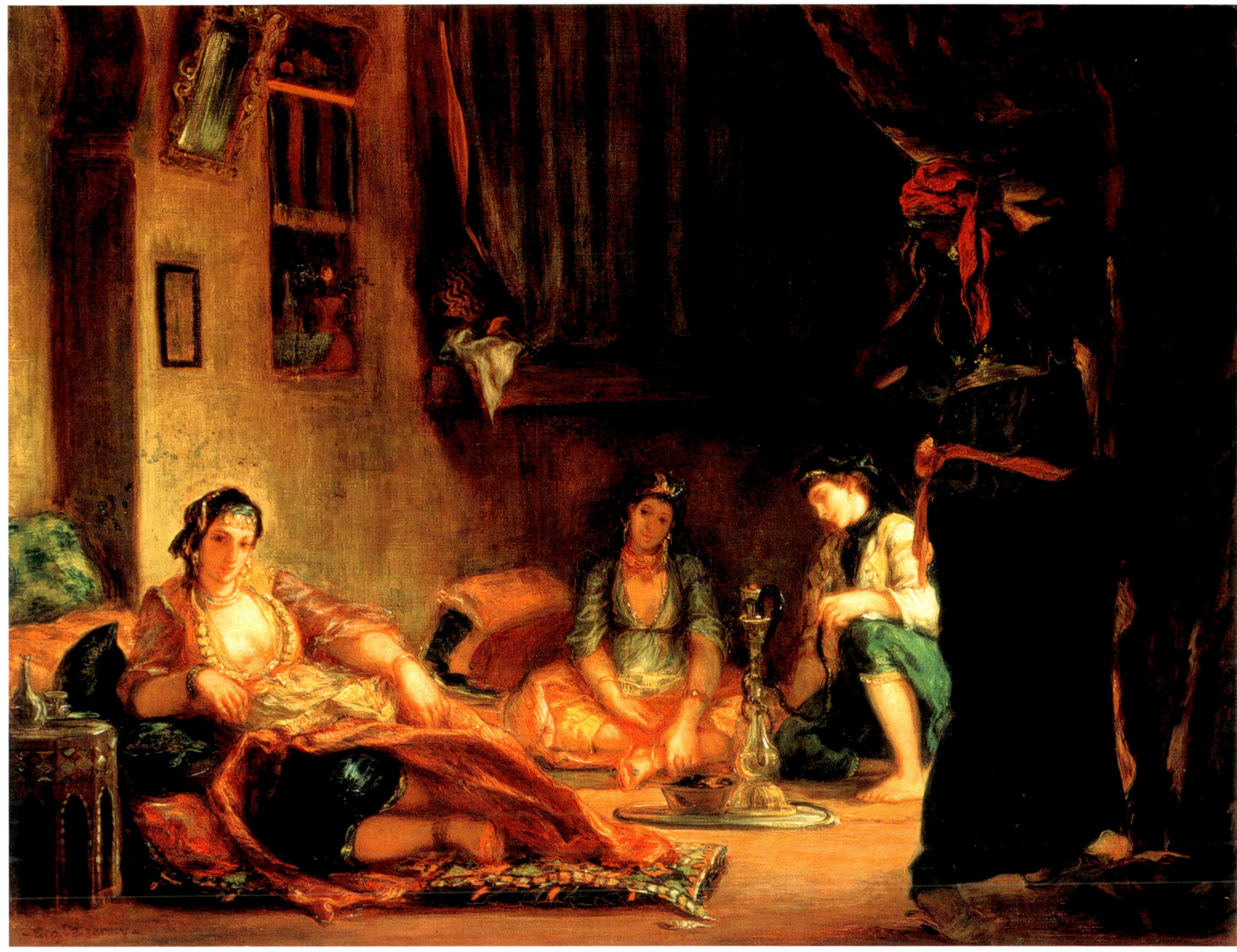

plate 116

Eugène Delacroix (1790-1863)
Women of Algiers in their apartment (The odalisques), 1849
Montpellier, Musée Fabre

'What I dream of in my best moments is not so much striking colour effects as once more the half tones. And certainly the visit to the Montpellier gallery contributed to turning my ideas this way. For what touched me there even more than the magnificent Courbets, [...] were the portraits of Bruyas by Delacroix and by Ricard, then the "Daniel" and "Odalisques" by Delacroix, all in half tones. For this "Odalisques" is quite a different thing from those in the Louvre; it is mostly in violet tones. But in these half tones, what choice and what quality!' [801/604].

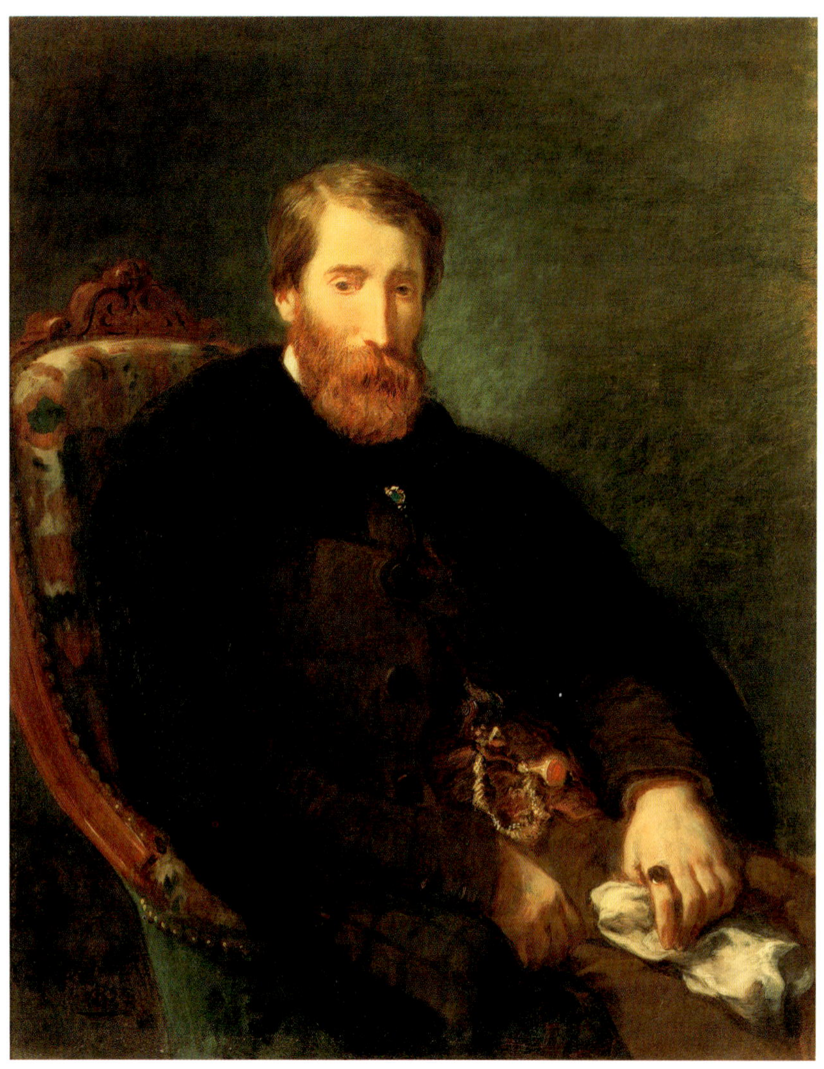

plate 117

Eugène Delacroix (1798-1863)
Portrait of Alfred Bruyas, 1853
Montpellier, Musée Fabre

'Bruyas was a benefactor of artists, I shall say no more to you than that. In the portrait by Delacroix he is a gentleman with red beard and hair, confoundedly like you or me, and made me think of that poem by De Musset – "Wherever I touched the earth, a wretch clad in black came and sat by us, looking at us like a brother"' [730/564].

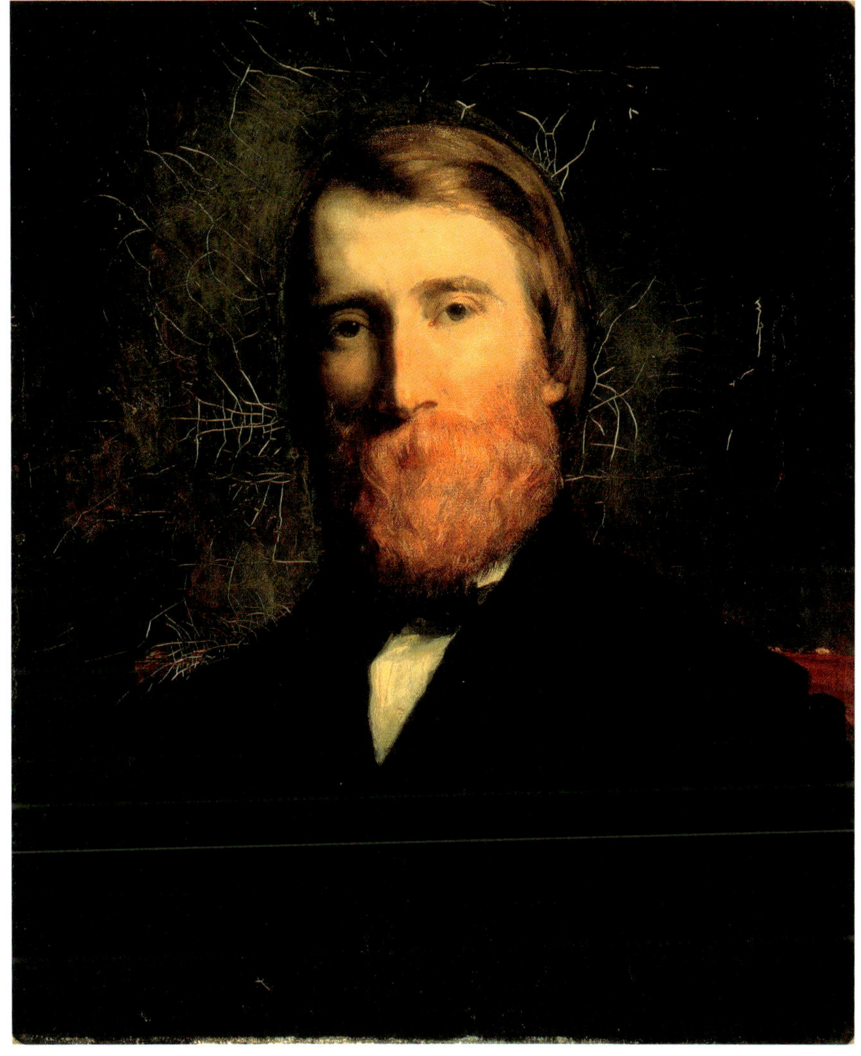

plate 118

Gustave Ricard (1823-1875)
Portrait of Alfred Bruyas, c. 1855-57
Montpellier, Musée Fabre

'I think that if one day you see the Bruyas Gallery at Montpellier, I think that then nothing will move you more than Bruyas himself when you realise, from his purchases, what he tried to be to artists. It is rather disheartening when you see some portraits of him, his face is so heartbroken and obviously frustrated. [...] The only serene portraits are the Delacroixs and the Ricards' [799/602].

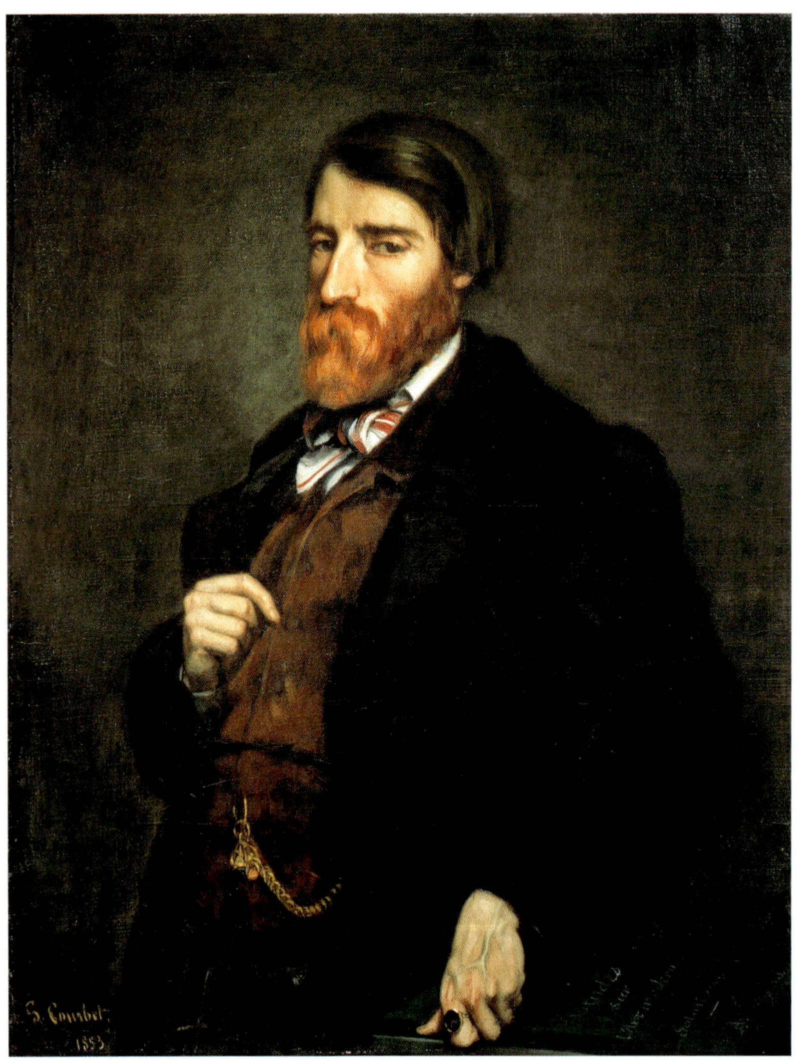

plate 119

Gustave Courbet (1819-1877)
Portrait of Alfred Bruyas, called 'Tableau-Solution', 1853
Montpellier, Musée Fabre

'Gauguin and I went to Montpellier yesterday to see the museum there
and especially the Bruyas room. [...] There are a lot of portraits of Bruyas,
by Delacroix, Ricard, Courbet, Cabanel, Couture, Verdier, Tassaert, and
others' [730/564].

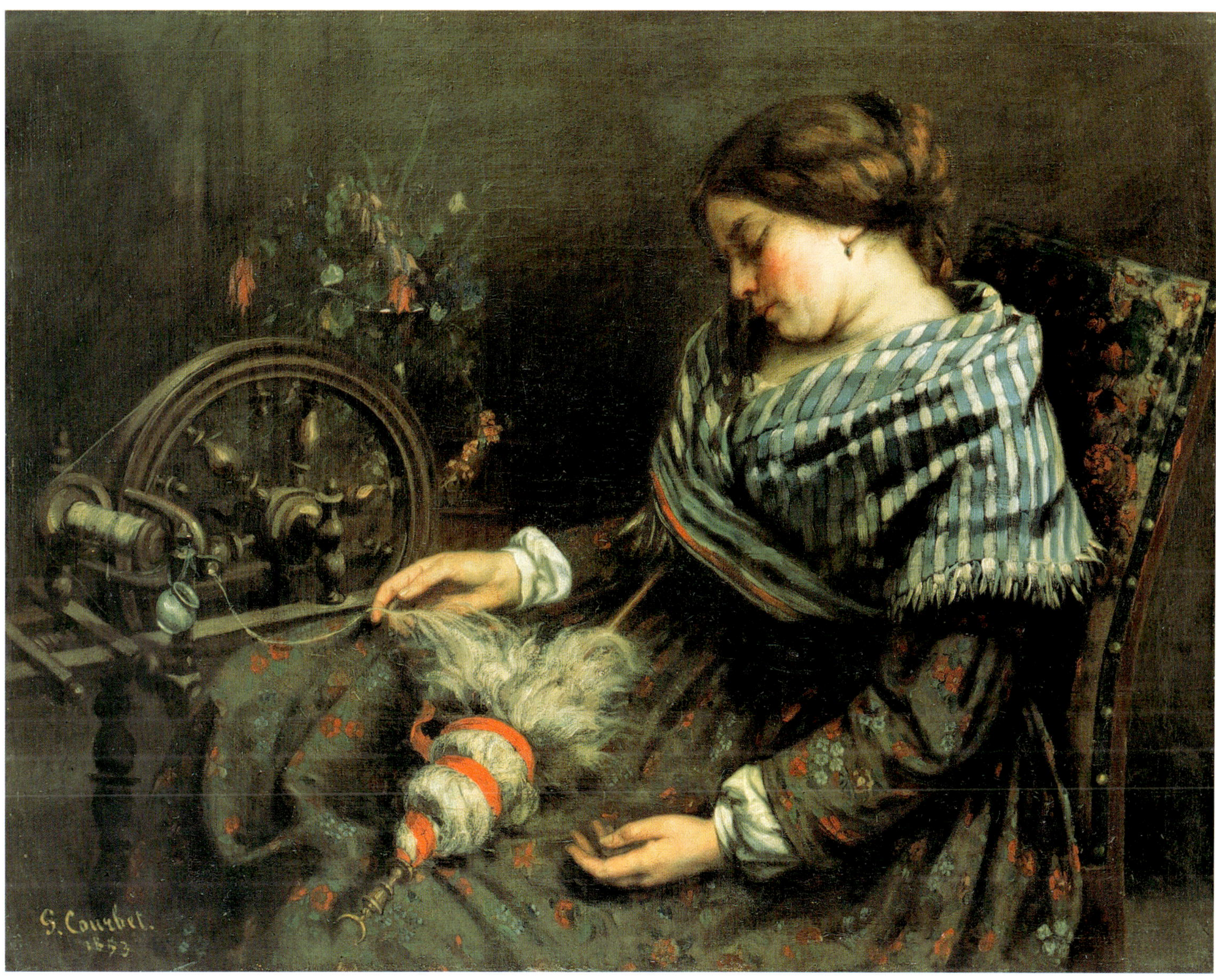

plate 120

Gustave Courbet (1819-1877)
The sleeping spinner, 1853
Montpellier, Musée Fabre

'Gauguin and I went to Montpellier yesterday to see the museum there
and especially the Bruyas room. [...] Courbet: first, the "Village girls", magnificent, a woman seen from behind, another lying on the ground in a landscape, second, the "Woman spinning", superb, and a whole heap more
Courbets' [730/564].

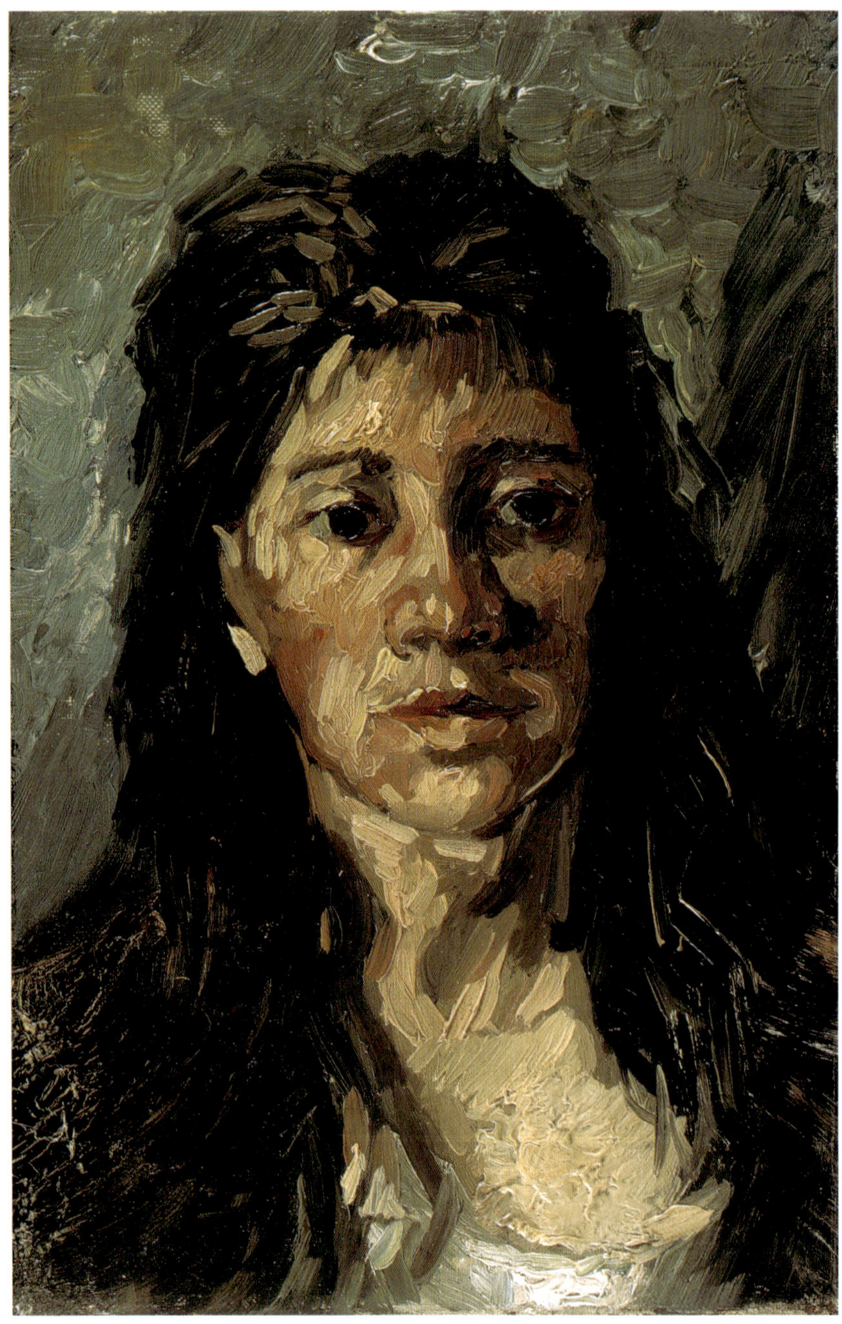

plate 121

Vincent van Gogh (1853-1890)
Head of a woman (F 206 JH 972), 1885
Amsterdam, Van Gogh Museum (Vincent van Gogh Foundation)

'I must write you again to tell you that I have continued with models.
I have made two fairly large heads, by way of trial for a portrait. First, that
old man whom I wrote to you about, a kind of head like V. Hugo's; then
also a study of a woman. In the woman's portrait I have brought lighter
tones into the flesh, *white* tinted with carmine, vermilion, yellow and a light
background of grey-yellow' [550/439].

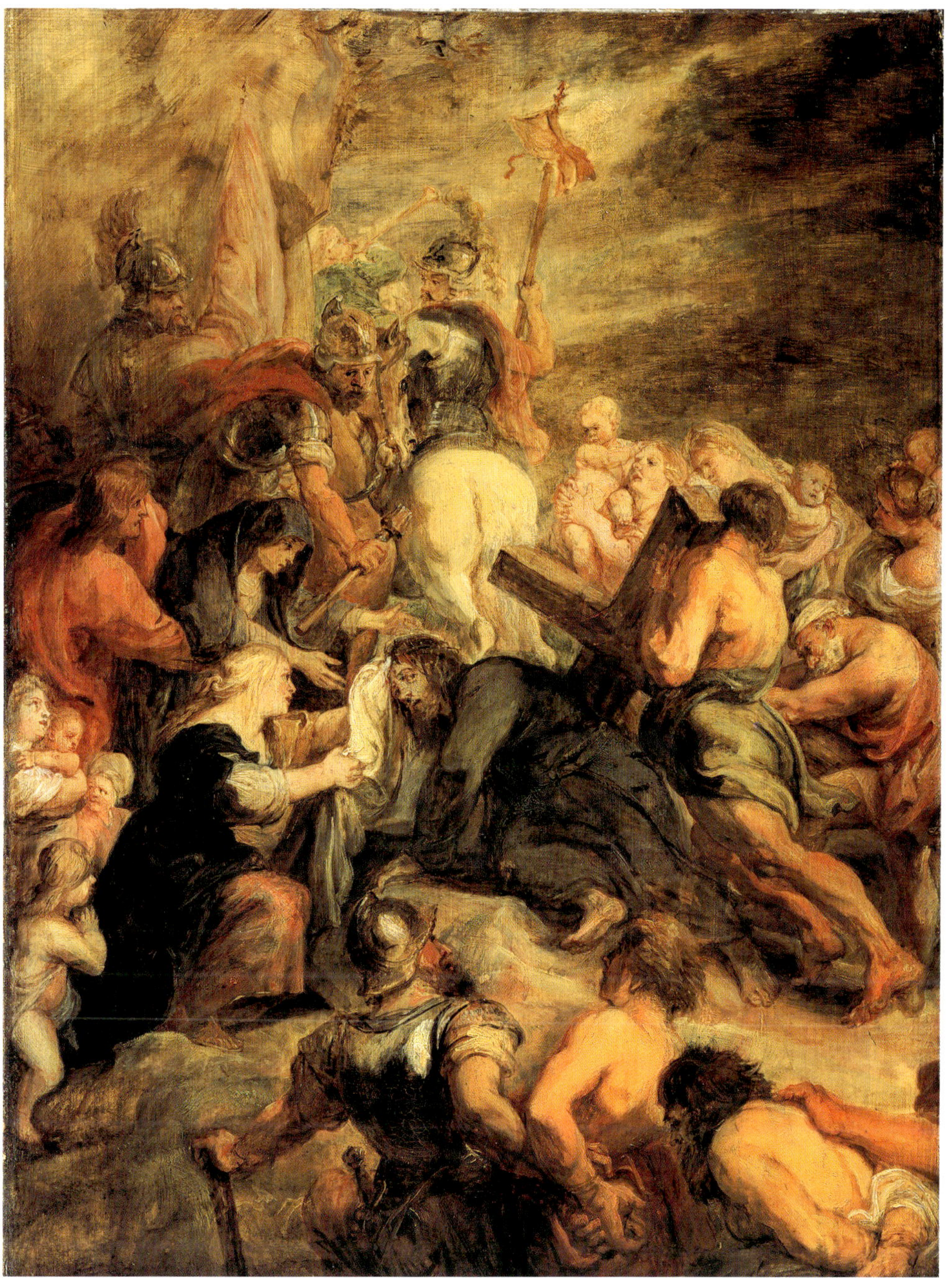

plate 122

Peter Paul Rubens (1577-1640)
The carrying of the cross
Amsterdam, Rijksmuseum

'Now I saw a sketch by Rubens and a sketch by Diaz as well, almost at the
same time as it were. They were not alike, but what they have in common
is the belief that colour expresses form if well applied and in harmony'
[538/427].

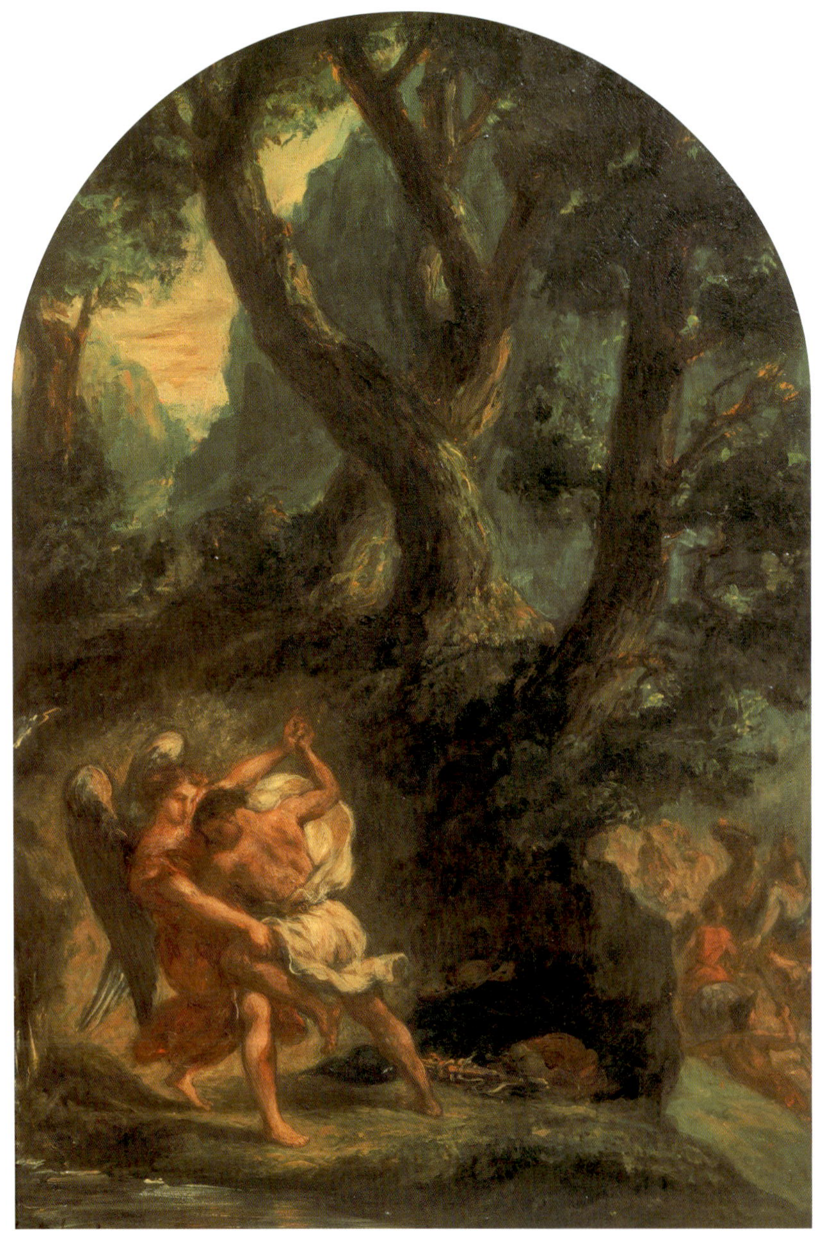

plate 123

Eugène Delacroix (1798-1863)
Jacob wrestling with the angel, c. 1850-56
Vienna, Österreichische Galerie Belvedere

'Therefore I very often use the ochres as I did in the old days. I know
quite well that the studies in the last package, drawn with long sinuous
lines, were not what they ought to have been; however I beg you to
believe that in landscape I am going on trying to mass things by means of
a drawing style which tries to express the interlocking of the masses. Do
you happen to remember that landscape by Delacroix – "Jacob wrestling
with the angel"?' [818/613].

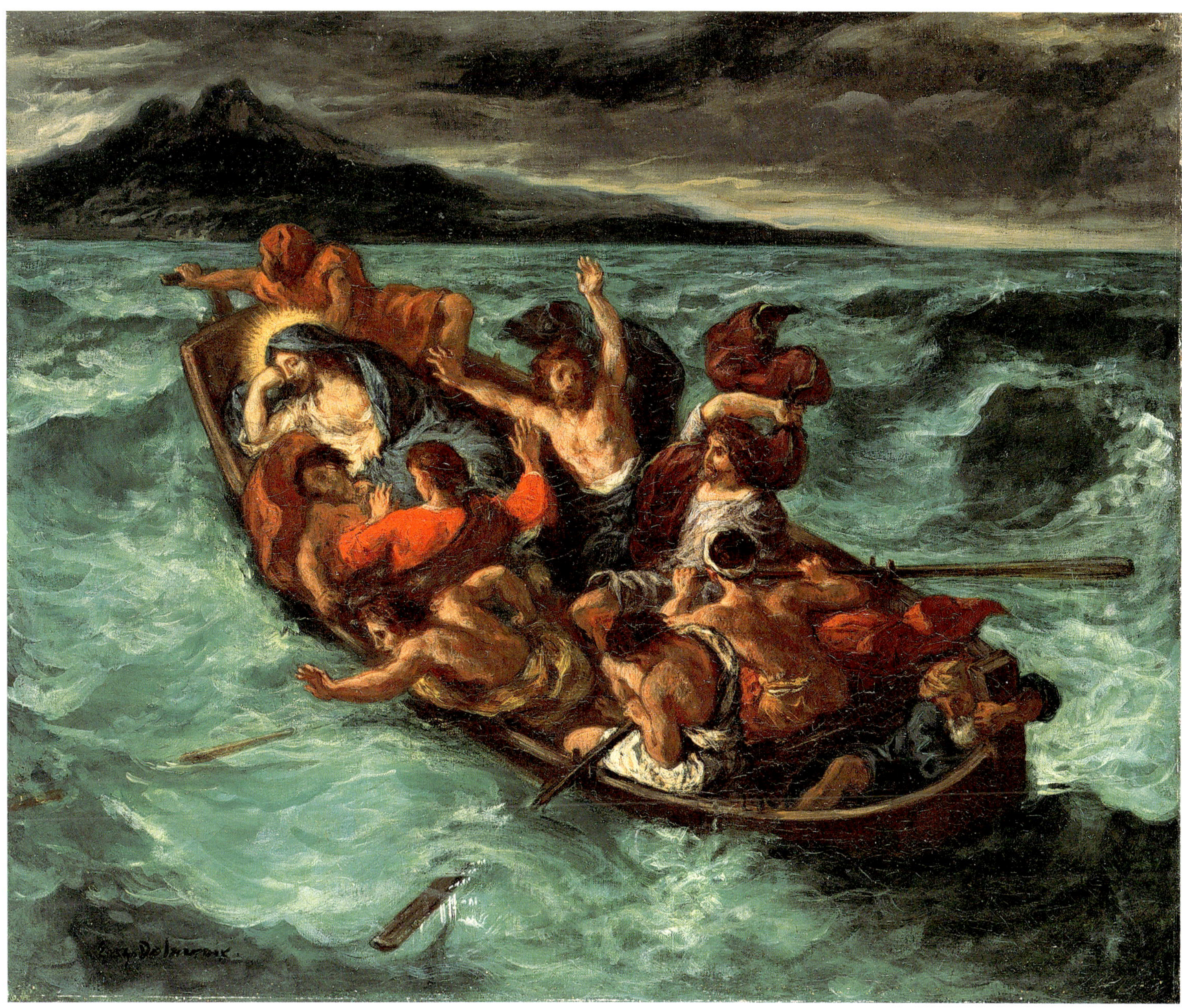

plate 124

Eugène Delacroix (1798-1863)
Christ asleep during the tempest, c. 1853
New York, The Metropolitan Museum of Art, Bequest of Mrs H.O.
Havemeyer, 1929, The H.O. Havemeyer Collection

'Oh, what a beautiful painting that is by Eug. Delacroix, Christ in the boat
on the Sea of Gennesaret! He – with his pale lemon-yellow aureole, sleeping, luminous in the dramatic purple, dark-blue, blood-red patch of the
group of bewildered disciples – on that terrible emerald-green sea, rising,
rising, right to the top of the frame. Ah, what an inspired conception!'
[635/B8].

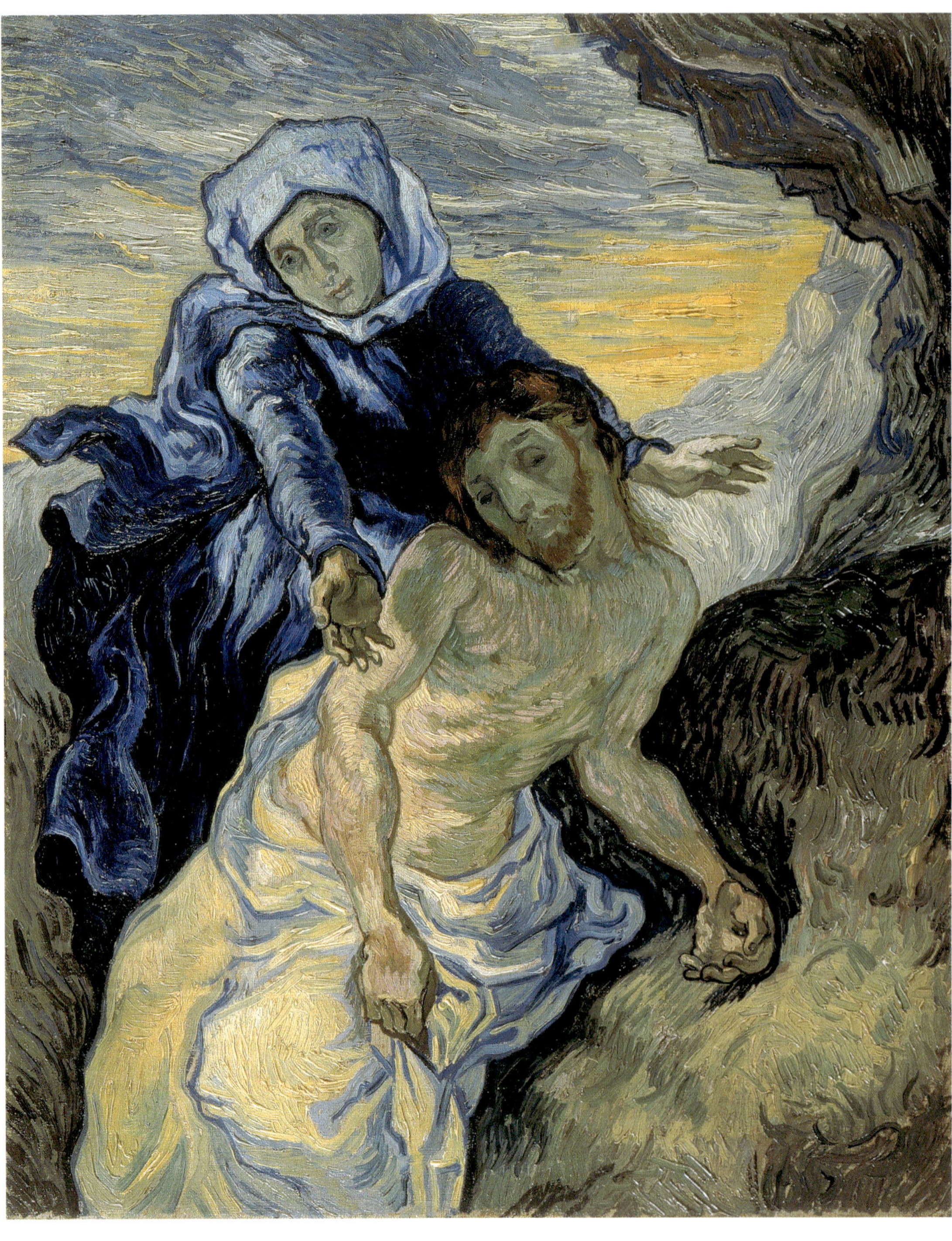

plate 125

Vincent van Gogh (1853-1890)
Pietà (after Delacroix) (F 630 JH 1775), 1889
Amsterdam, Van Gogh Museum (Vincent van Gogh Foundation)

'Work is going very well, I am discovering things I have sought in vain for years, and, aware of that, I am constantly reminded of that saying of Delacroix's you know, that he discovered painting when he had neither breath nor teeth left. Oh well, with my mental illness, I think of so many other artists suffering mentally, and tell myself that it doesn't stop one from carrying on one's trade as painter as if nothing had gone wrong. [...] I am not indifferent, and even as I suffer, religious thoughts sometimes give me great consolation. I had a piece of bad luck during my illness – that lithograph of Delacroix's, La Pietà, along with some other sheets, fell into some oil and paint and was ruined. I was sad about it – so I have been busy painting it and you will see it one day on a size 5 or 6 canvas. I have made a copy of it which I think has some feeling' [802/605].

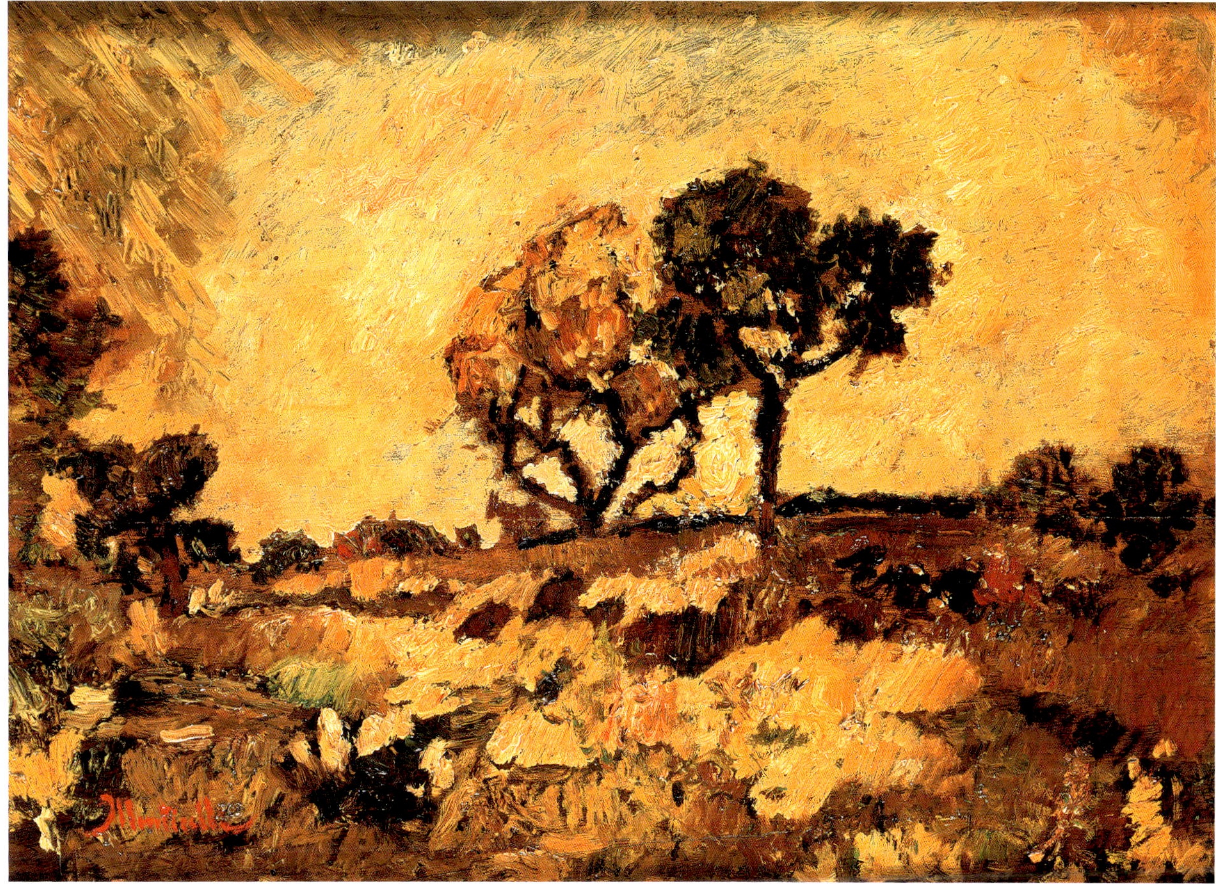

plate 126

Adolphe-Joseph Monticelli (1824-1886)
Sunset, c. 1882-84
London, The National Gallery

'You remember that fine landscape by Monticelli which we saw at Delare-
beyrette's, of a tree on some rocks against a sunset? There are many
effects like that just now, only I can never be outside at the hour of sunset, but for that I should have tried one of them myself' [810/610].

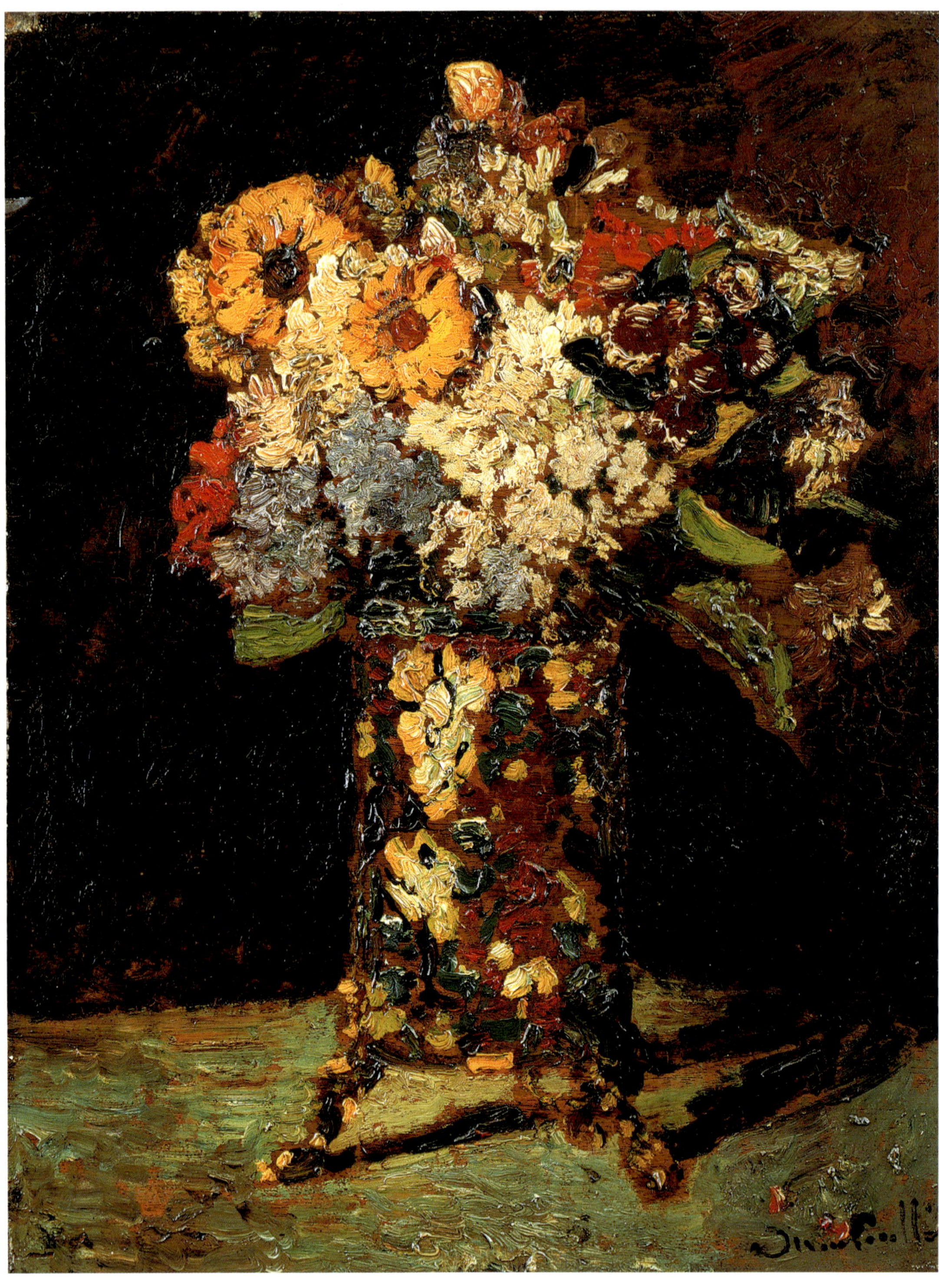

plate 127

Adolphe-Joseph Monticelli (1824-1886)
Vase with flowers, c. 1875
Amsterdam, Van Gogh Museum (Vincent van Gogh Foundation)

'What if you were to say to him that in our collection we have a bunch of flowers which is a better piece of painting and more beautiful than one by Diaz? That Monticelli sometimes made a bunch of flowers an excuse for gathering together in a single panel the whole range of his richest and most perfectly balanced tones? And that you must go straight to Delacroix to find anything equal to his orchestration of colours' [591/471].

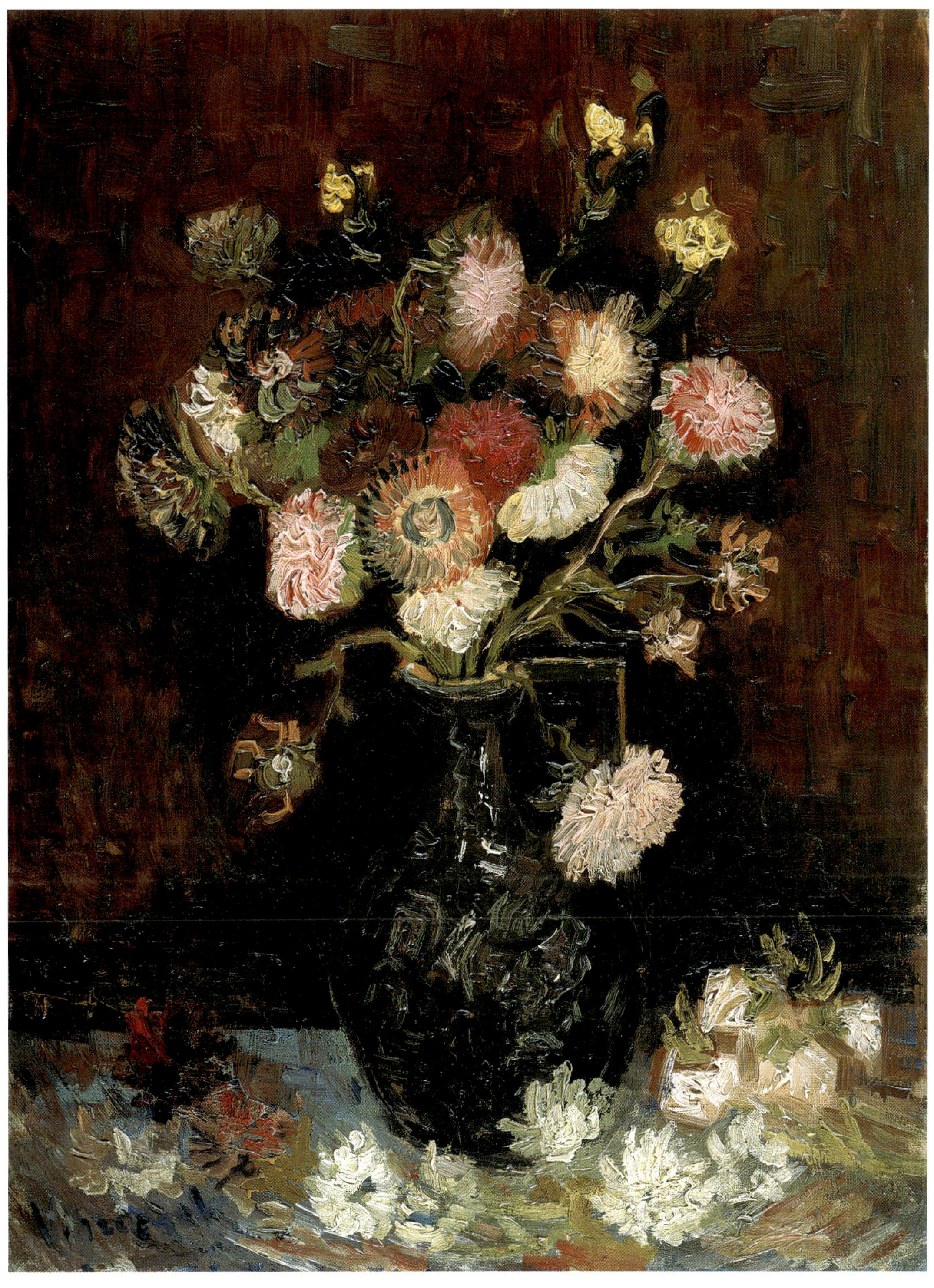

plate 128

Vincent van Gogh (1853-1890)
Vase with Chinese asters (F 234 JH 1168), 1886
Amsterdam, Van Gogh Museum (Vincent van Gogh Foundation)

'And now for what regards what I myself have been doing. I have lacked money for paying models, else I had entirely given myself to figure painting, but I have made a series of colour studies in painting simply flowers: red poppies, blue corn flowers and myosotys. white and rose roses, yellow chrysantemums – seeking oppositions of blue with orange, red & green, yellow and violet, seeking LES TONS ROMPUS ET NEUTRES [broken and neutral tones] to harmonise brutal extremes. Trying to render intense COLOUR and not a grey harmony' [572/459a; letter written in English].

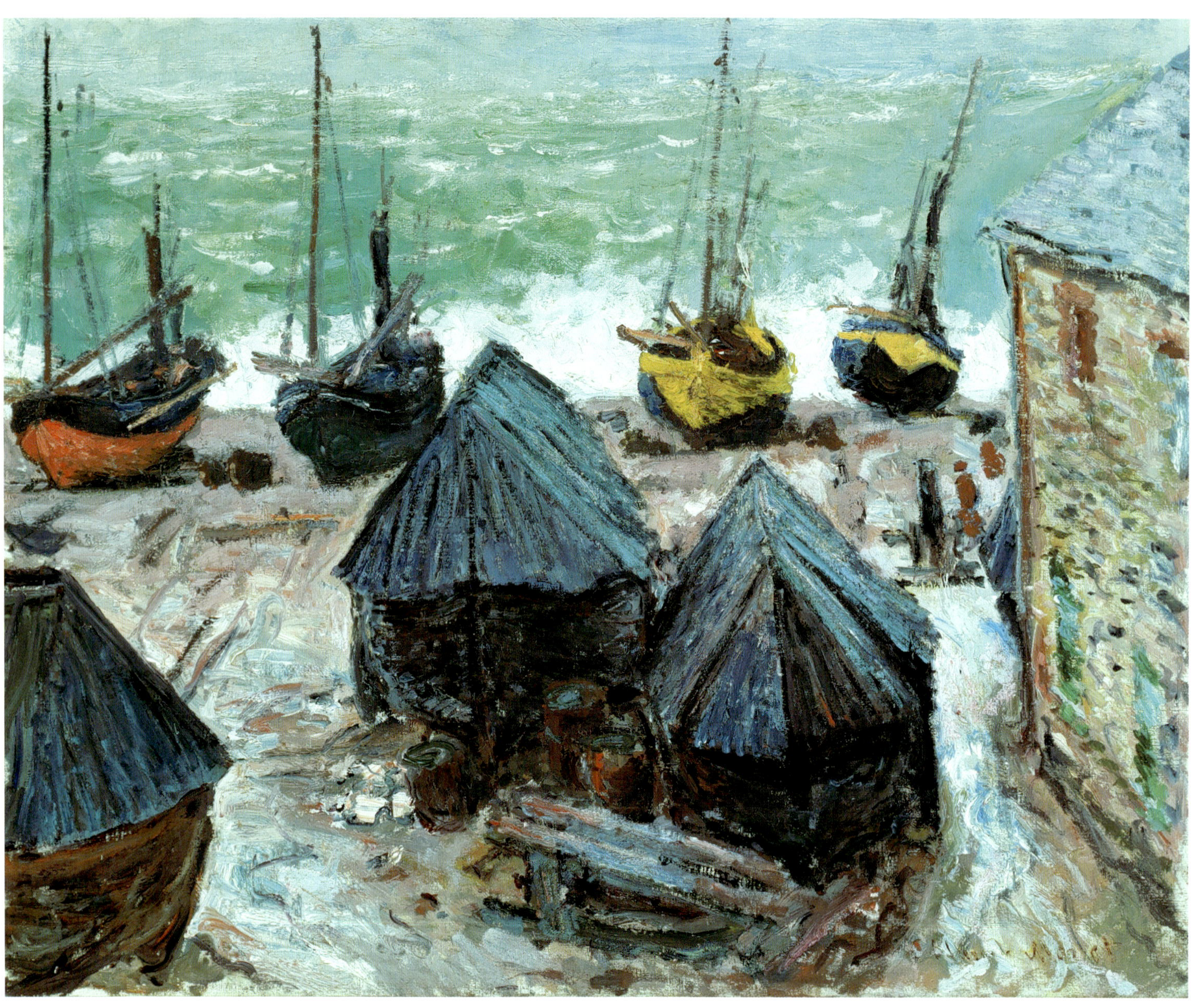

plate 129

Claude Monet (1840-1926)
Boats on the beach, Etretat, 1885
The Art Institute of Chicago, Charles H. and Mary F.S. Worcester
Collection

'The carriages are painted like a Monticelli, with spots of impasto. You used
to have a very fine Claude Monet showing four coloured boats on a
beach. Well, here they are carriages, but the composition is in the same
style' [708/552].

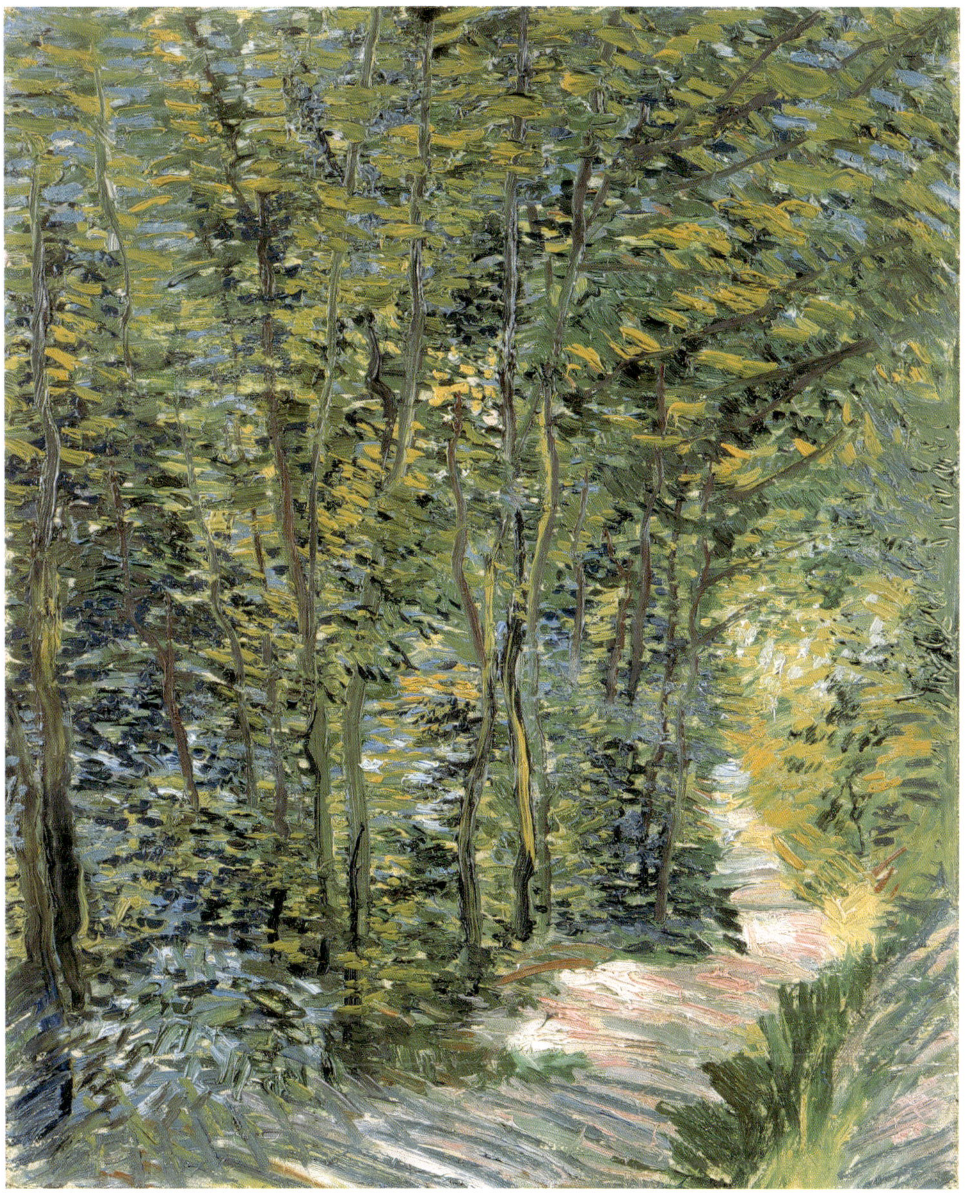

plate 130

Vincent van Gogh (1853-1890)
Woodland path (F 309 JH 1315), 1887
Amsterdam, Van Gogh Museum (Vincent van Gogh Foundation)

'Last year I painted almost nothing but flowers so as to get used to colours other than grey, namely pink, soft or bright green, light blue, violet,
yellow, orange, glorious red. And when I was painting landscapes at
Asnières this summer, I saw more colour in them than before' [576/W1].

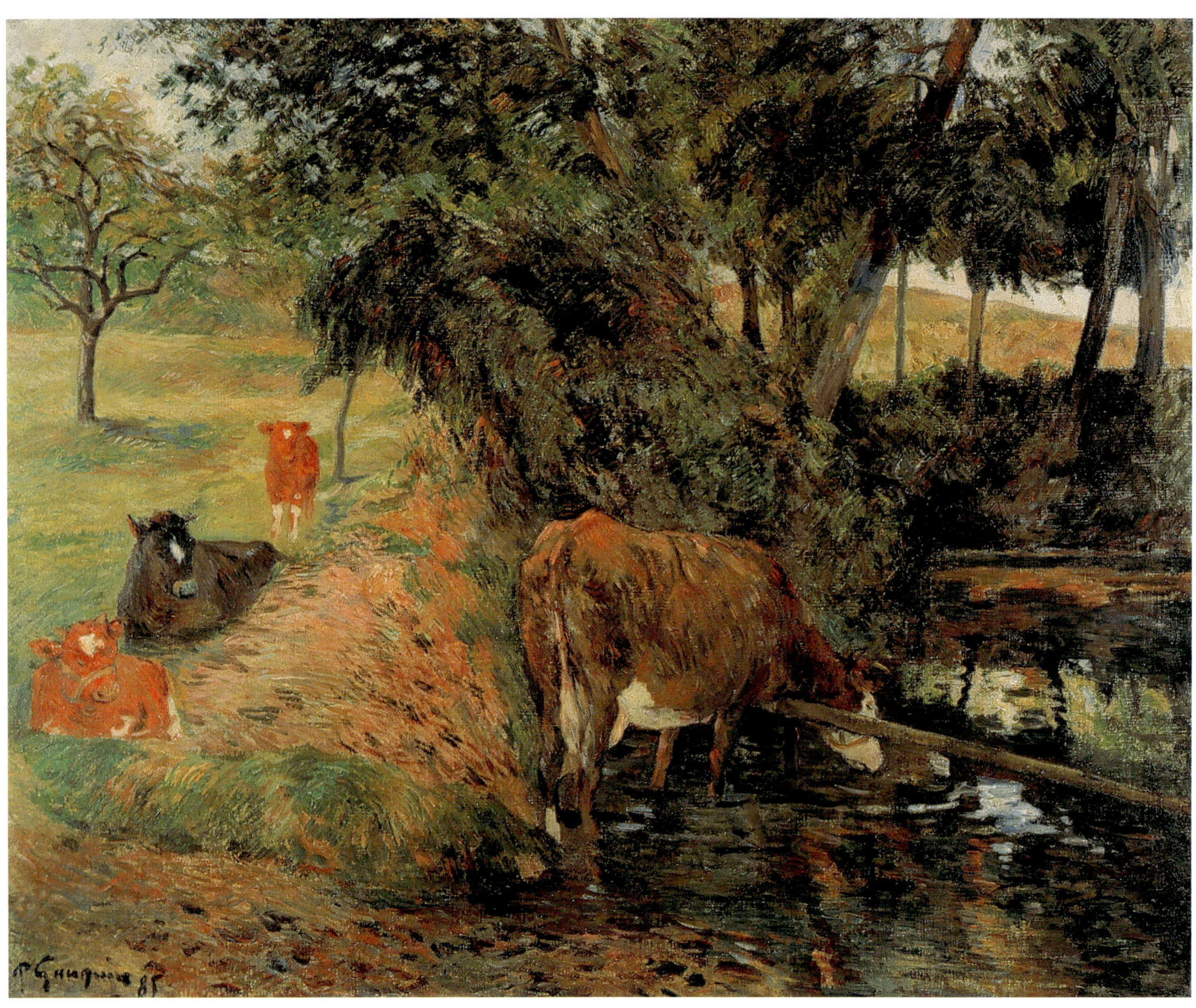

plate 131

Paul Gauguin (1848-1903)
Resting cows, 1885
Rotterdam, Museum Boijmans Van Beuningen

'You are damned right to think of Gauguin. [...] Everything his hands make
has a gentle, pitiful, astonishing character. People don't understand him yet,
and it pains him so much that he does not sell anything, just like other
true poets' [614/B5].

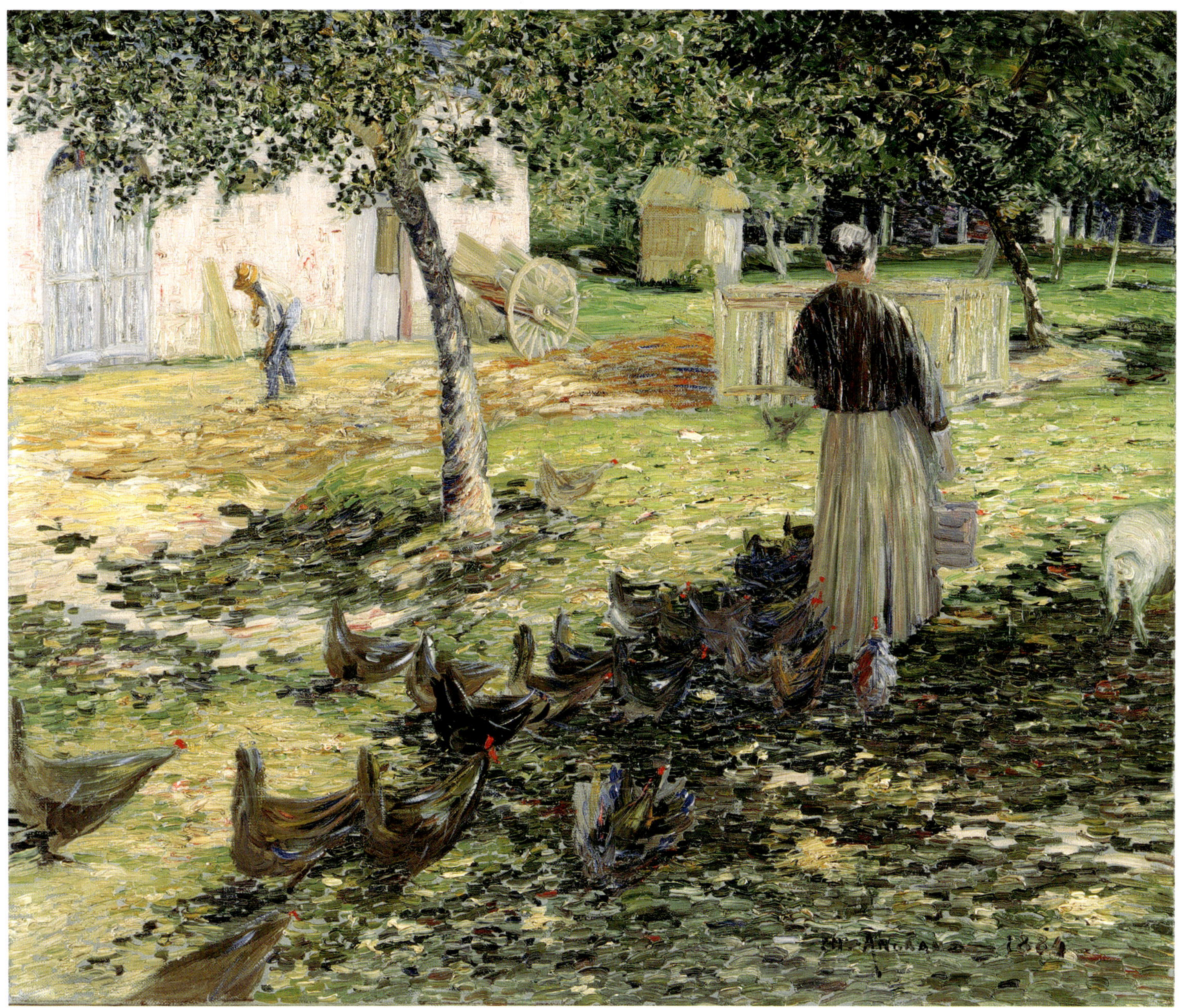

plate 132

Charles Angrand (1854-1926)
Feeding the chickens, 1884
Copenhagen, Ny Carlsberg Glyptotek

'I saw your "Young girl with chickens" at Tanguy's again. That's the very
study I want to exchange with you' [573/-, to Angrand].

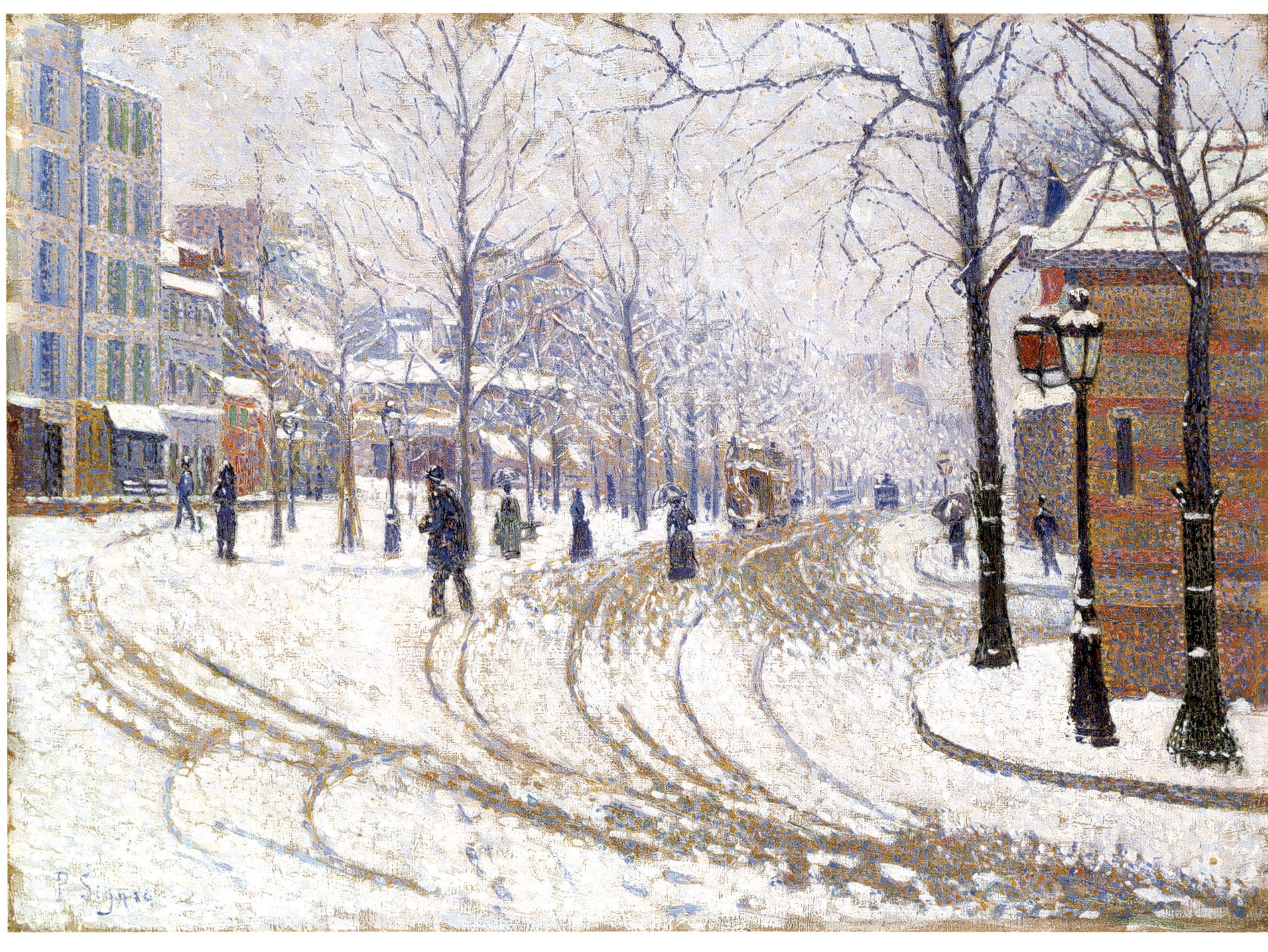

plate 133

Paul Signac (1863-1935)
Snow, Boulevard de Clichy, 1886
The Minneapolis Institute of Arts, Bequest of Putnam Dana McMillan

'As for stippling and making halos and other things, I think they are real discoveries, but we can already predict that this technique will not become a universal dogma any more than any other. That is another reason why Seurat's "Grande Jatte", the landscapes with broad stippling by Signac and Anquetin's boat, will in time become even more personal and even more original' [673/528].

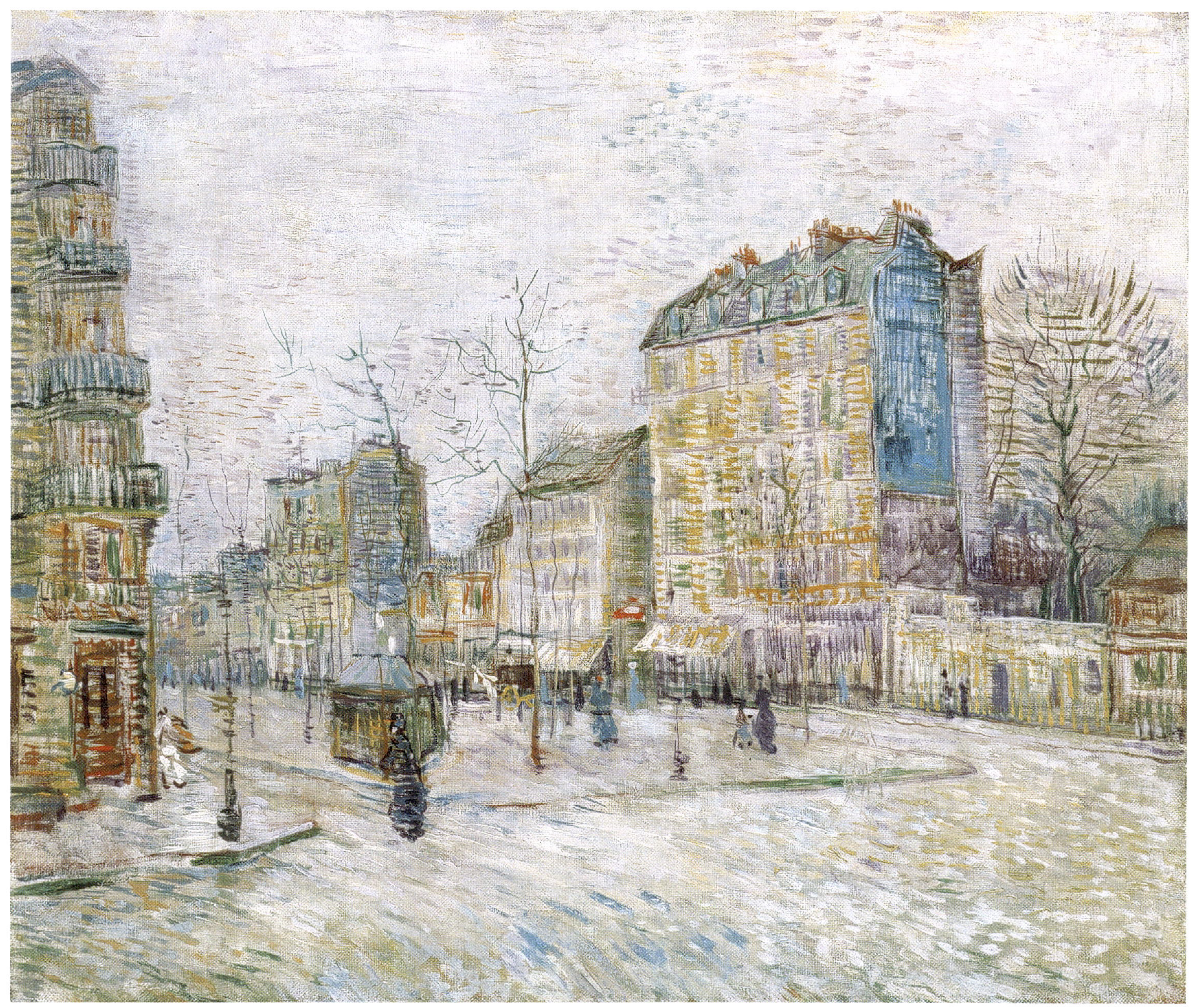

plate 134

Vincent van Gogh (1853-1890)
Boulevard de Clichy (F 292 JH 1219), 1887
Amsterdam, Van Gogh Museum (Vincent van Gogh Foundation)

'It was Sunday today, almost a spring day. This morning I took a long walk alone, going everywhere – through the city, in the park, along the boulevards. The weather was such that I think in the country they will have heard the lark sing for the first time. In short, there was something of resurrection in the atmosphere' [564/453].

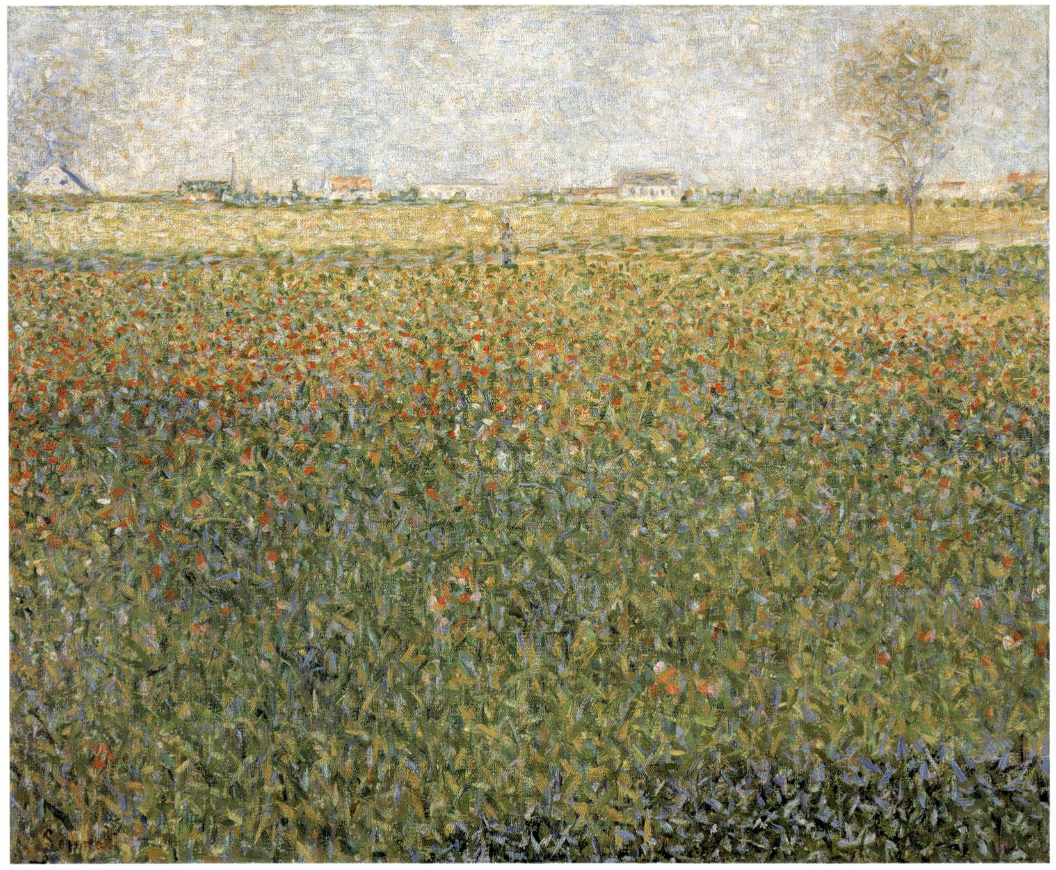

plate 135

Georges Seurat (1859-1891)
La Luzerne, Saint-Denis, 1885-86
Edinburgh, National Galleries of Scotland

'What is Seurat doing? I should not dare to show him the studies already
sent, but the ones of the sunflowers, and the cabarets, and the gardens,
I would like him to see those. I often think of his method, though I do not
follow it at all; but he is an original colourist, and Signac too, though to
a different degree, their stippling is a new discovery, and in any event I like
them very much' [687/539].

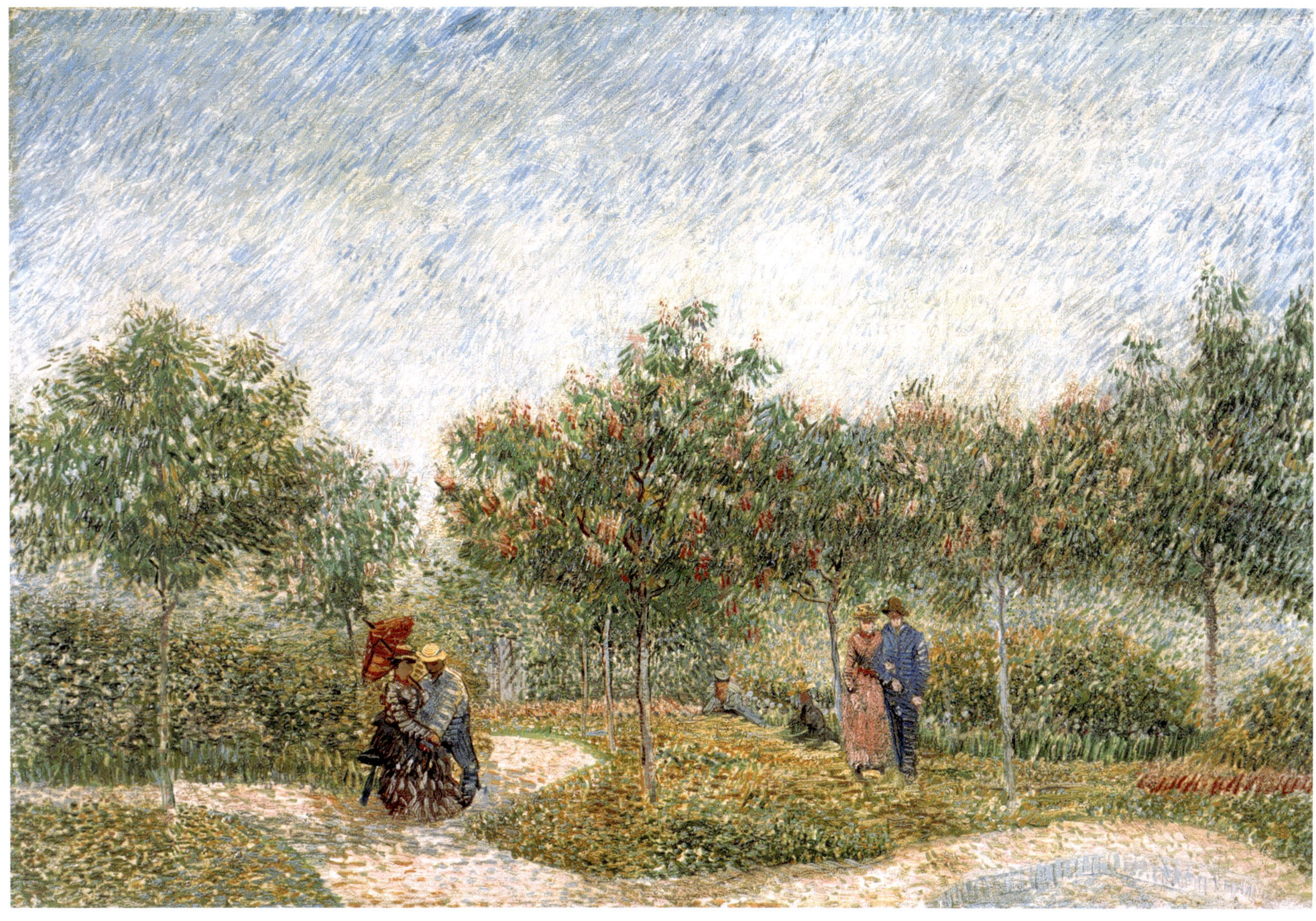

plate 136

Vincent van Gogh (1853-1890)
Courting couples in the Voyer d'Argenson Park in Asnières (F 314 JH 1258), 1887
Amsterdam, Van Gogh Museum (Vincent van Gogh Foundation)

'I saw Tanguy yesterday and he has put a canvas I've just done in the window. I've done four since you left and I've got a big one under way.
I realise that these big, long canvases are hard to sell, but later on people
will see that there's fresh air and a good mood in them. Now the whole
lot would do well as a decoration for a dining room or a country house'
[575/462].

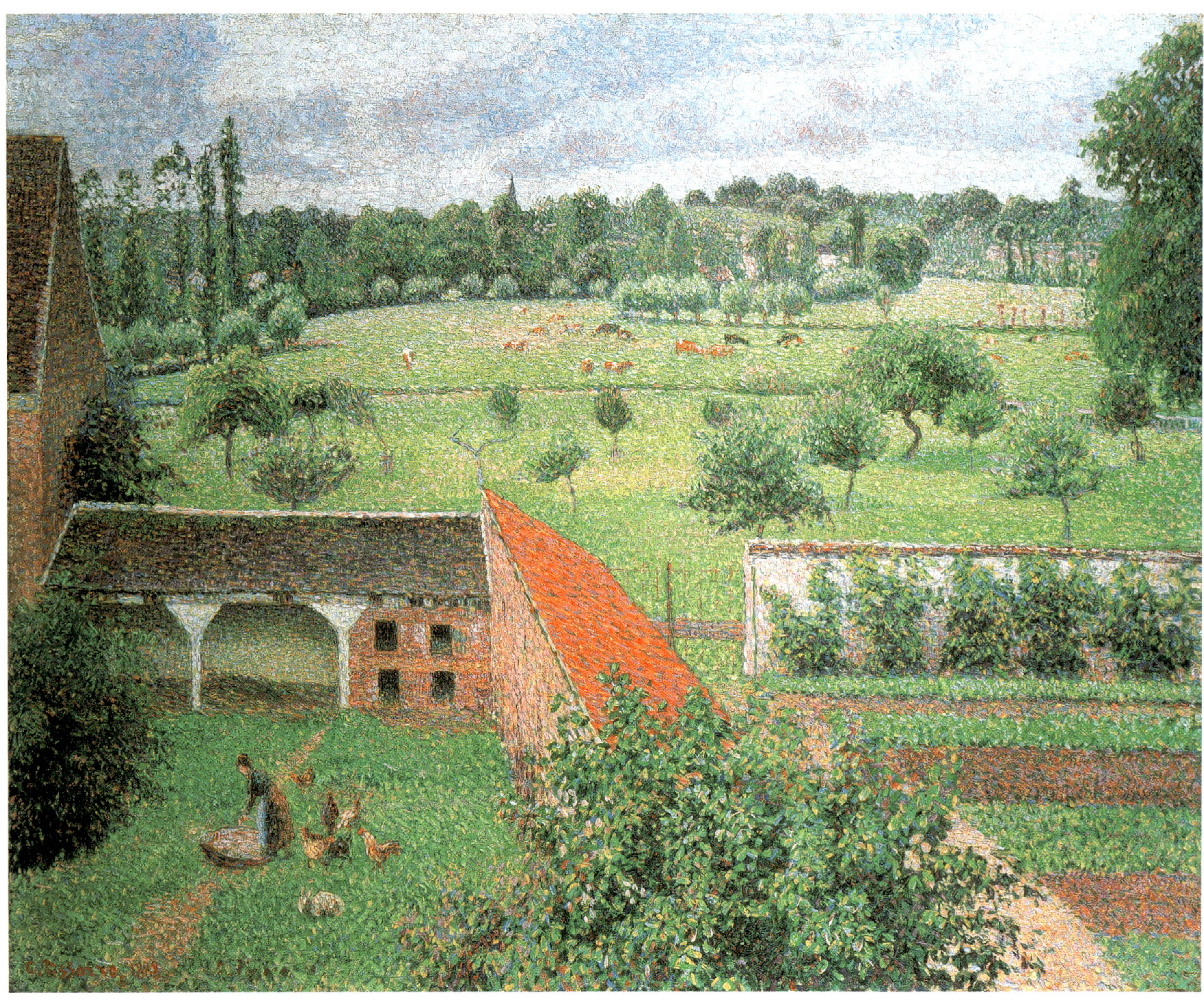

plate 137

Camille Pissarro (1830-1903)

View from my window in cloudy weather, 1886-88

Oxford, Ashmolean Museum of Art and Archaeology

'What Pissarro says is true, you must boldly exaggerate the effects of
either harmony or discord which colours produce. It is the same as in
drawing – the drawing, accurate colour, is perhaps not the essential thing
to aim at, because the reflection of reality in a mirror, if it could be caught,
colour and all, would not be a painting at all, nothing more than a photograph' [623/500].

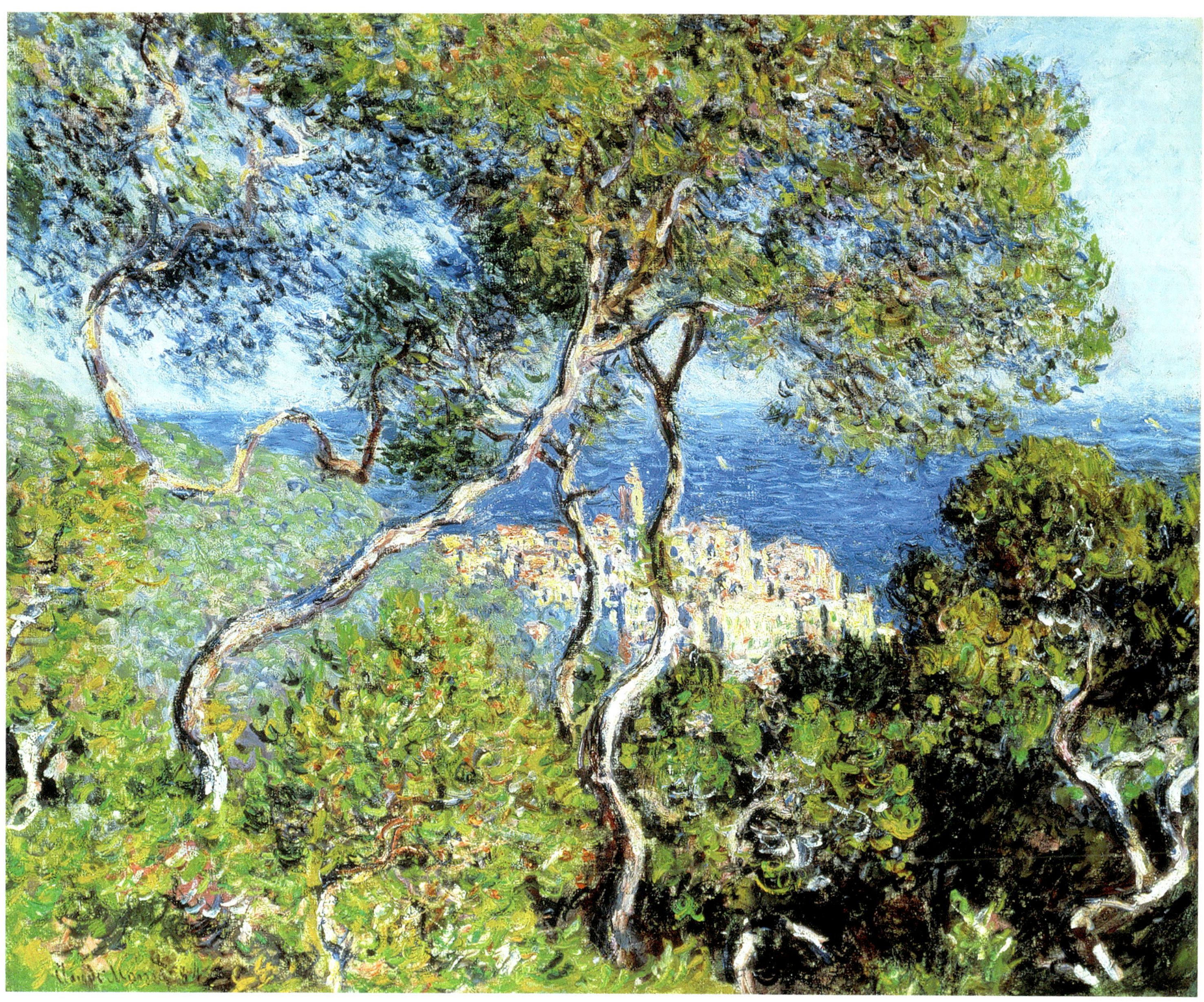

plate 138

Claude Monet (1840-1926)
Bordighera, 1884
The Art Institute of Chicago, Potter Palmer Collection

'Odd, but one evening recently at Mont Majour I saw a red sunset, its rays
falling on the trunks and foliage of pines growing among a jumble of rocks,
colouring the trunks and foliage with fiery orange, while the other pines in
the distance stood out in Prussian blue against a sky of tender blue-green,
cerulean. It was just the effect of that Claude Monet; it was superb. The
white sand and the layers of white rocks under the trees took on tints of
blue' [617/492].

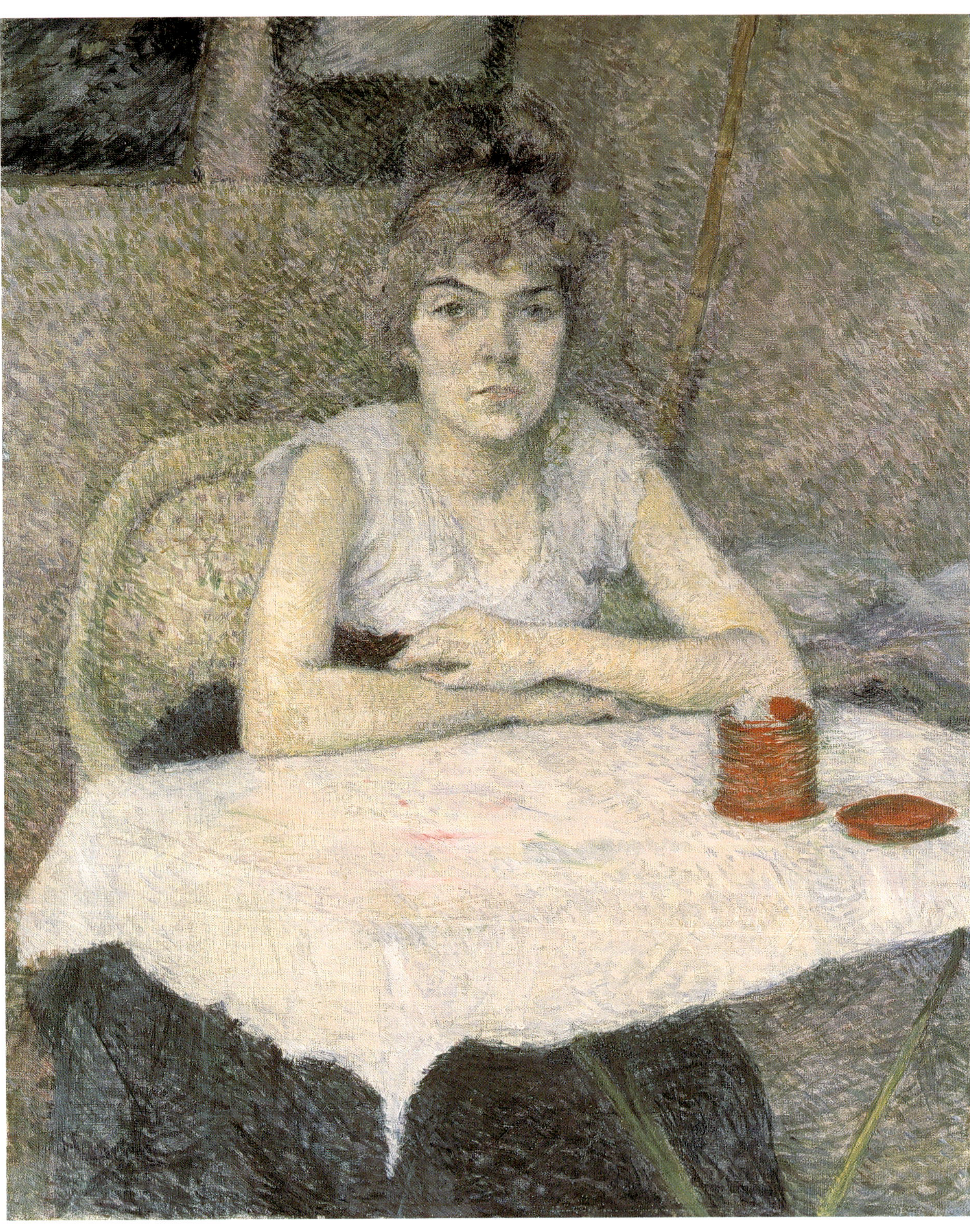

plate 139

Henri de Toulouse-Lautrec (1864-1901)
Young woman at a table, 'Poudre de riz', 1887
Amsterdam, Van Gogh Museum (Vincent van Gogh Foundation)

'I do not think that my peasant would wrong the De Lautrec in your pos-session, and I even believe the De Lautrec would appear even more distin-guished by the mutual contrast, and that on the other hand my painting would gain by the odd juxtaposition, because that sun-steeped, sunburned quality, tanned and air-swept, would show up still more effectively beside all that face powder and elegance' [663/520].

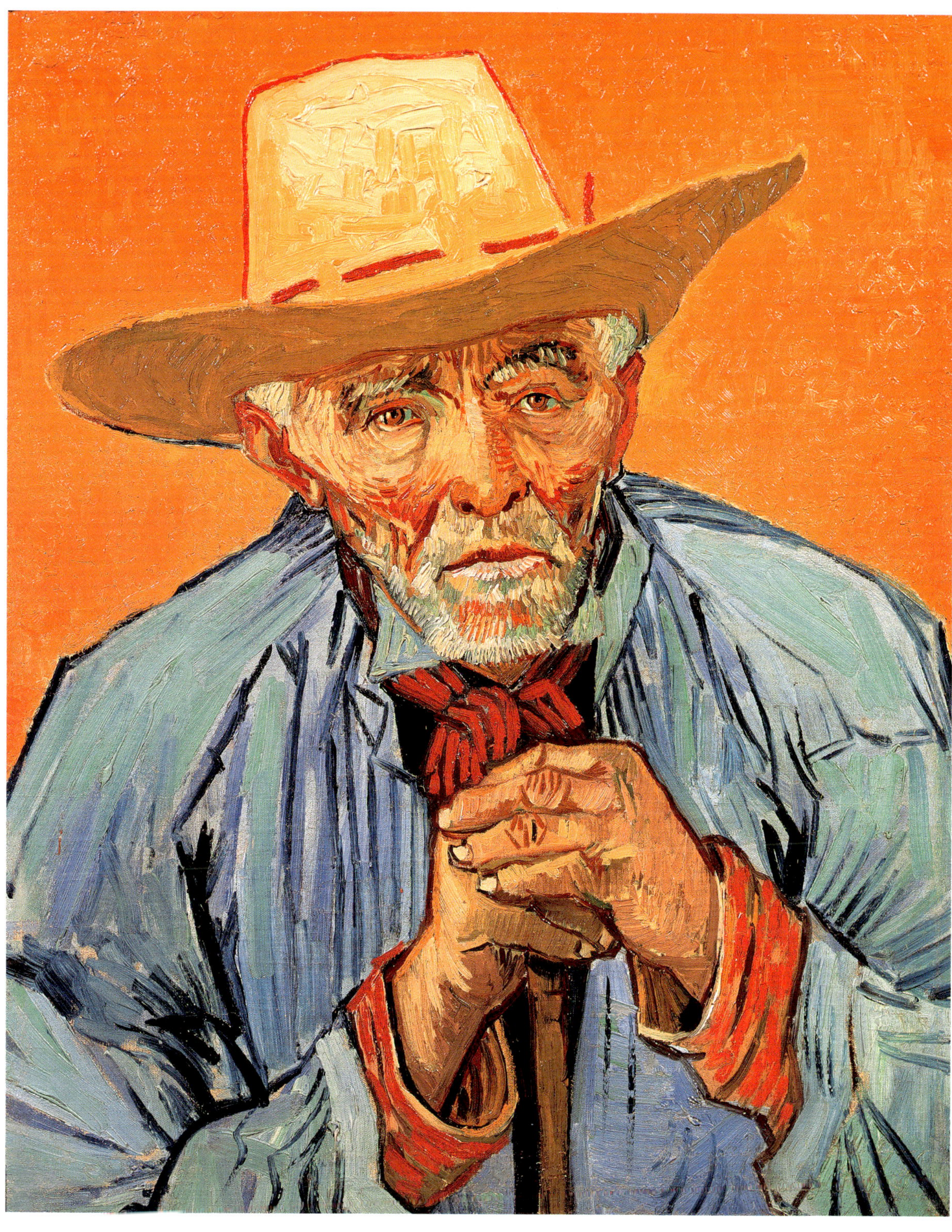

plate 140

Vincent van Gogh (1853-1890)
Portrait of Patience Escalier (F 444 JH 1563), 1888
Private collection

'I have two models this week: an Arlésienne and the old peasant. I am doing him this time against a background of vivid orange which, although it does not pretend to be the trompe l'oeil of a red sunset, may nevertheless be a suggestion of one' [675/529].

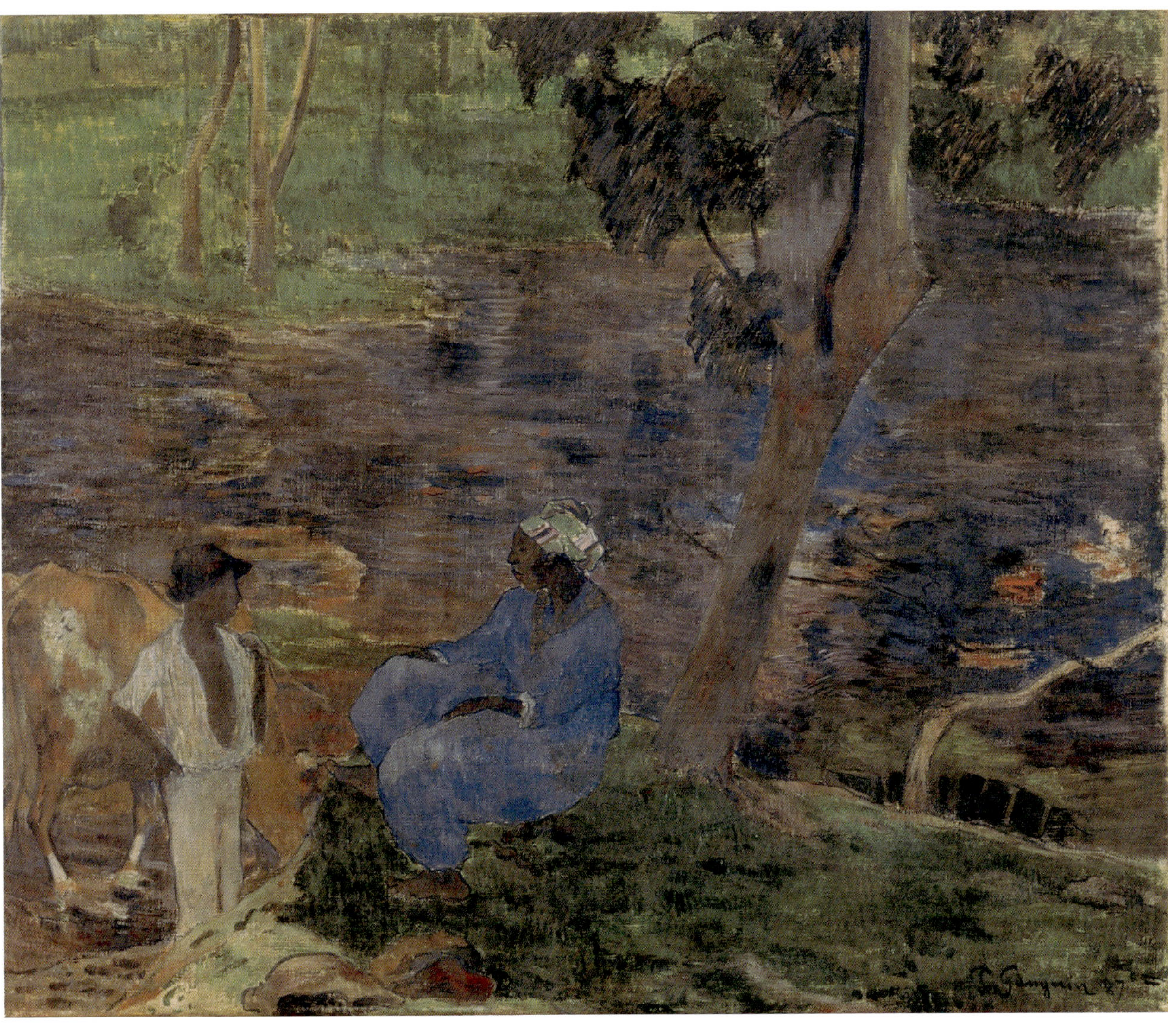

plate 141

Paul Gauguin (1848-1903)
On the shore of the lake at Martinique, 1887
Amsterdam, Van Gogh Museum (Vincent van Gogh Foundation)

'We have a second painting of his besides, which he exchanged for one of
my studies, a dried river with purple mud and pools of water mirroring
the pure cobalt blue of the sky, green grass, a Negro boy with a red-and-
white cow, a Negress in blue, and a patch of green forest. He is a fellow
who works like one possessed, and he does all sorts of things' [657/W5].

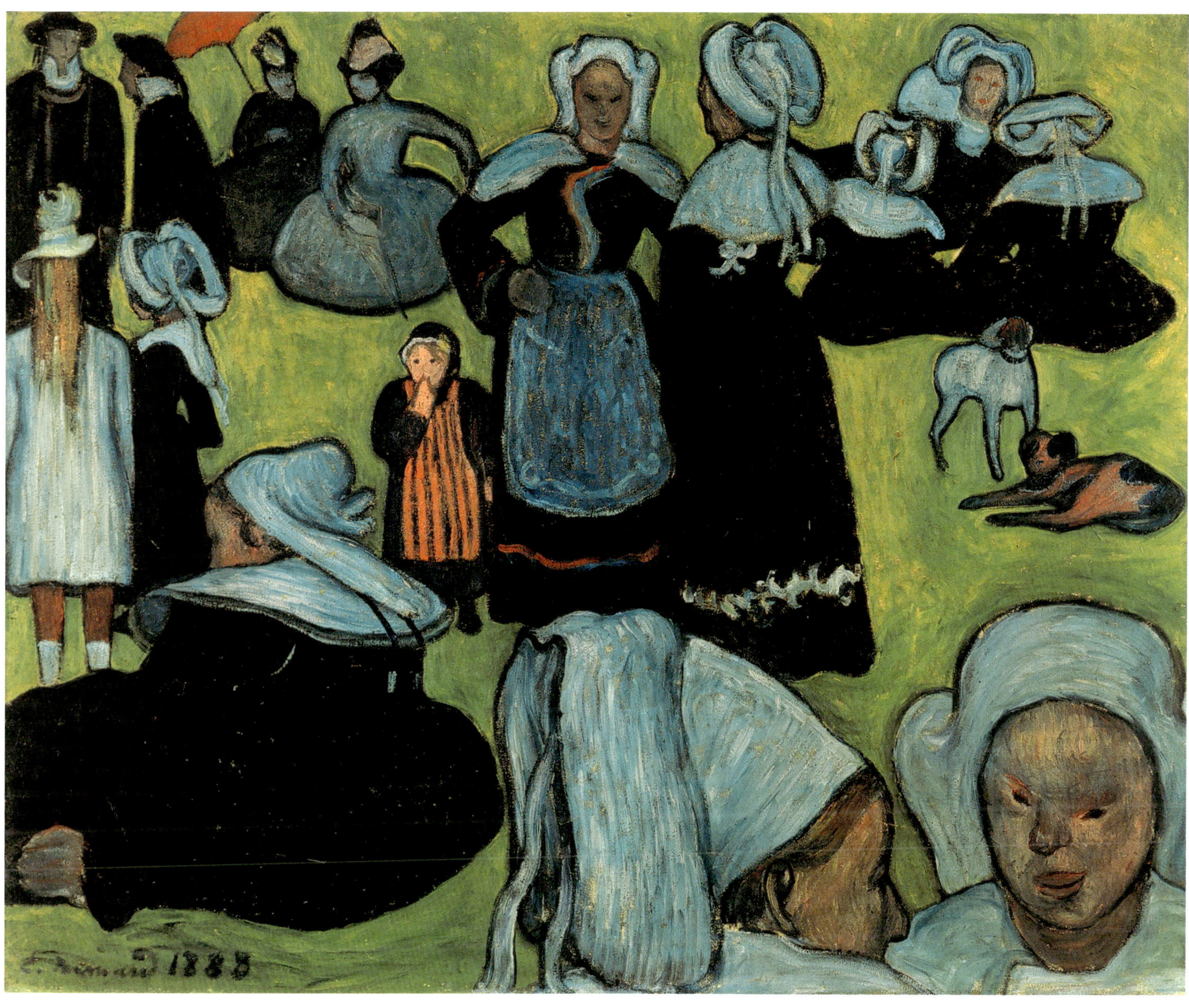

plate 142

Emile Bernard (1868-1941)
Breton women in the meadow, 1888
Private collection

'You ask me who Bernard is – he is a young painter – certainly no older than twenty – very original. He is trying to do elegant modern figures in the manner of the ancient Greek and Egyptian art, a gracefulness in the expressive motions, a charm in consequence of his daring colours.

I saw a painting of his of a Sunday afternoon in Brittany, Breton peasant women, children, peasants, dogs strolling about in a very green meadow; the clothes are black and red, the women's caps white. But in this crowd there are also two ladies, the one dressed in red, the other in bottle green; they make it a very modern thing. Ask Theo to show you the water-colour that I made after the painting; it is so original that I wanted to have a copy of it' [829/W16].

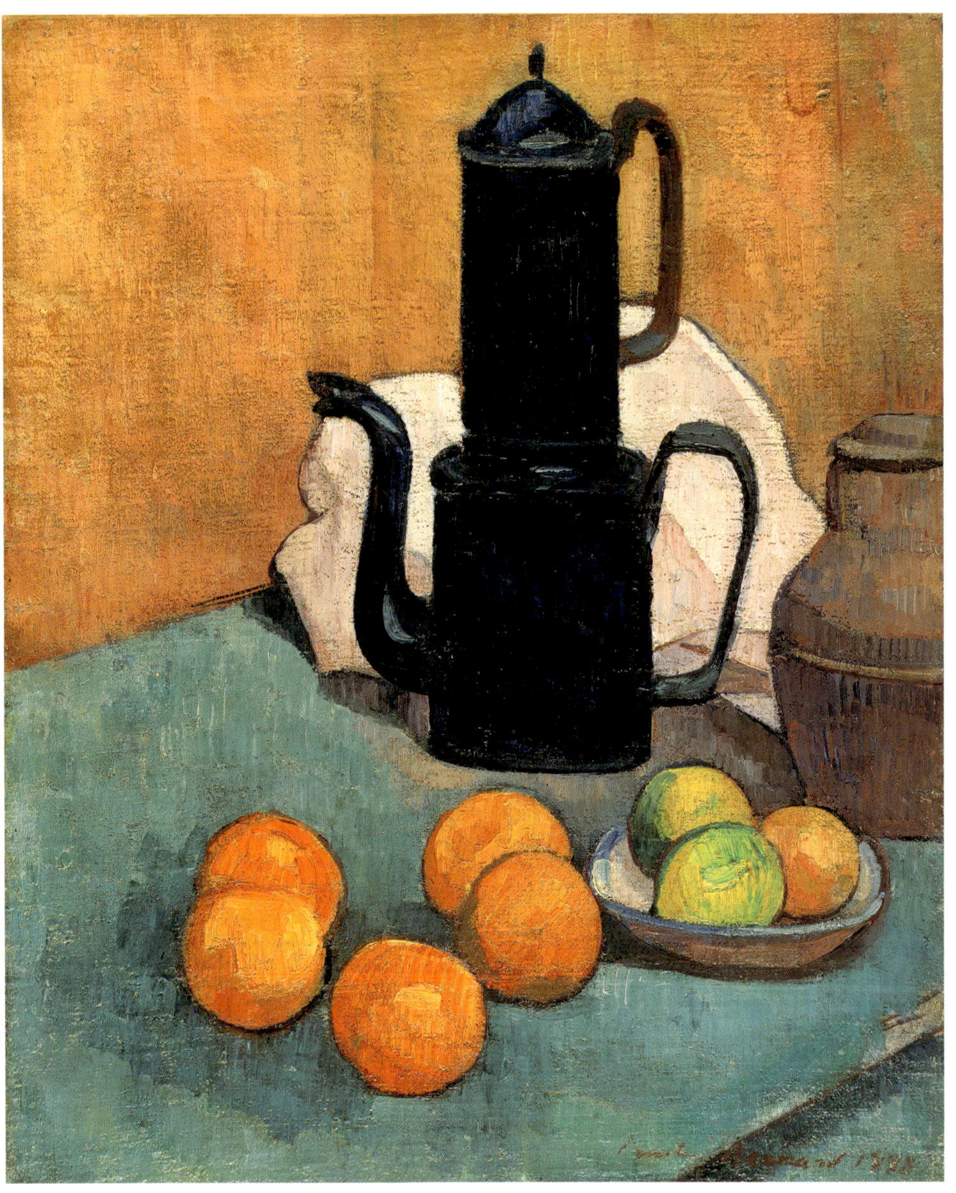

plate 143

Emile Bernard (1868-1941)
The blue coffeepot, 1888
Kunsthalle Bremen

'But I must speak to you again first of all about yourself, the two still lifes you have done and the two portraits of your grandmother. Have you ever done anything better than that, and have you ever been more yourself and a personality? I think not. [...] Do you know why I like these 3 or 4 studies so much? Because of that unknown quality of deliberateness, of great wisdom, that inexpressible quality of being steady and firm and self-assured of which they give evidence. You have never been closer to Rembrandt, old fellow, than in these studies' [659/B14].

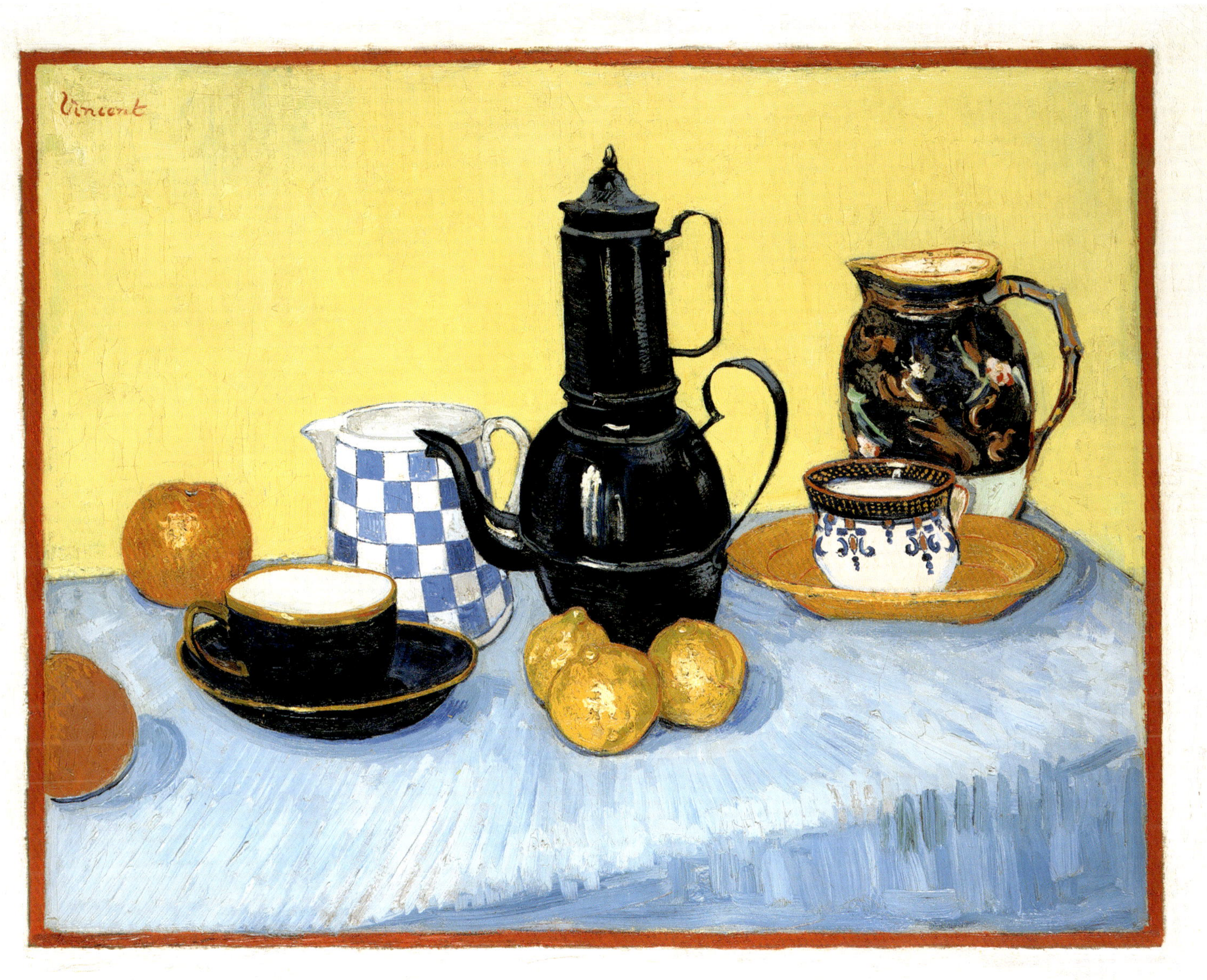

plate 144

Vincent van Gogh (1853-1890)
Still life with coffeepot (F 410 JH 1426), 1888
Private collection

'I have done a still life of a blue-enamelled iron coffee pot, a royal blue cup and saucer, a milk jug with pale cobalt and white checks, a cup with orange and blue patterns on a white ground, a blue majolica jug decorated with green, brown and pink flowers and leaves. The whole on a blue tablecloth, against a yellow background, and among this crockery two oranges and three lemons. So it is a variation of blues, enlivened by a series of yellows that go as far as orange' [614/B5].

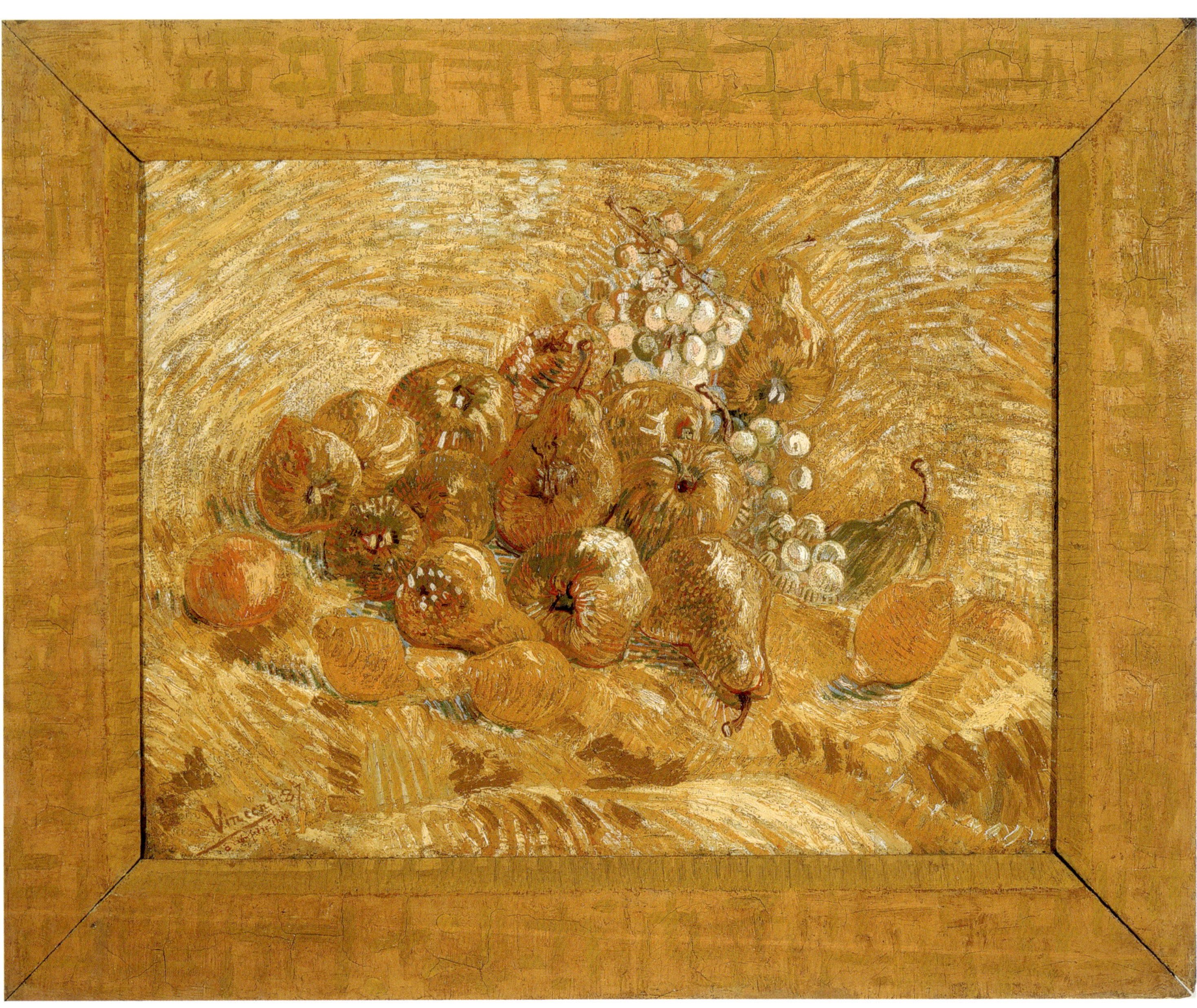

plate 145

Vincent van Gogh (1853-1890)
Still life with quinces and lemons (F 383 JH 1339), 1887
Amsterdam, Van Gogh Museum (Vincent van Gogh Foundation)

'The sunflowers are getting on, there is a new bouquet of 14 flowers on a green-yellow ground, so it is exactly the same effect – but in a larger size, a 30 canvas – as a still life with quinces and lemons that you already have – but in the sunflowers the painting is much simpler' [673/528].

plate 146

Louis Anquetin (1861-1932)
Avenue de Clichy, 1887
Hartford, Wadsworth Atheneum Museum of Art, The Ella Gallup Sumner and Mary Catlin Sumner Collection Fund

'The exhibition of prints that I had at the Tambourin influenced Anquetin and Bernard a good deal, but it was such a disaster! As for the trouble we took over the second exhibition in the room on Boulevard de Clichy, I regret it less: Bernard sold his first painting there, and Anquetin sold a study' [644/510].

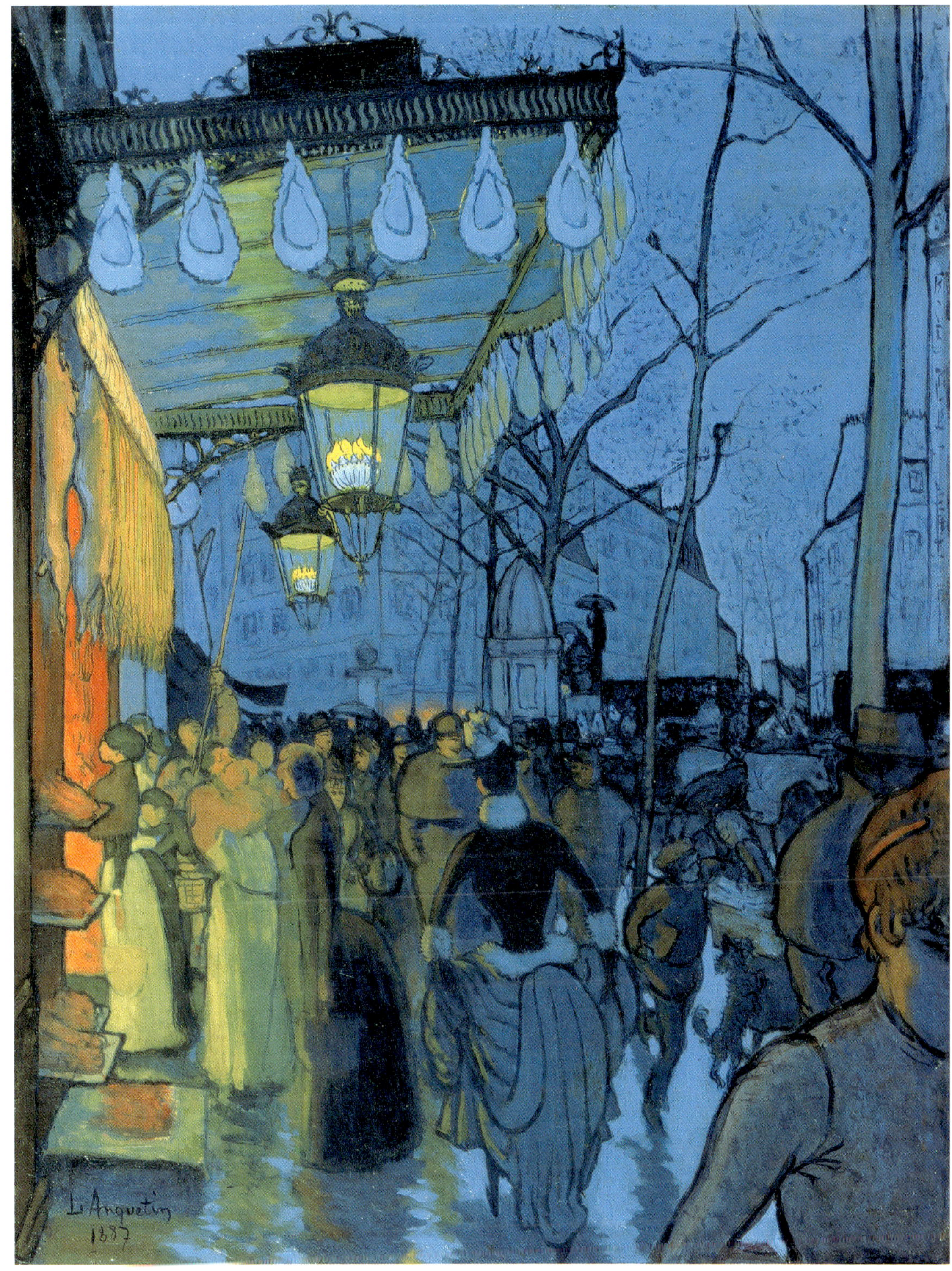

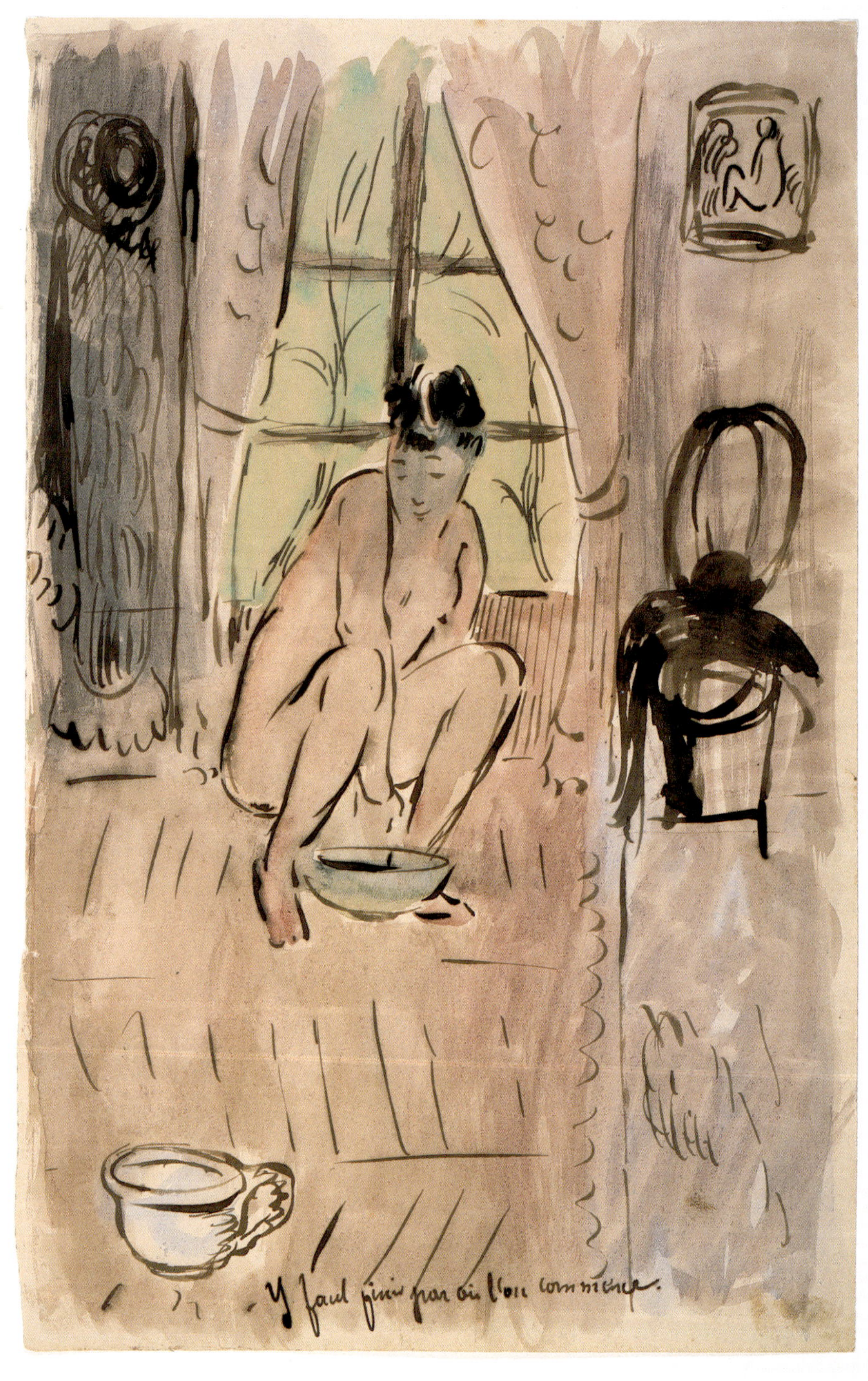

plate 147

Emile Bernard (1868-1941)

At the brothel: a prostitute making her toilet, 1887
Amsterdam, Van Gogh Museum (Vincent van Gogh Foundation)

'And now that I have started thanking you, I thank you furthermore for the batch of sketches entitled "At the brothel". Bravo! It seems to me that the woman washing herself and the one saying, "There is none other like me when it comes to exhausting a man," are the best; the others are grimacing too much, and above all they are done too vaguely, they are too little living flesh, not built up sufficiently. But no matter, these other ones too are something quite new and interesting. At the brothel! Yes, that's what one ought to do, and I assure you that I for one am almost jealous of the damned fine opportunity you will have of going there in your uniform, – which these good little women dote on' [702/B19].

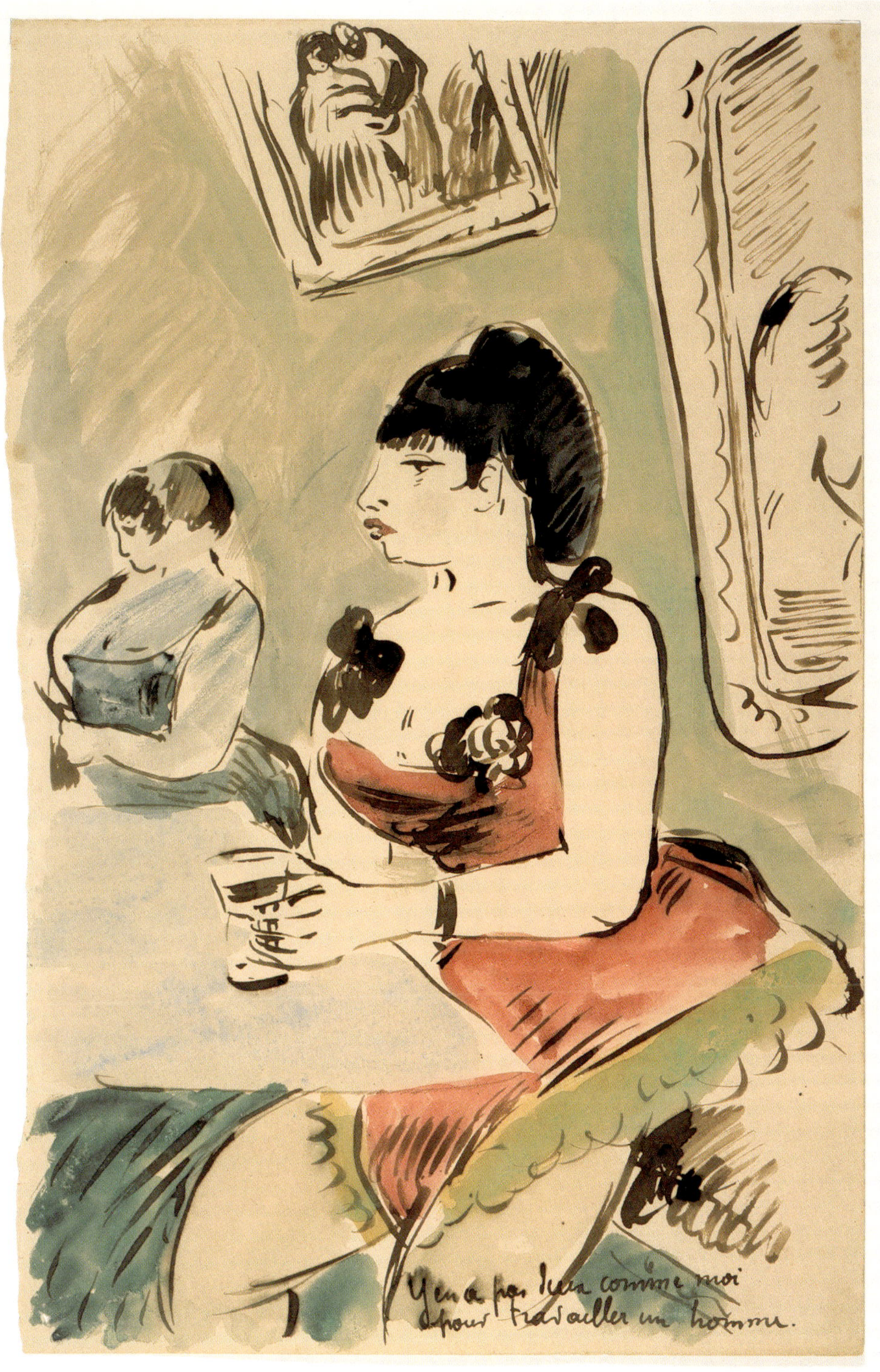

plate 148

Emile Bernard (1868-1941)
At the brothel: two prostitutes at table, 1887
Amsterdam, Van Gogh Museum (Vincent van Gogh Foundation)

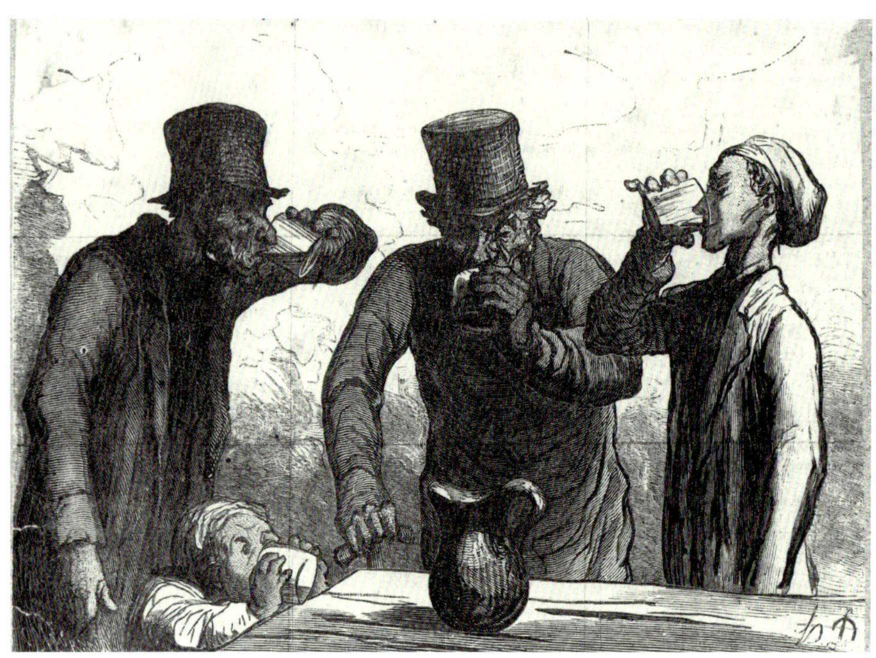

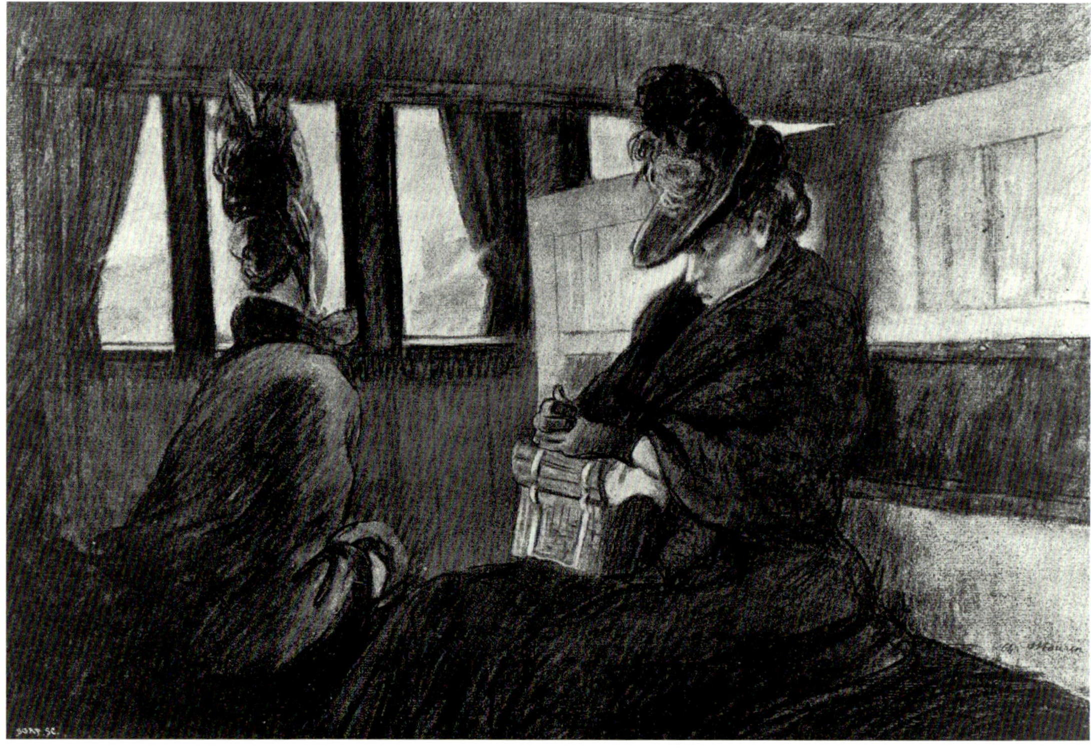

plate 149

After **Honoré Daumier** (1808-1879)
The four ages of a drinker, 1865-66
Amsterdam, Van Gogh Museum (Vincent van Gogh Foundation)

'I have always thought "The four ages of a drinker" by Daumier one of
his most beautiful things. There is as much soul in it as in a Degroux'
[267/R13].

plate 150

After **Charles Maurin** (1856-1914)
Before the accident, 1888
Amsterdam, Van Gogh Museum (Vincent van Gogh Foundation)

'I also received Maurin's drawing, which is magnificent. That man is a great
artist' [686/538].

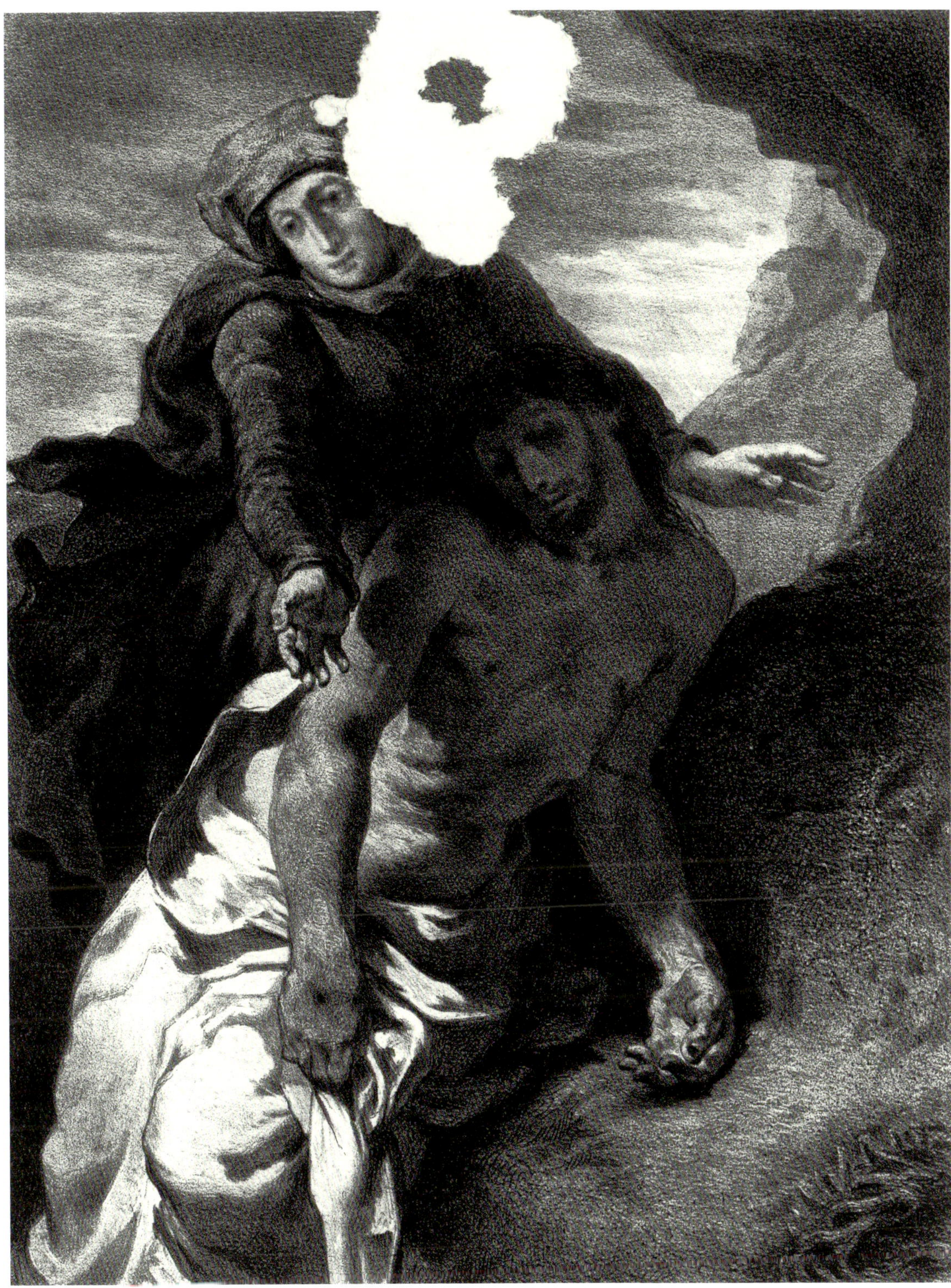

plate 151

After **Eugène Delacroix** (1798-1863)
Pietà, c. 1850
Amsterdam, Van Gogh Museum (Vincent van Gogh Foundation)

'If you come across Delacroix's "Pietà" again, [...] please get as many of
them as you can' [690/542].

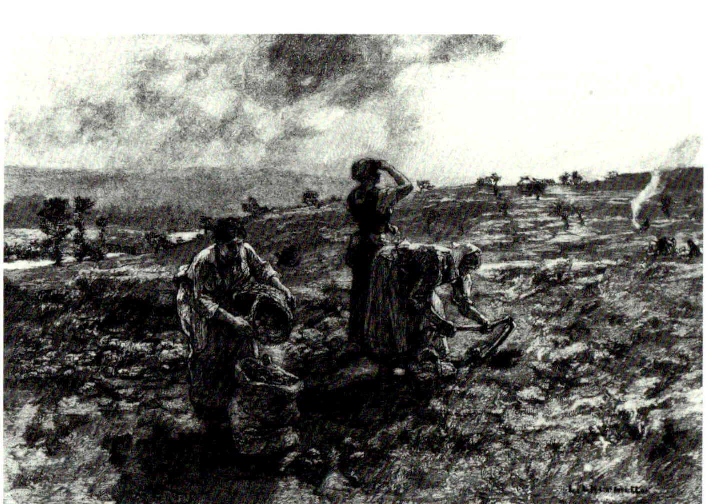

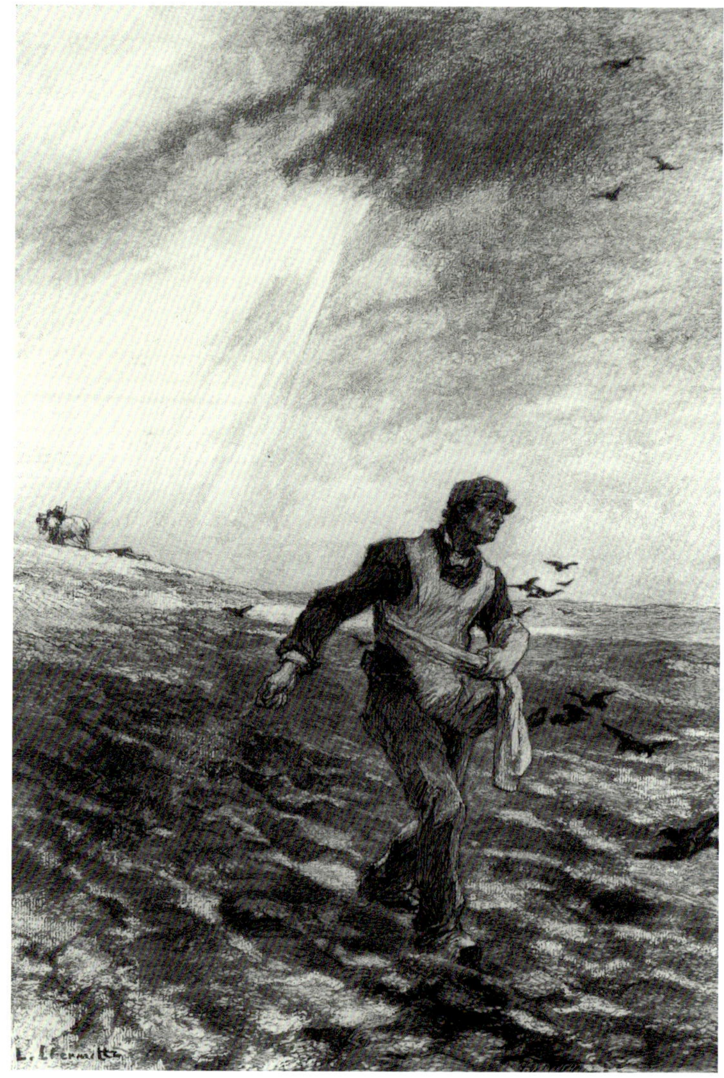

plate 152

After **Léon Lhermitte** (1844-1925)
Rural labours. October: lifting potatoes, 1885
Amsterdam, Van Gogh Museum (Vincent van Gogh Foundation)

'If *Le Monde Illustré* gives a composition of his every month – this one is part of a series, "The months on the land" – then I would very much like to have the whole series, and I shall be very glad if you will send them' [488/395].

plate 153

After **Léon Lhermitte** (1844-1925)
Rural labours. November: the sower, 1886
Amsterdam, Van Gogh Museum (Vincent van Gogh Foundation)

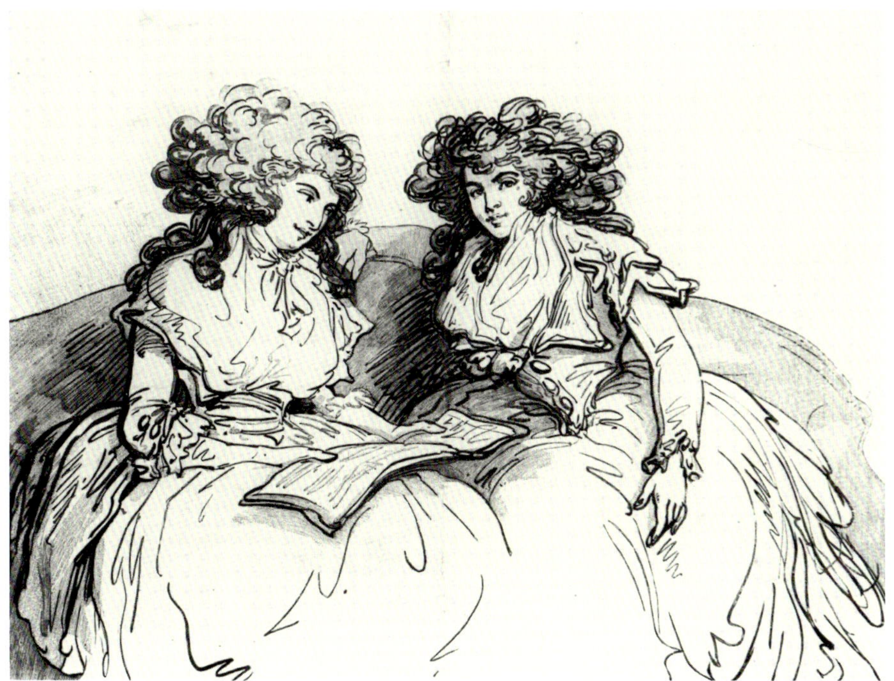

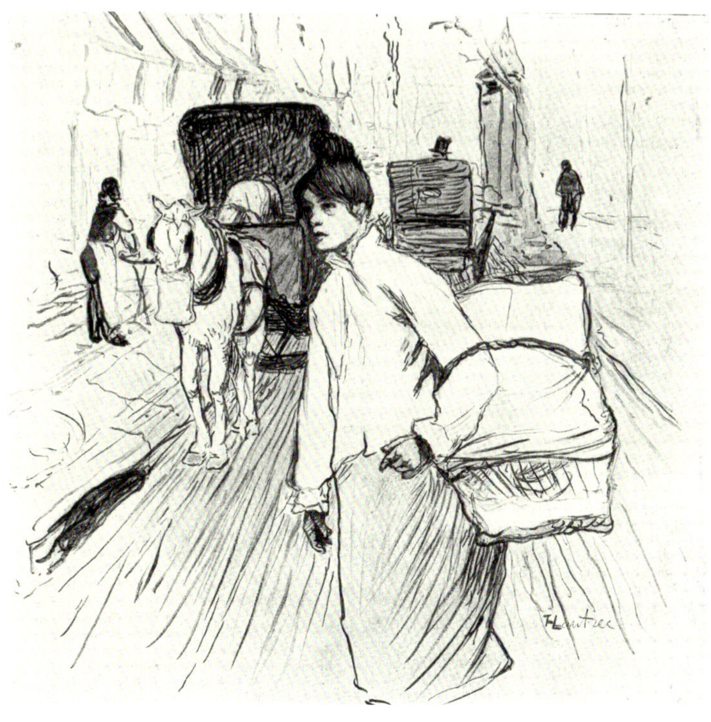

plate 154

After **Thomas Rowlandson** (1756-1827)
A difficult affair, 1888
Amsterdam, Van Gogh Museum (Vincent van Gogh Foundation)

'At the first opportunity I will send you an engraving after a drawing by
Rowlandson, representing two women, as beautiful as a Fragonard or
a Goya' [664/522].

plate 155

After **Henrl de Toulouse-Lautrec** (1864-1901)
The washerwoman, 1888
Amsterdam, Van Gogh Museum (Vincent van Gogh Foundation)

'The Lautrecs have just come, I think they are beautiful' [641/505].

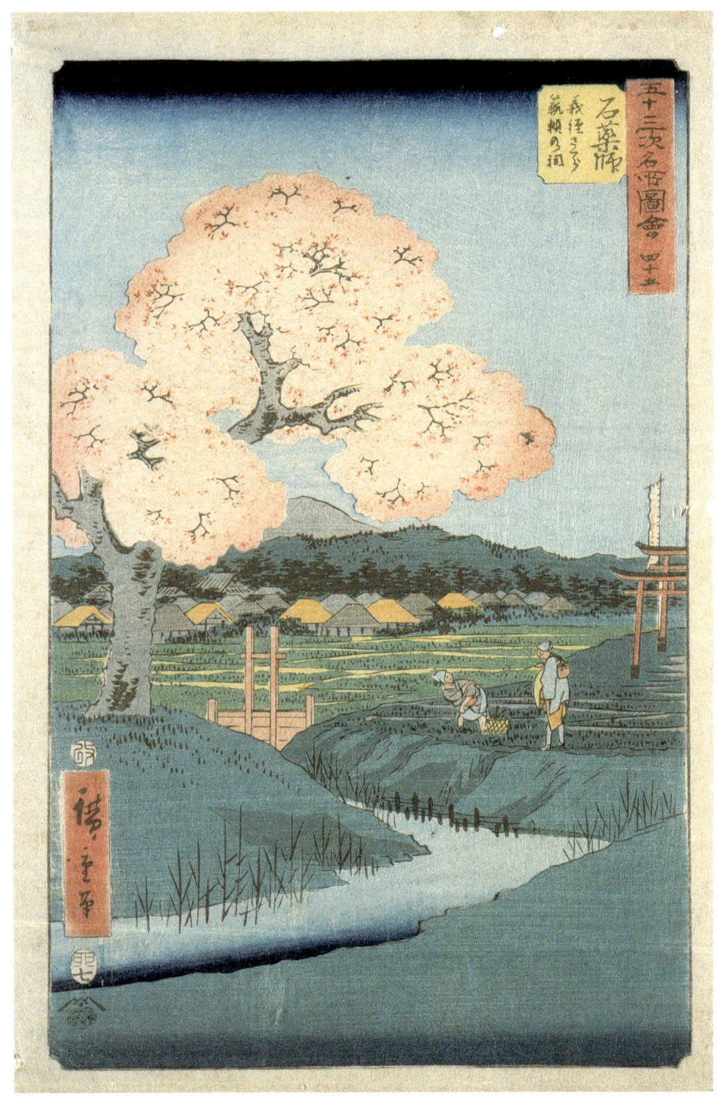

plate 156

Utagawa Hiroshige (1797-1858)

Ishiyakushi: the Yoshitsune cherry tree near the Noriyori shrine, 1855

Amsterdam, Van Gogh Museum (Vincent van Gogh Foundation)

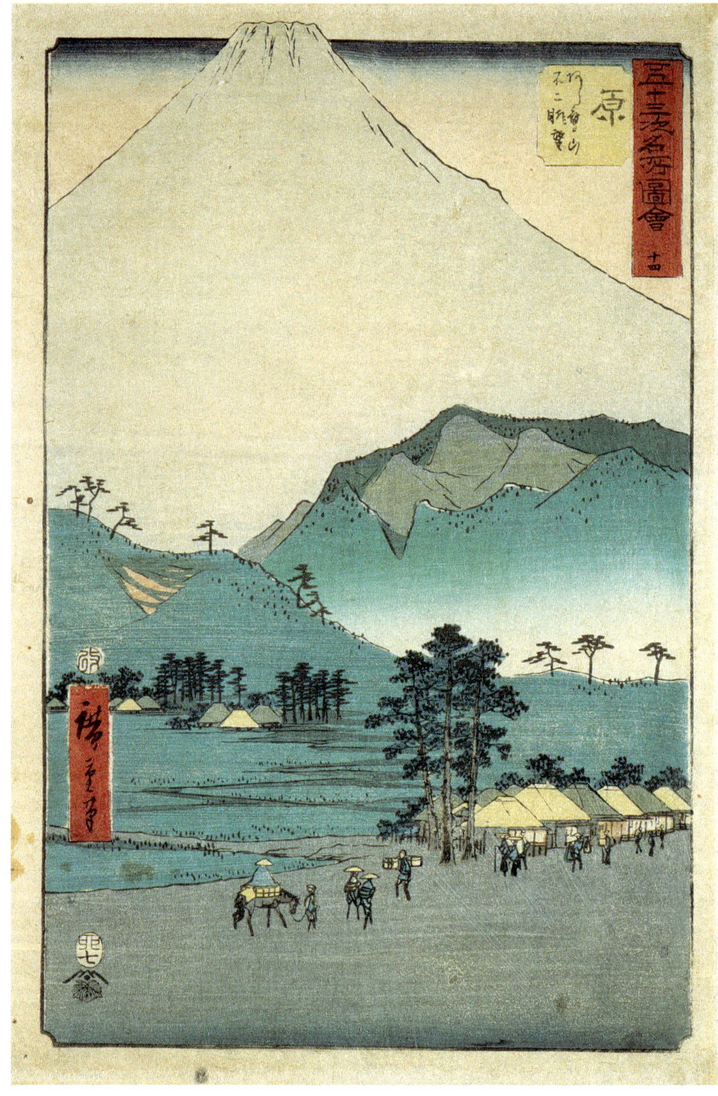

plate 157

Utagawa Hiroshige (1797-1858)

Hara: Mount Fuji and Ashitaka mountain in close-up, 1855

Amsterdam, Van Gogh Museum (Vincent van Gogh Foundation)

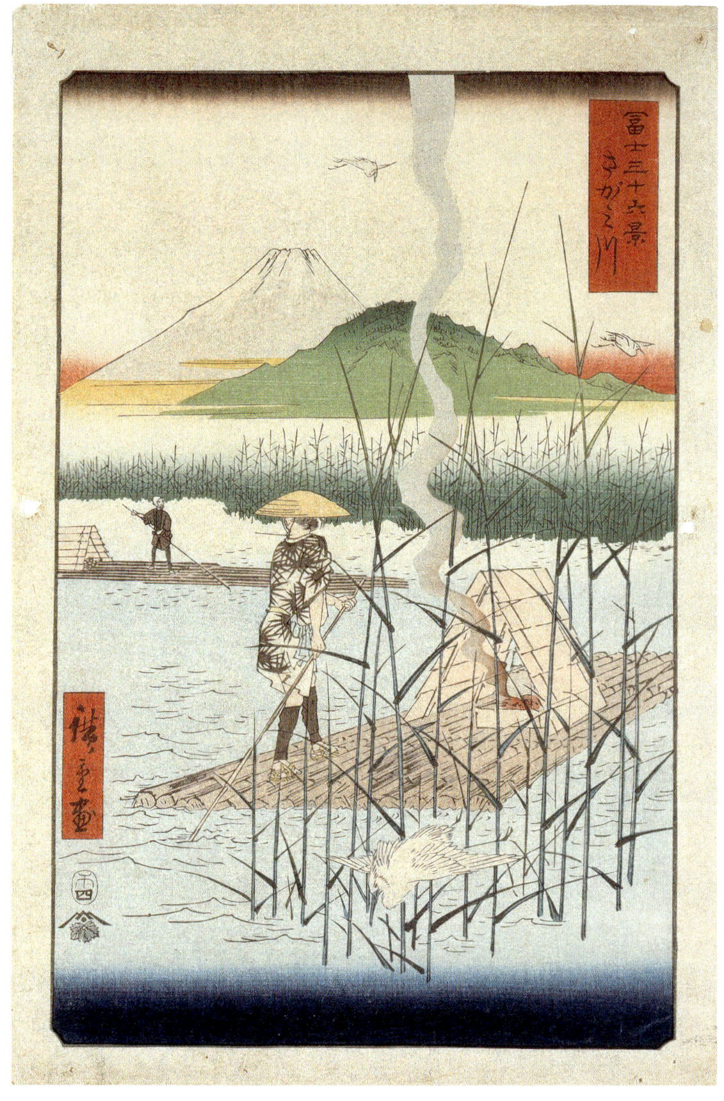

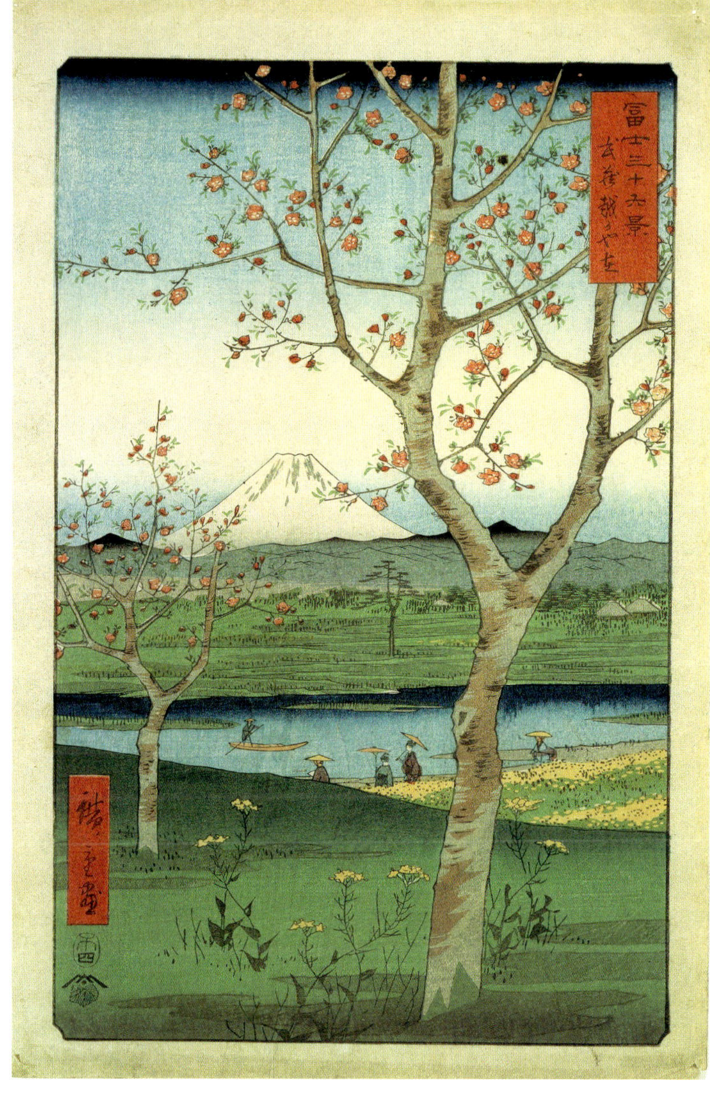

plate 158

Utagawa Hiroshige (1797-1858)

Fuji from the Sagami river, 1858

Amsterdam, Van Gogh Museum (Vincent van Gogh Foundation)

plate 159

Utagawa Hiroshige (1797-1858)

Fuji seen from the outskirts of Koshigaya in Musashi province, 1858

Amsterdam, Van Gogh Museum (Vincent van Gogh Foundation)

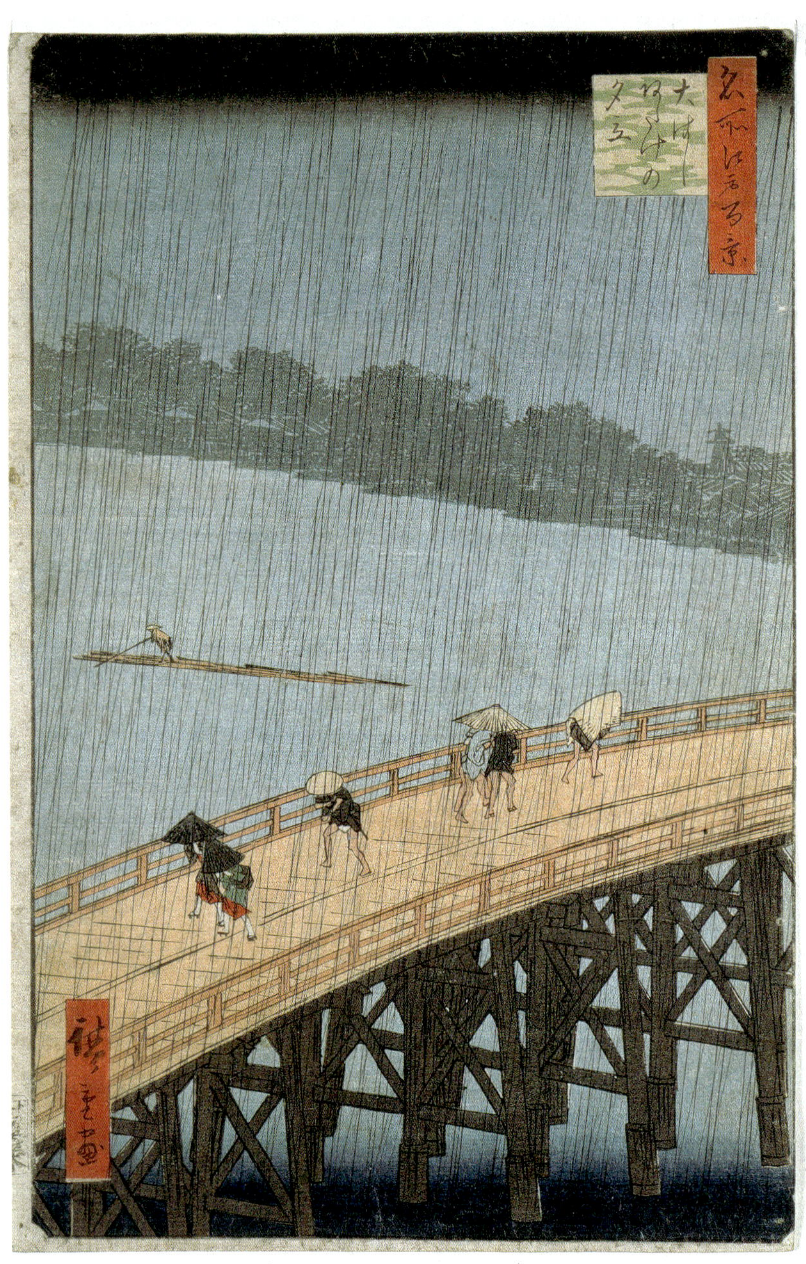

plate 160

Utagawa Hiroshige (1797-1858)
Sudden shower on the Great Bridge near Atake, 1857
Amsterdam, Van Gogh Museum (Vincent van Gogh Foundation)

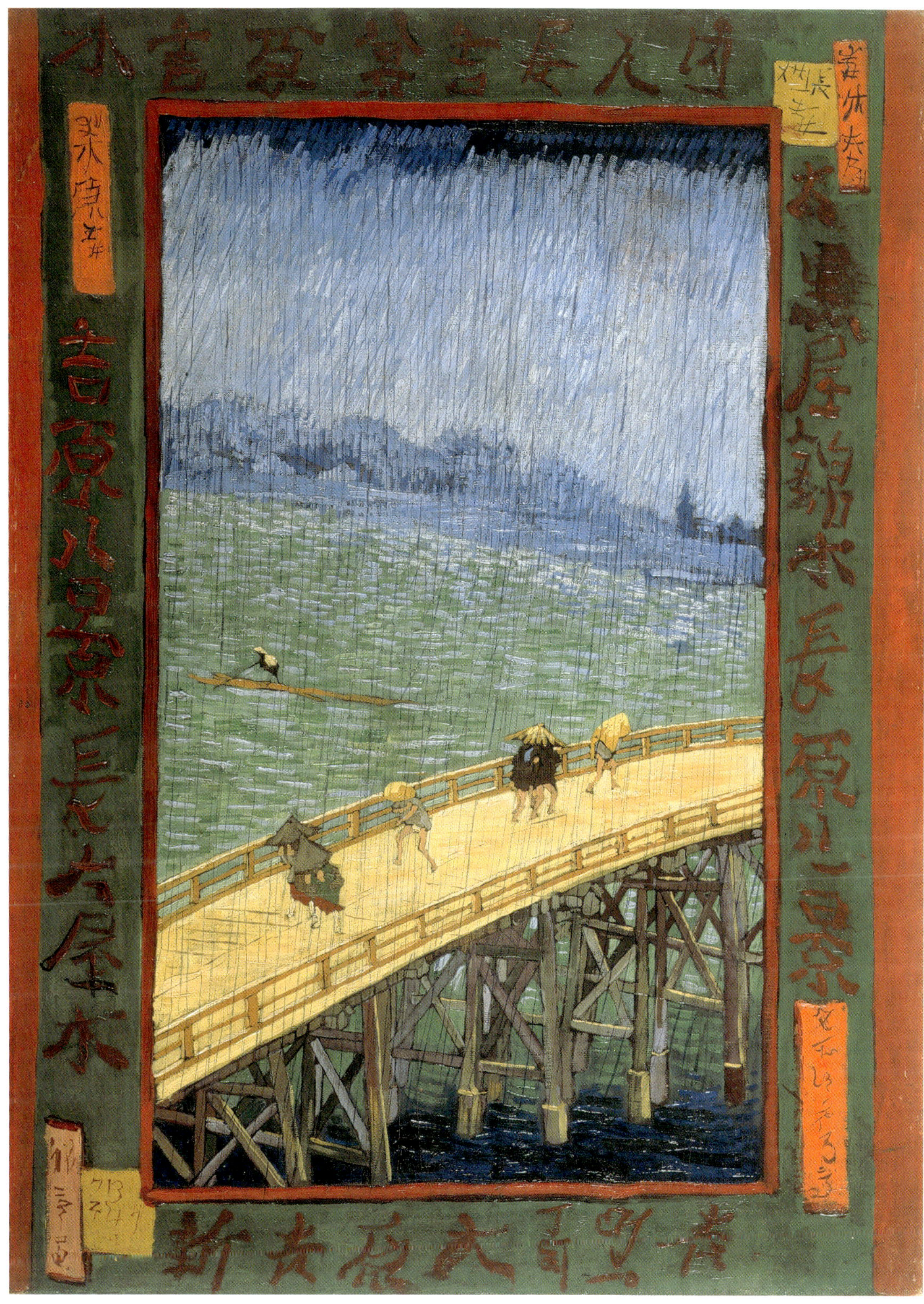

plate 161

Vincent van Gogh (1853-1890)
Bridge in the rain (after Hiroshige) (F 372 JH 1297), 1887
Amsterdam, Van Gogh Museum (Vincent van Gogh Foundation)

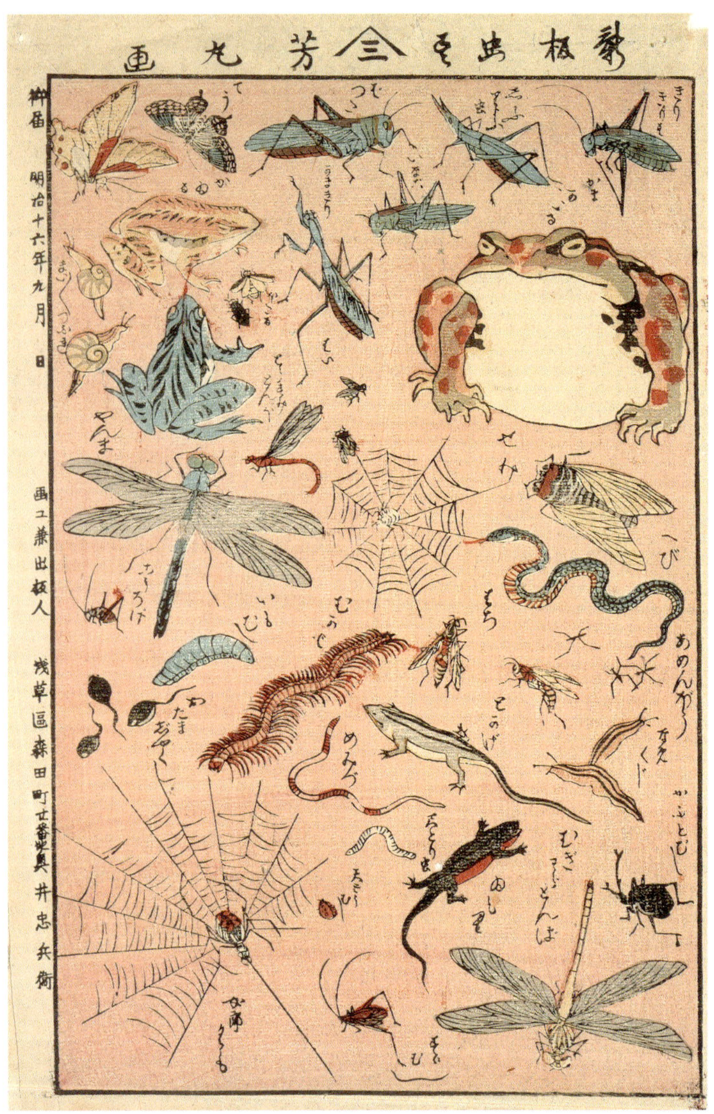

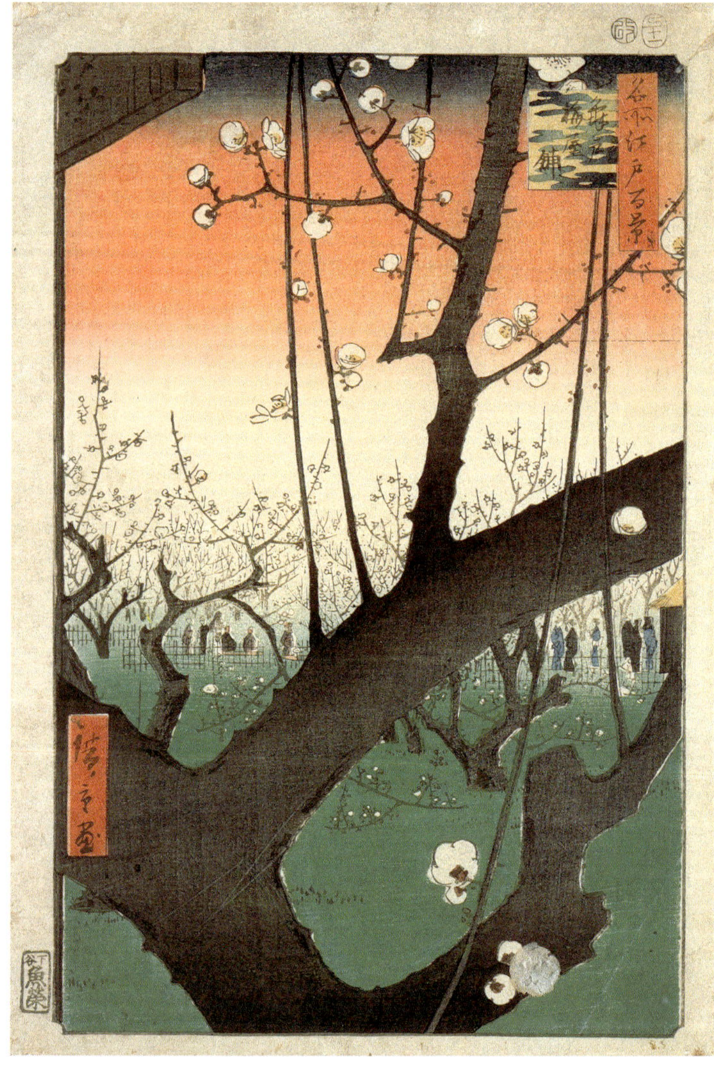

plate 162

Utagawa Yoshimaru (1844-1907)
New prints of worms and insects, 1883
Amsterdam, Van Gogh Museum (Vincent van Gogh Foundation)

plate 163

Utagawa Hiroshige (1797-1858)
The plum tree teahouse at Kameido, 1857
Amsterdam, Van Gogh Museum (Vincent van Gogh Foundation)

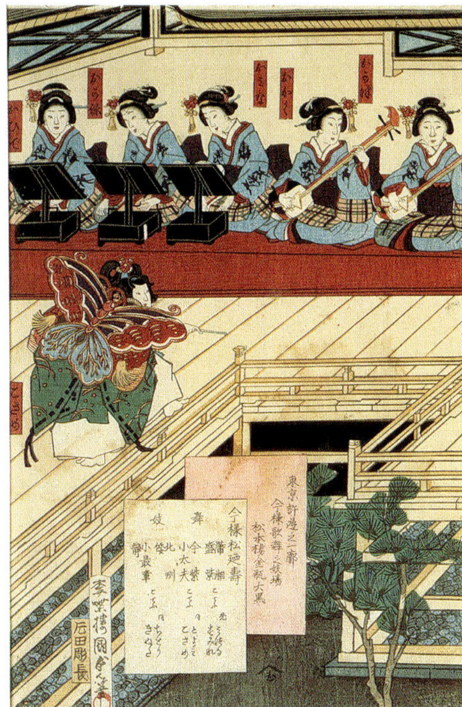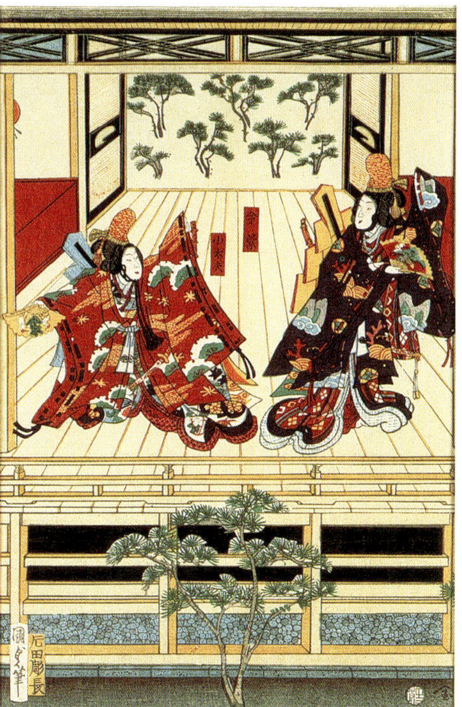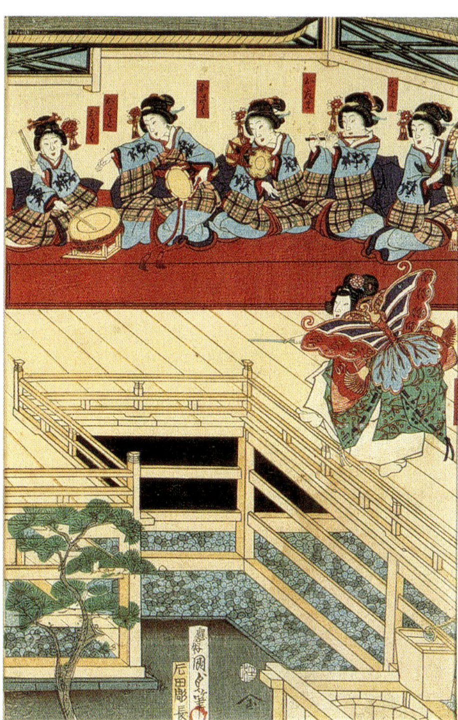

plate 164

Utagawa Kunisada II (1823-1880)
The Matsumotorō theatre in the Tokyo entertainment district, 1870
Amsterdam, Van Gogh Museum (Vincent van Gogh Foundation)

'Among them I think the cabaret in two sheets, with the line of violet girl musicians against the yellow illuminated wall is very beautiful – I did not know that print' [689/540].

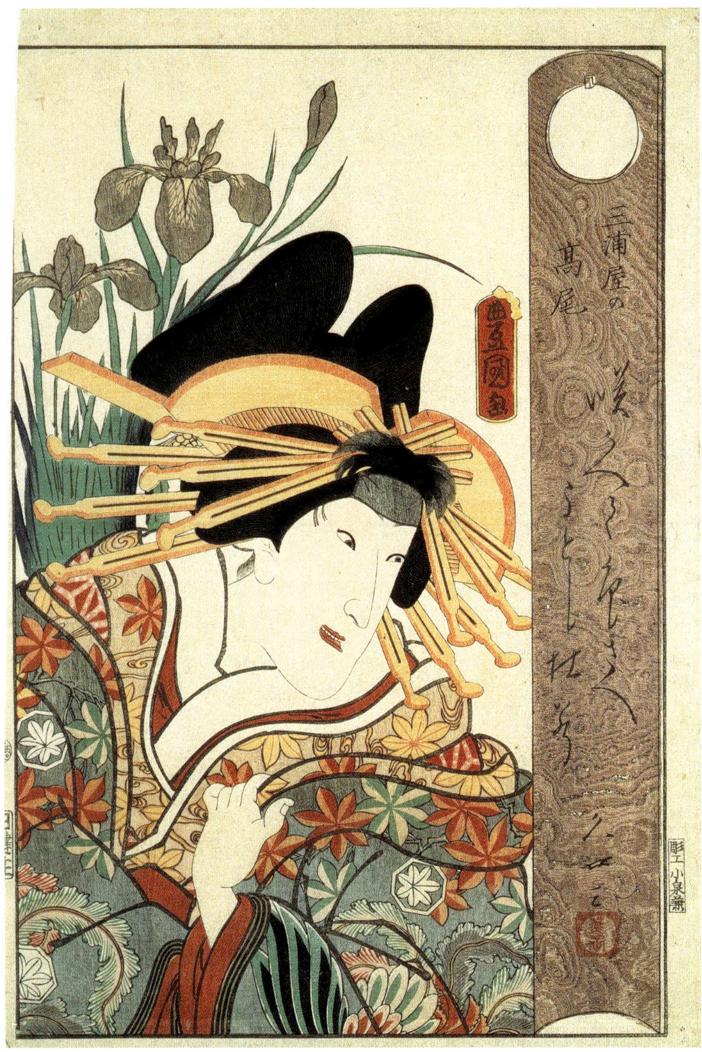

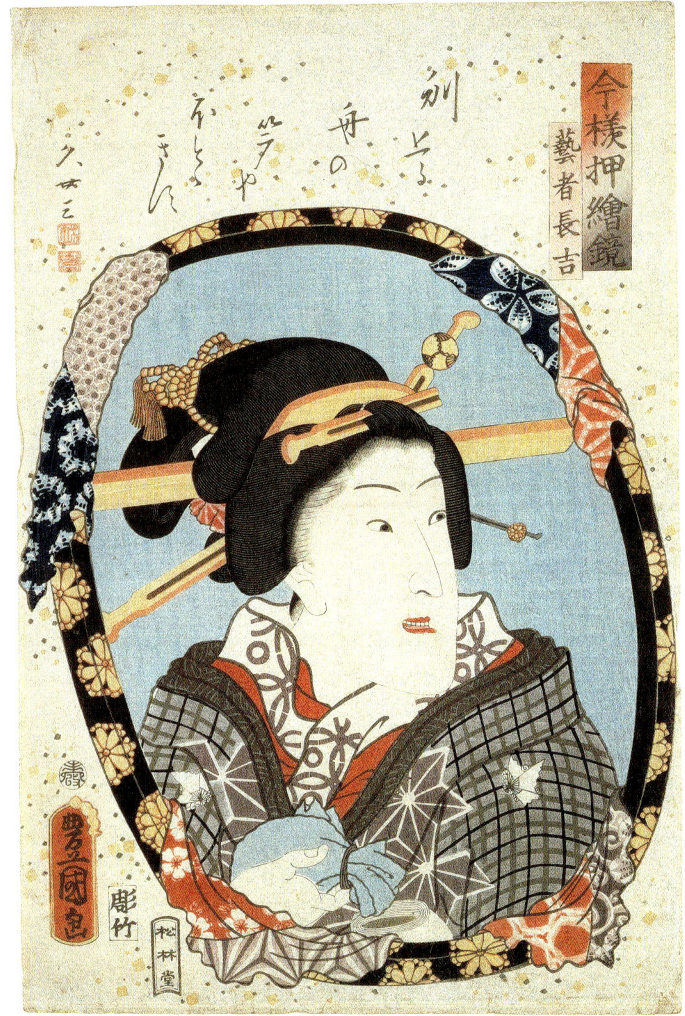

plate 165

Utagawa Kunisada (Toyokuni III) (1786-1864)

The courtesan Takao of the Miuraya, 1861

Amsterdam, Van Gogh Museum (Vincent van Gogh Foundation)

plate 166

Utagawa Kunisada (Toyokuni III) (1786-1864)

An actor as the geisha Chokichi, 1859

Amsterdam, Van Gogh Museum (Vincent van Gogh Foundation)

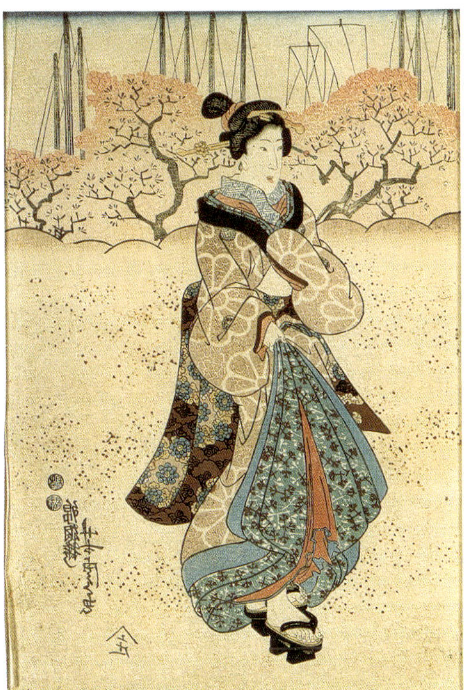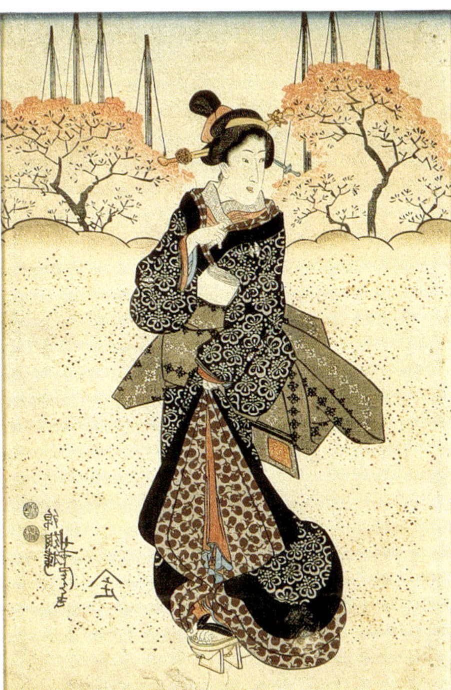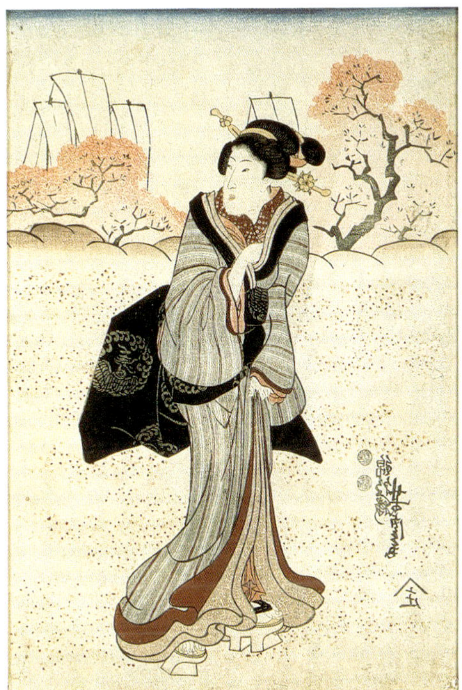

plate 167

Utagawa Yoshitora (active c. 1845-1880)

Three women, 1847-48

Amsterdam, Van Gogh Museum (Vincent van Gogh Foundation)

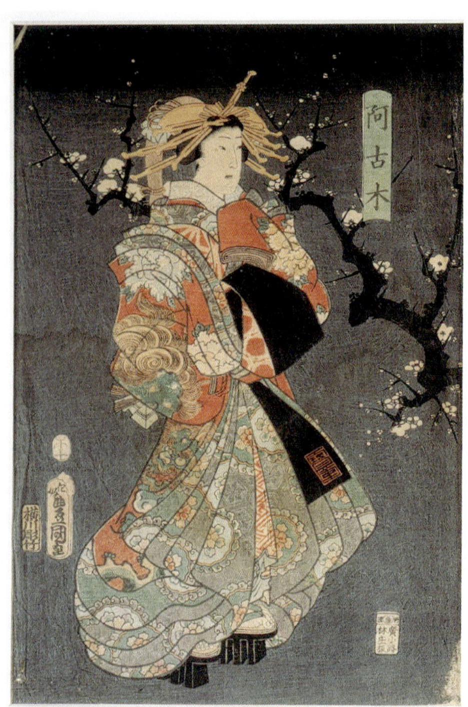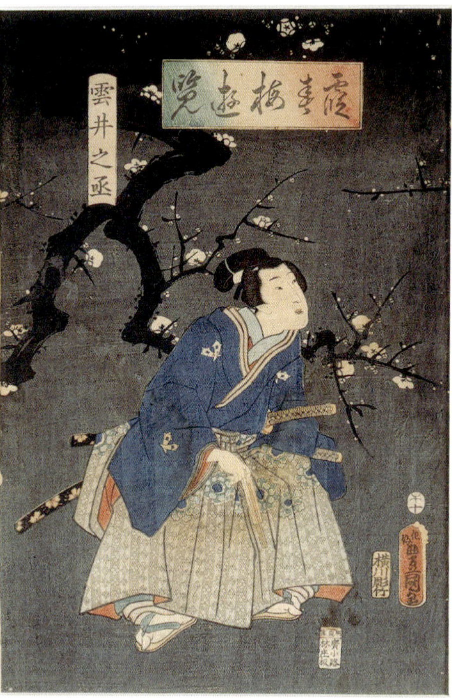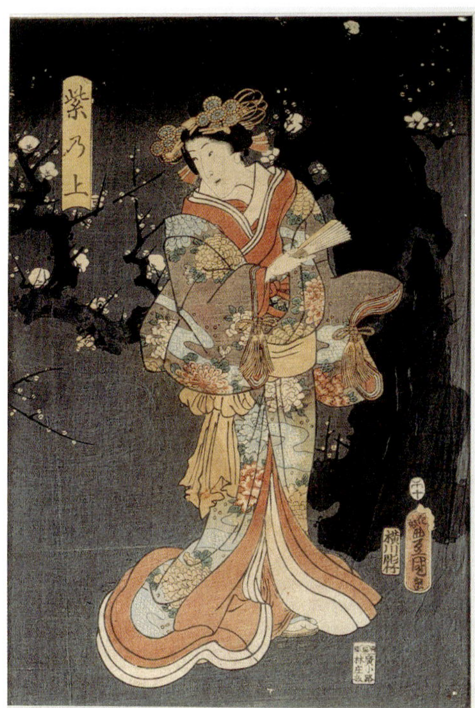

plate 168

Utagawa Kunisada (Toyokuni III) (1786-1864)

Enjoying the spring plum blossom in the haze, 1858

Amsterdam, Van Gogh Museum (Vincent van Gogh Foundation)

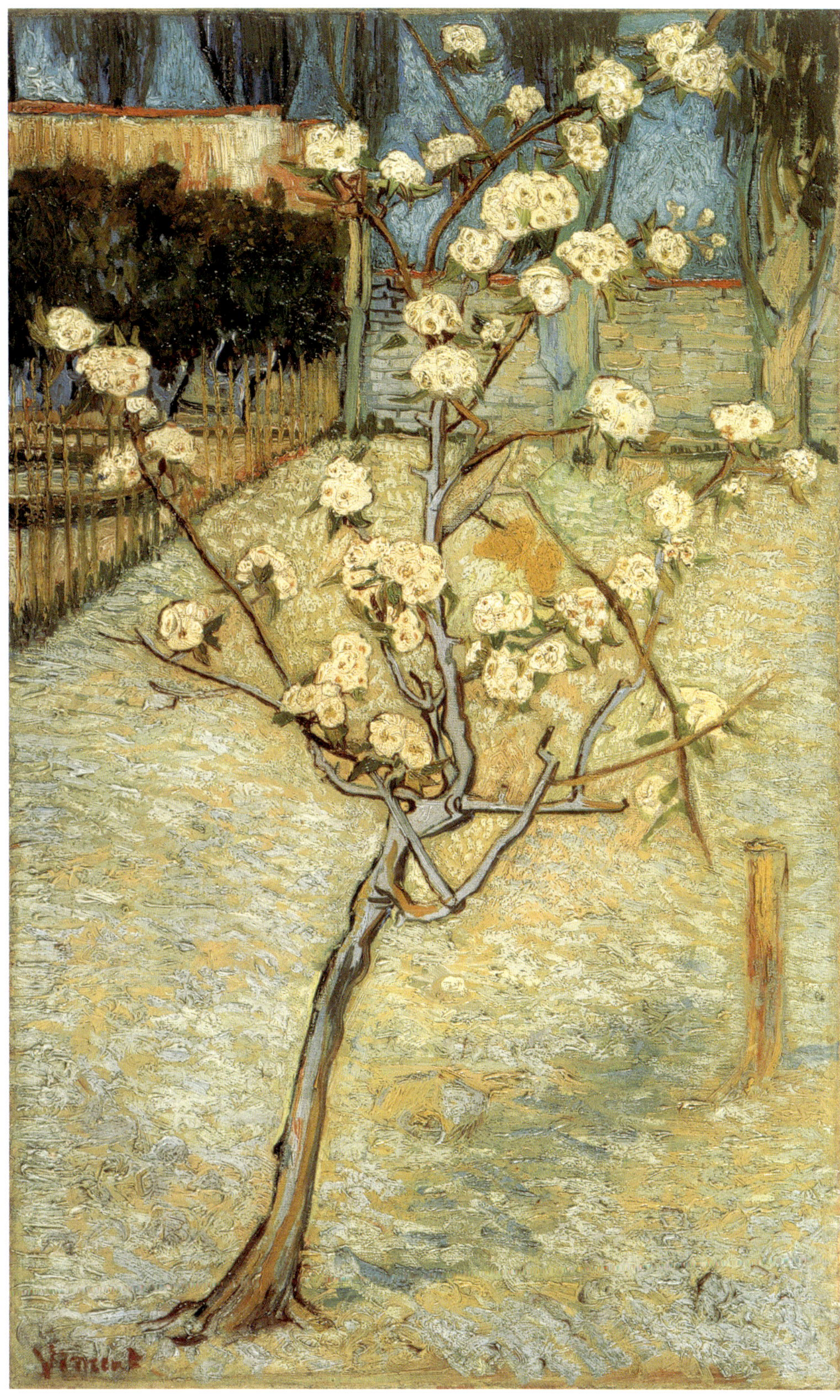

plate 169

Vincent van Gogh (1853-1890)
Small pear tree in blossom (F 405 JH 1394), 1888
Amsterdam, Van Gogh Museum (Vincent van Gogh Foundation)

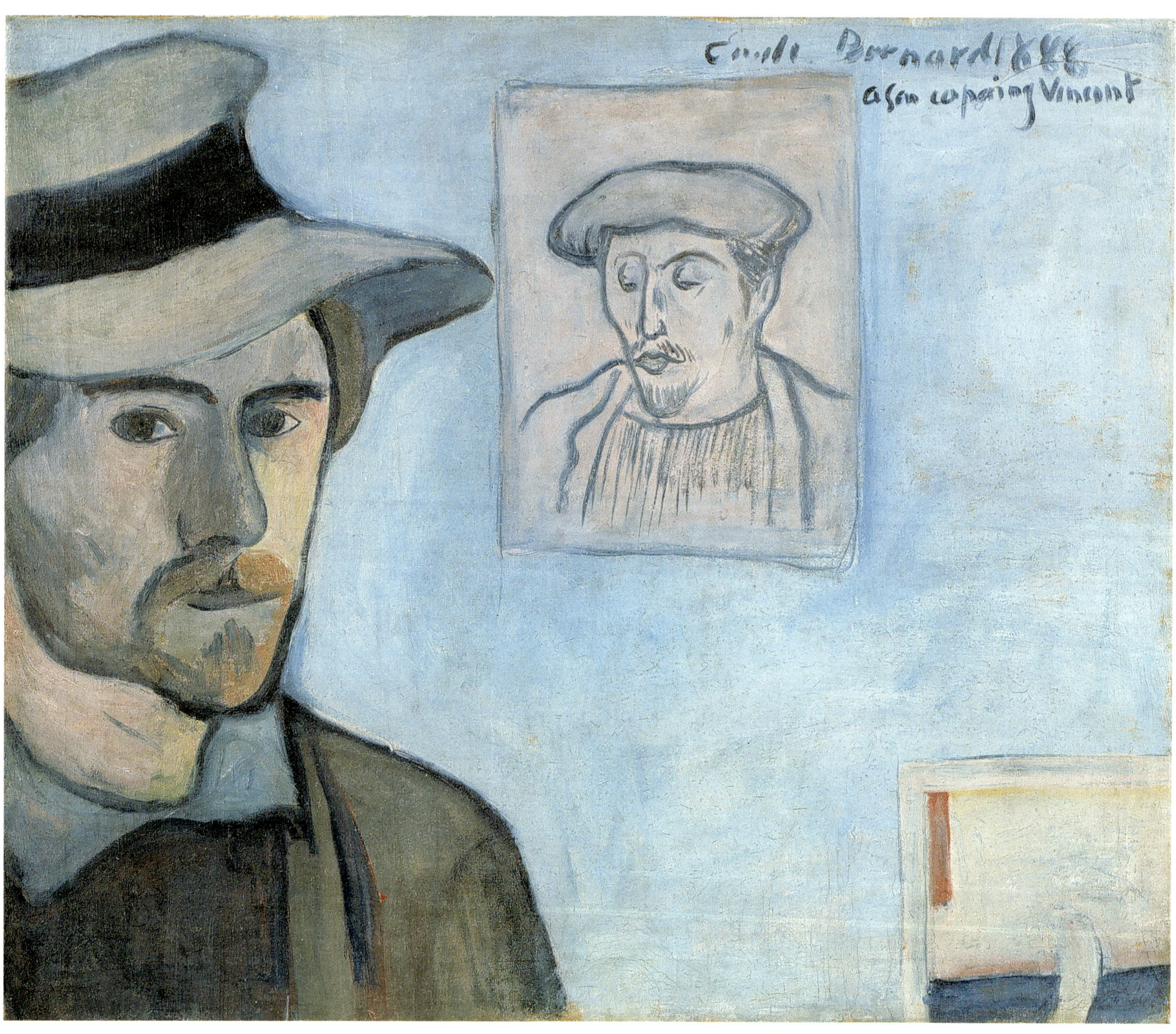

plate 170

Emile Bernard (1868-1941)
Self-portrait with portrait of Gauguin, 1888
Amsterdam, Van Gogh Museum (Vincent van Gogh Foundation)

'Now I have just received the portrait of Gauguin by himself and the portrait of Bernard by Bernard and in the background of the portrait of Gauguin there is Bernard's on the wall, and vice versa. The Gauguin is of
course remarkable at first, but I very much like Bernard's painting. It is just
a painter's idea, a few abrupt tones, a few dark lines, but it has style like
a real, real Manet' [701/545].

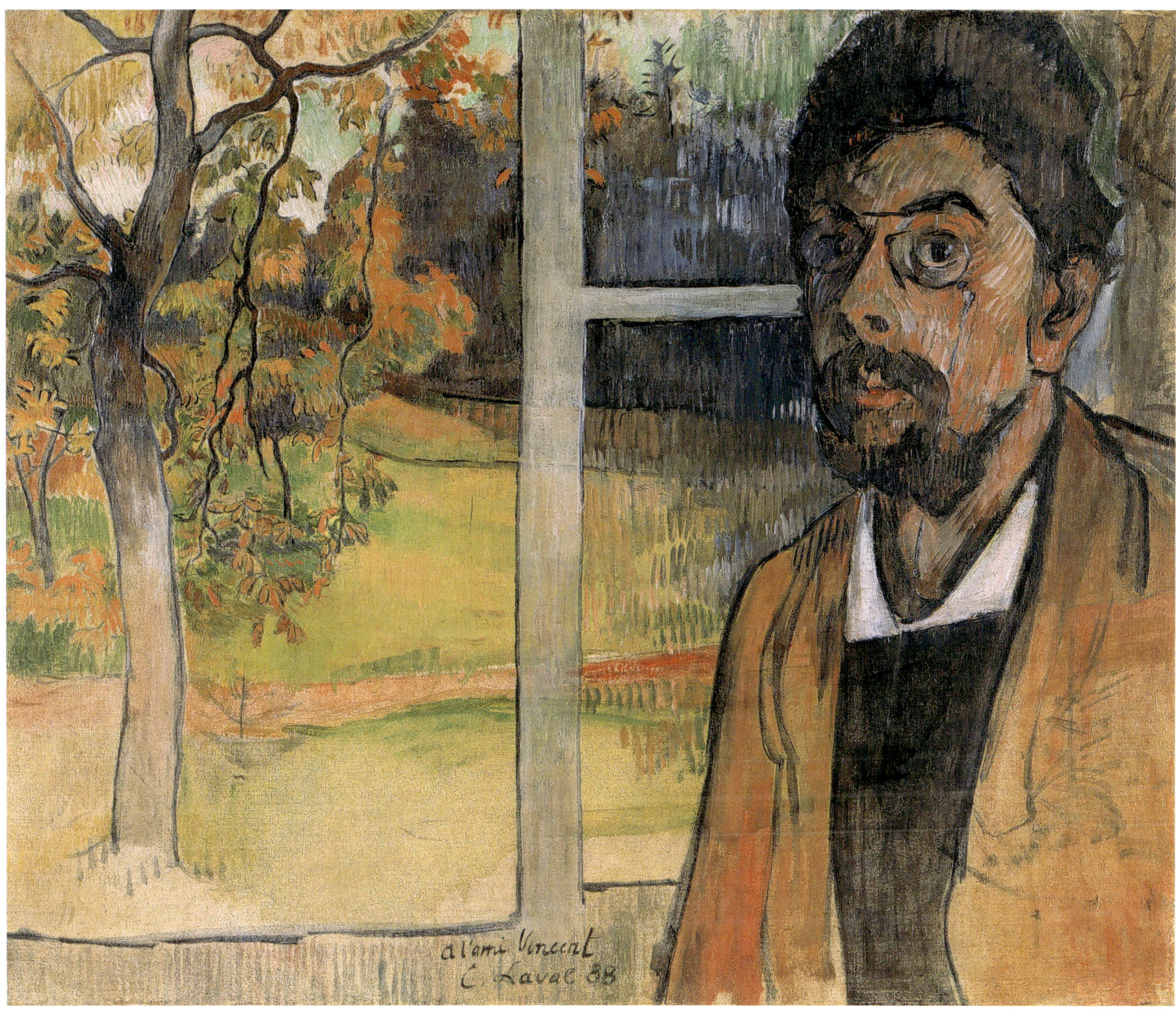

plate 171

Charles Laval (1862-1894)
Self-portrait, 1888
Amsterdam, Van Gogh Museum (Vincent van Gogh Foundation)

'You will also be pleased to hear that we have an addition to the collection of portraits of artists. The self-portrait by Laval, extremely good. [...] The portrait of Laval is very bold, very distinguished, and will be just one of the paintings you speak of, those one gets hold of before other people have recognised the talents' [724/562].

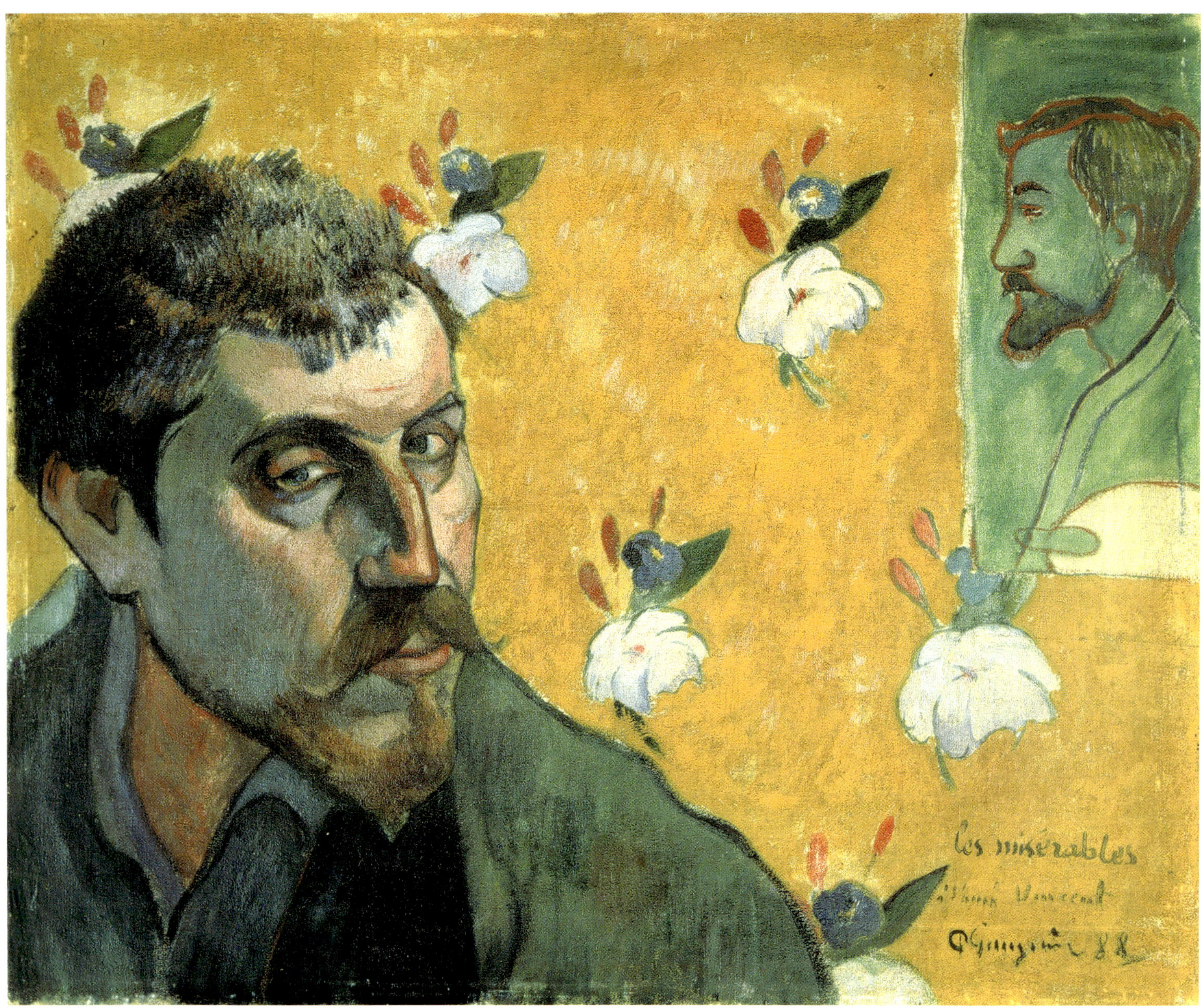

plate 172

Paul Gauguin (1848-1903)
Self-portrait with portrait of Bernard, 'Les misérables', 1888
Amsterdam, Van Gogh Museum (Vincent van Gogh Foundation)

'The Gauguin is more studied, carried further. That, along with what he
says in his letter, gave me absolutely the impression of its representing
a prisoner. Not a shadow of gaiety. Absolutely nothing of the flesh, but one
can confidently put that down to his determination to make a melancholy
effect, the flesh in the shadows has gone a dismal blue. [...] What Gauguin's
portrait says to me above all is that he must not go on like this, he must
console himself, he must again become the richer Gauguin of the
"Negresses"' [701/545].

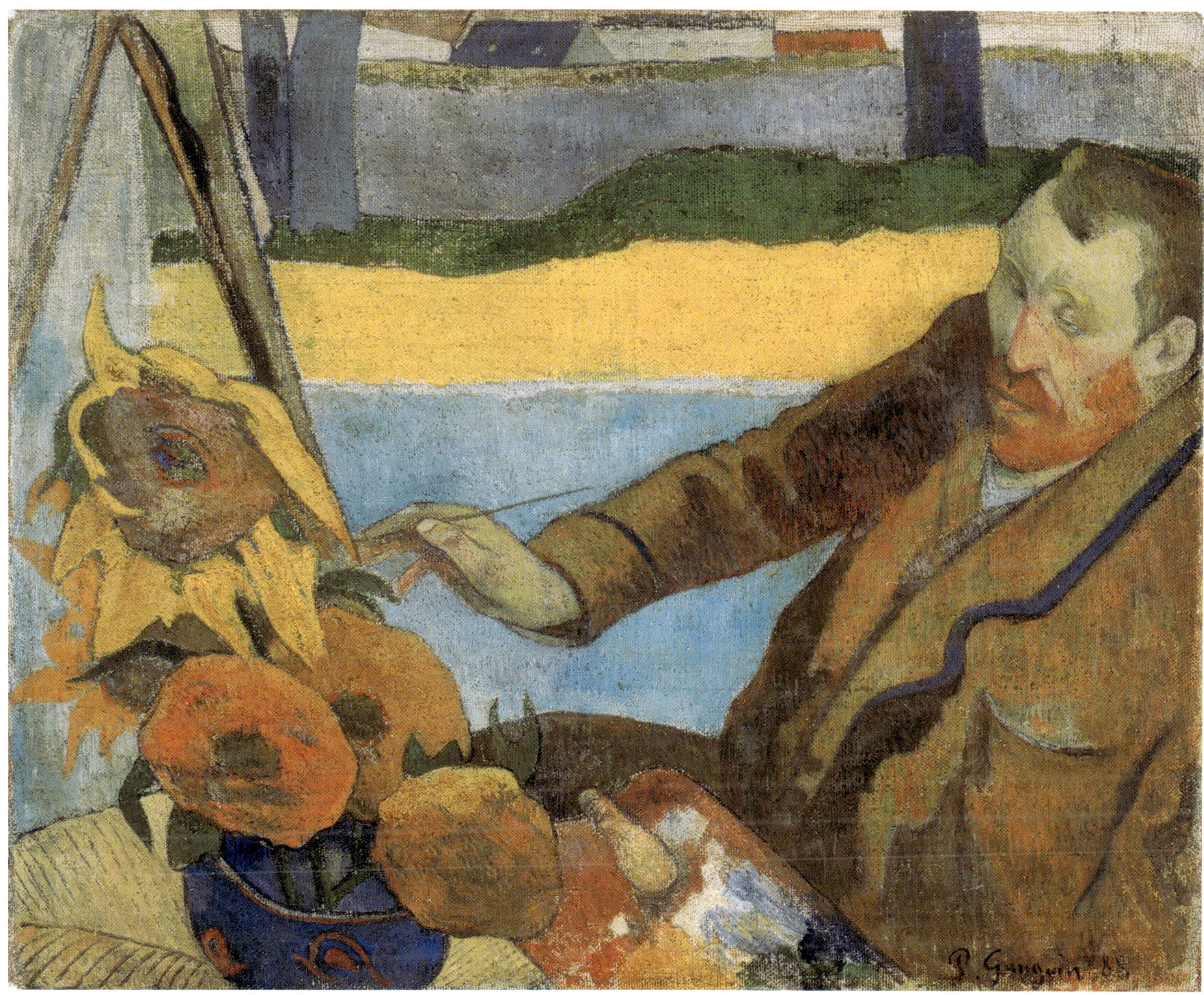

plate 173

Paul Gauguin (1840-1903)
Portrait of Van Gogh painting sunflowers, 1888
Amsterdam, Van Gogh Museum (Vincent van Gogh Foundation)

'Have you seen that portrait he did of me painting sunflowers? My face has certainly brightened up since then, but it was really me, extremely tired and charged with electricity as I was then' [802/605].

Compiled by Nienke Bakker

1853
30 March Born in Groot-Zundert, eldest son of Theodorus van Gogh and Anna Cornelia van Gogh-Carbentus.

1857
1 May Birth of his brother Theo.

1869
July Appointed junior apprentice at Goupil & Cie in The Hague. In this capacity becomes acquainted with a number of private collections, including that of the Hague industrialist Jacobson. Probably visits the Mauritshuis regularly. Collects photographs, photo-engravings and prints sold by Goupil.

1872
September Start of his (surviving) correspondence with Theo.
August-October Visits the Salon and the Palais Ducal in Brussels.

1873
January Pays a Sunday visit to his uncle Cor van Gogh, an art dealer in Amsterdam. Views his collection of paintings and drawings and visits the museums, among them the Trippenhuis.
2 March Sees the Dutch contribution to the upcoming World's Fair in Vienna at the artists' society Arti et Amicitiae in Amsterdam.
June Stays several days in Paris prior to his transfer to the London branch of Goupil's. Visits the Goupil gallery, the Salon, the Louvre and the Musée du Luxembourg, and meets the Belgian painter César de Cock.
July Reads Michelet's *L'amour*. Sends Theo a print after Weissenbruch's *View of the Trekvliet* (plate 2), a location with fond memories for both brothers.
August Visits the summer exhibition of the Royal Academy and the Dulwich Picture Gallery. During his stay in London he also goes to see the British Museum, the National Gallery (Rembrandt, *Self-portrait*, (plate 72)) and the Wallace Collection. Admires *The valley farm* by Constable (plate 5) at the South Kensington Museum (now the Victoria & Albert Museum).
12 September Sees work by Belgian artists at the London International Exhibition.
October Rereads the poems of Longfellow.

1874
June Visits the summer exhibition of the Royal Academy.
October-December Transferred briefly to Goupil's headquarters in Paris; he then returns to London.

1875
January Visits the winter exhibition of old masters at the Royal Academy, with, among other works, *The lamentation of Christ* (Rembrandt workshop (plate 69)) and works by Ruisdael, Hals and Rubens.
February Compiles an album for Theo of poems and prose fragments by Heine, Uhland, Sainte-Beuve, Carlyle, Michelet and Goethe among others.
Spring Sees Matthijs Maris's *The Nieuwe Haarlemse Sluis on the Singel, called 'Souvenir d'Amsterdam'* at a London gallery (plate 4).
May Again transferred to Goupil's headquarters in Paris. During his stay in the French capital he puts together an album for Matthijs Maris, with poems by Uhland, Heine and Goethe and fairytales by Andersen in verse.
Visits the Salon and the Corot retrospective at the Ecole des Beaux-Arts (e.g. *The agony in the garden* (plate 12)). Regularly goes to the Louvre on Sunday (Rembrandt, Ruisdael) and to the Musée du Luxembourg, where he is particularly impressed by the work of Millet, Jules Breton and Daubigny.
Creates his own album of reproductions and original graphic works by, among others, Dupré, Rousseau, Jacob Maris and Bosboom.

June Admires drawings and pastels by Millet from the Gavet Collection at a sale-exhibition in the Hôtel Drouot (among them *Woodcutter and his wife preparing faggots* and *Vineyard labourer resting* (plates 50, 53)).
October Advises Theo to read the work of Erckmann-Chatrian, particularly *Le conscrit*, *Waterloo*, *L'ami Fritz* and *Madame Thérèse*.
December Advises Theo to get rid of his books of poetry by authors such as Heine and Uhland.

1876
February Reads George Eliot's *Scenes of clerical life*.
April Dismissed from Goupil & Cie. From mid-April finds employment as a teacher in Ramsgate, and from mid-July as an assistant preacher in Isleworth.
June Sees portraits by, among others, Holbein, Rembrandt and Titian at Hampton Court Palace.
October Reads Souvestre's *Le philosophe sous les toits*.
November Visits the Obach family in London, where he sees a painting (or sketch) by Boughton of *The pilgrim's progress* (cf. plate 7). Had already read Bunyan's book of the same title.

1877
January-April Works for the booksellers Blussé & Van Braam in Dordrecht.
16 February Goes with his father to the Dordrechts Museum to see the paintings of Ary Scheffer (plates 8-9). Repeats the visit a short time later with Theo.
18 March Together with Theo visits the Museum Van der Hoop in Amsterdam. Sends his brother *Musées de la Hollande* by Thoré-Bürger, which he himself had read while in London.
May Moves to Amsterdam to prepare himself for his theological studies.
June Transcribes a passage from *La jeunesse de Cromwell* by Lamartine, a work he had much admired while in London.
August Reads Fénelon's *Les aventures de Télémaque*.
September Transcribes the whole French version of Thomas à Kempis's *De imitatione Christi* and reads Bossuet's *Oraisons funèbres*.
On 7 September goes twice to the Trippenhuis with his friend Harry Gladwell from Paris, whom he also advises to visit Haarlem to look at the paintings of Frans Hals. He himself had seen them together with Theo.
Pays another visit to the Trippenhuis later in the month to see the Rembrandt etchings.
October
Reads Dickens's *A tale of two cities* and Carlyle's *The French Revolution*.

1878
April Reads Michelet's *L'histoire de la Révolution française*.
July Abandons his theological studies and moves to Laken (Brussels), where he trains as a lay preacher.
15 November Meets Theo in Brussels. Together they visit the Museum voor Schone Kunsten, where they see work by De Groux, Leys and Coosemans.
December Leaves for the Borinage to work as an evangelist among the miners.

1879
June Reads Beecher Stowe's *Uncle Tom's cabin* and Dickens's *Hard times*.

1880
Winter Reads Hugo's *Le dernier jour d'un condamné* and Shakespeare's *Henry IV* and *King Lear*.
March Travels on foot to Courrières (in northern France) and sees the studio of Jules Breton. Decides to start drawing again.
August Devotes himself entirely to his draughtsmanship, with the aim of finding work as an illustrator. Moves to Brussels. Makes many copies of, among other works, prints after Millet.
October On Theo's advice pays visits to the painters Roelofs and Van Rappard.

1881

February Takes drawing lessons from a painter, probably Madiol. Starts collecting prints again.

March Sees the painting *Return of the conscript* and the drawing *The drunkard*, both by De Groux, in the museum in Brussels. Works in Van Rappard's studio. Sees an exhibition of watercolours.

April Returns to his parents' house in Etten.

Spring-Summer Reads a number of French and English novels, among them *Shirley* and *Jane Eyre* by Charlotte Brontë, *Illusions perdues* and *Le père Goriot* by Balzac, and the Goncourts' *Gavarni – L'homme et l'oeuvre*.

August Visits his cousin by marriage Anton Mauve in The Hague. Meets De Bock and goes with him to the Panorama Mesdag and the sixth exhibition of the Hollandsche Teeken-Maatschappij, the local draughtsmen's club. Shows his studies to Bosboom. Sees Fabritius's *Portrait of a man* in the museum in Rotterdam.

December Moves to The Hague following an altercation with his parents.

1882

Takes drawing and painting lessons with Mauve and advice from Weissenbruch. Van de Sande Bakhuyzen and Blommers also visit his studio. Often draws in the street in the company of Breitner.

March Reads Sensier's *La vie et l'oeuvre de J.-F. Millet*. At Goupil's sees paintings destined for the Salon and is particularly impressed by Jozef Israëls's *Old friends* (plate 65) and Mauve's *Fishing boat on the beach* (plate 68)**.**

Summer Reads Zola's *Une page d'amour*, quickly followed by *Le ventre de Paris*, *Nana*, *La curée*, *La faute de l'abbé Mouret*, *Son excellence Eugène Rougon* and *L'assommoir*.

June Reports to Theo that his collection now comprises around 1,000 prints, mainly from English and French illustrated magazines.

July Visits an exhibition of French art from private collections (e.g. the Mesdag and Post collections) at the Academie van Beeldende Kunsten in The Hague, with, among other works, *The descent of the cattle in the high Jura mountains* by Rousseau (plate 37) and Dupré's *Autumn* (plate 36).

August Visits the seventh exhibition of the Hollandsche Teeken-Maatschappij, which includes pieces by Mauve and Israëls, and a showing of work from the Koninklijk Genootschap van Nederlandsche Aquarellisten, a watercolourists' society.

Autumn Reads, among other works, Erckmann-Chatrian's *Les deux frères*, Daudet's *Les rois en exil* and *Le Nabab*, Zola's *Pot-bouille* and Hugo's *Quatre-vingt-treize*. Practises lithography in the hope of finding work as an illustrator.

1883

January Buys ten bound volumes of *The Graphic*.

Spring Reads Eliot's *Middlemarch* and Carlyle's *Sartor resartus*. Rereads Hugo's *Notre Dame de Paris* and *Les misérables*. Writes admiringly of Ruisdael's *View of Haarlem with bleaching grounds* in the Mauritshuis (plate 30).

May Visits Van Rappard at his studio in Utrecht to look at his work.

June-July Paints with Van der Weele in the dunes and works in De Bock's studio in Scheveningen

August Visits the second exhibition of work from the Koninklijk Genootschap van Nederlandsche Aquarellisten, held in the Gotische Zaal in The Hague.

September Departs for Drenthe, where he stays in Nieuw-Amsterdam and Hoogeveen.

October Reads Carlyle's *On heroes, hero-worship and the heroic in history*.

December Goes to Nuenen, where he once again moves in with his parents.

1884

February-March Transcribes the poems of François Coppée and Jules Breton in letters to Theo and Van Rappard.

March Reads Eliot's *Felix Holt, the radical*.

Summer Reads Blanc's *Les artistes de mon temps* and *Grammaire des arts du dessin* and Fromentin's *Les maîtres d'autrefois: Belgique – Hollande*.

Autumn Gives lessons in still-life painting to Kerssemakers, Hermans and Van de Wakker.

1885

April Reads Gigoux's *Causeries sur les artistes de mon temps*.

May-July In a written debate with Theo criticises Uhde's Salon painting *Suffer little children to come unto me* (plate 11).

September Reads Silvestre's *Eugène Delacroix: documents nouveaux* and Bracquemond's *Du dessin et de la couleur*.

October Has read the Goncourts' *Chérie*.
Stays three days with Kerssemakers in Amsterdam; they visit the Rijksmuseum, the Museum Van der Hoop and the Fodor Collection. Writes with great enthusiasm of Rembrandt's *Jewish bride* and *The syndics of the drapers' guild*; (a copy after) Hals's *The fool* (plate 109); Israëls's *At the churchyard* (plate 64); Van Goyen's *Landscape with two oaks* (plate 111); Rubens's *Carrying of the cross* (plate 122); (a copy after) Cuyp's *View of Dordrecht at sunset* (plate 110) and Decamps's *A shepherd with his flock* (plate 41).
Discusses the use of black and white in his letters to Theo, repeatedly using examples from the Dutch old masters.

November Reads the Goncourts' *L'art du* XVIIIe *siècle*.

24 November Moves to Antwerp. Sees the frescoes by Leys in the dining room of the artist's house, and visits the Musée Ancien (Rubens, Hals, Rembrandt and Jordaens) and the Musée Moderne (both collections now in the Koninklijk Museum voor Schone Kunsten).

December Regularly visits the Musée Ancien to study the heads of Hals and Rubens. Sees two collections of modern art: a show of paintings bought for the lottery at the Antwerp World's Fair, and an exhibition of works for sale.

1886

January Sees *The crucifixion (Golgotha)* by Francken de Jonge in the Sint Andrieskerk and the recent acquisitions of the Musée Moderne. Visits the Onze-Lieve-Vrouwekerk to see the *Crucifixion* and *Descent from the cross* by Rubens.
Takes lessons in figure painting and drawing after plaster casts at the local art academy.

c. 1 March Arrives in Paris and moves in with Theo.
During his stay in Paris he sees two works by Delacroix that make a lasting impression on him: the wall painting *Jacob wrestling with the angel* in the church of Saint-Sulpice (see (plate 123)) and the ceiling paintings in the Apollo Gallery in the Louvre.

15 May-15 June Probably visits the eighth and last impressionist exhibition, which includes, among other works, Gauguin's *Resting cows* (plate 131), Camille Pissarro's *View from my window in cloudy weather* (plate 137) and works by Seurat and Signac.

early June Together with Theo visits the sale-exhibition of the Saulnier Collection in the Hôtel Drouot, which includes works by Corot, Millet, Rousseau, Diaz and Manet among others. Particularly admires *Christ asleep during the tempest* by Delacroix (plate 124).

15 June-July Probably visits the 5e Exposition internationale de peinture et sculpture at the Galerie Georges Petit (with work by Monet and Renoir).

August In a letter to Theo cites from Voltaire's *Candide*, which he had likely just finished reading.

21 August-21 September Probably visits the 2e Exposition des Indépendants (with work by Angrand, Lucien Pissarro, Seurat and Signac among others).

Autumn-winter Works at the studio of Fernand Cormon, where he meets Bernard and Toulouse-Lautrec.

October Exchanges work with Bernard and through him meets Anquetin. Meets Angrand at the shop of the colour merchant Père Tanguy. Suggests they make an exchange: one of his own works for Angrand's *Feeding the chickens* (plate 132); Angrand refuses.

November Theo introduces him to Camille Pissarro and his son, Lucien, and he meets Gauguin following the latter's return from Brittany.

December Together with Toulouse-Lautrec visits the exhibition of the latter's work at Aristide Bruant's theatre Le Mirliton.

1887

January Meets Signac at Tanguy's.

February-March Organises an exhibition of Japanese prints at the Café du Tambourin.

March Together with Bernard and Anquetin pays a visit to the shop of Siegfried Bing to show them the latter's collection of Japanese prints. Frequents Bing's premises, where there was much Asian art on display.

26 March-3 May Probably visits the 3ᵉ Exposition des Indépendants, with, among other works, Signac's *Snow, Boulevard de Clichy* (plate 133) and work by Angrand, Lucien Pissarro and Seurat.

April-May Works with Signac at Asnières.

May-June Together with Theo visits the 6ᵉ Exposition internationale de peinture et sculpture at the Galerie Georges Petit, where he sees *Modern man* (plate 82) and *Prehistoric man* (plate 83) by Besnard and Monet's *Bordighera* (plate 138). Undoubtedly also goes to the Millet retrospective at the Ecole des Beaux-Arts.

Summer Exhibits several paintings at the Café du Tambourin.

Reads contemporary French literature, in particular Zola, Flaubert, Maupassant, the Goncourts, Richepin, Daudet and Huysmans.

Autumn Works with Bernard at the latter's studio in Asnières. Each paints portraits of Tanguy ((plate 88) and (fig. 122)). Exchanges *Basket with apples (Dedicated to Lucien Pissarro)* (F 378 JH 1340) with Lucien Pissarro for several of his woodcuts.

November-December Organises the Exposition du Petit Boulevard at the Grand Bouillon-Restaurant du Chalet, with work by Anquetin (*Avenue de Clichy* (plate 146)), Bernard, Koning, Toulouse-Lautrec and himself. Meets Seurat and exchanges with Gauguin two studies of sunflowers for the latter's *On the shore of the lake at Martinique* (plate 141).

20 November-20 December Together with Theo visits the Puvis de Chavannes retrospective at the Durand-Ruel gallery; among the works on display is the *Portrait of Eugène Benon* (plate 90).

November 1887-January 1888 Exhibits with Seurat and Signac at André Antoine's Théâtre Libre.

December Undoubtedly visits the exhibition of work by Gauguin, Guillaumin and Pissarro organised by Theo at the Boussod, Valadon & Cie gallery on the Boulevard Montmartre, and probably also the exhibition of work by Anquetin, Camille Pissarro and Seurat at the offices of *La Revue Indépendante*.

1888

January Undoubtedly visits the exhibition of pastels by Edgar Degas and paintings by Gauguin organised by Theo at Boussod, Valadon & Cie.

Theo acquires Toulouse-Lautrec's *Young woman at a table, 'Poudre de riz'* (plate 139).

January-February Probably visits the exhibition of work by Angrand, Seurat and Signac at the offices of *La Revue Indépendante*.

Visits Seurat's studio on 19 February, together with Theo, to see his most recent work; a few hours later he leaves for Arles.

Visits the Musée Réattu and antiquities museum in Arles. Had already read Daudet's *Tartarin de Tarascon* and soon begins *Tartarin sur les Alpes*.

March Meets the Danish painter Mourier-Petersen. Reads Maupassant's *Pierre et Jean*.

May Rents the Yellow House in Arles, with the aim of setting up an artists' colony. Expresses his hope that Gauguin will soon join him in the south.

July Reads Loti's *Madame Chrysanthème* and Balzac's *César Birotteau*. Forms the plan to reread all of Balzac's novels. Meets the Belgian painter Boch.

October Receives the self-portraits Bernard (plate 170) and Gauguin (plate 172) have painted at his request. Bernard also sends him a series of drawings entitled *At the brothel* (plates 147-148).

23 October Gauguin arrives in Arles.

Autumn Reports to Theo on his collaboration with Gauguin, whom he greatly admires, both as a person and as an artist. Is very impressed by Bernard's *Breton women in the meadow* (plate 142), which Gauguin brought with him, and makes a watercolour after it (F 1422 JH 1654).

December Together with Gauguin visits the Musée Fabre in Montpellier. Admires the portraits of Bruyas by Courbet (plate 119) and Delacroix (plate 117), Courbet's *Sleeping spinner* (plate 120) and Delacroix's *Women of Algiers in their apartment (The odalisques)* (plate 116).

23 December Gauguin returns to Paris.

1889

Repeatedly cites Flaubert's *Bouvard et Pécuchet* and Voltaire's *Candide* in his letters.

January Gauguin gives his *Portrait of Van Gogh painting sunflowers* to Theo (plate 173).

23 March Signac visits him in Arles; he makes him a gift of *Plate with two red herrings* (F 510 JH 1661).

June-July Rereads Voltaire's *Zadig, ou la destinée* and reads Shakespeare's history plays and *Measure for measure*.

September-October Makes copies in colour after prints by Millet (plates 49, 54), Delacroix (plate 125) and Rembrandt.

Exhibits two paintings at the 5ᵉ Exposition des Indépendants. Asks Theo if it would be possible for him to go and live with Camille Pissaro or one of their other artist friends.

November Harshly criticises Bernard's religious paintings, of which he has received photographs.

1890

January-February Exhibits work at the 7ᵉ Exposition des XX in Brussels with, among others, Lucien Pissarro, Toulouse-Lautrec and Signac.

March Represented with ten works at the Exposition des Indépendants in Paris.

April Asks Theo to send his *Cypresses* (F 620 JH 1748) as a thank-you gift to Aurier, author of a laudatory article on his work for the *Mercure de France*.

mid-May Visits Theo in Paris and together they go to the Salon du Champ-de-Mars. Is very impressed by Puvis de Chavannes's *Inter artes et naturam* (plate 94).

Travels on to Auvers, where he takes up residence at the Auberge Ravoux. Meets Dr Gachet and admires his collection of impressionist paintings (Pissarros and Cézannes, among others).

6 July Pays a brief visit to Theo in Paris and also meets with Aurier and Toulouse-Lautrec, whose portrait *Mademoiselle Dihau playing the piano* moves him (plate 87). Returns the same evening to Auvers.

27 July Shoots himself in the chest and dies two days later of his wounds.

Paintings and drawings

plate 132
Charles Angrand (1854-1926)
Feeding the chickens, 1884
Oil on canvas, 53.8 x 65 cm
Copenhagen, Ny Carlsberg Glyptotek

plate 146
Louis Anquetin (1861-1932)
Avenue de Clichy, 1887
Oil and paper on canvas,
69.2 x 55.5 cm
Hartford, Wadsworth Atheneum
Museum of Art, The Ella Gallup Sumner and Mary Catlin Sumner Collection Fund.

plate 32
Lodewijk Apol (1850-1936)
*A January evening in the woods of
The Hague*, 1875
Oil on canvas, 92 x 121 cm
Amsterdam, Rijksmuseum

plate 88 [not exhibited]
Emile Bernard (1868-1941)
Portrait of Père Tanguy, 1887
Oil on canvas, 36 x 31 cm
Basel, Kunstmuseum, Öffentliche
Kunstsammlung

plate 86
Emile Bernard (1868-1941)
Portrait of Bernard's grandmother, 1887
Oil on canvas, 53 x 64 cm
Amsterdam, Van Gogh Museum
(Vincent van Gogh Foundation)

plate 148
Emile Bernard (1868-1941)
At the brothel: two prostitutes at table,
1887
Watercolour, 40.5 x 26.9 cm
Amsterdam, Van Gogh Museum
(Vincent van Gogh Foundation)

plate 147
Emile Bernard (1868-1941)
*At the brothel: a prostitute making her
toilet*, 1887
Watercolour, 40.5 x 26.9 cm
Amsterdam, Van Gogh Museum
(Vincent van Gogh Foundation)

plate 143
Emile Bernard (1868-1941)
The blue coffeepot, 1888
Oil on canvas, 55 x 46 cm
Kunsthalle Bremen

plate 142
Emile Bernard (1868-1941)
Breton women in the meadow, 1888
Oil on canvas, 74 x 92 cm
Private collection

plate 170
Emile Bernard (1868-1941)
Self-portrait with portrait of Gauguin,
1888
Oil on canvas, 46 x 56 cm
Amsterdam, Van Gogh Museum
(Vincent van Gogh Foundation)

plate 14
Emile Bernard (1868-1941)
The road to Calvary, 1889
Oil on panel, 49 x 60 cm
Private collection

plate 82
Albert Besnard (1849-1934)
Modern man, c. 1884-86
Oil on canvas, 51 x 183 cm
Beauvais, Musée départemental de
l'Oise

plate 83
Albert Besnard (1849-1934)
Prehistoric man, c. 1887
Oil on canvas, 50 x 133 cm
Private collection

plate 115
School of **Sandro Botticelli**
(1447-1510)
The Virgin and Child with John the Baptist
Round panel, d. 75 cm
Paris, Musée du Louvre (on loan to
the Musée du Petit Palais, Avignon)

plate 7
George Henry Boughton
(1833-1905)
*God speed! Pilgrims setting out to
Canterbury*, 1874
Oil on canvas, 122 x 184 cm
Amsterdam, Van Gogh Museum

plate 33
Hippolyte Boulenger (1837-1874)
The Josapathwetering in Schaarbeek,
1868
Oil on panel, 110 x 85 cm
Antwerp, Koninklijk Museum voor
Schone Kunsten

plate 38
Jules Breton (1827-1906)
Evening, 1860
Oil on canvas, 89 x 117 cm
Paris, Musée d'Orsay (on loan to the
Hôtel de Ville, Cuisery)

plate 39 [not exhibited]
Jules Breton (1827-1906)
The feast of St John, 1875
Oil on canvas, 112 x 195 cm
Private collection

plate 40
Gustave Brion (1824-1877)
*Vosges peasants fleeing before the
invasion*, 1867
Oil on canvas, 105 x 173.5 cm
St Louis, Washington University Gallery of Art, Bequest of Charles Parsons,
1905

plate 5
John Constable (1776-1837)
The valley farm, 1835
Oil on canvas, 147 x 125 cm
London, Tate Gallery

plate 12
Camille Corot (1796-1875)
The agony in the garden, 1849
Oil on canvas, 242 x 156 cm
Langres, Musée d'art et d'histoire

plate 120 [not exhibited]
Gustave Courbet (1819-1877)
The sleeping spinner, 1853
Oil on canvas, 91 x 115 cm
Montpellier, Musée Fabre

plate 119 [not exhibited]
Gustave Courbet (1819-1877)
*Portrait of Alfred Bruyas, called 'Tableau-
Solution'*, 1853
Oil on canvas, 91 x 72 cm
Montpellier, Musée Fabre

plate 110
Copy after **Aelbert Cuyp**
(1620-1691)
View of Dordrecht at sunset,
18th century
Oil on canvas, 68 x 84.5 cm
Amsterdam, Rijksmuseum

plate 34
Charles-François Daubigny
(1817-1878)
The flood-gate at Optevoz, 1855
Oil on cancas, 92 x 162 cm
Paris, Musée du Louvre (on loan to
the Musée des Beaux-Arts, Rouen)

plate 35
Charles-François Daubigny
(1817-1878)
Spring, 1857
Oil on canvas, 96 x 193 cm
Paris, Musée du Louvre (on loan to
the Musée des Beaux-Arts, Chartres)

plate 41
Alexandre-Gabriel Decamps
(1803-1860)
A shepherd with his flock, 1843
Oil on canvas, 79 x 115 cm
Amsterdams Historisch Museum
(on loan to the Van Gogh Museum,
Amsterdam)

plate 10
Charles De Groux (1825-1870)
The paupers' pew, 1854
Oil on canvas, 137 x 102 cm
Brussels, Musées royaux des Beaux-
Arts de Belgique

plate 116 [not exhibited]
Eugène Delacroix (1798-1863)
*Women of Algiers in their apartment
(The odalisques)*, 1849
Oil on canvas, 84 x 111 cm
Montpellier, Musée Fabre

plate 123
Eugène Delacroix (1798-1863)
Jacob wrestling with the angel,
c. 1850-56
Oil on canvas, 57 x 40.5 cm
Vienna, Österreichische Galerie
Belvedere

plate 117
Eugène Delacroix (1798-1863)
Portrait of Alfred Bruyas, 1853
Oil on canvas, 116 x 89 cm
Montpellier, Musée Fabre

plate 124
Eugène Delacroix (1798-1863)
Christ asleep during the tempest, c. 1853
Oil on canvas, 50.8 x 61 cm
New York, The Metropolitan Museum
of Art, Bequest of Mrs H.O. Havemeyer, 1929, The H.O. Havemeyer
Collection

plate 36
Jules Dupré (1811-1889)
Autumn, c. 1865
Oil on canvas, 106 x 94 cm
The Hague, Museum Mesdag

plate 131
Paul Gauguin (1848-1903)
Resting cows, 1885
Oil on canvas, 64 x 80 cm
Rotterdam, Museum Boijmans
Van Beuningen

plate 141
Paul Gauguin (1848-1903)
On the shore of the lake at Martinique,
1887
Oil on canvas, 54 x 65 cm
Amsterdam, Van Gogh Museum
(Vincent van Gogh Foundation)

plate 172
Paul Gauguin (1848-1903)
*Self-portrait with portrait of Bernard,
'Les misérables'*, 1888
Oil on canvas, 45 x 55 cm
Amsterdam, Van Gogh Museum
(Vincent van Gogh Foundation)

plate 173
Paul Gauguin (1848-1903)
Portrait of Van Gogh painting sunflowers,
1888
Oil on canvas, 73 x 91 cm
Amsterdam, Van Gogh Museum
(Vincent van Gogh Foundation)

plate 66
Jean-Léon Gérôme (1824-1904)
The prisoner, 1861
Oil on panel, 45 x 78 cm
Nantes, Musée des Beaux-Arts

plate 1
Vincent van Gogh (1853-1890)
Winter, in life as well (after Jozef Israëls),
c. 1877
Watercolour, 15.6 x 22.4 cm
Private collection

plate 46
Vincent van Gogh (1853-1890)
The sower (after Millet) (F 830 JH 1),
1881
Drawing, 48 x 37 cm
Amsterdam, Van Gogh Museum
(Vincent van Gogh Foundation)

plate 67
Vincent van Gogh (1853-1890)
Old nag (F 1032 JH 368), 1883
Drawing, 51 x 64 cm
Amsterdam, Van Gogh Museum
(Vincent van Gogh Foundation)

plate 44
Vincent van Gogh (1853-1890)
The potato eaters (F 82 JH 764), 1885
Oil on canvas, 82 x 114 cm
Amsterdam, Van Gogh Museum
(Vincent van Gogh Foundation)

plate 13
Vincent van Gogh (1853-1890)
*The old church tower at Nuenen, 'The
peasants' churchyard'* (F 84 JH 772),
1885
Oil on canvas, 65 x 80 cm
Amsterdam, Van Gogh Museum
(Vincent van Gogh Foundation)

plate 42
Vincent van Gogh (1853-1890)
Digger in a potato field (F 1302 JH 859),
1885
Drawing, 54 x 41 cm
Amsterdam, Van Gogh Museum
(Vincent van Gogh Foundation)

plate 121
Vincent van Gogh (1853-1890)
Head of a woman (F 206 JH 972), 1885
Oil on canvas, 35 x 24 cm
Amsterdam, Van Gogh Museum
(Vincent van Gogh Foundation)

plate 128
Vincent van Gogh (1853-1890)
Vase with Chinese asters
(F 234 JH 1168), 1886
Oil on canvas, 61 x 46 cm
Amsterdam, Van Gogh Museum
(Vincent van Gogh Foundation)

plate 134
Vincent van Gogh (1853-1890)
Boulevard de Clichy (F 292 JH 1219),
1887
Oil on canvas, 46 x 55 cm
Amsterdam, Van Gogh Museum
(Vincent van Gogh Foundation)

plate 136
Vincent van Gogh (1853-1890)
*Courting couples in the Voyer d'Argenson
Park in Asnières* (F 314 JH 1258), 1887
Oil on canvas, 75 x 112 cm
Amsterdam, Van Gogh Museum
(Vincent van Gogh Foundation)

plate 130
Vincent van Gogh (1853-1890)
Woodland path (F 309 JH 1315), 1887
Oil on canvas, 46 x 38 cm
Amsterdam, Van Gogh Museum
(Vincent van Gogh Foundation)

plate 161
Vincent van Gogh (1853-1890)
Bridge in the rain (after Hiroshige)
(F 372 JH 1297), 1887
Oil on canvas, 73 x 54 cm
Amsterdam, Van Gogh Museum
(Vincent van Gogh Foundation)

plate 145
Vincent van Gogh (1853-1890)
Still life with quinces and lemons (F 383
JH 1339), 1887
Oil on canvas, 48 x 65 cm
Amsterdam, Van Gogh Museum
(Vincent van Gogh Foundation)

plate 89
Vincent van Gogh (1853-1890)
Portrait of Père Tanguy (F 1412
JH 1350), 1887-88
Drawing, 22 x 14 cm
Amsterdam, Van Gogh Museum
(Vincent van Gogh Foundation)

plate 73
Vincent van Gogh (1853-1890)
Self-portrait as an artist (F 522
JH 1356), 1888
Oil on canvas, 66 x 50 cm
Amsterdam, Van Gogh Museum
(Vincent van Gogh Foundation)

plate 169
Vincent van Gogh (1853-1890)
Small pear tree in blossom (F 405
JH 1394), 1888
Oil on canvas, 73 x 46 cm
Amsterdam, Van Gogh Museum
(Vincent van Gogh Foundation)

plate 113
Vincent van Gogh (1853-1890)
The harvest (F 412 JH 1440), 1888
Oil on canvas, 73 x 92 cm
Amsterdam, Van Gogh Museum
(Vincent van Gogh Foundation)

plate 47
Vincent van Gogh (1853-1890)
The sower with setting sun
(F 451 JH 1629), 1888
Oil on canvas, 32 x 40 cm
Amsterdam, Van Gogh Museum
(Vincent van Gogh Foundation)

plate 144
Vincent van Gogh (1853-1890)
Still life with coffeepot (F 410 JH 1426),
1888
Oil on canvas, 65 x 81 cm
Private collection

plate 140 [not exhibited]
Vincent van Gogh (1853-1890)
Portrait of Patience Escalier
(F 444 JH 1563), 1888
Oil on canvas, 69 x 56 cm
Private collection

plate 85
Vincent van Gogh (1853-1890)
Gauguin's chair (F 499 JH 1636), 1888
Oil on canvas, 90 x 72 cm
Amsterdam, Van Gogh Museum
(Vincent van Gogh Foundation)

plate 84
Vincent van Gogh (1853-1890)
Augustine Roulin ('La berceuse')
(F 507 JH 1672), 1888-89
Oil on canvas, 91 x 72 cm
Amsterdam, Stedelijk Museum
(on loan to the Van Gogh Museum,
Amsterdam)

plate 125
Vincent van Gogh (1853-1890)
Pietà (after Delacroix) (F 630 JH 1775),
1889
Oil on canvas, 73 x 60 cm
Amsterdam, Van Gogh Museum
(Vincent van Gogh Foundation)

plate 49
Vincent van Gogh (1853-1890)
The sheep-shearer (after Millet)
(F 634 JH 1787), 1889
Oil on canvas, 44 x 30 cm
Amsterdam, Van Gogh Museum
(Vincent van Gogh Foundation)

plate 54
Vincent van Gogh (1853-1890)
Night (after Millet) (F 647 JH 1834),
1889
Oil on canvas, 74 x 94 cm
Amsterdam, Van Gogh Museum
(Vincent van Gogh Foundation)

plate 15
Vincent van Gogh (1853-1890)
Olive grove (F 707 JH 1857), 1889
Oil on canvas, 73 x 92 cm
Amsterdam, Van Gogh Museum
(Vincent van Gogh Foundation)

plate 52
Vincent van Gogh (1853-1890)
*Snow-covered field with a harrow
(after Millet)* (F 632 JH 1882), 1890
Oil on canvas, 72 x 92 cm
Amsterdam, Van Gogh Museum
(Vincent van Gogh Foundation)

plate 51
Vincent van Gogh (1853-1890)
The woodcutter (after Millet)
(F 670 JH 1886), 1890
Oil on canvas, 44 x 25 cm
Amsterdam, Van Gogh Museum
(Vincent van Gogh Foundation)

plate 74
Vincent van Gogh (1853-1890)
The raising of Lazarus (after Rembrandt)
(F 677 JH 1972), 1890
Oil on canvas, 50 x 65 cm
Amsterdam, Van Gogh Museum
(Vincent van Gogh Foundation)

plate 29
Vincent van Gogh (1853-1890)
Wheat field under thunderclouds
(F 778 JH 2097), 1890
Oil on canvas, 50 x 100 cm
Amsterdam, Van Gogh Museum
(Vincent van Gogh Foundation)

plate 111
Jan van Goyen (1596-1656)
Landscape with two oaks, 1641
Oil on canvas, 88.5 x 110.5 cm
Amsterdam, Rijksmuseum

plate 109
Copy after **Frans Hals**
(1581/5-1666)
The fool
Oil on canvas, 67 x 60 cm
Amsterdam, Rijksmuseum

plate 6
William Holman Hunt (1827-1910)
The light of the world, 1851-56
Oil on canvas, 49.8 x 26.1 cm
Manchester, City Art Gallery

plate 64
Jozef Israëls (1824-1911)
At the churchyard, 1856
Oil on canvas, 244 x 178 cm
Amsterdam, Stedelijk Museum (on
loan to the Groninger Museum)

plate 65
Jozef Israëls (1824-1911)
Old friends, 1882
Oil on canvas, 132 x 174 cm
Philadelphia Museum of Art,
The William L. Elkins Collection

plate 112
Philips Koninck (1619-1688)
River landscape, 1676
Oil on canvas, 92.5 x 112 cm
Amsterdam, Rijksmuseum

plate 171
Charles Laval (1862-1894)
Self-portrait, 1888
Oil on canvas, 70 x 55 cm
Amsterdam, Van Gogh Museum
(Vincent van Gogh Foundation)

plate 4
Matthijs Maris (1839-1917)
*The Nieuwe Haarlemse Sluis on the
Singel, called ' Souvenir d'Amsterdam',*
1871
Oil on canvas, 46.5 x 35 cm
Amsterdam, Rijksmuseum

plate 68
Anton Mauve (1838-1888)
Fishing boat on the beach, 1882
Oil on canvas, 115 x 172 cm
The Hague, Gemeentemuseum

plate 92
Ernest Meissonier (1815-1871)
The draughtsman, 1855
Oil on panel, 20 x 14 cm
Musée National du Château de
Compiègne

plate 91
Ernest Meissonier (1815-1871)
Portrait of Pierre-Jules Hetzel, 1879
Oil on canvas, 32.6 x 23 cm
Meudon, Musée d'art et d'histoire

plate 43
Constantin Meunier (1831-1905)
The return of the miners, c. 1885
Oil on canvas, 132 x 238 cm
Private collection

plate 31
Georges Michel (1763-1843)
Three windmills
Oil on paper, 50.3 x 69.4 cm
The Hague, Museum Mesdag

plate 45
Jean-François Millet (1814-1875)
The sower, 1850
Oil on canvas, 106.6 x 82.6 cm
Boston, Museum of Fine Arts, Gift of
Quincy Adams Shaw through Quincy
Adams Shaw, Jr., and Mrs. Marian Shaw
Haughton

plate 48
Jean-François Millet (1814-1875)
Shearing sheep, c. 1860
Oil on canvas, 163.8 x 113 cm
Private collection

plate 50 [not exhibited]
Jean-François Millet (1814-1875)
*Woodcutter and his wife preparing
faggots,* 1866-68
Pastel, 49 x 34 cm
Private collection

plate 53
Jean-François Millet (1814-1875)
Vineyard labourer resting, 1869-70
Pastel, 70.5 x 84 cm
The Hague, Museum Mesdag

plate 138
Claude Monet (1840-1926)
Bordighera, 1884
Oil on canvas, 65 x 81 cm
The Art Institute of Chicago,
Potter Palmer Collection

plate 129
Claude Monet (1840-1926)
Boats on the beach, Etretat, 1885
Oil on canvas, 65.5 x 81.3 cm
The Art Institute of Chicago, Charles
H. and Mary F.S. Worcester Collection

plate 127
Adolphe-Joseph Monticelli
(1824-1886)
Vase with flowers, c. 1875
Oil on panel, 51 x 39 cm
Amsterdam, Van Gogh Museum
(Vincent van Gogh Foundation)

plate 126
Adolphe-Joseph Monticelli
(1824-1886)
Sunset, c. 1882-84
Oil on panel, 31.8 x 44.8 cm
London, The National Gallery

plate 137
Camille Pissarro (1830-1903)
View from my window in cloudy weather,
1886-88
Oil on canvas, 65 x 80 cm
Oxford, Ashmolean Museum of Art
and Archaeology

plate 90
Pierre Puvis de Chavannes
(1824-1898)
Portrait of Eugène Benon, 1882
Oil on canvas, 60.5 x 54.5 cm
Private collection

plate 94
Pierre Puvis de Chavannes
(1824-1898)
*Inter artes et naturam (Between art and
nature),* 1890
Oil on canvas, 40.3 x 113.7 cm
New York, The Metropolitan Museum
of Art, Gift of Mrs. Harry Payne
Bingham, 1958

plate 72
Rembrandt van Rijn (1606-1669)
Self-portrait, 1669
Oil on canvas, 86 x 70.5 cm
London, The National Gallery

plate 71
Workshop of **Rembrandt van Rijn**
(1606-1669)
The holy family at night, 1638-40
Oil on panel, 66.5 x 78 cm
Amsterdam, Rijksmuseum

plate 69
Workshop of **Rembrandt van Rijn**
(1606-1669)
The lamentation of Christ, c. 1650
Oil on canvas, 180.3 x 198.7 cm
Sarasota, John and Mable Ringling
Museum of Art, State Art Museum of
Florida, Bequest of John Ringling

plate 70
Follower of **Rembrandt van Rijn**
(1606-1669)
Christ in the house of Martha and Mary,
c. 1650
Drawing, 18.4 x 26.1 cm
London, British Museum

plate 118
Gustave Ricard (1823-1875)
Portrait of Alfred Bruyas, c. 1855-57
Oil on canvas, 62 x 50 cm
Montpellier, Musée Fabre

plate 114 [not exhibited]
Attributed to **Pietro da Rimini**
(14th century)
The death and assumption of the Virgin
Panel, 20 x 15 cm
Montpellier, Musée Fabre

plate 37
Théodore Rousseau (1812-1867)
The descent of the cattle in the high Jura mountains, c. 1834-35
Oil on canvas, 114 x 59.8 cm
The Hague, Museum Mesdag

plate 122
Peter Paul Rubens (1577-1640)
The carrying of the cross
Oil on panel, 74 x 55 cm
Amsterdam, Rijksmuseum

plate 30
Jacob van Ruisdael (1628/29-1682)
View of Haarlem with bleaching grounds
Oil on canvas, 55.5 x 62 cm
The Hague, Royal Cabinet of Paintings
Mauritshuis

plate 3
Jacob van Ruisdael (1628/29-1682)
The storm, c. 1660
Oil on canvas, 110 x 160 cm
Paris, Musée du Louvre

plate 93
Daniel Saubès (1855-1920) and
Léon Bonnat (1833-1922)
Portrait of Victor Hugo in 1879, 1903
Oil on canvas, 137 x 109.5 cm
Paris, Maison de Victor Hugo

plate 9
Ary Scheffer (1795-1858)
Christus consolator, 1837
Oil on canvas, 184 x 248 cm
Amsterdams Historisch Museum
(on loan to the Van Gogh Museum,
Amsterdam)

plate 8
Ary Scheffer (1795-1858)
The agony in the garden, 1839
Oil on canvas, 140 x 98 cm
Dordrechts Museum

plate 135
Georges Seurat (1859-1891)
La Luzerne, Saint-Denis, 1885-86
Oil on canvas, 65.3 x 81.3 cm
Edinburgh, National Galleries of
Scotland

plate 133
Paul Signac (1863-1935)
Snow, Boulevard de Clichy, 1886
Oil on canvas, 45.7 x 65.4 cm
The Minneapolis Institute of Arts,
Bequest of Putnam Dana McMillan

plate 139
Henri de Toulouse-Lautrec
(1864-1901)
Young woman at a table, 'Poudre de riz',
1887
Oil on canvas, 56 x 46 cm
Amsterdam, Van Gogh Museum
(Vincent van Gogh Foundation)

plate 87
Henri de Toulouse-Lautrec
(1864-1901)
Mademoiselle Dihau playing the piano,
1890
Oil on canvas, 68 x 48.5 cm
Albi, Musée Toulouse-Lautrec

plate 11
Fritz von Uhde (1848-1911)
Suffer little children to come unto me,
1884
Oil on canvas, 188 x 290.5 cm
Leipzig, Museum der bildenden Künste

plate 2
Johan Hendrik Weissenbruch
(1824-1903)
View of the Trekvliet, 1870
Oil on canvas, 65 x 100 cm
The Hague, Gemeentemuseum

Photographs and prints

plate 98
After **David Artz** (1837-1890)
Old people's home at Katwijk, 1882
Photogravure
Bordeaux, Musée Goupil

plate 17
After **Karl Bodmer** (1809-1893)
The Forest of Fontainebleau, 1859
Lithograph
Paris, Bibliothèque Nationale de
France, Cabinet des Estampes

plate 18
After **Karl Bodmer** (1809-1893)
Stags fighting, Forest of Fontainebleau,
1861
Lithograph
Paris, Bibliothèque Nationale de
France, Cabinet des Estampes

plate 22
Johannes Bosboom (1817-1891)
Carmelite playing the organ: cantabimus et psallemus, c. 1850
Lithograph
Amsterdam, Van Gogh Museum
(Vincent van Gogh Foundation)

plate 27
After **Gustave Brion** (1824-1877)
Grace before the meal, 1862
Engraving
Bordeaux, Musée Goupil

plate 16
After **Jan Brueghel the Elder**
(1568-1625)
Three mills, 1772
Engraving
Amsterdam, Rijksprentenkabinet

plate 19
Charles-François Daubigny
(1817-1878), after **Jacob van
Ruisdael**
*Dune landscape near Haarlem
(Le buisson)*, 1855
Etching
Paris, Bibliothèque Nationale de
France, Cabinet des Estampes

plate 107
Charles-François Daubigny
(1817-1878)
The large sheepfold, 1861
Etching
Amsterdam, Rijksprentenkabinet

plate 149
After **Honoré Daumier** (1808-1879)
The four ages of a drinker, 1865-66
Wood engraving
Amsterdam, Van Gogh Museum
(Vincent van Gogh Foundation)

plate 99
After **Honoré Daumier** (1808-1879)
Leaving the theatres, 1864-65
Wood engraving
Amsterdam, Van Gogh Museum
(Vincent van Gogh Foundation)

plate 151
After **Eugène Delacroix**
(1798-1863)
Pietà, c. 1850
Lithograph
Amsterdam, Van Gogh Museum
(Vincent van Gogh Foundation)

plate 100
After **Gustave Doré** (1832-1883)
Scripture reader in a night refuge,
1872-73
Wood engraving
Amsterdam, Van Gogh Museum
(Vincent van Gogh Foundation)

plate 105
After **Albrecht Dürer** (1471-1528)
Knight, death and devil, 1513
Engraving
Amsterdam, Rijksprentenkabinet

plate 97
After **Thomas Faed** (1826-1900)
Worn out, 1868
Mezzotint
London, British Museum

plate 28
After **Eugène Feyen** (1815-1908)
The honeymoon, 1869
Photograph
Bordeaux, Musée Goupil

plate 95
Mariano Fortuny y Carbó
(1838-1874)
*An Arab watching over the body of his
dead friend*, 1866
Etching
Amsterdam, Rijksprentenkabinet

plate 96
Mariano Fortuny y Carbó
(1838-1874)
The dead Kabyle, 1867
Etching
Amsterdam, Rijksprentenkabinet

plate 101
After Paul **Gavarni** (1804-1866)
Porters of the vegetable market, 1855
Wood engraving
Amsterdam, Van Gogh Museum
(Vincent van Gogh Foundation)

plate 20
After **Achille-Isidore Gilbert**
(1828-1899)
The late M. Corot, French painter, 1875
Wood engraving
Amsterdam, Van Gogh Museum
(Vincent van Gogh Foundation)

plate 21
After **Jules-Adolphe Goupil**
(1839-1883)
A young citizen of the Year V, 1878
Wood engraving
Amsterdam, Van Gogh Museum
(Vincent van Gogh Foundation)

plate 103
After **Sir Hubert von Herkomer**
(1849-1914)
Sunday at Chelsea hospital, 1871
Wood engraving
Amsterdam, Van Gogh Museum
(Vincent van Gogh Foundation)

plate 156
Utagawa Hiroshige (1797-1858)
*Ishiyakushi: the Yoshitsune cherry tree
near the Noriyori shrine,* 1855
Colour woodblock print
Amsterdam, Van Gogh Museum
(Vincent van Gogh Foundation)

plate 157
Utagawa Hiroshige (1797-1858)
*Hara: Mount Fuji and Ashitaka mountain
in close-up,* 1855
Colour woodblock print
Amsterdam, Van Gogh Museum
(Vincent van Gogh Foundation)

plate 158
Utagawa Hiroshige (1797-1858)
Fuji from the Sagami river, 1858
Colour woodblock print
Amsterdam, Van Gogh Museum
(Vincent van Gogh Foundation)

plate 159
Utagawa Hiroshige (1797-1858)
*Fuji seen from the outskirts of Koshigaya
in Musashi province,* 1858
Colour woodblock print
Amsterdam, Van Gogh Museum
(Vincent van Gogh Foundation)

plate 160
Utagawa Hiroshige (1797-1858)
*Sudden shower on the Great Bridge near
Atake,* 1857
Colour woodblock print
Amsterdam, Van Gogh Museum
(Vincent van Gogh Foundation)

plate 163
Utagawa Hiroshige (1797-1858)
The plum tree teahouse at Kameido,
1857
Colour woodblock print
Amsterdam, Van Gogh Museum
(Vincent van Gogh Foundation)

plate 104
Jozef Israëls (1824-1911)
Man lighting his pipe (The smoker)
Etching
Amsterdam, Rijksprentenkabinet

plate 165
Utagawa Kunisada (Toyokuni III)
(1786-1864)
The courtesan Takao of the Miuraya,
1861
Colour woodblock print
Amsterdam, Van Gogh Museum
(Vincent van Gogh Foundation)

plate 166
Utagawa Kunisada (Toyokuni III)
(1786-1864)
An actor as the geisha Chokichi, 1859
Colour woodblock print
Amsterdam, Van Gogh Museum
(Vincent van Gogh Foundation)

plate 168
Utagawa Kunisada (Toyokuni III)
(1786-1864)
*Enjoying the spring plum blossom in the
haze,* 1858
Colour woodblock print (triptych)
Amsterdam, Van Gogh Museum
(Vincent van Gogh Foundation)

plate 164
Utagawa Kunisada II (1823-1880)
*The Matsumotorō theatre in the Tokyo
entertainment district,* 1870
Colour woodblock print (triptych)
Amsterdam, Van Gogh Museum
(Vincent van Gogh Foundation)

plate 102
After **Auguste-André Lançon**
(1836-1885)
Gathering of ragpickers, 1872
Wood engraving
Amsterdam, Van Gogh Museum
(Vincent van Gogh Foundation)

plate 106
Alphonse Legros (1837-1911)
The lectern (The Spanish choristers),
1865
Etching
Amsterdam, Rijksprentenkabinet

plate 152
After **Léon Lhermitte** (1844-1925)
Rural labours. October: lifting potatoes,
1885
Wood engraving
Amsterdam, Van Gogh Museum
(Vincent van Gogh Foundation)

plate 153
After **Léon Lhermitte** (1844-1925)
Rural labours. November: the sower,
1886
Wood engraving
Amsterdam, Van Gogh Museum
(Vincent van Gogh Foundation)

plate 150
After **Charles Maurin** (1856-1914)
Before the accident, 1888
Lithograph
Amsterdam, Van Gogh Museum
(Vincent van Gogh Foundation)

plate 60
After **Jean-François Millet**
(1814-1875)
The sower, 1850
Etching
Amsterdam, Van Gogh Museum
(Vincent van Gogh Foundation)

plate 62
After **Jean-François Millet**
(1814-1875)
Men digging
Photograph
Amsterdam, Van Gogh Museum
(Vincent van Gogh Foundation)

plate 55
After **Jean-François Millet**
(1814-1875)
*The four times of the day. Morning:
going to work,* 1873
Wood engraving
Amsterdam, Van Gogh Museum
(Vincent van Gogh Foundation)

plate 56
After **Jean-François Millet**
The four times of the day. Noon: rest,
1873
Wood engraving
Amsterdam, Van Gogh Museum
(Vincent van Gogh Foundation)

plate 57
After **Jean-François Millet**
*The four times of the day. The end of
the day,* 1873
Wood engraving
Amsterdam, Van Gogh Museum
(Vincent van Gogh Foundation)

plate 58
After **Jean-François Millet**
*The four times of the day. Night:
the watch,* 1873
Wood engraving
Amsterdam, Van Gogh Museum
(Vincent van Gogh Foundation)

plate 63
After **Jean-François Millet**
(1814-1875)
The first steps, c. 1858
Photograph
Amsterdam, Van Gogh Museum
(Vincent van Gogh Foundation)

plate 61
After **Jean-François Millet**
(1814-1875)
The angelus, 1873
Etching
Amsterdam, Van Gogh Museum
(Vincent van Gogh Foundation)

plate 59
After **Jean-François Millet**
(1814-1875)
The labours of the fields, 1853 (series
of ten prints)
Wood engraving
Amsterdam, Van Gogh Museum
(Vincent van Gogh Foundation)

plate 79
Rembrandt van Rijn (1606-1669)
The blind fiddler, 1631
Etching
Amsterdam, Rijksprentenkabinet

plate 78
Rembrandt van Rijn (1606-1669)
The blindness of Tobit, 1651
Etching
Amsterdam, Rijksprentenkabinet

plate 80
Rembrandt van Rijn (1606-1669)
David in prayer, 1652
Etching
Amsterdam, Rijksprentenkabinet

plate 75
After **Rembrandt van Rijn**
(1606-1669)
The holy family at night, c. 1787
Etching
Paris, Bibliothèque Nationale de
France, Cabinet des Estampes

plate 81
After **Rembrandt van Rijn**
(1606-1669)
The raising of Lazarus
Etching
Amsterdam, Van Gogh Museum
(Vincent van Gogh Foundation)

plate 77
After **Rembrandt van Rijn**
(1606-1669)
Portrait of Jan Six, c. 1874-78
Engraving
Amsterdam, Rijksprentenkabinet

plate 76
After **Rembrandt van Rijn**
(1606-1669)
Christ at Emmaus, 1875
Engraving
Bordeaux, Musée Goupil

plate 25
After **Alfred Rethel** (1816-1859)
Cholera in Paris (Death as a foe), 1851
Wood engraving
Amsterdam, Rijksprentenkabinet

plate 26
After **Alfred Rethel** (1816-1859)
Death as a friend, 1851
Wood engraving
Amsterdam, Rijksprentenkabinet

plate 154
After **Thomas Rowlandson**
(1756-1827)
A difficult affair, 1888
Lithograph
Amsterdam, Van Gogh Museum
(Vincent van Gogh Foundation)

plate 24
After **Ary Scheffer** (1795-1858)
The holy women at the tomb, 1845
Photograph
Bordeaux, Musée Goupil

plate 23
After **Ary Scheffer** (1795-1858)
The prodigal son, 1857
Photograph
Bordeaux, Musée Goupil

plate 155
After **Henri de Toulouse-Lautrec**
(1864-1901)
The washerwoman, 1888
Lithograph
Amsterdam, Van Gogh Museum
(Vincent van Gogh Foundation)

plate 108
After **Frederick Walker** (1840-1875)
The wayfarers
Etching
London, British Museum

plate 162
Utagawa Yoshimaru (1844-1907)
New prints of worms and insects, 1883
Colour woodblock print
Amsterdam, Van Gogh Museum
(Vincent van Gogh Foundation)

plate 167
Utagawa Yoshitora
(active c. 1845-1880)
Three women, 1847-48
Colour woodblock print
Amsterdam, Van Gogh Museum
(Vincent van Gogh Foundation)

Austria
Vienna, Österreichische Galerie Belvedere

Belgium
Antwerp, Koninklijk Museum voor Schone Kunsten
Brussels, Musées royaux des Beaux-Arts de Belgique

Denmark
Copenhagen, Ny Carlsberg Glyptotek

France
Albi, Musée Toulouse-Lautrec
Avignon, Musée du Petit Palais (loan from the Musée du Louvre, Paris)
Beauvais, Musée départemental de l'Oise
Bordeaux, Musée Goupil
Chartres, Musée des Beaux-Arts (loan from the Musée du Louvre, Paris)
Compiègne, Musée National du Château de Compiègne
Cuisery, Hôtel de Ville (loan from the Musée d'Orsay, Paris)
Langres, Musée d'art et d'histoire (loan from the Fonds national d'Art contemporain, Puteaux)
Meudon, Musée d'art et d'histoire
Montpellier, Musée Fabre
Nantes, Musée des Beaux-Arts
Paris, Bibliothèque Nationale de France, Cabinet des Estampes
Paris, Maison de Victor Hugo
Paris, Musée du Louvre
Rouen, Musée des Beaux-Arts (loan from the Musée du Louvre, Paris)

Germany
Bremen, Kunsthalle Bremen
Leipzig, Museum der bildenden Künste

Great Britain
Edinburgh, National Galleries of Scotland
London, British Museum
London, The National Gallery
London, Tate Gallery
Manchester, City Art Gallery
Oxford, Ashmolean Museum of Art and Archaeology

The Netherlands
Amsterdams Historisch Museum
Amsterdam, Rijksmuseum
Amsterdam, Rijksprentenkabinet
Amsterdam, Stedelijk Museum
Dordrecht, Dordrechts Museum
Groningen, Groninger Museum (loan from the Stedelijk Museum, Amsterdam)
The Hague, Gemeentemuseum
The Hague, Royal Cabinet of Paintings Mauritshuis
The Hague, Museum Mesdag
Rotterdam, Museum Boijmans Van Beuningen

Switzerland
Basel, Kunstmuseum, Öffentliche Kunstsammlung

United States
Boston, Museum of Fine Arts
The Art Institute of Chicago
Hartford, Wadsworth Atheneum Museum of Art
St Louis, Washington University Gallery of Art
The Minneapolis Institute of Arts
New York, The Metropolitan Museum of Art
Philadelphia Museum of Art
Sarasota, The John and Mable Ringling Museum of Art, State Art Museum of Florida

Exhibition

Coordination / Andreas Blühm

Curators / Andreas Blühm, Sjraar van Heugten, Chris Stolwijk,
with the assistance of Nienke Bakker

Registrars / Martine Kilburn, Aly Noordermeer, Sara Verboven

Secretaries / Esther Hoofwijk, Adrie Kok

Design / The Office of Thierry W. Despont, New York

Lighting design / Johnson Schwinghammer Lighting, New York

Exhibition installation / Iris Vormgeving, Amsterdam

Graphic design / Frederik de Wal, Schelluinen

Insurance / AON Artscope Nederland Fine Art Insurance,
Amsterdam

Catalogue

Editors / Sjraar van Heugten, Leo Jansen, Chris Stolwijk

Authors / Nienke Bakker, Joan Greer, Sjraar van Heugten,
Cornelia Homburg, Leo Jansen, Hans Luijten, Chris Stolwijk,
Evert van Uitert, Wouter van der Veen, Roelie Zwikker

Production / Tijdsbeeld, Ghent, Ronny Gobyn (director),
assisted by Petra Gunst, Kristin van Damme and Barbara
Costermans (Tijdgeest, Ghent)

Copy editing / Michael Reaburn

Final editing / Chris Stolwijk

Research assistance / Nienke Bakker

English translation / Rachel Esner, Michael Hoyle

Manager of publications / Suzanne Bogman

Design / Frederik de Wal, Schelluinen

Typesetting, printing and colour separations / Die Keure,
Bruges

Binding / Splichal, Turnhout

Photography

All photographs are courtesy of the institutions or persons
owning the work reproduced. With special thanks to:
Martin Bühler, plate 88; Cussac/Speltdoorn, figs. 72, 88, plate 10;
Frédéric Jaulmes, plates 114, 116-120; Photos-Contact, plate 92;
Thijs Quispel, figs. 20, 32, 52, 58, 65-66, plates 39, 43, 90; Réunion
des Musées Nationaux (photos J.G. Berizzi, Gérard Blot, Bulloz,
C. Jean, Hervé Lewandowski, Jean Schormans), figs. 11, 15, 22,
27, 38, 43, 50, 55, 70, 71, 73, 84-86, 138, plates 3, 34, 38, 66, 92,
115; Trustees of Princeton University, fig. 116; Elke Walford, fig.
76; Washington, National Gallery of Art (Board of Trustees),
figs. 81, 126.

Main sponsor

Rabobank